The HISTORY *and* POWER *of* WRITING

The

HISTORY

and

POWER

of

WRITING

Henri-Jean Martin

Translated by Lydia G. Cochrane

The University of Chicago Press

Chicago and London

HENRI-JEAN MARTIN is professor at the Ecole des chartes and director of studies at the Ecole pratique des hautes études (IVe section). He has written many works on the history and sociology of the book.

The author has made a number of additions and corrections to the French edition of *L'histoire et pouvoirs de l'écrit* for this publication in English. The University of Chicago Press and the translator wish to thank Professor Martin for his courtesy in reviewing the text of this translation.

This book has been supported by a grant from the National Endowment for the Humanities, an independent federal agency.

Originally published as *Histoire et pouvoirs de l'écrit,* © Librairie Académique Perrin, 1988

THE UNIVERSITY OF CHICAGO PRESS, CHICAGO 60637
THE UNIVERSITY OF CHICAGO PRESS, LTD., LONDON

Printed in the United States of America

03   02   01   00   99   98   97   96   95   94   2   3   4   5

ISBN: 0-226-50835-8 (cloth)

Library of Congress Cataloging-in-Publication Data

Martin, Henri Jean, 1924–
    [Histoire et pouvoirs de l'écrit. English]
    The history and power of writing / Henri-Jean Martin ; translated by Lydia G. Cochrane.
        p.   cm.
    Includes bibliographical references and index.
    1. Writing—History.   2. Printing—History.   3. Books and reading—History.   4. Written communication—History.   I. Title.
    Z40.M3713   1994
    411'.09—dc20   93-26718

⊚ The paper used in this publication meets the minimum requirements of the American National Standard for Information Sciences—Permanence of Paper for Printed Library Materials, ANSI Z39.48-1984.

Contents

Foreword

Writing—that pinnacle of the Word—treated here by the finest scholar of the book (he has devoted four full decades of a life of learning to it; he has sought, paradoxically found, and founded a school; and he has inspired what has been done in this domain) is inscribed in the motivation behind the series entitled *Histoire et Décadence,* a series that has already had an illustrious beginning with Gabriel Camps, who led us out of the "Lost Paradise" with his *La préhistoire. A la recherche du paradis perdu,* and with François Caron, who exorcised fascination with decline in our industrial societies in his *La résistible déclin des sociétés industrielles.* Need I recall the ambitious aim of this project? To integrate the counterflux into the great thrust of history that until now—*tanto monta, monta tanto*—is, like Life itself, vectorially ascendant. From one millennium to another humanity has increased in numbers and in command of a greater mass of information. Until today it has succeeded in overcoming setbacks, counterflux, declines, and moments of decadence in the spirit of "Reculer pour mieux sauter" (hesitating before leaping forward). The series entitled *Histoire et Décadence* has had a clear intent, which was to integrate the risk of decadence into the chaotically, painfully, dangerously upward *processus* of the human Adventure. We have decided to look squarely at what people have done their best to forget or ignore, indeed, at what they have condemned, as if value judgments had any place in historical discourse.

There are in history felicitous moments for this sort of observation—moments or places in which one sees the ebb tide as if under a magnifying glass, in which one measures better the price that was paid, the sacrifice required for any advance, the death required for life, the negentropy for an entropy accrued elsewhere. Gabriel Camps has enabled us to grasp this in a "Prehistory" that was, globally, conquest, growth, and explosion. We have seen the same process with François Caron in the great technological and industrial changes of the nineteenth and twentieth centuries. We will soon follow it to a Rome in decline, and we will see it in the wide oscillations of the evolution of China. Seen from one angle, the Neolithic revolution—"in the sweat of thy face shalt thou eat bread"—tore an already numerous humanity from the delights of a lost paradise of relatively somnolent and effortless abundance. The decline of Rome saved us from the destiny of China; it was the price we paid—our "reculer pour mieux sau-ter." The thought of the infant political science of the Enlightenment fed on Rome. There is a vast difference between Montesquieu's vision, Gibbon's vision, and our own. They wrote of grandeur and decadence; we think in terms of ebb, retreat, withdrawal, and breakdown as the only way to reach a new level one notch higher.

With Henri-Jean Martin we leave the *hic et nunc* of Narrative for an ex-ploration of the whole of history. If writing is the spearhead of linguistic change, writing—quite obviously—cannot be dissociated from the word, and as far back as we explore our collective memory the Word (*Ha Dabar*) is humankind.

If the first tool dates back three million years, the first modulated cry bearing a message was nearly as old. The hand and the tool advanced at nearly the same pace as the face and language. But thanks to the tool the hand has made a stronger imprint on buried memory. When we try to conceive the progress of language we are reduced to weighing the conse-quences of cranial development in the frontal lobes in our prehuman, fos-silized ancestors. The first tomb is a Language; funeral rites are a treatise in metaphysics. It is clear that the dossier preceded writing just as abstract art preceded figurative art. Personal adornment, sculpted stones, brushes made with animal hairs, fairly regular series of scratches, dots, and hatch marks go back fifty thousand years; Lascaux dates back fifteen thousand years; Altamira even fewer. Such figurations of an awareness of death by contemporary hands are fascinating. Henri-Jean Martin is right to mention them; they cast a shadowy and intriguing light on the whole of history. The first lesson that I might draw from these traces concerns Language. The dual nature of language in the spoken and the written word, a duality reflected in sound and sign, in the ear and the mouth, and in the hand and the eye, goes back to the twilight eras of time. Although writing is re-cent—*homo faber* is three million years old and *homo scribens* only five thousand years old—and although writing separated from sound only a mere two centuries ago (that is, before sound caught up again), commu-nication by signs and the collaboration of the sign in the elaboration of thought are nearly as old as the Word.

From the first tomb, hence from when man became fully human, it is clear that the slash mark and the dot were connected with speech.

The *second lesson* is that of a strange chronology. We need to take the history of the stages of the Written Word, as Henri-Jean Martin has recon-

structed that history from the evolution of writing as an object, and super-
impose it on the reference points and grids we are accustomed to.

Five thousand years ago (forty thousand years after the first tomb, five
thousand years after the first city, Jericho), the very first writings appeared
in Egypt, in Mesopotamia, and in China. At first, we have the mark, which
corresponded to "man's need to visualize his interpretations of the external
world by fixing them." A schematic house plan symbolized the house.
There was a long road from the graphic symbol to the first rudimentary
writing, and there was no writing without numbers.

Writing followed the first grains of wheat over four continents and
through three millennia. It all began in the Fertile Crescent with "calculators," small clay objects that date back seven thousand years and that
served to count sheep. The oldest function of the most archaic of all forms
of writing resembles the knot in a handkerchief: it was a "mnemonic device comparable, in the final analysis, to file cards." The *quipus* of Peru
were to some extent of the same nature. These individual aids to memory
"would lose all meaning in the eyes of anyone unfamiliar with their
context."

Is a collection of pictograms (1,500 of them in the case of the ancient
Sumerian tablets) already a writing system comprehensible without
knowledge of the language? As a whole it is rudimentary, polysemic, difficult to decipher, and not very handy for expressing abstractions. Those
first proto-writings were sumptuous memory aids—the stage of the Na-
huatls at the moment of the Spanish conquest. They have given rise to a
false debate: writing *lato sensu*, yes; *stricto sensu*, no. I prefer to reserve that
word for what seems to me its true birth.

For me, writing changes and becomes itself with phonetic representation, when the sign no longer simply designates an object but a sound.
Ancient Sumerian was a strongly monosyllabic language with agglutinating tendencies, as was Chinese when writing emerged in China. Pho-
netization permitted a reduction in the number of signs; the writing
material used—clay—commanded the use of fewer signs. The Akkadians
adapted cuneiform, using it to transcribe a Semitic language. Like the Chinese system of ideograms, cuneiform persisted because of what it transmitted beyond words, and it lasted long after the appearance of a much
more efficient system, the consonantal writing on papyrus used by the
Aramaeans.

But the true inventors of Writing were the Egyptians, both by right of priority and by the immediate emergence of phonetic representation. Let us pause a moment by the cradle of Writing. The Egyptians were the first to take the only truly capital step, but by what strange aberration, when they were so close to the solution, did they fail to move over the threshold between an unarticulated phonetism and a consonant alphabet? Admittedly, hieroglyphics already bore a graphic symbolism. Hieratic and demotic writing simplified the system but without breaking with it. There is more to these writing systems (and to the Chinese system, a fortiori) than just words. In China the first signs arose out of an interest in divination fully as much as out of a need to calculate and stimulate memory. These strongly symbolic writing systems have the property of solidifying and functioning according to a logic of their own totally disconnected from the flux of words. The young Chinese learns his first signs faster, but after an entire lifetime of learning he will never know all the signs.

This is why the Alphabet was the first important offshoot in the history of signs, words, modes of communication, and thought.

The Alphabet that so simplified matters was a humble affair: is it an exaggeration to call it the first gift of the barbarians? The story is a strange one. The alphabet came from Indo-Europeans and Semites—yes, from barbarians. Because the Hittites were not included in the symbolic networks that sacralized the signs of an extremely ancient writing—cuneiform, hieroglyphics, and ideograms—let us leave them aside. All sorts of things that originated elsewhere have been attributed to them, including iron and a prototype for future alphabets. The Linear A in Crete is composed of eighty-five signs standing for syllables and a good number of ideograms. Japanese is a good comparison. The true alphabet was Phoenician and Greek. The Egyptians had managed to isolate consonants; the next task was one of simplification and systemization. Next came the consonantal writing of all the Semitic languages, a marvelous mnemotechnic system that leaves vowels to memory and imagination. Its amphibology was eliminated by vowel points in Hebrew and was palliated in Arabic by extensive recitation of the Koran. It was the Greeks who thought of adding vowels to the consonants. When the Latin variant of the Greek system arose, the job was done.

Not so fast: What job? Two long millennia had to pass before the nineteenth century, when writing became what it is today—the near totality of Language—and when the triumph of a unifying national language made written language the only remaining literature and the only language. The history of writing by no means concerns pure spirit; writing is first and

foremost material. Its destiny was always closely linked to the physiology
of the hand, back, and eye and to the physical nature of writing materials—from fresh clay to wood and from bark to the palm leaf—that is, until
the arrival of Papyrus, the first universal Panacea.

Ancient civilization was as dependent on papyrus as we are on personal
computers. Until recently, no one realized this was so: admittedly Antiquity was not good at writing. Orality occupied a place that Frances A. Yates
was the first to help us to understand. Let me recapitulate: poetry, discourse, dialogue—the summits of ancient literature, from the *Iliad* to the
Bible and the Platonic dialogues—were speech; they had been said well
before they were written. One cannot read and write simultaneously;
people did not write, they dictated. The notebook close to hand is a constant exercise in memory. In a word, ancient thought required the constant
exercise of memory aided by the *scriptura continua* of scroll books. Perhaps
it is not the least lesson of this important book that it shows a curious
progression: the further we go back into antiquity the more difficult reading is. Look at the letters stuck together without punctuation, paragraphs,
or capital and lowercase letters: we see an airless, murky forest of leggy
sticks. It is as if the scribe had wanted to prevent any other reading than
reading out loud, a reading method confirmed in tens—better, in hundreds—of texts. As I read Henri-Jean Martin, a strange thought comes into
my head when I contemplate the paradoxical triumph, in the first and
second centuries, of this unreadable *scriptura continua* in the Mediterranean
basin, where the corpus of Inscriptions inclines us to think that the number
of people capable of deciphering them was relatively high. This paradoxical
triumph operated as a barrier to keep writing from forging ahead of its
oratorical referent. What gave value to writing was that it was rare, and its
rarity confined it within dense, rhythmic forms. What gave value to writing
was not only, nor principally, that it was writing, but rather that it was a
dense and compact discourse made to exercise memory. Ancient literature
tended to write down only what could be learned by heart.

It was not so much that the ancients lacked means; rather, they lacked
the need and the desire. That fact struck Henri Irénée Marrou, who, to my
knowledge, drew no conclusion from it. The Modernization of the Book,
the first of the great changes that led to the rotary press and photocompo-
sition in the span of some eighteen centuries, came with the use of parchment as a writing material and with the rational disposition of the book in
codex form, with cut and sewn sheets. This first advance was a gift from
late antiquity. It was, so to speak, the gift of the Ebb, a backwash of cre-

ation, a backward step taken by people capable of reading and doubtless of recitation.

What better expression could there be of the idea that the roots of a new advance in writing and a new relationship between the oral and the written were concomitant with an ebb tide that came within inches of a near-total loss of the keys to the code? It is understandable that historians befuddled by the decline of ancient written culture have failed to see that the humble technological roots of the Revolution of the Book lay in the trough of that decadence.

Nearly everything had to be relearned in full humility: Latin, the language of writing, which no longer coincided with the language currently spoken; letters, which evolved toward more readable shapes; majuscule and minuscule letters, which became differentiated while modest blank spaces appeared in the written line. It hardly matters that these facilitating devices were only a palliative for weaker skills, as if poverty, the loss of a richness, had established the critical mass needed for launching a spiral of change. Henri-Jean Martin shows us an unusual dimension of Scholastic knowledge in its awkward manipulation of an impoverished language.

The century of the great take-off was the fourteenth, the century of Paper and the first outpouring of reading in the vernacular. The new start happened *then*, it took off full tilt and foreshadowed all that followed.

But why put off your pleasure any more? I would like only to call your attention to the paradoxical chronology of the written. The great century of writing, the fourteenth, was also a century of impoverishment and retreat, thanks to the plague and to losses in the human fabric of society. The sixteenth century echoed the third. Decidedly, writing thrives on crisis.

I wonder if this paradox is not juxtaposing things of a different nature. There is a higher level: the practice of silent reading with the eyes alone became general in the thirteenth century. It was made possible by a more open presentation of texts that a decline in reading had made necessary. Scholasticism engendered humanism as its own counterpoint. And, as I have suggested elsewhere, intellectual history resulted from a tension between two approaches: first, the approach of the logician and of the university establishment (nominalist Scholasticism), which was detached from the text, seemed freer, but was in fact prematurely rigid; second, the philological approach, which remained close to the ground level of an immediate historical sense of the texts that had come from the preservation of an ancient Wisdom, a global Knowledge, a Word from the Beyond.

I must add, spontaneously and almost in contradiction to what I have just said, that the needs that led to printing make me think of an internal barbarian invasion. Everything started with paper. Paper permitted . . . a more commodious administration. Paper relieved memory; it permitted the recruitment of a "proletariat" who read neither much nor well, of *homines scribentes* not broken to the subtle arts of the memory. And paper used for political and commercial purposes . . . led to a rudimentary and mediocre literacy among awkward decipherers incapable of understanding Latin. If printing, which the Chinese had invented without ever doing anything with it (as with other innovations that went nowhere), developed in Latin Christendom rather than elsewhere, it was as a procedure for the diffusion for prayers and pious images and for a new access to God. The prayer of reading was a rudimentary sort of reading in the vernacular.

The paradox of printing was also a paradoxical shift in ends: invented to peddle broadsheets in German fairs, its triumph was Gutenberg's forty-two-line Bible.

The print revolution of the fifteenth century accomplished two things: it produced increasing numbers of flyers and broadsheets, and it helped solidify the gains of critical humanism. Thanks to the correction of proofs the book gained first in improved quality, then in increased speed and power. Printing at first served to proliferate low-cost broadsides and slim anthologies that were half text and half pictures and that helped readers with a newly acquired and hesitant literacy in the vernacular to acquire a nonliturgical relationship with God.

It is clear that without "salvation by Printing Alone" the success of the Protestant Reformation—even the Reformation itself—would have been unthinkable. Writing lies at the heart of Christianity, where it plays a secondary but highly comprehensible role: Christianity is a relationship with a Word—better, with a History—that gives history its meaning. Ancient writing was simply a mnemonic. Interpreting the shock of the sixteenth century as a clash between tradition and writing is a superficial view that barely touches the surface of things. The shock occurred within tradition; it was a conflict at the heart of a tradition centering on a way for bringing recollection to the surface of memory.

I would place the real destabilization of tradition at the beginning of the seventeenth century. More than by the Americas or by disenchantment, the intellectual universe was turned upside down by glass from Venice and Holland—the glass that served to make astronomical lenses, then telescopes and microscopes. In one century the sheer volume of information increased more than it had in ten thousand years. It was the multiplication of information that brought an end to the first writing that had stretched from cuneiform to the Gutenberg Bible, a writing that was an artificial device to aid the "Arts of Memory."

Turning points as important as this have to be taken slowly and gradually. No one took notes during the interminable sessions of the Parlement de Dijon during the proceedings for the rehabilitation of Lally-Tollendal in 1783. Taking notes would have raised eyebrows because the members of that Parlement, who had been trained in the rhetoric of the "good fathers," still knew how to use the Arts of Memory. The literary genres of the century of Louis XIV—epic poetry, tragedy, sermons—were still genres of the memorized and declaimed word.

The short reign of the Gutenberg Galaxy began at this turning point, the reign of an almost cancerous relationship of writing at the heart of the Empire of Discourse.

In the realm of orthotic devices for the brain the revolution brought on by microprocessors was of the same order of magnitude as cuneiform imprinted on soft clay or Gutenberg's punches. I refuse to weep for a lost paradise. Admittedly, the "losses" column is crowded as we approach the revolution brought about by the media and the computer. As in all things, "il faut reculer pour mieux sauter." There is no gain without loss.

Henri-Jean Martin's *The History and Power of Writing* is one of the greatest history books ever written. It speaks of the art of better use of the nearly untapped powers of the brain, that humble receptor for thought. I promise you a captivating voyage in his company.

Pierre Chaunu
de l'Institut

Acknowledgments

I wish to express my gratitude to Pierre Chaunu, who persuaded me to offer to the public the results of reflection that began in 1968. I would never have dared to undertake a work of this scope if I had not been assured of finding aid and friendship when it came to discussing sectors of this vast history not within my areas of special competence. My thanks thus go to Robert Marichal and André Vernet, to Guy Beaujouan, Jean Bottéro, Jean Irigoin, Claude Nicolet, Colette Sirat, Jean Vezin, Wladimir Vodoff, Brigitte Mondrain, and to my colleagues of the quatrième section of the Ecole Pratique des Hautes Etudes, who provided me with much information. I also thank my colleagues of the Ecole des Chartes, Pascale Bourgain, Robert-Henri Bautier, Jacques Monfrin, Emmanuel Poulle, and Bernard Barbiche. Many thanks as well to Roger Chartier, Jacques Fontaine, Robert Fossier, Frédéric Barbier, François Dupuigrenet Desroussilles, Jean and Geneviève Hasenohr, Yvonne Martin, Jacques Breton, Matei Cazacu, Dominique Coq, Jean-Pierre Drège, and Marianne Grivel, and also to Gilbert Ouy and Ezio Ornato. Thanks also to Patrick Kessel for his judicious advice and, finally, to Bruno Delmas, professor at the Ecole des Chartes and directeur des études of the Institut national des techniques documentaires, my co-author for chapter 10 of this volume, for which he provided the greater part of the documentation. And, lest I forget those who are no longer with us, I offer grateful remembrance to Lucien Febvre, who, at one of our last meetings, pointed out to me the way I am attempting to follow today, to Father François de Dainville, ever present for me, and to Michel de Certeau, who gave me advice even in his last illness.

I owe much to all of these. Nonetheless, once I was alone before my paper or my word-processor, it was I who had to compose, make decisions, take stands. Thus I alone am responsible for the inevitable errors that may crop up in this study.

H.-J. M.

One
Writing Systems

A ll history is first chronology. And anyone imprudent enough to risk studying the chronology of writing alternates ceaselessly between vertigo and myopia.

Let us begin with Gabriel Camps's *La préhistoire*, which will help us to situate the appearance of writing on the scale of the human adventure.[1] Ramapithecus left the forest for the savanna some twelve million years ago. Lucy, the oldest and most illustrious of the Australopithecus, was born some three million years ago. Australopithecus lived for two million years. Pithecanthropus erectus lived between 500,000 and 100,000 B.C. They mastered fire around 400,000 B.C. and from about 250,000 practiced the "Levallois" technique for forming stone tools by striking off flakes that implies a form of conceptual thought. Neanderthal man (roughly 100,000–30,000 B.C.) was capable of reflective thought. Finally, after 35,000 B.C. came Cro-Magnon man, who ushered in *Homo sapiens sapiens,* which is what we are.

At this point history accelerates. The "Neolithic revolution" happened some 10,000 years ago—just yesterday. The appearance of writing, which in some respects signaled the end of that era, goes back just a little more than five thousand years—which is practically today. If we were to write the annals of humanity and reserve the same space for each millennium, the historical period, the age of *homo scribens,* would barely fill the last page of the book. Vertigo and myopia: it makes one's head swim, but how short-sighted it is to reduce humankind's acts to this short span of historic time! Vertigo sets in again when we look back at the scale of those five thousand years: from 3200 to 1500 B.C., picto-ideographic systems pursued their long reign and continued for another 1,500 years. Our system of alphabetic writing was widespread in Greece at least eight centuries before the common era; as for Gutenberg, he lived only a little over five centuries ago. The era on which he put his mark would thus correspond to five lines in our annals. Our contemporary mass media would appear only in the last line, with telecommunications occupying no more space than a final "?".

Still, time is only relative. It goes faster as our lifetime goes on, and many of our contemporaries view the exponential acceleration of history today as humanity's race toward its own last judgment. Does this not obligate us to interrogate the past to try to understand what we are becoming? And, in particular, to seek to comprehend the mission of writing and the role of the logic of writing in the series of evolutions that saw man lose many of his original gifts as he acquired the knowledge and tools that enabled him to dominate nature?

SPEECH AND THE SIGN

Speaking and writing seem to us such natural acts that at first it seems inconceivable that they are the most complex inventions ever achieved by the human brain. And, in the last analysis, the most fundamental (in the full sense of the term), since they gave man mental tools that made all the rest possible.

This is true of language. We would love to know more precisely in what period and by what processes our most distant ancestors managed to acquire the intellectual faculty of conceiving symbols, combining them, and expressing them by gestures and sounds (Gabriel Camps). Unfortunately, no one can ever explain to us how early man managed to appropriate this form of mastery over things and beings, which implies a capacity to define them and to communicate experiences and decisions to fellow creatures.

Let me at least attempt to pose the problem. The human brain can be likened to a machine that functions on several levels, the higher of which provide the faculties of abstraction and synthesis. The skeletal remains that have come down to us seem to show that the most primitive anthropoids already had human characteristics, even if their brain cavities were smaller than our own and their frontal lobes smaller in proportion to the rest of their brains. Nonetheless, the evolution that was set off among the hominids when they adopted an upright position, thus liberating the hands and enabling the mouth, no longer needed for grasping, to take on other uses, favored what André Leroi-Gourhan has called the opening of the cortical fan. It freed the rear of the cranium, which could become more rounded. The midbrain contracted into a tighter curve. The facial mass eventually became less prominent, the jaw became more detached, and the forehead became higher and broader. Thus the zones of the middle cortex, which control language, could expand notably even before enlarged frontal lobes favored the exercise of higher brain functions.[2]

Thus the Word came into being during a period that perhaps lasted longer than a million years. Although the continual extension of the surface of the cortex during this long evolution was certainly the cause and not the consequence of an increasing social integration, it nonetheless furnished the first men with better means for survival, defense, and attack. Undeniably, all progress was then conditioned by a dual technology involving the hand and the tool first and the face and language second. It is equally undeniable that developments in speech were closely connected with developments in actions, thus connected with tools, whose making required increasingly complex sets of operations. We will never know whether Australopithecus could already pronounce a few words referring to a concrete reality, nor can we measure the slow progress of speech in *Homo erectus.*

What should instead be emphasized is the acceleration that preceded the dawn of historic time. There is increasing evidence that in the Upper Paleolithic man conquered the means for speculative thought. Somewhat earlier than 50,000 B.C., for example, he began to bury his dead—a first indication that he now situated himself in a greater time span and a first sure manifestation of preoccupations of a religious nature. In roughly the same epoch he began picking up stones and shells that seemed to him curious, as if in quest of the fantastic in nature. Similarly he began to make decorative objects, to sculpt stones, bones, or wood with the aid of flint, to scrape ocher and manganese to make coloring agents, and to use animal hairs to make brushes. From about 50,000 to 30,000 B.C. he limited his efforts to incising more or less regular series of lines, dots, or hatch marks. Beginning between 35,000 and 25,000 B.C. he practiced a figurative art still limited to parts of the body, the most explicit forms of which were ovoid female shapes and animal heads and forequarters. Only very gradually did these figures come to be organized into the realism that we see in the great monuments of cave painting: Lascaux is no older than 15,000 B.C.; Altamira and Niaux date only from 13,000 to 8000 B.C. When the people of the Neolithic became sedentary, the hunters' art disappeared, thus ending the first of the artistic cycles leading from abstraction and symbolism to an increasingly detailed but colder realism.

At the outset, the prehistoric artist attempted to translate inner rhythms or an abstract vision of perceptible realities. His art only very gradually came to resemble nature: at first, parts or attributes seemed to symbolize the whole, with the result that the oldest graphic manifestations resemble writing as much as works of art. He eventually seized the essence of each object, and he succeeded in rendering receding perspective in remarkable attempts at schematization that must have been closely associated with efforts at verbal definition. These artists were not interested in showing all figures on the same scale, and like the Greeks, who depicted the gods as larger than men, they could give a gigantic size to the animals whose role in their imagery they probably considered essential. Even granting that the overall design of their compositions was guided by aesthetic and decorative concerns, we feel that their groupings obey a logic that escapes us and that corresponds to forms of symbolic organization that have nothing to do with our own representation of space or the linear conception of time that we have learned from writing.

His artistic activities permit us to surmise that man in the later Upper Paleolithic had mastered some form of language. The languages of primitive peoples today often show relational systems of a structural subtlety far superior to that of our written languages and that correspond to visions of the world that differ from our own. Unfortunately no one will ever know the language or languages spoken by the populations who occupied what is now France and Spain toward the end of the ice age. In particular, we cannot know how those languages expressed the notions of what we call space and time.

Recourse to graphic expression seems to have represented man's need to give visual form to his interpretations of the external world; to fix those interpretations and make them concrete in order to define them better; to take possession of them, communicate with the superior forces, and transmit what he had learned to his fellows.

This, then, is the universe of signs and symbols. Used from prehistoric times to establish relations with other people, they have been used with increasing frequency since the invention of writing (which is, after all, simply one system of signs among many others) and with even greater frequency with the advent of audiovisual techniques.

In reality everything became symbol or sign for man as he became part of a cohesive milieu. His posture, his clothing, and his ornaments all reflected the place he occupied within the community. A schematic drawing of a house symbolized relations among those who occupied it just as naturally as a symbol for the city expressed the social order that should reign in it. Similarly, individuals' names evoked membership in a family or a group and the existence of privileged ties with the beings and forces those names once designated.

Thus the symbol, the instrument for socialization par excellence, is the source of all means of communication. It underlies a good number of systems of signs. One example is the totem pole. There is a pole from British

Columbia in the Musée de l'Homme in Paris that is sixteen meters high and whose sculpted figures represent the genealogy of a chief of the Otter Totem. Or there were staffs used to denote command. Many primitive societies used them, and we are still familiar with their latter-day forms such as the royal scepter or the marshall's baton, but also the bishop's and the abbot's crosier, originally a shepherd's crook and the emblem of the Good Shepherd. There are also message sticks, sticks that tell a tale or recall a genealogy, or the aboriginal Australian churingas that, Leroi-Gourhan has remarked, resemble certain prehistoric carved objects. Such objects, marked with notches or covered with incised or painted signs, usually in the form of geometric designs, undoubtedly had a mnemonic value and helped the orator or the officiant (who, it seems, followed the designs with his finger as he spoke or chanted) to establish contact with what was represented abstractly on them and to evoke them better.

Many other examples could be cited. In the Marquesas Islands there are string games that accompany the recitation of genealogies or the innumerable couplets of songs. In worlds still dominated by magical thought, these are instruments for the evocation of remembered things that in some ways (the paradox should not be stretched too far) prefigure the arts of memory of classical antiquity and the rosary. Can these primitive systems be called language? Certainly. Herodotus has left us an illuminating anecdote in this regard. One day, King Darius received from the Scythians a frog, a mouse, a bird, and some arrows. He at first interpreted this gift as a form of homage, but his father-in-law, more perspicacious than he, revealed its real meaning: "Unless you hide in the swamps like a frog or under the ground like a mouse, or take to the air like a bird, we will pierce you with our arrows." This anecdote shows the polysemy of the language of objects when they undergo no coding. Among the first examples of such codes are marks of possession. They appear with seals, before writing but in the same milieus as writing. As time went by, possession marks took on the characteristics of escutcheons, shop signs, or even brand names. They soon "spoke" directly, for example when the thing depicted corresponded to a proper name. They also could bear multiple symbols and at times became abstract. As such signs became codified and simplified within societies more ruled by reason, however, they lost their evocative resonance, somewhat in the same way that depictions of ancient myths lost resonance when their forms were developed in the Renaissance. Such depictions are evidence of the universality of a certain form of wisdom, and they became a game for wits fond of devising emblems and a pretext for most of the painters who made use of them. By the Counter-Reformation they had become strictly codified in the iconologies of Cesare Ripa and his imitators. Their symbolism was stripped away but, as if in compensation, they could be grasped more rapidly than the written texts they illustrated.

These are of course well-known facts, but they lead us to wonder whether the Gospel according to St. John is really right in proclaiming that "In the beginning was the Word." The Dogon people may be wiser, since they often feel the need to draw before they explain, and they proclaim the primacy of drawing over speech in their myth of the creation:

> God, in creating, thought: before naming things, he drew them in his creative intention. . . . Creation, as it was offered to man, bore the mark of this divine intention, which he attempts to decipher and whose symbols he in turn reproduces. . . . It was by naming things that man affirmed his hold over them. If there had been no human consciousness to receive it and reproduce it, the divine word would have remained without response, hence without life.[3]

If we take all this into account, we can see that the primitive anthropoid, who had to learn to master and organize his acts in order to make tools and survive, must have expressed himself with gestures as much as words. And that *Homo sapiens,* endowed with reflective thought, was able to develop both graphic schematization and verbal conceptualization as he attempted to analyze the universe. As a representation of external realities, graphic communication seems more objective, or at any rate more concrete, than linguistic communication. By gathering data together in a globalizing vision, graphic means can also transcribe and dispose those data according to a logic that has nothing to do with our notions of figuration and perspective. Just as speech must use abstract symbols to express visible realities, the image needs a concretizing symbolic system to transcribe abstract notions. Deciphering the image thus requires a more active participation on the part of the receiver, and it offers larger possibilities of interpretation, thanks to the polysemy of pictorial representations.

One can of course imagine graphic languages—let us not call them writing systems or scripts—that would owe nothing to speech and that would offer their own forms of logic. This has been attempted repeatedly, at times with success. Nonetheless any form of writing that attempts to go beyond perceptible reality and to testify to all of human experience cannot avoid trying to realize the difficult combination of coded graphic representation on a two-dimensional surface and speech, which unfolds in time. As we shall see, this is a difficult marriage in which one party must always impose its law on the other.

THE BIRTH OF WRITING: IDEOGRAPHIC SYSTEMS

Writing, as it is generally understood, appeared on four continents over three millennia. Many of the systems that were elaborated remain unknown to us; others have disappeared, leaving no descendants. There is for example the as-yet undeciphered writing system of Harappa and Mohenjo Daro on the Indus River (late third–early second millennium); there are the Mesoamerican "near writings" that arose, as best we know, during the first century B.C. and were wiped out by the Spanish conquest. Still other systems—those of the Middle East, the oldest of which date from the end of the fourth millennium—have founded linguistic families that continue from one branch to another to our own day. Another system, the Chinese, has continued almost unchanged in the East, and it has served as a model for other peoples, notably the Japanese. Can one find a common context for the rise of these systems?

The first thing to note—and it takes us back to the Paleolithic era, sending us first to the Middle East—is that toward the eleventh and twelfth millennia, climate changes brought an end to the glacial era. This meant that man, who until then had turned most of his energies to adapting to nature, could attempt to dominate it. Communication techniques and ways to transmit knowledge took on greater importance. While Magdalenian art disappeared as if engulfed, the natural milieu in which the fate of humanity was at stake was totally renewed. Hunting and gathering civilizations thrived. Then, in the eighth millennium, came the greatest change human society has ever known: the "Neolithic revolution."

It was long thought that an increased population's need to find enough to eat was what incited man to move from the predator stage to that of producer, and that settling down in one place, the logical consequence of that change, had itself engendered fixed agglomerations. Events appear to have followed a somewhat more complex course. It has been discovered that as early as the tenth century—hence before this process began—stable villages were constituted in Anatolia and in Palestine. Sedentary cultures thus appear to have been the result (at least to some extent) of a way of thinking occurring when groups that had habitually broken up when they began to be too numerous resolved their contradictions as their society was already beginning to change.

From that moment on, human thought was concentrated in towns and cities around which exploitation of the soil had already been established. Henceforth space and time, which ruled human activities more and more strictly, were measured from fixed centers above which the celestial vault seemed to turn. It was certainly not by chance that the first known writing systems—systems that took the flux of words unfolding in time and transcribed them along a line in space—arose within societies in which the new form of organization was most accentuated. Writing arose among agricultural peoples, usually peoples settled along the banks of fertilizing rivers or on lands whose intensive cultivation required a clear division of labor and a rigorous hierarchy. And it arose in city-states dominated by a theocracy.

Mesopotamia

We can follow this process in the ancient Near East.[4] In the eighth millennium agriculture began to be practiced in fertile terrain in Anatolia and near the Persian Gulf. These populations practiced seed selection and cultivated wild grains, the origin of our first cereals. First sheep then goats were domesticated in Iran as early as the ninth or the eighth millennium. Oxen came next (sixth millennium). At the same time, people began to make ceramics, they learned how to construct square-cornered houses, and, since they had acquired a sense of yield and return, they attempted to foresee future needs by stocking their excess produce more systematically and by developing production for trade.

At this point their minds were occupied by three main concerns: finding appropriate ways to count or measure their goods, specifying clearly and indisputably the terms and the outcomes of increasingly complex transactions, and foreseeing the future.

In southern Anatolian agglomerations dating from the seventh millennium, incised seals for impressing identifying marks have been found, and excavations, for example, in a seventh-millennium Neolithic village at Qualaat Djarmo in Iraqi Kurdistan, have unearthed small clay objects that some have held to be toys but that seem more likely to be counting pieces much like the tokens or pebbles still used in a good number of primitive societies. It is quite conceivable that people attempted to devise better systems of graphic notation in such milieus, but if such attempts were to succeed they needed a stable climate and social stability. Fortunately this occurred in the sixth millennium in southern Mesopotamia, south of the site of the first known irrigation works at Tell es-Sawan and near modern

Samarra. During the sixth millennium the region was conquered by Sumerians, a people of unknown origin and of an agglutinating and monosyllabic language. Gradually the Akkadians, a nomadic people who spoke a Semitic language, settled among them. The result was city-states like Uruk, where the royal couple was worshiped as the incarnation of a divine couple.

It was not from Uruk, however, but from the city of Susa farther to the west that we can best grasp (thanks to recent discoveries) why writing arose in that region. When the city was founded, the rich plain of Sus was a dependency of a "high country" on the Iranian plateau called Elam. Stylistically advanced vases were made there that bear a figured decoration that had nothing to do with writing. When the city declined it was attached to Uruk, which made it part of a larger whole and encouraged the development of exchanges over a vast geographical area. From then on procedures for registering transactions and managing an accumulating wealth proliferated. One of the first of these was the use of cylindrical seals more as signs to sanction an agreement between contracting parties than as personal marks. Around 3500 B.C. clay seals known as *bullae* appeared, some of which enclosed *calculi* in a variety of shapes to represent specific quantities of foodstuffs. It became customary to mark notches on these wrappings to indicate the quantities involved and to impress each *bulla* with a seal. Certain *calculi* found in Susa represent objects (pitchers) or animals (ox heads); the accompanying notches and bars expressed the counts in the sexagesimal system. There are also clay tablets from Susa bearing the imprint of a seal accompanied by figures that may be a simplification of the system of *bullae*. A new stage appeared in Uruk during those same years. The tablets excavated in the temple of the goddess Inanna contain not only notches of various sorts but also pictograms obviously intended for remembering business transactions. The signs that can be identified (usually quite simple ones) evoke easily recognizable objects: a head or other part of a human or animal body, an ear of grain, or a garden represented by a rectangle and two trees drawn without perspective, as was customary in Sumerian art.

These tablets are far from explicit to those who examine them today. Although we have some comprehension of the number system they employ, we cannot know whether the graphic signs that accompany them correspond to a foodstuff or to the name of a person taking part in the eventual transaction. Nor can we grasp the exact nature of the operation they note. According to Jean Bottéro they may be mnemonics comparable, in the final analysis, to file cards that, when removed from their file box, lose all meaning in the eyes of someone unfamiliar with the context.

Very soon, however, the Mesopotamians made this system into a true script. One of the major obstacles to the development of pictographic writing is the proliferation of signs: the early tablets of the Sumerians show at least 1,500 pictograms. Also, it was difficult to indicate abstract notions by such concrete means. This led to giving each sign other related values. The sign of the lower part of the head thus represented the mouth, nose, and teeth, but also speech or a shout. Similarly, a foot also indicated walking, standing, and so forth. In other cases two pictograms were joined to express a new idea: the mouth and bread signified the action of eating; the eye plus water denoted tears. Finally, some signs were added to another sign to show how the first sign should be interpreted: thus the sign for a plow coupled with the sign for wood signified the implement; coupled with the symbol for man it represented the plowman.

In principle a system of this sort offers the advantage of being universally comprehensible no matter what language the sender and the receiver speak, provided that they are acquainted with the symbol used in that social system and with the thing it refers to. Two parallel lines to evoke amity and two crossed lines to express enmity were equally accessible (or inaccessible) to all. Somewhat less accessible was the pubic triangle that traditionally evoked the woman, which, joined to the three hills that evoked the mountains (hence the foreign lands beyond) signified a woman imported from abroad or a female slave. To cite another example, the notion of "king" was rendered by the sign for "man" and the sign for "great," which originally depicted a fly-swatter, the emblem of royal grandeur.

It was possible to jog the memory by this sort of juxtaposition of notions but not to construct a language capable of clearly imparting new information or, for instance, movement or relationship among beings and things. In other words, to use Aristotelian terms, it could render substances better than accidents. Thus if people wanted to avoid the drawbacks of using two languages, each with its own form of logic, they would have to base their writing system on spoken language, and that meant phonetism.

In order to understand the use of phonetic symbols in Sumerian writing we need to know something about spoken Sumerian. First, Sumerian was a largely monosyllabic language and contained a large number of homophones. The sound *du*, for example, had at least eleven meanings, each expressed by a different ideogram. (Modern languages do much the same thing when they use different spellings to distinguish between homophones.) Second, Sumerian was an agglutinating language that expressed grammatical relationships by juxtaposing to invariable "full words" symbols for prefixes, affixes, and suffixes (called "hollow words") that had no meaning in themselves but that corresponded to sounds.

The first traces of phonetism found to date appear in a tablet from Djemdet-Nasr perhaps composed only a century after the first known tablets. Two pictograms that seem to give the name of the greatest of the Mesopotamian gods, En-lil (Lord Wind) are followed by an arrow. Since the arrow was sounded *ti* in Sumerian and is a homophone of *ti*, "life," scholars have deduced that it was a proper noun that followed the Sumerian rules of anthroponymy and placed the person in question under the protection of the god En-lil. Thus the sign might be rendered as "Lord-Wind-Vivify."

Although it was an essential discovery, this ingenious expedient—and let me hasten to add that other peoples used it wherever pictographic writing reached this same stage of development—was considered only a convenient way to specify certain bits of information. For example, it permitted the transcription of words of foreign origin by a technique resembling that of the rebus. It also helped to indicate the meaning of certain polysemic ideograms by indicating their pronunciation, and it helped to express shades of meaning and to increase linguistic precision. On certain occasions, for instance, a plural came to be shown not by reproducing the same sign several times, as was customary, but by adding a sign corresponding to the suffix *mesh*, which indicated a plural in the spoken language. For a very long time, however—until the age of Eannatum of Lagash (ca. 2400 B.C.)—morphological elements were only exceptionally designated by phonetic signs.

These methods permitted a considerable reduction in the number of signs—roughly 800 at the height of Fara (ca. 2600 B.C.). The system evolved, however, after the latter half of the third millennium, thanks especially to its use by other peoples. Around 2350 B.C., when the Akkadians became the majority in the population and took over, their scribes undertook a more systematic notation of their eastern Semitic language, which used three consonants in a fixed order to form the invariable root of every word and to serve as a support for a variety of vowels. The Akkadians adapted Sumerian writing and respected its principles: they retained the system of ideograms (at least in certain cases) and simply read them in their own language. Above all, however, they drew up a syllabary adapted to their language by giving a sound value to ideograms that had no independent meaning. They also enriched the Sumerian system in a variety of other ways and attempted to find devices for transcribing (at least approximately) sounds in their language that did not exist in Sumerian.

This is the history of the first known writing, albeit in too rapid and schematic an overview. Many lacunae of course persist in the extant documentation on the origins of writing, and new discoveries might make it necessary to revise one interpretation or another. I might note that in the first pictograms the scribes utilized a system of symbolic reference and notional interpretation that preexisted the thing represented. This fact has led one scholar, Jean-Marie Durand, to reject the version of the appearance of writing that I have just presented. Durand says:

> The production of writing certainly did not respond to a need based in utility, as has naively been thought by projecting back to its origins the use that was subsequently made of it. Indeed, the creation of writing was, at its origins, merely a technique corrupted—to wit, going one step beyond reading the message inscribed by the gods on divinatory materials, [a process] that was given concrete form in the choice of a new writing material and in the creation of a system of original signs to codify what exists. Then the text due to human initiative appeared.

For Durand the rational management of goods and a recourse to calculation preceded discourse about them. This means, Durand explains, that the first known texts are

> not "redactions in themselves," which would leave one to suppose that they qualify as memoranda, but in fact are "discourses for others." This becomes evident on examination of the first texts concerning land sales: difficulties arose concerning the acquisition of a parcel of land that had originally been community property. Thus the text was the magical means that prevented the parties from going back on an agreement, and it proclaimed this in the most solemn manner possible. The writing material used for sales contracts was often stone, an extremely rare commodity in Mesopotamia but one that was often chosen so the event would be kept in mind. Finally, this text was often deposited in a temple.[5]

One might of course wonder to what extent the Sumerians were truly the initiators of this system, given that the use of pictograms comes naturally to man. It seems, moreover, that clay replaced stone, and, as we shall see, the use of clay tablets led to the schematization of cuneiform writing. It would also be somewhat paradoxical to deny that writing developed in Sumer above all in response to new needs of an essentially economic sort and in an epoch in which increased wealth, the concentration of wealth, and accelerated exchanges made it necessary to keep accounts.

The script that developed in this manner became extraordinarily complex, since in principle the same sign could have several ideographic meanings and several phonetic values. It was deciphered more than it was read; nevertheless, it was used (more often, it is true, in simplified forms) for more than three thousand years. From Sumer it spread throughout the Middle Euphrates region, and it gained wide diffusion thanks to the military enterprises of the Semitic dynasty of Agade. When the Sumerians gained the upper hand once more they produced a true literature. In the long run the Sumerians merged into the Akkadian mass, but their language, like Latin in Europe, remained the language of religious and literary culture until the end of Mesopotamian civilization. It was thanks to cuneiform writing that Akkadian became understood throughout the Middle East. The vehicle for a number of imperialisms, it served not only to note languages as different as Sumerian and Akkadian but also Eblaite (Syria, third millennium), Elamitic (second to the first millennium), Hurrian (northern Mesopotamia, particularly in the second millennium), and Urartian (Armenia, first millennium), and, more sporadically, Palaic (an Indo-European dialect, Turkey, first millennium), Hittite (Anatolia, mid-second millennium), and a number of other languages. Finally, it contributed to the constitution of the Ugaritic alphabet (Syria, fourteen–thirteenth centuries B.C.) and the Old Persian syllabary alphabet (southwest Iran, fifth–third centuries B.C.).

Cuneiform writing transmitted an entire cultural tradition through the generations. It is not too surprising that the Mesopotamians and those in their sway remained loyal to their traditional system, even when (in the latter half of the second millennium) other apparently simpler writing systems appeared—notably the consonantal writing on papyrus used by the Aramaeans, who were becoming an omnipresent ethnic group in the Near East. As in all societies, there were several hierarchies in the small world of the scribes who practiced cuneiform. People who specialized in practical tasks did not need to know the arcane complexities of a rich graphic system, which means that complexity did not seem (for example to the Akkadians) to be a defect. Complexity permitted ingenious shortcuts by the use of ideograms, or it permitted syllables to be spelled out phonetically.

Moreover it could render vowels as well as all the consonants, unlike new systems that seemed more like mnemonic devices in this respect. We can see that the study and assimilation of this material accumulated over millennia required an ongoing initiation. Interplay among the various levels of language and recourse to rare ideograms were taken as ways to hide access to superior truths from the noninitiate, particularly since the original Sumerian notion that every simple sign corresponded to a concept or a group of ideas and every complex sign to a speculation could be discerned, like a watermark, in the fabric of the written text. The Akkadians used writing as something like a grid for comprehension of the world, just as the constellations were "the writing of the heavens." Writing seemed to them a form of wisdom come down from time immemorial (René Labat).

One example of how the Akkadian scribes used the ambiguities of their originally Sumerian script to draw conclusions in conformity with their own logic is the *Poem of Creation*. This work ends with a paraphrased enumeration of the fifty names that the gods who became subjects of the god Marduk gave to him, each of which corresponds to an appellation (nearly all of Sumerian origin) that speaks of his destiny.

In tablets found in Ashurbanipal's library scribes offered a sort of gloss on this text to show that the explanations in the poem were simply ways to render those names more explicit. To this end they used their bilingual training to list the Sumerian terms and their Akkadian equivalents in parallel columns. This supposes that at least in certain cases all Sumerian graphs of a given sign could be taken as semantically equivalent. Thus the cuneiform sign for a star could be read equally well as *dingir* or *an* and could be understood semantically as "God," "What is superior" or "dominant," and could even be extended to concepts like "lord," "government," and so forth. Hence by following this system one could demonstrate that the name "Asari" showed that Marduk was simultaneously "Giver of agriculture," "Founder of the land roll," "Creator of cereals and fibers," and "Producer of all that grows green." This was in no way a learned game but rather a treatise *De divinis nominibus,* to use a Latin expression, and an interpretation of sacred texts. Those who had elaborated this method of investigation undoubtedly believed that they had found a key to learning, a rule of logic, and a law of knowledge and of the acquisition of truth.[6]

The long history of the earliest known writing system places us at the heart of problems that we will have to confront throughout this book. The boon granted to cuneiform writing, as we have seen, was to have benefited from the continuity of civilization in Mesopotamia. Cuneiform took hold throughout the Middle East thanks to the dynamism of Mesopotamian merchants but also to the might of the imperialisms it served. Today it seems enormously complex. But the concreteness that its pictographic origins provided, its associations of ideas, and the interplay between image and word of its ideograms were perfectly suited to the logic of the peoples who invented and used it.

All writing is tied to the form of thought of the civilization that created it and to which its destiny is linked. The peoples of the Middle East adopted and modified cuneiform writing as long as Mesopotamia remained a living source of energy. The history of the decadence and disappearance of cuneiform corresponded to alliances among other dynamic economic powers and other imperialisms. At that point cuneiform returned to its source, the land of Sumer, dying where it had been born some three thousand years before.

Egypt

Writing appeared in Egypt around 3150 B.C.,[7] thus, if current chronologies are accurate, one or two centuries after it appeared in Sumer. Because the two lands had close relations some have spoken of borrowing, but it might be a case of independent creation in two neighboring societies that had reached a comparable stage of development.

Egypt accomplished its agrarian revolution later than Mesopotamia (in the fifth millennium), but it soon caught up. Small states had grown up on the banks of the Nile under the aegis of totemic powers who later peopled the pharaonic pantheon, and there were artisans highly skilled in cutting stone and sculpting ivory.

The appearance of writing, which coincided with the upsurge of an entire civilization, marked the point of maturity of a way of life. We find it difficult to imagine that the Egyptians, who must have been just as interested in counting their wealth as the Sumerians, did not utilize writing for this purpose from the start. We have nothing to attest to such interests, however, before the third millennium, perhaps because by the fourth millennium scribes were already using papyrus, a highly perishable medium. Thus we have bookkeeping tablets excavated from the sands of Mesopotamia, and the banks of the Nile have furnished marked pottery, slate cosmetic palettes, stone club-heads, funerary steles, ivory tablets, cylindrical seals and imprints on jar-stoppers, and rock graffiti. This means we have clear evidence that, before the paintings and the sculptures of the great pharaonic tombs were made, hieroglyphs arose out of a systemization of the graphic techniques of earlier times.

This is illustrated by one of the oldest known documents bearing Egyptian characters, the palette of King Narmer, a sovereign held to have unified Egypt who reigned around 3150 B.C. The palette uses a variety of symbolic techniques. On one side Narmer is shown wearing the high headdress that later signaled the pharaohs' domination over southern Egypt. He brandishes a mace over an enemy whom he holds kneeling before him. Next to him a hawk—the god Horus—plunges the head of another enemy into a swamp symbolized by a clump of reeds. The lower part of the palette depicts two defeated adversaries, accompanied by identifying signs. On the other side of the stone two men hold ropes restraining two feline creatures with long and intertwined necks who may represent dangers surmounted. On the upper portion Narmer, this time wearing the crown of the delta lands, advances accompanied by dignitaries and preceded by four bearers of standards depicting animal heads. Two rows of decapitated enemies are piled up before the procession. At the bottom, a bull, the incarnation of royal might, tramples an enemy and destroys a fortress.[8]

This object served as an enormous commemorative medal whose graphic conventions and schematization attest to a very advanced social symbolism. The palette also bears written legends on both sides of its upper portions. Inside a royal palace represented by a few conventional lines there are two characters, a catfish and a sculptor's chisel, which gave the phonetic values *n'r* and *mr,* or the consonant framework of the famous sovereign's name. A group of hieroglyphs including the same signs placed above one personage in the royal suite tells us that he is Narmer's sandal-bearer.

Thus from the outset the Egyptians seem to have created a writing system that used phonetics and included signs to represent consonants either in isolation or in groups of two or three. There was nothing to prevent Egyptian scribes from creating a consonantal alphabet, as the Phoenicians, for example, were to do later. The Egyptians preferred to put phonetism to the service of a graphic symbolism, in particular in their religious and historical texts—which makes their solemn writing, hieroglyphics, a paradise for semiologists.

Like cuneiform characters, hieroglyphs can have the value of ideograms, phonograms, or determinatives. The sign for the sun-god provides a simple example. Since the ideogram (the solar disc) might cause confusion because it also meant "day" and was thus a polyphone, two phonograms were added to it, a human mouth for *r* and a forearm in profile for the aspirated laryngeal consonant *ayin*, thus providing the consonantal skeleton of the name (a third and final consonant was left out).

Although the system was complicated—it used 760 signs, 220 of which were in current use under the Middle Kingdom—it permitted the scribes to avoid all ambiguity.

In principle, hieroglyphic writing is read from right to left either in vertical columns or in horizontal lines. Words are not separated from one another, but a line or a column does not end in the middle of a word. Each sign is divided into quadrants, small invisible squares of equal size, each one of which can contain two signs arranged horizontally or vertically, four small signs, or even one larger sign and two small ones.

We need to pause a moment over the figures that these signs represented. They offer us a complete repertory of everything to be found in the Nile Valley, from the weather to the landscape, from men to animals, from agricultural products to "manufactured" objects, and of course including the gods. Taken together they suggest innumerable concordances and symbolic values. The rules for inserting these characters into the quadrants show that the signs did not correspond to the size of the represented object. The giraffe is shown no bigger than the scarab. There were two good reasons for this: first, the represented object's importance as a sign had no relation to its actual size; second, the system allowed every figure (represented without regard to the laws of perspective) to be as clear and immediately comprehensible as the signs placed by the sides of highways or in public places today.

These rules—or rather these conventions—were applied with a flexibility surprising to anyone accustomed to the rigidity of modern phonetic writing systems. The scribe could vary a sign that he had to repeat several times, as if to personalize it. For example, when two people were talking he could reverse the signs attached to one person and point them in the direction of that person's interlocutor. Scribes also shifted the place of signs within a word for aesthetic reasons (graphic metathesis). Similarly certain words such as "king" or "god" were placed before other words that would normally be pronounced first in such expressions as "servant of the king" or "priest of the god." In a like spirit the lines and columns of inscriptions on a stele might change direction, either for aesthetic reasons or in order to adapt them to a representation such as the image of a god. On other occasions bas-reliefs show an interpenetration between the representation of personages or scenes and the legends that accompany them. All this is proof that the Egyptians held the hieroglyphs to be living representations of reality much more than abstract signs charged with a transcription of spoken discourse.

The scribes were quite naturally urged to use all the resources of a system in which each sign could take on different ideographic or phonetic values and to invent variations that would highlight the parallel between the language of speech and the language of images. Pascal Vernus offers an illustration of this procedure:

> Here is an example of writing games: The god Toum (*TeMW*), a solar demiurge, will be written "sportingly" (to use the English school term) with the aid of the sign of the scarab, which in this case stands for T, and the sign for water, read MW, the combination giving *TeMW* thus the consonant structure of the name of the god. At the same time the group obtained is the image of the rising sun, often figured as a scarab who pushes the sun between his feet as he emerges from the primordial ocean, like Toum at the birth of the world. The signifying function of the image is displayed here on two levels: that of the conventional sign that bears the sound and that of the image.[9]

Hieroglyphic writing was undeniably solemn. The Egyptians used simpler writing systems, first hieratic then demotic, especially to note utilitarian texts on papyrus. The orthographic refinements just discussed are seen only occasionally during the Dynastic period, but they proliferated during the Ptolemaic epoch, when a lettered clergy enlarged the repertory of signs from about 760 to several thousand. These were not simple stylistic exercises, however. The Egyptians believed that the images used to write a text could develop superior truths by constituting a metalanguage capable, in the final analysis, of revealing the text's internal ideology. For them, speech and image were linked to the substance of the being that they reproduced or designated.

They believed in the creative virtue of words and in their dangerous power. After all, Isis had become mistress of the universe by forcing Ra, the old sun-god, to reveal his name to her, by which she could disarm him. Personal names, which normally included an invocation to or a relationship with the divine powers, were not simple signs of identification. It was for a good reason that the god Thoth, the patron of scribes and master of the hieroglyphs who was secretary to the gods and knew their speech, was reputed to be a dangerous magician. The writing of a word had the same powers as the word itself, and this was equally true of images, which, according to an extremely ancient belief, were endowed with a life of their own.

Thus the images, inscriptions, and portraits to be seen painted or carved on the temples and the tombs were not representations or remembrances of disappeared realities but living realities that profited the gods and the dead. Keys to survival, they had no need to be looked at or read in order to be animated with their own existence. By the same token we can understand why so many reliefs, statues, and inscriptions were damaged. Destroying the effigy or the name of a dead enemy was an effective way to kill a second time, eliminate him definitively, and take from him all power to do harm. Conversely, the scrolls bearing the name of a dead pharaoh were often carefully hidden in order to assure his survival, and in the subterranean apartments of the royal tombs scribes and artists put arrows through the signs reputed to be dangerous, or amputated certain of their parts to render them harmless.

The Greeks and Romans perhaps did not always understand that hieroglyphics were a form of writing when they saw the immense monuments that lined the Nile Valley. They saw them instead as traces of an ancient and secret wisdom. Throughout the centuries those monuments have been interrogated in an attempt to understand the power and the secret of the images and their language. Moreover, how many statues were (and continue to be) destroyed? How many inscriptions were (and still are) defaced by successive civilizations to announce reforms, revolutions, and victories? How many inscriptions did those civilizations put in places where they could not be read? And who among us has not paused before pronouncing or writing a definitive word?

Why should such behavior exist? And why should it be so persistent if not because it corresponds to the natural mechanisms of human thought?

China

Writing appeared in China, as it did in Mesopotamia and in Egypt, when a people—in this case the Hua—became agricultural and sedentary. In the case of China this came at the price of a hard-won conquest of the lower basin of the Huang Ho or Yellow River.[10] According to tradition, three emperors played a particular role in the birth of writing. One, Fu Hsi, was thought to have invented divination by casting yarrow stalks and interpreting the designs they made. The second, Shen Nung, supposedly taught the use of a tally system of lengths of string, perhaps resembling the *quipus* of the Incas, to register events, keep accounts, and possibly seal contracts. Finally, Cang Ji, a minister of the third emperor, Huang Ti, was reputed to have invented writing "after having studied the celestial bodies and their formation and the natural objects around him, in particular the tracks of birds and animals" (Vandermeersch).

All this is legend. But two things stand out. First, the earliest procedures for notation arose in China for the purpose of divination but also out of a need to calculate and keep accounts. Second and more important, writing had to express something of the natural order of the world. In Chinese, the word *wen,* antonyms for which are *wu,* "warrior," and *zhi,* "raw material, not yet polished or decorated," signifies a "set of marks," the simple written character, but it also refers to the vein in stone or the grain in wood, to bird tracks, to the tracings on a tortoise shell, and, by extension, to literature, courtesy, and manners.

A lucky find made toward the end of the nineteenth century helps us to grasp the sense of these accounts. In 1899 a flood of the Yuan River in Hunan province, not far from the Yellow River, uncovered some three thousand pieces of tortoise shell and deer shoulder-bones on which the shamans of the court of the Shang dynasty in An-yang (fourteenth century B.C.) had traced inscriptions using some 600 different signs, considered the first known characters in Chinese writing.

Before someone left on a voyage, or before the harvest, the shamans interrogated the ancestors for their advice by heating previously prepared pieces of tortoise shell or bone. After these objects cracked under the heat, the shaman would interpret the crack marks, giving his interpretation in signs inscribed on the other face of the shell or the bone. On the basis of these "oracle bones" and similar evidence, and after comparison with decorations on prehistoric pottery (some of which dates back to the fifth millennium) and above all with bronze inscriptions of the age of the Chou people in the west (eleventh century–70 B.C.), Léon Vandermeersch has proposed the following interpretation of the origins of Chinese writing.

1. Paleographic analysis of the sign corresponding to the verb *yue* seems to represent an instrument that Vandermeersch calls a *porte-écrit,* a "writing bearer." This sign, which is accompanied by a hand in the graph of the word *shi* (shaman, soothsayer) and which appears in a number of archaic signs where it bears the notion of "charm" or "prayer," reveals the existence in ancient epochs of important ceremonies implying recourse to magico-religious writings. During such ceremonies, the *shi* who manipulated the "writing bearer" probably used it to show the magic formulas to

the spirits. After first communicating royal decisions to the transcendent powers that gave them force, he was responsible for notifying the interested parties. We have every reason to think that this personage was both a scribe and a grand master of divinatory science.

2. Most paleographers agree in recognizing the markings on prehistoric pottery as the prototypes of Chinese characters. In particular they find a graphic filiation between these stylized and abstract signs and the stylized decoration of bronzes, notably the sacrificial vases of the Yin and Chou epochs (sixteenth–seventh centuries B.C.), which depict the combined supernatural forces of the spirits to be conciliated.

3. Writing proper is thought to have branched off from this evolving process at a time still to be determined. Its motivation was an attempt at analysis inspired by the cult of the ancestors and applied to the divination techniques discussed above. The inscriptions carved on bones and turtle shells after inspection of the fissures were held to follow a kind of diagram and to express "the act or the events whose supernatural repercussions were the object of divination and whose hidden cosmological structure was revealed in the mysterious lines of the divinatory diagram."[11]

Thus the first goal of Chinese writing was to furnish not an instrument of communication, strictly speaking, but a tool for symbolization. Symbolization was originally conceived of as similar to an algorithm—"giving this word a very broad sense, as with an instrument (made up of a system of graphic symbols) serving to support an effort to structure the representations" (Vandermeersch). The shamans' efforts were not guided by the idea of noting down a linguistic utterance, even when they used procedures for phonetic notation. Thus whatever its relations with the existing language might have been, that algorithm could not evolve into a simple notation of that language; rather it constituted something like another, parallel language. It would be more accurate to speak of the creation of a written language, not simply of a writing system.

We can well imagine how ambiguous the relations between the Chinese language and this sort of script were, and for how many millennia.

From the start the Chinese language lent itself particularly well to the use of an ideographic system. Phonemes, the natural minimal unit of all alphabetical systems, have only a limited autonomy in Chinese, given that each phoneme has to occupy a set position within the syllable. Chinese, an agglutinating language, was largely monosyllabic in the classical epoch, so the basic unit was the syllable (there were many more syllables than in modern Chinese). Because each syllable had at least one meaning of its own, it probably seemed natural to express each of these meanings in an appropriate ideogram. With time, however, many meanings tended to merge—an evolution that is not exclusive to Chinese. Polysyllabic words proliferated thanks to the juxtaposition of two words to create a new word whose meaning often had only a remote connection with its constituent parts. The word for "notebook"—*benzi*—for instance, was made up of the word *ben*, "root," "origin," "source," and the very common nominal suffix *zi*.

The syllable and the character were entities that remained on different levels; even now everyday Chinese has only 1,250 syllables whereas modern dictionaries list from 3,500 to 9,000 characters. Those characters can be simple or complex. The simple ones represent things or symbols—numbers, for example. At one time signs offering a schematic image of a concrete reality, they now have only a distant relationship with their primitive representation. The original representation remains implicit in them, however, and it is always explained in the schools. Complex forms do not necessarily include any phonetic element: for example, the sign for *ri*, "sun," and the sign *yue*, "moon," when juxtaposed read *ming*, "light," and the term *wu*, "military," is transcribed by the sign for *zhi*, "stop," followed by the sign for *si*, "halberd." The most frequent complex forms do involve a phonetic element, however, a character that no longer has its ideographic meaning but that keeps its sound and is preceded by a "key" that gives a rough idea of what the word refers to. For example, *sang*, "throat," is rendered by the key *kou*, "mouth," and the character for *sang*, "mulberry tree." This system gives no real indication of how the word that is written in this fashion is pronounced because the language has evolved through time but the phonetic characters have not changed. Thus if a phonetic element is common to two words, all it indicates is that at one time and in certain dialects the words were pronounced in roughly the same way. Modern languages have a similar problem with the relationship between the spelling and the pronunciation of certain words.[12]

All this points to several conclusions concerning the "defense and illustration" of this sort of writing.

First, a European child normally learns to read alphabetic writing, with all its implied abstraction and apprenticeship in phonetism, around the age of five; the Chinese child is capable of recognizing the sense of certain characters by the age of two, but he has to memorize thousands of signs and grasp their combined meanings before he can read an ordinary text.

Second, writing is available to the Chinese to complete speech and render it more explicit. Because homophones are in principle represented by different signs a Chinese speaker can trace the corresponding sign in the hollow of his hand or write it down on a scrap of paper if his interlocutor has not understood the sense of a word. This procedure permits two people who speak dialects that differ as much (in the European context) as French and Portuguese to achieve a minimal mutual comprehension.

Thanks to its origins, Chinese script expresses totally different preoccupations from alphabetic writing systems. It reflects the mentality of a people for whom superior wisdom lies in a conformity with nature, but who esteem abstraction as the path to the comprehension and interpretation of nature. After all, certain of the essential elements of Chinese philosophy arose from the study of divinatory hexagrams, which to some extent express the invisible world. The Chinese turned very early to schematizing and stylizing their characters, and they conceived of their writing as a bit like an algebra. In large part originally designed (as far as we can tell) for communication with the spirits and the gods, this writing system long remained the privilege of shamans and scribes who were charged with redacting and promulgating royal decisions and who, as guardians of the rites, assisted the sovereigns in religious ceremonies. It was probably in the eighth century B.C. that the function of "tablet-maker," soothsayer, and astronomer was extended to the composition of the royal annals, which remained a ritual act. The redaction of the first penal code in a text cast in bronze vessels in 535 was still a promulgation of *verba sacra*. Thus writing in China was only very slowly detached from the powers of rite and religion—a process completed by the period of the warring kingdoms (fifth–third centuries B.C.) when Confucianism and Taoism developed. When peace was reestablished and the empire was unified in 221 B.C., political centralization moved writing from the world of the soothsayer to that of the various sorts of "technicians" that the state needed in all branches of its administration, from military arts to agronomy, fiscal policy, penal law, and diplomacy. Politics became increasingly dissociated from religion, and more materialistic kinds of thought flourished.

As the emperors worked to shatter the particular interests that had blossomed under anarchy they imposed a single order for everything concerned with communication and exchange—weights and measures, coinage, even the axle-span of carts and wagons. Writing was a necessary part of this standardization, particularly since the language had evolved and regional written codes had proliferated. This was the reason for the first great imperial reform of the graphic system. Li Si, minister of the emperor Ch'in Shih Huang, drew up a list of three thousand characters to form a manual whose use was obligatory for all scribes. The use of "key" characters was systematized, and the contours of the characters were simplified. Soon after, a great many books (literary and religious texts in particular) were burned.

Thus writing tended to become a simple instrument for communicating and recording thought. It nonetheless retained all the prestige that its religious origins had conferred on it. The emperors who had put the ancient ritualism and aristocratic moral code in the service of the state intended to do the same with writing. The emperors served as guardians of graphic norms, in part because among their essential functions was to give every individual his name and his rank, in part because written symbols represented or evoked all beings in the universe. Henceforth only the emperor had the power to forbid the use of certain signs or put new ones into circulation, and "a great amount of political activity was dedicated to the appropriation of names and the choice of propitious characters to designate eras, divinities, official buildings, cities, functions, etc." (Gernet).

Words still had a certain power. Like portraits, the names of families or individuals were held to contain more or less hidden truths. Complex characters were broken down "into simple elements that served to form oracular phrases or prophetic pronouncements" (Gernet). The characters for "happiness" and "longevity" were ceaselessly reproduced, and writings or other forms of witness to faith addressed to the gods were burned or buried so they could make their way to heaven or the bowels of the earth.

The art of calligraphy was also considered of particular importance. To quote a first century A.D. author, "If speech is the voice of the spirit, writing is the drawing of the spirit." Thus calligraphy was an integral part of an art of painting in China that privileged the line and demanded that the artist animate his drawing with the breath of life. The art of writing became a form of asceticism; when, after a long apprenticeship, the practitioner had mastered his art, he needed to work in a favorable climate before nature and among friends in order to reach awareness of his own rhythms in the visible world.

Can one go farther? Anne-Marie Christin, in an article to which I owe a debt of gratitude,[13] has recalled that the spoken word supposes the account of an "I" who is receiver but also referent. It thus supposes a sort of liberation that is all the more violent because the speaker is absent when the word passes through the channel of writing. Seeing a landscape, contemplating nature, and graphically interpreting nature do not suppose the same tensions, but they require an effort of synthesis in which the personality tends to dissolve. Because it is made up of images the ideographic page demands a certain effort of reorganization that is all the more active because all the characters that compose it are rich in ambiguities. It resembles the form of Taoist mysticism that prefers the contemplation of nature to speech.

We can see why for millennia the Chinese have refused to abandon the ideograms they have enriched with so many meanings. We will also have to admit that even alphabetic writing is not merely abstract, disembodied signs. It was a Chinese of the T'ang era (seventh–tenth centuries A.D.) who wrote, "When customs change, writing changes." This formula could be adopted by all scribes, copyists, scriveners, and calligraphers everywhere and in all times. We shall have ample opportunity to return to it.

Precolumbian America

The beginnings of Precolumbian "near writings" resemble those of the systems just discussed.[14]

The Mayas began to settle in one area toward the middle of the second millennium in what is now Guatemala and surrounding lands. At the same time, not far from there, the Olmecs founded a flourishing civilization characterized by great temples and monumental sculpture. It was only in the first century B.C., however, that the first traces of glyptic writing appeared in those regions among peoples who built great temples without knowing either the wheel or the potter's wheel and who learned to work metal only later. Mayan hieroglyphs (which were used in books as well as being carved in stone) served above all to register the passage of time and the influences of the gods who governed the various time divisions. They contain extraordinarily accurate calculations elaborated by astronomer priests that have been deciphered even though we have no definitive key to the Mayan graphic system. Thus most Mayan inscriptions still retain much of their mystery.

We know somewhat more about the writing of the Aztecs. They became established in the Valley of Mexico during the fourteenth century A.D., and they developed a brilliant civilization. They knew and practiced the technique of ideograms, and shortly before the Spanish conquest they even used phonetic signs. They seem to have used pictography more than other systems, and they used great quantities of a material somewhat like paper for writing down their laws, rules for domestic economy, and tax rolls as well as for setting down their mythology, their calendar, and their ritual (William H. Prescott).

All their achievements were doomed to oblivion by the Spanish conquest. Hernán Cortés's troops, the Catholic clergy, and the Inquisition all did their best to annihilate everything that they considered superstition. For good measure they burned their victims' entire archives, so that all that has come down to us is three Maya manuscripts and some fifteen Aztec texts. We know these peoples only by what remains of their monuments, by texts written by some of their number after the conquest, by historical accounts from Spanish authors, often well informed, or by reports addressed to the sovereigns in Madrid.

Some scholars have expressed surprise at the primitive character of the writing systems used by peoples who built so well. Their architects, the heroes of isolated communities that disappeared or were replaced by others, differed from their counterparts in the Middle East in that they were never stimulated by a need to develop new techniques of communication to catch up with or surpass neighboring communities. It is senseless to wonder what these peoples' graphic systems would have become if another civilization had not been brutally imposed on them. The example of China clearly shows that the path to the alphabet was not ineluctable for a written civilization, although I might note that members of the aristocracy were astonishingly quick to learn the alphabetic writing of the conquistadores, a quickness that provided the Spanish with a ready means for wiping out the "idolatry" deeply rooted in Mesoamerican pictograms.

Nearly everywhere the great ideographic writing systems appeared first and at a precise moment in the evolution of human societies. They came out of a systemization of the image, and they remained linked to their pictographic origins even when, in one way or another, spoken discourse imposed the use of a phonetism that in turn often led to new developments.

Born within cultures dominated by animism, these scripts were ill equipped to discriminate between the reality of the signified and the signifier. Moreover the use of the ideogram imposed polysemies and relations that were not necessarily those of the word represented. Hence the multivalent language of those systems provided a constant temptation to seek the hidden realities of the invisible world.

The evidence that has come down to us to date leaves a great many questions unanswered. The most obvious of these concerns the first appearance of writing. If we are to believe the Mesopotamian documents, writing arose in Sumer out of a need to keep business accounts. This is a response that the Western historian immediately finds satisfactory, but the absence of tablets of other sorts does not mean that from the outset the Sumerians did not also write for other purposes and in ways that would give us better insight into how the social symbolization employed in the signs that figure on the tablets was constituted. Conversely, only indirect and much later evidence demonstrably shows that in very early times the Egyptians and the Chinese also had bookkeeping, fiscal, and administrative documents (which have now completely disappeared). This is perhaps a fine example of a false problem, in the sense that a society creates a writing system when it has attained a certain level of development, when the concentration of its population reaches a new high, and when it attempts to respond to a global acceleration in communications (in the broadest sense of the term).

In any event one thing is quite clear. Initially an instrument of power in the hands of small groups of priests, soothsayers, and scribes serving a deified monarch, writing was above all a means to domination and to the establishment of hierarchy, hence it was the expression of the ideology of a limited elite. Whether it also served what is conveniently called "progress" remains to be seen. The question is as ambiguous as the term "progress" itself, but it is one that we will have to attempt to answer.

THE COMING OF THE ALPHABET

New types of writing emerged in a quite different context during the second millennium B.C. on the fringes of the Assyro-Babylonian lands, which were forced to defend themselves from incursions of the Amorites and the Hurrians sweeping down from the Caucasus. At the same time, new fortunes were building in the eastern Mediterranean basin.[15]

The history of Hittite writing provides a revealing prologue to that development. That Indo-European population felt no need to adopt writing in their Anatolian villages, even when Assyrian merchants came among them using simplified cuneiform syllabaries for their commercial correspondence. The Hittites' attitude changed when energetic kings strove to unify them in face of the Hurrian threat. These sovereigns probably laid the foundations of the administration that their new state needed, calling on the aid of specialists captured during a raid on Babylon. Their scribes then noted the languages of the region, redacted a large number of acts that display a fine flair for legal niceties, kept their archives carefully, and translated the classics of Mesopotamian literature. However, they showed little creative spirit.

This imported writing was insufficient to give the Hittites a cultural personality. Still, by the fifteenth century B.C. they were using a hieroglyphic system for seals and inscriptions that seems totally their own creation. The system initially served to note the names and titles of deities and important figures, often along with a representation of those same figures. It later included phonetic elements as well, and its unmistakable characters were scattered on commemorative monuments and the walls of temples over the fairly vast area of the expansion of Hittite power. Used for cultural ends, it outlasted that power for some time.[16]

The Aegean Sea and the Greek world were awakening during the same period. The prosperity of Crete had been building since the third millennium, and from between 2000 and 1200 B.C. there were at least three types of writing that succeeded one another in the area.[17]

The first system was a script resembling hieroglyphics, probably used ca. 2000–1650 B.C. It is known particularly from extremely short texts inscribed on stone seals of a variety of forms and from vases, bars, and clay tablets found at Knossos and Mallia. The palace bureaucracy probably used this procedure (and its successors) for accounting and record-keeping.

The second system had a very different aspect and is known as linear A. It is made up of eighty-five signs, a good number of ideograms, and marks that seem to correspond to numbers. It appears on clay tablets (apparently used for accounting), vases, seals, and various documents, on which the characters are sometimes written in ink, and it has been found in a number of sites in Crete.

The third system was the famous linear B, which seems to have derived from linear A and is usually dated 1450–1200 B.C. It also had from eighty-five to ninety signs, and it used a hundred or so ideograms. The only tablets that have been found in Crete using this writing were in the palace at Knossos, but tablets have also been found on the Greek mainland in the palace of Nestor in Pylos (where they were hardened by fire when the palace burned) and in Mycenae. Further to the north signs of this type have been found on vases, notably from Thebes.[18]

Although the Cretan hieroglyphs and linear A are still undeciphered, we have good reason to think that these writings transcribed the original language of the Cretans. Soon after World War II, two British scholars, Michael Ventris and John Chadwick, showed that linear B was a syllabic writing system and that it served to record the earliest known Greek dialect, Mycenaean. Presumably, the Hellenes who invaded Crete in the fifteenth century had the writing of the place adapted to their speech. If we add that all these unbaked clay tablets were not made to be conserved and have only come down to us by accident and thanks to luck, we can deduce that this graphic system was widely diffused.

Another essential part of the picture comes from Cyprus, which was famous in antiquity for its copper mines and its commercial activity. The writing system used there toward the end of the second millennium remains undeciphered but seems related to Cretan. Later, after a gap of several centuries, a syllabary system emerged for noting the Greek dialect of Cyprus. Ancient methods could be remarkably persistent: that system continued to be used through the classical period and disappeared only in the third century B.C.

Thus writing was practiced in the Aegean world even before the arrival of the Greeks, and the Greeks used syllabary techniques before Homer. Linear B, in particular, seems to have been in wide use, and there is no reason not to suppose that the Mycenaeans, like the Cypriots, used wood plaques or skins to write on. The use of this script was limited, however: aside for a few painted inscriptions on vases it was used primarily to keep accounts. Most of the vestiges that have been discovered to date attest to the administrative activities of the palaces of Knossos, Pylos, or Mycenae. Mycenaean merchants may also have used writing, but unlike in the Eastern civilizations that used ideograms no monumental inscription records the deeds of the sovereigns, publishes their decisions, or perpetuates the memory of their dead (Olivier Masson).

It was not the Greek world that was preparing the future but the Middle East, in the lands bordering the eastern Mediterranean. Nearly everywhere from Mesopotamia to the Mediterranean and from Anatolia to the Sinai Peninsula the Semites who made up the base of the population had created city-states that struggled to resist invaders and were subject to rival imperialisms. Other Semites, however, had built the city of Ugarit (not far from the current Latakia) near the mouth of the Orontes River. Further to the south still other Semites who took the name of Phoenicians brought prosperity to the ports of Sidon, Tyre, Berytus, and Byblos, cities at the foot of the Lebanon Mountains, whose cedar wood they exported. These were fiercely independent mercantile cities little inclined to unite in an empire, though they accepted distant protection. Above all they looked to the sea and were guided by an extremely acute practical sense.

This is the setting in which the earliest known phonetic alphabets were developed. They were consonantal alphabets that transcribed only the roots of Semitic words, thus they were highly adaptable to other Semitic languages. We do not know when and how this system was perfected. Because the peoples who used this alphabet wrote on papyrus sheets that time has destroyed, our physical evidence of it is extremely sparse, not always decipherable, and made up largely of tablets and inscriptions.[19] The earliest example of the Phoenician consonant alphabet is in the royal inscriptions of Byblos, the most famous of which, from the sarcophagus of King Ahiram, dates from approximately 1000 B.C. These inscriptions show that this alphabet was fully formed by that time, and a few words incised on bronze arrowheads even permit us to date it back at least to the twelfth century B.C.

This was only the beginning. Excavations started in 1929 of the site of ancient Ugarit at Ras Shamra, near Latakia, unearthed not only cuneiform tablets with Akkadian texts but others bearing a small number of other signs also in cuneiform. Soon deciphered, they were revealed to use an alphabet of some thirty characters for a wide variety of texts that could be dated as fourteenth- and thirteenth-century writings—myths, legends, rituals, letters, contracts, bookkeeping records, and so forth—all written in the language of Ugarit. Moreover, the system was widely used, and the alphabet was later simplified and reduced to twenty-two signs to note a variety of languages, Semitic and non-Semitic, throughout Palestine.

Evidence seems to indicate that the Ugaritic alphabet preceded the Byblos alphabet. Can we take alphabets still further back in time? It is presently impossible to draw sure conclusions from the disparate corpus that is called "the Protocanaanite documents" or from the pseudo-hieroglyphics of Byblos that have eluded decipherers. The same is less true of the inscriptions called "Protosinaitic" that have caused so much ink to flow since they were discovered.

These are brief inscriptions found in the Sinai Peninsula on the site of Serabit el Khadim, where Egyptian, Asiatic, and (often) Semitic workers, toiling under high-ranking Egyptians, came from time to time to work the turquoise mines. The inscriptions are situated near other inscriptions in Egyptian hieroglyphics near a rock temple dedicated to the goddess Hathor, the protectress of mines; they are apparently in an unknown writing system of some thirty-five signs of pictographic or geometric aspect, and they can be dated at least as far back as the fifteenth century B.C. Although scholars have not yet satisfactorily deciphered these texts, a British Egyptologist, Alan H. Gardiner, supposed them to note West Semitic texts. Gardiner argued that they use acrophony—that is, each sign stands for the initial phoneme of the word for the object symbolized in the pictograph. Thus this script transcribed *aleph* by a house, which was said *alph;* the sign for *beth* was an egg, etc. Gardiner also suggested that this practice conformed to very ancient naming practices pointing to a pictographic origin of the alphabet. Thus one sequence of four or five signs that returns several times in these inscriptions should be read *lbᶜlt* or *bᶜlt*, a familiar Semitic word for "lady" or "mistress" and a perfectly logical designation for the goddess Hathor.[20]

I need not insist on the fragility of this sort of speculative construction and will leave it to the specialists to debate the origins—Mesopotamian? Egyptian? autonomous?—of the Phoenician alphabet. Let me simply reiterate that the Egyptians succeeded in isolating consonants but did not use them as the basis for a simplified system. Some have suggested that the Egyptian scribes did not want to exploit this possibility for fear of losing their power. This hypothesis is too simplistic. Writing systems, which are anchored in the minds of peoples in a determined area and are enriched by accretions brought by successive generations, die only when the civilizations that secreted them die. Thus it seems normal that new systems should grow up in a new context on the fringes of the domains of the systems that preceded them. This happened repeatedly during the second millennium B.C., as we have seen, from Anatolia to Crete, Syria and Palestine, and in Mycenae and Cyprus. It is what was to happen in the Far East when Japan invented two syllabaries to complete the Chinese characters and when the Koreans invented an extremely simple alphabetic writing that for centuries they refrained from putting into current use.

One cannot help but be struck by the degree of abstraction of a consonantal system that isolates and represents only the roots of words. It is contrary to the spirit of traditional ideographic procedures and their strictly concrete corresponding forms of thought—as one glance at the mathematical reasoning of the Mesopotamian sages will show. A genuine mental revolution took place when that degree of abstraction was achieved and writing was directly attached to speech. Nor is it surprising that it was the Phoenicians who brought off that revolution. Unlike Hittite hieroglyphs (to pick one example) their writing was not created to celebrate a national pantheon. Rather it was a technique for merchants who used skins or papyrus and a cut reed to inscribe the simplest possible signs as a way to keep their business accounts and to communicate over long distances. This move may have been one of the Phoenicians' commercial innovations, realized as they were about to swarm throughout the Mediterranean. Unfortunately, the essentially perishable nature of their writing materials prevents further speculation.

Consonantal writing had a rapid and lasting success. It very soon became the writing of all the peoples of the Canaanite language group—Phoenicians, Moabites, and Hebrews—and, in particular, of the Aramaeans, a people who played an essential role in the Middle East. It was Aramaean scribes who administered the empire of Cyrus the Great (in their own language and using their own writing) after he took Babylon in 539 B.C. Between the fifth and the third centuries, Aramaic even tended to supplant Akkadian, Phoenician, and Hebrew (which became a religious language). This means that Aramaic inscriptions range from Asia Minor to Pakistan and the Punjab, and there is even some thought that Indian graphic systems may be of Semitic inspiration. Similarly a number of peoples of Iranian origin and even the Indo-European and Altaic populations of central and northern Asia—Uighurs, Mongols, and Kalmucks—adopted systems inspired by the Aramaic alphabet.

Further to the south, various forms of consonantal writing were introduced in the Arabian Peninsula. The first evidence of such writing dates from the seventh century B.C. but may descend from models predating Phoenician writing. The consonant system reached as far as Abyssinia, where in the fourth century it produced the Ethiopian syllabary. It was only in the sixth century A.D., however, that the nomad Arab groups in the Syro-Mesopotamian steppes immediately adjoining Arabia, who had begun to organize into semi-independent kingdoms, adopted the cursive script of Nabataean writing. The first center of this culture appears to have been Petra, to the south of Jerusalem, an important stop on the caravan route that once reached from Medina to Damascus. Next a graphic system appeared that served the needs of the merchants of Mecca and was used in the primitive Islamic state to assure the smooth operation of a growing administration and to guard the original purity of the text of the Koran. From that moment on, the destiny of that writing system was tied to the Muslim religion and to Arab imperialism.

The Arabs welcomed converts, and they subjected peoples who refused complete assimilation into Islam and drew tribute from them. In the domain of language and writing they applied very strict rules. The Koran, the word of God, could be read only in its original text, as Allah had dictated it to Mohammed (hence it had to be read in classical Arabic). It was even prohibited to copy it in anything but its canonical form. To this day children learn to read and write classical Arabic, which continues to be spoken among the learned, thus assuring the unity of the Muslim world.

Beginning with the caliphate of Abd al-Malik (685–705), Arabic became the sole official administrative language in the conquered lands, which meant that Arabic culture was soon dominant in the Fertile Crescent (although isolated islands of Aramaean culture remained). Arabic linguistic dominance was established somewhat less rapidly in Egypt, especially in Upper Egypt, where Coptic was spoken. It occurred even more slowly in Berber lands, and it was very incomplete in Spain. All these regions thus used Arabic writing, with written Coptic being limited to religious use by Christians. The only exception was the Jews, who used Hebrew characters to note the Arabic they spoke. Not only were Muslims obliged to read and study the Koran in its Arabic text; those who lived in regions where national languages had persisted had to learn to read and write Arabic as well. The graphic system of written Arabic was applied to Persian, for instance, and Pahlavi (Middle Persian) script, which had been in use up to that point, was eliminated. The same thing happened to Afghan, also an Iranian language. Arabic script was even used to note Turkish and several Altaic languages. Its sphere extended to China and India, and it was even used in areas as remote from its source as Malaysia and black Africa.[21]

The appearance of consonantal writing brought on an important revolution. When the art of writing emerged from the closed circles of the scribes, the palaces and the temples, and the merchants, its use spread. Simple shepherds in the deserts of Arabia could carve graffiti even before the coming of Islam. A writing system centered on consonants permitted religions of the Book to flourish, and in turn they favored teaching and the diffusion of reading. When the written word and the divine Word eventually joined forces they encouraged religions in which an invisible God was known by his Word alone. Thus it is not by accident that the Bible shows God's chosen people struggling to combat the Golden Calf, or that Muslims tended to prohibit all representation in their art. Because they used the same word for "create" and "paint," Muslims felt that an image could be called to life, thus that the artist took to himself a power that belonged only to Allah.

While the Phoenician merchants and mariners were spreading out through the Mediterranean, Greece was emerging from a long period of troubles during which Mycenaean civilization had been destroyed by a new wave of Hellenic invaders. It was during that period, perhaps in the ninth or eighth centuries, that the Greek alphabet—the ancestor of modern Western alphabets—appeared.[22]

The originality of the Greek system lay in its precision. Syllabic writing systems had to make do with approximations. The word χρυσός (khrusos; "gold"), for example, was rendered in Mycenaean by ku-ru-sou; the word δρυτόμοι (drutomoi; "woodcutters") by du-ru-to-mo. As the Phoenician alphabet was constituted, it was unable to transcribe Greek satisfactorily because many syllables in Greek were vowels, and Greek adjectives, nouns, and verbs had inflections that required accurate rendering. Hence the need to complete the Phoenician alphabet and to change its character in order to make it over into an essentially phonographic system. The result is familiar to all. Assigning particular graphemes to represent vowels was made easier because certain consonant sounds in West Semitic languages had weakened in Greek, freeing the corresponding signs for other uses. The consonant function of the semi-vowels w and y had by and large disappeared, which furnished the Y (upsilon) and the I (iota). The w kept its value as a consonant in certain dialects, where it took the form of the F (digamma). For the other vowels, the A (alpha), the O (omicron), and the E (epsilon), the Greeks used the Semitic laryngeal consonants. The letter alep, which noted the laryngeal occlusive, was used for A (α); the letter ayin, which noted a sounded aspirated laryngeal, was used for O (o), and the letter he, which noted an unsounded aspirated laryngeal, was used for E (Michel Lejeune). Similarly, the xi (ξ) was derived from a Semitic letter, the såmek, but the phi, (φ) the chi (χ), and the psi (ψ) were Greek creations (of obscure origin), whereas the tau (T, τ) was borrowed directly from the Semitic alphabet and the upsilon (Y, υ), a graphic variant of the F (digamma), was moved to the end of the alphabet before the φ (phi), the χ (chi), and the ψ (psi) were added. Finally (and still according to Michel Lejeune), the sin became the Σ (sigma), the sade serving as a sibilant in place of the sigma in certain Greek alphabets.

Very soon, however, the Greeks felt that these signs were insufficiently precise and used special signs to note the timbre and length of certain vowels. The H (*êta*), a sign first borrowed as a mark of initial aspiration, which, to contrast with the E (*epsilon*), and a new sign, the Ω (*omega*), was created to accompany the O (*omicron*). Moreover, the changes in their language led the Greeks to reserve the Y (*upsilon*) for the sound *ü* and to adopt the graph OY to represent the sound *u* (in English *oo*) in dialects like Boetian that still retained this reconstituted phoneme. They also wrote the closed long "e" as a diphthong.

It would be extremely interesting to know when this system was elaborated. Unfortunately the Greek world, which has bequeathed us such a rich literature through later intermediaries, left practically no direct evidence of the beginnings of its writing system aside from some inscriptions on stone or a few signs painted on clay pottery, all later than the eighth century. Thus it is simple conjecture that Greece's innovative alphabet resulted from contacts with the Phoenician world. Merchants have often been credited with adopting or adapting Phoenician writing and with spreading its use in the Greek world, but economists doubt that writing was much used in the forms of commerce practiced at the time. Keeping in mind that traders differed little from other groups in the Hellenic cities, we can conclude that the alphabet caught on in response to a wide variety of needs, a question to which I shall return.[23] It is also conceivable that the new system was a learned construction, but the documents that have come down to us attest the existence of a number of local alphabets that show differences hard to explain. They also show a high degree of coincidence. In ancient Greece, a nation broken up into particularist city-states, writing was not fully unified until the fourth century, when the Ionian alphabet, called "of Miletus," was officially adopted in Athens (403 B.C.). Finally, the first known inscriptions were written (as were Phoenician inscriptions) from right to left, or they were in "boustrophedon" style, reversing direction like oxen plowing. Greek began to be written from left to right only well into the sixth century.

Thus writing reached a new stage. Unlike purely consonantal systems, the Greek alphabet attempted to break down spoken discourse into sounds, the indivisible atoms of speech. The results were imperfect because not all the letters utilized corresponded to true audible phonemes (occlusives, for example, cannot be pronounced alone) (James Février). In principle, however, the Greek alphabet attempted to provide an accurate copy of spoken discourse. Furthermore, with a few modifications to its list of signs it permitted notation of any language.

The question arises whether this new and totally analytical form of writing engendered new forms of thought. It is easy to recognize decisive innovations concentrated in the three fields of geometry, geography, and medicine. These disciplines broke with precedents known in the civilizations of the Near East to place graphic practices at the center of their activity (Marcel Détienne). Thus geometry was invented, a discipline in which figures and arguments have equal weight. Pure graphics in its operations and its instruments, with Euclid's *Elements* geometry became a wholly written science "in which the writing of the demonstration has already made a selection, retaining only the logical sequences." Anaximander dared to draw the inhabited earth, and he created the geographical map, an exercise requiring a high degree of schematization. Hippocratic medicine developed, inspiring a number of treatises composed for written publication and authors who relied on writing to lend accuracy and pertinence to their descriptions of illnesses.[24] When Plato created the doctrine of ideas he was simply developing these ways of looking at things. Any system has its drawbacks. By linking sound and the letter as closely as possible (one word originally expressed both notions in Greek), the Greeks privileged what was heard over what was meant. This resulted in a tendency among Attic epigraphists to place equally spaced letters in regular columns irrespective of the form of the individual sign. It also resulted in the Greek scribes' long-standing hostility toward abbreviations and in their slowness to adopt cursive scripts. The tendency of alphabetic writing to transmit the flow of spoken discourse was so strong that it long neglected to separate words and sentences. Finally, it never proved capable of expressing anything more than language, so that it was ill-suited to the task when it was called on to break out of the framework of language. This limitation is particularly noticeable in our own century.

This system, which gave the West its form of logic, was marked from the outset by an interest in efficiency. It was certainly not by chance that coinage, in the common sense of the term, first appeared in the sixth century B.C. on the banks of the Pactolus River in Lydia, the legendary land of Gyges and the kingdom of Croesus, where caravans arrived from central Asia, at a time when the Greek cities of the Asia Minor coast, Miletus in particular, were striking "private" money. Money arose not long after a writing system that strove to be universal, and money was to become the spur and motive force for everything in the West. As Jacques Gernet has emphasized, this implies ways of thinking totally different from the Chinese, for example:

It seems to me personally that there is a fairly strict relationship between the mentality that permitted the invention of a uniform money and the invention of the alphabet. I believe that it would be possible to demonstrate that money did not have the same functions in China and in the ancient civilizations of the Mediterranean basin. In any event, in China it was never conceived of as the measure of all things and a sort of common denominator, but rather as a sort of goods on the same level as cereals and cloth and on a different level, treasures and precious objects.[25]

A simple history of writing systems could stop here. This system's conquest of the universe, however, was only beginning.

Born with the Greek city, the alphabet as we conceive it today became under Alexander the Great the instrument of a new imperialism and the symbol of an intellectual superiority. By the same token it relegated Aramaic writing and its derivatives to the rank of symbols of resistance among nations at the edge of Hellenized regions.

Many peoples took the system that the Greeks had elaborated and adapted it to their own language. This was particularly true in Lemnos and in Etruria, where signs inspired by Greek letters were put to the service of languages that probably were closely related to Greek—signs that we can read without fully comprehending them. The Etruscans seem to have used writing largely for religious purposes. According to Cicero (*De divinatione*) they bequeathed their sacred texts to the Romans, who held the Etruscan religion to be the religion of the Book par excellence.[26]

The peoples of Italy, on whom the Indo-European invaders of the later second millennium had imposed their idiom, borrowed writing not from the Greeks but from the Etruscans. The Latins, for their part, began to note their language during the second half of the seventh century B.C. The Latin alphabet initially had twenty letters including the sounded consonants B and D, borrowed from archaic Etruscan, and the vowel O, which Etruscan later eliminated. Its evolution seems deliberate, as if thought through by a class of professional scribes. In the sixth century the *digamma* became the F and the unsounded aspirate VH lost its second element. The G appeared during the third century. Writing, which had rarely been used up to that point, became more common under the influence of such men as Livius Andronicus, Plautus, and Ennius, and especially in contact with Hellenism, but the number of inscriptions increased only slowly. The art of writing seems to have served for some time as an instrument of power kept in the hands of an oligarchy. Roman conquests later enormously extended the use of writing, which became more and more common in the administration of an increasingly vast empire.

This slow assimilation helps us to understand why writing (and for even greater reason, inscription, which aimed at fixing memory for all eternity) retained a magical aspect in Rome—a magic that writing has never totally lost. This was truer in Rome than in Greece, for example. Like the sculptures on Trajan's Column, certain monumental inscriptions do not seem to have been conceived to be deciphered. Above all they contribute to keeping alive the memory of a departed person who pursues a reduced life in the beyond and who is periodically reanimated by sacrifices and libations. On different level the bas-reliefs on the sarcophagi of the imperial epoch that show the intellectual life of the deceased—who are shown reading, declaiming, and so forth—are testimony to the eminent value that writing had taken on in the life of Romans of that age. Especially when they show children, such scenes take on a symbolic meaning and a religious overtone. The idea had developed that intellectual pursuits in this life assured the deceased a participation in the divine and a true immortality. Thus the child prodigy, the cultivated man, and even more the poet or the scholar were treated as heroes.

The long history of the conquests of the Greek and Latin alphabets throughout the centuries and an enumeration of their adaptations lie beyond the scope of this book. I will not even pose the problem, for instance, of the role of the Greek model in the elaboration of the Indian and Ethiopian writing systems.[27] We do need to recall, however, how religion and certain forms of nationalism elicited new systems of writing and on occasion made them prosper.

Egypt in the time of the Ptolemies was by and large Hellenized. For that reason certain Egyptians attempted to use the Greek alphabet to transcribe their language, particularly since it was easier to write than Egyptian scripts. In the third century, after a number of individual attempts and experiments, a system was devised—Coptic script—based on the Greek alphabet with the addition of a certain number of signs borrowed from demotic. Coptic script permitted notation of various dialects of the Coptic language, the last stage of the Egyptian language. It doubtless served for other purposes than the sacred and liturgical texts, the writings of the sects, and the books of piety that we know today. The Arab conquest interrupted its course, and today the Coptic language and Coptic script are used only by the Coptic church.

In other cases evangelizers had a notable part in creating new writing systems. Bishop Ulfilas (Wulfila in Gothic; A.D. 311–84) created a Gothic script on the basis of the Greek alphabet so that his West Gothic compatriots could know the Bible, which he had undertaken to translate. Although this system had only a limited success, the same was not true of two others, Armenian and Cyrillic, which helped a people or a group of peoples to assert their personality.

Emperor Theodosius abandoned Armenia at the end of the fourth century, thus sealing its destiny for centuries to come.[28] Several western provinces remained within the sway of the Eastern Roman Empire and seemed destined for Hellenization, but the greater part of Armenia had become a royal fief of the Sassanid dynasty of Persian kings who practiced Mazdakism, the principal rival of Christianity in that region. Since the Persians could hardly allow the Armenians to remain culturally linked to Byzantium, learned and religious circles had to speak Syriac and study in Syrian schools, and royal acts that until then had been redacted in Greek or in Syriac began to be written in Pahlavi, the official language of the Sassanids. Writing thus became inaccessible to people not conversant with those foreign cultures. St. Sahac, the patriarch, and King Vramshapuh encouraged various attempts to constitute a national writing system, but the merit of having resolved the problem falls to St. Mesrop Machtots. Mesrop had studied Greek literature in his youth, after which he served as "chancellor of the ordinances of the sovereign" and custodian of the royal archives until he went to evangelize the province of Siunia. He studied with the Syriac bishop Daniel, who lived in Mesopotamia, but he noticed that the letters that Daniel used "were insufficient to spell the syllables of the Armenian language." After taking counsel with a group of scribes in Edessa who were working on an analogous project, Mesrop elaborated an alphabet of thirty-six signs inspired by the Greek system but with the addition of Semitic characters. Thus he brought into being what the linguist Antoine Meillet called a veritable masterpiece:

> Each of the phonemes in Armenian is noted by its own sign, and the system was so well established that it furnished the Armenian nation with a definitive expression of phonetism, an expression that has persisted to our own day without having to undergo any change [and] without having to submit to any improvement, for it was perfect at the start[29]

Armed with this tool, Mesrop and Sahac supervised a team of scholars who translated the Bible into the national language, thus giving a new impetus to evangelization. We shall see how, with the backing of merchant patrons, the Armenian clergy used this same alphabet ten centuries later to set up typographical workshops in Europe that provided books that helped the Armenian people safeguard their cultural cohesion and resist Roman Catholic encouragement—also by circulating books—to attach the Armenian church to Rome.

The history of Cyrillic writing is more complex.[30] In the ninth century, the Slavs who occupied the greater part of the Balkans bore down on the Byzantine empire to the south of them, while in the north they were in contact with the West. They began to group into principalities, the largest of which were the Moravian kingdom, which included Czechs and Slovaks, and the kingdom of Bulgaria (where the Slavs gradually assimilated their Bulgar conquerors), which covered a large area toward the end of this period, to the point of controlling the commercial routes connecting Byzantium to Russia and northern Europe. The evangelization of the Bulgars is connected with the names of two brothers, Methodius and Constantine, the latter becoming a monk on his deathbed and taking the name of Cyril. Born in Thessalonica as sons of a Byzantine government official, the two brothers had served ten years in the Byzantine administration when Methodius became a monk and his younger brother Constantine went to Constantinople to continue his studies. Under the protection of Photius, the patriarch of Constantinople, whom he served as librarian, Constantine's career as a scholar and professor was interrupted by diplomatic missions to the Middle East and Asia. When Ratislav of Moravia requested a bishop to instruct his people (862), the emperor designated Constantine and his brother. The hagiographers report that Constantine-Cyril was seized with sudden inspiration and invented a system of writing to note Slavic. It is more probable that he had begun working out this system several years earlier, when he had retreated to the monastery in Bithynia that his brother served as abbot, and where there were a number of Slavs (855).

In all probability, what Constantine-Cyril spontaneously invented was not the writing system that has inaccurately been called "Cyrillic" but rather Glagolitic. Like Armenian, this system of thirty-six signs earned the admiration of Antoine Meillet. Unfortunately, its creator, who wanted to differentiate it as much as possible from the Greek and Roman alphabets, if not from the Hebrew, designed a set of rather round letters, using circles, triangles, and crosses that perhaps evoke eternity, the Trinity, and Christ's sacrifice but that are generally considered ugly and awkward.

Constantine-Cyril and Methodius used this system with great success during their missions in Moravia and Pannonia; during the same period they wrote a liturgy in a composite language largely inspired by the Macedonian dialect. Their initiative, which must have seemed daring even to the Byzantines, was bound to displease Rome, even though it implied no direct attachment of the new church to Constantinople. When the Hungarian invasions definitively cut off the Moravians and the Pannonians from Byzantium the disciples of Cyril and Methodius were obliged to move, with their alphabet, to Bulgaria, where they found a Slavic people strongly impregnated with Greek culture but eager to maintain their independence from Byzantium. The learned men of the country, who knew Greek and had often attempted to note their language in Greek script, probably found the new letters extremely ugly, but they adopted its phonetic system. Czar Boris, who had been baptized in 864 but had no intention of establishing close ties with his powerful neighbor, gave the disciples of Cyril and Methodius a warm welcome and encouraged the adoption of a writing system that would permit the development of a Slavic rite. Thus an alphabet came to be elaborated and adopted (893) in which all the letters, within the limits of practicality, were written on the model of Greek uncials. When the Russians converted to Christianity in the following century they chose Cyrillic script, and the evolution of Russian society from the twelfth to the fourteenth centuries brought a genuine "graphic explosion" (at least in certain regions), as evidenced by discoveries made in those areas since 1951 and by a wide variety of documents inscribed on birch bark.

After a long career, Glagolitic writing stopped being used, except for religious purposes in certain dioceses of Bosnia and Dalmatia (Croatia). The Cyrillic alphabet was adopted by all Orthodox Slavs and served to note their literary language. Most of the Slavs who rallied to Rome rejected it, however, which created the paradoxical situation in ex-Yugoslavia, where two peoples who speak the same language write in different scripts, the Serbs in Cyrillic and the Croats with Roman characters. Finally, as is known, the ex-Soviet Union did much to put into writing the languages spoken by the peoples within its borders, for the most part noting them in adaptations of the Cyrillic alphabet, while Russian became the language of culture throughout the Soviet Union.

I might go on to speak, for instance, of the efforts of Western mission-aries, colonizers, and scholars to adapt the Roman alphabet to the many languages of the world, but the moment has come to sum up. The histories of the Armenian and Cyrillic scripts attest that the creation of a new sys-tem—at any rate, a phonetic written system—is above all a deliberate act on the part of a group. Similarly, the reform of a writing system—including an ideographic system, as the Chinese can testify—requires an act of gov-ernment, thus a concerted policy. Graphic convention, which generates law in the face of custom, is itself a form of law. At the same time, however, writing—even more than texts and languages—constitutes the soul of a society, precisely by its testimony to the immutable: it is difficult to bring about change, even orthographic change. This means that the disappear-ance of a system and its replacement mark the death of a civilization. Fi-nally, contemporary experience proves that no system can be said to be a culminating moment linked to the triumph of Western logic. It also proves that writing that seems illogical and poorly adapted to a language is not necessarily a cultural handicap. Far from it: look at Japan.

Two
The Written and the Spoken Word

Writing systems are not disembodied, and written messages from past times are objects that speak more than one language. Dug out from the soil, discovered in tombs, or transmitted from generation to generation, they often seem odd to us and a far cry from our modern books. By their very aspect they remind us that the shape of written signs depends on the material on which they are written. When signs are written with care they attest to an interest in proclamation and durability; when they are cursive they show that a society was familiar with writing. When they are laid out without separations they remind us that our modern page layouts are recent acquisitions. When they are written on scrolls the text unfolds like a film. When only a small number of characters appears on each page rapid reading proves impossible. Hence all these odd objects need careful scrutiny before we can begin to understand what the always ambiguous relationship between speech and text may have been in their own time.

WRITING MATERIALS

More than anything else, the study of writing materials reminds us that the greatest civilizations are mortal. Quite often the civilizations that utilized perishable materials are known to us only by carved and graven inscriptions. The solemn graphic style of those inscriptions bears little relation to the style used for everyday writing (of which even graffiti—when we have them—give us only a distorted image).

The search for materials has always created a problem. Natural substances, wood in particular, were tried first. The Chinese ideogram standing for a book seems initially to have represented slices of bamboo, and the Latin term *liber* also suggests wood or bark. Egypt, Cyprus, and many other places used wooden tablets, prepared in various ways. Bark—birch bark in particular—long served the same purpose in India and especially in Russia. Indian manuscripts were inscribed on palm leaves until modern times.

Even when it was carefully prepared, wood received signs poorly, and it was difficult to reuse. Hence wooden tablets came to be covered with a layer of wax that could be written on with a stylus. This was a technique widely used in the West up to early modern times for keeping accounts and making first drafts, but because the wax surface was eminently perishable, writing on waxed tablets ordinarily served only for provisional notation.

In both the West and the East the societies that succeeded one another were obliged to seek other solutions. In Mesopotamia, as we have seen, men who had already learned how to make and paint pottery found it natural to use clay to make writing tablets. A number of peoples of the Middle East and the Aegean world followed their example. Clay presented certain problems, however. Scribes with a jar full of damp clay at their side fashioned a lump into the form they wanted, then traced signs on one or both faces while the clay was still malleable. The tablet was then dried in the sun or baked in a kiln so it would last longer. Bas-reliefs and paintings often show standing scribes writing on a clay tablet held in the hollow of the hand. If they worked on a larger tablet they had to place it on a board. Their pictograms, which at first they traced with a pointed tool, had curves that were difficult to make on fresh clay and that tended to be distorted as the clay dried. The scribes gradually left off tracing their signs and instead learned to imprint lines and wedges with the aid of a reed cut for that purpose, thus producing the form of writing we call cuneiform.

Very early—from the epoch of Shuruppak (now Fara; ca. 2600 B.C.) and perhaps even before—the signs took a ninety-degree turn to the left, a phenomenon that often occurred in cursive writings. The direction of the writing changed as well: instead of proceeding in vertical columns from right to left, the characters came to be aligned from left to right, one line following the other. Writing on clay later diversified and tended toward simplification, but inscriptions on stone or metal kept a vertical layout and their decorative graphic styles.

Although these graphic techniques do not permit recognition of the scribe's hand they do reflect the psychology of each successive epoch. For example the Code of Hammurabi, the greatest king of the first Babylonian dynasty, appears as a graphic illustration of a stable regime, "imposing on everyone the clear and serene will of a powerful administrator."[1] The writing of the warrior kings of Assur and Niniveh reflects their soldierly conquering spirit; its triumphant parallels and right angles mark the subjection of the sign to a sort of military discipline (Jean Nougayrol).[2]

The peoples of the Middle East used a good many other materials, but the clay tablet guaranteed them a degree of durability even though clay deteriorates over the very long term. This means that archaeologists have been able to recover intact entire buried libraries and archives.

Excavations carried out from 1973 to 1976 on the acropolis of Tell Mardikh, sixty kilometers from Alep, have laid bare the royal palace of Ebla (2400–2250 B.C.). Nearly seventeen thousand tablets have been found there in the palace administrative quarter, the audience court, and the archives. The findings include documents of all sorts—economic, financial, lexical, historic, literary, agrarian, and more—and they show how an active court organized commercial caravans, collected taxes and tribute, received reports and state correspondence, and instructed messengers and sent them out on missions. They reveal a hitherto unknown form of proto-Syriac civilization, the discovery of which upset a number of notions that were considered definitive acquisitions.[3]

In 1893 a discovery was made at a site some one hundred kilometers south of Babylon at Nippur (now Niffer), the site of a temple library that had already produced twenty-three thousand tablets dating from the twenty-third century B.C. The new find, some 730 terra cotta tablets from the years 445–403 B.C., was excavated from a chamber measuring roughly 5.5 × 2.75 meters. It permitted a reconstruction of the activities and the commercial methods of the Murašû family, a large family of Babylonian businessmen of Jewish origin.[4]

The clay tablet was a heavy and relatively cumbersome medium, but cuneiform writing permitted a large number of signs to be crowded onto a small surface. This means that above all the cuneiform clay tablet was an aid to memorization. Tradition weighs so heavily on communication that for several millennia the clay tablet fulfilled its function successfully for the businessmen of the Middle East, and where it was most firmly established many merchants continued to use it well after consonantal writing on papyrus had become the rule in lands newer to writing.

Like bamboo in the Far East and in Southeast Asia or the agave plant in Mexico, the papyrus served a large number of purposes in Egypt. Its roots could be sucked; it could be used to make sails for boats, sandals, loin-cloths, woven baskets, and even the hulls of light boats.

This member of the cyperaceae family was a swamp plant that grew in clumps at times nearly ten feet high. It found its ideal habitat in the Nile River delta, where it gave rise to a bustling industry.[5] Attempts to break the Egyptian monopoly by cultivating papyrus in Syria, Babylon, and (much later) Sicily were only moderately successful.

Because Egyptian sources say little about how paper was obtained from the papyrus plant, we have to turn to Pliny's *Natural History* for information. The fibrous pith of the stalk was cut into thin strips as much as 40 centimeters long. These strips were then laid down in close-set rows on a damp tablet and covered with another similar layer laid down in the opposite direction. The resulting sheet was beaten gently with a mallet and left to dry in the sun. Next it was smoothed with an ivory or shell tool. Finally a number of these sheets (usually twenty) were glued end to end to form a scroll.

Flexible, solid, and of a brilliant ivory white, papyrus paper felt like silk to the touch. The scribes used a cut reed dipped in ink to write on it. The Egyptians seem to have used papyrus very early, given that inscriptions from the first dynasty (ca. 3100–ca. 2700) show a scribe with his writing tools and a scroll. The only sample we have from that epoch is one virgin papyrus (of good quality, however) found in the tomb of a functionary. The first documents written on papyrus sheets are no older than the fifth dynasty (ca. 2500–2350). The famous squatting scribe in the Musée du Louvre dates from about 2400 B.C., and the "oldest book in the world," the Pruss papyrus, which contains texts from the fifth dynasty, seems to have been copied in hieratic script as late as 2000–1900 B.C.

It is not clear when this prestigious material moved beyond its country of origin. It is generally believed that the Akkadians knew papyrus in the sixteenth century B.C. and that the Phoenicians, who had close relations with Egypt, used it and traded it at least from the eleventh century. Mesopotamian bas-reliefs and frescoes rather frequently show two scribes side by side taking notes, the Assyrian scribe writing on a clay tablet and an Aramaean scribe writing on a scroll that may have been made of papyrus or of leather. Some of the Dead Sea scrolls are written on metal or papyrus, but most are written on skins, which leads us to the conclusion that leather was widely used in the Middle East, where papyrus must have been rare and expensive.

The Greeks must have had papyrus by the seventh century B.C., given that Greek mercenaries and merchants had flocked to Egypt and had made Naucratis a great commercial center. Although Herodotus mentions the papyrus plant in his description of Egypt he does not add that it served to make paper. The first mention of it in a Greek text appears in the *Anabasis,* where Xenophon describes a shipwreck off the coast of Thrace of a ship carrying bales of papyrus sheets that had already been used on one side and were undoubtedly on their way to that distant region to be reused on the verso. Alphonse Dain remarks:

> To tell the truth, until the mid-fourth century the Greeks lacked
> a common, inexpensive writing material accessible to all. In a
> word, the Greeks had no paper. We need to insist on this point.
> The average Greek wrote on anything at hand, and first on pot-
> tery fragments—*ostraca*. We have all seen the picture in our
> schoolbooks of the sherd on which an ordinary Athenian had
> written the name of Themistocles to vote for his ostracism. In a
> later age, in the time of Ptolemy, an ode of Sappho was written
> on a pottery fragment. . . . The ordinary person in Greece used
> quite perishable materials for his private purposes, materials
> that have left only very few authentic fragments. They wrote on
> waxed tablets, bits of leather or pieces of skin—one document
> was written on snakeskin. They used thin plates of lead and
> later sheets of gold and silver; lead was preferred for formulaic
> incantations.[6]

This means that in the Greek world the status of the written text was not
at all what one might think. When the alphabet appeared everyone could
use writing as he wished and as he understood it, and writing left the
dwellings of princes and the closed circles of the scribes. It soon appeared
on the walls as inscriptions, and after 650 B.C., when legislators gave written form to the law, it gained a new status. As Marcel Détienne put it,
writing became "a publicity agent" and a "constituent in the political
field." Henceforth, to make sure that all would submit to its will, the city
made its rules monumental and visible.

> A complex organization served to support [the rules] in the Pry-
> taneum, the place for political decisions: [there were] writing
> tables set up in the center of the public space [and] written signs
> lauding the independence of writing. But also affirming a will
> to act, to transform public life, to impose new practices,
> whether in the city's intervention in blood crimes or in the as-
> sembly's obligation to accept the will of the majority.[7]

This demonstrates that the importance of public inscriptions in the ancient
city was clearly to assert a presence more than to be read. We must also
remember that the scarcity of writing materials for individual use was so
acute and the role of oral teaching so important that disciples jealously
conserved the works of the great masters in single copies, eventually accompanied by the works of their respective commentators. Aristotle's
works, which spent long years stored in a cave, would probably have dis-

appeared if they had not been bought by an intelligent bibliophile. The greatest innovation in materials occurred with the large-scale introduction of papyrus into Greece after the fourth century as a result of the Ptolemies' support of exportation. From that time on libraries developed, but so did commerce in books, traces of which can be found in Athens in the fifth century. As a result, the true appearance of the book, in the sense in which we understand the term today, came when the material on which the text was written was itself the object of large-scale production and became a trade commodity.

More than in classical Greece, writing seems to have been omnipresent in Rome beginning in the late Republic, as Claude Nicolet has demonstrated:

> Despite the overwhelming importance of eloquence and oral techniques, we should not forget that nearly all the operations and circumstances of civic life involved the frequent use of writing. Declarations to the censor were copied on to registers; texts of proposed laws were posted up, as were the names of candidates for office. Voting-tablets were used, on which the elector himself had to inscribe a few letters at least. . . . We never hear of a Roman citizen being at a loss when called on to vote in an election (contrast Plutarch's story of the Athenian peasant asking Aristides to write his own name on an *ostrakon*) or, as in some new democracies at the present day, of ballots on which the candidates are distinguished for the benefit of the illiterate by different colours, pictures of animals etc. Such indications give the impression of what may almost be called a clerical civilization. This, of course, may be accounted for in two alternative ways. We may deduce from it that only a privileged minority generally took part in civic life, since it could not be fully lived without a fairly high degree of literacy. . . . Or, on the contrary, we may note the various signs that most of the citizen body took a remarkably large part in the different forms of communal life and, since this involved the use of writing, we may infer that the proportion of literates in the population, including that of Romanized Italy, was unusually high.[8]

Anyone who walked the streets of a Roman city would encounter abundant evidence of the omnipresence of writing, in dedications and honorific inscriptions incised on the monuments, in altars at street crossings, in boundary stones that showed the limits of a jurisdiction, in markers for the aqueducts that crisscrossed the city, in authorizations to construct granted by public administrations or institutions, not to mention the *Forma Urbis*, the marble map of Rome in the Forum of Peace in the age of Septimius Severus, or the many lost written pieces—posters, signs, and placards carried on sticks during processions (Mireille Corbier). Writing provided a spectacle lacking in the medieval city (Armando Petrucci). The excavations in Pompeii and Herculaneum, buried as a result of the eruption of Vesuvius on 24 August in A.D. 79, confirm this observation. In Pompeii a number of "electoral posters" have been found painted on walls. Innumerable graffiti attest to a high degree of day-to-day familiarity with writing and to a broad-based acquaintance with poets like Ovid and Propertius. Pompeii, which had strong ties with Greece and was bilingual, as were many cities of the Roman world, had several elementary schools that functioned largely outdoors, with somewhat rustic equipment, and traces have been found of more advanced educational institutions. It is true that the fine ladies of the city had slaves to write for them when they went to call on their bankers. Everyone did his own bookkeeping, however: one baker had his portrait painted holding a *volumen* while his spouse made preparations to use a writing tablet. The number of literate citizens seems to have been high, and many slaves were trained to write. We can find "fine hands" even among the gladiators who, like all the elite troops, were probably not the brutes that they are so often imagined to have been. Furthermore, the evidence from Pompeii can be compared with indications in the archives of a second-century company of *auxilii* found in the desert of Libya. These archives, written on papyrus sheets and *ostraca*, show that the Roman troops had almost as much red tape as modern armies (Robert Marichal).[9] It is possible that the literacy rate was no higher in the Roman legions than it was in the regiments of the Napoleonic Empire in which Jean-Roch Coignet served: obliged to learn to read before he could be promoted to corporal, when he retired as a captain Coignet wrote his memoirs phonetically.

Publishing and the book trade were also developed in ancient Rome. Atticus, Cicero's correspondent, was also his bookseller. Atticus kept a fairly large number of slaves who could copy books in Greek and on occasion in Latin as well, and at times he used correctors to revise a text. We do not know how big a "press run" an "edition" of a work might have, but we do know (from a letter of Pliny the Elder) that Regulus's eulogy of his young son was distributed in thousands of copies and that authors often revised their texts in view of a second edition.

Once a new work had come out, it took its place on the racks of one of the bookstores in the busiest quarters of the city. New publications were publicized by posters and flyers and extracts might even be circulated. The company of booksellers was sought after, and men of letters often frequented their shops. Under the Empire the larger provincial cities had their own bookshops, enabling Horace to boast that his *Ars poetica* was sold on the banks of the Bosphorus, in Spain, in Gaul, and in Africa. Propertius expressed satisfaction at being read in the frigid lands of the North, and Martial at having readers among the young people and the elderly ladies of Vienne on the banks of the Rhône. Pliny states that Varro was read in all corners of the earth, and Ovid consoled himself in exile with the thought that his works traveled west through the empire to reach Rome and Italy.[10]

Lest these few remarks be misleading, if one could calculate annual papyrus production in the Nile Valley the figure would surely be well below the production figures of fourteenth-century paper mills. The Roman administration made increasing use of papyrus under the Empire, and it took care to keep its administrative offices supplied: the *Scriptura historiae Augustae* tells us that a decree of Emperor Aurelian (third century A.D.) stated that Egypt was to deliver to Rome, in perpetuity and as a tax in kind, papyrus, linen, hemp, and glass. Always a scarce and precious commodity, papyrus paper was still for the most part reserved for record-keeping and accounts, for authenticated documents, and for the final draft of official acts. This meant that only the richest citizens could amass even a few *volumina*, as attested by finds in Pompeii and Herculaneum. One might well wonder whether the major merchants often used papyrus. Moreover we know that important people had slaves to write their letters for them on waxed tablets. Similarly a good number of contracts between private persons were drawn up on two tablets attached like a diptych and then closed and sealed to avoid fraud. Innumerable sums written on walls, on wooden tablets, or on *ostraca* have also been found in the four corners of the empire. Classical societies, where the literacy rate was high (at least in certain milieus and certain sectors) seem never to have found a way to procure sufficient quantities of an appropriate writing material—until the appearance of parchment.

Parchment began to compete with papyrus in the West between the first and the fourth centuries A.D.[11]

From time immemorial animal skins had served to write on. According to an ancient tradition, the technique for making parchment from skins was invented by the inhabitants of Pergamum after Ptolemy V Epiphanes, the king of Egypt, had prohibited the exportation of papyrus out of jealousy over the founding of the library of Pergamum by King Eumenes II (197–158 B.C.). This is why an edict of Diocletian (301) called parchment *membrana pergamena* and St. Jerome (A.D. 330–420) called it *pergamenum*.

Parchment was made by taking the skins of sheep, goats, or calves and first scraping them clean, removing the hairs, and rubbing them smooth with pumice. The skins were then washed, dressed with chalk, and the surfaces were finished with a lime-based wash. Vellum was made of the skin of a stillborn or very young animal and was known for its suppleness, thinness, and the absence of the imperfections that dotted the skins where the bulbous hair roots of the adult animal were removed. Large-scale manufacture of parchment as a replacement for papyrus most probably began when it became obvious that papyrus production was insufficient. Parchment was widely used in the early Middle Ages when communication routes with Egypt were disrupted. Although less prestigious than papyrus, it offered a good number of advantages: more resistant, it defied time, and it began to be used soon after the appearance of the codex.

One inestimable advantage of parchment was that it could be produced in the West, thus freeing Europe from the vagaries of papyrus shipments from the Middle East and decentralizing the production of writing materials. Still, it was only a palliative. Although it has become fashionable to refute the somewhat whimsical calculation that one manuscript cost the lives of an entire flock of animals, it nonetheless took two hundred skins to make the Souvigny Bible, which contains 392 large-format leaves measuring roughly 560 × 390 mm). It was a material that could meet demand only in an era in which the use of writing was extremely limited. Moreover its preparation required a certain technological know-how. Thus, in order to economize, old parchments were washed and reused, producing the famous palimpsests on which the older text appears faintly under the new, to the great delight of paleographers.

For a long time papyrus continued to be used in the East. Private records were often written on papyrus up to the sixth century A.D., and it was not until 676, after the Arabs had taken over Egypt, that the Merovingian chancery gave it up. The pontifical chancery continued to use papyrus until the ninth century, for the most part using Sicilian-grown stock.

During this time a far greater revolution was in the making in the Orient.

The Chinese, who normally used thin wooden boards or bamboo strips to write on, began very early to write on textiles as well, silk in particular. The invention of paper—that is, of a substance made of vegetable fibers reduced to a pulp, placed in molds or forms and then dried—is traditionally attributed to Cai Lun, a government official and director of the imperial workshops who wrote a report on the subject to the emperor-regent in A.D. 105. Scholars have recently found shreds of paper, one of them made of various fibers (hemp, ramie) dating from the first century A.D., which would put the discovery of paper back two centuries. Thus Cai Lun's contribution was probably to encourage the use of paper instead of silk cloth.[12]

After that date the Chinese made constant improvements in paper, which was a valuable commodity. Its use spread to Korea, Vietnam, and Japan, then throughout the Orient. It reached the Arab world, apparently with men of the Caliph of Baghdad acting as intermediaries after they had been imprisoned by the Chinese and had learned the secrets of the fabrication of paper from their captors (early eighth century). Gradually Baghdad, Persia, Armenia, and Syria became active centers for manufacturing and exporting paper, and the Byzantines began to write their books on Syro-Iranian paper starting in the eighth century and their acts starting in the eleventh. The Arabs carried the art of papermaking into Egypt, where papyrus culture was on the decline, and then on into Morocco: there were four hundred paper mills in Fez in the twelfth century. Thus the disciples of Mohammed had an inexhaustible supply available for the development of their culture and the extension of their administration.

CREATING A TEXT

The way a document was presented—whether words were considered significant entities and separated from one another; whether texts were punctuated and broken up into sentences and paragraphs or not—allows us a better comprehension of the relations between speech and writing within any given society and over the course of history.

The first case in point is Sumerian, a vernacular language that became a language of culture after the definitive triumph of the Akkadians. Mesopotamian writing, as we have seen, was set down in vertical columns, in principle reading from right to left, on the surface of clay tablets. These columns were initially divided into circled sections—"cartouches"—reading from top to bottom, in each one of which signs were inscribed for groups of words that together bore a message. Here is what Jean-Marie Durand has to say about this arrangement:

> Given that the archaic cartouche represents a unit of meaning,
> it is logical that the scribe, the moment he notes only what his
> space allows him, arranges his signs in the inscribed space not
> according to their order of pronunciation but according to a cri-
> terion of filling [the space] that could be qualified as either aes-
> thetic or utilitarian. Thus one sees that, from the point of view
> of reading, one must first take on the comprehension of the
> cartouche in an archaic text; what is understood is not a series
> of words but the set of signifiers that make up [the cartouche].[13]

The scribe had to determine the length of his text according to the format
of the tablet, the dimensions of the tablet, and the number of cartouches
available, and what he inscribed quite naturally functioned as an aid to
memory that might bear more than one meaning, particularly in the case
of literary compositions. This form of writing later lost its compartments,
and the cartouches were replaced by horizontal lines. When this happened the scribe was limited only by the size of the tablet, and in fact he
occasionally carried the text over onto its sides. He was also freer to develop the contents of the document that he was transcribing. This occurred
in a period when spoken Sumerian was beginning to be forgotten. This
means that an archaic Sumerian tablet can be distinguished from a later
copy by its incomplete redaction. As Jean-Marie Durand puts it, "Progress
in the notation of a Sumerian text went in the direction of a more and
more thorough explicitation, moving from pure ellipsis to total phonetic
notation."[14] Conceivably, the scribes who performed that explicitation interpreted a given text in different ways, one of which was eventually consecrated as the vulgate in the Recent era (first millennium). If this is
accurate, progress in the notation of Sumerian was tied to the fact that the
Sumerian language had ceased to be the vernacular and had become
the language of culture—a pattern that we will encounter repeatedly in
the course of this book.

I shall not return to hieroglyphics, but I need to add a note on Egyptian
writing systems before passing on to Oriental writing.[15] From the time of
the Middle Kingdom writing systems less monumental than hieroglyphics—hieratic, then demotic—were written to be read from right to left,
without word separation or punctuation.[16] Someone from Western culture
(unless he is a specialist) might find this all the more surprising because
these were systems for writing rapidly. How could such messages be deciphered with any sort of fluency?

Oriental writing systems—Chinese and Japanese—will help answer that question. In principle all Chinese characters were inscribed inside an imaginary square of uniform size. Traditionally they were aligned in vertical columns reading from right to left with no separation between the words. A horizontal disposition was also in early use.[17] The People's Republic of China has adopted a horizontal layout but the Japanese continue to use the traditional style (although not exclusively) in published books.

For a long time Chinese and Japanese texts were not punctuated and the end of a sentence was not marked, which makes the reading of classical Chinese books written in the traditional manner seem to us extremely arduous. In the past, however, when oral teaching was the rule, reading must have been guided by the rhythm of the phrases. Similarly, deciphering juridical and technical works or administrative documents must have been aided by acquaintance with the stereotyped formulas they contained. Certain administrative documents had a number of blank spaces that undoubtedly aided comprehension of the text. We need to remember, though, that for tens of centuries the Chinese have practiced forms of fluent reading and ways of setting down a text that seem to us singularly primitive. Indeed, they may not have given thought to the problem. They continue to use an ideographic system, in Japan completed by syllabaries, to express languages that are admittedly of a completely different structure from our own, and they do so at no cost to rapidity of reading or agility in their thought processes: quite the contrary.[18]

When we examine the oldest texts in alphabetic writing we can see that in consonantal writing systems the need to separate words for reading aloud seems to have led scribes to separate words in the written text as well. As James Février says in connection with Phoenician script:

> It is the perfect type of the consonantal script—of abstract writing, if you prefer. It is also and in a certain sense a script of words since every word, with the exception of a few extremely brief particles, is separated from the others by a vertical bar. If Phoenician writing, even more than Egyptian and above all more than Sumero-Akkadian, rigorously separated words, it was because the abstract nature [and] the very imprecision of that written notation necessitated the distinction of words in order to vocalize them. Consonantal scripts were to remain faithful to this need during their entire existence. Doubtless in most Phoenician epigraphic texts, once the epoch of archaic

Phoenician had passed (and in great part under the influence of Greek epigraphy), the separative signs tended to disappear, but they subsisted sporadically and we find them again in Neo-Punic and especially in Paleo-Hebraic until the second century B.C. Furthermore, when writing cursively, the Aramaeans were apt to separate words with a small space; they even went a good deal farther and for certain letters created special forms for final letters to warn the reader that he was at the end of a word. The custom has persisted, what is more, in the last descendant of Aramaean writing, Arabic, given that Arabic script is an Aramaic script.[19]

The Greeks, who had taken Phoenician writing or a system close to it as their inspiration for an alphabet, at first separated words in their inscriptions with a bar or one or more points. They then stopped doing so, as if it seemed to them unnecessary.

The problem of textual disposition in the two alphabets that were the direct sources of our civilization, the Greek and the Latin, takes us back to Egypt, where most of the papyri pertinent to the question have been found. The "Timotheus papyrus," one of the oldest known Greek manuscripts, found in a tomb in the Nile Valley, contains a work to be sung to cithara accompaniment entitled *The Persians* written by a certain Timotheus of Miletus (ca. 400 B.C.). The scroll, which we can date to the late fourth century B.C., is composed of sheets measuring 19 × 22 centimeters. The fifth column, conserved intact, is made up of twenty-seven lines of unequal length, since the copyist did not follow the metric pattern of the poem. Copied in a regular hand, this text is nonetheless noted in *scriptura continua* with no break between words or punctuation except for a "paragraph" line with the figure of a bird and a "coronis" separating the account of a battle and the poet's commentary. It goes without saying that the work shows no trace of either breathings or accents.[20]

The manuscripts of the great classical Greek texts must have been presented in much the same way. We know, however, that after the death of Alexander (323 B.C.) and the division of his empire, Ptolemy I, a Macedonian, managed to make Egypt the leading power in the eastern Mediterranean. He and his successors were not content to develop Egypt's economy (notably, by massive exportation of papyrus); they also made Alexandria a major center of Greek thought. In particular, they charged scholars, men of letters, poets, and grammarians with gathering together all the Hellenic masterworks, and they employed a throng of copyists. Their palace library contained some 490,000 scrolls and the library of the Serapeum 42,800.

When the soldiers of Emperor Aurelian burned the library of the Museum in A.D. 273 a good many masterworks were lost, but the texts that survived in copies made from original manuscripts in Alexandria and in Pergamum, whose rulers had similar policies, give witness to an immense effort of standardization and revision.

Standardization primarily concerned the dimensions and the contents of the scrolls, which could not be stored in infinite quantities. Although an occasional lover of letters might order a copy made with large margins on a scroll 40 centimeters wide or a "dwarf" barely 5 centimeters wide, most of the *volumina* measured 25 centimeters by some 7 to 10 meters in length, which means they could contain relatively extensive texts. Division into books and chapters, not originally practiced, began to appear. [21]

At the same time, grammarians and copyists took on the enormous task of text revision. Beginning in the first century A.D. they were largely responsible for the modifications discernible on the papyri that have come down to us. These ancient books were generally written in particularly clear and elegant characters the quality and size of which depended on how much the scribe was paid. The lines normally contained a limited number of full characters—in poetry one line of epic hexameter, iambic trimeter, or dramatic declamatory verse; in prose usually twenty to thirty letters per line. Relatively short lines made it easier to grasp the text by eye or to read it aloud.

The texts were usually written in *scriptura continua*. Furthermore, a trend toward standardization influenced by the text editors in the library of Alexandria led to the appearance of a certain number of diacritical marks. Diacriticals helped the reader to separate sentences and paragraphs and to pronounce and accentuate words correctly. Thus breathings and accents arose. Similarly, a point on the line between letters at mid-height or on a level with the tops of letters sometimes separated phrases and indicated paragraph breaks. The two points that initially signaled the end of a sentence later showed a change of speaker in a dialogue. Finally, a horizontal line under the letters beginning a line served very early to indicate the end of a sentence or a paragraph and the beginning of a new paragraph. Only very occasionally dramatic dialogue used abbreviations to show who was speaking. Finally, the most famous works were accompanied by explanatory scholia. [22]

Thus the basis for ancient punctuation, as far as it went, was essentially rhetorical, unlike modern punctuation (in German in particular), where punctuation reflects logical analysis. In reality, although ancient grammarians elaborated a syntax of words, the appearance of a syntax of propositions had to wait for the labors of the medieval grammarians and the eventual accomplishments of the grammarians of Port-Royal—another proof of the importance of the art of oratory in antiquity.

We know less about how the classical Latin manuscripts were redacted. If we can give credence to the inscriptions and the few Latin papyri available to us, the Latins separated words by dots up to the second or third centuries A.D., after which *scriptura continua* came into general use. Punctuation was not unknown, but it was never given any great importance, although at a very early date the jurists adopted systems of reference. Thus copyists transcribing a literary text did little more than guide reading by setting off divisions in the discourse by a change of line and by writing the first letters of the new paragraph into the left-hand margin, outside the vertical justification of the text. A pause for rhetorical reasons was often marked by a blank space within a line.

The problem of Latin punctuation is infinitely complex and still not well understood. I cannot go into it further here except to recall that St. Jerome worked out a particularly painstaking system of punctuation to facilitate the reading of sacred texts for friars with relatively little instruction. In a famous passage from his preface to the text of Isaiah, he says that he had borrowed "the practice of Demosthenes and Cicero, who both wrote in prose not in verse, of transcribing their texts *per cola et commata* for the convenience of readers." The meaning of "per cola et commata" is not easy to define, however (Jean Vezin). The term seems to refer to breaking the text up into brief phrases containing a complete idea that can easily be grasped by the eye, perhaps at one glance.[23]

It is also important to know how Latin understood the Greek words *colon, comma,* and *periodos.* Among Latin grammarians and theoreticians these terms seem to designate parts of the sentence rather than punctuation marks. The punctuation mark par excellence was for them the period or point (*punctus*), while the *distinctio* designated a pause or, more exactly, a particular sort of pause. The *colon* designated a part of a phrase complete in all its grammatical parts and, in metrics, a part of a strophe with the proper number of feet. The *comma* designated an incised phrase, a brief, complete clause in prose, or a break in metrical texts. These terms were first applied to forms of punctuation by Donatus (fourth century), who differentiated among the "distinction" (a dot on a level with the letters), which marked a stop at the end of a sentence, and two ways to mark lesser pauses, the "subdistinction" (a dot by the base of the letters), and the "middle distinction" (at the midpoint of the letters). This form of punctuation was linked with breathing, thus with reading aloud, which means that it was based on oratory more than on meaning. Donatus' works were widely consulted and commented, in particular by Servius and Diomedes. St. Jerome was a pupil of Donatus, and we can suppose that he punctuated in the fashion of his times by placing dots at various distances from the base line. Composition *in colis et commatibus* also seems to have referred to a layout of the text analogous to that of verse. It is extremely difficult to ascertain exactly what that layout was, but it seems that certain texts, particularly those for use in the schools, were presented in ways that highlighted the composition of the oratorical phrase and that resembled the layout of certain poetic texts in distichs or triplets with the first line set in or out from the margin in relation to the others. Still, the papyri that have come down to us show that many texts of the first centuries of the Common Era were not punctuated. For the rest, we must hope that Pascale Bourgain, who kindly gave me a note on the subject, will soon enlighten us with a study on the concepts of Latin grammarians.[24]

We need to turn to how a manuscript was constituted and presented to the reader, beginning with the *liber archetypus,* the author's manuscript on the basis of which (in principle) other direct copies were made. This sort of manuscript was written by a highly specialized slave, the *librarius,* for whose services there was keen competition and who might on occasion be lent to a friend. It was his task to carry out the physical redaction of the work and devise its page layout. The *librarius* first wrote his fair copy of the text on separate sheets, oiled their backs to protect them against mites and mildew, and glued them end to end to form a *volumen.* Next he smoothed the two edges of the rolled scroll with a pumice stone, then he attached the first and last sheets to a cylindrical stick, the *umbilicus,* the two ends of which had been painted, blackened, and decorated with ivory disks (*cornua*). He then made a title slip (*titulus*) by writing the name of the author and the title of the work on a band of fine parchment (*membranula*) and attached it to the scroll. Finally he placed the scroll in a parchment envelope or wrapping that he colored purple.

The Latin *volumen* was thus a precious object. As a general rule, it was some 6 to 8 meters long, like its Greek counterpart. The text was written on it in parallel columns of between 15 and 30 characters to the line, each column being 25 to 45 lines long, which made "pages" of from 300 to

1,350 signs, as compared with today's typewritten page of somewhat more than 1,500 characters or a printed page of the present work of some 3,000 characters (including the spaces that do not exist in a manuscript text written in *scriptura continua*). This means that each *volumen* contained a text notably shorter than that of a slim book today.[25]

This sort of scroll was meant to be unrolled as the reader passed from one set of columns to the other, hence reading was necessarily "continuous." Should the reader care to return to a previous passage or jump ahead to a later one, he had the irritating task of manipulating this elegant and somewhat fragile object. Consulting a specific passage was made even more complicated because there was no table of contents and no index. Pliny is credited with having first thought to place something like a table of contents, written on a special scroll, at the head of the volumes of his *Natural History*, which he conceived as an encyclopedic work.

The appearance of the codex—the work presented on pages written on both sides rather than on one side of a continuous scroll—was undoubtedly the most important revolution in the book in the Common Era.

The first trace of the codex comes from six epigrams of Martial (40–103 A.D.) written, according to Jean Mallon, to serve as labels for six codices distributed by lottery and containing the works of Homer, Virgil, Cicero, Livy, Ovid, and Martial himself. The poet expresses admiration that such immense works could be enclosed in such a reduced space. He stresses that these new books do not encumber libraries, can be used conveniently on a voyage, and can be held in one hand. His wonder seems to indicate that they were then a novelty. One might think that from the outset all codices were made of parchment, but the oldest of them (admittedly, found in Egypt), use papyrus as well. Rare exceptions aside, the oldest codices date from the third and fourth centuries. We can thus suppose that the traditional public remained faithful to the elegant *volumen*. Christians preferred the new form, however, for preserving their sacred texts and the writings of their doctors because it made the works easier to consult. They also preferred parchment, which was more resistant and durable than papyrus paper.[26]

The effects of this revolution were felt only in the long term. Heirs to ancient traditions, the oldest codices in our libraries usually chose the most compact form possible. It was only during the Carolingian Renaissance, when Latin had ceased to be considered a current spoken language, that the copyists attempted to reproduce texts more correctly and to insert punctuation into them. Furthermore it took a long process of development and the advent of another renaissance, that of the eleventh and twelfth centuries, before each word was represented as a separate entity on the written page.

WRITING

It should hardly be necessary to recall that the art of writing requires physical operations in which the hand must respond automatically to commands given by the brain after the brain has accomplished a particularly complex set of analyses. The history of writing helps us to understand both the relationship between the scriptor and the text and the diachronic evolution of the morphology of signs.

First the scribes. Bas-reliefs, paintings, and statuettes show them at work. In Mesopotamia they are represented holding a tablet, a papyrus, or a leather scroll in one hand and a reed or a stylus in the other. Usually standing, they take notes facing a sovereign or, on a somewhat humbler plane, a high functionary or an accountant. The position is singularly uncomfortable, but it was used only for taking dictation. We can also see Egyptian scribes crouching to write on a papyrus or a leather scroll spread out on their knees; or sitting on one leg, the other knee up, writing either on a hand-held tablet or on a papyrus spread out on their thigh.[27]

A bas-relief from Ostia shows two scribes taking dictation from a third scribe, all three of them seated before low tables on which waxed tablets are piled up. Is this simply an exception? In any event a number of illuminations before the thirteenth century show authors writing on a tablet resting on their knees. One statue in the royal portal of Chartres Cathedral (twelfth century) gives a singularly precise portrait of a scribe tracing letters on a portable desk posed on his knees. Finally, a fourteenth-century statue from Verona (now in London) shows a person seated taking notes on a board placed in front of him and connected to the back of his chair by two movable arms.[28]

The calligraphers and illuminators who worked on valuable manuscripts were probably never satisfied with such incommodious installations. Still it is clear that the desk, as we know it, was not commonly used until around the thirteenth century. Hence the innumerable complaints from copyists that such work tires the entire body. This is proof that writing practices that we take for granted resulted from a process of perfecting physical techniques that took several civilizations and innumerable generations. These techniques (and here we must focus on Western Europe or be lost among generalizations) produced Latin writing.

We need to begin by noting that there are gaps in the history of Latin writing. Because papyrus paper was an extremely fragile material, Latin manuscripts—rare exceptions aside—have been lost. There are even fewer Latin manuscripts on papyrus than Greek manuscripts. This means that the history of Latin writing must depend upon inscriptions on stone, *ostraca,* graffiti, and notes taken on waxed tablets, to which we can add, after the Common Era, shreds of papyrus and scraps of parchment. This continued to be true up to the triumph of Christianity and the barbarian invasions or until the fourth and especially the fifth centuries. When our immediate ancestors thought of the Roman alphabet they had in mind the capital letters that they could see on the facades of monuments that still stood before them.

If there is a problem regarding sources there is also a problem of method. For a long time, the paleographers who studied Greek and Latin writing were primarily interested in classification, so they strove to name (or to "label") each variety that they thought they had isolated. Next—as always—they attempted to justify their nomenclature by defining the graphic properties corresponding to each name. This may perhaps have been the most urgent task at hand, but they tended to forget that a writing style is an ongoing creation on the part of living beings. Today's specialists have quite other preoccupations. They are aware that writing is in constant evolution and that changes depended upon three things: the writing instrument utilized and the size of its tip; the writing material and its position in relation to the writer; and the order in which marks were made on the sheet, which is called the *ductus.* [29]

The paleographer's task is far from easy because writing is never consistent in any one epoch or region. There are formal hands, the canonized legacy of past traditions and habits, that emanated from the great chanceries, and there are usually cursive hands in constant evolution that may some day become canonized and provide a model that will be distorted in its turn. Furthermore, in all societies of the manuscript, styles differed according to milieu and the sort of text they noted. The result is a broad variety of recognizable models all of which reflect their civilization and require an extremely complex process of decipherment. These are essential matters that most historians unfamiliar with paleographic techniques carefully avoid and leave to a handful of specialists whose work they seldom know.

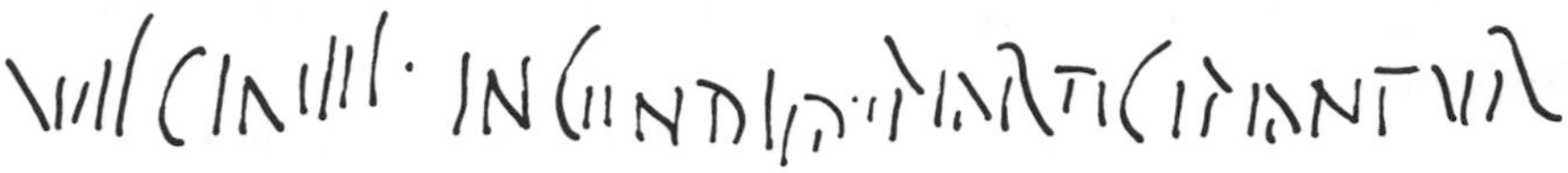

Fig. 1.   Cursive Latin. Pompeii, graffito, immediately prior to 80 B.C.: *veicinei, incendia, participantur*.

Fig. 2.   Cursive Latin. Pompeii, graffito, ca. 60 A.D.: *amoris ignes, si sentieres . . .* (Figs. 1 and 2 taken from Marichal, "L'écriture latine," 205).

The relevant hypotheses are always fragile and regularly challenged. The terrain is mined, but let us advance into it. The first documents that we have in Latin scripts are inscriptions. Their capital letters are easy to decipher, but for a long time they seem cold, as if a peasant's language was producing a peasant's writing. The influence of the highly refined style of the Greek stone-engravers was felt only centuries later, and Latin letters graven in stone were not habitually given serifs until the first century. After all, Cicero makes a point of being unaware of the work of Hellenic artists. Moreover, we do not know at what point the Romans were sufficiently familiar with writing to use (or have their slaves use) a cursive hand. Waxed tablets found in Pompeii and written by professionals bear traces of letters that still corresponded to archaic traditions, but graffiti from that same city show that the Latins made extraordinary advances between 80 and 30 B.C., passing from a stiff and fairly rudimentary cursive to a supple, broad, and elegant one (figs. 1 and 2).

Urbanitas replaced *rusticitas* in a society in which knowledge of writing, as Robert Marichal points out, was indispensable to the citizen.[30]

The still heterogeneous materials available in the period nonetheless show that Greek and Latin writing was singularly homogeneous throughout the empire from the North Sea to the Sahara and from the Euphrates to Spain in any one epoch. If the documents (for the most part from military sources) are to be believed, this is striking proof of the intensity of exchanges and communications throughout this vast space. It also shows the coherence and force of penetration of a culture that managed to persuade the majority of the Gauls to forsake their language in only a few centuries and that taught their Gallic elite not only the language of their Latin conquerors but also their written culture.

Writing evolved nonetheless. I shall limit myself to a rapid review of the theories of Jean Mallon, which specialists use as a basis for discussion. Mallon gave final expression to his long study of the question in a film of a high degree of scholarly rigor, *Ductus, ou la formation de l'alphabet moderne,* presented for the first time in 1976. In this film Mallon used the medium of the cinema to trace the execution of graphic strokes and to show how their long-term evolution slowed or accelerated. Emmanuel Poulle, professor of paleography at the Ecole des Chartes, summarizes Mallon's conclusions:

> One can see how, as if in a logical progression, the dominant horizontality of writing, which leads letters to open towards the right and tip toward the left, transformed painstaking calligraphy [*écriture à main posée*] into a cursive script called "classical common writing," then how, in the second century, changes in the technical conditions of the act of writing led to a shift of the angle of the thick strokes that, applied to cursive scripts, created a new common writing. As this change was taking place, the most famous specimens of writing that antiquity has left to us parade before our eyes in all their graphic diversity: the *Epitome* of Livy and the *De bellis macedonicis,* that "miserable scrap of parchment" of a few square centimeters that is both the most ancient evidence of the codex and the essential evidence of a graphic situation from which the new writing was to spring.[31]

We can see how a primordial manner of writing made of carefully formed capital letters, now lost, could have served (and according to Jean Mallon did serve) as a model for both a more conservative, formal writing that emphasized thick strokes and thin strokes and was used in books and official acts, and the old cursive script (the "classical common writing" mentioned above), which was smaller, lighter, and more cursive (fig. 3).

This script was characterized by a systematic elongation upward and toward the left of oblique strokes drawn from left to right. Particularly visible in the letter A, this form of negligence became an elegance and a stylization

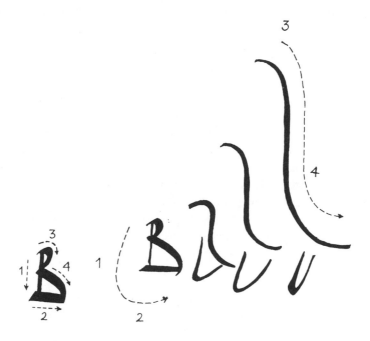

Fig. 3.   The effects of *ductus*: changes in the capital B (taken from Mallon, *Paléo-graphie romaine*, 34).

and was even introduced into epigraphy. It reflects the somewhat Baroque aesthetic of elegant circles in imperial Rome in the time of Tiberius or Nero. Thus, as Robert Marichal points out, it is mistaken to call it "rustic" (*rustica*); to the contrary, it is *urbanissima*. [32]

In the third century, however, a new graphic type developed, doubtless as a result of a series of transformations that had begun as early as the first century (new common script; Mallon's "common writing"). Through the centuries it replaced the older script ("classical common writing") to which it bore no relation. Comparison of sketches of the same word, *praefectus*, written in the two "common" scripts clearly shows how different they were (figs. 4 and 5).

The new writing style may perhaps have resulted chiefly from a change in the angle of writing in which the sheet came to be tilted toward the left, as the orientation of the thick strokes seems to show. This change in angle brought on a change in the *ductus* of the letters, certain of which came to look quite modern, but it also resulted in more vertical stems, some of

Fig. 4. *Praefectus*, classical common writing, first century.

Fig. 5. *Praefectus*, new common writing, fourth century (figs. 4 and 5 taken from Poulle, "Une histoire de l'écriture," 144).

which now had ascenders and descenders stretching more decidedly above and below the body of the letters. This characteristic led some scholars to call this hand a primitive minuscule, a notion that Jean Mallon contests, arguing (rightly) that many other hands also show the characteristics of minuscule.[33]

Be that as it may, nothing is ever immutable where writing is concerned, and the appearance of the new cursive script was only a stage in a complex history. Emmanuel Poulle tells us why:

> During the last centuries of the Empire and in the barbarian era the subtle interplay, on the one hand of distortions linked to the action of cursivity, which developed certain morphological elements exaggeratedly (to the point of caricature) and, on the other hand, of stylized canonizations of those distortions as well as reciprocal influences that operated among the various branches issuing from the same trunk—the new common writing—led to the appearance of that masterpiece of medieval calligraphy that was Carolingian minuscule.[34]

The importance of the appearance of minuscule can hardly be emphasized too much. Robert Marichal explains:

> In relation to the capital the minuscule is an absolute advance: it is much more readable. Legibility is not something relative: oculists [and] type-font designers have drawn objective laws of legibility from the mechanism of reading and a comparison of different type styles, and the primitive minuscule conforms to [those laws] much better than the capital. Certain characters have shafts that rise above or descend below the body of the letters; each word has a silhouette of its own. The top portion

of the body of each letter is more differentiated from the other
letters than with capitals; the eye can recognize them more
easily when it follows the upper part of the line, as is the case
in rapid reading.[35]

It is surely not a coincidence that this graphic mutation began with the
success of the codex at the time of the third-century crisis that resulted in
enormous changes in the Roman world in the reign of Diocletian. It was a
time when classical Latin itself was undergoing profound changes and
when Christianity, increasingly widespread in the West, adopted Latin over
Greek as its liturgical language. Compared with radical change of such
scope the evolution of a few pen strokes would certainly not have merited
more than passing mention here if this shift in long-standing habits of
hand, eye, and the mind did not reflect profound transformations in Roman society.

Still, under the Empire there were nearly infinite variations in writing
styles in the Latin world. Not only did cursive hands change but more
solemn and calligraphic styles developed as well. Where books were concerned these styles were the various forms of rustic script or square capitals
that derived from the graphic system of the first century and continued to
be used for copying manuscripts at least until the sixth century. The uncial
and the half-uncial, an almost perfect "minuscule," accompanied the new
cursive script. Finally, although the old cursive script (the "classical common writing") disappeared little by little, the imperial Roman chancery,
which was just as conservative as all great chanceries, continued unper-
turbed to write in a stylized "celestial" version of the old script whose
calligraphy was elongated out of all measure. The emperors Valentinian II
and Valens warned their proconsul in Africa not to allow his administrators
to counterfeit this version (A.D. 367). This made for great variety, a phenomenon that we shall encounter again.

This apparent diversity should not mask an essential fact first noted by
Emmanuel Poulle that concerns a break in the way the letters were executed in all writing styles:

> Throughout this history of Latin writing, from the first monu-
> ments that we can interrogate up to Carolingian minuscule and
> even much later, until the fourteenth century, one thing re-
> mains constant: the fragmented execution of each letter. This
> was a major fact of civilization, even if it appears clearly only in
> a cursive or negligent hand, and it alone can explain the depen-
> dent relations that were established between a given form in the

original capital alphabet and the corresponding and apparently aberrant form in the cursive alphabet, as Mallon has demonstrated in a now classic article on the letter B. This fragmentation persisted in the hands that Mallon called "linked" [*liées*], a term one can accept only if we acknowledge that such hands respected a necessarily fragmented execution of each letter. The combination of two contingencies at first sight contradictory—on the one hand a morphological definition according to which each letter must be executed in two or three strokes and, on the other hand, the economy of the graphic gesture that encourages the hand to reduce the number of times it raises the pen—this combination, I say, produces the characteristic phenomenon of ligatures from head to foot, a system in which the last part of a letter is linked to the first part of the following letter while the two parts of the second are separated by a similar connection. There is something impressive in noting that eight centuries later the same causes produce the same effects: between the cursive but fragmented ligatures characteristic of the group [of letters] "test" as found in a testament on papyrus of the sixth century and in a diocesan legal document [*une charte d'officialité*] of the thirteenth century there is a remarkable identity of structure that testifies, above and beyond appearances, to the continuity of graphic gestures during more than a millennium.[36]

WAYS OF WRITING AND READING

All these matters pose the essential problem of the relationship between the written and the spoken word in ancient societies, notably among the Greeks and the Romans.

We can draw one clear conclusion: the texts discussed thus far—those redacted in alphabetical scripts but probably those in ideographic systems as well—were meant to be read aloud. The "tool words" that are so numerous in Greek and Latin were all the more precious because they permitted the reader to mark progress from one proposition to another. Above all, the rhythm observed in the arrangement of short and long syllables marked the articulation of the period, notably in Latin. Later, the accent indicating higher pitch rather than quantity played a comparable role. Latin sources furnish innumerable proofs of reading aloud in this manner. This is why the scholar Joseph Balogh, in an article written in 1926, could gather passages from such authors as Lucian, Suetonius, Horace, and Ovid that attest to silent reading being considered unusual at the time.[37] The most explicit text is from St. Augustine. Speaking of St. Ambrose in the *Confessions* (6.3) he says:

> When he was reading, his eyes ran over the page and his heart perceived the sense, but his voice and tongue were silent. He did not restrict access to anyone coming in, nor was it customary even for a visitor to be announced. Very often when we were there, we saw him silently reading and never otherwise. After sitting for a long time in silence (for who would dare to burden him in such intent concentration?) we used to go away. We supposed that in the brief time he could find for his mind's refreshment, free from the hubbub of other people's troubles, he would not want to be invited to consider another problem. We wondered if he read silently perhaps to protect himself in case he had a hearer interested and intent on the matter, to whom he might have to expound the text being read if it contained difficulties, or who might wish to debate some difficult questions. If his time were used up in that way, he would get through fewer books than he wished. Besides, the need to preserve his voice, which used easily to become hoarse, could have been a very fair reason for silent reading. Whatever motive he had for his habit, this man had a good reason for what he did. (Trans. Henry Chadwick, 1991)

The texts that Joseph Balogh and his followers presented prompted polemics that have recently been revived. Various interpretations might be put on these texts or other passages cited—from Horace, for example—to attest that silent reading was practiced in antiquity. For Armando Petrucci, to cite one dissenting voice, highly varied forms of reading existed at that time:

> In reality, as everyone knows, the custom of *tacite legere* was already known in the ancient world (Horace *Satires* 2.5.68), and where the early Middle Ages are concerned the situation is a good deal more complex than it seems at first sight. It is in fact possible to distinguish three techniques of reading that were widely diffused and consciously used for different purposes: silent reading, *in silentio*; reading in a low voice called "murmur" or "rumination," which aided meditation and served as a tool for memorization; finally, vocalized reading that, as in antiquity, demanded a particular technique and was quite similar to the practice of liturgical recitation or chant.[38]

Each of these techniques corresponded to a precise function, but beyond a doubt the practice of *scriptura continua* was connected with a concept of reading aimed primarily at the declamation of literary texts—a concept quite evidently linked with teaching methods. Henri-Irénée Marrou, the author of a classic work on education in ancient Greece and Rome, is of help here. [39]

With the democratization of Hellenic society came a corresponding growth of schools for free boys and girls. We know about the methods elaborated in these schools, which were used throughout the Hellenic world and taken up by the Romans, thanks to documents found in Egypt. The schoolmasters of the time practiced a strictly analytic pedagogy, in appearance perfectly logical, that was praised by authors as late as St. Augustine and St. Ambrose. Pupils first recited by heart the names of the letters in order—an exercise with added significance because the letters served as symbols for cosmic elements. Once this vocabulary was assimilated the children passed on to recognition of the corresponding signs, then of syllables of two and three letters, where they had to name the characters before pronouncing the resulting combination. Next they worked on words of two syllables, then on longer words. Rare and complicated terms were preferred because they added to the challenge. Then they moved without transition from reading phrases or short texts to reading selections (also committed to memory) from recognized authors such as Homer and Euripides. Unlike later schoolchildren in the Christian West, they also learned to write on waxed or unwaxed wooden tablets. They also practiced manual *comput*—that is, they did simple calculations with their fingers or with tokens—and they had to be able to write numbers and fractions.

Henri-Irénée Marrou calls this pedagogy summary and brutal, and in many ways it resembles the methods in practice until recently in certain countries of the Middle East or North Africa. Indeed, it required the child to remain passive and it seems to have relied exclusively on fear and emulation for motivation. The method offered little enrichment, and it is hardly surprising that pupils progressed very slowly or that their real education took place elsewhere in the many contacts that daily life provided in the ancient city. At least when young Romans got out of school they could write their names, inscribe the names of electoral candidates, decipher a practical text, and do simple sums.

Many did not stop with elementary schooling and went on to take lessons from a grammarian. Whatever the limits of ancient grammar, after such training the pupil could analyze the structure of discourse and recognize correct forms, for example, of verb tenses. Thus at a relatively advanced age he was equipped to manipulate the language. As a practical exercise and an initiation to traditional culture he had to study the works of the great classical authors. This could prove a delicate operation as the language and vocabulary of such authors were antiquated or specialized (particularly in poetry), but having to compare two levels of language must necessarily have sharpened his sense of precision and broadened his field of knowledge.

One specific exercise seems to have been the end-point of all these labors: an "expressive reading" of texts that were also committed to memory. All the documents agree to show that the traditional ways in which texts were written made careful preparation for this sort of reading imperative. Papyri have even been found in Egypt on which the student separated words to show accentuation and broke them into syllables to aid in scansion. When we add that the third part of ancient education was based on the study of rhetoric, we must admit that, at the time, writing was conceived as a simple means for fixing and memorizing spoken discourse and that the higher goal of all instruction was initiation to the art of eloquence in a society dominated by the prestige of the orator.

These attitudes had consequences of enormous importance for the intellectual realm, first concerning the way literary works were composed. If we remember that the art of writing, fine writing as well as speed-writing, was the specialty of slaves or freedmen, we might wonder to what extent Latin authors, among whom *dictare* at times seems synonymous with composition, practiced a form of oral composition. In fact the notables of ancient Rome (like executives today) dictated official notes, memoirs, reports, and letters; Caesar, like Napoleon later, kept several secretaries occupied at once. Since signatures were not known, men of that rank often added a short note in their own hand at the end of a missive (Cicero's *Vale*). They wrote confidential texts and personal letters in their own hand.

Still, this was hardly the epoch of Balzac or Proust. Pliny tells us that he worked late into the night because he needed darkness and silence in order to concentrate. He composed his text mentally, memorized it, and dictated it the following morning. He was of course acting just like intellectuals today who prefer to "sleep on" a problem or reflect on it overnight in the thought that "the night brings counsel." Pliny undoubtedly memorized not only his text but also the rhythms and cadences that he wanted to give to his text. Yet the same Pliny took along tablets and styli when he went hunting and put them to use during long waits by the nets while the beaters were flushing the game. Virgil spent his mornings meditating on the verses that he later dictated to his secretary. He then took them back and corrected and organized them during the course of the day, probably working alone. Horace recommends frequent use of the blunt end of the stylus to rub out what one has just written (*Satires* 1.10.74–75).

Cicero declares (*De oratore* I.33.150–53) that a carefully meditated speech was still inferior to a written composition that was the fruit of assiduous labor. He adds that thoughts and brilliant expressions flow spontaneously to the tip of the stylus. Quintilian declared himself opposed to dictation.

All in all Latin authors who composed works to be spoken were certainly inconvenienced in certain phases of their work by the fact that it is extremely difficult to declaim a text as one is writing it. They seem normally to have begun by taking notes (*notare, adnotare*). Next they drew up a detailed outline or a first draft (*formare*). Then they dictated the text, paying special attention to its rhythms and periods. Finally they reread and corrected the final version (*emendare*).

The importance of the art of oratory in Rome—and of these methods of composition and reading—reflects the place that rhetoric occupied in Latin discourse. One result is that in spite of the adage *res, non verba*, Latin spoken discourse tended to be verbose. Another is that Romans paid little attention to the material organization of a manuscript into phrases, paragraphs, and chapters, or to following an outline or presenting the text so that its divisions were obvious at a glance. Consequently certain works seem to us negligent and poorly organized. It undoubtedly bothered the Romans less than it does us that Cicero's *De oratore* is a patchwork of separate and disparate texts. Even though Seneca's works are constructed according to strict and scholarly rules they nonetheless seem to us somewhat scattered; and, as Henri-Irénée Marrou has demonstrated, themes and ideas are mingled in St. Augustine. The development of a topic was interrupted before the limits of the reader's attention span were reached, and the topic was picked up again later. Incidental materials and digressions were inserted to amuse the listener. There were innumerable repetitions, but they were not the result of negligence; rather, they reminded the reader-listener, who often read the scroll one sequence at a time, of what was essential, and they lessened his tendency to be distracted.

These methods were bound to influence the ways that classical antiquity remembered and reasoned. In order to get a closer grasp of these ways of thinking we need first to examine the various styles of reading aloud. In a society in which writing was used in the most ordinary daily occurrences there must have been many men who could read faster than their lips could move when they were reading something relating to specific matters in a familiar context—posters, business letters, simple correspondence, or contracts and official or juridical acts in which repetition and stereotyped formulas aided comprehension of the message. Truly cultivated people seem to have been able to read literary works in a genuinely cursive manner. Martial tells us, for example, that the most studious men carried a book in a string bag when they went hunting; Pliny states that Minerva could be encountered in the woods just as easily as Diana; Horace took reading matter to his country house. Catullus did the same when he went to Verona, and booksellers made copies of works that could be read on voyages.

Still, there is much that we do not know. Were these men reading or rereading? We should also remember that the rhythm of the phrases guided reading and contributed much to the pleasure of the reader-listener, and we know that physicians in antiquity recommended to their patients who needed exercise that they read, just as they recommended walking, running, or playing ball games. This proves that at the time reading implied an involvement of the entire body, which helps to explain why Greeks and Romans so often had texts read to them by a special servant. Notables listened to poetry recitations during banquets, and in certain periods they went to hear an author or a lecturer read some new literary work at *recitationes publicae* that somewhat resembled the literary *cénacles* of nineteenth-century France. This fashion, which spread first under Claudius and Nero and again under Domitian, occurred in an age when the orator no longer played an important role in the city and when authors addressed a public more restricted than the entire citizen body. Nonetheless, we have to admire the culture and the attention span of men capable of appreciating on simple hearing the refinement and the subtlety of works as dense and allusive as those of Tacitus.

It is difficult to measure the effects of the barbarian invasions on reading. According to Armando Petrucci, copyists were recruited among the less-gifted monks, and the little care that they took to facilitate the task of their readers shows that such copies were made above all in order to conserve the work. Still, people continued to read aloud. The Christians' respect for sacred texts led them to intone as they read, maintaining a predetermined and regular rhythm. As Father Jean Leclercq says:

With regard to literature, a fundamental observation must be made here; in the Middle Ages, as in antiquity, they read usually, not as today, principally with the eyes, but with the lips, pronouncing what they saw, and with the ears, listening to the words pronounced, hearing what is called the "voices of the pages." It is a real acoustical reading; *legere* means at the same time *audire*. . . . No doubt, silent reading, or reading in a low voice, was not unknown; in that case it is designated by expressions like those of St. Benedict: *tacite legere* or *legere sibi*.

Leclercq concludes:

This results in more than a visual memory of the written words. What results is a muscular memory of the words pronounced and an aural memory of the words heard. . . . This repeated mastication of the divine words is sometimes described by the use of the theme of spiritual nutrition.[40]

Because both the act of writing and the act of reading obligated people to subject their actions to the operations of thought in an endless two-way exchange, they long found it difficult (for a number of reasons) to grasp that a written text could be independent of speech. Their auditive memory was more highly developed than our own, and often it was aided by the rhythm of set formulas that facilitated retention of what was read or heard.

To what extent did the practices and attitudes of the ancient Greeks and Romans resemble those still current in the East, particularly among the Arabs, who in so many respects were the heirs of ancient culture? The Arabs used a consonantal script that separated words but did not punctuate or indicate capital letters. This form of writing corresponded to a highly rhythmic form of reading aloud accompanied by body movement. The Arabs had an astonishing capacity to memorize and to learn by aural repetition, but they found it difficult to take notes during lessons and indeed notes were normally dictated. Like the ancient Greeks and Romans, the Arabs were highly skilled in rhetoric, but by the same token the development of their critical spirit was hampered. This may explain why even today in the Arab world there are periodic demands for a reform of their graphic system.

Three
Speech and Letters

A ll societies of the oral tradition have their laws, their legends, and their myths. The safeguarding of these things is entrusted to leaders who render justice and to specialists—priests, shamans, poets, and other guardians of collective memory who are inspired by the breath of the divine spirit.

It can happen that writing is introduced into such milieus for precise and limited ends. The Gauls used Greek writing to keep the accounts of their cities or to draw up lists, but their druids refused to use it to set down—thus to divulge—the secrets of their religion. Still the appearance of writing was usually connected with changes in which tribes and clans merged into a larger whole and developed an urban civilization. When this happened, the new system of communication was imposed in all domains, interfering with traditional mechanisms. This in turn led to a break with the past, a redistribution of tasks, and eventually the rise of new forms of logic. The radical changes set in motion in this manner were felt only gradually, however, by processes that we need to examine.

THE WRITING OF THE LAW: CUSTOM AND LAW

Very early in history, writing served to remind people of the debts and obligations that they contracted with one another. The history of proof in contractual matters illustrates the changes in ways of thinking that this process brought.

In traditional societies the juridical act—in classical Latin the *negotium* or manifestation of a will implying an intent to create, transform, or do away with rights or promises—was expressed by some solemn act, usually by symbolic gestures and words exchanged under the eyes of the gods who guaranteed the operation and in the presence of witnesses who would keep it in memory. In Mesopotamia, for example, someone who sold a plot of land would transfer a lump of dirt to the buyer or throw a lump of dirt to the ground, breaking it as a sign of dispossession. A comparable ritual occurred in the West among certain barbarian peoples of the early Middle Ages.[1]

Spoken words pass, witnesses die, but a written text remains. Moreover many contracts had clauses with specifics that were important to remember. There were problems involved with written contracts, though. First, according to the primitive mentality, the act redacted on such an occasion had to reflect the symbolic gesture that linked the contracting parties during the solemn ceremony; second, any document of the sort was juridically valid only if it was "authentic"—that is, if it bore the required signs of validation.

To satisfy these two conditions the Mesopotamian debtor recognized the obligation that he had contracted by placing a personal mark (as if he were abandoning a part of his person) on the damp clay of the tablet—a fingerprint, the imprint of part of his cloak or of a amulet button attached to his cloak, or above all an imprint of a cylinder seal, which even predated writing and was charged with a symbolic force closely associated with the name and the person of its owner. On occasion the contracting parties were so eager to avoid falsification that they sealed up the tablet witnessing the act inside a clay envelope that at times bore the text of the contract in even more explicit terms and offered more space for affixing signs of validity for the simple reason that an envelope is always bigger than its contents.[2]

How was this new form of proof regarded in a society accustomed to heeding the word of living witnesses? Babylonian judges sometimes spoke of the contents of a tablet as its "mouth" or said that they had "heard" the tablet.[3] There was never any question of setting up an opposition between the dead speech of the tablet and the living speech of persons present: anyone who "denied" his seal was severely punished. Thus it was also out of the question to compare the probatory force of these different forms of witness: in this sort of society oral tradition and written tradition appear inextricably mixed.

Not all ancient cultures utilized and assimilated the principle of the written contract with equal ease. The Greeks, a merchant people, are reputed to have soon become past masters in such affairs, but even they did not use writing with genuine consistency until the fourth century B.C. The written act was recognized in the law of the time only in extremely specific sectors, commerce between cities and maritime law, for instance, and although in Athens written testimony gradually replaced oral testimony as proof of a contractual agreement, writing nonetheless had only probative value. As late as Justinian's compilers, the Romans retained the *stipulatio* in their contracts—questions and responses that followed a time-honored pattern and recalled the eminently oral and solemn nature of this sort of agreement (called *de verbis*, what is more). If we add that for a long time orality remained equally important in procedural matters it is clear that in many domains the Latin people long gave more importance to speech than to writing, resembling the Germans in that respect more than they did Semitic peoples.[4]

Be that as it may, in increasingly secularized societies the need to effect incontestable transactions resulted in a growing role for public power, the source of authority on which, in the last analysis, the authenticity of the act depended. Hence the appearance of a corps of public notaries (that took many forms) and the rise of the notion of registration. Greek law was quick to reach this stage and to offer private individuals institutions to facilitate the authentification of contracts, first by noting them on rolls, then by the redaction of the originals in public offices. Rome, on the other hand, reached this stage only rather late. We are told that it was only in the third century A.D. that professional scriveners, or tabellions, appeared, and in the later Empire they were placed under the supervision of the public powers. It was only under Constantine that a number of central, provincial, or municipal administrative bodies were granted the right to record the acts or declarations of private individuals or to register contracts and deliver certified copies of them.[5]

One consequence of this slow advance in writing in the domain of contracts was the rise of a new category of scribes placed under the sign of power whose activities gave those who held power domination over people and things. Soon after written contracts had become the rule, however, the barbarians invaded the Empire, but once the system had been set up it was never totally forgotten, and it is quite probable that the medieval notarial system was based on it.

In a parallel evolution, law became distinct from custom. Following Henri Lévy-Bruhl, we need to keep in mind several essential notions.[6] Since all life in common supposes juridical rules custom is, as a consequence, the primitive and normal model for the formation of the law. It consists of the repeated use of a rule applied to a specific case; it arises within the group without notice; it seems to be the direct product of the collective consciousness. Preexisting its formulation, it is revealed only when it is violated. Therefore it has no birth certificate and is apt to evolve, in spite of heavy hindrances, at the same time that society evolves; it can thus be applied in an extremely supple manner. It is of course closely connected with religion in traditional societies and thus it constitutes something like a secret conserved by an oligarchy. Law, on the other hand, has an author: the competent power, which marks it with its seal, as it would a birth certificate, since [law] is promulgated by means of specific procedures. Rare exceptions aside, it is written. Thus it cannot evolve and is only replaced by another law.

In this domain as in others the effects of recourse to writing were felt only over the long term. Let us return to Mesopotamia, to the most famous of the law codes, the Code of Hammurabi, as we can contemplate it in the Louvre, inscribed ca. 1760 B.C. on a diorite stele found in Susa, where an Elamite king brought it after the sack of Babylon. We see here the sun-god Shamash dictating his law to the king, but although inspired by the gods the law is not a religious law. After the prologue, in which the king invokes divine authority and affirms his own obligations as dispenser of justice and protector, comes a series of short articles treating concrete cases for which the king gives a juridical solution. These cases concern the most common sorts of questions—justice, procedure, penal law, land ownership and rights of usage, contracts, marriage, family, succession. By a logic natural for the time and place it moves from one topic to the other by association of ideas: from the field to the garden, from the garden to the house, from the husband to the wife, from the wife to the child. Finally an epilogue proffers curses to anyone violating these laws.[7]

We can see here the difficulties that Mesopotamian scribes encountered when they wrote the law. Although Sumero-Akkadian writing was perfectly adapted to writing contracts (even complex ones), it lacked the precision needed for definition and for distinguishing between abstract notions. *Arnum,* for example, meant "offense" or "sin," but it also expressed the penalty inflicted; *dinum,* according to context, meant "judiciary litigation," "trial," "sentence," and even "law"; separate categories of thieves could be distinguished, but it was impossible to define theft in the abstract.[8]

Hammurabi's code fits into a clearly defined context. A self-declared "rule of peace" that extended the military and political deeds of the sovereign to other lands, it was designed to facilitate the fusion of Sumer and Akkad and the absorption of recently conquered territories. It made no claim to replace custom but tended to conserve a good part of the previous law by bringing unity to customs pertaining to specific points. At the same time the ruler seems to have intervened to seek a more equal justice, a tendency often explicit in similar written "laws."[9]

In Mesopotamia the king, the vicar of the country's god, held the right to interpret custom. In primitive Greece that right was held by the king (*basileus*), who was the head of the clan (*genos*). It passed to the king of the city when the city replaced the clans. God's representative among men, the Greek king enjoyed the protection of Themis, who inspired him and gave him clairvoyance although, as Nestor explains in the *Iliad* 9.97–103, he might consult the elders and the people before making a decision.

The growth of the urban population in the seventh century B.C. reinforced the powers of the city leaders to the detriment of the clans. According to tradition, when the popular classes demanded that the fundamental rules governing society be set down, inspired legislators did so—Lycurgus, "bringer of light," in Sparta, and in Athens Draco, the "serpent god" who watched over the Acropolis. These sage redactors of ancestral custom reportedly had no intention of suppressing custom, which long remained the rule in jurisprudence: one of the decrees of Lycurgus is supposed to have gone so far as to prohibit "written law." [10]

In Greece the shift from custom to written law was attached to the name of Solon (ca. 630–ca. 560 B.C.). Henceforth the laws of the city were redacted by legislators and tyrants, the successors of the inspired legislators. Later, in the fifth and fourth centuries, the people participated in the elaboration of the law, custom then being evoked only to complete or (when necessary) correct the law.

This revolution—for that is what it was—could be accomplished only when a certain number of concepts took on a deeper meaning. The notion of law appears in Homer only in the term *thēmis* (*tithémaï*, to pose), which at first evoked judgment inspired by the gods but also referred to the stable rules posed by the gods, and in the term *dikē* (from *dikazeïn*, to judge), which expressed first "judgment" then the general idea of the law. Hence Hesiod presents Themis, the daughter of Earth and Sky, the spouse of Zeus, and the mother of three daughters, Discipline, Peace, and Justice (*Dikē*), whose mission it was to point out the unjust to her father, while *nomos* became the law as prescribed by the gods. With Heraclitus of Ephesus (ca. 500 B.C.) juridical notions became secularized and *nomos* came to mean the law received by the City. Finally, although the Sophists denied the existence of a superior order, claiming that justice and truth flow from a law that can vary from people to people and land to land, Plato held justice to be innate in man and Aristotle held that human laws, though precarious, are universal law made explicit. [11]

Henceforth the written law opposed custom. The law was made by the ruler or resulted from a democratic decision. It was fallible and might appear contrary to natural law, which explains the indictments of the law in Sophocles' *Antigone* and *Oedipus Rex*. The Greeks, who secularized the law, discovered how to pose the essential problems when the use of writing gradually led them to isolate the abstract concepts that are one aspect of the mental equipment of *homo scribens*.

It was the Roman people who defined the forms of written law that we know and that are still practiced in some parts of the world today. An Indo-European people, the Romans formed a strongly structured society from the start, and their principal priesthoods, represented by the flamens of Jupiter, Mars, and Quirinus, reflected the traditional system of a society divided into priests, warriors, and peasants. The Etruscans, Rome's neighbors and long its dominators, gave Rome early knowledge of the writings of the Etruscan priestly caste and bequeathed a portion of their sacred books to Rome. We do not know precisely how the pontifex maximus took over from the kings at their fall; in historical times we see the pontifex acting as a counselor to the magistrates and the Senate in matters having to do with the cult and with religious affairs. Sacred knowledge was deposited in him: it was the pontifex maximus who fixed the calendar, set the wording of invocations, and knew the proper prayers for every circumstance. The pontifical "college" that he headed served as guardian of the general welfare; it kept the sacred books, in early years had exclusive possession of the formulas for initiating juridical proceedings, and controlled the judicial calendar. The pontifex maximus was thus master of trials. Founding his power on the keeping of ongoing records—formularies, rituals, and minutes (*Acta Pontificum*), notes on juridical matters (*Commentarii*), and registers of important facts (*Annales*)—he figured as the guardian of the city.[12]

The Republic challenged this power based in custom. According to tradition the tribune Terentius Arsa led a demand to have the decemvirs charged with redacting "laws" (after consultation with the elders). The result was the Law of the Twelve Tables—so-called, legend tells us, because they were posted on twelve painted wooden planks. Whatever the truth of the tale, writing was thenceforth used to protect the people against an oligarchy. The original purpose of the Twelve Tables, however, was to set down a limited number of customary laws, together with decisions regarding the social crisis that had prompted their writing. The pontiffs long remained the masters of customary law and, even more important, of its application. It was only when Appius Claudius was censor (312–307 B.C.) that the *arcana*—the formulas for legal proceedings, the dates of propitious days, and so forth—were finally divulged. Toward the mid-third century the first plebeian pontifex maximus, Tiberius Coruncanius, began to give public consultations. Candidates for magistracies soon imitated his example as a means of forming an electoral clientele. Since public life was in the hands of the nobility, juridical science long remained the privilege of the great families, and it was imbued with the spirit of tradition. Things changed with the end of the Republic: with the breakup of the priestly colleges knights, *municipes*, and freedmen (many provincials among them) became jurists.[13]

The Romans may have been peasants with a penchant for formalism but that did not make them legislators, at least not at the start. Practitioners more than theorists, they were sensitive to the law when it became poorly adapted to circumstances or when the passage of time made it totally inappropriate. Their merit was to have attached particular importance to jurisprudence and to have created a doctrine that permitted the interpretation of texts. As their domination spread and their relations with foreigners increased they eventually felt the need, particularly in the domain of obligations, to create a *jus gentium* to accompany the *jus civile* and founded (they thought) in natural reason.

The earliest Roman jurists were practitioners with a triple mission: *respondere, cavere,* and *agere*—that is, they acted as consultants, they redacted acts, and they served as guides and leaders for judges and factions. They also composed theoretical works. Schooled by the most famous dialecticians and rhetoricians of their day—the ones whose works we know at least in part—they tackled the fundamental problems of the law. Since they also practiced law, their methods were casuistic, reflecting practical concerns and resembling those of the Stoic moralists. Their role was an essential one, largely because their interpretations often went beyond the texts to offer new solutions to fill in the gaps in legislation.

The jurists originally derived their authority not only from their learning but also from the fact that they were members of the aristocracy. Later, when recruitment to their numbers broadened, Augustus reinforced the authority of certain jurists by granting them the *jus respondendi* so that they could hand down consultations *ex auctoritate principis*, thus providing a body of legal opinion that judges welcomed (at least when the opinions were not contradictory).

We have knowledge of quite a few texts of the great Roman jurisconsults.

They are elementary treatises in systematic form: rules to be learned by heart, commentaries on law in the form of writings on practice, and general treatises or manuals for the use of government officials. The most famous of them are Ulpian's *Regulae* and Gaius's *Institutes.* Unfortunately we have few texts that are more than fragments appearing in the compilations of the late Empire or elements incorporated into the "barbarian laws" of the sixth century.[14]

Well-established doctrine fostered the development of a broad and coherent set of laws brought together in the Byzantine codifications, notably under Justinian (sixth century A.D.). These compilations provided a conceptualization of human relations that was the result of centuries of reflection and experience and that the medieval West had the incomparable good fortune to recover when the time came.

The ancient Latin legislative texts rarely reached the Middle Ages in their original form. After the division of the Empire in A.D. 395 access to the whole body of laws given by Constantine and his successors became extremely difficult since they were scattered among the archives of four prefectures and a number of provinces. The emperor of the Eastern Roman Empire, Theodosius II, reached an agreement with the emperor of the West, Valentinian III, to charge a sixteen-member commission to redact a general collection of new laws by pruning and correcting the texts of imperial constitutions. This became the Theodosian Code, which took effect January 1, 439.

A century later Justinian, also emperor of the Eastern Roman Empire, undertook an even greater task when he decided to encourage reform in his administration by collecting and adapting all the constitutions rendered since Hadrian, adding to them the more important opinions of classical jurisconsults. The work was carried out by commissions working under the direction of the indispensable Tribonian. The *Codex constitutionum* (A.D. 528–29, revised in 534) was divided into twelve books that were in turn subdivided into titles and laws, all arranged under headings and presented in chronological order. The *Code* included a selection of imperial constitutions, often abridged and combined, along with decisions relating to specific cases; the *Pandects* or *Digest*, also divided into books and headings, was a vast collection of decisions handed down by the most famous jurisconsults since the beginning of the Empire; the *Institutes*, a work conceived as a basic law text without citations to the sources of its extracts, was published 21 May 533 and had the force of law; the *Novels* or new laws were promulgated from 533 to 565.[15]

The rise of written law did not mean that custom ceased to be the essential and even, in a sense, the only source of law. Here too writing offered advantages but also disadvantages. Writing liberated custom from a secrecy that the dominant groups in traditional societies had guarded jealously, but it gave rise to new dominant groups. I need not recall the power that knowledge of the key to ideograms gave to a very small number of Mesopotamian or Egyptian scribes. What is important to note is the extent to which the rise of written law, closely linked with the growth of administration, contributed to modifying the internal equilibrium of society under the Roman Empire, especially in the third century when the emperor became sole master of the law. Henceforth, as the Senate declined, true power passed to the administrative offices and especially to their jurists and their redactors. The reign of the chanceries was beginning; its end is not yet in sight.

ORAL TRADITION AND WRITTEN TRADITION

The druids who opposed writing because they did not want their legends and the secrets of their religion set down or divulged did not take that stand without good reasons. Although the world owes the literatures that we know to the use of writing there was a price to be paid.

The most illustrious case in point is that of the Homeric poems. No poet has ever been more revered throughout the ages. The men of classical antiquity used Homer's works as the basis of their children's education; Byzantium then took them up, and after the Renaissance the entire West saluted the genius of the blind bard. During the Enlightenment, however, Giambattista Vico in Italy and Christian von Wolff in Germany expressed doubts that Homer had ever existed. With an incredible audacity they took Homer's name to be some sort of symbol for poetic genius and saw his immortal creations as the collective work of an entire school of Ionian poets of the twelfth to the eighth centuries B.C., later condensed and refined.[16] Could anyone deny the mission of genius in literary creation with greater impudence? Vico and Wolff caused a great stir, which has continued nearly to our own day. Nonetheless, they had solid arguments to back them up when they questioned the very existence of Homer. The siege of Troy occurred in the thirteenth century B.C., whereas everything seems to indicate that the *Iliad* and the *Odyssey* could not have been written down until the eighth century B.C. How were those epics elaborated and transmitted during that long period of the Greek "Middle Ages?" On examination they prove to be composite works. Since they tell a story that gives prominent roles to the Achaeans, they could be taken to be of Achaean origin, yet they reflect forms of civilization that are Dorian—that is, that speak of the people who destroyed the power of the Achaeans, who were the victors in the Trojan War.

Scholarship during the last fifty years permits a better grasp of the possible genesis of those works than Vico and Wolff could have had. All studies agree that in the society responsible for classical Greek culture the narratives and myths that explained the world were cast in a poetic mold. Specialists like Milman Parry, A. B. Lord, and their followers had the idea of seeking out the Yugoslav bards, the last living epic poets in Europe. They heard such men creating their works as they performed, not merely with words but using formulas to embroider on such traditional themes as anger, vengeance, and combat. They found that thanks to this method the poets of oral cultures could still improvise on a subject, develop it, memorize thousands of lines of verse, and recreate them in recitation, although no two versions were an exact replica of one another. These poets brought an equal facility to the epic poem, the work song, or even a funeral chant resembling the one Mérimée tells us that Colomba improvised in early nineteenth-century Corsica.[17]

Thus within traditional societies there were forms of literary creation that called on individual invention and imagination. A number of examples still exist outside Europe. For people of oral tradition, however, composing, learning, and transmitting are forms of activity that blend together, and any individual's work is ceaselessly modified, reworked, and in a sense recreated every time it is performed. Ultimately it becomes an anonymous work.

To return to the *Iliad* and the *Odyssey*, linguistic and stylistic analysis reveals the frequent recurrence of groups of words that seem ready-made for dactylic hexameters. One example is in the qualifiers that accompany the name of the hero. One can also find the traditional themes of this genre of literature in these two works and can point out recurrent techniques of composition. Thus the Homeric poems represent the legacy of oral traditions transmitted from one century to another by generations of *aoidos* like the singers pictured in those works, men playing their citharas and singing, whose descendants, like the Homeridae of Chios, claim Homer as an ancestor. Furthermore it is generally accepted today that the Homeric epics cannot be held to be single, self-contained works. According to Pierre Chantraine the plot of the *Iliad* leads us to think that a primitive nucleus of the work centered on the defeat of the Achaeans. This defeat, brought on by the anger of Achilles, prompted Zeus to intervene, thus leading to the actions of Patrocles, the vengeance of Achilles, and the death of Hector. Perhaps originally these classical themes of anger and vengeance even formed the basis for separate poems. In any event, although certain lays make up the heart of the primitive work, others are not part of the original composition and are later additions, perhaps composed in order to change an *Achilleiad* into a *Trojan War.* [18]

It would be interesting to know when these various songs were assembled and whether parts of the text were set down in writing even before the appearance of alphabetical writing (perhaps in some late form of linear B). We can imagine great banquets lasting several days during which one bard after another sang poems, perhaps from the same cycle—a scenario that in no way excludes the notion that an artist of genius wrote down the cycle. Like *The Song of Roland* in a later age, the *Iliad* and the *Odyssey,* in this interpretation, are in a sense the legacy of a society of oral culture bequeathed to a new world in which writing was imposing its law. All subsequent works among the Greeks and the Latins had an author and a birth certificate as soon as they were written. The work could undergo only minor changes, usually as the result of a more careful job of producing the physical text. The mythic epic gave way to the historical narrative and the work of fiction. As early as the sixth century B.C. Hesiod attempted to put Greek myths into a rational chronological order, while at the same time new visions of time and space began to emerge. Anaximander and Hecataeus used techniques from Babylonia and Egypt to draw the first maps of the world. Soon historiography was born, some say developing out of local chronicle, others, out of a search for the most likely version of events drawn from a variety of sources. Herodotus, for example, who was interested in explaining the role of Athens, incorporated elements from the history of that city into his own work. With Thucydides past events began to be traced from written documents rather than by relying on traditions revised through the ages by oral transmission.[19]

The Romans found it difficult to follow the example of Greece. The origins of certain elements in Latin poetry can probably be traced to the Romans' religious practices.[20] All invocations to the gods, for instance, were made in rhythmic verse; sacrifices were performed to the sound of the flute; and the *vates* who composed the rhythmic verse banded together in powerful "corporations" (as did the *tubicinae,* the musicians). The Latin literature that we know began to develop only in the third century B.C. and was largely of Hellenic inspiration. Andronicus, who was carried off during the siege of Taranto in 272 B.C. and fell to the lot of the Livian family, played a well-known role in that evolution. When he was freed, Andronicus became a friend of his former master and the preceptor of his children, for whose benefit he translated the *Odyssey*. Next came Ennius, who was also born near Taranto and who took it upon himself to compose a Roman national epic.

Still, the Latins had known writing since the seventh or the sixth century B.C. and the pontiffs, the guardians of the sacred books, kept Rome's archives, as we have seen. The archives were burned by the Gauls in 390 but they probably were reconstituted. Thus one might suppose that Livy (59? B.C.–A.D. 17) had available dependable sources for his history of Rome. But in the eighteenth century a scholar, Louis de Beaufort, the tutor of the princes of Hesse-Homburg, made an astonishing discovery. As Georges Dumézil tells it: "He sifted the sources which [Livy and Dionysus of Halicarnassus] list, rejected as nonexistent or falsified the *Annales Maximi* of the pontiffs, the *libri lintei,* and the Tables of the Censors, and allowed to stand only the Memorial of the Families, which, however, he challenged as being brazenly misleading."[21]

This means that the pontifical archives were fakes, odd as that seemed. The statements of the Latin historians, which were based on ancient traditions, reflected the hesitation they felt when the moment came to set down religious tradition. The early introduction of writing among the Roman people may help to explain both the meticulous ritual of ancient Roman law and the poverty of the Roman national myths.

That state of affairs in turn helps us to understand certain aspects of religious evolution in ancient Rome. In their city, which had become the greatest metropolis of the Mediterranean and the capital of an immense empire, and throughout Italy, where Greek was often spoken, the national gods simply co-opted the legends of their Hellenic cousins. Various sorts of mystic cults from the East also took root, which meant that it was fashionable to scorn some of the cults of the common people. At the same time a desire to return to the ancient virtues of the Latin race and a fear of seeing traditions lost incited scholars such as Varro (116–27 B.C.) to become early "folklorists,"[22] as is always the case whenever a culture begins to admire what Michel de Certeau called "the beauty of death."

After the end of the civil wars Augustus put all forms of religious propaganda and even the gods to the service of his reconstruction program.

These were the circumstances in which the greatest poets, Virgil first among them, sought inspiration in Greco-Latin traditions.[23] But how can we deny that such works, composed in the context of a concerted policy, codified and rationalized what formerly had been considered inspired by the gods and sacred (Georges Dumézil)? Despite some artificiality, in the long run this movement resulted in putting the imperial cult on a relatively solid basis.

The ancient myths did not disappear. Neither Homer nor Virgil were forgotten during the Middle Ages. The history of myths is a tale of eternal return, and other legends came along and were added to those of Greece and Rome. The heroes of antiquity stood next to King Arthur and Charlemagne among the Nine Worthies (*les Neuf Preux*). Later Petrarch and Boccaccio rediscovered the *Iliad* and the *Odyssey*. In the Renaissance, the tableaux vivants presented before sovereigns at their solemn entries were filled with allusions to classical mythology. Ovid was read with passionate interest and French poets sought Trojan ancestors for the Franks. For centuries Greco-Roman mythology would continue to inspire painters and artists, and an entire literature—the literature of emblems—would attempt to explain that mythology with the aid of images. Sheer play, of course, took an increasing part in all this. Still, the history of French classical literature shows that the men of those times were still persuaded that mythology contained elements of an ancient wisdom. They were not the last to think so.

Thus the myths created by oral tradition survived, and they still survive in spite of reforms aimed at their elimination. Better, they are renewed, so strong is the hold of symbolic imagination. If myths of our own century are so poor it is perhaps because a society cannot give more than it has.

WRITING AND SPEECH IN ANCIENT THOUGHT

Writing is neither necessary nor sufficient to turn societies upside down. It is not indispensable to certain forms of technological progress: think of Neanderthal man. When writing is introduced artificially into traditional societies out of contact with the rest of the world it is soon forgotten. In partially literate societies it can be used only to keep alive a literal knowledge of a sacred belief within a priestly caste. Finally, it has hardly any role in relations within primary groups like the family, but it tends to control secondary groups by secreting a bureaucracy. It is not revolutionary, but it appears every time that a revolution in communications and exchanges prompts a fusion into a larger whole. When this occurs it accelerates the changes set in motion within that society. There are two reasons for this. The first is that culture is nothing but what the thought of successive generations has produced; it permits the storage of that thought. As Jack Goody has observed (in a work with a particularly suggestive title in French translation, *La raison graphique*), this means that skeptical individuals ready to question certain rites can exist within traditional groups, but a skeptical current can develop there only to the extent that it takes root and crystallizes around a stable supporting structure that accumulates ideas and observations.[24] The second reason is that writing casts speech onto a two-dimensional space and fixes it there, thus permitting speech to be an object of reflection outside of any context. Furthermore, because it visualizes discourse, writing prompts new sorts of connections in the reasoning process. This means that the new medium surpasses its initial object and comes to have a role of its own in the linked stages of the cognitive process.

Like the ethnologist, the historian must make sure not to set up a binary opposition—as Goody says, a "Great Dichotomy"—between cultures, between oral cultures and cultures of writing for instance. Why? First, because each graphic system has its own logic and dynamism. Next, because the relation of man to the spoken and the written word has never stopped changing through the course of time. Finally, because speech and writing belong to the same global system of social communication and share its tasks in an always precarious equilibrium.[25]

The "first linguistics" saw writing as a reflection of spoken discourse. Ferdinand de Saussure states:

> Language and writing are two distinct systems of signs; the second exists for the sole purpose of representing the first. The linguistic object is not both the written and the spoken forms of words; the spoken forms alone constitute the object. But the spoken word is so intimately bound to its written image that the latter manages to usurp the main role. People attach even more importance to the written image of a vocal sign than to the sign itself. A similar mistake would be in thinking that more can be learned about someone by looking at his photograph than by viewing him directly. This illusion . . . has always existed.[26]

What we have learned about the role of the image in the appearance of the first writing systems contradicts these assertions, and the only writing whose origins are to some extent known, Sumero-Akkadian, seems to have been developed not to reproduce a preexistent spoken discourse but to commit to memory concrete bits of information. This quite naturally led the Mesopotamian scribes to make a science of the art of organizing a list and using a clay surface to make selections and reclassifications in tables arranged in columns. Administrative lists, inventories, and accounts testify to their ingenuity. Above all the complexity of their script soon led them to make up lists of signs, lists that are true lexicographical compendia. These lexicons exclude verbs and adjectives to concentrate on the nouns that, in their minds, were closely connected with existence and reality. Not only did such lists provide materials for a number of specific definitions, they suggested ways to classify reality that extended to the ordering of all things.[27]

For the Mesopotamian scribes the appearance of writing was connected with their need to develop their calculation skills, but in both calculation and writing they failed to achieve generalization and abstraction. The mathematical documents they elaborated were essentially collections of problems. The oldest of these tablets gave direct answers to specific questions such as how to calculate the length, width, or area of a field. They offered simple aids in the form of tables for multiplication, division, or square-root tables, in certain series even giving exponential or logarithmic relations. But that is as far as they went in abstraction. Thus a tablet is apt to give a set of problems all of the same type differing only in numerical quantities, without ever stating or demonstrating a general mathematical principle. Despite their remarkable achievements in developing systems of calculation, the Babylonians were no more capable of defining general mathematical principles than they were of formulating a general definition of the notion of theft.[28] The Egyptians showed comparable tendencies: they are reputed to have taught geometry to the Greeks but they too concentrated on furnishing solutions to concrete problems.

Similarly, Babylonian astronomy, although highly developed, remained primarily within the context of an astral religion. The astronomers of Babylon followed the progress of the stars, not for their inherent interest, but because they represented divinities to whose movements men's destinies were linked. The scribes who performed those observations for the kings and whose responsibilities were religious and terrestrial did indeed acquire precise knowledge of certain phenomena, but they remained arithmeticians and showed no interest in developing geometrical models. The attitude of the Greeks was totally different: for them the universe was inscribed in mathematical formulas.[29]

Ideograms also had a logic of their own. The writing systems that used them involved things and were based on a principle of semantic reconciliation that permitted the more learned scribes to shift from one meaning to another. It is hardly surprising that the science they turned to for an explanation of things was divination, the science that revealed connections between words and things, proper names and the deductions that could be drawn from them, the reality of the written word and the message it transmitted. In linguistic terms, it offered the possibility of dissecting the signifier to advance knowledge of the signified.[30]

It would also be interesting to know to what extent continued use of the last of the great ideographic systems—Chinese—contributed to giving some peoples of the Far East a mentality different from that of Europeans. In asking that question we need to remember that the languages they speak, Chinese in particular, differ fundamentally from our own. Joseph Needham has contrasted the Greeks' attempt to explain natural phenomena by an investigation of their causes to the associative thought processes of the Chinese. Similarly, Jacques Gernet has shown that the Chinese reacted to the writings and the message of the missionaries in ways that often reflected differences in mental categories and mental frameworks both in questions of the relation of politics to religion and of the role of reflective awareness and spontaneity in the moral realm. These differences were particularly clear in the refusal of the Chinese to distinguish a level of stable truth separate from the world of phenomena and the rationale of sense perception. Gernet also stresses how difficult it was for missionaries speaking in Chinese to explain that the concrete and the singular are fundamentally different from the abstract and the general. He concludes from this that their mutual incomprehension was due to the difficulty of expressing in a agglutinating language ideas that had been formulated in an inflected language on the model of Latin or Greek.[31]

The role of writing seems secondary in this sort of debate. One simple conclusion might be that each of these two types of language eventually found its deepest characteristics reflected in the writing system it now uses. This might explain why the Chinese have kept their ideograms, while the Semitic peoples and Indo-Europeans of the Middle East eventually adopted various sorts of alphabets.

With the alphabet the stylus captured and imitated the flow of speech by taking speech as the model for written signs. Among the Greeks this innovation seems to have been accompanied by a revolution that was all the more profound because Greek society was rapidly evolving when it passed from a nearly exclusively oral culture to use of an easily accessible writing system. We need to pause and think about that a bit. As in all primitive societies, up to that point the Greeks believed that divine powers and occult forces intervened directly in the life of men. The poet, like his cousin the soothsayer, was inspired by the gods and possessed by divine delirium. Blinded by the light, as legend tells us Homer was, he saw into the invisible. The knowledge or the wisdom that the goddess Memory dispensed to both the poet and the soothsayer was a divinatory omniscience. Time did not exist for either of these figures, and in Hesiod memory reigned not only over what had been but over what was and what was yet to be. The poet had to undergo a harsh apprenticeship memorizing plots, themes, and formulas and learning genealogies, which were the archives of peoples without writing and which allowed them to establish order among heroes and gods. The poet had something like an unmediated experience of past worlds; he unveiled the past as the soothsayer unveiled the future. As Jean-Pierre Vernant put it, the poet's realm was "not his own personal past, nor even the past in general as if it were an empty framework quite independent of the events taking place within it, but rather the 'olden days' with all their own particular content and quality—for example, the heroic age, or, even further back, the primeval age or original time." [32]

The Greeks broke only very gradually with poetic expression and all that it implied. Athenians of the age of Pericles and the grand tragedians still limited their definition of cultivated men to those who had been formed in the disciplines of the *Mousikē,* the domain of the Muses, the word *Grammatikos* coming into use only in the fourth century, when it indicated, without cultural implications, a person who knew how to read. It was not until the age of Plato (428/27–348/47 B.C.) that language had evolved to the point of permitting easy manipulation of abstract concepts. [33]

Plato, who lived in a world in which the domain of writing was like an island of literacy surrounded by peoples of oral tradition, was perfectly aware of the revolutionary changes taking place in Greece. This makes the passages in his dialogues in which he speaks of writing all the more interesting.

The *Phaedrus* gives a summary of his point of view. Young Phaedrus has brought with him a manuscript of a speech by Lysias, a highly artificial rhetorical exercise full of virtuosity. Socrates easily demonstrates that this piece of so-called literature totally lacks authenticity and serious purpose. He delivers a closely argued criticism of the art of the Sophists, which he contrasts with a rhetoric founded on dialectic. What follows is the famous fable in which Socrates tells how writing was invented by Theuth, the ibis-god of Naucratis, who was also the father of calculation, geometry, and astronomy, not to mention backgammon and dicing. This is how Theuth presents his discovery to the pharaoh Thamus:

> To him came Theuth, and revealed his arts, saying that they ought to be passed on to the Egyptians in general. . . . When it came to writing Theuth said, "Here, O king, is a branch of learning that will make the people of Egypt wiser and improve their memories; my discovery provides a recipe for memory and wisdom." But the king answered and said, "O man full of arts, to one is it given to create the things of art, and to another to judge what measure of harm or profit they have for those that shall employ them. And so it is that you, by reason of your tender regard for the writing that is your offspring, have declared the very opposite of its true effect. If men learn this, it will implant forgetfulness in their souls: they will cease to exercise memory because they rely on that which is written, calling things to remembrance no longer from within themselves, but by means of external marks; what you have discovered is a recipe not for memory, but for reminder. And it is no true wisdom that you offer your disciples, but only its semblance; for by telling them of many things without teaching them you will make them seem to know much, while for the most part they know nothing; and as men filled, not with wisdom, but with the conceit of wisdom, they will be a burden to their fellows." [34]

According to Plato true opinions acquired during the course of previous existences are awakened when we cannot answer a question. Thus learning is equivalent to remembering, and the mission of the memory is to permit access to the world of ideas and to achieve union with the divine. This vision perhaps helps to explain Plato's mistrust of the new "artificial" memory. His arguments against it are well known:

> You know, Phaedrus, that's the strange thing about writing, which makes it truly analogous to painting. The painter's products stand before us as though they were alive: but if you question them, they maintain a most majestic silence. It is the same

with written words: they seem to talk to you as though they were intelligent, but if you ask them anything about what they say, from a desire to be instructed, they go on telling you just the same thing for ever. And once a thing is put in writing, the composition, whatever it may be, drifts all over the place, getting into the hands not only of those who understand it, but equally of those who have no business with it; it doesn't know how to address the right people, and not address the wrong. And when it is ill-treated and unfairly abused it always needs its parent to come to its help, being unable to defend or help itself.[35]

Plato does not sing the praises of traditional oral culture, though. Rather he criticizes the immorality of the tales that mothers and nurses told children in their most impressionable years, and he denounces mythological tales in which gods and heroes fight for utterly trivial reasons, change their appearance like magicians, and repeatedly resort to ruses and lies. In a well-known passage in the *Republic* (3.396) he declares his downright hostility toward the inspired poet, to whom he prefers the legislator:

Suppose, then, that an individual clever enough to assume any character and give imitations of anything and everything should visit our country and offer to perform his compositions, we shall bow down before a being with such miraculous powers of giving pleasure; but we shall tell him that we are not allowed to have any such person in our commonwealth; we shall crown him with fillets of wool, anoint his head with myrrh, and conduct him to the borders of some other country. For our own benefit, we shall employ the poets and story-tellers of the more austere and less attractive type, who will reproduce only the manner of a person of high character and, in the substance of their discourse, conform to those rules we laid down when we began the education of our warriors.[36]

Plato's mistrust of both writing and the "inspired poet" needs to be returned to a context in which the relations between speech and writing were not what seems natural to us today. The alphabet was born in the ancient city, and it had favored the growth of democracy in that setting, but communication in Greek society nevertheless remained essentially oral. Discussion was considered indispensable as a way to hold the collectivity together. It alone permitted compromise and peaceful settlement of conflict; it alone permitted deliberation before a collective decision could be reached. Similarly debate was seen as the best means for attaining truth and wisdom, and nothing could replace the word of the master. This is why a statesman had to be an orator capable of swaying crowds.

That attitude was to some extent symbolized by the fact that the word *logos* had multiple meanings ranging from "speech" to "reason." By the same token language was conceived as an instrument of human relations, even as a means for domination over others, rather than as revelatory of being. Plato, who criticized the tradition that based education on the study of Homeric verse, also disapproved of the teaching of the Sophists, who went from city to city teaching rich and wellborn young people eager to get ahead in the world how to triumph over their adversaries or improvise speeches in which they appeared competent in matters about which they knew little or nothing. The instruction of the Sophists, based on purely formal procedures, enabled the orator to demonstrate a point or its contrary; their methods included ways to conceal or invert the true nature of relationships. Plato considered this a genuine misdirection of the mission of philosophy. The search for public success encouraged this sort of rhetorician to think that the power of discourse lay in its excellence even when it obviously ran counter to fact.[37]

It is clear why Plato contrasted those who love true *logoi* (the philosophers) and those who produce only copies or appearances of them. It is just as clear why, in the seventh letter attributed to him, Plato denounced Denys, the young tyrant of Syracuse, for having had the audacity to present his philosophy in a book, or why Plato preferred the dialogue, a poetic transcription of the progress of the spirit in the search for truth, as a means of expression. Thus Plato's rejection of written philosophy and his much reiterated proclamation of the preeminence of oral expression make us wonder about the relationship between his own written work and his oral teaching.

One wonders whether Plato was not using this rejection of writing as a way of making a hermeneutic appeal for its proper use. How can we deny that underlying his theories there is an implicit vision of the written word and a logic of the division of labor that reflects the logic of the alphabet? Writing forcibly removed speech from the instant. By the same token it invited the sage to distinguish the truth (*epistēmē*) from received opinion (*doxa*). By making language an object of reflection, writing permitted the Master of the Academy to note that language had by no means been conceived or organized by some philosopher's legislation. Thus language was of no help in attaining the essence of things. This explains the reflections in the *Cratylus*, where Plato states that knowledge of the truth of things must be first be apprehended in relation to things like language that are only its image. This is what made dialectic, the science of reasoning, necessary. It is characteristic of Plato that as his life advanced he accorded less importance to reminiscence and insisted more and more on the two procedures of dialectical method summarized in three famous passages from the *Phaedrus*. The basic principles are these:

> The first is that in which we bring a dispersed plurality under a single form, seeing it all together; the purpose being to define so-and-so, and thus to make plain whatever may be chosen as the topic for exposition.

> The second procedure [is] the reverse of the other, whereby we are enabled to divide into forms, following the objective articulation; we are not to attempt to hack off parts like a clumsy butcher.

> I am myself a lover of these divisions and collections, that I may gain the power to speak and to think; and whenever I deem another man able to discern an objective unity and plurality, I follow "in his footsteps where he leadeth as a god." [38]

Since Plato held that thought is made by joining separate elements it is hardly surprising that he compared the dialectician's task of analysis and synthesis to children's efforts to learn their letters, then to decipher increasingly complex syllables, and finally to understand words and phrases. The two processes seemed to him quite evidently based on the same technique. [39]

Such efforts could lead only to a classification of the sciences and a hierarchization of knowledge. Plato was led in this direction by his proposal for a program of education to form citizens, particularly the citizens promoted to philosophic dignity who would be leaders. As an aristocrat he thought it appropriate to make them warriors by a exposure to a balanced program of gymnastics and music to teach them control over their bodies. Although Plato admitted that certain qualities of verbal expression were indispensable, he saw the real problem of education as detaching the child's mind from the world of the senses so that he could attain the world of the intelligible, the higher degree of abstraction. Hence the need to study mathematics. Plato followed the lead of Hippias of Elis and the Pythagoreans, who had already proposed a *quadrivium* based on the study of arithmetic, geometry, acoustics, and astronomy, and limited himself to adding solid geometry, which was beginning to have an important place in the schools thanks to Theaetetus and Eudoxus. Only after such studies (which lasted until the age of thirty) should the student have access to the study of dialectic.

We need to return to Aristotle (384/85–322 B.C.) for the final word on these matters. For Aristotle, knowing and acting, even acting intelligently, were not identical functions in man; a value judgment between something good and something bad (thus to be avoided) was not the same thing as a judgment concerning existence or truth. This helps us to understand Aristotle's division of the sciences, which perhaps corresponded to a curriculum, into the poetic sciences (from *poïein*, to do or make), which concerned the art by which things are made, the practical sciences (from *praxis*), which like ethics concerned the activity of the agent unconnected with its results, and the theoretical sciences (from *theōria*), the object of which was knowledge for its own sake.[40]

This view suggests a hierarchy of knowledge that we have inherited. At the summit were mathematics, the abstract science par excellence, and physics, the "first philosophy." At least this conception recognized that the natural sciences and technologies had a certain dignity.

Paradoxically, logic had no place of its own in this hierarchy, probably because it was an *organon* (an instrument), to use the expression of Aristotle's commentators at the beginning of the early modern period. Still, the great philosopher was himself above all a logician, which meant that he paid special attention to language while Plato was content simply to talk about it.

Contrary to what Plato states at the end of the *Cratylus*, Aristotle thought that the philosopher could not escape words. Although he was just as severe as Plato on the immorality of Sophists and rhetoricians, their very indifference to truth in their discourse made it all the more necessary to dismantle the mechanisms of their argumentation. Realizing that the very nature of language led to its misuse, Aristotle took up the study of linguistic forms and structures in order to spring their traps (Pierre Aubenque). Hence the ambiguity inherent in Aristotle's dialectic. For example he cited as a "proof" the confidence that an orator can inspire and he studied the formal techniques of persuasion and showed how to appeal to the passions, but when he reduced rhetoric to a simple theory (what is commonly called rhetoric is an application of that theory), he saw it only as a method for discerning the arguments put forward about the problem under discussion, the premises of which were simple opinions and so merely plausible (Léon Robin). Thus the discipline of rhetoric no longer concerned a search for truth but only coherence in discourse. Since the aim of philosophy must be to attain truth, Aristotle studied (particularly in the *Analytics*) the conditions of demonstrative knowledge, the essential parts of which were terms, propositions, and syllogisms.[41]

In the last analysis Aristotle defined man as a speaking animal, and in his *Categories* and his *Topics* he attempted to set rules for meaningful discussion. The *Categories* make obvious use of linguistic analysis, given that Aristotle's categories for the analysis of thought are basically those of the Greek language. Critics have periodically reproached Aristotle for moving in the universe of discourse rather than in that of reason and for having occasionally adopted somewhat naive positions, as Charles Serrus said, by "simply making explicit a certain metaphysics spontaneously present in the Greek language."[42]

At least Aristotle had the merit of revealing the ambiguity of speech, which is always torn between reason and passion. He also was the first to attempt to impose univocality in the practice of language—that is, to suggest the need to give only one meaning to each word in a phrase. He achieved a secularization of speech, which in his hands, stripped of myth and poeticization, became a manipulable instrument.[43]

Obviously, Aristotle's analysis was dependent upon a comparison between spoken and written discourse. It did not aim at dissociating the two, though, and thanks especially to the syllogism it furnished a solid framework for coherent oral debate. Thus it represented one of antiquity's most valuable gifts to the modern world.

Like their Greek neighbors the Romans remained primarily a people of spoken discourse. Under the Republic, as in Athens, the orator was the city's guide. In Rome, the term *orator* originally had the technical meaning of one who speaks solemnly in public. The function of Rome's heralds and ambassadors, the *fetiales* and the *oratores publici*, consisted especially in pronouncing declarations of war by calling the gods to witness that the enemy had broken commitments. Their speech had religious efficacy. Similarly, the *patres* (who were also the senators), consulted by the king of Rome before he declared war, responded in ritual formulas.

It was quite natural that the orator should have a central place in Cicero's reflections. In Cicero's view the Greeks had practiced a theoretical *sapientia* that his fellow citizens had put into action in both law and custom. Thus a glorious advance sanctioned by social institutions made the citizen first a soldier, then an orator and statesman, and finally a thinker.[44]

As in Greece this conception arose out of an urban setting. Spectacle was everywhere, not only in the theater but also in the Forum and in the law courts. There the Mediterranean public who crowded around a lawyer could give an expert evaluation of his performance. Like the actor the lawyer carefully cultivated his diction and adapted the rhythm of his speech to his aims, eliciting pathos, reaching for the sublime, speaking confidentially, or using sarcasm or the powers of seduction. He used other resources as well, twisting his toga or accompanying his speech with gestures calculated to raise a laugh, move his hearers to tears, or elicit their approval.

Eloquence was a weapon not only for the lawyer but also for the magistrate and the statesman. It made the orator conscious of his mission as a mediator and the bearer of a form of wisdom. Cato's reiterated definition of the orator—*vir bonus, dicendi peritus*—stresses that he must be *bonus*, a bearer of the national virtues. After the civil wars Cicero still saw that same eloquence as the last rampart of the Republic and a means for putting the Senate on guard and for rallying the people. He stated his theories at some length: the orator pledges himself to virtue and to his sworn oath (*fides*); he must manifest *gravitas* in all its seriousness and weight; he must display the *dignitas* that generates consideration. When he does so it is because he is also a *patronus* who must not only defend his clients but also give an example to the young people who come to him for instruction. This was a prideful program and one that conferred *auctoritas* on those who followed it. In Ciceronian philosophy authority was one of the faces of power, the other being *potestas*.

Eloquence thus procured one of the most evident forms of superiority, but Cicero saw it as a demanding mistress. The orator must have all styles at his command from the sublime to the joking; he must practice all genres from eulogy to discussion; he must appeal to all sentiments in order to vary and adapt what he had to say. Furthermore he had to have encyclopedic knowledge in order to be able to raise his argument to the level of general ideas that embraced all particular cases. Just as a flutist could not perform without a flute, an orator could not be eloquent without a crowd to hear him, thus the great writer who proclaimed his faith in the rectitude of popular judgment held that cultivated listeners should cede to that judgment. Hence the simplicity and universality of Cicero's language, so often admired. As someone "in the trade," he tended to glorify his profession, thus he declared that when the judges were not up to the task the lawyer must embody Roman wisdom, and he tended to present confrontations between lawyers as loyal combat. The eclecticism of Cicero's philosophy did little to resolve the tension between ancient ethics and ancient rhetoric. Experience had taught him that to win a case a lawyer's plea must appeal to the passions. In the course of his career a lawyer often had to plead a case for and against the same person. Since Cicero was well acquainted with the law courts, which sought verisimilitude more than certitude, he left it to the judges to find out the truth, limiting the lawyer's province to what was likely. Although Cicero admired Plato, he found it difficult to reconcile him with the Sophists, and he attempted to eliminate what bothered him in Plato's Stoic doctrine. In other words, there were a number of ambiguities in a thought that in fact gave action priority over principle.

It has become fashionable to denounce Cicero's pride, to stress the ambiguity of his philosophy, and to note the failure of his politics. It has also been suggested, not without reason, that he was not a major mind. Nonetheless, the adventure of the last of the great orators of antiquity was only beginning on that day in 43 B.C. when Octavian and Antony had him assassinated. Like Homer, and because he too represented a unique moment in the relationship between speech and writing, Cicero furnished an unequaled model. It was particularly from him that scholars of the Renaissance learned their first lessons in style, language, and thought. Never has a writer been so studied, translated, and plagiarized: only very recently have his works (in fact if not in theory) been removed from school curricula.

The art of oratory by no means disappeared from Rome with the Republic. The emperors themselves practiced it, if only to harangue their troops. The Senate continued to debate, the magistrates to discourse with ritual pomp, the lawyers to plead their cases. As Romanization spread with the Empire, Roman customs and fashions spread to the provinces. Similarly, the elite of the Latin or Latinized young in the West, like their Hellenized counterparts in the East, frequented the schools of rhetoric.

Early on, however, Romans began to distinguish between the *indocti*, the rough common people, and the *docti*, a relatively cultivated public that usually had long years of study behind them. At times the *docti* were in sufficient number in the court for Cicero to address them directly (in spite of the democratic principles we have just seen). In the classical age the "learned" included a number of provincial notables who proved eager to meet famous authors when they came to Rome.

Also very early, as soon as what might properly be called writers began to appear, literary "micro-milieus" grew up. The oldest of these Roman circles in which literary exchange took place grouped around Scipio Africanus (235–183 B.C.), whose adopted grandson, Scipio Aemilianus, grew up under the tutelage of Laelius Sapiens. Authors of modest origins such as Terence, the son of a slave, were welcomed into this circle. The members of such groups were Hellenized and fond of elegant and literate correspondence; they often exchanged brief poems—*nugae*—when they met, just like the *précieux* of seventeenth-century France. The women who reigned over such groups—Precia and Lesbia in the days of Cicero and Catullus—fostered careers and helped authors to win fortune.

Thus the Roman man of letters was born. He was of course never independent. Epic poetry centered on noble historiography, the theater depended on the patronage of the great families who sponsored the *ludi,* and even elegant poetry and the familiar ode never totally ceased being commissioned verse (Jean-Marie André). With the Empire, writers were invited to put their art to the service of the reconstruction of a Roman ideology. This is where Maecenas entered the picture.[45] A singular and complex person, like many of those who have taken on the role to which he bequeathed his name, this knight from an aristocratic Etruscan family was both the friend and the factotum of Octavian (later Augustus), but he refused all official posts. He received Roman lettered society, Virgil in particular, in his magnificent dwelling on the Esquiline. He warbled with Horace in his park and gave him a villa in the Sabine Hills. A mediocre poet with baroque tastes, jealous by nature and at times arrogant, Maecenas understood the force of public opinion. Before Actium he urged Horace to abandon light verse for the aesthetic of *virtus.* After Actium he became the patron of the highest forms of poetry, preached triumphant lyricism, and contributed greatly to developing the heroic talent of Virgil. In partial disgrace after 22 B.C., he played the role of the disinterested lover of the Muses and left direction of the world of letters to Augustus. He seems to have been torn between the demands of the patron, a role he appears not to have enjoyed, and a certain belief in *ingenium* and in the natural liberty of the artist. Still, his fits of bad humor had already led Horace to dream of some form of social status for the writer. In a word, Maecenas would today be an excellent literary editor of a publishing house, extremely courteous but firm.

This was the setting in which Horace wrote his *Odes,* a work of national inspiration in which he glorified ideas dear to Augustus, and later he glorified the emperor himself. It was in that same climate that Virgil's *Georgics* were written to celebrate a return to the land, labor, and homeland, the reestablishment of peace, and the "predestined" man who presided over it all.

There has been extensive debate on the scope of this restoration, and the question of the extent to which the Romans believed in their myths has often been raised. Be that as it may, their poets were extremely popular. Virgil received a standing ovation one day as he entered the amphitheater, and Ovid's verse (in somewhat garbled form) has been found among the graffiti in Pompeii. More and more, however, the writers and orators of the Empire tended to address a more cultivated public. People flocked to the public sessions in which rhetoricians exhibited their pupils, and orators launched a fashion for recitals in which they showed off their talents before a select audience. Authors and professional readers presented new works (or new in principle) in *recitationes publicae.* [46]

Was the art of oratory in decline? The discourses of the *delatores* who functioned as public prosecutors in Rome still attracted great crowds. It would even be hazardous to be too quick to denounce imperial censorship when the Sophists rather directly criticized the emperors' acts in certain periods. Nonetheless, the orator was no longer at the center of political life and the heroes admired by the throng henceforth tended to be from the circus or the games—which explains why Nero and Domitian took it into their heads to perform there themselves, just as certain political figures of our own day insist on displaying their music-hall talents on television. It is certain that the imperial power brought a good deal of pressure to bear not only on writers' works but also on lawyers' arguments and orators' harangues.[47]

This was the climate in which Tacitus (A.D. ca. 56–ca. 120) composed his celebrated *Dialogus de oratoribus* in which he denounced (in moderate terms, however) the decline of eloquence and stated that it had come to occupy a less important place in a state in which "governmental deliberations belong, not to the incompetent throng but to one man alone, the wisest of all." Relations between the orator and his public were impure, Tacitus continued, because his art furnished ruses that permitted him to dominate his listeners; thus the reign of eloquence had developed unreasoning passions. Furthermore, the stormy relations between Nero and Seneca made Tacitus pessimistic about the likelihood that the Sage would ever govern the Prince. The Sage would thus liberate himself by consenting to the designs of the gods and arming himself with courage, the Stoics' weapon, throughout his lifetime. The historian (who could not be sure of being a sage) of course had duties toward other men, but henceforth he tended to address the many *doctissimi* of the age and adjust his style accordingly. When writers such as Seneca or Tacitus addressed a cultivated audience they abandoned Ciceronian periods and elegant conjunctions to practice an "abbreviated" style. Make no mistake, however: the easy structure and style of their works may at times surprise us but they were worked out in scholarly fashion. This is true, for instance, of Seneca's dialogues, which follow the rules of a very elaborate rhetoric with which his public was familiar. We may at times find disconcerting the density of information that Tacitus packs into his historical works, but the cultivated listener of his times was accustomed to the techniques of oral recitation, could seize every allusion, and understood and appreciated the lesson in wisdom that was being offered to him. By the same token, however, this style worsened the split in Roman society between the elite and the rest of the population.[48]

The oligarchy of the Republic had reduced administrative personnel to the minimum. By reason of its nature the imperial regime tended to fill in the gaps, enlarge administrative bodies, and multiply services, hence there was a need to recruit increasing numbers of competent personnel.

Imperial policies over five centuries are beyond the scope of this work, but we need to ask to what extent Roman rhetorical formation and literary tradition, which continued to provide the foundation of classical culture, could prove satisfactory in this new state of affairs despite their much-criticized formality and conventionality.

As the Empire evolved and jurisprudence advanced, more and more jurists (whose formation included rhetoric) were called upon to fill administrative posts. Hadrian, for example, introduced jurists into the imperial council, where they were its most stable element, and there was hardly a jurist of any renown who had not served the emperor in one way or another. However when Hadrian reorganized the chancery (up to that time it had been staffed by freedmen), he appointed the historian Suetonius as director of the office *a litteris* (charged with sending letters). Although, as has often been pointed out, Pliny the Younger (like Tacitus) had difficulties with certain juridical problems, he pursued a career as a magistrate and held high administrative posts. Nonetheless the young people who followed this sort of career usually had made their reputations as lawyers after completing their rhetorical studies. This introduction to the law certainly provided them with as good an education as the young *maîtres des requêtes* of great families "of the robe" in eighteenth-century France or certain bureaucrats in France today who have come out of the Ecole nationale d'administration.[49]

The state in the late Empire was even more reliant on its dual base of the army and an increasingly tentacular bureaucracy. This meant that schools proliferated, particularly in the East. They attracted large numbers of students and furnished a great many administrative officials. Professors had perhaps never had greater authority than during this period when ancient culture seemed to be sinking into barbarity. The last emperors, soldiers of fortune, were the champions of that culture. Thus Valentinian I, a Pannonian, called the Bordeaux poet and rhetorician Ausonius to be tutor to his son, Gratian, who gave his former tutor the important post of praetorian prefect when he in turn became emperor.[50]

Thus the cult of rhetoric, discourse, and letters survived to the bitter end—a cult that the senators had promoted in years gone by and continued to respect in the third century when they left the cities to take refuge in their country estates, and that the Christians respected as well. Professors in the schools of Autun could promise a fine career to their pupils. One would like to know more about the mass of officials who crowded the offices of the imperial administration. Henri-Irénée Marrou has written on the popularization of stenographic techniques characteristic of scribal activities during that period. Perhaps a new type of relationship with writing developed in the late Roman Empire that we will never know, given the total destruction of the archives of the time. However that may be, the cultural system based on the techniques of the art of oratory created by the senatorial elites of the Republic lasted only as long as the Empire. However, it left descendants.[51]

RELIGIONS OF THE BOOK

The power that words had over things seemed apparent to primitive populations. We can decipher funerary inscriptions nearly everywhere in which the dead or their loved ones ask that their names be pronounced or that an offering prayer containing their names be read aloud, almost as if that could make them live again. We are also aware of the power of magical formulas. For the Egyptians the gods had only to speak to create, a notion that we also find in the first verses of the Bible.

Egypt made a priestly science of such concepts.[52] Since language contained a cosmic force, words that resembled one another could not do so fortuitously. This may explain the systematic exploitation of the richly evocative possibilities of hieroglyphic script and its seemingly immutable principles, but it also explains the efforts made to enrich it with new signs. Hieroglyphics were charged with magical values. There are burial vaults in the Nile Valley covered with inscriptions not put there to be deciphered once the tombs were sealed but that nonetheless had full efficacy. The same concepts led to the defacement of statues from former times in periods of crisis; they explain why signs for dangerous things were slashed in two in the subterranean apartments and why certain statues and inscriptions were held to possess curative virtues. In a similar spirit, Jews, who in one section of the Psalms refrained from writing the name of God, still wash their hands before and after they have touched the Torah, so formidable is the Word of the Lord. In the *Cratylus* Plato states that words are not born of simple convenience but made by analogy with the very nature of things, hence one must study their genealogy.

It would be tempting to pass with no transition to the attitude of the Hebrews as they fled from Egypt and when, following the orders of Yahweh, they constructed the Ark of the Covenant to contain the Tables of the Law that he had just given. It would also be tempting to contrast traditional polytheism with the religion of the one God, who from the outset, even before the Book, was the God of Scripture. But the passage in Deuteronomy that relates this story is a late work, and monotheism was the result of a slow conquest. It was a way for Israel to preserve its personality in the face of the many temptations to synchretism in the land of Canaan. Thus the Old Testament reflects the slow gestation of a people who began as an aggregate of tribes and gives the history of its relations with God, whose chosen people it was. All genres and epochs mingle in the Old Testament. It contains the verse of a nomadic people, popular and religious songs of all sorts, mythical tales based in the cosmogony of the Middle East, oral traditions concerning national origins, prophecies, legislative and sacerdotal documents at times bearing traces of laws and institutions that came from other nations and other ages, liturgical pieces, annals or chronicles, collections of proverbs written down long after their first appearance, moralizing texts often inspired by outside sources, and tales and romanticized fiction. [53]

The Old Testament is a library, the result of a series of redactions and revisions over more than a thousand years; it reflects a constant interpenetration between an ongoing oral tradition and periodically updated written versions. The Torah, the Law of the Jews (for Christians, the Pentateuch)—the five books of Genesis, Exodus, Leviticus, Numbers, and Deuteronomy—provides a case in point. Long attributed to Moses, it is in fact a collective work in which we can recognize extremely ancient traditions preserved in sanctuaries and transmitted by tale-tellers or simply repeated among the people as generations passed, progressively modified, and grouped into cycles when the traditions came to be written down.

Like many other peoples, the Hebrews used poetry first. Magical poems like Joshua's curses, proofs of the power that speech had at the time, come from the oldest period, as do the two great narratives, the "Book of the Wars of Yahweh" and the "Book of the Just." Certain portions were perhaps written down in the time of the Judges (twelfth and eleventh centuries B.C.), and that way of preserving tradition developed with the establishment of the monarchy, when David conquered Jerusalem around the year 1000 and the Temple of Solomon was built around 950 B.C. The king had a minister who functioned, in classical fashion, as both personal secretary and secretary of state, and his administration included a good number of scribes. This is the age to which the official texts inserted into certain narrations belong: annals, chronicles, and the history of the reign of David found in the Book of Kings in which the misfortunes of the aging sovereign are related in a relatively independent manner and which seems to have been set down a good while after the events related. The death of Solomon split up his kingdom, and Israel to the north and Judah to the south were set up as independent states. The two oldest currents that we can discern in the Pentateuch come from that period. Current J, in which God is called Yahweh from the name revealed to Moses, seems to come from the south, whereas Current E, in which God is called Elohim, probably came from the north.

The Assyrian attacks on Israel and the fall of its capital, Samaria, in 722 B.C. meant that Jerusalem fell heir to the legacy of the north. Hence the E and J currents merged, probably around the end of the period of the kings. A desire to fight contamination by other religions and to ward off dangers from the outside then made it imperative to maintain cohesion among God's people. One result in the time of King Josiah was legislation that attempted to proclaim the Temple of Jerusalem the sole sanctuary of Yahweh. This was the context of the "discovery" by a secretary of the king of the Book of Deuteronomy in that temple (probably in 622 B.C.). In Deuteronomy 4:2, Moses declares: "You must add nothing to what I command you, and take nothing from it, but keep the commandments of Yahweh your God just as I lay them down for you." Josiah, horror-struck that his people had been unfaithful to the Law for so long, brought them together to read the work to them and had them contract a new covenant with their Lord. We do not know when this text had actually been elaborated (perhaps in the north in the eighth century B.C.). At that time, a school of redactors may have undertaken the task of merging versions J and E, their labors furnishing the D current of the critics.

These redactions had been greatly influenced by the prophetic movement. There were in fact a number of prophets who proclaimed the Word of Yahweh around the Temple. "Inspired" poets, they were also the critics and counselors of kings, and their mission was to remind the chosen people of the demands of the Lord and to incite them to obey and to love Him. As orators and preachers the prophets were men of the oral tradition, but what they had to say was often noted down, and on occasion they engaged in literary skirmishes. Thus God told Jeremiah to note down the warnings that had proliferated in the last twenty-five years, to mark the date and urge the Jews to repent now that Jerusalem was threatened. But the king of Judah tore up the scroll that was read to him, the city was taken and the Temple destroyed, and the Hebrews were deported en masse to Babylon (586 B.C.). Nonetheless Yahweh, mounted on his chariot, appeared to Ezekiel in 593, ordered him to prophesy, and, to give him inspiration, had him eat a scroll covered with lamentations. Ezekiel was the product of a priestly family and he was quite familiar with Phoenician and Mesopotamian literature. When all had come to pass, he described his vision of the Temple restored and religion triumphant. With him prophecy at times resembled articles of law. Religious force compensated for the failure of the temporal power, and the priestly scribes who were the leaders of the dispersed communities took on the task of writing down the rites of the cult as they had been practiced in Jerusalem. Thus the Babylonian Captivity corresponded to an episode of intense literary creation, and the redaction of the priestly code persisted long after the Jews returned to Palestine in 538 B.C. Since this current (known as 5P) was last in date, it gave the Pentateuch its definitive framework and on occasion has been thought its original nucleus.

As the Pentateuch was being constituted in this manner a series of redactors did their best to adapt the texts of their predecessors, at the risk of offering differing descriptions and interpretations of the same events. Thus we find two descriptions of the Creation, the first of which (in the beginning of the Book of Genesis) springs from the priestly tradition. Similarly, there are two descriptions of the Flood and two Decalogues, one Yahwist and the other Elohist, neither of which contains ten articles; one supposedly written by God himself and the other dictated to Moses after he broke the first tablet of the Ten Commandments in his indignation at seeing the Jews worshiping the Golden Calf. In later passages the priestly current can be discerned at the end of Exodus, throughout Leviticus, and in the better part of Numbers. The nucleus of Deuteronomy, which is the text found under Josiah, is framed by a discourse attributed to Moses that was also inspired by the priestly tradition (the last chapters of the book aside).

Thus the use of writing developed among the Jews as it did elsewhere from the moment when tribes and clans tended to merge into a greater whole. Writing helped the kings to put order into their administration and to levy taxes, and as early as the eighth century Isaiah denounced kings who promulgated iniquitous decrees and wrote oppressive rescripts depriving the poor of justice and despoiling the widow and the orphan. The sovereign, however, was not the source of the law. All he could do was to have the assembly of the people approve the successive texts of the Law given by Yahweh, which Scripture traditionally attached to the revelation received by Moses. In reality Hebrew law remained customary, and the elders of the cities long played an essential role in the courts.

The richness of the Bible came from the incessant dialogue between the chosen people and their God, in particular from the idea that the history of that people was not the result of a series of chance occurrences but rather of the will of Yahweh, who punished his people for their faults before raising them up again in his goodness. Everything began to change after the Exile. The line of the great prophets died out, and in the fifth century B.C. Malachi, for instance, seems less a spokesman for a superior will than a moralizing preacher operating by intuition, objections, arguments, and responses. Moreover the redaction of the priestly code was coming to an end and a new era was beginning in which new writings of a different nature, more on the terrain of wisdom and practical piety, were being added to the sacred texts. Henceforth the scribes, whose importance had grown during the Exile, were in command. These men of letters, the product of a broad variety of backgrounds, are often connected in the Old Testament with the notion of wisdom. They read and commented on the Torah in the synagogues, and they became the prime interpreters of the Law. Grouped in colleges, the most learned of them discussed actions to be taken and transmitted their thought to their disciples. They played an essential role in the law courts and were indispensable in the administration and in diplomacy. Solomon, to whom so many writings are attributed, seems to have been a scribe-king, and Esdras, the priest-scribe and learned interpreter of the commandments of Yahweh whose name remains connected with the history of the Torah, was their model. Such persons could translate the sacred texts from Hebrew into Aramaic (the only language the post-exilic masses spoke), and they not only took an interest in the *hallakah*—the law—but also in the *hagadah* —the history of their people. They also played a leading role in the redaction of wisdom literature, and they annotated or composed a mass of texts, commentaries, and translations (*targums*), as seen in the Dead Sea Scrolls. Nonetheless the Jews long remained essentially people of the spoken word, and in both their disputations and their teaching they appealed, by and large, to oral memory. It was not until the time of Vespasian (A.D. 9–79) that the canon of the Bible was closed, conforming to the traditions of Judaic piety, and only around A.D. 200 was the *mishnah*, the commentary on the Pentateuch that Pharisee tradition saw as originating in Moses, given written form. The Jews' great collections, the Eastern and the Western Talmud, were cast in definitive written form only in the fourth and fifth centuries A.D.

The history of the New Testament is an even more typical illustration of the close connection between oral tradition and written tradition.[54] According to the opinions most broadly accepted today, Jesus was born in 7/6 B.C. His public life lasted approximately three years, and we can date the Passion in the year 30. Paul converted around 34, and his first mission can be situated between 45 and 48. The Letter to the Thessalonians dates from the year 50; the First Letter to the Corinthians was written between 54 and 57. By that time, Christianity was spreading throughout the Mediterranean basin. Peter was probably martyred in 64 or 67, and Paul decapitated in 67 or soon after. Titus besieged and captured Jerusalem and took the city in 70, after which most of its inhabitants were killed, sold, or sentenced to forced labor. Still, St. Irenaeus, writing in the latter half of the second century, has this to say about the writing of the Gospels:

> Thus Matthew published among the Hebrews and in their own language a written form of Gospel in the epoch in which Peter and Paul were evangelizing Rome and founding the church there. After their death Mark, the disciple and interpreter of Peter, also transmitted to us in writing what Peter preached. Luke, the companion of Paul, consigned in a book the Gospel that the latter preached. Then John, the disciple of the Lord, the very one who had rested on his bosom, also published the Gospel while he was sojourning in Ephesus in Asia. (Irenaeus *Contra haereses* 3.1.1)

Ecclesiastical tradition attested in the second century A.D. thus attributes the Synoptic Gospels to three specific persons: Matthew, a publican who had belonged to the "college" of the twelve apostles and whose work, first written in the "Hebrew language" (that is, in Aramaic), was later the basis for the Greek version that is the only one we know; Mark, a disciple from Jerusalem; and Luke, a physician perhaps born in Antioch, who also wrote the Acts of the Apostles. The texts of these three Gospels offer a kinship that makes them generally held to have come from a common source or to have been inspired by one another. There is a tendency today to place the Gospel according to Mark at about the time of the death of Peter and before the fall of Jerusalem, while the Greek texts of Matthew and Luke are doubtless slightly later in their final redaction, although both by their style and their redaction they seem earlier than the letters of Paul. Finally, the Gospel according to John and the other later Johannine texts received definitive form at a later date.

As for the evangelists' sources of inspiration, tradition has identified two rival tendencies. The first is that of the exegetes who seek to determine the relations between the Gospels of Mark, Luke, and Matthew and attempt to establish the existence of presynoptic documents. The second is that of the champions of the oral tradition who once excluded all notion of a common literary dependence on a sole previous Gospel and held that the catechesis of the primitive church had rapidly become stereotyped because of the poverty of the Aramaic language and the laws of continual repetition. Today we are better informed, thanks to advances made by German scholars. Specialists in Aramaic have used stylistic studies—studies of the phrase rhythms, mnemonic procedures, key words, inclusions, word displacements, and so forth—to determine more precisely the exact role that this form of tradition may have played in the writing down of the Synoptic Gospels. The critics still fail to agree on the extent and the duration of this influence, and also on the possible existence of earlier written sources in Aramaic.

The exegetes' patient and painstaking labors also give us a better understanding of the climate of opinion in which the redaction of the New Testament may have taken place. During Jesus' lifetime Palestine was the site of many spiritual currents; it had close connections with the Hellenistic world, was subject to Roman domination, and more than ever it was a land of encounters and contacts. Writing was widespread there, notably within the Jewish world. Speech was still dominant, of course, particularly in matters involving disputation, instruction, or religious propaganda. Furthermore, as we have seen, all that writing did in the orthodox Jewish world was to select, fix, and consecrate oral traditions (often ancient ones) that it seemed useful to set down to consolidate the faith. The same was the case with the New Testament, which without a doubt represents a part of the "functional" literature of the earliest Christian communities. If we consider the term "church" as referring to the actual assembly in which the first Christians became aware of their common call and sought to establish connections with all others who responded to the same vocation, we can consider that church gatherings were where the first Christian literature was elaborated (the term "literature" being understood to include not only written but also oral compositions, still easily retained in these milieus where auditory memory remained well developed). Nonetheless, we need to distinguish among several different "places" for the "production" of such texts. First there were the synagogues, for as long as Christians were admitted to them, or the spaces around the portals of the Temple, where Christians often were to be found. Other narratives were repeated in private meetings between followers of the new belief, notably in their houses, where they listened to the teachings of the apostles and broke bread together. Still other texts were composed for preaching missions during which the Gospel was preached to larger and larger crowds, first of Jews, then of Samaritans, and finally of pagans. Thus with time and thanks to reiteration traditions developed that were nourished by the memory of Jesus but had their own ends and functions. It is probable that when the apostles left a community that they had founded they gave the congregation a written summary of their sermons. The narration, ceaselessly repeated, of the death and resurrection of Christ, the *Kerygma* or "Good News," seems to have been set down in writing at an early date. Similarly, the sayings of Jesus were memorized, repeated orally, and soon written down. Next came composite writings, not to mention the epistles, whose circulation gave cohesion to the widely dispersed churches and which were gradually collected together. A liturgy eventually developed, complete with sacred formulas, prayers, and canticles.

The shift from the oral tradition to the written tradition seems to have occurred within some thirty years, an exceptionally short span of time. However, the way in which the Gospels were elaborated helps us to see that they cannot be said to represent an objective narrative of the life and sayings of Jesus, few of which have come down to us. The Gospels are a codification of texts primarily designed to spread the faith, and they tell only a part of what the apostles and those who had approached the Messiah knew of him. Proof of this is the last sentence in the Gospel according to St. John: "There were many other things that Jesus did; if all were written down, the world itself, I suppose, would not hold all the books that would have to be written." This explains why Christians at first recognized only the Old Testament as their Holy Scripture and became aware of the rise of a New Testament only later.

The one God of Israel continued to be the god of one people. After an initial period of uncertainty Christianity asserted its universality, the first time that a religion had done so. As it spread through the Mediterranean basin with an astonishing rapidity, Christianity maintained its unity and developed its doctrines only by recourse to writing. Furthermore, the only way it could conquer the Roman Empire was by appealing to Greek and Latin culture.[55]

Thus a new form of Greco-Latin literature developed in the age of the Fathers of the church. Christian authors trained by the techniques of classical schooling, the rules of rhetoric in particular, often raised the question of whether they should read so many classical texts imbued with "superstition" and authorize others to read them. Most of them thought knowledge of such reading matter not only indispensable to their own intellectual formation but also a necessary tool for converting the pagans by using concepts and arguments borrowed from their own philosophers— Plato and the Stoics for the most part. St. Basil wrote a brief treatise on the utility of profane letters, and St. Jerome, taking inspiration from Deuteronomy, compared pagan culture to a captive whom a Jew could take to wife on the condition that her head be shaved and her nails cut.

The definitive battle between Christianity and paganism was launched during the fourth century when Constantine, the first Christian emperor, accorded freedom of worship to the adepts of the new law (A.D. 312). It resulted at the century's end in the rout of the pagans, who defended themselves with some dignity. The Council of Nicaea, which proclaimed the consubstantiality of the Father and the Son, unleashed a phase of intense doctrinal activity. It is hardly surprising that the greatest Fathers of the church were grouped in one generation: among the Greeks, St. Basil (330–79), his brother St. Gregory of Nyssa (335–95), St. Gregory of Nazianzus (ca. 328–89), and St. John Chrysostom (ca. 347–407); among the Latins, St. Ambrose (333–97), St. Jerome (347–419), and St. Augustine (354–430).

The Christian authors of the early centuries were surprisingly prolix. The prize goes to the Alexandrian Origen (ca. 185–ca. 253/255), to whom St. Epiphanius attributes two thousand writings (St. Epiphanius' own bibliography, by St. Jerome, lists eight hundred entries). Authors like these worked without respite, but thanks to wealthy patrons they had an army of scriveners who knew shorthand and to whom they could dictate their compositions, which explains negligences of style, overladen phrases, and brusque shifts of topic. St. Jerome worked in just this manner: he translated the Book of Tobit in one day, the Book of Esther in one night, and he admitted that he could not stop to reflect when he saw the scrivener before him, awaiting his word with raised stylus. A number of sermons and homilies (with notations of the hearers' reactions) were taken down by stenographers placed among the crowd, traces of whose work remain in definitive versions of the texts.

This was the climate in which the doctrines of the Catholic Church were elaborated, but that climate also included incessant controversy and the claims of a number of heresies. Like any other institution, the church needed an indisputable source for the dogma it adopted, and that source was necessarily revelation, transmitted from generation to generation by the paths of tradition and still living in its bosom.

Before going on we need to recall what was meant by "tradition." [56] The Littré *Dictionnaire de la langue française,* an apostle of secularity, gives tradition as "the action by which one transfers something to someone"; it is "the transmission of historical facts, religious doctrines, legends from age to age by oral means and without authentic and written proof." The definition continues, "particularly in the Catholic Church, transmission from century to century of the knowledge of things concerning Religion and that are not in the Holy Scripture." Tradition, however, is not limited to the transmission of previous materials by the intermediary of living beings and institutions; on its way it also integrates new givens or principles. Thus tradition is renewal, re-creation of the values of a community. By the same token it cannot depend on mere human forces, and it normally draws its authority from supernatural forces, as with the solemn contracts of customary law.

Tradition is thus connected with the prestige of the past. It proceeds from the myth of the Golden Age and the Platonic idea of a need to return to primordial forces in the face of a continual decadence. It appears (and rightly so) primarily as a mode of transmission proper to societies with an oral culture. This statement needs qualification, however: we have seen, for example, that the codification of custom did not hinder a revolution in custom in ancient societies, and we know that, in spite of the triumph of law, tradition remains, even in today's society, the essential source of law. Was the same thing true in the Christian religion?

The oral tradition reigned supreme at the origins of Christianity. It was what Jesus had in mind when he told the apostles to spread the Good News, and St. Paul, who had not known Jesus directly but was in contact with him through personal revelations, declared, "It was God who decided that we were fit to be entrusted with the Good News." Because he may have written the better part of his letters when the first versions of the Gospels had not yet appeared, Paul indicates in his Second Letter to the Thessalonians, "Stand firm then, brothers, and keep the traditions that we taught you, whether by word of mouth or by letter." He tells his disciple Timothy, "You have heard everything that I teach in public; hand it on to reliable people so that they in turn will be able to teach others." This was how what is commonly called the apostolic tradition came to be established. But that tradition concerned more than a narration of human events. As with the Jews and the Old Testament, what was needed was to point out the day-by-day consequences of the divine message, which was how it differed from the Gnostic heresy, which spoke of a secret teaching communicated by Jesus to a few apostles and transmitted to a handful of the "perfect." Moreover as time passed and Gospels that the church considered apocryphal spread, witnesses to Jesus' message became increasingly vague and increasingly subject to caution. Heresies prompted the problem of legitimacy, and St. Irenaeus attempted to show that the only incontestable criterion of legitimacy was the apostolic succession of bishops, the bishop of Rome in particular, whose church had been founded by Peter and Paul. At the same time lists of authorized texts (the Gospels in particular) began to circulate.

Thus the notion of tradition was formed within the Catholic Church. As soon as a truth had to be transmitted from one generation to another by mortal men, "tradition," in the active sense, came to indicate a sacred trust that must be guarded faithfully. This did not mean that the Holy Spirit did not continue to explain the inexhaustible content of that deposited trust and bring it to life in a world in perpetual evolution. St. Irenaeus, contrasting that notion to the Gnosis, explained that "true gnosis" was "the doctrine of the apostles and the ancient order ($\sigma\nu\sigma\tau\eta\mu\alpha$) of the Church throughout the whole world, the distinctive (recognizable) mark of the Body of Christ, which consists in the chain of succession by which the bishops, through tradition, have established a Church in every place." Father Congar concluded from this:

> It is in this, says Irenaeus, that true gnosis consists. This *gnosis* which St. Paul insisted the faithful should be filled with, remained an ideal in the early Church. It is a spiritual gift which has as its object or content the knowledge of the ways of God, the understanding of the great saving acts accomplished by Christ and of their proclamation in scripture. Tradition and gnosis are related as means and end. Both come from the Holy Spirit, both presuppose life in the Church, the receptacle of the Spirit. The Church is, says St. Irenaeus, like a beautiful vase to which the spirit communicates unceasingly a superabundance of youth while renewing, also, the deposit it contains.[57]

From that point on, the Fathers of the church ceaselessly asserted that the church was the unique depository of the truth, which the apostles had passed on to it, because only the church was inhabited by the Holy Spirit. Although the notion of tradition had been formulated before the notion of apostolic succession, the principle according to which ministers had authority to teach the faithful in continuity from the apostles can be found, in one way or another, in all ancient documents (Yves Congar). Thus one could justify the appearance of traditions not attested by Scripture, notably those concerning liturgical customs, which the ecclesiastical authors defend by appealing to their antiquity or their universal presence and acceptance. The Protestant Reformation later severely criticized and denied the apostolic character of these traditions.

The difficulties inherent in setting down prophetic revelation in writing are even clearer in the history of the Koran than in that of the New Testament.[58]

For Muslims, the Koran (in Arabic, Qur'an) was nothing less than the transmission "in clear Arabic language" of a divine archetype kept in Heaven from all eternity and graven on "the guarded Tablet." That archetype was revealed to Mohammed (A.D. 570−632) in a series of visions, the first of which occurred in 612, and Mohammed stated explicitly that he had done nothing but transmit the message of Allah, adding nothing and removing nothing. Mohammed was probably illiterate, and he informed his entourage of the divine discourse orally. The very term "Qur'an" (and the verb from which it was taken, *qu'ran*) originally meant vocalized recitation, not a written book. It was only after the Hegira (622) that certain disciples of the Master began to inscribe fragments of what they had heard on camel shoulder-bones, bits of leather, or any other materials that came to hand. After the death of the Prophet, the Koranic revelations were gathered into a number of corpora, the most important of which was collected by the first caliph, Abu Bakr. Later, the third caliph, 'Uthman (645−65), enlarged this corpus, drew up a vulgate from it, and, in order to put a stop to disputes, ordered the destruction of all the writings set down during the Prophet's lifetime.

This move aroused a storm of criticism. Some of Mohammed's companions were indignant that their contributions had been left out. The Shiites accused the caliphs responsible for the compilation of having intentionally eliminated the passages demonstrating the legitimacy of claims to spiritual leadership of the fourth caliph, Ali, Mohammed's son-in-law and cousin, who was assassinated. Furthermore, the 114 *suras* (chapters) that made up the work were arranged in order of length, according to what seems to have been Arabic custom, ignoring all logic and chronology. This structure posed problems, but the theologians claimed it was divinely inspired. Moreover every *sura* juxtaposed revelations from different epochs. Above all the limitations of Arabic writing made interpretation difficult. In the seventh century, written Arabic allowed only for notation of the consonantal framework of words plus the three long vowels ē, ū, and ī, omitting short vowels. One sign was used to note consonants that were articulated very differently, and there was no indication of the function of certain words or the articulation of the phrases. A graphic system of this sort obviously lent itself to varying interpretations, and it furnished little more than a guide to memory for repeating aloud a text that had already been memorized. Thus it did not substitute for oral tradition. In the eighth and ninth centuries the extension of Islam to populations who did not speak Arabic and could hardly be expected to guess at what had been left out prompted a series of improvements aimed at clarifying the reading of the text. Grammatical studies were developing during the same period, and the copyists of Koranic texts tended to abandon the angular and monumental Kufic script in favor of a handsome, rounded cursive. This was still not enough to remove all the ambiguities of the original system.

There are thus characteristics of Arabic script that explain the tenacious survival of reading aloud and of memorization of the Koran and that justify the role of a body of readers charged with restoring the contents of the sacred text to its full integrity. Under these conditions, a vulgate could be read and accepted with slight variants. After the ninth century such variants were thought to correspond to seven "chains" established by scholars whose authority was recognized, and the various interpretations of the divine Word were considered a form of enrichment that permitted better rendering of its hidden truths (Régis Blachère).

The Koran, like Judeo-Christian scriptural texts, arose in lands in which speech preceded letters within populations who knew writing but nevertheless remained within an oral tradition. Muslims may also have felt some fear in noting down the word of God. Is there any reason to criticize the disciples of Allah who admitted that all speech is polysemic when Christians were doing their utmost to make speech seem univocal?

Four

The Death and Resurrection of Written Culture

Any break cripples chronology. Setting the end of classical antiquity at A.D. 476 under the pretext that a barbarian prince deposed the last Roman emperor of the West, Romulus Augustulus, in that year of disgrace, is a break neither worse nor more satisfactory than any other. In any event it should serve to remind us that the Eastern Roman Empire survived for nearly another thousand years, and that the death agony of classical culture continued in the West at least until the eighth century. It is even hard to say whether Charlemagne was an emperor in the Roman fashion or the first ruler of a society on its way to something new.

Hence we have arrived at a critical moment in the history of writing—a moment of decline par excellence: that of Rome. And at a period whose unity is factitious—the Middle Ages. We will see a series of centuries in which writing survived only with the aid of religion, in which the Carolingian "renaissance" provided a sustained underlying note, and in which new invasions brought writing close to the zero point. Then in the late tenth century we will see the brusque awakening of a world that seemed regenerated. Through all this time the *translatio studii*, a transmission of knowledge that has raised much controversy, nonetheless preserved the essence of the classical heritage and enabled northern Europe to discover it once more. In other words, as always, we shall see a change that took place on the fringes of an older culture, with newcomers gaining a better mastery of the techniques of writing. All this happened before the great Renaissance of the fifteenth century, when, to the east of territory that was the old Romania printing appeared and provided a point of departure for many new changes.

The Impact of the Barbarians

There is a price to pay for decline. The great invasions often began in insidious ways when entire peoples came to seek refuge behind the Roman *limes* and the populations of the Roman Empire welcomed auxiliary troops who were willing to do their fighting for them. Raids became more frequent, and eventually the Empire had to make room for occupation troops and their families. The economic and moral weakening of the Empire delivered its western half to the barbarians. After the catastrophic fifth century, the century of great waves of invaders, the *pax romana* seemed to be reestablished, especially in the more profoundly Romanized and less massively occupied southern portion of Europe. After the German conquest the populations kept their monuments, their baths, and their theaters. They continued to use scriveners to draw up the usual acts, which they deposited, as before, in the archives of the municipalities. Some acts were still posted up in Rome or Ravenna, and sale contracts, acts of donation, and wills were still drafted according to formulas carefully regulated by the jurists. The school system continued to function, much of the middle class received the usual elementary instruction, and aristocrats continued to frequent grammar schools and schools of rhetoric.[1] Nonetheless everything had changed. The barbarians were there in their midst with their chiefs, their assemblies, and their traditional culture. The barbarians knew writing, certainly. Had not some of them created runes, mostly for magical purposes? And had not missionaries given the Goths a writing system of their own?[2] The Goths could not see that it had much use, though, except in particular situations. Their only juridical rules were their own customs, transmitted orally. They had systems of real and solemn contracts for transactions that concluded by swearing to superior powers in the presence of witnesses. They had their legends, their poems, and their songs, and they preferred a warlike moral training at the court of their rulers, where the virtues and the exploits of their ancestors were taught, to the rhetoricians' schools. Furthermore, when they converted en masse to Christianity during the fifth century, most of them adopted Arianism, which means that they had their own clergy—often well organized—were hostile to Catholicism, and were inclined to accept the laws of the Empire forbidding intermarriage between Romans and barbarians.

Nonetheless these peoples were ready to accept the fiction of the Empire, and their recently implanted kings had every interest in reassuring the populations that they had subjected. Those rulers quite naturally thought it good policy to offer the local elites certain forms of collaboration. Some Romans, the poet Apollinaris Sidonius, for instance, refused collaboration as best they could, but others sought to become part of the new order and to influence its evolution.[3] Theodoric the Great, king of the Ostrogoths, reigned over the north of Italy. At one point a hostage at the court in Constantinople, Theodoric posed as the champion of Romania, and he gathered together in his court in Ravenna an elite of administrators and Latin men of letters along with his own warriors, Germanic poets, and Arian prelates. Boethius, a great Hellenist from an illustrious family that had rallied to the Ostrogoths, shone in this company. Proclaimed consul, then *magister palatii,* Boethius was later suspected of conspiring with the emperor of the East, the persecutor of Arians, and was thrown in prison, tortured, and executed. Cassiodorus, also from a family of notables who had rallied to the Ostrogothic monarchy, passed part of his life at court laden with honors before he was taken prisoner by Belisarius, Justinian's general and the conqueror of Italy, and taken off to Constantinople. It is tempting to wonder what life was like for these refined men of letters at the court of a barbarian king and what sorts of relations they might have had with poets from a totally different world. At least they attempted to teach their conquerors some aspects of classical culture. Cassiodorus wrote a flattering *Historia Gothorum* inspired by the legends of the Goths as much as by Roman historical sources, and he did his best to present the Gothic kings as combating Rome against their will. Cassiodorus also wrote or supervised the drafting of a number of official documents that later served as models for many medieval chanceries. As for Boethius, his abundant and varied collected works included not only theological treatises but commentaries on great Greek and Latin philosophers. He wrote his famous *De consolatione philosophiae* while in prison. Using a dialectical method inspired by Aristotle's late Neoplatonic commentators, he consoled himself at the thought of his approaching death by recalling arguments in favor of the existence of a profoundly good and providential God.[4] In this way Boethius served as an intermediary between the wisdom of antiquity and the Christian thought of the Middle Ages, and he helped to elaborate—at times in tragic circumstances—the legacy of classical knowledge in works all the more important for being perfectly adapted to a new world in formation.

The coexistence in the same territory of ethnic groups with different customs and traditions posed more urgent problems. For instance, it was important to know which law had priority. As a general rule laws of the dominant group pertained: and individuals were judged under their own law, although when barbarian and Latin law clashed, the system that prevailed varied according to the region or the epoch. Another problem was to know those laws. Heedful of the need to adapt the work of the last Roman emperors, Alaric, a Visigoth, Gundobad, a Burgundian, and Theodoric, an Ostrogoth, all established "breviaries" of Roman law for the use of their Roman subjects. The barbarians also understood that contact with Romanized populations threatened their customs with contamination, if not replacement, if the customs, too, were not written down. Such "codes" of law redacted by order of the sovereign by Roman jurisconsults (who necessarily influenced their interpretation), in reality remained customs. They evolved as society evolved, and they required periodic revision with the aid of the people's assembly, whose role (along with the king's) was essential in such matters. Gradually, however, revision ceased, and as generations passed the people began to forget and judges came to lack the training that would enable them to read the texts on which they were supposedly basing their decisions.[5]

The situation changed in different ways from one region to another. Byzantium's reconquest of part of Italy and of certain Mediterranean coastal areas favored the survival there of what remained of classical culture. In Visigothic Spain, where the invaders had been relatively few in number, the written act continued to serve as the usual way to handle social transactions. After King Reccared converted to Catholicism (587) and after the Third Council of Toledo, the Germanic aristocracy turned to classical culture and the sovereigns protected letters. This was the climate in which Isidore of Seville lived. Granted easy access to the great classical texts in a land with a long-standing and lively Latin tradition, Isidore compiled with passion whatever came his way. His great work, the uncompleted encyclopedia of origins, or *Etymologiae*, seems a desperate effort to give order to the knowledge and activities of his age. This gigantic labor, moving incessantly between the secular and the sacred, was to make Isidore the most frequently consulted author of the early Middle Ages, and it won him a place in the fourth heaven of Dante's *Paradiso*, where his name was emblazoned ahead of those of the Venerable Bede and Richard of Saint-Victor.[6]

North of the Loire the Frankish warriors and herders remained faithful to their traditions. The Salians had barbarized Austrasia but Neustria was less profoundly affected. Clovis's conversion to Catholicism broke down a number of barriers between the Franks and the Gallo-Romans, and the Merovingian conquest of the south of France helped to win over the Frankish aristocracy to written culture. Chilperic, whose sinister portrait Gregory of Tours has left us, played the enlightened ruler. He composed hymns in imitation of the poet Sedulius, dabbled in theology, and seemed to have wanted to reform the alphabet, in imitation of the emperor Claudius, but probably also as a way to note the new sounds that had appeared in the pronunciation of vulgar Latin. Chilperic is even reputed to have ordered that texts be rubbed off old parchments with pumice stone so that new texts could be written on them. The legend of the Trojan origins of the Franks seems to date from the same epoch: echoes of it can be found in the chronicle of Frankish history supposedly written by Fredegarius.

Princes and aristocrats displayed their taste for song and for religious litera-ture, and the court of young King Dagobert was a genuine center of cul-ture. Every man of letters is closely dependent upon the society in which he lives, and this rule was even truer of Gregory of Tours (534–94) than of Isidore of Seville. Gregory, an aristocrat of Gallo-Roman origin im-mersed from early youth in a bustling milieu of strong barbaric influences, seems nearly a caricature of the classical tradition. His grammar was fan-ciful and his style rough. Above all his *Historia Francorum* shows little ca-pacity for discerning connections of cause and effect, and faith alone cannot explain the credulity and naiveté of his lives of the saints and his *Miracula*. [7]

It would be interesting to know all the stages of this very slow disinte-gration. Rulers everywhere maintained chanceries, at times active ones that attempted to keep up ancient traditions and that produced letters and texts of a legislative or regulatory nature. The redaction of private acts as well long showed a close filiation with the redaction of the acts of Roman times. Nonetheless, although some of the oldest medieval deeds have au-tograph subscriptions and signatures, after the seventh and eighth centu-ries autography became more and more the exception, save in strongly Romanized regions like Septimania. If a person initiating an act or the witnesses to the act could not hold a pen even to trace a cross, they were invited to touch the parchment (the *manufirmatio*). Scribes lost sight of the real meaning of the formulas they recopied; deviations arose, particularly in the tenth century, when the conclusion of a juridical act is described in a third-person narrative of a solemn ceremonial. As in the case of other legal instruments, the probative value of such notices depended on the lists of witnesses they furnished. [8]

Still, writing kept its prestige throughout the centuries. The texts of the ancient laws were recopied and consulted even when they were increas-ingly inappropriate. Rolls continued to be drawn up for the collection of taxes that grew out of the Roman system. The new masters found it harder and harder to keep the tax registers up-to-date. The barbarians refused to pay these taxes, and the disappearance of public services was no incite-ment. Gregory of Tours reports that Chilperic threw the tax rolls of the city of Tours into the fire rather than displease the great St. Martin. [9] Good King Dagobert sent his political enemies to collect the taxes in the hope that they would not return. Rulers began to reside on their *villae*, living on the revenues from their domains. At least they did not abandon written book-keeping: they probably kept registers like the ones that have been found

for St. Martin of Tours. Furthermore, the masters of great domains continued to have copies made of the inventories of their goods, copies known to
specialists by their late Latin name, *polyptychae.*

More important than the common heritage were the deep cleavages that
marked Europe with an indelible stamp. The more Romanized western
Mediterranean world from Italy through southern France to Spain remained loyal to a shared conception of written matter and saw Latin as the
mother tongue of all culture. Soon a dividing line separated those more
southern lands that remained loyal to written law from the lands of customary law of the North. Also soon, the West confirmed the law that newcomers build new forms of thought on the basis of the acquisitions of older
peoples. A renascence that had begun on the shores of the Mediterranean
blossomed in northern lands.

During this period a new church—pontifical, monastic, and missionary—was becoming organized. It would pick up the heritage of classical
antiquity, adapt it, and effect its transfer to northern lands. The founders of
the first monasteries, which were created in Italy in the fifth century, admittedly had totally different objectives in mind. Their aim was to form a
militia dedicated to prayer and asceticism. They reserved a place of honor
for psalmody, which filled those who sang with the Word of God. Contrary
to ancient habits, every monk was to devote long hours to individual reading. The Rule established by St. Benedict specified that in summer three
hours of the day must be reserved for reading and in winter two, that every
monk had to read one volume *in extenso* during Lent, and that monks must
carry a small book with them when they traveled and open it during halts.
This impregnation was to be reinforced by reading aloud during meals and
before compline.[10]

Thus psalmody developed. It was a science of reading aloud; a form of
rhythmic reading in which the reader avoided any personal interpretation
and acquired what might be called a muscular memory of the divine Word.
This sort of reading was undoubtedly interspersed with pauses for meditation and a better comprehension of the passage that had just been read. It
was an exercise that required more concentration than was customary for
the age; it was in fact so arduous that St. Benedict stipulated that two older
monks must supervise the reading "work" of the younger monks and report them if they were lazy.

It was soon deemed necessary to encourage the study of Scripture in the monasteries, following the example of the Byzantine monks. After Cassiodorus abandoned secular life in 537, he organized a monastic group at Vivarium, where he tried to persuade the monks that he had brought there not only to read sacred works but also to copy them. He insisted that the monks learn the rudiments of profane letters—in other words, that they have the appropriate intellectual baggage—as a way to reach a better understanding of sacred works. In communicating a taste for intellectual work to his companions, Cassiodorus was careful not to condemn pagan authors; rather he stressed that the classics should be read not in and of themselves but as a means for attaining a better comprehension of Holy Scripture and the works of the church Fathers. To assemble the necessary materials he had manuscripts brought from Africa at great expense, and he had them stored in nine cabinets. This was a modest beginning, as Pierre Courcelle has remarked, but it was a beginning.[11]

Soon a new chapter in the history of the *translatio studii* began in northern Europe. When the Romans retreated from the British Isles, Latin culture took refuge further west in the regions in which the Celts had settled when the German invaders chased them out of England. Left to its own devices in a land without cities, the Irish church regrouped into monasteries whose abbots, often, were also bishops of the surrounding territory. Under their direction the monks pursued an asceticism much like that of the East and studied sacred texts. In their isolation their Latin kept its full purity. They had no scruples about studying the liberal arts, notably grammar and rhetoric, but their specialty was ecclesiastical reckoning (drawing up the church calendar, fixing the date of Easter, and so forth). Hence these apparently closed milieus (but in which relations with Byzantium had never been totally broken) produced a flourishing but strange and mannerist style that in some aspects recalls classical Asian qualities; a style of proliferating periphrases and epithets, perhaps influenced by national oral traditions. Along with this florid writing style they cultivated the illuminator's and the goldsmith's arts, making extensive use of spirals, interlaced motifs, and highly stylized human and animal figures.

There were also newcomers to be converted—Angles, Jutes, and Saxons. The initiative came from Rome, where Gregory the Great had become pope. Understanding that his mission was to evangelize the barbarian peoples, in 596 he sent a small group of monks to settle in Kent. Soon after the Irish joined the first missionaries with efforts of their own, until finally the British Isles were wholly Christianized though divided between the Irish and the Roman traditions. The British Isles were unified under Rome in 663, thus forming a nucleus for further growth free of the weight of old habits at the edges of the ancient Latin cultural universe. One result of this movement was that a group of peoples adopted a language totally foreign to them as their language of sacred culture. Very soon schools prospered beside the churches. A disciple of masters who were illustrious in their own right, Bede entered the monastery of Jarrow in 685 at the age of thirteen. He later wrote a *Historia ecclesiastica gentis Anglorum*, biblical commentaries reliant on the church Fathers, treatises on spelling, measures, and ecclesiastical reckoning, and a *De natura rerum* in some ways comparable to the *Etymologiae* of Isidore of Seville but purged of all reflections of the cosmogony of classical antiquity. Thus Bede laid the foundations for a scholastic tradition that subordinated culture to religion, mistrusted tricks of dialectics, rhetoric, and speculation, and concentrated on clarifying scriptural texts with the help of grammar and on studying ecclesiastical reckoning, grammar, and astrology.[12]

This renewal of island cultures at a time when the Arabs were seizing the greater part of the Iberian peninsula and ravaging the southwest of France shifted the Continent's center of gravity toward the northeast. Contact increased between the British Isles and Europe, along the coast and moving up the great rivers. This proved a help to the Irish and Anglo-Saxon monks when they in turn took up missionary work, and it contributed much to the creation of a network of abbeys that henceforth formed the nerve centers of Western Christendom.

The newly founded abbeys and monasteries could never have become the centers for study and copying that they did if they had not initially received the materials they needed from elsewhere and then kept up exchanges with the outside. In the fifth century the Irish encouraged the importation of books from the Continent, and they welcomed pupils from other lands. Thanks to Gregory the Great, Rome became the next important purveyor of materials. The first missionaries that he sent to England took with them not only liturgical trappings and ornaments but books— probably liturgical works. A later pope sent two scholars, Theodore of Tarsus, a Greek, and Adrian, an African, to educate a native clergy, and they undoubtedly stocked up on the necessary texts before their departure. Similarly, Benedict Biscop, a thane of the king of Northumbria who had made the decision to serve God, went to Rome in 673–75 (the first of five such voyages), bringing back a large number of manuscripts. Close ties were established between the Anglo-Saxons and the Holy See, and both texts and men went back and forth between the British Isles and Rome.

Between these two poles the abbeys of the Continent were the crossroads of a variety of influences. In 632, not long after its founding, the
monastery of Fleury-sur-Loire received relics of St. Benedict from Monte
Cassino, and it continued to have close relations with that great Italian
monastery; similarly, the monastery of Corbie acquired a number of manuscripts from pilgrims returning from Italy. Nearly everywhere abbots and
monks interested in gathering manuscripts had them copied and sent from
sister houses in Italy or England. These new establishments and the cathedral libraries were indispensable intermediaries for rescuing secular texts,
which tended to disappear along with the culture they represented. Nothing symbolizes the importance and the fragility of this sort of exchange
better than the history of one known manuscript of the Fifth Decade of
Livy's *Annals*. This manuscript, probably copied in Italy in the fifth century,
passed into England in the seventh or eighth century; later it was taken to
Frisia by a missionary, and it ended up in Lorsch Abbey, where a sixteenth-
century humanist discovered it and published it.[13]

❖

Thus it is hardly a coincidence if the revival of the West arose in the region
between the Meuse and the Rhine rivers in Austrasia. This land was the
birthplace of the Carolingian dynasty, whose aristocracy was nearly completely illiterate and whose clergy, according to its reformer, the Anglo-
Saxon Wynfrid, was particularly ignorant and corrupt. The revival quite
obviously happened as the result of a cultural appeal to outside forces on
the part of a people who had reached maturity through previous contacts.
No Frank figures in the first small group of men of letters that Charlemagne
assembled around him to give luster to his reign. Like many other conquerors, he used both violence and seduction to attract the people he
needed. He retained Paul the Deacon, who had come to beg a pardon for
a brother who had been compromised in a conspiracy. After the capitula-
tion of the Lombard King Desiderius, Charlemagne brought back the aged
and knowledgeable Peter of Pisa and Paulinus, whom he made bishop of
Aquileia. He took in Spanish scholars who were fleeing the Arabs and
made one of them, Theodulf, bishop of Orléans and another, Agobard,
archbishop of Lyons. Above all, Charlemagne succeeded in attracting Alcuin, an Anglo-Saxon scholar who had taught at York but who, at the age
of fifty, was only a deacon and abbot of a small monastery. Charlemagne
assured him a brilliant career.[14]

The most striking (but also the most ephemeral) results of Charlemagne's efforts can perhaps be measured in the decoration of the palace in Aachen and in some of the prestigious manuscripts made for the sovereigns and their entourage. Both bear witness to an indisputable familiarity with classical art. The revival of the imperial ideology also shows that Rome and its culture had struck profound echoes among these barbarians of the North, who probably drew more inspiration from the sight of the proud monuments that still stood in the cities of the West and the prestige of the Byzantine emperor than from texts alone. We need to guard against too idyllic a view of the Palatine Academy, a circle of poets and great personages particularly active during the late eighth century whose members each chose a name borrowed from classical antiquity or Scripture. Grammar and astronomy were debated in the Academy in the presence of courtiers and young nobles who had come to complete their education and serve the sovereign at what has been called (somewhat erroneously) the Palace School. Charlemagne himself contributed to these animated debates, but his own level of culture was highly questionable. Einhard's flattering life of the glorious sovereign (a close imitation of Suetonius' *Lives of the Twelve Caesars*) states that Charlemagne could express himself with equal ease in Latin and in his native tongue (a Germanic dialect), but Einhard admits that Charlemagne understood Greek better than he spoke it. How much hyperbole is there in this portrait? The emperor certainly must have understood the distorted Latin of his subjects who spoke a Romance tongue. He certainly read Latin. We are left wondering, though, when Einhard himself adds that Charlemagne learned to write late in life, working at night when he could not sleep with slate boards or sheets of parchment that had been placed near his bed, and that he never became truly proficient.[15]

One might regard the efforts to develop the use of writing during this period with some skepticism. Admittedly, the chanceries of the Carolingian monarchs were extremely busy. Diplomas proliferated, particularly writs to establish proof of private rights, but there is no trace of the sort of written nominations to high office (to a countship, for example) that can be found for the sixth and early seventh centuries. Charlemagne rearranged and republished the old legal dispositions concerning the church and the state and added new decrees. He issued a proclamation in Italy in 787 affirming that the written law was superior to oral custom, and after his coronation he attempted to have the laws of his various peoples set down. He also encouraged a revival of writing in diplomacy and administration. Nonetheless, his capitularies were never drafted as carefully as the diplomas were, and the documents that have come down to us bear no trace of validation. The essential act in the legislative process thus seems to have been the "word" (*verbum*) by which the sovereign made known, solemnly or informally, a decision that the diet may have previously considered on the basis of a simple oral report. The written document that resulted often took the form of a memorandum, thus it seems to have been a device for giving public notice of a decision rather than a document that had force of law.[16]

Any change in this domain was hindered by an increasing inability to write Latin in lay circles. Forms of administrative correspondence did exist, but the documents addressed to the Palace were frequently drafted incorrectly and the questions addressed to the counts and their responses show clearly that on both sides an appropriate intellectual formation was so obviously lacking that writing did not always result in communication. On occasion the *missi* even specify that envoys sent by the counts to bring back their instructions had to be capable of understanding what would be explained to them.

It is clear that Charlemagne and his successors struggled against odds. The Merovingians had lay chancery officials to redact documents but it became the rule to replace them with clerics, many of them future prelates and men who, quite naturally, were loyal to the chapel and to its head, the arch-chaplain. Furthermore, when in the reign of Louis the Pious the arch-chancellor freed himself from this subjection to the arch-chaplain, it was for reasons of personal aggrandizement rather than to supervise the redaction of acts, which continued to be done by clerics.[17]

The men of those times had something quite different in mind when it came to restoring written culture. Their intent was to use a common learned language—Latin—to gain an acquaintance with and a better comprehension of Scripture, and to perpetuate correct and uniform performance of rites and sacraments for the glory of God and the unity of the West. This was the predominant motivation behind Charlemagne's educational policies, which simply brought order and system to long-standing efforts to prepare a competent clergy. In the *Admonitio generalis* of 789 Charlemagne insisted (as his father had before him) on the need to teach the clergy the "Roman" style of chanting as it was done in the *Schola cantorum* founded in Rome by Gregory the Great. Recalling that he had established cantors in Metz and in Soissons, Charlemagne decreed that every church must send a choirmaster to study with those cantors and correct the antiphonaries. Every church and every monastery was to teach the

Psalms, the *notae Tironianae* (a shorthand system), singing, ecclesiastical reckoning, and grammar. They were also to keep corrected copies of books and make sure that no one corrupted a text when reading or copying it.[18]

The aim of this educational program was to prepare priests to serve the altar. The schoolchild's first reading texts were the Pater, the Credo, and the Psalms in Latin, which he had to know how to intone. He was also taught the rudiments of Gregorian chant and the readings of the Mass. The teaching of writing was of secondary importance—a pedagogical view that became firmly ingrained and that contributed to producing, well into the eighteenth century, semi-literates who could decipher a text but could not write.

Charlemagne was fully aware that the clergy needed a good knowledge of written Latin. In a letter written some years after the *Admonitio* and addressed to the bishops and the abbots he stressed that grammar alone permitted penetration of the meaning of Scripture. He was referring to a specific pedagogical model. The pupil must be introduced to the study of Latin through elementary texts like the *Catonis Disticha*, the *Fables* of Phaedrus and Avianus, and Alcuin's *Praecepta vivendi*. He then learned practical vocabulary through the use of glossaries based on the *Etymologiae* of Isidore of Seville, and he used Donatus' short grammar as his basic textbook. The study of grammar in the broader sense also included learning one's letters, learning words, learning "punctuation" (really the art of reading aloud), and studying the figures of speech and prosody with the aid of the *De nuptiis Mercurii et Philologiae*, written in the fifth century by Martianus Capella. The aim of all this was to prepare for the monastic *lectio divina*. By following this program the student could acquire basic notions of rhetoric and dialectic and an introduction to ecclesiastical reckoning.

These methods, spread in large part by Alcuin from the Abbey of Saint Martin in Tours, helped to raise the level of studies in religious circles throughout northern Gaul and Germany. Henceforth clerics in search of instruction went from one abbey or cathedral school to another to hear the leading masters comment on sacred texts and (on occasion) offer genuine theological instruction or the rudiments of philosophy. Bishops and abbots, who were often kin, corresponded from one institution to another, exchanging letters of humanist inspiration and manuscripts. In this manner a few superior minds had access to a coherent abstract thought and produced some works that have resisted the ravages of time.

Although this intellectual revival was the work of small groups it had an undeniable importance. The scribes of the period concentrated on the copying of liturgical texts, but they were not limited to these. A fragment of a catalogue of the Palatine Library written in 790 by an Italian shows that the classical works contained in that library could also be found in the collections of many of the great French and German abbeys—a clear indication of concerted efforts. All scholars who have edited texts know how often they have used Carolingian manuscripts or copies of manuscripts made in that period. Beyond a doubt the Carolingian renaissance was an essential link in the *translatio studii*. [19]

We need to turn next to the documents themselves, and to the writing styles. Some traces of confusion are visible after the barbarian invasions of the fifth century; then, in the total collapse between the sixth and the seventh century, the "landscape" of writing seems overwhelmed and fragmented. In Italy the writing styles of the chapter workshops in Verona, Vercelli, and Lucca remained fairly close to what they had been, but there was also the "Beneventine" script of Monte Cassino. In Spain, Visigothic showed a degree of unity, while new scripts appeared in Ireland and in England: a majuscule with short ascenders, heavy thick strokes, and marked serifs, and a pointed minuscule. These models spread with the missionaries to the abbeys of Luxeuil, Saint Gall, and Bobbio. In Merovingian France the acts of the sovereigns were written in a tortuous and complicated hand with haphazard ligatures, while monastic and episcopal workshops presented an enormous variety of hands.

Faced with this much diversity, the paleographers of yesteryear concentrated primarily on classifying this bewildering array of styles, attempting to describe their peculiarities and giving them somewhat romantic national names such as Lombardic, Visigothic, Anglo-Saxon, or Merovingian. They may have thought that these scripts reflected deep-seated tendencies in each of these peoples, a particularly tempting notion that perhaps was even justified in the case of the highly characteristic decoration of Irish manuscripts.

There is a good reason for this attitude. In those years the scholars who scrutinized the documents of the early Middle Ages had not yet given more than a passing glance at the graffiti of Pompeii and were unaware of the work of the papyrologists. Consciously or unconsciously thinking of ancient writing systems in terms of inscriptions on monuments, they were put off by the look of old parchments, and they attached little importance to *ductus*, the direction and sequence in which letters were written that gave a written hand its structure. Thus they failed to see that the contours of the scripts that they dubbed national were of the same inspiration as Roman writing. The way the barbarian kingdoms were constituted had simply set up a graphic compartmentalization in a Europe where goods, men, and written matter gradually stopped circulating and where the various *scriptoria* had evolved independently, each one seeking to affirm its own style.

The appearance of Carolingian letters was the last act in the long drama of classical writing. The Carolingian script was prepared gradually during the eighth century with the appearance of minuscules written with separated letters rather than cursively. Once again, a graphic reform announced a renascence, but for all its unity and sobriety Carolingian minuscule triumphed over regional styles only during the ninth century.[20]

It is easy to image how this shift occurred. The concentration of the art of writing in the cathedral complex and the abbey had at first encouraged a compartmentalization that was subsequently eliminated as the networks of communication from one institution to another tightened. Charlemagne and his successors encouraged the re-creation of graphic unity as an expression of their own desire for political universality. They prompted a far-reaching revolution, but one that had its limits. Morphologically, the Carolingian script seems to owe much, directly or indirectly, to the half-uncial. Technically, it was a total success and a clear advance in legibility. It is characteristic of the scribes who perfected it that they also developed systems of punctuation to facilitate reading and recital of the texts that they copied in a language and a syntax that were increasingly foreign to their contemporaries, even in Romance-speaking lands. These copyists were precursors of the humanists and the fathers of our modern Roman letters. Nonetheless, from the point of view of *ductus* their writing was in no way a point of arrival or even an advance. As with the writing of the ancient Latins, its characteristic feature was a writing of letters in several strokes, which means that the similarity between that script and our modern writing styles, in which each letter is written as a whole, is only apparent.

NEW DEPARTURES

The Carolingian achievements were fragile enough, but in the ninth century new waves of invaders rushed into Charlemagne's former empire, now split up into several parts. The Saracens moved into the south; the Hungarians into the east, and the Vikings into the north. In a ravaged Europe the Germanic lands, less stricken, seemed to come into their own, starting with Saxony. The Ottonian dynasty moved out to defeat the Slavs and the Hungarians and to claim the imperial title. Otto III settled in Rome in 998. Educated as a priest, he sent copyists to Bobbio and to Reims and he instituted a search for the works of the great Latin historians and for memories of Roman glory. Lettered prelates and cultivated princes gravitated around him. He protected Gerbert, a monk of the Abbey of Saint-Géraud in Aurillac who had studied mathematics in Catalonia (a region in contact with the Arabs) and had taught the future King Robert the Pious in Reims before becoming archbishop of Ravenna, then pope under the name of Sylvester II. At the same time the abbeys of Richenau and Saint Gall flourished unaffected by the invaders, while further to the north the great episcopal schools of Utrecht and Cologne won a brilliant reputation. The somewhat rough illuminations of Ottonian manuscripts are a good illustration of these last glimmers of the Carolingian renaissance in regions that had been relatively untouched.[21]

Revival was not destined to spread out from Germanic lands. Toward the end of the tenth century the invaders were either in retreat or had become integrated into a world they had found to their liking. The Western world may have been terrorized, but it revived nonetheless. A Burgundian monk, Raoul (or Radulfus) Glaber claimed he had seen the Devil (who looked just like the many portrayals of him soon to be seen in cloister capitals). He also stated in his *Historiae* that three years before the year 1000 an enormous dragon had been seen in the sky "coming out of the northern regions and moving toward the south, throwing off bolts of lightning." Just then a severe famine affected the entire Roman world. But "as the third year after the year 1000 approached, church buildings were being rebuilt in nearly all the earth, but especially in Italy and in Gaul." The Romanesque age was on its way.[22]

Such men had an astonishing destiny: in the depths of adversity they found the memory and the vitality needed to make a new start on the basis of extremely ancient acquisitions that at times had been preserved as if by miracle. Moreover, in a tightly compartmentalized world they managed to learn new ways to behave and to survive, thanks to a series of technological innovations. It is hardly surprising that a revival of symbol and image figured prominently in the art of this Europe that was finding its personality once more. With the tenth century great abbeys and cathedral churches rose up under the supervision of prelate-builders, and stone churches decorated with a host of statues appeared in both towns and villages. A large number of influences intersected and mingled in the art that had sprung up so suddenly—there were ancient traditions inspired by Roman ruins and enhanced by the vision of the Carolingian epoch, there were borrowings from Byzantium and Islam, and there were contributions from the barbarian invaders. An entire fauna of lions, bulls, anthropomorphic monsters, griffins, and centaurs—extremely ancient forms drawn from collective memory—appeared everywhere, even on knights' shields. This profusion was dominated by high learned concepts that made visible the ordered harmony of the world and turned not only architecture and the figurative arts but also music and liturgy into an initiation into higher things.[23] The result was a closed and introverted aesthetic destined for the learned, but also a profusion of representations in which everything was language and pedagogy from the deadly sins sculpted on the capitals in the cloisters to God enthroned in majesty and the depictions of divine mysteries carved into the tympanum of the churches, or the scenes from Scripture and the lives of the saints and images of divine majesty in the frescoes of church apses and choirs transformed into vast picture albums.

Thus there was a revival of the image, the form of collective communication that enables the illiterate to contemplate what they are unable to grasp through writing. Nonetheless, the feudal society that was coming into being between the eighth and the eleventh centuries remained strictly traditional. Vassalic rites continued to make use of the three typical symbolic elements of word, act, and object. Homage, for example, involved both a declaration, the vassal's sworn engagement, and a gesture, when the vassal placed his joined hands between his lord's. Sworn loyalty was sealed with a kiss on the mouth, an exchange of saliva and vital force, and with an oath sworn on the Bible and on holy relics. When a great lord invested a vassal with a fief he gave his man symbolic objects—a branch or a piece of turf to symbolize a landholding, a rod to grant power, or a knife or a sword to symbolize the right to employ violence.[24]

Northern France was the epicenter of these revolutionary changes, but northern Italy, which had suffered relatively less destruction, enjoyed a new prosperity once better times returned. Northern Italian merchants traveled all the routes of Europe, they encouraged active industries in their own fast-growing cities, and they soon found themselves at the center of complex networks of an increasing variety of commercial operations. Italy had been profoundly marked by writing and had never totally forgotten the many uses that could be made of it. In Italy one could still find schoolmasters, physicians, jurists, and above all public notaries. Admittedly, the Roman scrivener-notaries only barely survived south of Rome, and even in Rome they had degenerated to become public writers of various sorts. Northern Italy still had notaries, however, men of diverse origins and often attached to the new authorities: bishops, abbots, counts, and cities. Kings of Lombardy, King Berengar (888–915) and King Hugo (926–45), launched an effort to unify their land, and ever since the Carolingian conquest the Lombard kingdom had had a well-organized "sacred palace." Emilia and Tuscany soon had an educated and competent administrative personnel as well. As if symbolically, the basilicas of the Prado were built over the tombs of notaries who had worked on the shores of the Venetian lagoon when Venice was still a village.[25]

This competent personnel permitted the early development of relatively complex commercial techniques. In the eleventh century, first in Venice and Genoa and then elsewhere, contracts for orders began to appear that spread risks and profits between the merchant who took to the seas and his financial backers. Next came a wide variety of partnership contracts between land merchants, and even insurance systems. Operations like these forced the notaries to sharpen their methods. They developed the habit of taking notes in the presence of clients before they drew up contracts, and in the twelfth century, when Genoa became a great mercantile port, the notaries of the city began to use a register in which they entered their notes so they could have a written record of them. By the same token, the draft copy of an act came to be considered the original, and the versions sent out simply authentic copies. Next, only the most prestigious authorities—the pope, the emperor, and, after Philip the Fair, the king of France—had the right to nominate public notaries in the regions of public law in the south of Europe. Thus a simpler and, all things considered, more efficient system than that of ancient Rome came into being and once more placed written proof under the protection of the most powerful public authorities.[26]

Gradually associations of various sorts began to be formed on the shores of the Mediterranean, grouping together the businessmen of one family or one city and creating diversified networks through correspondence. The principal difficulty in this sort of system was to maintain a balance that would assure every member in every place access to the necessary means of payment. The complexity of the monetary systems explains why the earliest banks grew out of a need not for credit but for an exchange service. Alternately money changers, lenders, and borrowers, the great merchants found themselves obligated to use increasingly abstract written instruments in their long-distance commerce, in order to fulfill a need to guarantee payments and facilitate the granting of credit. This in turn hastened the circulation of goods and, in the long run, created wealth.

This was how the techniques that were to regulate the management of business affairs throughout the early modern period got their start between the thirteenth and the fifteenth centuries. The bill of exchange appeared some time between 1275 and 1350. At first a document drawn up before a notary, by the mid-fourteenth century it functioned more like a letter missive. In this form of contract (unknown in Roman law) the "giver" furnished a certain sum of money or its equivalent in merchandise to the "taker," and in exchange he received a long-term promise to pay. Thus it was both a credit operation (but with payment shifted to another place) and a money-changing transaction. All contracts of this sort involved these two closely connected operations. When it came due, this sort of contract might also produce a profit for someone who could juggle rates of exchange in different places and through time. It permitted vast speculations. In the sixteenth century it was further developed by the practice of endorsement, and innumerable kinds of negotiable instruments developed out of it in the nineteenth century.[27]

Accounting methods kept pace. The great merchants of Italy added to an accounting of their cash balance (cash expenditures and receipts) accounting techniques on behalf of third parties (credits and debits), net-worth accounting, and finally profit-and-loss accounting. Because they wanted to enable interested parties to be able to read their accounts from their own points of view (monies owed and owing), the merchants reversed the order of their own cash transaction accounts and, in a spirit of symmetry, subtracted sums credited to the account. This was the birth of double-entry bookkeeping, a procedure seemingly just as unnatural as alphabetical arrangement, which also came to be nearly universally adopted during the same period. Both techniques marked the triumph of specific forms of the logic of writing.

Soon these new techniques spread outside Italy, thanks notably to the Lombard merchants who frequented the fairs of Champagne, where they met other merchants—Flemish merchants in particular. When maritime trade developed along the shores of the Baltic and the North Sea, Bruges became a major center of European trade and the place where Venetian and Genoese traders met their counterparts of the Hanseatic League. There one could meet pawnbrokers of Lombard origin (who were treated with some scorn), money-changers (who were treated with consideration), and the merchant bankers who represented the great Italian companies and dealt with sovereigns as equals. Thus thanks to the use of writing, Europe began to be organized between two great centers of urban civilization. Nonetheless, the practices whose rise we have been following long remained within an extremely small world, and major commercial figures continued for centuries to carry on their affairs with much more rudimentary methods.

At the same time, however, other regions that had remained essentially agricultural witnessed a return to writing by other paths and with other goals. This was the case in France, where land clearing had developed, the population had increased greatly, and commercial and other exchanges had come to be organized. Relations among individuals and among groups had grown more frequent and more complex, with the result that the traditional gestures, now too frequent and as if polyvalent, had lost their prestige. Solemn contracts came to seem imprecise and poorly adapted to circumstances, first in the eyes of the merchants and the landowners (who, to cite one practice, were still were using systems of land rents that dated back to the years 1125–50), then in the eyes of a large part of the population. Economic progress, which made it easier to procure hides carefully prepared to make parchment, dies, seals, ink, and wax, made possible an increased use of writing, just as writing had become indispensable to relieve an overburdened memory. The common people, who were still of a more primitive mentality, accepted writing as something with magical powers that could set down the Word of God, keep the memory of the dead in funerary inscriptions, and invoke God and the celestial powers from crosses and shrines by country roads.

Henceforth the written act seemed to be the best way to define individual rights and duties precisely and compellingly. In the eleventh century there was an increase in the number of the various sorts of documents that go by the name of *chartes* in French; by the late twelfth century customs that hitherto had been transmitted orally began to be written down. Since the clergy had monopolized the practice of writing, lay lords had to turn to them, for example asking an ecclesiastical institution to draw up the papers for donations to their benefit. Gradually, however, lords created chanceries by attracting to their service clerics who also functioned as their chaplains. Many of these men were not very well educated, and when asked to translate into Latin instructions that had been given to them in their own language they drafted their Latin versions with the aid of whatever models they had at hand, stumbling over a word or an expression here and there. In the lands of *langue d'Oc* in the eleventh century one can even find passages transcribed in dialect, and the same thing happened in regions of *langue d'oil* a century later. As a result, it was customary to write a number of documents of this sort in the vulgar tongue.[28]

The first Capetians seem to have had only a modest "office" with only a few scribes working, in theory, under the authority of the archbishop of Reims, who traditionally had the title of archchancellor. These monarchs held real authority only over their own domains, and within the limits of their jurisdiction the lords who held title to the great feudal domains issued diplomas and charters analogous to the royal diplomas. Things began to change around 1060, when Philip I named the bishop of Paris as his chancellor. When the king went to Poitiers in 1076 his royal seal remained in Paris, thus indicating that an embryo of the institution of the monarchy already existed. Later an increase in the number of acts passed in the royal chancery coincided with the growth of royal authority, as in France at the time of Philip Augustus and later of Philip the Fair.

The royal administration also became more important, a pattern that held true in all lands. The king's court, long a shifting body composed of the vassals who happened to be present, became better organized and eventually gave way to a royal council of competent men who enjoyed the king's trust and whose functions gradually became specialized. In England the Exchequer, the financial organ of the monarchy, developed even before the king's council; in France a judicial subdivision of the council formed, and in 1239 it took the name of *Pallamentum,* or Parlement, soon subdividing into chambers. Other courts followed, among them the Chambre des comptes or auditor's office. There were also increasing numbers of officials on the local level. In England in the shires (which became counties after the Norman conquest), there were sheriffs, then escheators named by the king, then coroners elected by the county court. Similarly, *prévôts* appeared in France in the eleventh century, and royal judges toured the provinces beginning with the reign of Philip Augustus. Called *baillis* in the north and *sénéchaux* in the south, these judges eventually remained fixed in one place, where they performed administrative, judiciary, and financial functions above the level of the *prévôts* and were assisted by lieutenants, lawyers, and king's prosecutors. Later they were freed from their financial responsibilities by the *receveurs.* Finally, in the fourteenth century, *élus* (elected judges) and *généraux de finance* (tax collectors) appeared.[29]

The full extent of this change can best be measured in England. The Anglo-Saxon kings had already developed a form of original culture in Britain that utilized neither Latin nor the vernacular idioms but an official language—Anglo-Saxon—that was also used, as we have seen, to popularize certain great texts of clerical culture and to set down the national poetry. Are we to attribute the relative scarcity (only some two thousand pieces have come down to us) of archival documents emanating from Harold's dynasty to the massive destruction that took place after the fall of the Anglo-Saxon monarchy? Edward the Confessor, the last king of his race, was also the only one to use a royal seal. Still, William the Conqueror, who had no chancery in Normandy, ordered a census taken of people and beasts after his victory. Hence the famous *Domesday Book,* which so struck people's imaginations that it launched a tradition, obligingly spread by the supporters of the new monarchy, that the invaders from the Continent had introduced writing into their new land. In any event, there is little doubt that the disturbances accompanying the establishment of a new order did much to encourage the use of writing. During the twelfth century autograph documents, letters missive, and briefs proliferated. Change was particularly rapid between 1140 and 1160, a period in which the number of letters sent seems to have tripled, to judge from what has come down to us. Thus we can estimate in the hundreds of thousands and perhaps at more than a million the number of acts concerning the sale or granting of lands to peasants or serfs that were redacted during the thirteenth century. During that period, the French language competed with Latin for a primacy that French had won at Hastings, before English triumphed over them both. It is hardly surprising that toward the end of that period King Edward I ordered the lords to produce the acts that justified the franchises or privileges conceded to them. Henceforth even illiterate peasants had to submit to the rule of writing, but this revolution induced a mental turmoil that could lead to resistance, as in the anecdote about the count who, when ordered to prove his rights, answered by producing an old and rusty sword that his ancestors had wielded at the Battle of Hastings.[30]

When it comes to measuring the power of the written word, nothing can replace an examination of the documents themselves.[31]

Let us look first at the documents that were most highly charged with meaning, the acts by which men attempted to regulate their juridical relations: decisions of public authorities, judgments handed down by the courts, and contracts drawn up between private individuals. Such documents aimed at validation and authentification, hence their origin and content had to be unambiguous. This explains the importance of the notion of the original document. As we have seen, in lands of written law, notaries' minutes were soon taken to be true originals of contracts, with engrossed fair copies that might be delivered to the interested parties being considered simply as authenticated copies. These were exceptional cases, but as a general rule the originals of public acts were delivered to the beneficiaries, who were expected to keep them.

In a society still marked by traditional forms of the contract these documents must have seemed to reflect the word of the emitting party and to serve as a physical affirmation of the solemnity of such engagements. The documents themselves varied enormously in appearance: they were written on the "noble" side of the parchment, the underside of the hide, carefully whitened with chalk, on a sheet whose dimensions depended less on the length of the text than on the power of the authority from which it emanated and especially on the nature and the importance of the decision. The charter redacted by the chaplain of a minor lord seems modest indeed beside the diplomas or letters patent of a powerful sovereign. In the older royal diplomas, for example, the first line of the text, including an invocation to divine power, the name and title of the sovereign, and the salutation, is usually written in closely spaced and spidery letters with particularly elongated ascenders. More generally speaking, from late antiquity the scribes of the great chanceries proclaimed their affiliation with time and tradition by affecting a deliberately archaic script, schematizing the contours of their letters and stylizing them by lengthening the ascenders and decorating them with extraneous elements. This mannerism could reach the point of artifice and strive for prestige through illegibility. This was already true of the *litterae coelestes* of the Roman imperial chancery; it was just as true of the *bollatica* of the Vatican in the early twentieth century, in which only the thick strokes of the letters are drawn in, with the result that the only way to decipher the text is by squinting.

The physical aspect of the document is not what mattered most, however. In order to take on their full value such documents had to be an integral part of the authority from which they emanated; they had to bear appropriate and incontestable signs of the agreement reached by the contracting parties and, in certain cases, the mark of the witnesses. It is difficult for a modern reader to imagine the problems this raised at a time when the autograph signature, in the modern sense, did not yet exist. As in classical antiquity, the Middle Ages long had to make do with a subscription or a seal. The subscription was the form most currently used in the early Middle Ages. At first it took the form of an autograph declaration by the person involved that included his or her name, the verb *subscribere* in a personal form, and a formula explaining the reasons for the act. The Merovingian sovereigns, who had some instruction, wrote their names at the bottom of their precepts with a formula of this sort added in their hand or another's. If a great personage did not know how to write, someone else would write the subscription and he would add a *signum*—a sign—such as a cross. Under Pepin the Short a simple cross surrounded by a legend functioned as the royal *signum*. Later the monarch's monogram was substituted for this cross; under Charlemagne it was drawn by a notary, in certain cases with the emperor simply marking his approval with a pen stroke, after which the notary drew the whole *signum*. The autograph signature disappeared almost completely in the tenth century: as Georges Tessier has said, "Neglect of the notion of autograph is one of the most characteristic phenomena of the decline of the written act before the seal came to give it back its validity and efficacy." [32]

The seal had been known from earliest antiquity and had never been totally forgotten, but for some time only sovereigns used it to validate an occasional act. Others began to use seals in the late eleventh century, and their use spread gradually. In France bishops used seals sooner than lay lords, and they were used earlier in northern France than in the Midi. The use of seals became universal in the early thirteenth century, when commoners and humble beneficed clergy had a seal, as did communities and jurisdictions. We can understand that these symbolic objects whose images "spoke" so clearly must have seemed to men of the age an unambiguous affirmation of a personality or a will. They had exactly the same value as a signature today (Georges Tessier). Certain seals that belonged to more public physical or moral entities came to have special force. They were called "authentic seals," but there were a number of degrees in that form of authenticity. [33]

Authentication was accomplished in two ways: southern Europe preferred the use of notaries and northern Europe the use of the seal. Private persons in northern Europe who wanted to draw up a probative written contract without appending to it a list of witnesses capable of initiating judicial action in case of contestation turned to their lay lord, if he held a *sceau notoire*, or recognized seal, to their bishop, or even to their sovereign. That person then had an act drawn up to register the declared intent of the parties present and had the act sealed with his own seal, thus giving physical proof of his quality as a privileged witness. Soon clerks' offices sprang up near the courts of law that held the "graciously accorded" jurisdiction—*juridiction gracieuse*—to handle cases involving private persons. In the north of France, the courts of the *officialités* and the *baillages* had such offices, as did certain large cities outside France. This was the origin of scriveners' offices in northern Europe, which only very slowly caught up to the higher technical level of the notaries in the south.

An act was not born by spontaneous generation. Its elaboration and its publication were part of a chain of operations leading from the issuing to the receiving parties in which a number of people had a role to play.

Since Mabillon's path-breaking work in Latin paleography, these mechanisms have been studied with singular perspicacity by austere specialists who have made a veritable science of the study of diplomas and charters, the science of diplomatics. In a number of ways their work prefigured that of analysts of communication techniques today. What do such men have to tell us about writing?

First, that every writ that establishes rules for relations among men (in Latin, *instrumentum*) rests on a juridical act (*negotium*). Hence one must distinguish carefully between the *actio*—the accomplishment of the juridical act—and the *conscriptio*—its setting down in writing.

According to the theory most widely accepted by jurists today, a juridical act was valid irrespective of the means that its author had chosen to manifest his (or her) will. In other words, in principle the act was "perfect" without having been written down, and writing it down had only a probative value. Nonetheless, the "diplomatists" observe that in practice the existence of the act was linked with its being set down. As time went by, this formality became indispensable for testaments, donations, marriage contracts, and mortgage contracts. Rare exceptions aside, the law has also always been written since the Middle Ages. Thus the "dispositive" value of written acts appears to have involved the gradual conquest of a certain form of power on the part of secretaries and notaries, incontestably the ancestors of the innumerable drafting specialists in modern administrations.[34]

We have many indications of how responsibilities were assigned in the elaboration of an act. To cite only one example, certain royal letters patent bear a formula written on the fold by the notary and signed with his name, stating the authority by which he received the order to draft the document. We might compare this custom to the initials placed on executive letters today to indicate who typed the letter and who wrote it, if not the signatory.

As early as the Middle Ages there was a division of labor within a sovereign's council and his chancery. In the case of an act under *juridiction gracieuse* the various phases of the *actio* were as follows: First the basic document, the request, was delivered directly or indirectly to the ruler, then was transmitted to the appropriate official, who would initiate proceedings. In the council of the king of France, for example, this might be a *maître des requêtes*. Next came consultation with or action by third parties—important persons who supported the petition, counselors who gave their advice, and of course witnesses. In due course a decision was reached and, when appropriate, the order was given to draft a corresponding act. When the pope assented to a formal petition he wrote *fiat* on the request, but the document still had to be copied into a register and then passed on to the officials of the chancery responsible for drawing up the actual act. Often the order might come from someone who held authority for a particular matter rather than from the sovereign himself. In France this might be the chancellor or a *maître des requêtes,* the Conseil de la Chambre des requêtes, the Parlement, or the Chambre des comptes. The next phase was that of the *conscriptio.* The king's notaries and secretaries wrote up a draft called "minute," which was passed on to be transcribed by a calligrapher. Next an official of the chancery checked the act one last time to be sure that its form followed the rules and its content was consistent with the intent (*recognitio*). Then came the validation, the essential part of which was affixing the seal. In France that operation was performed in the Chancellerie and by the chancellor himself during sessions known as *audiences du sceau.* In the course of these the chancellor could question the interested parties, if they were present, should a problem arise.[35]

An increased use of writing led, as if ineluctably, to the rise of administrative bodies and procedures involving a division of labor. Those who controlled use of the pen in these operations had an almost measurable power from the outset. We can see why the thirteenth-century kings of France feared the power of the chancellor, who was traditionally chosen from among the great lords of the kingdom, and why a king sometimes chose to leave the post vacant. Later the *garde des Sceaux,* originally an official of a much more modest rank, picked up the title of chancellor, and under the ancien régime he became the second most important person in the state. To this day the minister of justice in France is also keeper of the seal, and

by tradition he precedes his colleagues. Certain of the "notary clerks" became singularly important. After 1316 three of their number were attached
to the person of the king as *clercs du secret*. Toward the end of the fourteenth
century other clerks had exclusive rights to control letters relating to expenditures. The kings put so much trust in such men that in 1547 King
Henry II put four of them in charge of expediting state affairs. This is how
the posts of secretary of state and minister of the king of France were created in the ancien régime.

The number of acts and letters increased to the point that the chancery
officials began to give them a less and less solemn form. In the twelfth
century, under Philip the Fair, letters patent appeared to join the diploma.
Various categories of letters patent were established, sealed with different
colors of wax according to the presumed duration of the declarations they
contained. Next came sealed letters, missive letters, and *lettres de cachet*
sealed with the modest seal of a simple chamberlain—the *sceau du secret*—rather than that of the chancery. At the same time, the clerks-notary
of the king, who had been no more than ten in number in 1285, grew to
a body of thirty in 1316, forty-eight in 1320, fifty-nine in 1361, and
seventy-nine in 1418. Robert-Henri Bautier has calculated that in the reign
of Philip VI (1328–50) some twenty thousand letters sealed with the great
seal emerged from their offices and fifteen thousand more were sealed with
the *sceau du secret*. [36]

The chancery was not the only organism of the French monarchy in
which the use of writing increased. More and more, matters brought up
before the Parlement and requiring additional inquiry involved an *arrêt
d'appointement* obligating the parties to produce written reports. Such reports, called *productions*, were deposited with the office of the clerk of the
court by the *procureur* (the state's attorney), after which they were passed
on to a *conseiller* who drafted the document on the basis of which the full
chamber deliberated. The Grande Chambre eventually came to delegate
such matters to a special chamber, the Chambre des enquêtes. This meant
that the numbers of the *procureurs* charged with preparing such dossiers
increased enormously, and the offices of the clerk of the court to the Parlement of Paris and the provincial parlements established specialized subsec-
tions staffed with an entire roster of court clerks, notaries, and secretaries.
The number of registers of the Parlement of Paris increased tenfold between
1320 and 1360. Unlike the chancery officials, the members of the Parlement developed the habit of keeping a record not only of all their decisions
but also of their principal deliberations, and they had copies made of all

the acts communicated to them by the sovereign in case they should need to refer to them later. At first this registration was conceived as a formality, but eventually it provided an opportunity to make observations on the content of the acts and, on occasion, to demonstrate the Parlement's refusal to conform to the royal decisions by not registering them. This was the origin of the *droit de remontrance* that so often led the sovereigns of the ancien régime to preside at a *lit de justice* to command the court to register and observe the contested decisions. Henceforth, however, it was within the scribe's powers to refuse to write something down.[37]

The further growth of writing in France during the thirteenth and fourteenth centuries is beyond the scope of this study. Let me simply recall that it was in that period that parish priests began to keep registers to note baptisms, marriages, and burials. The first known parish registers in France are those of Givry, near Chalon-sur-Saône, covering burials from 1336 to 1357 and marriages from 1344 to 1348. Thus civil registry was born.[38]

Once again, writing hands went through various stages, both in their general aspect and their *ductus*.

Cursive writing hands, which had disappeared in the seventh century, first returned in Italy. A more connected and rapid hand appeared there as early as the twelfth century, in particular in the pontifical chancery. In the thirteenth century, notaries, merchants, and of course men of letters began to feel the press of time and to note texts with a running hand. This is a sure indication, as Henri Pirenne noted some time ago, of the use of writing in the most ordinary acts of life.[39]

The evolution of writing hands in northern Europe was somewhat different. The Roman script inherited from the Carolingians tended to change form: the contour of the letters began to be broken; lateral compression became more and more pronounced and eventually resulted in a clear verticality. According to Jacques Boussard this revolution was a fashion that Anglo-Saxon scribes transmitted to their Continental colleagues, and G. I. Lieftinck is undoubtedly correct when he states that this fashion reflected a search for a more compressed text. It also became habitual to separate words more, and the broken curves that appeared around 1210 to 1230 may also have been an attempt to give words greater individuality to make them easier to read. In the Romanesque era letters were treated as separate entities inserted into a whole, but the breaks and ligatures of the new writing reflected the skeleton of the word. Thus the new hand derived from the same sort of spirit as Gothic architecture, in which every detail is conceived to emphasize the basic structure of the building.

In both northern and southern regions the continuing need to write faster brought not only a return to cursive but incessant change. Informal scripts gradually penetrated the written style of books, and bastard or mixed hands developed. The best known of these is the *lettre bâtarde* that appeared in the fourteenth century at the court of France and was frequently used in manuscripts in the vulgar tongue. It can be found in a more baroque and elaborate form in the court of Burgundy, where it bore a resemblance (as has often been remarked) to flamboyant Gothic architecture. Emmanuel Poulle has recently suggested that the cursive form of this script used in the chancery of France marked an essential moment in the evolution of writing styles. Notaries began to abandon the system that had predominated since classical antiquity of linking the head of one letter to the foot of the next, which forced a hurried writer to pick up his pen to make the second stroke of certain letters, the *r* and the *s* in particular. In mixed writing the personnel of the French chancery seems instead to have preferred to link strokes within the letter. Thus we can see the beginnings of tenacious efforts over two centuries, through a number of seemingly minor modifications, to change the order of strokes in the letter so as to enter into and exit from each in a way that moved naturally from the *ductus* of the one to that of the next. Of course ancient traditions long persisted, notably in the "satanic" writing hands of notarial minutes in the sixteenth and seventeenth centuries that are so difficult to decipher. It made little difference that the humanists' innovations moved in precisely the opposite direction, starting from the ancient Carolingian script. Cursive writing styles were freed in an evolution that began in the fourteenth century. Our modern handwriting is the result.[40]

The rise of the autograph signature was an extremely important addition to the dynamic changes that took place in fifteenth-century writing. From the eleventh to the twelfth centuries, as we have seen, the autograph disappeared in the validation of acts. Only public notaries so validated their *minutes* (drafts) and their *grosses* (engrossed fair copies), marking them not only with an autograph signature that they attempted to make uniquely their own but with a hand-drawn *seing*, a characteristic mark or device. Though the scriveners who redacted acts for the chanceries did not actually sign documents, they were sufficiently accustomed to working with a pen to develop distinctive hands, and they began to place autograph notes and their names in the margins of the original of acts. Rulers eventually did the same. The first king of France to sign his name on acts was John the Good. Soon the signature of the sovereign came to complete and even replace the seal, which nonetheless is used to this day for the most solemn sort of documents. Soon everyone who could handle a pen learned to trace his or her name, with varying degrees of success, rather than be reduced to marking documents with an x or a cross.

THE REVIVAL OF SPECULATIVE THOUGHT

Accelerated commercial exchange increases wealth and opens new horizons. It is accompanied by new investments of intellectual capital and gives rise to new ways of thinking.

Europe in the eleventh century was no exception to this rule, and the revival of the use of writing for practical purposes appears to have been closely connected with a return to the legacy of classical culture and a renewal of speculative thought. This movement was of course clerical. Its promoters were men of the church concerned with endowing the new society with appropriate forms of thought but also with communicating the divine message to the illiterate masses. They were philosophers and theologians, thus they were at times the authors of spiritual works and almost always preachers.

The first phase of this revival came at the same time as renewed commercial exchanges in Italy. It emerged on the plains of the Po Valley, a region that had suffered relatively little destruction, and its primary source was a tension, exacerbated during the reign of the Ottonian emperors, between the spiritual and the temporal. From the time of Charlemagne the same tension had incited the pope and his champions to draw arguments from Roman law and even to forge documents, the most famous of which is Constantine's supposed donation of Rome to the pope. Thus while the Lombard merchants were taking to the road all over Europe, Bologna knew its finest hour. Bologna lay surrounded by fertile wheat fields at the crossroads of the main routes to Rome, Pisa, and Pavia; it stood near the borders of Byzantine, Lombard, and Roman influence, at the heart of the territories later disputed between Guelphs and Ghibellines. Its law school, which probably grew out of an earlier school of the liberal arts, owed its first success to law studies in the age of Gregory VII. The law school was organized by Irnerius, the ancestor of glossators and a man close to Countess Matilda, at whose fortress castle of Canossa Pope Gregory VII received the penance of Emperor Henry IV. This was the start of the greatest juridical university in Christendom.[41]

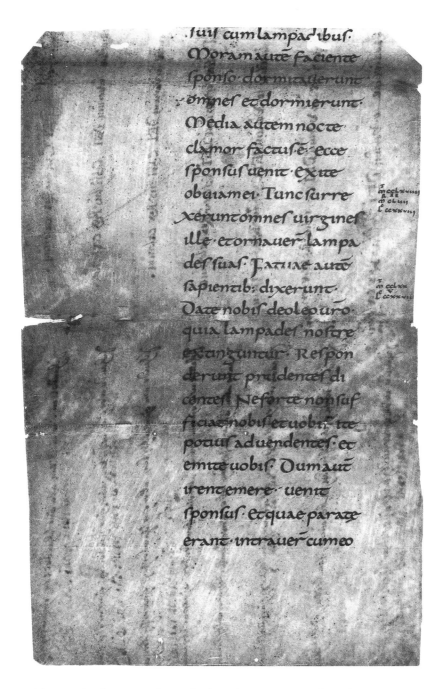

Manuscript fragment from the New Testament, written in a
Carolingian hand of Tours. Ninth century.

.De Bello Ciuili Sille & Marij./

Bello Sociali nundum confumato R̄
q̄ noxiū ciuile et mitridaticū q̄d
triginta: alij quadraginta annis g̃
comemorant bella funefta comota fu
Anno Sexcenteffimo fexageffimo fecun
Sila igitur cum contra mitridatem
Confil cum exeratu effet acceffurus
rius contra eundem Mitridatem .fepti
fibi confulatum dari poftulauit: quod
egre ferens uel papiens ut erat inuer
impatiens atq̃ fupbus cum quatuor leg̃
ante urbem confedit: quam cū intraff
mariū cum multis fibi adherentibus
curia foro atq̃ Capitolio uulgo necatis
cutus eft: Marius uo fugiens in mitur
fibus paludibus fe abdidit Deinde comp
& Minturnas ductus incarceratufq̃ de
uinculis liberatus in Africam tranffugi
& inde continuo Romā regreffuf eft:
fe Cinne Confuli Senatorio & Gneo ca
boni comiunxit. Nan ad profligandam

Johannes de Crivellis, *Compendium historiae romanae,* written in
humanistic hand. Italy, 1464.

uniuersam rem publicam tres legiones Marius, et vnam exercitus Cneius carbo, alia
uo Sertorius & terciam cinna partes
sortiti sunt. Igitur marius colonia hosti-
ensem ingressus omnia genera libidinis
auaricie et crudelitatis exercuit. Pompe-
ius qui horis erat inimicus et paulo ante
cum Sartorio sic pugnauerat fulmine per-
cussus interijt: eius uo exercitus pestile-
tia consumptus est. de quo quadraginta
uirorum mortua fuisse: Sex uo milia ab
Octauio consule oblata dicuntur. Postea
marius ipe Ancium et Aritui ciuitates
hostiliter capit: Singulorumque bona dirri-
pit. postea cum fugitiuis et Cinna consul cum legionibus urbem ingressi usque
nobilissimos senatus et plurimos consu-
lares uiros interfecerunt: Q uorum tantus
fuit numerus ut pocius libeat subtice
que dolendo comemorare. Nam capita in-
terfectorum conuiuiis capitolijs et rostris

Thomas Aquinas, *Commentaries*. Note pecia mark at lower right edge of the page. France, ca. 1300.

Johannes Balbus, *Catholicon*. Johannes Gutenberg, Mainz, 1460.

St. John, *Apocalypse.* Page from a hand-colored block book.
Swabia [?], ca. 1470.

Illustration from Terence, *Comoedia*. Jean Trechsel, Lyons, 29 August, 1493.

Itaq; ,quas pueri miferimus ad te lucubra
tiones noftras , numerare aliquas poffumus; quas adolefcentes, non poffumus :
quo in confilio nobis diutius permanen
dum effe non puto: nam ut interdum nó
loqui moderati hominis eft; fic femper
filere cum eo , quem diligas, perignaui:
neq; Hercule; fi in officio permanfimus
in prima aetate ; debemus nunc , tanq̃
inexercitati hiftriones , in fecundo , aut
tertio actu corruiffe. praefertim cum
aemulatio tuorum ftudiorum Angéle
nos non excitare modo languentes poffit,
fed etiam incendere; quippe , qui multa,
et praeclara habuimus a te femper, habe
múfq; quotidie et confuetudinis noftrae
teftimonia, et doctrinae tuae. Quare fi
cuti pueri fcriptiunculas noftras, quafi la
ctentis ingenii acerbitatem , detulimus
ad te; fic nunc deinceps etiam ad te adole
fcentiae noftrae primos foetus deferemus;
non quo me ipfe plus ames; nam iam id

Pietro Bembo, *De Aetna*. Aldus Manutius, Venice, February, 1495/6.

fieri poſſe uix puto : ſed plane quia ita debemus inter nos : neq; enim arbitror cario
rem fuiſſe ulli quenquam ; q̃ tu ſis mihi.
Sed de his et diximus aliâs ſatis multa; et
ſaepe dicemus: nũc autem ; quoniam iam
quotidie fere accidit poſtea, q̃ e Sicilia ego,
et tu reuerſi ſumus; ut de Aetnae incendi-
is interrogaremuſ ab iis, quibus notum
eſt illa nos ſatis diligenter perſpexiſſe ; ut
ea tandem moleſtia careremus; placuit mi
hi eum ſermonem conſcribere; quem
cum Bernardo parente habui paucis poſt
diebus, q̃ rediiſſemus; ad quem reiicien-
di eſſent ii, qui nos deinceps quippiam
de Aetna poſtularent. Itaq; confeci librũ;
quo uterq; noſtrum cõmuniter uteretur:
nã cum eſſemus in Noniano ; et pater ſe
(ut ſolebat) ante atrium in ripam Pluuici
contuliſſet ; acceſſi ad eũ progreſſo iam in
meridianas horas die: ubi ea, quae locuti
ſum⁹ inter nos, fere iſta ſũt. Tibi uero nũc
oratione utriuſq; noſtrũ, tanq̃ habeatur,

A ii

P·O·N·in septimum Aeneidos librum,
argumentum·

S eptimus Aeneam reddit fatalibus aruis·
H ic quoq; Caietam se pelit,tum deinde profectus
L aurentum uenit·hanc uerbis cognouit Iuli
F atalem terram,mensas en uescimur,inquit·
C entum oratores,ueniam pacemq; petentes
A d regem mittunt lecti tum sorte Latinum·
Q ui cum pace etiam natae conubia pactus,
H oc sorte Alecto Iunonis dissipat ira,
C oncurrunt dictis,quamuis pia fata repugnent.
B elli causa facit uiolatus uulnere ceruus·
T um gentes sociae arma parãt,fremit arma inuentus·

P·V·M·AENEIDOS LIBER
SEPTIMVS·

V quoq; littoribus nostris Aenea
nutrix
t   A eternam moriens famam Caiet
dedisti.
E t nũc seruat honos sedem tuam,
ossáq; nomen
H esperia in magna(siqua est ea gloria)signat·
A t pius exequiis Aeneas rite solutis,
A ggere composito tumuli,postquam alta quierunt
A equora,tendit iter uelis,portumq; relinquit·
A spirant aurae in noctem,nec candida cursum
L una negat,splendet tremulo sub lumine pontus.
P roxima Circaeae raduntur littora terrae,

D ives in accessos ubi solis filia lucos
A ssiduo resonat cantu,tectisq; superbis
V rit odoratam nocturna in lumina cedrum,
A rguto tenues percurrens pectine telas.
H inc exaudiri gemitus,iraeq; leonum
V incla recusantum,et sera sub nocte rudentum,
S etigeriq; sues,atq; in praesepibus ursi
S aeuire,ac formae magnorum ululare luporum·
Q uos hominum ex facie Dea saeua potentibus herbis
I nduerat Circe in uultus,ac terga ferarum,
Q uae ne monstra pii paterentur talia Troes,
D elati in portus,neu littora dira subirent,
N eptunus uentis impleuit uela secundis,
A tq; fugam dedit,et praeter uada feruida uexit.
I amq; rubescebat radiis mare,et aethere ab alto
A urora in roseis fulgebat lutea bigis,
C um uenti posuere,omnis q; repente resedit
F latus,et in lento luctantur marmore tonsae,
A tq; hic Aeneas ingentem ex aequore lucum
P rospicit,hunc inter fluuio Tyberinus amoeno
V orticibus rapidis,et multa flauus arena
I n mare prorumpit,uariae circumq; supráq;
A ssuetae ripis uólucres,et fluminis alueo
A ethera mulcebant cantu,lucoq; uolabant.
F lectere iter sociis,terraeq; auertere proras
I mperat,et laetus fluuio succedit opaco·
N unc age,qui reges Erato,quae tempora rerum,
Q uis latio antiquo fuerit status,aduena classem
C um primum Ausoniis exercitus appulit oris
E xpediam,et primae renocabo exordia pugnae·

L iii

❧AETATVM❧

**Mundi Septem supputatio, per Carolum Bouillum
Samarobrinū, ad Franciscum Molinū virū clariss͂i,
& Regiorū eleemosynarum principem.**

*Prelum
Ascēsianū.*

Venundatur Iodoco Badio Ascensio.

Charles de Boucelles, *Aetatum mundi septem supputatio.* . . . This title
page shows a typical printing shop of the sixteenth century, with
an inker, pressman, and type setter. I. Badio, Paris [1520].

Cozax etc. Hic mitio se plurimu esse sollicitu oñdit de filio eschino adoptiuo que nõ rediisse a scena reti uit. Mit. o stozax serue sic dicte ab odoze. Na stozax gen' est aromatis ut Plin.ait.huc aut stozax nõ debat corã sed. vocabat ut sciret ubi nã esset oñs ei' eschinus:cui seruiebat volēte mitione quo seruo nõ respõdēte subdit pronūciatiue poti' ch interrogatiue ut vult. Do.quasi secū cõquerens loquif eschin nõ rediie hac nocte a cena nech ch ... seruulog ch ierāt.i.iuerāt aduersuz.i.obuiā illi rediit inch pfecto certe boies sup. dicit hoc vulgo sup.tanch hoc dictū sepe i oze populo sit.Si abiis scda psona p ter tia.i.si sit aliqs absens uspiã.i.uich hoc est i ali quo loco. Na nusch z nuspiã z uich z uspiam ch ide signat dicitur t in loco z ad locū aut si ces ses.i.si sis ociosus ibi.i.ubi tu sis absens sati est.i.meli' est ea mala euentre.i.cõtingere tibi: ch mala uroz dicit in te.i.cõtra te z ch mala ipa irata cogitat in aio ch illa euenire tibi que pa rētes pspitij.i.benignii in aio inch suo cogitat. Si cesses.i.sis cessatoz et ociosus alicubi uroz aut cogitat te amare.i.amoze alicui' puelle ee captu aut cogitat tete.i.tespm amari.i. p amo rē ab aliqua detineri aut cogitat te potare.i. potui in dulgere atch cogitat te obsequi.i.mo re gerere aio tuo.i.explere tuū oim obiectatiõe aliqua chã cupiueris:z cogitat bn esse tibi soli cū male sit tibi.i.cogitat ch sol'z uas capis deli tias quo tpe male se bs uroz. In oib' aut bis pdictis mitio uidet alique alloch cū tñ sol' ch quif.z sc.õa psonauriff p tertia.ego mitio ch co gito.q.d.mala tñ.i. quas habeo cogitationes malas.f.z hoc lege interrogatiue z ea oia cogi to eã ob rech fil' nõ rediit:z nūc chb' reb'ma lis.f.sollicitoz.i.veroz anri' suz z sollicit' inter rogatiue etiã pnūciãdo z exclamatiue.ocinde sobfūgit chb'reb' sollicitef.f.bis malis reb'vez ne.i.ut p ch aut ille inueniet:seu frixerit:seu frigus nimtiuz sit passus pp ch male habuerit nech redire potuerit. Na morboz frigus potif simū est gtm.i.sollicitoz inch ne.i.est aut cecide rit uspiã.i.in aliqo pcipuū. Na ër uspiã ad lo cū oz aut ch perfregerit aliqd.i.habeat aliqo mēbrū fractū. Na ut Laure.val.bz tregit bra chiū significat habeo brachiū fractū.filr fregi naue.i.nauis mea fracta est. Uab iteriecto ir rideris se ne.i.utrū verū est sup.quēch z aliqué boies instituere in aio.i.pponere sibi aut col locare in mēte:aut parare.i.cõparare cõsilare zbere:acqrere seu in aio disponere aliqd chõ sit ch art' z.i.dilecti' quod ipse bõ qui istituit est cha rus sibi pf.at ch hic eschin' nõ est nat' ez me. i.nõ est fil' me' naturalis:sed ez fratre. Is sez frater Demea est studio.i.voluntate z animi ap plicatione adeo.i.valde seu nimiuz dissimili.i. diuersa sã iude.i.iã eo tepoze quod sequif.f.ab adolescētia.i.a iuuentute ego secut sum.i.ama ui tanch magistrã bene beatech viuēdi:ut disci puli sequunt preceptozū documēta quib' ad hereant:propterea sectatozes dicunt. Ego er go secutus sum hanc vitã urbanã.i.huc modū viuēdi in urbe clemente.i.que reddit homines

Aditio seneȝ.

In hac pzima scena qõ plogus pmisit argumētu narrat opoz tunech vita aspera cum leni:pater mitis cū seuerissimo cõparatur. Oftendit etiã se Aditio admodum esse sollicitum de Eschino filio adoptiuo quod nondum de scena besterna redierat: simulch lenita te potius ch asperitate aut vi instituendos liberos pfcribit.

Cozax non rediit hac nocte a scena eschi nus nech seruulozum quisch qui aduozsum ierant pfecto hoc vere dicūt:si absis uspiã aut ibi si cesses euenire ea satius est que in te uroz dicit z in aio cogitat irata ch illa que parētes pzopicij. Uzori cesses aut te amare cogitat aut tete amari:aut potare at ch aio obsequi:et tibi bene esse soli cū sibi sit male. Ego (chz nõ rediit fil') que cogito:quib' nūc sollicitoz reb' ne ille asserit:aut uspiaz ceciderit aut perfregerit aliqd. Uah.quēch ne hoiem instituere in aio aut parare chõ si charius:ch ipse est sibi:atqui ez me nat' hic nõ est:sed ez fratre:is adeo dissimili studio est. Iam ab adolescentia ego hāc clemētē vitãuzbanā atch ociū secutus sum:z chõ fortunatū isti putat uzorē nunch habui. Ille cõtra hec oia ruri agere vitã.semp parce ac duriter se hre uzorem duxit:uzorem clementes:ut pallida mozs. Dicitur enim clemens qui colit mētē quod maxime sit in uzbibus:atch secutus sum ocium uzbanum.i.securitatem seu tranquillitatem u:bis:z nunch habui uzorē sed uixi uita celibe quod.i.nõ ducere uzorē.isti.i.qui a me dissentiunt putant esse fortunati.i. plurimū felicitatis habens z propterea vocant hanc vitã celibem quasi celitem. Ille frater contra.i.eduerso nisi ute uingere contra hec omnia predicta:sed melius est ut sic dicatur. Ille cõtra elegit sup.hec omnia siue secutus est hec omnia que sequunt:videlicet agere vitã.i.viuere ruri.in datino aduerbialiter.i.in agris:z habere se.i.se gerere semper par ecid est tenaciter chtum ad seruandum:ac duriter id est aspere:acerbe chtum ad laborem.Ipse frater duxit uzorem duo filij nati sunt ez eo z uzore quam duxit iude id est ez quibus filijs(ut vult Dona.)ego optaui mihi.i. assumi

---

Terence, *Comedie*. Printed book with a glossed text and illustrations.
Jacob Myt, London, October, 1525. (The Wing Foundation)

Henceforth the awakening and reorganizing West sought the great texts of classical antiquity that it had lost. The *Pandects*, forgotten for centuries, are reputed to have been found in a sixth-century manuscript that the Pisans took when they defeated Amalfi (which was allied to the Byzantines) and that was transferred in the sixteenth century to the Biblioteca Laurenziana in Florence. A search for canon-law texts in Italian libraries led Gratian (around 1140) to compile his *Concordia discordantium canonum*, the very title of which is an entire program. Written law was alive once more, and with its rebirth there appeared a new personage, the jurisconsult, counselor to cities and princes.[42]

During its long dormancy the West had lost contact with many other texts, notably with most of Aristotle's works. Europeans quite logically went to seek for them (and for other precious works) among the Greeks and at the confines of Islam. Above all, they were interested in understanding and assimilating the learning of the Arabs. Very early, Gerbert went to the abbey of Santa Maria de Ripoll to seek information on Arabic learning and, in the absence of decisive proof to the contrary, he can be credited with first popularizing Arabic numerals and the astrolabe in the Latin world. Also very early, medicine emerged from its torpor thanks to the school at Salerno founded (tradition tells us) by four masters, Salernus, a Latin, Pontus, a Greek, Adela, an Arab, and Helenus, a Jew. It was in the twelfth century, however, that interest in Arabic culture increased all along a contact zone whose strongest points were Spain and Sicily. In his desire to know more about Muslim religion (with the aim of refuting it better), Peter the Venerable, the abbot of Cluny, commissioned a translation of the Koran, made around 1140–43 by a team of Christian scholars that also included a Jew and a Muslim. People of many sorts—statesmen, clerics, but also merchants and adventurers—traveled far and wide to procure sought-after texts. One of these was Adelard of Bath. Born in England, Adelard studied music in Tours and played the cithara before the queen of France; after teaching in Laon, he went to Sicily, and from there to Palestine and Syria. Eventually he returned to England, where he exercised his accounting skills, perhaps in the office of the Exchequer.[43] Another was Leonardo Fibonacci of Pisa, an eminent mathematician who had spent his youth in Algiers, where his father served as consul general and was an active merchant and a manuscript-hunter.

The immense task of retrieving ancient texts was not completed until the early thirteenth century. As it turned out, nearly all the grammatical, hagiographic, and theological texts came from Byzantium, which also provided two Platonic dialogues and a portion of the works of Euclid, Proclus, and Hero of Alexandria. Westerners often preferred to seek Greek texts through the Muslims in an age when Arab scientific knowledge seemed a more fitting heir to Greek learning than Byzantium, where texts had simply been conserved. This explains the success of translations made in Spain with the aid of Spanish scholars and the borrowing of a large number of Arabic scientific and technical terms that came into Western vocabularies.[44]

Some monastic schools still continued to flourish during this same time, and cities were reviving in a Europe that was much more heavily populated than it had been in Roman times. News flowed into the towns and discussion was no farther than the nearest street corner. Guibert de Nogent, who stated that in his childhood (around 1066) no schoolmasters were to be found in small towns and hardly any in the cities, observed fifty years later that there were so many schools that even the poorest student could attend one. I need not retrace the history of this revival, except to note that throughout Europe cathedral chapters that had been reorganized according to the Gregorian reforms encouraged new cathedral schools under the direction of a *scholasticus*. More and more young people went from one city to another in search of famous teachers. The professors of Tournai at one time made that city a "new Athens." Then came the turn of Laon with Anselm, the "master of masters," then of Auxerre, Bourges, and, outside France, of Durham and Toledo. In the eleventh century Chartres stood out as one of the liveliest centers of learning, first under the bishop Fulbert and the canonist Yves de Chartres, then, in the twelfth century, with Bernard de Chartres, Guillaume de Conches, Gilbert de La Porrée, and Thierry de Chartres. Paris soon began to attract both masters and students. While Abelard was pursuing his tumultuous career there, Thierry de Chartres and Gilbert de La Porrée came to Paris to teach, as did English scholars like Adam du Petit-Pont, John of Salisbury, and Robert of Melun and Italians like Peter Lombard. Henceforth students flocked to the banks of the Seine from the four corners of Europe.[45]

The medieval university system came to be organized during the same period. Teaching in Paris at first took place in the cloister of Notre-Dame; it then spread to the cloisters of the nearby abbeys of Saint-Victor, Sainte-Geneviève, and Saint-Marcel; later it moved to various places on the slopes of the Montagne Sainte-Geneviève. Instruction also diversified to cover grammar, law, medicine, rhetoric, and dialectic as well as theology. Often foreigners, both masters and students organized into corporations on the urban model, first in Paris and Bologna, but also in Oxford (when Henry II forbade his subjects to go to the Continent to seek instruction), and later in Montpellier, Padua, Cambridge, Naples, Toulouse, Salamanca, and Valladolid. The teachers dominated some of the institutions organized during this period; in others the students commanded. These pragmatically derived infrastructures were all minimal and flexible: the masters first taught in rooms that they rented, then in colleges set up for poor students or members of religious orders or congregations. Ceremonies took place in the cloisters and the churches. The course of studies was extremely long. Although students at the Faculty of Arts in Paris could finish the seven years of the *cursus* by the time they were between the ages of twenty-two and twenty-five, students in Bologna, who had often had some practical experience before coming to study, might be the same age as a master of arts. The theology students of the collège de Sorbonne were usually from twenty-four to thirty-five years of age, and doctors of theology were normally over thirty-eight years of age when they completed their studies.

Given the atmosphere of constant confrontation that reigned in European cities, it would have been extraordinary if there had been no clashes between those who believed in the revived logic of writing and those who sought to serve God and enter into direct contact with him.

This eternal debate between the intellectual and the prophet was made flesh in Abelard and St. Bernard. The son of a Breton knight, Abelard was arrogant and aggressive. In his struggle for supremacy over Guillaume de Champeaux he conceived of dispute as a combat in which the loser bit the dust and the winner carried off the booty (in the form of the defeated professor's clientele). His love affair with Heloise began as a scientific experiment in seduction. Caught in his own trap, Abelard, a man who had seemed to think himself pure spirit, was terror-stricken to see the consequences that his act was to have on his career as a cleric. After the irreparable act of his castration, the entire affair ended in literary sublimation. Intellectuals of his time had a confidence in the infallibility of a well-conducted argument that we have learned to temper. A pure intellectual, Abelard attempted reconcile the texts of Scripture and the apparently contradictory opinions of the Fathers of the church. To that end he studied the language of those authors with care, trying to take into account copyists' errors and the existence of apocryphal texts, and he attempted to show how certain theologians (St. Augustine, for example) had changed their points of view during their lifetime. He also demonstrated the need to develop a science of language in order to determine the adequacy of words to express reality. In the debate on universals, the great quarrel of the age, Abelard opposed both Roscelin, the nominalist, and Guillaume de Champeaux, the realist. He presented a complete exposé of the problem and proposed a solution that was, as Etienne Gilson put it, "doubtless disputable, but assuredly rigorous and new."[46]

We can imagine the anger that seized some people when they heard problems of faith discussed with cold logic in this manner, and we can understand the reaction of St. Bernard, the prophet of the Second Crusade, to Abelard, the prideful intellectual. A mystic and a man of action, Bernard had devoted his life to a different search for God and to quite different combats. An aristocrat born in the country and a solitary by vocation, he was horrified when he first came into contact with the schools of Paris, when he gave his famous sermon against the modern Babylon. Bernard did not hesitate to use "political" means to silence Abelard. Like Bossuet, whom he recalls from more than one point of view, Bernard had the temperament of an inquisitor and an orator. A "literary" author if ever there was one, nourished on the *lectio divina* and the Fathers of the church, he refused to quote the authors of classical antiquity. His style was elegant and easy, however. His chief means of expression were public letters and sermons, forms chosen in the interest of being clearly understood and as ways to move his auditors. He has left more than 350 sermons, some given before large crowds of people whom he wanted to enflame and others before small groups of monks. We have them in their Latin versions, but at least some sermons must have been given in French. A man fond of direct contact with listeners, Bernard undoubtedly did not compose all these texts in advance. Some seem to be from his pen, but others were most probably written from an outline he furnished to the team of notaries that he employed or were reconstituted after the fact from notes taken as he preached. St. Bernard's rhetoric was thus in a sense Ciceronian. The written word and logical analysis of discourse did not have the same meaning for him as for Abelard.[47]

The dual functions of the medieval intellectual were incarnate in Abelard and St. Bernard. Above all a man of the church, the intellectual had to be a theologian skilled in textual analysis and able to construct faultless arguments. A pastor and a leader of men, he also had to be a preacher capable of swaying and converting crowds. The scholarly exercises that gave him that dual formation were summarized in the lapidary formula, *legere, disputare, praedicare*. Teaching, shaped by the need to understand and interpret Scripture, was based primarily on the study and interrogation of authorities. Each faculty had its own. In the Faculty of the Arts, for example, they were Priscian and Donatus for grammar, Cicero's *De inventione* and *Rhetorica ad Herennium* and Quintilian's *Institutio oratoria* for rhetoric, and Porphyry, Boethius, and Aristotle for dialectic. The reader of one of these works was expected to begin with a detailed examination of the text, word by word and phrase by phrase. Only after this lengthy exercise could he discuss the underlying meaning of what he had dissected, summarize it, or, when appropriate, offer his own thoughts on it.

Methods were even more rigid in the noblest faculty, the Faculty of Theology, to which the student gained access only after completing the curriculum of the Faculty of Arts. After several years following the teaching of the master, the student was received as a bachelor in theology and could himself explicate the Bible, limiting his lessons to its literal meaning. He could become a *bachelier sentenciaire* (sententiary bachelor) by offering as proof of mastery an interpretation of passages of his choosing from Peter Lombard's *Sentences*. Part of his presentation had to be a discussion of arguments for and against the question posed, after which he was permitted to offer his own conclusions. The master who read Scripture, however, was quite naturally prompted to raise problems and, following the methods of the times, to translate them into questions, suggesting counterarguments and raising objections, which he then attempted to answer. He might judge it opportune to present this latter part of his course as a special exercise that displayed his superior knowledge and that of his more advanced disciples. This was the formal debate or "disputation," in which objectors and respondents faced off as in a tournament, with the professor acting as arbiter and, in certain cases, imposing his own resolution (*determinatio*) of the question. In the lesson following this oratorical joust, the master would return to the problems that had been raised, put the arguments into order, and give his own overall conclusion, also called a "determination." The most solemn disputes, the quodlibetic debates, normally included other doctors and their disciples. In this exercise the master, aided only by his "bachelor," answered a variety of questions in what Father Palémon Glorieux has compared to a press conference. Finally, on the next available "reading" day, he would sum up the debate before his usual, more restricted, audience.[48]

The most solemn activities in the University of Paris were thus oral debates in which each participant had to be on constant guard to keep his arguments from being distorted in a persistent use of the dialectic method. When we add that both masters and advanced students were obligated to give sermons in Latin at which attendance was also obligatory for all students and that many of them also preached in the churches and other religious institutions of the city, it is clear that the chief objective of a theologian's formation was to prepare him to dispense correct doctrine to large audiences.

Medieval university methods can be explained by the social context of the times. When young men, often of modest origin and rural background, arrived at the schools, they knew practically nothing about the written word and the practice of writing. They first needed to be initiated into a new language of an implacable logic and learn not only to understand it but to manipulate it. They were expected to assimilate notions up to then totally foreign to them, using texts that often had been composed more than a millennium earlier and must have seemed to come from another world. Abstraction was a long and difficult conquest. By dint of long efforts to master spoken discourse they learned to construct a rational argument with the aid of a restricted vocabulary of carefully defined notions. Hence the importance of the *quadrivium*—the disciplines of language—and the recognized preeminence of grammar, which had been promoted to the rank of a superior discipline in virtue of the persistent and latent idea that there were correspondences between the laws of language and the laws of thought. In the last analysis the Scholastic method was an attempt, doggedly pursued, to analyze written authorities, to draw a lesson from them, and to pass on that lesson by means of reading, disputation, and sermons in a world where speech remained the highest form of communication. This goes far to explain the weighty arguments and the impersonal style of most medieval theologians.

In order to understand what part writing played in all this, we need to open a manuscript of Scholastic theology. It is copied in a small, broken hand that bristles with abbreviations. Every page was supposed to be compact and full, to the point of filling a blank space by recopying a passage that had already been written, but carefully leaving out the punctuation to tell the reader not to waste his time on it. But we can also see signs, often made with colored ink, that highlight new arguments and clarify the overall structure of the text.[49]

The organization of St. Thomas's *Summa theologica* is exemplary in this regard. The copyist indicates its component parts at the head of the work, and every part, every treatise, and every question is preceded by a summary. Each article, the basic unit in this hierarchical structure, has a title beginning *utrum* (whether). Alternative possibilities are followed by series of objections, the first of which is introduced by the formula *videtur quod non* (it would seem not) and each of the following by *praeterea* (furthermore). Then, after the formula *sed contra* (but to the contrary), an argument (usually only one) against the point originally raised gives an answer to the question. In the body of the article, introduced by *respondeo dicendum* (I answer saying), each objection is refuted in order, preceded each time by *ad primam, ad secundam,* and so forth (Robert Marichal).

The same psychology and the same fondness for subdivision and articulation underlay this system, double-entry bookkeeping, with its written refinements, the complex organization of university sermons and Dominican preaching, and the broken writing of the Gothic period. Even more, as Erwin Panofsky and Robert Marichal have demonstrated, the very structure of Thomistic logic derives from the same technique as the Gothic vault, in which opposing thrusts are balanced by a keystone.

St. Thomas could not have composed his monumental work so rapidly if this framework had not been available. Nonetheless, the texts that he composed needed to be read and reread, and indeed the Scholastic method required the reader to make incessant journeys back and forth on the page to assimilate the master's thought. The copyists took great care to punctuate such texts, not just to guide the inflection of the voice but to aid comprehension. The same aim led to concentrating the greatest possible amount of text on one page and to a search for a density that expressed more than a simple desire to save parchment. Hence the systematic use of conventional abbreviations, which, like ideograms, permit the reader to grasp a notion at a glance. The word and its precise and technical significance gained predominance over the syllable-by-syllable deciphering preached in classical antiquity. Although the new system undoubtedly facilitated the work of students skilled in its complexities, on the whole it was conceived to manipulate only a relatively reduced number of abstractions. Thus it reflected a society in which each "micromilieu" had its own vocabulary and language.

As soon as all knowledge depended on systematic reference to a growing number of authorities, memory and reading—even cursive reading—were not enough. Reference works were needed. All civilizations had some indexing system—we need only think of Mesopotamia. The Roman jurists were past masters at it. Furthermore, beginning in the third century the codex permitted Christians to add to the books of the Bible "capitulations" listing the subjects mentioned in them. Eusebius of Caesarea (ca. 260–340) conceived of a system to establish a parallel life of Jesus from the four Gospels. These two inventions, however, seemed to suffice for centuries, so that when a number of procedures for indexation and classification appeared between the eleventh and the thirteenth centuries they reflected a real revolution in scholars' working methods that is in some ways comparable to the revolutionary effects that electronic data banks have had on scholarship today. It is worth thinking about. Gratian's *Decretum* and Peter Lombard's *Sententiae* were works of a totally new conception. Peter Lombard even declared that he had compiled his book so that people who sought information would not have to waste their time searching through a large number of works to pick out quotations. Efforts were also made to facilitate the consultation of manuscripts. A summary of chapters appeared with increasing frequency at the head of a work; a running title headed each folio; colored letters or "signs" helped to locate a given passage; quotations were marked (for example with two points that prefigured quotation marks) or the name of the person being quoted was sometimes given in the margin in a sort of "headline." Thus while St. Bernard, some years before, was delighted to have his listeners or his readers launch into lengthy studies if they wanted to understand his thought, Peter Lombard was pleased that his carefully codified presentation would facilitate the work of his readers. Furthermore, there were a number of other systems that I cannot dwell upon here that simplified the work of the learned by the use of page glosses.[50]

These systems seem natural and elementary to our eyes, but some contemporaries found them surprising and resisted them. Papias, who worked in northern Italy in the mid-eleventh century, compiled the first work arranged in alphabetical order, an *Elementorum doctrinae Erudimentum*, a sort of encyclopedia whose original presentation copyists at times misunderstood, since it used a system of letters of different sizes, placed in the margins, to guide the reader. Papias had no immediate imitators, but the appearance of a series of *Distinctiones* that listed the various meanings of words repeated in different places in Scripture drew a sharp reaction from theologians who found this procedure the antithesis of reason and contrary to an order of nature fixed by God (Richard H. Rouse). In their eyes it risked opening the door to totally arbitrary reconstructions. Such methods were too convenient to be abandoned, however. The Cistercians showed themselves to be great compilers of indices, and they devised a system for locating an entry based on a division of the page into zones with corresponding letters placed in the margins—a procedure that remained in constant use until well into the Renaissance.

Such changes in the ways in which a text was apprehended were truly revolutionary, and specialists agree that they took place primarily in the fourteenth century, at a time when texts and instruments for consulting texts were proliferating, as was written matter of all sorts. All this implied new attitudes toward writing and above all new ways of reading. Henceforth the reader looked at a page rather than listening to a text, and his eyes moved over the two-dimensional surface seeking a particular word or scanning for reference points or colored letters. By the same token, any reasoned argument was as if detached from the realms of God and men and took on an objective existence. The written text became amoral because it became detached from the writing process and no longer demanded that the reader take on responsibility for it by reading it aloud. This may have facilitated heretical propositions. No wonder the philosophers of that age, even more than in Plato's times, questioned the relations between words and things and the reality of ideas.

Thus there was a revolution that was the daughter of the alphabet and the mother of printing. Texts were accumulated, no longer primarily in human memory but through the aid of external instruments. That meant, however, that they were open to a quantitative evaluation, a calculation of the profit to be gained. What then was the "book capacity" of the medieval intellectual?

The history of the book and the history of libraries will help to answer that question. With the enormous increase in study, the period during which most texts were reproduced in monasteries came to an end. Henceforth texts were recopied and sold by booksellers and stationers under rules set by the university authorities. The latter made sure that "just" prices were charged; more important, they made sure that the texts were not corrupted. In order to facilitate the work of both the copyists and the students, *exemplaria*—carefully corrected manuscripts—were rented out one quire at a time. This system may seem to us primitive, but for centuries it proved totally satisfactory, so much so that the stock of available school texts grew in succeeding generations. Nonetheless, the manuscript remained a rare and expensive commodity because, until the appearance of paper, parchment was costly enough to dampen the zeal of most students. This meant that when a friar from one of the mendicant orders arrived at the university with four works on long-term loan from his order—a Bible, Peter Comestor's *Ecclesiastical History*, the *Sententiae* of Peter Lombard, and St. Thomas's *Summa theologica* for the Dominicans or St. Bonaventura's *Summa* for the Franciscans—he was considered affluent. According to university regulations, students were supposed to have one course-book for every three students, but one might well wonder how they could possibly have procured them. Fortunately, the "required texts" remained very few. In the fourteenth century, only some two hundred *exemplaria* circulated in Paris. In 1338 the library of the Sorbonne, the richest library in Christendom, had only 338 books for consultation chained to its reading desks and 1,728 works for loan in its registers, 300 of which were listed as lost. The collections of the other colleges of the period included no more than three hundred works, among them the great basic texts.[51]

The medieval university student's attitude toward the book was nothing like our own. When they sat down to read a page they struggled with every word and every phrase until they had totally assimilated it. Still, the relative scarcity of books had consequences: one of them—as is always the case when books are scarce—was specialization. A theologian would probably not have understood the vocabulary or the abbreviations of a jurist or a physician, let alone his thought. Each discipline had a highly precise but extremely limited vocabulary. Students could certainly not have read all classical Latin texts fluently. Although now they could consult a work by scanning it, they had undeniably lost the immense auditive memory of traditional societies that reading aloud had enabled the Greeks and Romans to retain. It was an age of micromilieus, each one of which, as we shall see, had its writing style and its internal communication networks and each one of which functioned as if in a closed circuit.

THE WRITING OF NATIONAL LITERATURES

At the same time that a new form of clerical culture was developing, the various peoples of Europe were beginning to write in vernacular languages and to put down on parchment both their literature and their customs. They set in motion a rupture with the mechanisms of oral tradition and they prepared the conversion to the logic of writing. The only way to grasp this change—a change that moved the West out of the category of a partially literate society (which is what it had been for centuries)—is to look first at the linguistic situation of Europe at the time. Germanic dialects had held their ground east of the Rhine and had gained ground in some territories toward the northwest and the west, while the Anglo-Saxon invaders had imposed their language on most of England. Celtic idioms were now spoken only in Ireland, Scotland, Wales, and Cornwall, as well as in Brittany, where refugees from the British Isles had flocked. Elsewhere the barbarians had adopted the language of the peoples they conquered. But in Romania—the former Byzantine Empire, now broken up into separate regions—spoken languages had gradually drifted away from classical or post-classical Latin to arrive at languages of a totally different structure.[52]

When Charlemagne revived the Roman Empire, people became acutely aware of languages, and the schoolbooks tell us (somewhat erroneously) that the Strasbourg Oaths in 842 marked the birth of the French and German languages.

It is a familiar story: Two of the sons of Louis the Pious, Louis and Charles, opposed another son, Lothaire, and sealed their alliance during a solemn meeting near Strasbourg. Since they wanted to be sure that their respective armies would understand them, they first harangued them in their own languages—Louis's troops in Tudesque and Charles's in Romance. Next they both swore alliance in the language of the other one's troops, after which the armies swore a similar oath in their own languages. The words spoken on that occasion were set down in Nithard's *History of the Sons of Louis the Pious.* The oaths were probably judged of enough importance to have been agreed upon and written down beforehand and preserved in the archives of the two sovereigns, where Nithard must have found them.[53]

Writing posed quite different problems for the various groups in Europe. The majority of the Germanic populations as well as the Celts who had escaped Romanization held to oral traditions that had never died. Romanized peoples long saw Latin as the learned form of their own spoken languages, in somewhat the way that contemporary Arabic speakers view literary Arabic. The barbarians who had contact with Greek or Latin culture only rarely thought writing useful, but they were not systematically hostile to it and even used it in certain cases. Caesar tells us that the Gauls, for example, used Greek characters to keep their cities' accounts, and the Helvetes noted on tablets the names of emigrants gathered to invade Gaul—338,000 of them, so it seems.[54] After coming into contact with Rome, the Germans worked out a system of runes that they used to write inscriptions on stone, metal, or wood, not only for magical purposes but also to remember an event or communicate a message, and even to write fragments of poetry. The Celts in the British Isles had comparable writing systems, and Irish missionaries left notes and glosses in their own language on the margins of Latin manuscripts in Bobbio and in Wurzburg. Finally, the Ostrogoths used writing on occasion, after Ulfilas had introduced it among them as an aid to their evangelization, to subscribe to acts redacted in Latin in the parts of northern Italy that they occupied.

One interesting question is the attitude of the Catholic Church in its long struggle against the barbarians' Arian national clergies. As we have seen, missionaries trained in Byzantium created alphabets in order to evangelize the Goths, the Armenians, and the Slavs in their own languages, but Roman Catholics refused to give up the Latin language that had guaranteed their cohesion and their domination. When the Germanic clergy was obligated to learn Latin, all but a few exceptional individuals felt a need for bilingual glossaries. One such was the famous *Abrogans* compiled around 770 at the instigation of the bishop of Freising. Similarly, bilingual versions have been found of the Rule of St. Benedict and of hymns, and there were translations of the common prayers, a Rhenish Frankish version of the *De Fide catholica ex Vetere et Novo Testamento contra Judaeos* of Isidore of Seville, and a version of a harmony of the Gospels made around 830 in the Abbey of Fulda. [55] Thus throughout Europe we can find works written in the vernacular if we look for them, and we know that the barbarians had written laws (written in Latin) for the use of their Romanized subjects. They do not seem to have written down their traditional tales, their poetry, or their songs, which were part of another system. As we have seen, Caesar relates that the druids consistently refused to write down their legends, and as the Christian religion triumphed it prohibited (in Germany, for example) the transcription of pagan traditions.

The end of the "old Germanic legends" is typical. When Germany opened up to Christianity, thus to clerical culture, it was penetrated by multiple influences and only in northern Europe and Iceland were the old traditions conserved. When missionaries reached those lands and they became more thoroughly Christianized, Snorri Sturluson, one of the most prestigious of the Icelandic chiefs and himself the author of a saga, composed (between 1220 and 1240) a sort of manual of poetics for the use of young skalds, lest they forget the metaphor systems and conventional denominations of the traditional poetry. His work also included fragments of older works and even entire works, some of which date from the seventh century. Snorri Sturluson got around the unavoidable problem of allusion to pagan mythology by presenting mythology euhemeristically, stating that the ancient gods were men given divinity by tradition. Thus the *Edda* was born, which, in its Scandinavian written versions, permits us to admire the beauties of an already moribund culture.[56]

Charlemagne did several things to preserve the history of his people. According to Einhard, he ordered the transcription of the very ancient poems celebrating the oldest kings of his race, and he even ordered the compilation of a grammar of the Frankish language. All that has come down to us is (perhaps) a few fragments of an epic song conserved in the Abbey of Fulda, the *Hildebranslied,* which tells of the deeds of Odoacer and Theodoric. The only historical enterprise of this kind that bore fruit was that of Alfred the Great in the late ninth century. Noting that many of his subjects could read Anglo-Saxon but that knowledge of Latin was waning, Alfred had a number of standard texts translated for the use of the children of his aristocracy—a *Cura pastoralis,* the histories of the Venerable Bede, Paulus Orosius, and Gregory the Great, as well as the *Soliloquies* attributed to St. Augustine. Anglo-Saxon became the official language of his kingdom, and epic texts were written down (we have them in eleventh- and twelfth-century copies but they surely date from much older times).[57] Nearly all the known texts in the Germanic language before the eleventh century were written by clerics and reflect their curiosity or their religious interests. The six thousand lines of the *Heliand,* written in Saxon dialect verse, have probably survived because the work was inspired by the Bible. Ecclesiastical milieus also began to produce texts in Romance. A manuscript from the Abbey of Saint-Amand, near Valenciennes, bears on its last folios twenty-eight lines of rhythmic verse from the *Cantilène de sainte Eulalie,* influenced by Prudentius, and a poem in Rhenish Frankish, the *Ludwigslied,* celebrating the exploits of King Louis III at the battle of Saucourt in 881.[58]

What conclusions can we draw from the few relics that chance has granted us? First, that people probably knew how to write in the various vernacular languages a good deal earlier than has been thought. But what part did oral traditions play in the various lands of Europe? To what extent could epic narrative forms develop or revive in lands of Romance language that had been profoundly marked by Latin culture? And how, for example, did preachers prepare their sermons in the vernacular? These are the questions to which we shall turn next.

❖

The definitive break with oral composition techniques and the oral tradition began in France when the Romance *chansons de geste* were written down.

How did this change take place? The first evidence we have comes from the physical aspect of the manuscripts. A dozen are small in format and written in one column without superfluous decoration. The oldest are a manuscript in the Royal Library of Brussels, which can be dated from 1130 and contains 661 lines of octosyllabic verse of *Gormont et Isambart,* and the Oxford manuscript of the *Chanson de Roland* (Digby 23), somewhat later in date. These modest volumes have been called "jongleurs' manuscripts," though with little justification. There are also manuscripts of later cyclical works that bring together separate texts on a related topic, probably compiled for aristocratic libraries.

These narratives embroider on ancient and real events: the attack on the Abbey of Saint-Riquier by the Normans in 881 for *Gormont et Isambart;* an ambush set for Charlemagne's troops on their return from an expedition in Spain (778) for the *Chanson de Roland;* the history of a Frank who became the count of Toulouse and earned glory but was defeated by the Saracens at the gates of Carcassonne for the *Chanson de Guillaume d'Orange.* In nearly every case the epic crystallizes around a hero, according to the rules of the genre. All or nearly all the characters and historical events go back to the Carolingian epoch, never beyond. The psychology of the heroes and the view of the vassal's role and the royal system have nothing Carolingian about them, referring instead to feudal values and to the vicissitudes of Capetian society, its first, as yet powerless, kings, and its restless barons.

On the level of composition these poems seem to follow a formal technique that Jean Rychner has described.[59] They are divided into lays of decasyllabic or octosyllabic (on occasion, hendacasyllabic) verse using assonance or rhyme, and they seem to have been intoned rather than actually sung. From their many attention-catching expressions ("oyez," "écoutez") and from reiterated statements that the singer has to interrupt the story because of the late hour or because he needs rest, it is clear that such works were meant to be declaimed or spoken. At times the jongleur states that he is addressing gentlemen, but what mountebank does not flatter his listeners in that manner? Everything indicates that the chansons de geste were elaborated in aristocratic milieus but were destined for an eventual larger public.

Their genesis remains a mystery. Despite the studies of Edmond Faral on the jongleurs, those who conceived and sang such works are just as much of a mystery as the origin of the works themselves.[60] Documents may be lacking, but the hypothesis-makers have gone at the question with whole-hearted energy.

One of these was Léon Gauthier, who wrote during the Second Empire. In Gautier's view the Romance epic was Germanic in essence; with Gaston Paris, he sought their origins in *cantilènes* like the *Ludwigslied*. With the Franco-Prussian war in 1870−71 Gauthier repatriated the French epic and declared it wholly Romance. Philip August Becker and Joseph Bédier later declared it wholly Capetian. An inspired writer, Bédier evoked the world in which the jongleur recited—and later jongleurs modified—his version of such tales. Above all Bédier found the theme of the Crusade everywhere; he gathered internal evidence that the memory of epic heroes was attached to pilgrimage churches; he proclaimed that "in the beginning was the road and the sanctuary." After World War II, some of the most perspicacious scholars were seeking indications of their manner of composition in the texts themselves, and Ramón Menéndez Pidal traced the legend of Roland after the Carolingian period. Even more recently Italo Siciliano devastated the theory-makers by explaining that a style highly reliant on formulas is not obligatorily a guarantee of oral composition. Hence his declaration, "In the beginning was the caste."[61]

The debate may be eternal: in any event, the chanson de geste appeared in the form in which we know it in the eleventh century and it flourished in the twelfth century, the very high point of feudalism, whose ideology it transposed. But the chief problem lies, as it always has, in judging how great a share of the creative process to attribute to collective creation and how much to the person who wielded the pen when the legend was noted down. To what extent did the writer simply join scattered songs into a coherent whole? These are the same questions we had for the Homeric poems. The least we can say is that the evolution of a society that valued entertainment (just as Ionian society had in the distant past) facilitated a proliferation of poets and reciters, many if not nearly all of whom were clerics by training. It is clear that these men drew on sources of inspiration within the feudal aristocracy and its traditions, but it is equally clear that they put their works—at least their epic songs—in contact with the people, whose reactions must have had some influence on them. It is hardly surprising, then, that sovereigns and great feudal lords take a leading role in these narratives, even when there is an implied criticism in their depiction. The people are present everywhere, however, because the people function as a judge and are the principal support of an ideology in which the monarch is shown, through the legendary figure of Charlemagne, to be work-ing for unity, peace, and order. In the last analysis, the chansons de geste represent a form of mythic interpretation of the feudal system and a popu-lar and clerical vision of its ideal operation. Once again, these poems were a legacy from an essentially oral tradition to a society turning in the direc-tion of the written word.

A highly elaborated form of lyric poetry appeared in the Pays d'Oc around the year 1100. After the jongleur came the troubadour, and after him the trouvère and the minnesinger.[62]

We need to sketch the scene, even at the risk of indulging in imagery. The troubadour arrived, dressed with a certain elegance, after the passing of winter, the dead season for things of the spirit, festivity, and warfare. If his voice was fine, a troubadour might himself sing his compositions, but ordinarily he left that chore to a jongleur dressed in particolored clothes who accompanied his recitation with a harp, a drum, a viol, or castanets. Of the 450 troubadours who have been identified, some were mighty lords (one was William of Aquitaine, the grandfather of the illustrious Eleanor); others were loyal feudal lords or honest knights; some were clerics and burghers. Some, finally, were of extremely modest origin, as was Bernard de Ventadour, whose mother was the baker in the château of Ventadour and who may have been one of Eleanor of Aquitaine's lovers.

At the center of this sung poetry was the *canson*. The troubadour might strive for simplicity in his style; frequently he sought to show his virtuosity by the richness of his rhymes (*trobar ric*); at other times he gave his verse an aristocratic cast by use of a hermetic, allusive style full of double mean-ings (*trobar clus*). Or he might abandon the *canson* for the *sirventes*, satiric verse, the *ensenhamen*, moral verse with a lesson for living to offer the child, the damsel, the squire, the knight, or the jongleur. Or he might prefer the *tenson*, a discussion in dialogue, the *planh*, or complaint, the *partimen*, a game involving taking sides, the *pastorelle* or pastoral, the *alba* or morning song, or the *descort*, a learned but not strictly ordered sort of poem.

Thus a refined poetry arose that was constructed in accordance with precise norms by authors who had read all of Ovid. It was verse obviously destined for a public able to appreciate its subtleties, and it was sung in the medieval fortress, a center of attraction for landless nobles and young vas-sals come to complete their social and military education. The cult of the Lady, following the rules of courtly love, undeniably had a symbolic value in a setting of that sort. Let me support, without insisting on the point, Erich Köhler's thesis that the aim of courtly lyric poetry was to make use of a common ideal to neutralize a persisting tension between the higher feudal aristocracy and the lower nobility in a system that members of the upper bourgeoisie at times tried to join.[63]

As long as the feudal system flourished the troubadours had admirers and imitators in the Pays d'Oil and, soon, throughout Europe, from Italy to the north and from Portugal to Germany. It was then that a new genre, the verse romance, sprang up in northern France. This was at first a sort of marvelous tale in which a large number of episodes were strung together or intermingled, often thanks to the device of the quest, and in which the characters had a unique psychology unlike the stereotypes of traditional epic literature. It was a tightly governed and learned literature popular in lordly and princely courts; Eleanor of Aquitaine, the wife of King Louis VII of France and later of Henry II Plantagenet, and her children played an essential role in the acceptance and diffusion of the genre. Once again, there are difficult problems of transfer for the historian interested in tracing the source of such works. Many of these romances are qualified as classical: there is the Romance of Alexander, the first version of which dates from the eleventh century, the Romance of Thebes inspired by Statius, the Romance of Troy, and the *Aeneas*, whose characters reflect the spirit of the barons and the knights for whom they were composed in line with a principle stated by Chrétien de Troyes that chivalry was a legacy from Greece and Rome. Other works used tales and legends also found in the East: *Barlaam et Josaphat* was a Christianized version of the life of Buddha borrowed from a Greek romance translated into Latin in the tenth century; the *Lai de l'oiselet* was based on an Oriental apologue; the *Dit de l'unicorne* came from a fable of Indian origin known as far away as Japan.[64]

These were undeniably learned works, composed in an age in which the Crusades had developed relations with Byzantium and an interest in classical antiquity and the East. The same poets who adapted these tales also used Celtic legends, however, and we might well wonder by what channels these had reached them.[65]

Which brings us to the problem of the origins of the Arthurian legends. There is no doubt that Geoffrey of Monmouth played an essential role. A cleric of Welsh origin, protected by Robert of Gloucester (who was himself the son of Henry I Beauclerc and a Welsh concubine), Geoffrey amplified the meager information that he had found in his predecessors, Gildas, the Venerable Bede, Nennius, and William of Malmesbury, to write his own

Historia regnum Britanniae. Geoffrey's work, which immediately circulated among the Anglo-Norman and even the French courts, narrates the history of the kings of Britain from the arrival of the first of their number, Brutus, three generations after the fall of Troy, to the last, Caedwalla, who died in 689. The principal hero of the history is Arthur, however, an ancient Welsh chieftain whom Geoffrey depicts chasing the Saxons out of England in the sixth century and conquering a part of the Continent.

Edmond Faral has shown that Geoffrey, who was denounced as a forger even in the twelfth century, used his imagination to make vast improvements in the written, but probably also oral, sources that he had chosen to exploit. The least we can say is that his history reminds us, once again, of the incessant exchanges that took place between the oral tradition and clerical literature—as in the lives of the saints. Everything indicates, however, that the Arthurian legend soon spread throughout Europe. The adventure of Queen Guinevere, for instance, appeared in statues on the tympanum of the cathedral of Modena around 1120. We know that Eleanor of Aquitaine heard Celtic bards at her father's court in Poitiers, and Marie de France tells us herself that her lays were inspired by the songs of Breton harpers. But the first Arthurian romance, the *Roman de Brut,* was simply an adaptation by a cleric, Wace, of the *History* of Geoffrey of Monmouth (1155), and Chrétien de Troyes relates that he found the story of the Grail in a manuscript supposedly given to him by his protector, Philippe d'Alsace. Thus we get the impression that the courtly authors integrated Celtic traditions into their imaginary universe with the encouragement of the Plantagenets, at a time when the Welsh courts were losing their original personality through contact with the Normans, but we do not know by what channels they received those traditions. It is probable that clerics noted down this fast-disappearing form of literature. Unfortunately the few modest volumes that give us snatches of these works are no older than the thirteenth century, so a link is missing in the history of this transfer.

During this same age German feudal society was becoming aware of the chansons de geste and the French romances, and German singers and poets turned toward the few ancient sources in their own land that had not been totally eliminated by time and Christianization, in particular the sources of the epic of the Nibelungen. This complex work joins and merges several different narratives. One tells of the exploits and the death of the young Siegfried, a story probably known in fairly brief songs; another relates the death of the Burgundian kings, who probably furnished subject matter for an earlier epic around 1160. Although it is not signed, the long poem was almost certainly composed by an Austrian man of letters soon after the year 1200. Later sources, in particular in Norway, show how that writer could compose a Christian work on the basis of pagan tales, because the hero Siegfried and his enemy Hagen were probably originally mythical beings symbolizing light and dark, and Brunhild, at first a Valkyrie and the daughter of Odin, became the virgin queen of Iceland. The various stages of transformation that the epic underwent after that period are of less interest to us. As it had happened long before with the Homeric poems, more recently with the *Chanson de Roland*, and, to a certain extent, with the Arthurian romances, when the Nibelungen epic was set down in writing it resulted in a masterwork that was something like a testament that passed on a legacy of oral traditions whose days were numbered.[66]

The victory of writing is often only apparent. First, because writing exists only by right of previous speech, thought or spoken, and its first aim is to set down spoken discourse in visual form. Next, because in a certain sense written discourse remains spoken when it is conceived to be recited in public. Last, because poetry was primarily spoken, at least in the West.

All this was confirmed during the Middle Ages, as Paul Zumthor has often reminded us.[67] As is always the case, the literary message passed along through a series of operations that are familiar to specialists in communications: production, transmission, reception, storage, and repetition. In a society that practices writing, each of these operations occurs either through oral/aural sensory channels or through writing, which involves sight. Midway through the shift that interests us here, during the eleventh to the thirteenth centuries in particular, when literary works continued to be spoken in public, there came a moment that Zumthor has called "performance." This is a moment in which the voice is important (as are silences) but gesture and stance are also involved, as they are in the sermon. Any performance is a spectacle, and needs to take place in an appropriate place: for the chanson de geste, that place was the fairgrounds, the courtyard of the château, where we can easily imagine a jongleur declaiming the *Chanson de Roland,* or the great hall of the château, where the troubadour and his jongleur came to present their latest *canson.* As an "auditive" object, the utterance cannot be dissociated from the process of uttering it, and the very notions of author and actor tend to blend. One result is that, if writing had not intervened more and more directly in the transmission of the message, the West might have arrived at a search for formal perfection comparable to that of the Japanese Nō drama, where all the elements, from the sound of the musical instruments to the tone of the actors' voices and the pace of the discourse, contribute to the stylization.

The medieval poetic text was thus originally conceived to address a coherent collectivity rather than today's set of individuals who do not know one another and do not know the author of the book they read or the film they have come to see in a darkened hall. This means that the value of the work depended on the relationship that could be established between its author, its interpreter, and its public. It had to prove its worth at every performance. Quite often the actor in that performance was in a situation comparable to that of an actor in classical repertory theater today, who must transmit a message written for the system of reference of a bygone society. But the age of the manuscript was not the age of print, and the way a medieval work was composed bore little resemblance to our modern methods. In Breton romances Merlin the Enchanter does not himself write; secretaries who are often eminent personages note his words and assemble them. Another thing we do not know is whether courtly lyrics were always written before they were later gathered together in the songbooks thanks to which we know them. It is also clear that such transfers to writing occurred after a filtering process that it would be too simplistic to call censorship. More generally, orality continued to play an extremely important role in medieval literature. Even more, the notaries who recopied the texts seem not to have had any more compunction than the actors who performed them about introducing changes in them, if only to adapt them to the dialect spoken by a new audience. This means that when we have several manuscripts of a chanson de geste they present noticeably different versions. Like custom, and for comparable reasons, literary texts were not yet totally frozen by being written.

In the end, however, this was a game that writing always won. This is particularly clear regarding the romance. The product of two convergent traditions—the chanson de geste, from which it originally borrowed a number of procedures, and the historical chronicle or a certain kind of hagiography—and of the ancient epic, the romance arose at a time when history was definitively replacing myth in the national collective memory.

Romances were usually written by an author who had close relations with aristocratic protectors; at first it often used an octosyllabic verse form with alternating masculine and feminine couplets, a rhythmically weak form whose use emphasizes the gap between musical expression and the rational expression of speech.

Around 1220–30 we arrive at the triumph of prose. At the same time, a more systematic use of writing worked in favor of carefully constructed cyclical romance. As Ferdinand Lot pointed out some time ago, the Arthurian cycle came to center on Lancelot and the Grail, chronological logic was strictly respected, and characters who had become superfluous were eliminated in later episodes.[68] Thus the epic was replaced by a genre manifestly conceived to be read aloud in small groups or even alone in a murmur. Next, in the fourteenth and fifteenth centuries, because the language was changing and the people found it increasingly difficult to understand the old verse compositions—a sign of the times—"de-rhymers" (dérimeurs) put the chansons de geste and the verse romances into prose, quite clearly adapting them to new reading habits. It is characteristic of such men to state that verse prevented "speaking short," "being brief," and holding fast to the truth. According to them, versified narratives lied and prose was better suited to such stories and to history. They eliminated the old, familiar words, the epic clichés, the attention-getting devices, but also too-lengthy descriptions and psychological embroidery. Writing aimed at efficacy, which meant that it gave priority to the concrete and to action, but also to verisimilitude, hence to details of time and place.

Manuscripts confirm this trend even in their physical appearance. Manuscripts in prose, which were often commissioned for dynastic or political reasons and were written in an elegant hand, illuminated, and bound, could be beautiful objects that lent sacred aura to their contents. Like many modern luxury publications, however, their text is often faulty. Dérimeurs and copyists, at times the same person, might add a long prologue explaining and justifying their efforts to the reader in terms that often approach the language of publicity. More to the point, they divided their narrative into chapters preceded by headings announcing or summarizing their content. This provided natural breaks in reading, which by now was done among small groups or by lone individuals. It permitted the imagination to wander and meditation to take flight, and it established a dialogue with an author who, henceforth and ever more, remained invisible and mute.

COUNTERPOINT

A rich harvest of advances in writing occurred by the end of the fifteenth century: there was a return to written sources, a revival of commercial correspondence, the appearance of an administration dedicated to writing, a growth of speculative thought and spiritual literature, the development of techniques for abstract calculation and of procedures of classification and retrieval that obeyed a purely graphic logic, and, to end the list, the appearance of written national literatures. The harvest was so rich that one might imagine that our tale had ended and henceforth Europe was converted to writing, or that writing was the same for all peoples everywhere.

Nothing could be farther from the truth. First because the small world of writing was still compartmentalized. But also because that world was only one thin layer of society—some few hundred thousand clerics, merchants, notaries, scribes, and "writers." All around them there were tens of millions of men and women who continued to live and to think in the traditional mode. Let us try to see how so many groups and different milieus operated together.

We need to look first at the circulation of written information. Here we have a good indicator in writing hands, which varied enormously in this period, and which offer us something like a reflection of the groups that produced them. Gérard Isaac Lieftinck took on a nearly impossible task in his classification of the vast assortment of Gothic hands of the period.[69] This does not mean that a good paleographer cannot identify the source of a document or a manuscript at first glance. It is possible to guess, for example, that an act written in a cursive hand without embellishments comes from an Italian mercantile milieu, or that another in a more cramped hand was written by an Italian notary. Difficulties arise when we try to systematize such observations. István Hajnal has listed thirty-five types of chancery hands, noting identical tendencies in countries quite far apart, and he has attributed these similarities to scribes of different nationalities who had studied at the same university. Book hands are equally difficult to classify, in particular because periodically they were influenced by the writing styles in documents and updated.[70] The result was an immeasurable diversity of scripts. The picture is further complicated by a hierarchy of writing styles according to the degree of solemnity that a document or a book merited—a hierarchy that, disconcertingly enough, was observed only in the great chanceries and copyists' workshops, whereas elsewhere style depended on the whim of the scribe or the needs of the person writing. This means that there is no internal logic even in the names that fourteenth- and fifteenth-century writing masters gave to their models.

To examine specific cases, let us look at the most solemn volumes, liturgical books. It does not much matter whether we call their written style *textura, formata,* or *formata textualis;* such terms are scholars' quarrels and the secret garden of paleographers. All we need to note is that their calligraphy tends to be monumental and that it clearly attempts to stress the architecture and the structure of the letters by giving them an angular appearance. This writing style, which was originally intended for use in choir books that had to be read from a certain distance, remained stable for several centuries. It inspired the characters of the great Bibles: Gutenberg took one of these styles as his model. There are limitless gradations between these models and cursive book hands—*cursiva currens* or *notula,* depending on the specialist. The university manuscripts provide one coherent group of them. Their copyists hated empty space for the reasons we have seen, and their minuscule was relatively rapid: the Paris hand was chiseled as if into facets and was made up of broken lines whose fineness contrasts, as in the English style, with the thickness of the other strokes. The Bologna minuscule had more rounded curves, tended to avoid breaks, and quite evidently reflected a different sort of mind. As for the construction of the text as a whole, let me refer to what has already been said and simply recall that although the many conventional abbreviations facilitated a rapid grasp of information during reading, they slowed down writing. St. Thomas avoided them. During this period, finally, the chancery scribes, urged on by the need to produce ever more rapidly an ever-increasing number of originals and correspondence copies, created and then canonized increasingly functional forms that were often used for literary manuscripts aimed at lay readers as well. Every institution quite naturally wanted to affirm its own identity with its individual style.[71]

Not only were the scripts of the Gothic age highly diversified; their ceremonial forms grew more and more complex, resembling flamboyant Gothic architecture. There were different script families that were used according to the nature and destination of the text to be noted, and there were often variations within one script family connected with attempts to achieve greater solemnity or greater rapidity. One overall trait was a stylistic difference between the lands of northern Europe, where scripts showed the attraction of the Gothic and an affirmation reflected in verticality, and the styles in Latin lands that remained loyal to rounded letters and prefigured the humanist script. Thus each model had its public; each functioned as a "logo" to reflect the self-image of cultural micromilieus that remained relatively distinct from one another.

Most people who used writing had not yet reached the point of being sufficiently familiar with these writing styles to be able to use them for natural written expression. Missive letters had of course continued to be written since classical antiquity, and during the Carolingian age learned abbots had made them a literary exercise. But it was still out of the question to use correspondence for immediate and practical purposes. Nothing could replace the messenger, and a letter of Charles the Bald to the inhabitants of Barcelona is an exception. The redaction of letters began toward the end of the tenth century. We possess letters of Gerbert of Aurillac, Peter the Venerable, and St. Bernard, and the letters exchanged by Abelard and Heloise (the authenticity of which raises some questions) are famous.[72] Exceptions aside, these were still literary exercises on the part of men (or women) of letters, or even brief treatises addressed to a great personage and his entourage. Some "letters" do not even seem to have been sent to their apparent addressees, who thus become more like dedicatees. Sending correspondence posed a number of problems. The letters of Peter the Venerable were carried as opportunity arose by students, merchants, pilgrims, minstrels, and even great persons. On occasion Peter sent his correspondents a person entrusted with confidential information to be transmitted orally or who could supplement a written message with additional information and could receive a response. Should we find it surprising that the crusaders only exceptionally sent letters to France? In reality, if they had no model before their eyes even educated people long found it extremely difficult to put down on paper narratives or sentiments that touched them personally. The universities played an important role in private letter writing: they originated the *Artes dictandi*, the ancestors of modern epistolary manuals, which offered students examples for all the important events in life. These were still stylistic exercises, however, destined to make a good impression on a far-off relative financing the young man's studies.[73]

Writing nonetheless gained ground constantly. Its use spread in mercantile circles, where merchants occasionally added personal notations to their still stereotyped business language.[74] The great cities in Italy were already putting order into their correspondence (for example on the occasion of the fairs in Champagne), and the king of Persia granted free passage to

Florentine couriers in 1326. About that same time administrative correspondence came into being. Acts came to resemble and to be called letters
patent, letters missive, or sealed letters, for which the *Artes scribendi* offered
rigid models, imposing a *decorum* appropriate to every situation. This created a need for couriers to be sent regularly on public business, which led
to the rise of the postal service.

The church, a centralized institution with branches throughout Christendom, showed the way. As early as the fourteenth century the popes in
Avignon created a corps of couriers, horsemen and officials of fairly high
rank. The members of this corps were relatively few in number, however—forty or so around 1350—which meant that travelers were still
entrusted with letters and, above all, with answers. Next, professional
couriers appeared in Avignon who were paid by the trip or who worked
for one of the great commercial companies with which the Holy See maintained relations. This made it possible for a message to reach Paris from
Avignon in five or six days, Bruges in eight days, and Venice, Florence, or
Naples in from ten to fifteen days.

Other systems of communication arose. In France, by the late thirteenth
century, the University of Paris, which included students and professors
from all over Europe, had a service (also available to the public) for sending
letters and packages. Next, the courts and other juridical bodies used couriers to transmit the dossiers of cases transferred from one jurisdiction to
another. As in Italy, French merchants joined forces. This movement
reached its height in the fifteenth century, when Louis XI employed a large
number of horsemen—226 at the time of his death—and set up way stations along strategic routes supervised by functionaries who took the name
of *maîtres de postes* under the reign of Francis I. During that same period,
the Taxi family, originally from Bergamo, headed an organization under
the protection of the emperors that soon counted as many as twenty thousand horsemen and that served a good part of Europe.[75]

What were the relations between those who had mastered writing, those
who managed to write with some degree of difficulty, and the illiterate
masses?

A first reliable indication is in the connection between custom and law.
There were at the time innumerable customs that governed human relations within the various groups and communities. In the eleventh and
twelfth centuries there was a felt need to write down these rules. This hap-

pened first in Barcelona, then in Frisia, then throughout Europe. The first attempts to set down customs were made by individuals, legal practitioners for the most part; next, in the thirteenth century local or regional authorities ordered customs written down. Higher powers eventually intervened and written custom took on the force of law. In principle one could go no further, so customary law gradually "petrified."[76] As a corollary, the notion of "law" was recast. Under the influence of the Germanic invaders, the law had long been held to be immutable in the early Middle Ages. For the Germans, legislation consisted in reconstituting an order that the governing power served rather than created. Still, the Roman conception of law had not been completely forgotten in the Mediterranean world, and beginning in the eleventh century the Christian idea that sovereignty was a *ministerium* given by God favored a revival of legislative activity, in a world that no longer seemed totally static and in a universe whose order no longer seemed exclusively divine.[77] The need to control this shift dictated that new rules be established, and a fear of seeing everything change for the worse at the whim of events encouraged writing down the law. Henceforth the mission of the governing power was not only to defend the peace but also to govern and to legislate, and at a time when the revival of cities and economic difficulties raised juridical problems that had never been encountered before. It was not until the thirteenth century, however, that rulers began to express their will as it applied to all their subjects rather than dispensing favors or privileges to some of them. Law in France began to give priority to the monarch's laws over custom. Communications between those who made the law, using writing to pass judgment and raise taxes, and the masses that they were intent on governing was not without problems. The discourse of the law-makers, who had studied rhetoric, was primarily addressed to their peers; it was presented to others who might hear it as proof of a store of knowledge from which those others felt excluded. Administrative structures were weak, and solidarity among the dominant group often incited its members to twist the decisions they were supposed to apply. In principle the law was equal for all, but it became an instrument for inequality, as the history of taxation clearly shows.

The Italian cities devised systems for counting households and for assigning to each household something like a coefficient for estimating its wealth (Pisa, 1162; Lucca, 1182; Florence, 1202). Further progress was made with methods to count each family's movable and immovable goods (Toulouse, 1263), a move opposed by the wealthier families. Cadastral surveys appeared in the fifteenth century in Italy and in some cities of the south of France. In early fourteenth-century England King Edward I succeeded in making his subjects pay a real-estate tax proportional to their financial holdings. In France the size and the diversity of the French territory made the problem of taxation nearly insoluble. The attempts of Philip the Fair to establish a tax either on capital or on income (or simply by household) failed when his subjects proved incapable of the necessary evaluations. A census of households (still far from perfect) was finally achieved in 1328. The corresponding tax was eliminated by Charles V on his deathbed (1380), but it was replaced soon after by the *taille*. From the fifteenth century on, tallage was based on real property in the Midi, but northern France had a personal tax based on households.[78]

The chief question, in those days as in our own, was to decide on a tax base. Taxes in England were on an individual-quota basis and proportional to real-estate holdings, but fraud and dissimulation reduced the tax revenues from year to year. In France the taille was apportioned, and the amounts to be collected were divided among the *généralités*, then among the *élections*, and eventually among parishes. By using the harsh but efficacious procedure of applying collective responsibility in every community, the French governing powers made the collection of taxes easier but opened the door to all sorts of pressure and negotiation. Exemptions proliferated. The city of Florence succeeded in freeing its citizens from taxation by shifting the burden to the surrounding countryside. In England the clergy was exempt from the "percentage," as were the poor, whose numbers consequently rose with suspicious rapidity. In France, nobles and cities did not pay the taille, which became, as Bernard Guenée has said, an "execrated tax on the defenseless hinterland."[79] Writing was of course not responsible for all these social ills; all it did was help to spread them. What it comes down to is that the illiterate masses were the primary victims of a system that the use of writing had engendered.

A gulf was thus created between the "elites" who participated in written culture in one manner or another and the rest of the population. The relations between written and oral literature after this period are a particularly striking case in point. Written literature fed on oral literature: its composition and its manner of reading remained in great part spoken, but writing led its practitioners to break with the mechanisms of traditional transmission. In both France and Germany the epic disappeared when it engendered the chivalric romance. No return from the written to the oral seems to have taken place. This was true of popular tales as well, and the changes made when tales were written down are only exceptionally found in the tales that continued to be repeated orally up to this century. Except in certain regions of the Mediterranean where literacy rates remained low, oral literature thus tended to reflect only one aspect of society and to become residual, while people in "lettered" circles joined together to share the same reading matter and, later, to attend the same theatrical performances in symbolically closed spaces.[80]

We still need to look at one essential element: religion. Everything became more complicated with advances in writing. To begin with, because the church held that Revelation was not entirely contained in Scripture but also reposed in a living tradition that continued uninterrupted from the apostles.

Communication in the vast area of religion can be seen schematically: On one side there was God; on the other, the mass of the faithful. Between them stood the cleric, an initiate of a sacred language and an intercessor endowed with supernatural powers. Dogma—that is, the set of verities that were the objects of faith—issued from Revelation. It included both explicit and implicit truths. The theologians' mission was to clarify dogma under the supervision of the hierarchy, which drew conclusions from their findings; their debates were not to weaken the edifice of the church. The church was one, however, and the faithful participated in its life and in its evolution. Furthermore, love was the chief concern of the church, not theological dispute. It continued to draw enrichment from popular sources, as attested by the great number of cults, the invention of relics, and miracles. And in such matters, did not God prefer to address the humble? This meant that messages circulated in both directions. At the center stood the preacher, a man of several cultures, whose function was to make Sacred Doctrine accessible to all. One familiar aid to preaching lay in collections of *exempla* containing brief moralizing tales from a variety of sources, some from folklore (supernatural tales in particular), some of learned inspiration; the laity could also find edification in the painted or sculpted images in the churches.[81]

An organization such as the church could only be monolithic: as in all authoritarian societies, the Truth was one, just as God was one. But when bishops attacked one another, when scholars moved their doctrinal disagreements out of their own circles and appealed to a larger audience, when the clergy faltered or simply proved unequal to their task, or when any or all of these lost the ability to draw from humble sources of piety to guide and channel the aspirations of the masses, then heterodoxy threatened to crystallize and the seamless robe to tear. This was why compartmentalization was necessary and, as a last resort, censorship.

Censorship: finally we get to a topic that every reader of this book must have expected on first opening it. We need to go back quite far to see just what it entailed.

The most direct form of censorship and the one that strikes the imagination most vividly aims at destroying the cause of scandal, which means the speaker and the word, in the oral tradition, and the book after the coming of writing. The model that was always cited is in Acts 19. After St. Paul preached in Ephesus some of the Ephesians who had practiced magic piled up their spellbooks and set fire to them. This is censorship in a nearly perfect form. It is symbolic, first because it concerns practical works of an operative value that the fire turned into impalpable ashes (as it did many heretics and sorcerers); second because this was self-censorship and a ceremony was that intended to obliterate the works from memory, which is the highest form of censorship.

The Romans of classical times had used comparable forms of destruction against the Christians: the "traitors" (see the *Dictionnaire de théologie catholique*) were those who, willingly or unwillingly, turned liturgical objects or sacred books over to the temporal authorities.[82] When Christianity triumphed, the Catholic Church used coercion against the heresies that assailed it. After the Fathers of the Council of Nicaea condemned Arius and his doctrine (325), Emperor Constantine commanded that the books of Arius' sect be burned and prohibited the use of the term "Arian," replacing it with a term less shocking to orthodox ears, "Porphyrians." Procedures of that sort wiped out a number of heresies; many of the works of Origen, censured on several occasions, disappeared, not so much because they were destroyed as because their condemnation struck such horror and fear in potential readers that the works were no longer studied or copied.[83]

This was the beginning of a long series of book burnings. The most famous and the most massive during the Middle Ages were the pyres lit by the Parisian subjects of the saintly King Louis IX to burn Jewish books after the pope had anathematized the Talmud because it portrayed Jesus as a common criminal.[84] Such operations remained the exception, however. Normally censorship took other paths.

We are in the twelfth century. The West had once more begun to accumulate a capital of texts. More than ever the theologians' thought was nourished by the ancient philosophers, and Aristotle arrived, one volume after another, by way of the "impure" channel of Jews and Arabs and bearing their commentaries. The only way that right doctrine could be drawn from such instruments was by lengthy confrontation of opinions, which is what justified the *lectio* and the *disputatio*, the two main university exercises discussed above. In systems of that sort, the word is more important than the letter and the idea more important than the text. Scholars debated propositions, not books, and denunciation of adverse opinion was an integral part of a search for the truth. Denunciation became censorship only when it came from the ecclesiastical authority in one of its jurisdictions, and when this happened the aim was usually to correct someone's thought. It proved more efficacious to prohibit the teaching of a suspect doctrine or replace a teacher than to suppress a manuscript only some parts of which were blighted by error. When a manuscript was judged in error, the authorities simply attached a list of the suspect sections to the volume or marked the incriminated passages with a special sign, promising to eliminate them in later copies. The author himself sometimes took responsibility for making the necessary corrections in a text, as Gilbert de La Porrée seems to have been the first to do, in 1148.[85]

This system functioned nearly perfectly when Aristotle's *Metaphysics* and *Physics* penetrated into the West. Between 1200 and 1210 the bishops of the province of Sens, which included the capital of the kingdom, began to be concerned about the conclusions that certain masters of the Faculty of the Arts were drawing from these recently translated texts. They forbade them to be read (in the university sense) in public and private lessons, and ordered that the *Quaternuli* (doubtless the notebooks of a master, David of Dinant, who was probably also a physician) be brought to the bishop of Paris to be burned.[86] This censorship, which was confirmed by the statutes of the university in 1215, prompted a great deal of ink to flow. It was a benign censorship, however, to the extent that the incriminated works could be read and meditated in private, and they were even openly taught at the University of Toulouse between 1229 and 1245. When Averroës' commentaries became known, Gregory IX ordered a commission to examine what measures could be taken to permit Christians to study books that were not allowed to be taught, thus enriching their thought as the ancient Hebrews had enriched theirs with Egyptian learning. The affair was inconclusive, and the Faculty of Arts finally decreed, on its own initiative, that all of Aristotle's works could be put into the curriculum (1255). This created three opposing camps: the radical Aristotelians such as Siger of

Brabant and Boethius of Dacia, who became the champions of an autonomous philosophy not easily reconciled with Christianity; moderates like St. Thomas who wanted to reconcile all parties; and conservatives who evoked the authority of St. Augustine. To calm the dispute, the bishop of Paris, Etienne Tempier, published a list of thirteen propositions he judged to be heterodox (1270). On the pope's insistence, he then appointed a commission of inquiry, and on the basis of its findings Tempier published (in 1277) another denunciation of heterodox ideas listed in 219 articles. This condemnation, the most important in the Middle Ages, seems to its most recent historian, Roland Hissette, a hasty job inspired by the neo-Augustinians of the Faculty of Theology. It is unimportant for our purposes whether the censors twisted the thought of some of their adversaries or whether or not they were attacking St. Thomas. The measures taken by the hierarchy had attained tangible results. In the short term, the masters of the Faculty of Arts learned to distinguish more carefully between the content of the texts they studied and the conclusions they drew from them. The measures taken by spiritual authority, which expressed the theologians' mistrust of the intellectual domination of philosophy, had weighty consequences in the long term: their full effect was felt in the fifteenth century.[87] Thus, as long as books circulated among the learned the church held back its attacks or only made a symbolic gesture. When heresy threatened to crystallize, however, it attacked men.

Indeed, during the twelfth and thirteenth centuries vast spiritual movements were set in motion in the same mystical and prophetic current that launched the Crusades. Making their way along the trade routes, appearing first in commercial centers, and proclaiming a variety of objectives that often were pantheistic and nearly always anticlerical and antisacramentarian, these movements had as prophets inspired preachers whose only weapon for denouncing the visible and official church was the divine Word. It remains to be seen what they and their followers really knew of Scripture. It is not coincidental that the first form of dualism to appear in Europe—the Bogomils—originated in Bulgaria, a recently Christianized region close to Byzantium, where the Gospel had been diffused in translation into Old Slavonian (which, incidentally, was not the vulgar language of the land). In 1079, Gregory VII forbade the translation of the Bible into the vernacular in Bohemia, denouncing the dangers of free interpretation. For the Cathars, the Book par excellence was the New Testament (since they viewed the Old Testament as having been inspired in great part by the

Bad God). Among the Cathars, the Good Men, those by whom salvation came, were those who had the Book that contained the true Text (even though some of them were incapable of reading it, even in translation). They placed it, symbolically, on the head and the shoulders of the *impétrant* (the candidate) during their ceremony of *Consolamentum*. When they made converts by preaching or direct contact, the Cathar missioners were apt to lend the hesitant convert a volume to hasten the process. Similarly, the Cathars who preached the Good News were often escorted by a companion who read a passage from the Gospel on which the preacher commented. Identical Cathar propaganda pieces have been found in widely scattered places.[88] During the same period, Waldo, who came from a merchant background in Lyons similar to that of St. Francis in Assisi, preached from a vernacular translation of the Bible, and some illiterate members of his sect learned by heart what they could not decipher.[89]

One can sense the share that modest clerics (notaries in particular) might have had in all this—one example is the Authier family made famous by Emmanuel Le Roy Ladurie.[90] Clerics pose the classic problem of the possible connections between forms of learned culture and the culture known as "popular." The story of the Amalricians—the disciples of Amaury de Bène (Amalric of Bena)—as elucidated by Marie-Thérèse d'Alverny, is an enlightening case in point.

A dialectician who, like many of his contemporaries, knew how to apply the methods of logic and theology, Amalric of Bena quite certainly drew inspiration from Joachim of Flore and John Scotus Erigena when he gave the broadest possible interpretation to the notion of the mystical body of Christ. According to Amalric, every Christian should be held to be a true member of Christ. He was obliged to retract before his death in 1206, but his pupils had already spread his heterodox theories among the laity, winning over several dioceses from Troyes to Amiens. After the Amalricians had been denounced, due to an imprudent visionary, and their ranks penetrated by a spy, they were the object of intensive investigation. The records of the trial of some of their number show how theoretical teaching, poorly assimilated by only partially learned clerics, could produce strange resonances among the ignorant faithful who used what they heard to construct a religion more in line with their own aspirations and their mental universe. We can easily imagine the role played by conventicles in which the participants could air their thoughts even if they challenged the basic principles of received faith. To suppress this movement the church condemned Amalric of Bena's doctrine of love again in 1210 and removed his remains from consecrated ground. The *De divisione naturae* of John Scotus Erigena (a work more heterodox than heretic) was burned again in 1225, three centuries after the author's death. During this time, however, the doctrine of Amalric of Bena found enough champions among the learned to avoid new condemnations, but those who thought they could draw practical conclusions from those principles died at the stake or, if they retracted, spent the rest of their lives in prison.[91]

In the twelfth and thirteenth centuries, then, writing played only a secondary role in the diffusion of heresies. We do not even know, for example, if Amalric of Bena wrote his teachings down on parchment or if they were diffused orally. But it was already true that once the Book that transmitted the divine Word appeared in the vulgar tongue it was a weapon of redoubtable force that enabled clerics and semieducated laymen to demand from the learned the right to know and to speak. And the right to lead revolts against the established powers and authorities.

These demands could only grow as the use of writing increased. This is clearly visible during the second half of the fourteenth century and the beginning of the fifteenth, when the two first great modern heresies—those of John Wycliffe and of Jan Hus—got their start. Both ended in failure. Let us try to see why.

John Wycliffe (ca. 1330–84) was born into a family of modest means. After a long course of studies at Oxford he received his doctorate in philosophy, somewhat late in life (1372), and passed into the service of the king. England felt its position in Christendom was rather marginal, and the English hated the Avignon papacy both for its policies of centralization and for its efficient collection of taxes on English soil. Worse, Avignon was in league with England's enemies, the French. Already known for his anticlericalism, Wycliffe was sent to Bruges to participate in negotiations with the papal legates in an attempt to arrive at a financial *modus vivendi*. He then took to the pulpit to defend the interests of his Lancastrian protector, John of Gaunt, in some rather dubious causes. He proved a formidable preacher, but his attacks on the church brought him a citation to appear at St. Paul's before William Courtenay, his future archenemy and at the time bishop of London (February 1377). Things moved fast after that. Wycliffe published, piece after piece and book after book, the results of his meditations and his teaching in a series of hastily written and increasingly aggressive works. For the first time, a doctor elaborated a doctrine that counseled rupture. Above all, he denounced the failings of the church, corrupted since the time of Constantine by a search for temporal power, for having developed useless institutions and recommended sterile practices. A former nominalist converted to an extreme realism, Wycliffe attacked transubstantiation with particular vehemence. The consecrated host remained bread and Christ could not be physically present in it; he was simply inscribed in it, like a message on paper. Wycliffe mercilessly drew the consequences of his premises: Jesus could give himself only to the predestined, just as the Gospel could profit only the just. The church in its present state offered more evil than good. It could exercise only minor functions for the salvation of men, and since we cannot know to whom God speaks, the clergy should no longer hide Scripture but give it over, freed from its glosses and in everyday language, to the mass of the faithful. We can recognize in this language the servant of a king whose administration was increasing in efficiency. Wycliffe's emphasis on civil society, at the time in full expansion, is expressed in his proclamation that the active life was superior to the contemplative life and marriage to chastity. Above all, Wycliffe held that the visible church, which had become the body of the Antichrist, no longer had any connection with the community of the elect (the mystical bride of the Word), and that the church could be regenerated only by the temporal power, whose mission it was to make the law of the Gospel reign everywhere.[92]

The ecclesiastical authorities reacted swiftly. In 1377 the pope condemned eighteen articles drawn from Wycliffe's writings and demanded his arrest. He appealed to his friends at the University of Oxford, however, who concluded in his favor. The Great Schism saved him. Summoned to Lambeth in March 1378 by the bishop of London (the same Courtenay), he was invited to cease spreading false doctrines. The rupture came only in 1381–82, with the results of a university commission called by his enemies and a synod brought together by Courtenay. Forbidden to preach, Wycliffe retired to his rectorate at Lutterworth, compensating for his obligatory silence by a rage to write. After suffering a stroke, he passed on the torch (or rather, the pen) to his secretary, John Purvey, and died soon after in his bed. He was buried in holy ground in 1384.

The church's relatively mild treatment of Wycliffe can be explained by the university traditions of free discussion. It also shows the weaknesses of the official church. Moreover, Wycliffe had his partisans, and his enemies were aware of the importance of his early protectors. Courtenay avoided even mentioning his name in the condemnation of 1382. By that time, however, it was abundantly clear that Wycliffe's doctrine posed a threat to the established order. For years, in fact, poor priests, drawing their hostility toward the established church from the same sources as Wycliffe, went about preaching ideas close to those of the Waldensians, competing with the efforts of the mendicant monks. This is how the movement of the Lollards arose. Even more, 1380 had been the year of the famous Peasant Revolt, the occasion for John Ball's famous "When Adam delved and Eve span, who was then the gentleman?" Wycliffe immediately dissociated himself from this movement and seems not to have wanted any rapprochement with the popular preachers. He was certainly behind Nicholas Hereford's translation of the Bible, which followed the text of St. Jerome's translation almost word for word and was doubtless aimed, in its spirit, at aiding preachers and attacking the great lordly estates (not a total novelty). Above all an intellectual and called *doctor evangelicus* by his followers, Wycliffe was not eager to bring theological quarrels into the streets and marketplaces, and writings in the vernacular that have been attributed to him seem in many cases to have been the work of his disciples. They had a totally different attitude. Purvey, who gave a much more accessible translation of Holy Scripture, wrote a vast number of tracts aimed at a large public and drawn from Wycliffe's sermons. Most of the Lollard leaders, however, were modest chaplains, priests without a living, merchants of a certain substance, and artisans. One of these, William Smith, a vegetarian, an opponent of alcohol, and a self-taught man if ever there was one, learned to read and write late in life and wrote tracts invoking the Scriptures and the Fathers and condemning auricular confession, indulgences, and the cult of images. On the fringes of this world there were black-robed visionaries who proclaimed themselves "doctors of religion" and catered to the gentry or even to learned knights, some of whom owned copies of the *Roman de la Rose* or the *Poèmes* of Eustache Deschamps.[93]

Preaching was the best means for conquering followers, but many of the Lollards were capable of reading Scripture, works like the *Lay Folk's Mass Book,* and tracts. Writing in the vernacular was already frequent in orthodox circles, and here it became an instrument of propaganda and a tool for personal reflection. We often find references to gatherings in which the members of a household, joined by a few neighbors in the evening, listened while one of their number read and commented on the divine Word. It is no wonder that the ecclesiastical authorities took increasingly brutal measures. Inquisition commissions were set up in 1388–89 to seek out heretics and their books, while Courtenay pursued Wycliffe's disciples one by one. A good many universities abjured and profited from their abjuration, but resistance was stronger among the common folk. The Lollards went so far as to place placards on the doors of Parliament in 1395 summarizing their principal theses. At this point Thomas Arundel, who had replaced Courtenay as the archbishop of Canterbury, demanded that the monarchy decree that heretics would receive capital punishment. The measure was not passed until 1401, and William Sawkey, a priest, was the first to die at the stake. After that, Arundel launched (1407–8) thirteen propositions condemning unauthorized preachers, forbidding translations of the Bible without the agreement of the hierarchy, prohibiting the reading and teaching of Wycliffe's works pending further examination, and, above all, ordering the university authorities to inquire into the opinions of the members of their colleges and other institutions. In 1409, the commission that had been called in response to Arundel's demand condemned 267 errors in Wycliffe's works, which apparently were burned at Oxford the following year. These inquisitional measures made the Oxonians lose their taste for theological speculation once and for all. The Council of Rome in 1413 confirmed the condemnation of Wycliffe, and the Council of Constance ordered his remains removed from consecrated ground. His bones were thrown into the river that runs through Lutterworth.[94]

Wycliffe's movement had been doomed to fail from the moment the royal power joined forces with the church in 1382 in a move to avoid attracting contestation itself. In the end, the mendicant orders proved better armed to conquer the masses. Wycliffe's failure was the defeat of a counterpower that did not manage to impel recognition, primarily because the lay world of the written word had not yet acquired the autonomy that humanism was later to give it. Since they were part of the clerical world, the Oxford University scholars were doubtless poorly armed for drawing the consequences of the theological positions they had taken. The manuscript tradition was probably simply not enough to guarantee the coherence and unity of "activist" groups.

Be that as it may, by the end of the fourteenth century the true heirs of Wycliffe were no longer in England. His writings, carried to eastern Europe in the late fourteenth century by students returning home from Oxford, provided a doctrinal basis for a reform movement preached by no less a personage than the archbishop of Prague. Heresy in Bohemia found a leader in the person of Jan Hus. His movement was also the movement of a nation. I shall not repeat its history, except to note that it too ended in failure when the Council of Constance sentenced Jan Hus and Jerome of Prague to be burned at the stake (1415, 1417), after which came the Hussite wars and total collapse. Are we to impute this failure to the Czechs' isolation in a world unable, before the appearance of printing, to coordinate the heretical forces that were latent everywhere? This thesis has been argued a good many times. Since we cannot rewrite history, I shall simply pose the question.[95]

Five

The Arrival of Print

Techniques for the serial reproduction of multiple copies of texts by means of movable type appeared in Europe between 1430 and 1450, but comparable procedures had already been used in Korea for several decades. If I adopt the point of view of the West here, it is not out of intellectual shortsightedness but because it was from that part of the globe that typography conquered and imposed its logic on the entire world.

GERMANY'S MOMENT COMES

Renaissances are the daughters of depressions and crises, and they are brought forth in pain.[1] This was particularly true of the great Renaissance of the fifteenth century. Clouds had appeared on the horizon by the late thirteenth century. Were these due to demographic pressures that threatened an always precarious equilibrium in a "full" Europe? Were the looming misfortunes triggered by an abrupt change in climate? Whatever the reason, the first, still sporadic, food shortages began in 1305. Like the first ravages of the Hundred Years War (1337), they remained localized in France. Slowly, however, economic conditions worsened and everything seemed to fall apart: even ore deposits gave out in mines that had been easily exploited, and the mining techniques of the time were insufficient for pushing further. In 1348, when Genoese ships returning from the Crimea landed some sailors ill with the plague in Messina, it took only two years for the disease to spread to the greater part of the West. In the following years the plague continued to strike harder and harder, and although it abated in Germany, the Low Countries, and Spain in the late fourteenth century, there were parts of Europe that trembled for many years to come.

The age of Petrarch and Boccaccio was an age of anxiety. Boccaccio composed the *Decameron* in Fiesole, where he had taken refuge to avoid the "putrid miasmas" of Florence in the valley below. The population of Florence went from 110,000 in 1338 to 50,000 in 1350; the city then regained population slowly, reaching 70,000 or 80,000 around 1380. It took Europe until the late fifteenth century to fill in the gaps in its population. One result was a crisis in rural areas, in which mid-sized landholdings tended to fail. There were also wars for survival initiated by lords whose feudal revenues were sorely diminished and conflicts that were continued by profit-seeking soldiers of fortune who cared little for truces and peace treaties. The cities too were in crisis, and the dead were replaced by newcomers seeking an often illusory shelter within the city walls. Jacqueries and urban revolts of all sorts arose, led by sorcerers' apprentices who set "the small" against "the great." States invented taxation, but they were insufficiently armed to enforce a reign of order and justice. The church, to end the list, was also sick: the papacy was in Avignon and the Great Schism used up all its energies.

Despite all this, the peoples of Europe managed to live more or less as they had in the past and even to prepare the future. The deserted villages that made such a deep impression on the historians who discovered their desolation were more an indication of a new start than of depopulation. Infertile lands were abandoned; less wheat was produced and what was needed was imported at low prices from the Baltic while agriculture turned to more profitable crops. In Germany, Burgundy, and Italy, "strong" wines were produced, and the cultivation of flax increased in southern Germany. More livestock were raised: labor was scarce and more costly but husbandry required little manpower.

The woes of the times did not hold back technological progress. Quite the contrary. The fulling mill, invented in the thirteenth century, came into common use as workers became more scarce, and textile production techniques improved, silk weaving in particular. The mining industry devised methods for exploiting abandoned mines and opening new galleries, deeper mine shafts were dug that provided access to several galleries at once, and water was drained off by more powerful pumping systems. The production of iron was increased by improvements in smelting ovens that eventually led to the blast furnace. Procedures for rolling metals and for drawing wire were improved. Mines everywhere, from the Rhine to the Danube, searched out the precious metals that so aided the economy but also other metals such as the copper needed for casting cannons and, soon, for making engraving plates. In Styria an ore was discovered that contained a high proportion of copper mixed with silver-bearing lead, and in Nuremberg around 1425—not many years before Gutenberg began experimenting in Strasbourg—methods were developed to separate the silver from the lead and the copper and, perhaps, for isolating antimony.[2]

The economic downturn of the fourteenth century had incited the enterprising businessmen to defend their interests by perfecting their accounting methods and financial procedures. They found that commerce alone was not enough. Although the Medicis long concentrated on banking before cornering the market for the pontifical alum mines, Jacques Coeur in France, closely followed by the Fuggers in Augsburg and then Nuremberg, controlled what I am tempted to call an industrial complex. Similar figures, men with close connections with the mercantile world from which they had sprung, dominated the city-states of both Germany and Italy, and, in the courts of sovereigns whose realms were no longer expanding, their powerful presence challenged the feudal aristocracy.

In the early fifteenth century, when Europe was emerging from a period of woes that were felt more keenly in some regions than in others, the world was still made up of separate universes set off from one another by vast empty spaces. Africa, Europe's traditional source of precious metals, and the Americas, with their large populations, were still closed systems unknown to Europeans and unaware of one another. Western Europe received African gold and Asian spices and other valuable commodities through the Muslims. Separated from the great civilizations of the Far East by vast spaces or by rapidly shifting nomadic empires, Europe knew the East only through the reports of a handful of voyagers. The Mediterranean, once the center of a unified whole, had been split up since the seventh century and was bordered by three quite different societies, Muslim, Byzantine (with Slavic areas of influence), and Western European. Although there were contact zones and exchanges among them, these three cultures opposed one another more than they penetrated one another. Europe, finally mature, grasped the importance of Greek culture only after the emperor of the East, his back to the wall, had been forced to beg help from Rome, Venice had constructed its merchant empire on the debris of the Byzantine Empire, and refugees had flocked to Italy after the fall of Byzantium. Latin Christianity pushed toward the north and slowly eliminated paganism in Scandinavia, but in its bosom, from the Scottish Highlands to Sardinia, it contained small, self-contained, immutable worlds. Even more, although the peasants who made up the majority of the population lived under a variety of regimes, their horizon often extended no farther than two or three leagues from their villages, perhaps to the fairs and markets for which they might go to nearby towns. They knew the pope, however, and they had heard tell of the conflicts that rent the church. They also knew that beyond their lord they were subjects of a prince or a king, and in France as in England and soon in Spain, they became aware of being part of a homeland.

The ports of the North Sea and the Baltic pursued trade in a variety of ways, but even there the landscape was beginning to change. Bruges, the capital of the late Gothic world under the dukes of Burgundy, was the "Florence of the North." It had not yet suffered too much from the decline of the textile industry in Flanders (which was losing out to English and Dutch textile factories), it exported luxury items, and it was still a major business and commercial center. But its port was silting up and Antwerp was preparing to take its place. Henceforth the future belonged to the English and the Dutch, and they made life difficult for the merchants of the Hanseatic League.

France cut a pale figure in comparison. Wars lingered on, and the kingdom recovered only slowly from its wounds. France's Atlantic ports began to awaken, but in the interior large-scale trade no longer traveled its roads. The Hundred Years War had shifted trade routes toward the Alps and the Rhine corridor, and Lyons was not yet ready to be an important commercial center. It was Germany's moment.

Germany's power expanded rapidly in the fifteenth century. Mines founded its new wealth—mines in the Hartz mountains and in Bohemia, Hungary, and Styria. Luther was a miner's son. Cologne, the largest Germanic city of the Middle Ages and a city placed strategically near the Rhine delta, had stopped growing in the fourteenth century. Still, Westphalian roads started there, and its trade with Saxony and Silesia was increasing. Although the Hanseatic merchants no longer reigned supreme in the Baltic, the cities of southern Germany were growing rapidly. Augsburg, whose merchants had long traveled the routes of northern Italy, was first among them. In the 1320s, on the eve of the great crisis, the economy of Augsburg began to pick up thanks to the introduction into Swabia of techniques for weaving fustian, a less costly substitute for wool cloth made of a mixture of the linen that was cultivated locally and cotton imported from North Africa or Egypt. Social conflicts occurred in southern Germany, notably in 1368, but Augsburg patricians (unlike those of Cologne) made sure that the government was favorable to their business interests. During the fifteenth century the merchants advanced funds needed for the exploitation of the mines, and as lenders to the rulers they could buy metals at discount prices. Thanks to what they learned from the Italians, they mastered fund transfer techniques, thus laying the foundations of their later power.

Nuremberg became even more prosperous. It was the market city for Flemish textiles sold in central Germany; it traded in iron and in linen; it specialized in lending money at extremely high rates. In 1332 the Nuremberg merchants enjoyed special customs privileges in sixty-nine cities in Europe. In the early fifteenth century they increased their relations with Lübeck, then with France, and as far north as Livonia. Since Nuremberg lay at the crossroads of both north-south and east-west routes, its merchants profited fully from the flourishing mining activities that surrounded them. They became expert in metallurgy, thanks to their municipal ironworks, and they developed their arms manufacturing and specialized in hardware, cutlery, and, to some extent, goldsmithing.

Germany, a fragmented empire, had a dense but decentralized network of routes. A small number of men and commercial groups dominated the territory, and from the early fifteenth century Germany's prosperity spread to the West, as we shall see for Strasbourg. Because all new wealth, when it is based on effort and not on luck, engenders the form of capitalism that is intellectual activity, Germanic lands also experienced a remarkable intellectual revival. Europe was ready for Gutenberg.

CULTURAL MODELS IN A COMPARTMENTALIZED WORLD

It is difficult today to imagine what book culture might have been in societies that knew writing but not printing. Unlike our printed books, manuscripts were by definition unique. At the end of the Middle Ages an author often wrote with his own hand the presentation copy of a work he offered to a protector, and copyists, usually working on commission, grouped together in small, specialized workshops to reproduce texts for university professors, humanists, or pious laymen. The majority of the manuscripts in circulation, however, were collections of notes or copies that students, churchmen, or men of letters made for their own use, which subsequently passed from hand to hand. There was no "market," strictly speaking, for a new book, and each social group exploited the stock of works that the passing generations had accumulated in any given place. People usually were generous about lending the books they owned. New works circulated—slowly—among the author's protectors, friends, and correspondents.[3] The result was a variety of self-contained groups and cultural models that differed greatly from one epoch, one milieu, or one place to another. What were these groups and these models in the century of Gutenberg?

We need to turn first to the oldest libraries, those of the cathedrals and the long-established abbeys. There books emerged from the locked cabinets and conquered a place of their own after the revolution of the twelfth century. By the fifteenth century, books were housed in quarters that might be modest or cramped—over a chapel, for instance—but that were dedicated to book storage. Such spaces might contain hundreds of volumes arranged by categories in bookcases along the walls, forming a decor for the room that was already an expression of a cultural ideal. In the fifteenth-century frescoes in the chapter library at Le Puy, allegories of the liberal arts decorate the walls above books on the related subjects. Such libraries testify to the activity of venerable *scriptoria*. The chapter library in Lyons had copies of works that were transcribed there in the fifth century and annotated from generation to generation. The same is true of Monte Cassino, Saint Gall, and Reichenau. These basic collections included liturgical books, Bibles (glossed or not), classical authors, and works of the Fathers of the church. The humanists made their greatest discoveries in just such libraries, but we should not take too literally their explanations that they carried off precious manuscripts in order to save them from certain loss under the monks' negligent care: they needed to justify their thefts.

Many of these collections seem not to have changed for centuries. For example, the canons of the cathedral of Bayeux owned 74 valuable books carefully housed in coffers and 243 others laid out on shelves, but the collection gives the impression that the canons were unaware of Scholastic culture. In the Jura the Benedictines of Saint-Claude lived surrounded by liturgical works, Bibles, and the writings of the Fathers, most of them in extremely ancient copies. Some ecclesiastics seemed more open to newer ideas: the canons of Rouen Cathedral often bequeathed to their chapter the treatises on theology and canon law that they brought back from their studies in Paris. The same was true of the Abbey of Saint-Ouen, with the result that Joan of Arc's judges, who on occasion borrowed scriptural and classical texts, seem quite well educated. In 1480 the Abbey of Cîteau, which often sent its young monks to study in Paris at the Cisterican college, had a large and varied collection: 340 volumes kept in a room near the dormitory, 157 others in a nearby room, 748 more distributed among the choir, the chapels in the church, the deambulatories of the cloister, the chapter room, the schools, the novices' quarters, and the abbot's apartment. An inventory made in Clairvaux in 1506 lists 1,788 manuscripts (and only three printed works). This means that although some milieus were open to change during this period, others had closed themselves in as soon as manuscripts were produced in lay workshops rather than in monastic *scriptoria*. [4]

University collections had a quite different aspect. The largest of them, that of the Collège de Sorbonne, aimed at offering its readers accurate copies of the texts most useful to their studies, and they could be consulted at all times. An inventory made in 1338 declares that it had 338 *usuels*—noncirculating volumes chained to the reading desks lined up facing the twenty-six benches of the reading room. Among these volumes were grammars, Aristotle and his commentators, a few treatises on law (which was not the specialty of the Sorbonne), and above all many theological works—commentaries on Scripture, Peter Lombard's *Sententiae*, the works of the Fathers, relatively recent summas and treatises, and an entire series of collected sermons, since a theologian must know how to preach. A nearby storeroom contained a lending library—1,728 works (300 of them marked as lost)—that included roughly the same titles plus a few classical authors: Cicero, Valerius Maximus, Seneca, Solinus, Boethius, and the pseudo-Socratics. From the outset, the Sorbonne had received valuable manuscripts as bequests: Cicero's *Epistolae ad familiares,* Plato's *Phaedo,* and the *Elegies* of Tibullus and Propertius (of which Petrarch and Colluccio Salutati had copies made). The Sorbonne collection gave only a highly fragmentary vision of ancient thought, though, and it included practically no books in French, an errant *Roman de la Rose* excepted. For its time it was an exceptionally large collection: the libraries of the other colleges in Paris amounted at the most to a hundred or so books in the fifteenth century, and the same was true of Oxford and Cambridge. Hence university libraries provided a notably insufficient documentation that limited the horizons of masters and students alike. This explains why men of letters and ecclesiastics filled their wills with clauses leaving their friends and relations books. Books were working tools that, after solid studies, would provide access to honorable religious or secular careers.[5]

Most of the libraries of the mendicant orders were comparable to the university libraries. The Dominicans were fond of comparing their books to weapons, and they worked to give an exemplary organization to courses of study for their order. The novices and young brothers first received instruction in the monastery itself; they were then sent to interprovincial *studia theologica,* and finally, if appropriate, to a university. Each friar received a few basic works, as we have seen, before he left his province. Thus the Dominican (and the Franciscan) libraries were vast reserves of duplicate copies. By the same token, they kept to narrow areas of specialization. Their libraries in France and Italy only rarely contain the books of spirituality of the most illustrious members of their orders, although these same works can be found in female convents and among the Carthusians. The libraries of the mendicant orders also contained few works from classical antiquity.[6] One gets the feeling that certain prohibitions were in operation.

From 1350 to 1460 new models for libraries crystallized.[7] The oldest of these was the Franco-Burgundian princely model. It had been created almost from nothing by the sons of John the Good, the first bibliophile king of France, in the darkest years of the fourteenth century, when literary production had slackened. The three princes who were the most illustrious promoters of the library, Charles V, Philip the Bold, and Jean de Berry, shared their father's taste for rare books and fine illuminations. But the constitution of a *librairie,* at least for the first two of these men, fitted in with other interests. From the time of Philip the Fair a polemical literature had developed in France, and Charles V, who had had to take over the reins of government during his father's captivity (and who had to deal with Etienne Marcel) realized the importance of propaganda and the power of ideologies. His acts illustrate the problems posed by the growth of a secularized clerical culture in a society dominated by a feudal aristocracy. He gathered around him a team of translators, often illustrious ones—Nicole d'Oresme, Raoul de Presles, and the Carmelite Jehan Golein—so that he could add to the most famous national texts (the romances of the Charlemagne cycle and Breton romances, allegorical and satirical works, and pious tales) translations of Latin works of immediate utility to the king and his advisors such as Aristotle's *Ethics* and *Politics* and his *De caelo.* Charles V's collection also contained works of politics and astrology (in that age the science of predictions), some treatises on Roman or feudal law, *De proprietatibus rerum* (*On the Properties of Things,* a sort of encyclopedia of nature by Bartholomaeus Anglicus), the *Livre des profits ruraux et champêtres* of Pierre de Crescens, and multiple copies of Vegetius' *Epitoma rei militaris.* Housed near them were Plato's *Timaeus* and almost all of Seneca's works. In the religion section there were Bibles, liturgical books, the works of the Fathers, and above all St. Augustine's *City of God* and the *Soliloquies* attributed to him. For ancient history there were Livy, Valerius Maximus, and Flavius Josephus. There were also books of a more immediate interest: *Le songe du Verger,* an immense compilation treating current political and social problems, and a few long epics, *Florent et Octavien, Hugues Capet, Charles le Chauve,* and *Theseus de Cologne,* all of which served to provide the Valois dynasty with illustrious ancestors at a difficult moment in its history.

Thus Charles V encouraged something like a state humanism well suited to the spirit of the nation. Time has confirmed his choice, as witnessed by the long survival of the works he had translated. The experiment was cut short after him, however, and his library was dispersed under his son, the mad Charles VI. The library of the dukes of Burgundy, on the other hand, continued to be enlarged for more than a century. Lettered princes par excellence, the great dukes of the West brought "writers" to their court who had the combined the skills of the compiler, the translator, the copyist and engrosser, and even the illuminator. Such men translated works from classical antiquity and adapted the heroic romances, casting them in prose, bringing them up to date, and putting them to the service of the Burgundian cause, while ducal historians wrote chronicles to pass the glorious deeds of their masters to posterity. Thus the library of the dukes of Burgundy, like the royal library, had an important propaganda function and was central to a politics of munificence. The personality of the prince counted for much in the orientation of such collections, however. The collection of the dukes of Berry was primarily a picture gallery hidden between the pages of liturgical books. Charles d'Orléans preferred spirituality and poetry and King René, also a writer, poetry and allegory. Feudal lords great and small set out to imitate these models to the best of their abilities. One still cannot help being struck by how little French literature there was in French collections of the late Middle Ages.

Quite soon the merchant bourgeoisie in the cities of Italy, which was the most dynamic part of that society, understood that its children needed to learn to do more than to read their prayers and sing psalms, so they hired preceptors to teach what they considered indispensable: fluent reading, rapid writing, and fast and accurate counting. When the bourgeoisie took hold of power in the municipal governments, it gave the commune the task of organizing schools, and by 1338 Giovanni Villani could say of Florence, at the height of its powers: "The boys and girls who learn to read are about 10,000; the children who were learning calculation and mathematics in six schools were from 1,000 to 1,200; those who were learning grammar and logic in four great [more advanced] schools were from 550 to 600." When they came out of such schools budding young merchants honed their skills by working in the shops. While the merchants did their sums, first in Arabic numbers on loose sheets, then transcribed in Roman numerals in their registers, or while they wrote letters to their correspondents, messages arrived from the four corners of the earth exchanging news of wars or incoming ships, or organizing trips to distant places. On occasion a navigator might tell of his adventures: Christopher Columbus owed a good part of his store of knowledge and his intuitions to his contacts with the world of trade.[8]

Mercantile practices thus contributed to forging a new man, and business needs encouraged him to subject his existence to the operation of reason, for example, by adopting fixed references for measuring time since accounts started and ended at specific times. Clocks that rang at regular intervals first appeared.

The major traders and bankers were too busy for intellectual speculation, but they did not scorn it. They considered it the business of specialists—who necessarily were the men of letters to whom they had entrusted the administration of their cities. It is hardly surprising that Petrarch was the son of a notary in the pontifical chancery, or that Boccaccio belonged to a merchant family and himself at one point worked for the Bardi family; that, later, the "godfather" of humanism was Coluccio Salutati, who had a long career as a notary before becoming chancellor of Florence, or that Leonardo Bruni, who translated a number of famous Greek texts into Latin, later occupied that same post, as did Poggio Bracciolini, who discovered many classical texts.

The burghers' spirit of enterprise encouraged faith in the individual, and it led them to question their own reasons for action. In these rich regions full of the memories of classical antiquity, they saw their communes as the heirs of the ancient city, and they demanded lessons of universal wisdom from the classical authors. The promoters of humanism were less interested in reaching an understanding among specialists than in proposing a common ideal couched in a language that everyone could understand, a task made easier because their schools had never neglected the teaching of rhetoric. This was the only secret behind their enthusiasm for Cicero and their efforts to make their language a language of literature.

These intellectual leaders presented humanism as an abrupt break with a culture of their times that was too much under the influence of France (but what heads of a school do not affect noisy manifestos?), thus as a movement in continuity with the Italian past. The humanists were well aware that the Middle Ages had not waited for their arrival to interrogate classical texts, but they reproached the leaders of university culture with having consulted too few texts and texts too often corrupted by intermediaries, with twisting the thought of ancient authors in order to support their own doctrines, and even with being too often sastisfied with anthologies and extracts. Thus they set off to search the libraries of Europe for manuscripts of former times, and they uncovered a host of Latin works that had been forgotten or neglected. Just as Byzantium was crumbling, the humanists took on the task of restoring the heritage of Greeks letters, in particular by bringing their contemporaries the thought of Plato in the Latin translations of Marsilio Ficino, who worked under the protection of Cosimo de' Medici.[9]

Petrarch hoped to leave his books to an institution in Venice and thus to make them available to men of letters. The project came to naught, but Boccaccio bequeathed his collection to the Augustinians of Florence, and Coluccio Salutati completed this bequest. One decisive initiative was the renovation of the library of the monastery of San Marco in Florence, using the collection of the patrician and bibliophile Niccolò de' Niccoli as a point of departure for a collection gathered together by sixteen curators grouped around Cosimo de' Medici. This basic collection, which included a number of manuscripts of the great Greek and Latin texts, was installed in a graceful room with double rows of columns forming three naves. A peerless advisor was called on to classify and complete the collection: Tommaso Parentucelli of Sarzana, who, as Pope Nicholas V, later played an important role in founding the Vatican Library.[10]

The "canon" that Parentucelli established for the library of San Marco, which was to serve as a model for all later new libraries, gives a good idea of the humanists' vision of the ideal library. As tradition dictated, Parentucelli reserved the first two sections for Scripture and Patrology. Next came Philosophy and Scholastic Theology (which were by no means excluded), then Mathematics with Euclid's *Elements* and the *Arithmetic* of Boethius, then Geography with Ptolemy's treatise. Last came Humane Letters, divided into Grammar, Rhetoric, History, Poetry, and Philology. Only a restricted number of ancient authors were represented, and only five poets: Virgil, Ovid, Horace, Lucian, and Statius.[11]

There was nothing revolutionary in all this. The ideal that inspired this canon was primarily Christian; all it did was to make the collection less compartmentalized. The Viscontis did not hesitate to add to their collections the literary manuscripts that their French wives brought with them or had sent from France, and the Aragonese rulers of Naples added to their library the chivalric romances and the Provençal song collections that they had seized from their rebel vassals. But these princes of the Renaissance also showed their desire to complete tradition with the greatest possible number of classical tests, which eventually swelled the sections that we might call "techniques of expression" totally out of measure. Heeding the urging of their humanist friends, the princes often turned to a great Florentine bookseller, Vespasiano da Bisticci, who had agents on the lookout for texts all over Europe and employed a number of copyists to supply princely libraries: forty-five copyists worked to provide Cosimo de' Medici with the two hundred manuscripts he wanted when he founded the abbey of La Badia near Fiesole.[12]

Never had the adoption of a script been as charged with symbolic value as in Italy during this epoch. There too, Petrarch had shown the way. There is a famous passage in a letter addressed to his friend Boccaccio in which Petrarch explains that he was occupied with transcribing his *Letters*, "not in that loose and exuberant writing that befuddles the eyes and soon fatigues them, which is that of the scribes, or rather the painters of our times . . . but in another [hand], careful and clear, as if heedful of the sight, and neglecting nothing of writing and grammar."[13] Elsewhere the great humanist criticized the vertical compression of letters and the many abbreviations in the manuscripts of his time. Men of letters who deciphered Carolingian manuscripts were struck by how legible they were. Italians could do nothing to change the angular, closely spaced, and cramped Gothic hand of the theologians, but they always preferred rounder scripts closer to the Carolingian model. As Berthold Ullman observed, Petrarch and Coluccio Salutati, both of whom probably grew far-sighted with age, had reason to complain about some of the small-lettered graphic styles. Still, Petrarch himself always wrote in a rounded Gothic hand, and Salutati introduced only a small number of new forms, for the most part inspired by the manuscripts of the tenth and eleventh centuries with which he was familiar. The true creator of the humanist script was Poggio Bracciolini, working in the early fifteenth century. He merits the title of father of modern roman letters, and his friend Niccolò de' Niccoli perfected a somewhat slanted script that developed into italics. This was the rise of a script whose adoption became a sign of solidarity with the cultural program of its promoters.

These men had not servilely copied either the Carolingian letters or their eleventh- and twelfth-century heirs; rather, they improved them by introducing details from the Gothic script to which they were accustomed. Poggio's humanistic hand is more regular and more geometric than the Carolingian script; the ascenders are more regularly vertical and thick and the descenders have reduced serifs; the upper arches of the *m* and the *n* are slightly broken; the *g* is systematically recomposed to take the form it has in typography today; the *i* is more consistently dotted. All this led to a gain in legibility over the models that had inspired this script, which were in turn an advance over older forms of writing.

These innovators had before them a much more prestigious model for letters in the capitals of Roman inscriptions. They used mathematical calculations to analyze the ideal proportions of Roman capitals, and they used them as the capital letters of their new alphabet, with the result that their script combined (with mixed results) ancient capitals and artificially constructed minuscules, whereas the Gothic script was made up of a natural minuscule that, in its bastard form, prefigured the *ductus* of modern letters combined with an artificial capital letter inspired by classical uncials.

The humanists' innovations in the written aspect of the texts made even more sweeping changes. The Latin practiced in their times was by no means classical Latin, which meant that the humanists had some difficulty perceiving the exact meaning of many of the texts that they marvelled at but that were foreign to them—even when such texts inspired their own writings, at times felicitously. They picked out the faults and transcription errors in the ancient manuscripts they studied and they did their best to produce accurate texts, but their efforts were hindered by the lack of separation between words in the texts they read and by a punctuation system designed to guide the voice rather than to aid comprehension of the written phrase. In reaction they created some of the punctuation signs still used today. They invented quotation marks by borrowing from twelfth-century manuscripts the triangular sign that served to distinguish the text from the commentary and using it to replace the red underlinings of Gothic texts.[14] On occasion the humanists borrowed from Byzantine usages and picked up recent innovations to use commas and periods in the modern manner. Gasparino Barzizza seems to have been the first to use parentheses. Every man of letters had his own system, however, more or less inspired by that of his friends or his teachers, and we need to wait for the speed of printing for punctuation to become consistent.

The humanist movement could never have developed so harmoniously if it had not corresponded to the aspirations of the Italian elites. This was true of the patricians and the merchants of Florence, who, as Christian Bec has shown, at times owned a number of manuscripts: Bibles and missals, religious and mystical works, chivalric romances, but also such works as the *Divine Comedy* and the *Decameron*.[15] Florence was by no means exceptional, as the Sicilian example attests.

Henri Bresc has shown that in Sicily, although craftsmen and the more modest merchants owned only a few books, patricians and the feudal aristocracy at times owned twenty books or more, and physicians, doctors of law, and theologians owned more than forty books. Clerics oscillated between a canonical culture, a theological and philosophical formation, and an increasing sensitivity to classical antiquity, whereas patrician collections were divided between the law and a humanistic culture. To be sure, technical treatises abound in certain collections, which means that the law and (at times) medicine predominated. Still, most of these collections contained texts of Scripture, of the works of the Fathers, and above all, as in Florence, of St. Augustine, grammars, and classical authors. Finally, Latin culture did not totally eliminate chivalric culture in Sicilian collections, and of course Dante, Petrarch, and Boccaccio were always represented.[16]

If we add that recent studies have shown that libraries in Barcelona and Valencia show a similar distribution,[17] we can conclude that the merchants of the cities of the western Mediterranean combined a cultural advance with their commercial advance in ways that differed notably from libraries in France and England.

To return to France: the thirteenth century had been France's century of glory. The University of Paris reigned supreme in Europe, and the kings, like their English counterparts at Westminster, began to develop one of the first modern administrative centers in their palace in the Cité.[18] The notaries, secretaries, and magistrates who worked there revolutionized writing with the bastard cursive script. The woes of those times cannot be attributed only to the limited results of the cultural policies of the French and Burgundian rulers: there were structural reasons for the failure of those policies, reasons that still affect the way the French think.

France was less urbanized than other European lands, and an increased use of writing had not set off the same sort of revival in the educational system as it had in Italy. Lyons is a case in point. Lyons was a merchant city in constant contact with merchant cities south of the Alps, but the attempts of its bourgeoisie to develop elementary schools for their young and a *studium* to prepare jurists clashed with the positions of the church. French cities did not have "secular" schools, and French children continued to be educated as little clerics. Nearly everywhere, however, chapter schools offered secondary instruction. This was particularly true in Champagne, a privileged province, where there were *collèges* in Reims, Soissons, and Troyes. Masters, on occasion eminent ones, lectured on the elements of theology and law in Reims, a city that enjoyed special privileges and that welcomed the first French humanists. On the other hand, the bishop of Reims, Guy de Roye, opened a college in Paris for university students from his diocese, and regulations for the schools of Troyes show that as late as 1436 their course of studies concentrated on grammar. The college of Soissons was destroyed during the Hundred Years War. Hence most young townspeople had little schooling beyond the parish schools, which proliferated from northern France to Champagne and from Burgundy to Franche-Comté. Paris at the time had forty-one *régents* and twenty-two *maîtresses* (elementary school teachers) under the rule of a *chantre* (preceptor), as compared with only a dozen a century earlier.[19]

Thus an entire category of men grew up who, in principle, had received some instruction and who claimed clerical status, which gave them certain privileges, such as being judged by ecclesiastical courts.[20] Siméon Luce was the first to note, more than a century ago, that such men might have rather loose ties to the church: they were tonsured, but they could marry. Some became lawyers or scriveners, some were peasants, and some even exercised a manual trade. Some of them (it may be coincidence that they were almost all from Champagne) had astonishingly successful careers. One such was Nicolas, called "Coleçon le Crantinat," the son of a bondman of the lord of Baye. Enfranchised at the age of nine, he was tonsured and permitted to pursue university studies in Paris at the Collège de Beauvais. As Nicolas de Baye, he became archdeacon and clerk of the court of the Parlement of Paris. At his death he left not only valuable memoirs but more than two hundred volumes. The tax offices of Burgundy, which insisted on considering him merely an *homme de corps* like his father, seized his goods at his death, and his heirs could reclaim them only by producing the act of enfranchisement that the late Nicolas had had the prudence to keep, neatly filed among his records (Gilbert Ouy).

Another case in point is that of Jean Gerson. His father, Arnoul le Charlier, a free man, was a carter in a village near Rhetel. The care he took to give his children religious instruction makes us suspect that he was already a cleric. As for the future chancellor of the University of Paris, he must have gotten his first schooling in the primary school in his village. After being tonsured—"crowned"—by the archbishop of Reims, he was sent (at the age of thirteen) to Paris to the Collège de Navarre, which accepted "poor scholars" from Champagne (1377). His later career is well known.[21]

The church long gave such men a career. From the moment that the chancellor of France was a layman, however, dynasties of tonsured clerics sprang up. These servants of the state originally had no awareness of belonging to a separate social category, particularly since the sovereign gave and took away offices at will. At first, clerics who served the king pursued an ecclesiastical career at the same time. Secularization increased, however, because the king was intent on controlling his functionaries, and because it was in their interest to place themselves under his protection and safeguard, where they were not so easily dismissed. For quite some time the appointment of royal administrators alternated between designation and election, but eventually these procedures gave way to the buying and selling of offices, which quite naturally led to hereditary posts.

The king's notaries and secretaries were in constant contact with their colleagues at the court in Avignon, where the popes had established a large library and where Petrarch was often present. For such men Latin culture was a matter of professional competence, and fine style was a weapon, which meant that relations between them and the Italian men of letters were ambiguous. Paris kept its full prestige, and Petrarch, sent on a mission to John the Good in 1360, declared that he had come to France more prepared to learn than to teach. Seven years later, however, when Urban V returned the papacy to Italy, the French took that diplomatic defeat as a victory of rhetoric, and Petrarch piqued their amour-propre by proclaiming that no orators or poets were to be found outside the Italian peninsula. When Jean de Montreuil was sent with Miles de Dormans, the former chancellor of France, on a mission to Louis d'Anjou, who was fighting in Italy and was besieged inside Arezzo, he begged Coluccio Salutati, with whom he was negotiating, to send him model letters to untangle the nets of language for him, as for a newborn babe or a tame jay.[22]

Italian humanism soon penetrated France. In 1376–77, Charles V had Petrarch's *De remediis utriusque fortunae* translated, then Philippe de Mézières wrote a French version of Boccaccio's "Griselda" (1385). Next, Laurent de Premierfaict, a cleric from Champagne attached to the pontifical chancery, translated Boccaccio's *De casibus illustrium virorum* (1401) and the *Decameron*. After 1400 a French version of *De mulieribus claris* began to circulate, and later the French discovered the *Elegantiae linguae latinae*, which had an immense and lasting success. Still, it would be a mistake to reduce the movement that swept over France to a simple imitation of Italian models. French men of letters working at the Collège de Navarre in the entourage of Nicole d'Oresme soon set to work, and French scholars developed a theology founded on the reading of the Fathers. Etienne Gilson has observed that, if the Italians advanced from Cicero to St. Augustine, the French progressed from Augustine to Cicero. The French had different interests from the Italians, as Françoise Autrand has shown in connection with members of the Parlement under Charles VI.[23] Such men often owned sizable libraries for the time—over one hundred volumes—that reflect their concerns as jurists primarily preoccupied with problems concerning relations between the spiritual and the temporal. They may even have sought inspiration in ecclesiastical models for the organization of the state. They owned polemical books, but also books of hours, psalters, scriptural texts, Scholastic treatises, and the works of the Fathers. Their professional interests drew them toward rhetoric as well, and they often owned collections of letters or sermons. Some had more classical texts than others, but all were attracted to ecclesiastical history, which at times led them to Roman history. Above all, they were great readers of spiritual texts, from St. Augustine and St. Bernard to the lives of the saints by Jacobus de Voragine. Thus French learned circles form a precociously rigoristic "micromilieu" of an undeniable coherence.

Like all labels the terms "humanism" and "Renaissance," so often used in these contexts, invite misunderstanding. When historians discovered the "French humanism" of the late fourteen and early fifteenth centuries, they tended to see it as an "aborted renaissance." Guillaume Budé, the son of Jean Budé, royal notary and *grand audiencier* to the chancery, and grandson of Dreux, who had exercised the same functions, belonged to the milieu in which French humanism had developed a century before. After a brilliant start the movement had died down under Charles V around 1431. France was in crisis: after all, Joan of Arc was burned on 30 May 1431, and conflicting forces battered the land. It was only in the last third of the fifteenth century, when her wounds had begun to heal, that France reentered the European scene. Until that time, the Germanic world commanded.

From the late thirteenth century, the cultural system whose keystone was the University of Paris had begun to crack. The Dominican masters' grand attempts to unite natural theology and revealed theology into one solid synthesis prompted a growing number of reservations. Two English Franciscans, Duns Scotus (1266–1308) and William of Occam (1285–1349), encouraged by Oxford tradition to demand the certitudes of material evidence, reproached Thomism with taking probabilities as sure information and with claiming to reduce God's free will to rational laws. More radical than Duns Scotus, his elder, William of Occam consummated the rupture, scrutinizing with pitiless logic the abstract generalizations of his predecessors. Thus Nominalism took advantage of a period of disequilibrium to proclaim a divorce between theology and philosophy, encouraging a secularization of society, contributing to the liberation of scientific thought, and inciting the faithful to seek God by the paths of love rather than those of the intelligence.[24]

The decline of the University of Paris, increased use of writing, the formation of the state, and rising nationalism all urged rulers to create universities capable of forming the personnel they needed. Thus the twenty or so universities in existence around 1300, all situated southwest of an imaginary line drawn from Cambridge to Paris, were joined by some fifty new universities, at least half of them in Germanic, Slavic, and Scandinavian lands that until then had been blank spaces on the scholastic map. Unlike the older universities, which were usually founded in response to pressures from professors and students, the new ones were typically created by the secular authorities and subsequently approved by the papacy. This was the case in Prague (1347), Krakow (1369), Vienna (1364), Erfurt (1384), Heidelberg (1386), Cologne (1388), and, later, Uppsala (1477) and Copenhagen (1478). The new universities allowed impecunious young people to study closer to home, with the result that the student population in Germany rose from under one thousand around 1400 to more than four thousand in 1520. Furthermore, increased dissemination of university instruction encouraged both the expression of national opinions and the crystallization of heterodox theories—as with Jan Hus.[25]

At the same time, another aspect of the future was in preparation in the intensely urbanized region that stretched from the shores of the North Sea to the mid-Rhineland. It originated in forms of spirituality still present today and based on dialogue with God through images and books. Since the twelfth century, monks who were shut off from the world in their monasteries where they copied the spiritual writings of St. Augustine, St. Bernard, Hugh of St. Victor, or St. Bonaventure for their own edification had found it natural to jot down at the end of the text the reflections and meditations these works had inspired in them. These annotated texts formed new works that circulated, copy by copy, as if they had been written by the authors who had inspired them. This was the origin of a good many apocryphal works, the most famous of which are perhaps the *Meditations* and

Soliloquies attributed to St. Augustine, which derived directly from an abridged form of the *Confessions* of Jean de Fécamp (d. 1078) that continued in print form well into the seventeenth century.

City-dwellers came to feel that the traditional collective religious practices were insufficient, and the more devout among them yearned for an affective and personal relationship with the Savior for them too. Some also turned their backs on accumulating wealth and like Francis, the son of a rich Assisi merchant, chose the way of poverty. Pious associations, brotherhoods, and groups that rejected the discipline of the religious orders sprang up, at times giving rise to heterodox tendencies in their midst.

The mendicant orders had the mission of containing and guiding this movement. Their preachers played an essential and multiple role, teaching the lessons of the Gospel in simple terms, translating theological doctrine in ways that the faithful could understand, but also serving as directors of conscience for their sisters, the cloistered nuns, whose convents were hotbeds of mysticism. All through the Rhine Valley and particularly in Cologne a spiritual school grew up, Dominican for the most part and inspired by the teachings of the famous Master Eckhart (ca. 1260–ca. 1328), whose disciples, Johannes Tauler (d. 1361) and Heinrich Süse (d. 1365), left sermons and spiritual writings that circulated widely in both Latin and German versions. The Carthusians in Cologne, Strasbourg, Basel, and elsewhere were also active in the diffusion of this spiritual literature. The *Vita Christi*, a work that was to have an enormous influence and was attributed to one of their brothers, Ludolph of Saxony, was "launched" from the Carthusians' Strasbourg house. In France Jean Gerson combated the excesses of speculative theology and recommended to learned clerics that they take up mystical theology as well. Gerson wrote a number of treatises on doctrine aimed at the less-educated members of the clergy, and he exercised his moral authority to denounce deviate mystical currents and errors in doctrine. Gerson often sent correspondents copies of his works: for instance, he sent one bishop a manuscript of his *Miroir de l'âme* with the admonition to furnish all the parish priests in his diocese with a copy so that they could read it and comment on it from the pulpit instead of giving a sermon. The Carthusians of Basel, with whom Gerson had close connections, passed the same work from house to house within their order.[26]

In that tragic age when everyone had to be ready to face death at any moment, the spirituality of the laity was fed by images, but also and increasingly by the reading of pious works: the *Vita Christi* for the better educated, the *Golden Legend*, written toward the end of the previous century by the Italian Dominican Jacobus de Voragine, and, in particular, collections of prayers and books of hours from which the faithful read three times daily and that were so ever-present that some confessors held it a sin to skip daily reading.

Geneviève Hasenohr's studies remind us that ascetic literature in France developed enormously in the fourteenth and fifteenth centuries. Aside from the *Golden Legend,* the chief inspiration for the spirituality of the age, there were other works with an extremely wide circulation, to judge by the number of manuscript copies that have come down to us. Among them are *Le testament* of Jean de Meun (116 copies extant), the three *Pèlerinages* of Guillaume de Deguilleville (80 copies), Jean Gerson's *La médecine de l'âme* or *Science de bien mourir* (45 copies), and the *Doctrinal aux simples gens,* whose distribution was promoted by Guy de Roye (some 40 copies). Other popular works were those *Soliloquies* and *Meditations* attributed to St. Augustine and the *Sermon de la Passion* (some 30 copies). Added to these works were a number of allegorical texts about the Abbaye du Saint-Esprit and works to aid in the examination of conscience and preparation for confession. The laity were invited to practice the contemplative life in imitation of the religious orders, but they were also offered codes of morality and good conduct to sustain them in the active life. One has the impression that this flourishing production did not break down any real barriers. Gerson and the clerics who offered the laity works in the vernacular often seem unaware of anything they did not write themselves or that was not adapted from learned literature. This indifference (or ignorance?) seems tied to the conditions under which such works were produced. "Fine" manuscripts often came out of urban secular workshops under the direction of a stationer or were copied on individual commission in court circles. None of the works that reached the laity in France came from religious milieus or from the Brethren of the Common Life, as was the case in the Low Countries or in Germany, which means that many French spiritual texts seem to lack an institutional support or the backing of a great feudal family. Such works proliferated, but somewhat anarchically. Finally, although most of the manuscripts that have come down to us came from the upper aristocracy, the regular clergy, or the hospitals (where laymen and monks worked together), a certain number of manuscripts belonged to men of the law, to burghers, or to merchants, a fact that seems remarkable, given that a larger proportion of works from such laymen's collections must have been lost.[27]

This was the background of a devotional movement of exceptional breadth that arose at the same time as the development of mass education, starting in the Ijssel Valley around Zwolle and Deventer, two Dutch cities whose prosperity was linked to the textile industry.[28] The founder of this movement was Gerhard Groote (1340–84). Once his theological studies were behind him, Groote turned away from benefices and the contemplative life, preferring to preach, to denounce the vices of the clergy, and to work for the salvation of all humanity. He died young, but his friend Florentius Radewyns carried on his work. The Brethren of the Common Life that the two men founded was a new sort of confraternity that brought together clerics and laymen outside the monastic system, although the movement was backed up by a congregation of canons regular, the Congregation of Windesheim, created in 1387 in the monastery of that name, which often welcomed communities of the Brethren who wanted to enter the monastic life.

The Brethren and the canons regular practiced *devotio moderna*, a discipline and form of asceticism that concentrated on mastering the passions. Holding that the heart and the will can be educated, they preached forms of meditation based on readings. The Brethren copied and bound books for a living, and they moved on to produce works of their own, at first systematic anthologies of passages from works of the masters of spirituality, then original works, the most famous of which is the *Imitation of Christ*.

The Brethren of the Common Life spread their ideas by sermons, dialogues, books, and by example. If, like Gerson, they reacted against the intellectualism of the Nominalists, they nonetheless attached great importance to education, perhaps because some of them owed most of their knowledge to their activity as copyists and they were well aware of the lacunae in their own preparation. From the outset the Brethren had close connections with school circles in Holland. In 1374 Jean Celse, a friend of Gerhard Groote's, became rector of the school in Zwolle, which he made famous and which grew to have more than 1,200 students. The Brethren promoted school reform by introducing their own methods in a large number of schools in Flanders and the Rhine Valley.

Something similar was happening, as Paul Adam has demonstrated, in Sélestat. The Latin school there was under the control of both the parish and the magistracy. Reading, writing, calculation, and singing were taught, but also the rudiments of the *trivium* (grammar, rhetoric, and dialectic). Some students from Sélestat went to Heidelberg, where they met a young cleric from the diocese of Paderborn, Ludwig Dringenberg, a disciple of the Brethren, and they had him named rector of the school in Sélestat. Dringenberg accomplished wonders: he kept the previous manuals (notably, the grammars of Donatus and Alexandre de Villedieu), but he eliminated texts that he thought useless and shifted the teaching away from logic, glosses, and commentaries. He, like his former teachers, believed that nothing could replace direct contact with the texts, especially the works of the Fathers and of the authors of classical antiquity known for their moral elevation and their style. He interested his disciples in history, and he himself wrote a long poem celebrating the defeat of Charles the Bold, which makes him one of the founders of Alsatian humanism.

One should not exaggerate the levels of scholarly proficiency attained in such milieus. Nonetheless, the Brethren of the Common Life prefigured the modern private secondary school by dividing their students into groups of ten, practicing selective admissions, and forming eight class-levels. At times they had more than one hundred students in a school. It is easy to see why the people who made xylographic block books—booklets printed from wood blocks—and the first printshops so often produced elementary grammars, particularly in northern Europe, and why the Brethren themselves set up printing presses in their houses.

In the early fifteenth century, reform within the various orders of regular clergy spread throughout Germany, not without encountering tenacious resistance, however. Eighty "residences" of canons regular were affiliated with the Congregation of Windesheim, and many Benedictine abbeys awakened to the call of the Abbey of Bursfeld in the north and the Abbey of Melk in the south. Thus while the cities of southern Germany were enjoying prosperity, German lands as a whole became the scene of an intense effort to produce texts, as attested by the great catalogues, unfortunately still unfinished, of the inventories of German, Swiss, and Austrian medieval libraries.

To recapitulate: The Carthusians had created many houses in German lands, they copied a large number of texts for the glory of God, and they had thousands of manuscripts of all descriptions at Aggsbach, Salvatorsburg, and Buxheim, which at times they communicated to the outside world. Sisters and cloistered nuns, who did not always know Latin, built up libraries of pious vernacular works that might reach the lay masses, and on occasion they had workshops to do illumination, as did the Poor Clares of Cologne and the Cistercian nuns of Lechenthal, near Freiburg im Breisgau. The canons of Windesheim concentrated on copying learned works; the Brethren of the Common Life copied manuscripts for their own instruction, for the edification of their contemporaries, and to earn a living, using different writing styles for liturgical texts and vernacular works of "modern devotion." Activity in southern Germany seems to have been even more intense. The Benedictines of Saint Emeric, Tegernsee, and Scheyern employed professional scribes to copy sermons, theological and ascetic works, encyclopedias, and liturgical books. The library of Melk, for example, owned 794 manuscripts in 1450; at the end of the century, the monks at Tegernsee owned 1,794 manuscripts. Donations and bequests of books flowed into the abbeys of Saints Ulrich and Afra of Augsburg, Saint Egidius in Nuremberg, Michelsberg in Bamberg or Heiligenkreuz near Vienna, with the result that a number of religious houses east of the Rhine owned collections comparable, at least quantitatively, to those of Cîteaux and Clairvaux.[29]

There were difficulties: the copyists of the German universities, attracted by the concession of statutes modeled on those of the University of Paris, worked hastily at times and often produced inaccurate texts.[30] Furthermore, we do not know of great copying shops in Germany comparable to the ones in Italy. All that we know is that notaries and master writers in southern Germany worked to copy manuscripts on individual commission.

One way or another, the new elite gradually collected the indispensable works. Henrich Neithart of Ulm, for instance, began his university studies in Prague in 1391, earned his master of arts degree in Vienna in 1397, and then studied law in Bologna and Padua, receiving a doctorate in decretals in 1405. Over the years he served as a canon at the cathedrals of Augsburg, Freising, Constance, and Rich. During the course of his career he collected some three hundred manuscripts of all descriptions, among them a number of classical and humanist texts, which he bequeathed to the cathedral of Ulm on his death on the condition that they be housed in a small room over his family chapel. Or there was Amplonius Ratinck (1363–1435), who attended schools in Osnabrück and Soest before attending the universities of Prague, Cologne, Erfurt, and Vienna. He was named physician to the archbishop of Cologne, and in 1412 he traveled to Rome before becoming prebendary in Cologne, then dean of St. Victor's Cathedral in Mainz. In 1412 he founded a college at the University of Erfurt (from which he held a degree of doctor of medicine) and richly endowed it with books: 40 works of grammar, 37 of poetry, 27 of logic, 12 of rhetoric, 73 of mathematics, 63 of natural philosophy, 15 of metaphysics, 35 of philosophy, 100 of medicine, 16 of canon law, 6 of civil law, and 213 of theology. Among these manuscripts, which came from many parts of the German and Roman worlds (some from the cathedral library of Cologne), there were manuscripts dating from the Carolingian era. They helped to give Erfurt the largest stock of books in northern Germany (just as Prague had the most books in lands more to the south).

There was also Nicholas of Cusa, the most prominent man of letters in Germany in his time.[31] The son of a Moselle river-boatman, Nicholas studied in Deventer with the Brethren of the Common Life and in Heidelberg under Nominalist masters. In 1417 he left for Padua, where he earned his doctorate in canon law. In his career he was an indefatigable papal legate charged with promoting the religious reform of the regular clergy in Germany, a member of an embassy to Byzantium, one of the most heeded counselors of Pope Pius II, then, in 1449, a cardinal. This philosopher who was also a mystic and who left one of the largest bodies of works of the Renaissance took the time during the Council of Basel to comb German abbeys (Fulda in particular) to seek manuscripts of classical authors, as Poggio Bracciolini had done. Nicholas discovered twelve comedies of Plautus, Cicero's *De republica,* and books 1–4 of Tacitus' *Annales,* and he introduced his compatriots to Tacitus' *Germania.* In 1458 he gave his library to Kues, the city of his birth, where it can still be visited in a room in the hospital.

The city of Nuremberg, the cradle of the German metals industry, gives a good indication of the nationalistic enthusiasm that gripped the German bourgeois elite. It could boast of the library of the Benedictines of St. Egidius and of collections of equal size among the Franciscans and the Reformed Dominicans, who owned more than seven hundred volumes in German. There was also a collection of manuscripts in the New Hospital, and increasing numbers of works distributed among the parish churches. In 1446 The church of St. Sebald, for example, received a bequest of over two hundred volumes from the parish priest, Albrecht Fleimann. A number of chapels also had manuscript collections.

This was not enough, however, to satisfy a city whose administration already included well-informed humanists. In 1429–30, the magistrates in the City Hall began to plan another library. In 1443 a city judge who had studied in Prague bequeathed a sizable collection of juridical and religious texts to the new library. At about the same time Hartmann Schedel, who was born in Nuremberg in 1410, studied at the University of Leipzig, then studied medicine in Padua and became the personal physician of Frederick II of Brandenburg, of the bishop of Utrecht, and eventually of the bishop of Augsburg, was the central figure in a circle of men with a passionate interest in classical antiquity. A cleric and celibate, Schedel left his books to his nephew, also named Hartmann (1440–1516), who followed in his uncle's footsteps by compiling an enormous dossier of materials on which he based his *Nuremberg Chronicle*, the most famous incunablum. This documentation, which was bequeathed to the city in the age of Dürer and included nineteen thousand iconographic items, quite naturally found its niche in the City Hall. Thus immense amounts of material were accumulating in the century of Gutenberg and in the land in which the arts of engraving and printing were born.[32]

When Gutenberg began working in Strasbourg around 1434, the English had not yet been totally chased out of France. Byzantium fell twenty years later (1453), completing the amputation of the eastern half of Christendom. In the West, the unity of the church seemed nearly reestablished. Epidemics had finally been stifled, but they had left a good many regions bled dry. There were signs of new life in the western Mediterranean, however, and on the Atlantic coasts of the Continent. Southern Germany was waking up. Still, the revival was to become evident and universal only during the latter part of the century.

Writing was making indisputable progress, however, first in Italy, but also in England, where libraries were being founded, and in German lands and among the Slavs. At the same time, culture remained as compartmentalized as ever. Everyone drew on common sources of ancient literature, both pagan and Christian, and on a common liturgical and spiritual tradition, a common chivalric culture, and a common university tradition. Still, the various national and linguistic entities lived as if by different clocks, each seeming to follow its own model, as we have seen concerning education. Moreover, each milieu seemed closed in on itself, living in a world apart; each had also woven a system of references reaching beyond regional barriers. This was true, for example, of the small and very international world of the chanceries, of the aristocracy, and of chivalry, but it was also true of the various worlds of the monastic orders. I need not recall that the elites of that age moved about ceaselessly and that roads throughout the Continent were traveled not only by soldiers, adventurers, and merchants, even by artists and engineers, but also by churchmen. For the businessman and the painter, Bruges was comparable to Florence, if not to Lübeck or Barcelona (despite obvious differences in those cities). Similarly, masters and students found the same climate in university cities everywhere, and all ecclesiastical dignitaries of any importance went to Rome once the papacy was reestablished there.

Did the need to break down barriers that was keenly felt in a Germany catching up culturally engender printing there? Or was the invention of the art of typography an integral part of the technological progress that lay behind that catching-up process? This is the question to which we need to turn next.

TECHNOLOGICAL INNOVATIONS

One cannot separate the history of the techniques whose invention is attributed to Gutenberg from the history of the inventions that preceded or accompanied those same technological advances and whose origin raises closely related questions.

The first of these technologies is paper.[33] Invented in China and adopted by the Arabs in the eighth century, paper spread with Islam between the ninth and the eleventh centuries along the southern shores of the Mediterranean.[34] Paper penetrated into Muslim Spain by way of Cordoba and Toledo. Játiva, near Valencia, became an active production site at least by the twelfth century. Catalonia, an industrial region with relations with Italy, became an important center for the export of paper.

For information on how the Arabic and Spanish papers were made, we need to turn once more to the description of Mu'izz ibn Badis (1007–61), whose treatise has come to us in two slightly different versions, somewhat modified during the twelfth century. The raw materials used were hemp or linen, either in the natural state or in the form of used cordage and, most probably, rags. When the ropes had been untwisted, they (and the other materials) were cut up with scissors and the resulting pieces were put to soak in a lime solution, then rinsed clean and dried in the sun. This pulp was next placed in a mortar and carefully mashed, and the resulting slurry was transferred to a large basin and mixed with water. The papermaker then used a frame lined at the bottom with split reed stalks, on occasion tied to one another with horsehair, to dip out and spread a portion of this mix. When the water drained off, the resulting sheet was sized with a flour and starch coating to prevent it from soaking up ink.

The quality of the resulting product, which was very white and somewhat puffy, depended on the care and the skill of the papermaker. Papers sold in Bagdhad, Damascus, or Alexandria were reputed to be better than those made in the western Mediterranean. As in the East, Western papermakers lived grouped together in villages, and they supplied an enormous market that included the Byzantine Empire, whose chancery adopted the new material even as early as the mid-eleventh century. What is surprising is the complexity of the operations demanded by these techniques, which craftsmen never seem to have improved on, except perhaps in Spain, where mills and millstones were sometimes used to break down the rags into pulp, and where in certain cases the bottoms of the forms were reinforced with metal wires.

During that same period, the use of writing grew spectacularly in Europe, particularly in Italy. Paper was first used there in regions that had contacts with the Arab world such as Sicily, where first the Norman then the German chanceries continued a custom that may have gone back to the Muslim occupation of the late eleventh century. In the twelfth century Genoese notaries followed their example. At that point, Italian industrialists got to work. Around 1210 Arabic paper was imitated near Genoa, but it was above all in Fabriano that Western papermaking techniques were developed.[35] Situated in central Umbria, not far from Ancona, in a basin bordered by hills whose streams flowed into the Giano River, Fabriano owed its first prosperity to the forges that sprang up along the banks of the river. Were the papermaking procedures that appeared there borrowed from the Orient, thanks to contacts made during the First Crusade, as has often been imagined? Or were they perfected by local metallurgists with the backing of businessmen in the aim of competing with the Arabic and Spanish papermakers? Whatever their origin, an impressive number of innovations were realized in that microcosm between 1240 and 1280.

The innovations in papermaking that can be attributed to Fabriano are:

1. The pulping process. The Fabriano papermakers utilized water power to turn paddle wheels connected with geared camshafts that ran batteries of pounders reinforced with studs of various shapes depending on exactly how the pulp was to be treated. Given that Fabriano was also famous for its nails, tacks, and studs, it is obvious that these processes were a local innovation.

2. The form. The Fabriano papermakers replaced the bamboo used in the Far East and the reeds used for Arabic paper with brass wire so fine that it took tens of meters of it to line each form (thus implying sophisticated techniques of wire manufacturing).

3. Watermarks. It is not known whether the zigzag markings observable in certain Spanish papers were early watermarks. In any event, the first known real watermark (a small design in the paper made by attaching

shaped brass wire to the sheet frame) appears in paper made in Bologna in 1282 by an artisan from Fabriano.

4. Sizing. Fabriano papers were sized with animal sizing (gelatin), which gave a smoother surface than vegetable glue made of flour and starch.

The Fabriano papermakers were soon doing considerable business. Paper mills of the same type soon appeared in Bologna, then in Amalfi, Battaglia, Treviso, Padua, Pignerolo, Foligno, Sallo, and Colle. By the fourteenth century raw materials—cordage and rags—had become scarce in these early centers of paper production. The Senate of Venice, the Republic of Florence, and the Signoria of Genoa reserved to their own compatriots and their suppliers the right to collect rags in their territories. The products of these paper mills were actively traded by Lombard and Piedmontese merchants. They gave Spanish paper keen competition, even in southern France and in Spain itself, and paper could be found everywhere in the Mediterranean basin and even in northern Europe. These same traders encouraged the creation of paper mills around Avignon when the popes resided there.

Toward the middle of the fourteenth century, however, Champagne became active as a center of papermaking. The high calcium content of the local water probably made the process more difficult, but Paris was nearby, with its administrative offices, its university, and its abundant supply of rags, and when traders deserted the fairs of Champagne it did not stop papermakers in Troyes from taking over the paper market in the Low Countries. In the fourteenth and fifteenth centuries new paper mills were created all over France, first around Paris in Saint-Cloud and Essonnes, but also in Franche-Comté, in the Barrois, the Vosges, and in Auvergne, as well as in the Beaujolais and the Angoumois. The French paper industry, dominated by a handful of great traders who advanced the necessary funds to the papermakers and distributed what they produced, reigned supreme in Europe until the late seventeenth century.

As early as the late fourteenth century, however, the Germans set up paper mills of their own. In 1390 a powerful Nuremberg entrepreneur named Stromeyr organized a complex for making paper at the gates of the city, and it was followed by similar enterprises in Ravensburg (1393–94), Chemnitz (1408–25), Strasbourg (1445), and Basel. Brabant and Flanders had paper mills in the late fourteenth century, as did much of eastern Europe, England (in 1490), Austria (in 1498), and the northern Low Countries (in the sixteenth century).

The importance of this movement can hardly be exaggerated. Before paper became available, the hides of a veritable herd of young animals were required to make a single *in-folio* volume. After the fourteenth century, when the West had access to a writing material in seemingly unlimited quantities, the way was open for printing.

This revolution had its source in a movement toward industrial use of hydraulic power, and it seems to have been linked with progress in metallurgy. As is often the case, the techniques that were developed in Fabriano were hardly modified for several centuries. Toward the end of the seventeenth century, however, the Dutch invented a more vigorous and faster pulping process by fitting cylinders with cutting edges and using the wind power of the windmills of their flat land to turn them at.high speed in metal-reinforced vats. The French paper industry lost its supremacy, in part through the flight from France of large numbers of Protestant workers, in part through the monarchy's policy of imposing a return to traditional ways of making paper. The paper industry in France caught up only in the age of the Montgolfier brothers, whose ascents were made in paper balloons. On the eve of the French Revolution demand for paper was growing, and a bookkeeper for Diderot, Nicolas-Louis Robert, invented the first machine that produced paper in continuous sheets. This machine was later powered by a steam boiler, but the production of continuous-sheet paper spread only slowly, following demand in the early nineteenth century.[36]

When industrial methods could be used to produce a writing material—paper—an obvious next step was to reproduce images and texts in multiple copies. The Chinese had invented several ways to do this. The texts of their classics were customarily engraved on steles, as were inscriptions to commemorate a man or an event, and paper rubbings from these inscriptions were at times offered for sale. The Chinese also imprinted engraved seals into wax or on wet clay surfaces, first in intaglio, then, after ca. 500, in relief, and they also reproduced images and spells on silk and later on paper. The Chinese use of printed charms is at times surprising. The *Suishu*, a history of the Sui dynasty (581–617) written in the second quarter of the seventh century, tells of Taoist priests who printed charms bearing images of the constellations, the sun, or the moon, holding their breath while they did so to cure the sick. Buddhists thought that making multiple images—including statuettes of Buddha himself—was a way to

gain merit. Finally, we know that the Japanese empress Shōtoku attempted
to win the support of Buddhist monks during a revolt, perhaps in 764, by
ordering a million miniature pagodas made, each one of which contained
dharani (charms) printed on a paper 57 × 5.5 cm. that was rolled up to
form a small scroll. The technique of printing booklets from wood-blocks
(perfectly suited to an ideographic writing system) developed somewhat
later, reaching its first height in the twelfth and thirteenth centuries. Gigantic production figures could be realized with woodblocks: the bibliography
of books published in Japan before 1867 includes some six hundred thousand items, a number greater than all printed editions in any major European land of the time. It was also a procedure that permitted an image and
text to be printed together, unlike the typographic technique that triumphed in the West.[37]

Did the East teach the West the art of wood engraving? Or did the West,
which had excellent wood sculptors, simply reinvent a process that came
quite naturally? In any event, engraved wood blocks were used very early
in Europe for printing textiles, first with repeating motifs, then, from the
fourteenth century, with scenes, and this process seems to have been transferred without difficulty from one material to another to make paper
prints. Whatever the case, the first woodcuts on paper bearing a date go
back to the years from 1417 to 1437. A good many archival documents in
Italy, France, the Low Countries, and above all Germany mention printers
and their like (*Drucker, Briefdrucker, Formschneider*) or playing-card makers,
which indicates that the new technique was already quite widespread.

Given that each woodcut could print thousands of copies before it
showed too much wear to be usable, prints must have been produced in
enormous quantities and been quite common in their day, making the few
that have come down to us all the more exceptional. Still, we have some
ten thousand different pieces: they were glued to the covers of small boxes,
used, with other papers, to pad book bindings, used to illustrate manuscripts or printed pamphlets, hung on the walls of houses and preserved
by collectors in the past. Eight-tenths of these prints represent religious
subjects: crucifixions, scenes from the life of Jesus, Madonnas of all sorts,
indulgence themes like the Holy Face, the Mass of St. Gregory, and so on.
Above all we have confraternity images of travelers' patron saints like St.
Christopher or healing saints like St. Roch and St. Sebastian. Secular pieces
included playing cards, but also prints that depicted the Nine Worthies (*les
Neuf Preux*), who were extremely popular at the time, allegories on death

(*memento mori*), and the Ages of Man. Toward the end of the century, there were also tables showing how to recognize counterfeit coins, as well as satirical images. [38]

These woodcuts have often been studied; they present difficulties of interpretation that can be just as mysterious as their origin. Some have defied scholars: for example the same saintly abbot with his fingers pierced by leathermakers' awls has been identified in Dijon as St. Benignus, in Picardy as St. Quentin, in the Tyrol as St. Cassian, and in Westphalia (perhaps) as St. Erasmus. Style and provenance in these ceaselessly copied documents, and even the watermarks, which normally point to paper mills of the east of France or from Germany, can only support guesses. The most one can say is that many of these images came from monasteries in Bavaria (Reichenhall, Tegernsee, Ebersberg), in Upper Swabia (Buxheim, Inzighofen), and in Austria (Mondsee), although they may simply have been conserved with greater care there than elsewhere, and that they bear legends written in Latin, Flemish, and French attesting to an extremely wide distribution throughout central Europe.

Thus the first woodcuts may have been diffused from monasteries and pilgrimage sites, but the rise of wood engraving is quite obviously connected with the rising fortunes of the mercantile cities, where image-cutters, affiliated with the carpenters' and cabinetmakers' guild, may have found their best customers in confraternities. There is nothing surprising about this form of propaganda. Johan Huizinga's classic *Waning of the Middle Ages* has shown that manifestations of piety and devotional exercises multiplied increasingly toward the end of the Middle Ages. Men of that time wanted to give religious things a specific figuration that could be imprinted onto the popular mind like "pictures clearly outlined and vividly coloured." They nourished their yearning for sacred things with ultrarealistic representations, for instance of cadavers, that encouraged them to consider the fragility of human life. Thought was crystallized in images, aided by the preaching of the mendicant friars, who memorized their sermons with the aid of the arts of memory and sprinkled them with concrete exempla. People felt the need to give the sacred a material form, even at the risk of rigidity, in an age in which easel painting and tapestry tended to individualize and secularize representation for the wealthy, while the bourgeois, the clergy, and craftsmen used woodcuts to decorate their walls or their household objects. There was a proliferation of images that the most lucid theologians—Pierre d'Ailly, Nicholas of Clémanges, or Gerson, for example—often denounced as excessive. Sacred symbols may have been cheapened, but the image was ubiquitous.

Engravers soon put texts into their prints: phylacteries bearing words spoken by the personages they depicted or brief legends similar to the ones in stained-glass windows or frescoes. As early as the fourteenth century an increase in individual piety and a taste for images had created a demand for small, mass-produced illustrated religious manuscripts.[39] Naturally, wood engravers imitated works of this type in block-books of their own.

If we examine the corpus of xylographic booklets from the point of view of their function, we would have to mention first the single sheets and small books aimed at teaching prayers and the commandments. Thus there is a *Decalogue* showing a barefoot Carmelite preaching a sermon, an *Exercitium super Pater Noster* in which an angel (*Oratio*) is teaching a young friar the phrases of the Pater Noster, each one of which is illustrated and explained with a maxim or two taken from the *Pomerium* of Henri Bogaert, a Brother of the Common Life from the monastery of Groenendael. In a somewhat different spirit, there is the *Ars memorandi Novum Testamentum*, which probably originated in southern Germany for use in Bavarian monasteries and which employs all the resources of the ancient arts of memory, following the recommendations of St. Thomas. On one page it gives the titles of various episodes from the New Testament and on the facing page the symbol of one of the Evangelists surrounded by objects as a help in memorizing the episode (one such was a bucket to recall the story of the Good Samaritan).

Some of these booklets probably served as First Communion gifts, but they were also pedagogical materials for use in the schools, and even ways to explain a sermon. As such, they were comparable to the printed booklets studied by Paul Perdrizet. First came the illustrious *Biblia pauperum* ("The Bible of the Poor," an expression created by bibliophiles of the eighteenth century) and the *Speculum humanae Salvationis*. In both cases an image that used the layout of the twelfth-century Mosan enamels commented on a scene from the New Testament and showed how it was prefigured in the Old Testament. Neither of these works was totally new. The Bible of the Poor had been widely distributed in manuscript form in Germany from the early fourteenth century, while the *Speculum humanae Salvationis*, which arose in the fourteenth century in Swabia or in Alsace, in circles close to the Dominicans, may have been the work of Ludolph the Carthusian.

These two booklets were decorated with pen drawings. The *Ars moriendi,* which had an immense success, first as a block-book and then in printed form, came into being to illustrate a text known in three hundred manuscripts and only became an album of images after the appearance of engravings.

All these works seem to have been produced originally for students preparing for the clergy, for clerics (who may have used them in missionary work), or for pious laypeople. They included the *Defensorium inviolatae virginitatis Mariae,* a work inspired by a Dominican from southern Austria, Francesco Rezzano; the *Confessionale,* which was produced for the instruction of confessors; and a good many Passions, many of them published in Germany and which often included litanies and prayers for the canonical hours. Other booklets were produced for pilgrimages: there was a *Vita sancti Meinardi* for the pilgrimage to Einsiedeln, near Strasbourg, the *Vita sancti Servatii* for the pilgrimage to Maastricht, and a *Mirabilia Romae* for the many pilgrims who went to the Eternal City.

Some of these block-books, often from France, reflect somewhat more literary interests. There is a handsome *Cantique des cantiques,* and the famous *Apocalypse figurée,* which had circulated in a number of illustrated manuscripts, one of which was in the library of Charles V and another of which inspired the famous tapestries of the Apocalypse in Angers. Finally, there were the *Histoire des Neuf Preux,* printed on three large sheets, the *Oracles des sibylles sur la Nativité,* the *Passion,* and a number of calendars and astrological almanacs published everywhere from Germany to Lower Brittany, some of them presented as the work of famous professors to stimulate sales.

For a long time, scholarly opinion thought that these xylographic block-books preceded the first printed books. Today however, an examination of watermarks indicates that their moment of greatest popularity was after 1455, which means that they would have been a response on the part of wood engravers to the appearance of printing. I shall return to the question.

During this same period new types of prints were produced by other engravers trained as goldsmiths and familiar with the traditional graving and chasing tools of that profession.

The least common and perhaps the latest in date of these new techniques was cribbling, or giving relief to the printed portion of a print by punching light marks on the plate that showed as white dots in the finished piece. As with wood engraving, the metal engraver removed what he wanted to leave blank and left the lines or surfaces that would receive the ink. This procedure may seem perfectly logical, but it works the wrong way for a metal plate, which does not take ink easily and is hard to engrave. The artist used a burin to trace white lines on a black background, and he used stamps for details like small flowers or crosses that he wanted to make stand out in white. One could, of course, make a "positive" (black on white) image by doing just the opposite, carving out large surfaces and leaving fine lines, but that took a great deal of work. Hence most of the prints made with this technique have a nocturnal look to them even when the drawing is fine.

A much more important development was the invention in the mid-fifteenth century of copperplate engraving. Here the engraver took a copper plate and used a burin to incise thin lines that would receive ink. According to Max Lehrs' catalogue, 3,100 such engravings have come down to us, some 600 of which are signed with initials or a monogram. This process, perfected by goldsmiths and metal chasers, who long remained specialists in the technique, was used more for decorative motifs or works of art that circulated within a relatively refined public than it was for pious images.[40]

The origin of the first copperplate engravings is perhaps less mysterious than that of the earliest woodcuts, but it still poses a problem. The oldest identifiable master seems to have been the so-called Master of the Playing Cards, whose wild-looking men, women, plants, and animals reveal the hand of a talented draftsman. The presence of cyclamens and the watermarks in the sheets that have come down to us suggest that these engravings were made in the Lake Constance region, the place of origin, somewhat later, of the prolific "Master E. S." When we note that a *Flagellation of Christ* by an artist of the school of the Master of the Playing Cards is dated 1447, we can suppose that copperplate engraving arose in the area of the upper Rhine, and from there spread both down the Rhine and south to Italy.

But why did this new technique appear? There is quite evidently a close connection between the rise of copperplate engraving and the advances that had been made, in particular in the mines of Styria, not far from there, in processing ores to extract silver and copper. Copperplate engraving, however, was a much more delicate procedure than intaglio in wood. Although woodcuts could be printed with the use of a roller or a rudimentary press, copperplates required a cylindrical press that could exert enough pressure to force the paper to receive the ink from the incised portions of the copper plate. A cylindrical press bears some similarity to the machines used in metal-rolling mills, hence one might wonder whether this was not one of the many cases that the history of the age offers of technological transfer.

Like copperplate engraving, the printing techniques perfected between 1435 and 1450 derived from the arts of metalworking. To recall the basic principles of printing from movable type: small metal blocks with a character or a typographic sign carved into one end are placed in order in a frame (called a "form"), inked, and pressed so as to leave an impression on a sheet of paper. In order to do this it was essential to produce sets of characters of a strictly identical size on shafts of exactly the same height. Each sign was carved so that it would stand up on the top edge of a piece of extremely strong metal, usually steel. Next this "punch" was impressed into a matrix made of a softer metal such as lead or copper, and the matrix then served as a mold to cast sets of characters out of a mixture of lead, tin, and antimony. (Readers interested in the organization of an artisanal typographic workshop will find full information in Febvre and Martin, *The Coming of the Book.*)

Few inventions have as full a dossier as printing. Like all *causes célèbres,* however, there are still some mysteries connected with Gutenberg's discoveries.[41]

First, the narrative sources. They all mention the name of Gutenberg, be they the Mainz Chronicle, the letter of Guillaume Fichet to Robert Gaguin that figures in one of the first books printed in Paris (1472), the *Chronicle of Eusebius* published in Venice in 1482 by the German printer Erhard Ratdolt, or the Cologne Chronicle, published in 1499 by Ulrich Zell, who had learned his craft in Mainz. The first three texts present Gutenberg as the inventor of printing; the fourth adds:

> The noble art of printing was first invented in Germany, at Mainz on the Rhine. . . . It came to us in the year of our Lord 1440 and from then until 1450 the art and all that is connected with it was continually improved. Although that art was discovered in Mainz, as we have said, the first trials were carried out in Holland, in a Donatus printed there before that time.[42]

Thus the problem of the "Holland manner" was posed. Quite a bit later, in 1561, two men of letters in Haarlem state that the art of typography arose in their city. In 1566 the physician Hadrianus Junius attributed the invention to a native of the same city, Laurens Janszoon, called Coster (Sacristan), who, in theory, printed a *Speculum Salvationis*, a Donatus, and various other books using cast metal characters, until one of his servants stole his secret. There are also documents dating from 1445 and 1451 that mention the purchase in Cambrai and Bruges of a Donatus and a *Doctrinal* of Alexandre de Villedieu that may have been printed. Although copies of a Donatus and works on doctrine have been found that seem to have been printed in Holland, perhaps with sand-cast characters, closer examination shows them to have been printed well after Gutenberg's invention.[43]

Johannes Gensfleisch, called Gutenberg (from the name of a family estate named "The Good Mountain"—*Zu Guten Bergen*—was born between 1394 and 1400 in Mainz, where his father, a patrician, held an honorary post at the Mint, without necessarily having any functions connected with the goldsmith's art or the coining of money. Gutenberg may have been enrolled at the University of Erfurt from 1418 to 1420, during which time his father died. He had to leave his native city, probably around 1428, when the guilds revolted against the patriciate, to which his family belonged. What became of him next is unknown, but we pick up his traces next in Strasbourg in 1434, where he was a member of the goldsmiths' guild and appears to have been well-off. He was sued by a young lady for breach of promise of marriage, and he seems to have had a taste for punch. In 1436, he paid a goldsmith originally from Frankfurt, Hanns Dünne, the considerable sum of 100 florins in exchange for "things to do with printing" (*das zu dem drucken gehoret*). He also drew up a contract with a Strasbourg burgher, Andreas Dritzehn, promising to convey to him a procedure for polishing precious stones, which seems a quite conceivable notion in a city with a lively trade in the local semiprecious stones. Next Gutenberg signed another agreement, this time with Hans Riffe, the bailiff of Lichtenau, later joined by Dritzehn and a goldsmith named Andreas Heilmann, to exploit a new procedure for making mirrors to be sold at the Aachen fair. His partners demanded a share in his other "arts and enterprises" (*Künste und Afentur*). Gutenberg eventually agreed and received a notable sum of money. From that moment on, he and Dritzehn set to work furiously, calling on aid, when needed, from Heilmann and the women of the neighborhood. Andreas Dritzehn died on Christmas Day 1438, however, and when Gutenberg refused to take on Dritzehn's brothers and heirs as partners they sued.

We have the depositions of fifteen of the thirty-two witnesses cited by the two parties. The atmosphere they reflect is in many ways like that of the small teams who worked on photography in the nineteenth century or on the airplane in the early twentieth century, an atmosphere in which the team members, inspired by an indomitable faith, worked with their own hands, ready to sacrifice their last penny to achieve their goal and make their fortunes. This story has a quite different setting, however. The mirrors made by our associates were designed to be attached to the headgear of pilgrims after they had been exposed to the grace emanating from the relics that the clergy of Aachen put on public view on the balcony of the cathedral at certain times of the year. The depositions also tell us, however, that Gutenberg had insisted that no one could see the press that a turner had constructed for him or the machinery on which he was working, which Andreas Dritzehn had put in the house of his brother Claus. Not long before he died, what is more, Andreas Dritzehn had sent his servant Lorentz Beldeck to fetch the "forms" that his brother was keeping for him. But what can we infer from the testimony of that diligent and loyal servant?

> Lorentz Beldeck has deposed: that Johannes Gutenberg sent him, once, to the house of Claus Dritzehn, after the death of Andreas, his late brother, to tell Claus Dritzehn that he must show no one the press that he had under his guard, which the witness also did. He spoke to me, furthermore, and said that I was to take the trouble to go to the press and open it by means of two screws, for the pieces would then come apart from one another; these pieces were then to be placed in the press or under the press, and after that no one was to see or learn anything.[44]

Did Lorentz Beldeck know more that this? In any event, Claus Dritzehn accused him of concealing part of the truth. This sibylline dossier needs to be completed by a last piece of the puzzle, a suit opposing Andreas Dritzehn's two surviving brothers, Claus and Jörg, over his estate. One brother received a press—undoubtedly the press in question—and a "tool" for cutting (*das Scitzelzeug*), which may have been a device for polishing stones; the other brother received books, large and small. Were they printed by the Gutenberg press?

A German scholar, Professor Wolfgang Stromer von Reichenbach, may some day shed light on this mysterious affair.[45] Until then we might simply note that Strasbourg was not at the time a particularly dynamic city. Nonetheless, a number of artists and technicians had been attracted there to work on the cathedral, which had just been finished. There was also talk of holding a council at Strasbourg that would have attracted the elite of the Catholic literati, as the Council of Basel had done at an earlier date. The first "arts" that we see our engineer practicing, polishing precious or semiprecious stones and making mirrors (in particular, with the use of antimony) were specialties of Nuremberg. Had Gutenberg spent time in that capital of metallurgy? His third art demanded a considerable financial investment, and Dritzehn seems indeed to have poured a fortune into it, considering that he was not only paying for the "secret" but also buying materials for further experimentation and, perhaps, for initiating production. Dritzehn, Riffe, and Heilmann, who were members of the merchant group of the Ammeister, were among the few Strasbourg merchants connected with the international trade that branched out from southern Germany to the Low Countries, the Rhône Valley, and Lombardy, and we glimpse behind them the silhouette of a great merchant banker, Friedel von Seckingen, who represented German financial interests in Alsace and who lent the partners money against security and acted as guarantor for them in difficult moments. He also played a part in the very suit that interests us here. To all appearances, our men were part of a powerful cartel, perhaps headquartered in Nuremberg.

Gutenberg drops out of sight from 1444 to 1448. Will someone some day find traces of his presence in Holland, Basel, or Venice? In any event, precisely during those same years, two new inventors enter into the picture: Prokop Waldfoghel and Girard Ferrose, whom the documents call, respectively, a silversmith or goldsmith and a locksmith and clockmaker. Ferrose's career is hard to trace, but Professor von Stromer has given us a good idea of Waldfoghel's. Waldfoghel belonged to a family of German origin settled in Prague who were known as cutlery manufacturers between 1367 and 1418, when the family fortunes seem to have suffered from the Hussite wars. Prokop worked in metallurgy in Nuremberg in 1433 and 1434, and he undoubtedly learned there how lead, copper, and silver could be extracted from ores. In 1439 he acquired citizenship in Lucerne, which was not far from Basel, where his family had connections. We catch up with him in 1444 in Avignon, a traditional center for copyists and booksellers. He was then teaching "an art for writing artificially" (*ars scribendi artificialiter*) to a highly diverse group of persons: David Caderousse, a Jew, Manuel Vitalis, a bachelor decretalist from the diocese of Dax, Arnaud de

Coselhac, who was a friend of Vitalis's, and Georges de la Jardine, apparently a fairly wealthy Avignon burgher. Waldfoghel lived for most of this time with Ferrose, to whom he taught his "artificial writing," and who pawned a clock rather than relinquish a collection of tools they had in their house. The two men had other interests, however. Caderousse taught Waldfoghel a cold-water process for dyeing textiles (which may have been useful for making colored inks). Ferrose contracted to teach a sixteen-year-old from Troyes named Godini the arts of clockmaking and locksmithing, plus how to make bombards and *couleuvrines* (small cannons) and "all that he was skilled in." [46]

To judge by these documents, Waldfoghel and Ferrose were highly skilled technicians. They probably knew of Gutenberg's experiments, since a relative of Hans Riffe's, Walter Riffe, was a goldsmith in Strasbourg, where he lived near Gutenberg and had worked with him, and often visited Avignon during this period. Obviously, we would love to know exactly what was the procedure for artificial writing these two men used. Let us examine the dossier compiled toward the end of the nineteenth century by Abbé Requin. In 1446 Caderousse ordered twenty-seven Hebrew letters engraved in iron (*scissas in ferro*) and devices made of wood, tin, and iron. Furthermore, for two years he held 408 Latin letters as security on a loan. It is interesting that the two witnesses mentioned at the end of the contract are a locksmith from Avignon and a man from Troyes who made leather-punches. Moreover, an act dated 4 July 1444 describing materials that Vitalis left with Waldfoghel for safekeeping mentions two steel alphabets (*duo abecedaria callibis*), two iron forms (*formas ferreas*), forty-eight tin forms, and other objects relating to artificial writing (*ars scribendi artificialiter*). When Vitalis later withdrew from the partnership he sold machinery made of iron, steel, copper, brass, lead, tin, and wood. This would seem to suggest various parts of machinery that was already in operation, but it remains as mysterious as Gutenberg's equipment in Strasbourg.

When he was invited to return to Mainz in 1430 following an agreement between the corporations and the patriciate, Gutenberg did not respond. He was not wholly mistaken, given that his brother-in-law, who became the leader of the patrician party, had to flee to Frankfurt in 1444. But on 17 October 1448 Gutenberg signed an agreement in his city of birth, to which he had finally returned, contracting for a loan guaranteed by a

wealthy compatriot and kinsman, Arnoldt Gelthuss. He borrowed the considerable sum of 150 florins (at an interest of 5 percent), which he probably
used for setting up printing machinery. Next we meet another Mainz burgher, Johann Fust, who came from a family of wealthy merchant bankers
connected, it seems, with trade with Nuremberg. Originally a lawyer, Fust
later held titled offices, and a younger brother who later became burger-
meister is called an architect or a goldsmith. In 1450 Johann Fust lent
800 florins to our inventor (the price of a herd of 100 fat oxen) at 5 percent
interest so that Gutenberg could make "certain tools" (*Geczuge*), and in
1452 Fust promised Gutenberg an annuity of 300 florins for "book work"
(*Werk der Bucher*), an activity undertaken in their joint interest and for
which there were projected expenses for parchment, paper, and ink.

It seems obvious that our heroes had reached a phase in which great
things were happening, and the specialists agree that the work in progress
was the famous 42-line Bible, a perfectly realized masterpiece. The rest, as
the saying goes, is history. Fust accused Gutenberg of not having repaid the
sums he had advanced. He sued, and Gutenberg had to repay with interest
what remained of the capital that Fust had invested. Two years later, on
14 October 1457, the Mainz Psalter appeared, the first work dated and
signed by its backers, who were Fust and a newcomer, Peter Schoeffer.
Gutenberg had certainly been treated in a shoddy manner, and at this point
he was probably useless to the others, since they had passed on to the
phase of exploitation and profits. Gutenberg once more disappears from
the documents. In 1465, however, the new archbishop of Mainz, Adolph
of Nassau, ennobled him for personal services and promised him an annual
gift of a court costume, twenty measures of wheat, and two hogsheads of
wine for his household. Gutenberg seems to have continued to print, since
at his death the city received from the archbishop Gutenberg's forms, tools,
and other objects relating to printing.

A few words, finally, on the last to arrive in this puzzling story, Peter
Schoeffer. When he was still a student in Paris in 1449, Schoeffer copied a
manuscript of Aristotle in a magnificent hand that possibly prefigures the
type of the 1457 Psalter. He is cited as a witness in the 1455 suit, and he
appears to have been the engineer in his association with Fust, whose
daughter he married (and who died in 1467 on a trip to Paris). Schoeffer
died in 1502, but some years earlier he told Johannes Tritheim (according
to the latter, in any case) that with the aid of Fust, he had perfected the art
of typography, initiated by Gutenberg, by inventing an easier way to cast

characters. In the early sixteenth century one of his sons settled in Basel and became an important type merchant who sold fonts throughout Europe.

Tradition dictates that we move on from the invention of printing to examine the pieces without a printer's imprint from the earliest typographers and attempt to ascertain who printed what. I shall state from the outset that all who have ventured onto this unsure terrain have brought back no sure answers, although recent work on the printing of Giovanni Balbi's *Catholicon* has made some troubling discoveries regarding the methods of the first printers.[47]

What can we know of the motivations of our inventors and their clients from a list of such books and pamphlets? Let us turn to Seymour de Ricci's survey, which, although dated, has never been supplanted.[48] It shows fragments of short texts, often taken from the bindings of registers in the region around Mainz, the relics of a vanished and probably large output. We also find administrative pieces like the famous letters of indulgence. There was an obvious advantage to producing such documents mechanically: the intention was to collect as much money as possible, and by printing the necessary certificates they could be produced for less. Next we find calendars and almanacs. Both in the East and the West, they needed to be reproduced rapidly in the largest possible numbers at the beginning of every year. There were also a number of grammar texts—Donatuses—which picked up from the block-books and had an immense public, for reasons we have seen. Then there were the great print works: the 42-line Bible, which was designed as a symbol to impress the world and to prepare the conquest of a market; the 36-line Bible, probably from a rival printshop, Balbi's *Catholicon,* a sort of encyclopedia from the thirteenth century, and other famous monuments of print. From the outset, then, the art of typography had found its dual purpose: to produce circulars and common, short texts in quantity for a local public (this is perhaps what Gutenberg concentrated on at the end of his life); and to increase the number of books and lower their price in order to capture an immense potential market. This was what interested Fust and Schoeffer, who may have been better suited for this sort of commerce than Gutenberg.

Given the state of our knowledge, can we grasp the dynamics of the development of typography and its widespread use? Studies in the history of technology remind us that the invention of printing was one of an entire series of other, linked discoveries. Printing depended on the appearance of paper in Europe, and on the Fabriano metallurgists' invention of efficient machines (using water-powered camshaft mills, a relatively recent development) before it could transfer to paper—a first hybridization—the technique of printing textiles with woodblocks. This was how the idea arose of reproducing images and texts mechanically. It was not enough, however. The search for precious metals led metallurgists to devise a technique for extracting silver, copper, and lead from the ores in which they lay mixed, which made it profitable to exploit new veins. The potential of antimony was discovered. The men who achieved these advances were the first technicians of the modern age to deserve the title of engineers. Their notebooks, which Bertrand Gille has brought to light,[49] testify to a superabundant imagination well before Leonardo da Vinci. The first printers used the metallurgists' discoveries to study the properties of the metals that were now more readily available, and they explored ways to replicate metal objects using an alloy of lead, tin, and antimony that melted at a relatively low temperature. As we have seen with Waldfoghel, they also showed an interest in coloring agents that would enable them to make various colors of inks. It is hardly surprising that when copper plates became readily available people should think of using them rather than wood blocks when they wanted to make particularly fine engravings. Copper plates required a very powerful press, one fitted with rollers inspired by the technology of the sheet-metal rolling mills. Copperplate engraving probably already existed in the region of Lake Constance when Waldfoghel was staying in Lucerne, and one might wonder whether some of the same people were involved in the development of both copperplate engraving techniques and typography. We still do not know exactly what Gutenberg was trying to do in Strasbourg and what Waldfoghel succeeded in doing in Avignon. We do not even know exactly what sort of work Gutenberg was doing in Mainz. He was certainly aware of a technology already in use in Nuremberg; he had a background in the minting of coins and he had manufactured mirrors, so he was in an excellent position to think of decomposing a page and breaking it down into individual signs, then of recomposing it with the help of small metal blocks. Still, it is impossible to reconstruct the various trial attempts of these men, or to determine the part each one played. It is not the aim of this book to do so.

We would like to know, though, what those men thought would be the consequences of their acts. They may have dreamed of a better world, like Gabriel Martin, an inventor, who explained to me in 1938 that a "sound book" would be highly useful to the blind. We cannot be sure of this, however; it is perhaps symbolic that the same engineers who were teaching the "art of writing artificially" also taught their disciples to make cannons. Inventors' motivations are not necessarily of this world: their inventions are the offspring of the obsessed imagination of men who feed on utopias and sweep all obstacles from their path. This can produce what we call "progress," but, as we know more keenly today, there is a price to pay for every advance. This price would surely be less if the financiers and techno-crats, who always have the last word, could foresee the consequences of their decisions, and if their dreams of wealth and power could be guided more lucidly. But then, excessive audacity may be the price of movement, hence of life.

❖

Gutenberg and Waldfoghel are merely two minor local gods in the pan-theon of the demiurges who invented means of communication. By their side in the modest section reserved for printing there are other gods, older and wiser, not half so clever and, above all, less agitated. They lived in the Far East.[50]

The point of departure was the same: the use of paper to transfer images and texts. There was merit to be had simply by reproducing an image of the Buddha or a sutra; early European woodcuts, which often represented healing saints or saintly protectors of travelers, must surely have offered similar rewards. Easily cut blocks of soft wood made the xylographic book-let a perfect solution to the problem of the thousands of signs in Chinese writing. A press was not even needed to transfer such a text to paper, since a simple horsehair brush would do the trick and not even subject the plate to much wear. In lands where letters were drawn with loving calligraphy and the whisper of the brush on paper was appreciated, the fact that the same character had to be recut every time gave a talented engraver an opportunity for variety.

Very early, however, movable characters began to be used. In the elev-enth century the blacksmith and alchemist Pi Cheng is reported to have made movable type out of a fire-hardened mixture of clay and liquid glue, a technique that served to print a certain number of works under the Sung dynasty (960–1279). Next, probably in the early fourteenth century, the very prolific author of a treatise on agriculture and a number of technical works, Wang Tzhen, had sixty thousand individual wood characters cut, with which he printed (among other things) a local gazette in more than one hundred copies. China and Korea may both have had a certain number of works that were printed with metallic movable type as early as the twelfth and thirteenth centuries. In any event a work printed in 1377 and exhibited in 1972 at the Bibliothèque nationale in Paris entitled *Edifying Treatise of the Buddhist Patriarchs* seems to have been made in that fashion. A new dynasty, the Yi, came into power in "the land of the calm morning," now Korea, and its first king, T'aejo (1392–98) and his administration published an entire series of xylographic booklets. He seems to have had still other projects in mind. His successor, T'agong (1400–18), put out a royal command for casting movable characters in bronze in 1403. He justified his decree by noting the rapid wear of carved wooden blocks, the difficulty involved in importing books from China, and the need to codify and set down the new policies of his kingdom, now that Confucianism had replaced Buddhism as the state religion. It is a characteristic detail that this sovereign, who thought of himself as enlightened, decreed that the project be financed by the palace treasury rather than ask his people to bear the burden. The royal clan, the ministers, and certain high functionaries eventually had to pay a share. The king succeeded in his objective, and the royal printshop that was created by the decree used movable characters to produce printed books from 1409 to the nineteenth century.

The methods used in Korea have an almost hallucinatory similarity to Gutenberg's. "Punches" (in this case incised wooden cubes) were used to form a "matrix" in sand placed inside a metal "mold." The characters that were cast in this manner were made of bronze or, in some cases, of lead. Korean typography reached its height under King Sejong (1418–50), who also supported the development of artillery (a symbolic pairing) and copper coinage and whose artisans also made a great many convex bronze mirrors. Finally, the king commanded his palace scholars to devise an alphabet that would give his people greater access to the written word. In 1441 they produced a system based on Sanskrit that used eighteen consonants and ten vowels.[51]

Soon after that date the Chinese devised a procedure for using movable characters, but these brilliant initiatives produced no radical change. The Chinese remained faithful to xylographic booklets and the Koreans waited until the twentieth century to put their alphabet into common use. Large-scale initiatives in both China and Korea remained in the hands of the state or wealthy patrons; no dynamic market for books ever existed. More important, in his infinite wisdom King Sejong prohibited the sale of the books that were printed in his palace, which means that the several hundred copies that made up the "edition" of a work were distributed only to a handful of high dignitaries who were the masters and dispensers of things of the mind and the interpreters of the ideograms in that static society. This was at the same time that books printed in Mainz were spreading rapidly throughout Europe, where, within some thirty years, printshops sprang up everywhere under the aegis of a handful of bourgeois capitalists seeking profits. For centuries to come the East remained immutable while Europe, a small peninsula situated at the end of an immense continent, created a market in which thought could be bought, sold, and exchanged. We have to grant that for once there were virtues in capitalism, preferable, in the last analysis, to a society paralyzed by a rigid hierarchy that is often the twin of the process of statehood.

"CECI TUERA CELA"

But to return to the West: from the outset, printing satisfied two sorts of requirements. It was useful for information and administration, but also for culture. Thus it seems natural that it should have appeared in the Rhine region, at the heart of Europe and at the crossroads of several worlds.

The next step was to commercialize the invention. The 42-line Bible served as a sort of declaration of intent. It demonstrated that henceforth one could produce, in quantity and at relatively low cost, books exactly similar to handwritten manuscripts. The 1457 Psalter, which was conceived in much the same spirit and was updated after the Community of Buxheim had made textual revisions, bore the address of its printers and, in one extant copy, their mark—a sign of the times and the first example of printed publicity. It also contained the first known attempt to print initials in different colors rather than entering them by hand.

Fust and Schoeffer then set out to conquer the European market. Fust died in 1466 in Paris, where we find Schoeffer in 1468 and where the Mainz group had a storehouse and an agent. They also sold their books in Frankfurt, Lübeck, Angers, and Avignon, and Schoeffer also printed publicity posters, as did many of his imitators, for Mainz soon lost its monopoly. Had Gutenberg's work in Strasbourg left some trace? Did Bishop Ruprecht actively promote printing? In any event, in 1458 or 1459 a notary in the episcopal service named Johan Mentelin, who was also a calligrapher and who had lived in that city at least since 1447, opened a printshop there. Mentelin and his partner, Heinrich Eggestein, the bishop's vicar for juridical matters and Keeper of the Seal, made a pact to keep the new art a secret never to be revealed to anyone. During those same years some of Gutenberg's companions seem to have set up shop in Bamberg, where they may perhaps have printed the 36-line Bible. On the night of 27–28 October 1462, however, Mainz again became the scene of troubles when Adolph of Nassau's troops attacked and sacked the city. German typographers moved out all over Europe, as can be seen from the maps in *The Coming of the Book.* [52] In 1465 we can find Germans in Subiaco, not far from Rome, in 1466 they were in Rome itself and in Venice. There were presses in German lands as well: in 1465–66 in Cologne; then in Basel, Constance, and Augsburg, further to the south, in 1468; in Nuremberg in 1469; and in Beromunster in 1470. Paris had a press in 1470, Lyons in 1473. Around 1480 a pattern in the distribution of printshops begins to be clear: some fifteen were operating in the Low Countries (often under the influence of the Brethren of the Common Life); there were another twenty or so in southern Germany, and thirty or so in northern Italy. There were already presses in Seville, London, Copenhagen, Breslau, Prague, and Budapest. Afterwards, this vast space filled in with more printshops and reached as far as Danzig and Stockholm. There were more than 250 centers of the print trade by 1 January 1501, the fatal moment after which books, now out of their cradle, are no longer called incunabula. The estimated 27,000 known publications certainly represent more than ten million copies, circulated in less than two generations in a Europe whose population was under a hundred million. This would give a maximum of some few hundred thousand confirmed readers.

This diffusion, extremely rapid for its time, reminds us that like so many other inventions, the invention of typography was a revolution in communications. In an age in which exchanges were accelerating and markets were becoming unified from one end of Europe to the other, the Continent quite naturally developed ways to create an ideological superstructure that reflected the mentality of an emergent bourgeoisie. This process began in Germany.

No invention has struck people's imagination quite as much as the invention of printing, nor has any been as glorified by its contemporaries, precisely because it involved things of the mind. Gargantua writes to Pantagruel (1532) that printing was discovered as if by divine inspiration, while artillery and gunpowder, by countersuggestion, were diabolical works.[53] Rabelais may have been inspired by the classical *topos* contrasting the arts of peace and the arts of war; it would be interesting to know whether he was aware of the drama of Waldfoghel and Ferrose, which had taken place in Avignon, not far from Lyons. Later, Luther himself at times wondered whether he had been right to translate the Bible and put it into the hands of readers who drew conclusions that he condemned. He also worried, as did many humanists of his age, whether the proliferation of books would not encourage his contemporaries to read too superficially.

Three centuries later Claude Frollo, the archdeacon of the cathedral in Victor Hugo's novel, *Notre-Dame de Paris*, is paging through a copy of Peter Lombard's *Sentences* printed in Nuremberg when he pronounces the enigmatic phrase, "le livre tuera l'édifice" (the book will destroy the building).[54] In the section of his novel entitled "Ceci tuera cela" Hugo contemplates the heroine of his book and the cathedral, despoiled by the Revolution and a skeleton stripped of its statues (this was well before Viollet-le-Duc gave the church a face-lift). Hugo proclaims prophetically that printing would destroy the church and that "human thought, in changing its outward form, was also about to change its outward mode of expression; that the dominant idea of each generation would, in future, be embodied in a new material, a new fashion; that the book of stone, so solid and enduring, was to give way to the book of paper, more solid and enduring still." The book, which had spread everywhere thanks to printing, had become indestructible.

This is of course a poet speaking, but a poet who was aware of the potential connections between architectural construction and the structures of thought in an epoch. And who invites us to stop to reflect on what the West lost in exchange for the invention of printing.

First, it lost a certain form of the language of images, which began a long decline. We have seen how much the society of the waning Middle Ages—Gutenberg's society—was obsessed by images and by visual forms of representation, which often lent inspiration to poets and preachers. Prints and engravings came from that climate, and block-books, those unsuccessful rivals of the typographic book, different from their Oriental counterparts by remaining primarily stories told in images. Like stained-glass windows and church frescoes, to which they remained closely linked, block-books treated the texts engraved on their pages as simple explanations or glosses to their pictures. In most cases, text was not even needed for comprehension of a pictorial narrative.

Five years after the publication of the 42-line Bible Albrecht Pfister, secretary to the bishop of Bamberg, began to publish the first set of illustrated typographic books (1460–64).[55] At first, text and woodcuts were printed separately, but printers soon learned to place the engraved woodblocks inside the type forms and print them along with the text with one pull on the press bar. The works chosen to be published in this manner are signifi-cant: there was *Der Ackermann von Böhmen*, a dialogue between Death and a Bohemian plowman whose author, Johann von Saaz, had worked in several chanceries and possessed a solid culture; there was *Vier Historien*, the stories of Joseph, Ruth, Esther, and Tobit; there was *Der Edelste'n*, verse fables with morals by Ulrich Boner, the bailiff of a town in the canton of Berne and a Third Order Dominican; finally, there was a "Bible of the Poor." Each one of these works had several printings, and they seem to have been intended to illustrate sermons preached by friars of the mendi-cant orders in the German cities and towns.

The rapid rise of the printed book and, even more, of the illustrated book, was quite naturally upsetting to the wood engravers, who felt they were being exploited or pushed aside by keen competition. Around 1466 they attempted to prevent Günther Zainer from setting up a press in Augs-burg, then they did their best to prohibit any member of their guild, the corporation of cabinetmakers and carpenters, from illustrating his publi-cations.[56] This may be why no typographically printed book but Pfister's was illustrated in Germany before the series that Günther Zainer launched in Augsburg in 1471 and his brother Johann launched in 1472 in Ulm, a city that was at the time a center of production for playing cards. Their publications were almost immediately reprinted by printers in Nuremberg and Basel. Between 1471 and 1480, printers like these put out an entire library of illustrated books, among them *The Golden Legend*, the *Speculum vitae humanae* (Mirror of Human Life), the *Belial*, a moralizing apologetic work written by a holy bishop of Florence in the mid-fourteenth century in which the Devil brings Jesus to trial before God the Father, the *Historia destructionis Troiae* of Guido delle Colonne, fables of Aesop and other au-thors reworked by Heinrich Steinwell, a humanist physician of Ulm, as well as Boccaccio's *De claris mulieribus*, Petrarch's *Griselidis*, and Jean d'Ar-ras' *Mélusine*, all of which were offered in both Latin and German versions.

The illustrations in these volumes were still somewhat minimal: they were engraved in broad strokes, were intended to be colored by hand with watercolors, and were inspired more by the sorts of pen drawings found in a number of German manuscripts of the time than by traditional minia-tures. As time went by illustrations became finer, began to show shading (indicated by fairly rough hatching), and gained a degree of autonomy from hand-coloring, which at times disfigured them. At the same time the block-book industry, which had peaked between 1460 and 1475, disappeared.

The triumph of lead brought vast changes. Pfister's "Bible of the Poor," is a good example. The flexible page layout of the block-books, faithful reproductions of their manuscript models, contrasts strongly with the layout of the typographic text broken in the middle by a woodcut. In the typeset version the pictures are disorganized; they are simple additions to a text rather than, as formerly, a discreet recall of a known tradition to which the reader could refer if need be. Similarly, the four juxtaposed scenes showing an episode from the New Testament side by side with three prefigurations from the Old Testament that were set under a series of arches on the upper portion of each double page of the *Speculum humanae salvationis* in its xylographic version were now broken up into four isolated figures separated by commentaries following one another pell-mell rather than proceeding in parallel columns under their corresponding images. Finally, the illustrated Apocalypses, whose page layout, inspired by earlier manuscripts, recalls some of today's more ambitious comic strips, were soon replaced by albums of plates without text, the most famous of which is Dürer's, that reflect a totally different conception.

The disappearance of the xylographic book consummated the decline of a certain type of relations between text and image—relations that would be revived in the nineteenth century by new methods, notably lithography. By the same token, despite an occasional burst of new energy, the logic of lead slowly reduced allegorical language to a game. Henceforth the illustration placed at the head of the work became its publicity and its glorification. Throughout the text, the illustration or the plate was now merely a variation or a commentary on themes that the text developed. It retained some degree of autonomy only in scientific or technical works. At the same time, the printed book came to side with the elites. In the hands of the bourgeoisie, whose emergence was connected with the use of writing, it was an instrument of power used to combat the aristocracy. This is why romantic (and bourgeois) authors later glorified it, at times with a certain nostalgia for bygone days. Once again, we are forced to note that there is no such thing as an innocent medium.

❖

Little by little, the printed book ceased to be a simple reproduction of its manuscript model. There too it lost something in the process, as if in compensation for all that it had gained.

We need to ponder this point a bit. Until the appearance of printing the need to copy a text that one wanted to study or keep gave the copier an almost kinetic memory of its content and an almost physical familiarity with the author's intellectual methods and style, even his tics. It encouraged thinking along the same lines as the author—hence the apocryphal texts of the twelfth and thirteenth centuries discussed above. It also encouraged a form of dialogue that consisted in modernizing, even progressively and naturally modifying, a work in the vernacular. Finally, it led the scribe to correct (or add errors to) the versions of the great texts of classical antiquity that lay before his eyes and to give them a new form, notably by adding his own punctuation and diacritical marks. Handwriting styles that, like letter design, were in constant evolution helped the copyist to offer his own vision of the works of the past. The manuscript tradition, in operating as an intermediary between the oral tradition and the written tradition, eased the transition from the past into the present.

It is true that the first printers did their best to reproduce, as exactly as possible, the manuscripts with which they were familiar. They went as far as to reproduce some of their models line by line, or so it seems: the Bibliothèque municipale of Lyons conserves two copies of the Missel de Lyon, one a manuscript and the other printed in 1482 by Neumeister, which were owned by the same canon and decorated by the same miniaturist. The two are true twins: unless the viewer is a specialist, they are distinguishable from one other only by the color of their ink and the regularity of their characters, which are slightly larger in the manuscript version. Similarly, glossed texts, which until well into the sixteenth century often bear witness to the virtuosity and the patience of the compositors of those times, copy their original models with an unshakable fidelity for a clientele of conservative jurists. Painstaking care took time, however, hence it cost money. As long as new books were in competition with manuscripts they were treated as facsimiles of the older versions and the text was completed with hand-painted initials and rubrics. All that soon changed. Except for books for liturgical use, printers abandoned two-color printing, which required two passes through the press, each time masking the portion of the form to be printed in the other color. Hand decoration was also gradually eliminated, and rubrication and hand-colored initials were replaced by woodcut letters. Marginal rubrics to point out the articulation of the argument were no longer highlighted by lines of different colors according to section and subsection. At the same time there was a tendency to reduce page size, to squeeze lines of type closer, and to fill the page in order to trim costs. Little by little type sorts, the small lead blocks lined up like soldiers on parade, imposed their logic.[57] To facilitate the compositor's task, ligatures were eliminated and the range of letter styles was cut down, so that printers did not continually have to cut new alphabets.

Thus modern page formats are the result of a gestation period that took many centuries. The people who delight in glorifying Gutenberg and who talk so freely about "popular" reading matter would do well to take just one good look at the printed texts themselves. They are comprehensible only on rereading. Similarly, those who are so quick to proclaim that the printing press freed the great texts from the stranglehold of commentaries would do well to take the trouble to look at some of those as well: they know what such texts have gained, but they might also see what they have lost. An excellent case in point would be the Terence prepared in Lyons by Josse Bade for Trechsel in 1491. Not only does it offer an interpretation of Terence's comedies, but reading is guided by glosses on the speeches of the various characters. What high school or university student today would complain of guidance in studying a classical work that he or she can no longer understand or even have any instinctive feeling for? Even more, the somewhat mysterious illustrations interpreting the plays in an undeniably imaginary theater are no more a betrayal of the original than some much-applauded modern settings of the same works. They too have their strokes of genius: one such is the frontispiece of the Lyons Terence, which was used again for the Strasbourg and Paris editions. In it the spectators, rather than gazing toward the magical circle at the center of the theater, look out toward the world that the author rendered so well.

The works of the first generations of printers still reflect visions of times gone by. Soon the dynamism of printing encouraged a more fluent reading of a pared-down text, thus carrying the pruning process suggested by Petrarch to its logical extreme. We shall see what reason gained from the process. For the moment, however, I shall limit myself to noting, in this indictment that we must draw up if we are to be fair, that typography encouraged a divorce of the text from the image and of the present from the past. As the generations passed, it helped to give the most famous texts superstar status; they became codified heralds of an archaeologized knowledge written in dead languages. Only too often they responded to the interrogations and the reactions they prompted with an icy silence and, in conformity with the new spirit, they could be approached only by scholars armed with all the tools of erudition.

Six
The Reign of the Book

A round 1500 printing conquered Europe. It was to reign supreme over the continent for four centuries and move out to conquer the world. Since it owed its power to the commercial dynamism of the West it was subject to the laws of the market, and it governed intellectual life by those laws. Hence we need to review the mechanisms by which the book, that "merchandise," to use Lucien Febvre's expression, was able to tighten its hold on society and to organize its fields of awareness

THE LAW OF THE MARKET

Printing spread throughout Europe extremely rapidly. The protagonists of that conquest have been studied thoroughly and are now familiar figures. They were likely to be former journeymen or disciples of the first typographers in Mainz, and they often attended a university or had been trained as goldsmiths.[1] At this early stage the small teams of printers had to know how to do everything: cut type, cast letters, compose a text, work the press. Many of them were itinerant, halting for several months or several years wherever they found work, and eventually taking up residence in a town they thought propitious, where they founded a stable press.

The map of European publishing centers, some of which became dominant, gradually took shape. For a better understanding of how the market was organized, let us move to Paris, to the Montagne Sainte-Geneviève, in the mid-fifteenth century. While Gutenberg was working with Fust in Mainz, Peter Schoeffer was pursuing his studies in the Faculty of Arts in Paris (1449–52), as were a young Savoyard, Guillaume Fichet, and a young man from Stein, near Constance, Johann Heynlin. Fichet obtained his Arts degree in 1453; Heynlin in 1455, after which both were admitted to the Faculty of Theology. Around 1460, they may have encountered a fellow student from Lyons, a man considerably less advanced in his studies than they and never destined to be a great cleric, Barthélemy Buyer, whose father was a jurisconsult in Lyons and whose mother came from a family of merchant traders. These men undoubtedly had occasion to leaf through the new books from Mainz and to question Fust or his agents. In 1461–62 Fichet and Heynlin, who had continued their theological studies, were received as *socii sorbonici*, which meant that the Collège de Sorbonne assured them room and board and opened all its doors to them, including those of its library. There they could borrow classical texts as well as the theological works they needed for their studies. They joined the ranks of the traditionalists—the "Realists"—in opposition to the Occamites, the modernists of those times, and between 1464 and 1467, Heynlin supported the Realist cause in Basel, where he had been named dean of the Faculty of Arts. It is highly probable that in Basel he met Ulrich Gering, who matriculated in 1461, was received as a bachelor in 1467, and later qualified as a *magister* (master of arts), and perhaps also Michel Friburger, who took his degree in 1463 and probably learned the typographer's trade with Gering in Beromünster. In the meantime Heynlin had returned to Paris where he was elected rector of the university in 1467, and his friend Fichet, who received his doctorate in 1468, became rector the following year, also continuing as the librarian of the Collège de Sorbonne.[2]

Heynlin was clearly fond of traveling, for he took at least one more trip to Basel, probably to seek out typographers and materials. Thus the first book printed in Paris appeared even before the end of the year 1470; it was the *Epistolae* of Gasparino Barzizza, an Italian professor of rhetoric. The book bears the imprint of the Collège de Sorbonne and is signed by Gering, Friburger, and Martin Krantz (who had studied in Erfurt). Our printers, guided by Fichet and Heynlin, then launched a vast printing program, probably financed by Cardinal Rolin and, above all, by the duc de Bourbon. Among other works they produced a treatise on spelling by Barzizza, Fichet's *Rhétorique*, the *Elegantiae* of Lorenzo Valla, and a number of classical texts, among them Sallust's *History of the Jugurthine War*, and Cicero's *De oratore*. Thus Heynlin and Fichet used their positions at the Sorbonne to campaign for a better knowledge of ancient rhetoric and the ancient classical language. But while Heynlin was working to provide accurate texts, Fichet pursued his own route. During the winter of 1469–70 he was sent on an embassy to Galeazzo Maria Sforza, the duke of Milan, in order to ask him join a projected crusade against the Turks. Next, perhaps through another *socius sorbonicus*, Guillaume Baudin, ambassador of the king to Pope Paul II, Fichet established contact with Cardinal Bessarion, champion of the Eastern Christians, whose *Orationes* he published and whom he presented to Louis XI. The two men failed to persuade Louis to their cause, and they went to Rome, where Fichet pursued a somewhat modest career. A month later Heynlin, who had also received his doctorate, devoted all his energies to teaching. He later retired to the Carthusian monastery in Basel. At that point the first Parisian typographers, left to their own devices, had to change course. They moved to the rue Saint-Jacques at the sign of the Golden Sun, and they shifted their publishing strategies to works aimed at the large numbers of clerics and priests who frequented the Latin Quarter. At the same time they replaced the somewhat awkward Roman letters that they had used up to then with traditional Gothic letters.

Paris, the seat of the largest university in Europe, the capital of a vast kingdom, a city renowned for its luxury industries, and a major crossroads, offered signal advantages as a highly important center of publishing. Quite soon, printers who wanted to become established imitated the example of Gering and his companions. It seemed natural to settle in the Latin Quarter, which soon took on a new look. Booksellers' shops lined the rue Saint-Jacques, while printers and bookbinders settled in the streets and alleys nearby and the less-frequented colleges served as warehouses in which to store piles of books. Thus an entire neighborhood sprang up where hundreds of journeymen worked side by side: in the seventeenth and eighteenth centuries several thousand people—workers and their families—made their living from printing, bookbinding, and bookselling.

The rue Saint-Jacques district was not only near the Seine but the street was the largest merchant artery crossing Paris from south to north. Paper and book deliveries could reach it easily. All merchants tend to move closer to their clientele, however, and as the city developed and the university lost some of its importance the booksellers began to group toward the northern end of the street around the church of Saint-Séverin or on the bridges leading to Notre-Dame and towards the Châtelet. Other booksellers sold devotional works around the cathedral, and Claude Savreux, ever-faithful to Port-Royal, sold his books in one of the towers of the abbey in the seventeenth century. The booksellers specializing in new works and works of jurisprudence gathered near the merchants of luxury objects who set up their stalls (somewhat like the shops in a modern railroad station) along the walls and against the pillars of the corridors of the Palais de Justice, where magistrates, royal officials, lawyers, parties to a lawsuit, and elegant ladies who usually frequented the trials would be sure to pass. To end the list of booksellers, there were peddlers, authorized and unauthorized, and itinerant booksellers who gradually spread throughout the city, offering for sale administrative acts, brochures, pamphlets, and prohibited books. In the seventeenth century the Pont-Neuf became the principal rendezvous, and gazettes, inexpensive books, and engravings were sold on the nearby Quai des Augustins.[3]

Together these booksellers offered the Parisian public a respectable number of volumes: certainly more than one hundred thousand books were for sale from the shops along the rue Saint-Jacques in the eighteenth century, and in all probability there were tens of thousands more in the Palais de Justice despite the small size of the bookstalls. Nor was Paris unique: almost everywhere booksellers grouped near the law courts, and the Hall of Westminster, the Palais des Etats at The Hague, and the Royal Palace of Prague all had booksellers specializing in new publications. The cathedral, the bishop's palace, and the larger colleges were places where other bookshops were concentrated. There was of course less choice in the smaller cities, and readers often had to order most of the books they wanted, either from their local booksellers or directly from the printers.[4]

The presence of even a sizable local clientele was not enough to guarantee that a city would become a great publishing center. As the history of the book trade in Lyons proves, the essential elements lay elsewhere. Let us follow Barthélemy Buyer as he returned home after the death of his father. Like many merchant cities, Lyons at the time was a place where two worlds coexisted in near-total unawareness of one another. The right bank of the Saône, along the slopes of Fourvière, was still the realm of the canon-counts, noble and powerful personages most of whom lived there only episodically, for after making their way up the university ladder, they tended to try their luck at the pontifical court. Near them was the residence of the cardinal archbishop de Bourbon, a nephew of the learned bishop of Puy and of Duke Jean II, the protector of the Sorbonne press, whose court was at Moulins. The archbishop had built a palace in the Florentine style near the cathedral, replacing the somber fortress of Pierre-Scize built by his predecessors. A lover of art, he had no interest in what went on across the river, where the burghers had become masters of the commune, building their prosperity along with the bridges they built across the Saône and the Rhône to enable people and merchandise from the Empire and from Italy to pass into French lands. From its position between the Saône and the Rhône, Lyons, a river port, was connected with waterways that led from the Mediterranean toward northern France and, via the Loire, to the Atlantic. It had become an incomparable crossroads, and in the fifteenth century, after the fairs had guaranteed the city's prosperity, the rue Mercière where the merchants gathered became one vast warehouse.[5]

While the highly cultured canons and the bishop, a famous patron of the arts, turned their eyes elsewhere, Barthélemy Buyer was calculating his chances. There were a number of paper mills near the city, in particular around Trévoux. The fairs attracted money changers, and money began to flow into the city. Commercial routes were opening in all directions, but Lyons did not yet possess a solid industry. Sensing the importance of the potential market, Buyer took into his house near the church of Saint-Nizier a typographer whose name was Gallicized as Guillaume Le Roy and who came from around Liège and was fleeing unrest in that city. Buyer soon set to work other typographers of German origin: Martin Husz from Bottevar, Nicolas Philippe from Darmstadt, and Marcus Reinhart from Strasbourg. His plan was simple: to introduce on the French market translations of the illustrated editions that had proved so successful in the cities of southern Germany, and to carve a place for himself in the international market by publishing the most often used collections of texts on Roman and canon law. He gathered together a group of willing workers: a handful of monks and canons of the church of Saint-Augustin, who translated pious or moralizing texts, and a group of jurisconsults, most of whom had studied in Italy. He soon established a foothold in the Italian market and showed the redoubtable Venetians some competition. Next he opened a warehouse in Toulouse and set off on the road to Spain. His timing was good and he established a strong position not only in France south of the Loire but also as far as Madrid and Naples. The firm he founded prospered up to the turn of the nineteenth century.

Thus the absence of intense intellectual activity did not keep Lyons from becoming one of the major centers of publishing in Europe toward the end of the fifteenth century. Even more, during the height of the French Renaissance, the presence of a number of presses and the wealth of the Lyons bourgeoisie encouraged the flowering of an original literary movement. Henceforth, the book was to be produced and sold in large part in the great merchant cities, nearly all of them situated near river or sea ports. Venice—not Florence or Rome, capitals of culture and religion—long dominated the European market. And when activity in the Mediterranean area died down, it was Antwerp's turn, then Amsterdam's and, finally, London's.

The book became a product made in quantity and subject to the laws of the marketplace. Henceforth those who produced and sold books were to face problems of price—cost price and sale price—of optimal production figures, of financing, and of distribution. Let us take cost price first. It is traditionally divided into fixed costs, which are based on expenditures made once and for all independent of production volume, and variable costs, which are proportional to volume. In artisanal book production, the principal fixed-cost items were general expenses (work-space rental, amortization on equipment, etc.), composition and correction costs, press start-up costs, and, in some cases, illustrations. Variable costs were largely determined by the price of paper and ink, the cost of the actual printing, and wear and tear on the equipment—plus the cost of paper or board bindings, although the customer often bought a copy of a work unbound.[6]

In the artisanal industries raw materials—in this case, paper—were typically high in cost in comparison with manpower. This meant that variable costs remained high in relation to fixed costs, whereas in our own day the necessary expenses for photo-reproduction and illustrations and for setting up sophisticated machinery tend to make fixed costs considerably higher than variable costs. In that age it was relative easy to lower fixed costs to a negligible level and still keep pressruns low.

Printers, who were still competing with manuscript copyists, nonetheless had to put out relatively large editions if their prices were going to be low enough to be competitive. Editions were limited to 300 or 400 copies in the still unorganized market of the 1470s, but they soon rose to 600 copies. Books of erudition and theology long continued to be printed in around 800 copies, but books of current interest normally reached editions of 1,200 to 1,800 copies in France of the classical period. In England the agreements arrived at in 1587 between the members of the Stationers' Company and the compositors established the maximum figure for a pressrun at 1,500 copies for ordinary books and 3,000 for schoolbooks, catechisms, and grammars. Although these norms were raised in 1637, pressruns seems not to have been much higher than 2,000 copies in London during the seventeenth century.[7] Publications subsidized by the author could of course be published in editions of only a few hundred copies, and the pressrun of church books was quite naturally proportional to the numbers of the clergy for whom such works were destined. Finally, the demand for books of hours was so great that they often were printed in several thousand copies; school texts were also printed in impressive pressruns in eighteenth-century England; and almanacs were updated yearly and printed in enormous quantities: 72,000 for Collombat's *Almanach de la cour* in 1725.

The persistence of relatively small pressruns (exceptional cases aside) is largely explained by the booksellers' interest in not immobilizing their capital in an age in which the price of paper and bookbinding (when required) made up the greater part of the printer's expenses but expenses for composition and printing were relatively low. It was better business practice simply to take care that the remaining stock did not run out, reprinting the work when necessary, particularly when the earlier edition could be reproduced page by page, if not line by line. Thus the most common devotional works were reprinted periodically in the 1770s and 1780s in specialized printshops in Lorraine or Normandy in editions of 750 to 1,500 copies.[8]

Although the publication of a book represented an important investment, setting up a printshop was not overly costly. Seasoned lumber to make a press was in ready supply, and a press practically never wore out. The pressing screw represented the only notable expense, especially when it came to be made of metal rather than wood. Characters were more costly. Typographers used fonts of reduced size—100,000 to 200,000 sorts—which means that they were forced to reduce to a minimum the time they spent on correcting proofs, and even had to make corrections as they printed so they could reuse the same sorts. Still, when a font wore out it was possible to use the metal in the alloys for casting new ones. Thus the cost of even a well-equipped printshop was decidedly lower than the set-up cost for a well-stocked bookshop.

Financial backing was necessary before a book could be published, which created a need for patrons in the early stages of printing and later led to the role of merchant booksellers who invested their own money and operated much like a publisher today.[9]

In Germany leading merchants organized their own printshops at an even earlier date. This was already true of Fust, and it was also true of Peter Drach, a patrician from Speyer who seems to have had a particularly large printshop with outlets in Strasbourg, Frankfurt, Cologne, Leipzig, Augsburg, Prague, Brno, Olomouc, and elsewhere in the 1480s. The largest printer of the age was Anton Koberger of Nuremberg, Dürer's godfather, whose family, some of whom were goldsmiths, were wealthy bakers who had joined the patriciate. Anton knew all the humanists of southern Germany, and at times he had more than one hundred persons working in the group of firms he owned. He even set up a system for providing running water to his workshops so that his workers could dampen the printing paper and clean their forms. He had relations with a number of cities and owned book deposits in Lyons and in Paris.[10] Quite soon, however, these great entrepreneurs found it difficult to keep their presses working regularly. They jobbed out some print orders to other typographers: Koberger used the services of Amerbach in Basel in this fashion and those of certain Lyons printshops to whom he supplied woodcuts and perhaps even characters.

Unlike the French market, the German market long continued to be dominated by the great printer-booksellers. This is particularly evident in the period of the Reformation. The market was feverish, and the Wittenberg typographers were turning out the translation of the Bible that Luther produced, book after book, in a variety of formats and a large number of editions that printers there and elsewhere reprinted immediately. When calm returned, the market organized, and it became of the essence to set up some form of cooperation among booksellers to enable them to distribute their publications swiftly and at the least cost to places some distance away, in an age when couriers were relatively scarce and slow and bank transfers, as we know them today, were nonexistent.

The booksellers coped with these difficulties by large-scale barter. They all had official correspondents with whom they had particularly close connections, so they could make use of a limited number of sites to exchange not only items on their own lists but also their fellow citizens' books. In this manner, the businessmen of one city could band together to have an efficient system for distributing all their products.

The greatest advantage of this distribution system was its speed. Shipments were usually made as soon as books were printed, and copies were sent unbound, which meant they weighed less and could be bound in the style that prevailed in the place of arrival or according to the buyer's preference. Sheets were stacked and shipped in bales and bound books were shipped, for the most part, in barrels, sometimes with other commodities. When possible these bundles and barrels were shipped by water, which was less expensive, but at times carters who specialized in book-hauling were used. These shipping methods, which lasted well into the eighteenth century, required long and painstaking verification, and shipments might easily arrive damp and partially spoiled. The addressees frequently complained that they had been shipped unsalable works. Finally, the 10 to 25 percent discounts that the publisher granted (and which varied according to the payment terms and the house's confidence in the bookseller) led to long negotiations, and although in principle accounts had fixed deadlines, they were always in arrears. When an agreement was reached the account was paid off by a bill of exchange, and the major printers and booksellers used such occasions as an opportunity to engage in speculative operations that have left traces in the documents only when the results were catastrophic.[11]

Such methods helped shape the way the book trade was organized. In the largest centers—Venice, Paris, and Lyons, or, at a later date, Amsterdam or London—the most powerful booksellers constituted a sort of oligarchy. Most of them formed the habit of combining forces to publish an unusually large work, each taking his share of the copies and each lot bearing its own title page and publisher's imprint. Thus a number of ephemeral associations occurred, but there were also stable societies specializing in putting out a specific type of book, like the successive large companies of bookseller-printers in Lyons who published important works in civil and canon law. Later, during the Counter-Reformation, the power structure favored the establishment of Paris companies, which enjoyed exorbitant monopolies. In the late seventeenth century this prompted the Parisian publishers who specialized in new works to form the Compagnie du Palais, which served as a model for their competition in Amsterdam, where booksellers grouped together in the same way. Finally, in 1680, the major bookseller-printers of London formed a particularly dynamic association that controlled a large part of the British market and that was called "The Conger," a name derived both from the Latin verb *congere* (to act in concert) and from the eel, known for devouring smaller fry.

Each one of these societies had its leaders. In Renaissance Lyons, the major names were Vincent, La Porte, and Gabiano. Thanks to his many joint ventures, Jean Petit, the son of a wealthy butcher, had a hand in roughly one-fifth of all books published in Paris during the first third of the sixteenth century. Later Horace Cardon in Lyons and Sébastien Cramoisy in Paris dominated the publishing world of their day. Such men accumulated considerable fortunes, and they often served as magistrates of their cities. These success stories were the exception, however, and even when they were involved in large-scale business dealings, bookseller-printers usually remained people of modest wealth and position. Moreover, in this small world in which unity guaranteed strength, there was no rigorous division of labor. The master printers were often paid in kind for their work and reinvested their profits in editions that they put out themselves. Similarly, bookbinders often received unbound books in exchange for the books they had bound, and nearly all of them owned an assortment of books that they offered to private customers. At times they even operated as bookseller-printers themselves.

This system to encourage long-distance exchanges aimed above all at guaranteeing the widest possible distribution to everyone's list. It was a system dependent on a world of literati and settled ecclesiastics who shared a common learned language—Latin—and participated in a common culture. When the system was put to the service of the Catholic Church, it made it possible to launch "great enterprises"—large pressruns of works in multiple volumes—without incurring too much risk. It was a conservative system, reflecting an economic equilibrium and a political stability. The great bookseller-printers who concentrated on distribution such as Jean Petit or Sébastien Cramoisy (or such as Louis Hachette at a later date) could afford to publish new works only if they confirmed an established success. What is more, such men usually jobbed out print work and hardly ever introduced typographic innovations.

When it came time to rethink forms or texts and when a moral or intellectual crisis prompted a strong demand for innovative or contentious works, this system seemed unwieldy. Then new, more supple, less cumbersome "units of production" closer to the works' creators moved to the forefront, and the printer began to take a leadership role.

The most illustrious of these innovating printers were the ones who are usually called "humanist printers," Renaissance princes of an ephemeral realm. Aldo Manuzio (Aldus Manutius) was one of these.[12] Manutius was born in 1451, and he first pursued a long career as a man of letters and a pedagogue. A fervent Hellenist and a friend of Pico della Mirandola, that prince of universal learning, and preceptor to his nephews, Leonardo and Alberto Pio of Carpi, Aldus and his friend Pico both dreamed of a renewal of Italian society through contact with Greek thought. For several decades the literati of the Italian peninsula had sat at the feet of Byzantine refugees and had learned to venerate Plato, whose works Marsilio Ficino had just translated in Florence. It seemed a natural move to use the press to awaken minds and to exploit what appeared to be a potential market in order to help ideas crystallize more rapidly. In this aim Aldus chose to settle not in Florence near the Platonic Academy and under the protection of the Medicis, but rather in Venice, the metropolis of printing and the focal point of the book market. With more ideas than money and with the support of the princes of Carpi he managed to win the aid of the nephew of Agostino Barbarigo, the doge, and of Andrea Torresani, an important printer-bookseller who specialized in traditional works. The doge's nephew provided half the necessary funds and Torresani four-fifths of the rest, so that Aldus owned only one-tenth of the firm that was to bear his name. With the aid of Francesco Griffo, a type designer of genius, he recast the aesthetics of roman characters and succeeded in the delicate task of creating type for a Greek alphabet with accents and breathings. He produced thirty princeps editions of Greek authors with this type font, Aristotle among them, and presented Latin works in editions for cursive reading. Finally, taking as his model the handwriting of Niccolò de' Niccoli and the style of papal briefs, he created italic characters, and, with a privilege granted by the Senate of Venice for this invention, he used italics to increase the readability of both the Latin classics and contemporary works in Latin that he published in portable editions. Manutius was a creator of fashions: protected by patrons like Jean Grolier, the treasurer of the king of France for the conquered territory of Milan, he introduced Italian-style gilded bindings into France, and between 1494 and 1515 his four to six presses produced 117 editions, representing 130 volumes or a total of at least 120,000 books. Aldus acted more like a literary editor-publisher than a typographer, and on occasion he was away from his press for months at a time, for he dreamed of gathering Italian men of letters into one academy and of restoring Italy to its ancient glory through the cult of classical letters. He made Andrea Torresani a wealthy man, but, according to Erasmus, Aldus himself was a miser who offered his guests miserable fare when they were invited to dinner. More important, when he was over fifty Manutius married Torresani's daughter and belatedly founded a line of famous printers.

There were other humanist printers who, like Aldus Manutius, got their start with the help of the owners of traditional enterprises. One such was Josse Bade.[13] A Fleming and a former student of the Brethren of the Common Life and of the University of Louvain, Bade had stopped in Lyons on his return from the classic trip to Italy. In Lyons he learned typography and the correction of Latin texts, and he acted as a sort of "literary editor" for the printer Jean Trechsel, whose daughter he later married. Already known for his fine epistolary style, Bade moved on to Paris to seek his fortune, and there Jean Petit hired him to edit and correct texts and later helped him to found his own printshop. When Bade the humanist also became a master printer he published a number of works: short texts in good Latin for use in schools, editions of the classics, and devotional books inspired by the *devotio moderna*. At the start he often worked for Petit or in association with him or with other booksellers, but later he worked increasingly on his own, producing 750 editions between 1503 and 1535. His home became a gathering place for French and foreign scholars from Lefèvre d'Etaples and Guillaume Budé to Beatus Rhenanus and Erasmus (whom he eventually accused of being an advance scout for Luther and with whom he had a falling out).

In comparison with the bookseller, whose chief concern was to service a traditional market, the master printer often appeared as an innovator. This was the case when the humanist printers engendered the modern book, and it was to be the case whenever the need arose to circulate books of a revolutionary nature. When it came to clandestine literature, the typographer was always in advance of the bookseller, and the great "publishers" of the Reformation and the Enlightenment were nearly always first and foremost masters of printshops.[14]

The barter system and the solidarities it entailed, the booksellers' incessant travel, and the correspondence that they maintained made this small world a singularly homogeneous and mutually dependent society in which the ruin of one involved the ruin of others. In the eighteenth century, however, when other modes of payment became commonplace and clandestine works began to represent a larger part of the book trade, the climate began to change. "Bad risks" became notably more numerous, particularly in towns and smaller cities.

Work within the printshop required an even tighter solidarity. Printers seem to have worked as a team, with compositors assigned to specific presses. Soon, however, it became customary to take each worker who finished a task and put him to work on whatever was most urgent, which means that the workers switched from one task to another. They worked under extraordinary pressure fourteen hours a day to print from two thousand to three thousand sheets, a figure that amounts to a pressing every ten or fifteen seconds![15] Even if we accept these figures as theoretical (they appear in all the literature on the subject), the small teams of the artisanal age seem to have accomplished an enormous amount of work. Never for example did the humanist printers seem to have available more than from four to six presses (with the exception of Christophe Plantin, a rather special case). In the finest hours of Calvinist propaganda, Geneva counted only slightly more than twenty printshops with a total of thirty-four presses. Bonaventura Elzevier had only four presses in Leiden in 1651, and there were only twenty-nine presses in all of Leiden, which figured as a great European center. All of Holland had no more than some 150 presses in 1671. Paris in 1643-44 had only 183, divided among 76 printshops employing a total of 237 journeymen and 94 apprentices. In 1764, at the height of the Enlightenment, French provincial cities had 274 printshops, 697 presses, and somewhat more than 900 workers, while Paris in 1770 had 40 printshops and 389 presses worked by fewer than a thousand masters and typographers.[16]

The major problem for everyone was the irregularity of the work load, which required sudden reductions or increases in personnel from one season to another. At least in the eighteenth century each master printer had at his side a *prote*, a foreman on whom everything depended; he might also have had a small number of permanent *compagnons en conscience* who worked on stated tasks. The greater part of the work was done by temporary personnel. The journeyman or hired printer was often an *enfant de la balle*, the son of someone in the printing trade, but he might also be from a large family of minor notables. Restif de la Bretonne, for example, was the son of a tax-collector for a local lord. The aspiring printer had probably learned to read and write in a parish school, and he might have attended the first years of a *collège*, in which case he would know a little Latin, perhaps even Greek—indispensable skills for becoming a master printer in France after the late seventeenth century. During his apprenticeship, he would have been the drudge and the whipping boy of the shop, where he learned a specialized vocabulary and won a gradual initiation into the trade, punctuated by gifts he was expected to make and drinking bouts he was expected to pay for. When he in turn became a journeyman, he and his comrades might abandon the shop for several days, then return to finish the job by working straight through, Sundays and holidays included. Printers were proud of their skills, and in the sixteenth century they demanded the right to bear a sword as a way of showing that they were not involved in "mechanical" labor. Traditionally extremely politicized, they were among the first to enroll during the Wars of Religion or the conflicts of the Fronde. The instability of their profession encouraged them to play the adventurer, and once their apprenticeship had ended most of them embarked on a "tour of France" or an itinerant life elsewhere that might continue for a good part of their lives.[17] French journeymen, who were fond of sunshine, usually headed for the Midi, stopping in a city for a few days or several months as the opportunity arose. As long as the possibility existed, the more enterprising among them attempted to set up a printshop of their own at the first chance they had, usually in a small city that did not yet have a press. Great girl-chasers, they courted the burghers' daughters (on occasion, their wives, and especially their widows). Often they restricted their wanderings to one region, where they became well known. In constant correspondence with one another and careful to call a colleague "Monsieur," they often found lodgings where another printer had moved on, and they waited impatiently for the letter from a master requiring their services who would send them money for the "voyage" that would take them—not necessarily in all haste—to a new place of employment. They had no compunction about breaking a contract if something more advantageous turned up along the way, and at times they abandoned the shop simply for the pleasure of "scouring the countryside." These habits created a small, coherent milieu, and laid the groundwork for subversive propaganda networks.

There could be acute underlying tensions between the master and his family and the journeymen. The documents concerning strikes in the sixteenth century are already proof of these, as are the many polemical pamphlets of the seventeenth century. The situation seems to have become increasingly tense in Paris in the eighteenth century, however, particularly when master printers attempted to eliminate the traditional system of apprentices and journeymen (who appeared to the masters as future rivals) and replace them with simple hired help that did not aspire to become masters. The hired apprentices, who rose before dawn, and the typographers who soon joined them often detested the *prote*, the foreman under whose direction they worked, and they hated even more the master printer who often lived in or near the printshop with his family and, after rising at a late hour, would unfailingly berate them. The result, in the neighborhood of the Montagne Sainte-Geneviève, where printshops crowded together, was an atmosphere faithfully rendered in Nicolas Contat's *Anecdotes typographiques,* which Giles Barber has edited and Robert Darnton has studied.[18]

Contat, a hired apprentice employed by the aging printer Jacques Vincent, had his nerves set on edge by cats (some the pets of the printers and their wives) who howled all night long under his loft window. One fine day the workers slaughtered the cats and set up a mock court to try them in the courtyard of the house. Vincent's wife, whose special pet, La Grise, had disappeared, was particularly upset by these carryings-on, and Robert Darnton shows how the workers ridiculed their master, whose marital problems were known to all, and performed something like a verbal gang rape of his flighty wife.

THE ORGANIZATION OF SPACE IN EUROPE

By 1500 printing had conquered its space: a vast area of Western Europe stretching east to Stockholm, Danzig, Bohemia, and Hungary. Still, the typographic map of Europe was barely sketched in. Central and southern Germany, northern Italy, and southeast France were well dotted with printing establishments, but the conquest of Eastern Europe had barely begun. The Low Countries, which were already quite active, furnished only a regional clientele with school texts, devotional works, and novels in French or Flemish; England was still an export market for French and Flemish booksellers and printers; the presses of the Iberian peninsula, often run by Germans, also did little but supplement lists of books produced elsewhere. It took more than a century before printers had established modest printshops in smaller cities that produced works of regional or local interest and that functioned as distribution points for the larger centers.

From the fifteenth to the seventeenth centuries the major part of the business of the leading booksellers still was in learned works written in Latin destined for the libraries of men of letters and ecclesiastics in all countries. Every day the major firms that dominated the market wrote to their correspondents near and far to acknowledge the receipt of a shipment, enter an urgent order for volumes wanted by a client, propose a discount, demand extra sheets, or settle a debt through a bill of exchange. The publishers of new books—the humanist printers in particular—soon began to publish catalogues of their offerings, on occasion indicating the price of each work.

Still, nothing could replace direct contact. Every firm of any importance was run by two partners, usually a father and a son who traveled to visit the booksellers, settle accounts with the firm's correspondents, and look over the market. Even that was not enough when it came to drawing up the list of new publications and reprints, especially when any printer could reprint the publications of another printer (who of course might reply in kind). Hence the importance of fairs. Although information is scanty concerning the place of booksellers in the Lyons fairs, we are well informed concerning Frankfurt and Leipzig at a somewhat later date.[19] In 1555, when peace returned after thirty years of religious war, booksellers in German lands, which were divided into a number of small states with a decentralized economy, felt the need to coordinate their efforts and reorganize their market. For a long time, the Frankfurt fairs, which made a specialty of Latin works and, in principle, were open to all confessions, far outstripped the Leipzig fairs, and for fifty years or more Frankfurt was the meeting-place for representatives from of all the great publishing centers of Europe. From Naples to Amsterdam, from London and Antwerp to Lisbon, they met regularly in the Bücherstrasse—Book Street—to unpack their volumes, post the tables of contents of their new publications, and circulate lists of works they were offering for sale or were interested in acquiring. Amid the din of hawkers selling almanacs or pamphlets, authors and men of letters seeking employment went from one bookseller to another to offer their services.

Frankfurt thus became the place where the great religious and scholarly publications were "launched." In 1564 a bookseller from Augsburg, Georg Willer, had the idea of making up a catalogue of all the works offered for sale at the Frankfurt fair, and his idea was picked up by the organizers and was continued until the eighteenth century. Until about 1625 these repertories served as a bibliography of the current offerings of all European publishers; the twenty-five thousand or so titles with a German imprint and the twenty thousand other titles of foreign provenance give some notion of the scale of the international book trade. What exactly do these catalogues reveal? First, they show the astonishing prosperity of European publishing on the eve of the Thirty Years War. Second, they confirm that the church of the Counter-Reformation played an essential role in publishing in an age in which territories that had remained Catholic were becoming dotted with schools and convents. After the Council of Trent there was a concerted effort within the church to revise the Vulgate, provide accurate editions of the works of the Fathers of the church and of the decisions of the older councils, provide a wide variety of commentaries on Scripture, offer a reinvigorated theology and an adequate catechism, and, finally, adapt local liturgies to the Roman rite, which itself was revised on three occasions. Hence there was a particularly fruitful commerce among Catholics that rejected the Protestants as outsiders and reduced them to the role (a profitable role, as it turned out) of challengers. I shall have occasion to return to the subject.

All this helps us to understand the mechanism of exchanges within Europe. Each of the booksellers of the largest cities published his own list of the most sought-after works. Each had publications that he exchanged with others, the barter process leading them to accept the specialties of their trading partners. This encouraged booksellers to operate as wholesalers, distributing both their own editions and those of their correspondents among the retail booksellers of the region or the country that was their particular "territory." Paris printers organized networks in northern France, while their counterparts in Lyons dominated the regions south of the Loire. Similarly, Paris exported its books from Rouen (and often those published in Lyons as well) to the lands of northern Europe; Lyons maintained solid relations with Italy and the Iberian peninsula through Toulouse and Nantes; Antwerp held the keys to the Spanish Low Countries and, from the age of Plantin, to the entire Spanish empire; Venice was mistress of the trade in Italy (despite competition from Lyons) and had close contacts with Austria and southern Germany; Cologne—with Frankfurt—was the center for the distribution for Catholic publications in the Rhineland; and Leipzig already dominated trade with Eastern Europe.[20]

The printing and selling of books were nonetheless subject to the laws governing the general evolution of the European economy. As in other domains, Venice and the Italian cities still made a good showing, and in the late sixteenth century Venice remained the largest exporter at the Frankfurt market. Soon, however, Antwerp and its sister cities in the Low Countries made a sweeping entry onto the scene. Just as the Italian textile industry was collapsing in face of competition from the Low Countries, Italian publishing bowed to their superior strength, and behind the ultra-Catholic Antwerp the silhouettes of the Protestant cities of Leiden and Amsterdam (and later London) were looming, while Geneva was keeping a close eye on the decline of Lyons.

During the entire artisanal period, publishers in the Low Countries and French Switzerland enjoyed a very special situation. Economically they were powerful and dynamic, and they were well placed to act as intermediaries between France and German lands. Still, they did not draw on the hinterland needed to give a solid base to their prosperity. From time to time they created well-equipped printshops, but, like Japan in today's world, their survival depended upon their ability to export. The history of printing in Holland is characteristic from this point of view. Once they were free from the yoke of Spain, the Calvinist citizens of the United Provinces could neither enter into Catholic circuits nor count too much on their Lutheran neighbors in Germany. Despite these handicaps they used all their advantages to carve out a place for themselves in the international market. Among their talents was the business sense that inspired the first of the Elzeviers, a beadle in the newly founded University of Leiden who accumulated a stock of books by buying up the libraries of deceased professors and who procured ready cash by inventing book auctions. Another advantage was the Protestants' superiority in philology, which enabled the Leiden professors and their friends abroad to provide excellent critical editions of ancient authors. Still another was a talent for technological invention, which led Willem Janszoon Blaeu, formerly a "mechanic" for the astronomer Tycho Brahe, to set up a printshop in Amsterdam whose presses were capable of perfect reproduction of the large copper plates of the atlases he published. Blaeu also used a particularly black ink that made his press capable of printing clearly with nearly microscopic characters—hence his famous collection of classical authors in duodecimo-sized volumes and his series of "Republics" in a 24 mo. format, tiny volumes that are the ancestors of modern travel guides.

Just as the Counter-Reformation was losing energy, the Dutch, masters of the nonreligious book, penetrated the German and French markets. But the Thirty Years War, a product of the excesses of the Counter-Reformation, broke out in 1617. When either Catholic or Protestant princes won a victory in a ravaged Germany they merrily pillaged the library that had been the pride of their vanquished adversary or they carried off its contents as spoils of war. Outside Germany a somewhat artificial prosperity propped up by the Catholic Reformation for a time continued to buck the current, but recession spread throughout Europe. The market was flooded with folio volumes, and the great texts, formerly so eagerly sought, no longer found buyers. The booksellers of the largest centers, who until then had cooperated with one another within the book trade, embarked on a merciless war of pirated publications, striving to ruin one another in an attempt to survive. Italy closed in on itself, and when peace was reestablished in the Empire in 1648 the Venetians no longer traveled to Frankfurt. The Dutch dominated this singularly shrunken international market: Geneva attempted a revival; Paris and Lyons were in retreat. It was a pyrrhic victory, however, as the Latin book no longer "paid." As if symbolically, the powerful Stationers' Company in London eliminated its Latin stock in 1625. The time had come for national literatures in a cultural Europe that was breaking apart, if not shattering. In German lands that had long lain in ruins the Leipzig fairs organized by Saxon booksellers who specialized in vernacular publications gave the Frankfurt fairs increasing competition. In England the bookseller Andrew Maunsell compiled the first *Catalogue of English Printed Books* in 1595, and in France Father Jacob published a *Bibliographia Gallicana* and a *Bibliographia Parisina* between 1643 and 1653. Analogous efforts were made in the Spanish Netherlands and the

United Provinces. Thus a new deal was being prepared that would totally revise the rules of the game for the European book trade.[21]

Although the major booksellers had rapidly broken down the barriers separating the various literary milieus to organize pan-European circuits for publications in Latin, the constitution of circuits for national literatures was the result of an extremely slow gestation.

As early as 1471−72 a group of printers in Augsburg and Ulm launched a series of books of religious instruction and moral edification, along with works of fiction at times of a humanist cast. For the most part these works were designed to reinforce the lessons of the preachers among the urban middle classes, and they were abundantly illustrated with pictures to clarify texts published in both Latin and the vernacular. The only way that the printers could meet the cost of engraving these illustrations was to amortize them by massive reuse. As a result, printers who had originally worked with the clientele of their city or their region in mind began to rent out or sell their woodcuts, which were reused by colleagues in other cities who adapted the texts that went with them to their own dialect or language. In turn the success of these publications might be so great that still other booksellers had the illustrations copied by a local artisan, and in this way many of these works were soon translated and distributed throughout Europe. At the same time booksellers began to produce a good many chivalric romances, a genre that until that time had circulated primarily among the aristocracy and in the small world of the courts. Some (Antoine Vérard, formerly the head of a illumination workshop in Paris, or Colard Mansion in Bruges) began to illustrate these tales with engravings either from their existing stock or with others made for the occasion. Other booksellers who were particularly prosperous or who had support from patrons published sumptuously illustrated chronicles, the most famous of which were the *Nuremberg Chronicle* (Koberger, 1494) and *La mer des histoires* (Paris: Le Rouge, 1493; Lyons: Dupré, 1488−89).

It would be difficult to exaggerate the importance of the role such booksellers played. When they chose an item out of the stock of manuscripts in circulation they gave its text a survival that may have been unhoped for; conversely, they condemned other texts to oblivion. They often called upon translators or adapters for the works they selected, some of which became veritable best-sellers. One such was the famous *Shepherd's Calendar*, in reality simply a patchwork of passages from works well known in their day.

The booksellers had little effect on the process of literary composition, however, particularly as authors were gradually discovering the power of the press.[22]

During this time scholars were attempting to revive and circulate the great works of classical and Christian antiquity. As if in successive waves, the bookseller-printers first published the scholars' labors in large-sized editions, often with glosses, then in smaller portable editions in imitation of Aldus Manutius. Around 1530 Greek works as well as works in Latin became the fashion.[23] Scholars and writers were also producing large numbers of pedagogical works and books of neo-Latin poetry that gave them respect and celebrity in lettered circles. The moment came, however, when the market was saturated and something else had to be found. The humanists recalled Petrarch's lesson on the eminent dignity of national languages, which they took it on themselves to refine. Claude Nourry in Lyons, who until that point had been content to exhume and modernize traditional tales, launched Rabelais' *Pantagruel.*

The enterprising large-scale booksellers then plunged into the national market by offering a kind of literature aimed at a fairly well-educated lay public of government officials, wealthy merchants, and women. The history of Jean I de Tournes, a humanist printer of the new generation, gives a good idea of this new tendency. The grandson of a notary and the son of a goldsmith, Jean de Tournes was born in 1504. After travels (though we do not know just where), he signed up to work with Sébastien Gryphe.[24] He founded his own firm in Lyons (at roughly the same time that Dolet founded his), and it became a center for the translation of Latin and Greek texts, but also of Spanish and Italian works. De Tournes was the official publisher of poets of the Lyons school—Maurice Scève, Louise Labbé, and Pernette Du Guillet. He followed the fashion of placing an illustration in the center of the page of a small-format work, thus making the image more prominent than the text. This layout served him for the publication of two famous works, the *Métamorphoses d'Ovide figurées* and the *Quadrins historiques de la Bible,* illustrated by the official painter of Lyons, Bernard Salomon, and it not only did much to popularize these famous texts but created an iconography that was copied ceaselessly. In an effort to create a French typeface that could rival roman letters, De Tournes asked Bernard Salomon's son-in-law, Robert Granjon, to create characters for him: the result was the typeface known as *caractères de civilité,* a style that much resembles handwriting and was more readable for people seeking an introduction to book reading. Not incidentally the new typeface was used for books of religious propaganda. Although this script did not eliminate roman letters, it was used for centuries in the elementary schools of northern France and Flanders to help children learn to write who already knew how to read.

In 1517 Martin Luther, an Augustinian monk, posted his propositions against indulgences on the doors of the chapel of the Augustinians in Wittenberg. Almost immediately the first modern press campaigns were unleashed throughout Germany in a flood of competing posters, pamphlets, and caricatures. As if smitten by fever, the presses produced vastly increased numbers of books in Low German. They functioned at top capacity to distribute far and wide the works of the Reformer, his partisans, and his adversaries. Such works alone accounted for perhaps one-third of German publications in the years between 1518 and 1523, and some works, the *Betbuchlein*, or "Appeal To the Christian Nobility of the German Nation" for one, went through tens of reprints and reached a total of perhaps fifty thousand copies. It was Luther's translation of the Bible, however, that was the mainstay of the press. That it was not the first translation of the Bible mattered little: printed by Melchior Lotter in Wittenberg on three presses working simultaneously, the New Testament appeared in September 1522; it went through fourteen reprintings in that same city in the following two years, and it was reprinted sixty-six times in Augsburg, Basel, Strasbourg, and Leipzig. Overall it had eighty-seven editions in High German and nineteen in Low German. The Old Testament, which appeared next, book by book, had an equal success: there were a total of 410 editions of it between 1522 and 1546. Its success continued unabated: In Wittenberg Hans Lufft was responsible for producing thirty-six editions of the Old Testament from 1546 to 1580, so that Jean Crell was hardly exaggerating when he stated that Lufft alone distributed one hundred thousand copies of biblical texts between 1534 and 1574.[25]

We are talking about massive circulation figures that pushed aside the publishing of learned works, at least for a time. Germany, a land with a high literacy rate for the period, the motherland of printing, and in an earlier age over-equipped to supply the greater part of the European market, bore the full brunt of the first modern means of mass communication. Of course the Reformation had quite other origins. The demand for books was so great that the printshops of every city worked in all haste to satisfy a local or regional public visited by peddlers in the surrounding villages and rural areas. Such works encouraged forms of reading aloud in which those who could decipher a text would read to their family or to a circle of illiterate friends. The works gained in prestige from the mere fact of being printed; printing gave them something like a palpable existence and an implicit verity. In sixteenth-century Germany the Word of God gained in prestige as it was offered in several million volumes: reading was like a revelation hitherto known only in restricted circles which had transmitted no more than glimpses of it in sermons and readings during the Mass.

In this way a vast public began to have access to the book in Reformation Germany. Outside the learned circuits that connected scholars, local and regional circuits grew up that were closer to the wants of the population. At the same time a cleavage opened between regions won over to Lutheranism (or Calvinism) and southern lands that had remained faithful to the Roman Church and that would be inundated with a mass literature of their own during the Catholic revival.[26] We also need to keep in mind that the typographers of the artisanal age had little interest in producing large pressruns at one time, so that publishing success stories were defined by a high number of editions. This favored a fragmented market that encouraged particularism, a situation that reinforced some forms of a taste for reading but weakened literary creation in the national language.

The Reformation in France did not result in this sort of division. The competition among certain booksellers who attempted to use clandestine networks to crystallize opinion is beyond the scope of this volume.[27] Let me simply state that, as in so many other cases, no amount of repression could stifle the book and the messages that it was its function to transmit. Lutheran writings arrived in Paris through Basel, and they were immediately condemned by the Faculty of Theology and the Parlement. The booksellers of Basel responded by organizing barely clandestine relay stations that passed books from Lyons to Chalon-sur-Saône and from Paris to Nantes. At the same time the first bases for an underground struggle appeared outside France, first in Strasbourg from where Latin editions of Lutheran pamphlets were dispatched throughout France. Antwerp, another center of distribution, followed a policy often practiced even in our own day. The Most Catholic king tolerated the printing of heretical books aimed at "infecting" the kingdom of his Most Christian "brother" on the condition that they not be distributed in his own kingdom. One can easily see why French refugees soon dreamed of a "haven" where they could be sole masters of their acts beyond the reach of all police forces. On 4 November 1530 one of their leaders, Guillaume Farel, entered Neuchâtel, where he chased out the priests, and abolished the Catholic cult. He was soon joined by one of his old associates, Pierre de Vingle, the son of a *prote* from Lyons who had worked for Claude Nourry, had been a peddler in Haute-Provence, and had printed heretical works in Geneva under precarious conditions. Finally in safety, Vingle printed a translation of the Bible by Pierre-Robert Olivétan. He used the same type font, however, to print a small poster denouncing the horrors of the Mass. This modest handbill was distributed throughout Paris, where it set off an unprecedented repression. This was how the famous *affaire des placards* came to be written into history to provide an example of the cycles of provocation and repression that are all too familiar even today. Be that as it may, on 10 August 1535, the Mass was abolished in Geneva. Eleven months later, Calvin made his entry into the city and instituted a government of theocratic tendencies. The city, which at the time had only a few presses, soon received a throng of refugees, among them a number of people from the book trades. Conrad Bade, Josse Bade's son, arrived in 1549, and no less a personage than Robert Estienne in 1550. Some forty presses functioned in Protestant Geneva, most of them working to turn out works of religious propaganda. Support networks grew up among printers and booksellers who more or less openly supported their cause. In spite of all the laws and all the efforts of the royal police, peddlers who at times paid with their lives regularly provided French Protestants with the books they needed to nourish their faith.

This was how Geneva came to be a great publishing center. Large numbers of typographers and booksellers from Lyons took refuge there when the Catholic party won out in their city or, more simply, when work orders lagged. A great bookseller, Antoine Vincent, headed this movement. His activities still remain something of a mystery, and he seems to have had printed in Geneva the same books that he published under his imprint in Lyons. Once peace was restored the Genevans headed a network that furnished books to the French Protestant communities. That market did not suffice, however: the Geneva printers also published the works of heterodox Italians and, like the printers in Lyons, they specialized in works on medicine and the law. They figured prominently at the Frankfurt fairs, and they established privileged relations with their coreligionists in Holland. When the nature of the book trade obliged them to become wholesalers, they contributed greatly to furnishing books over a territory that stretched from the Spanish Franche-Comté to the French Dauphiné and reached into Huguenot Languedoc. The revocation of the Edict of Nantes cut into their business, but they achieved an astonishing comeback. Taking over from the last great publishers of the Counter-Reformation in Lyons and shamelessly putting a Lyons imprint (or that of some other more fantastic place) on their publications, they became specialists in Catholic theology and took over the Iberian market and its American dependencies. In our own days an ambassador of the Swiss Confederation who is also a learned bibliographer has demonstrated that the ecclesiastical libraries of Spain, Portugal, and South America often owned volumes that originated in Geneva printshops from firms that had printed a large number of heretical books and would soon contribute to the circulation of Voltaire's works.[28]

The crisis from 1630 to 1660 divided the history of the artisanal book into two quite different phases. Coming as it did at the moment when Europe was passing from expansion to recession, it marked the end of the euphoria of the Renaissance. It also prompted new ways in which national circuits occupied the territory—a territory that in turn subdivided and split into regional areas.

This means that modern vernacular literatures developed in societies that were closing in on themselves. France dominated the publishing world over Spain, which never had the presses that its writers deserved, Italy, which was undergoing an economic downturn, a ravaged Germany, and England, whose hour had not yet come. The seventeenth century in France was the century of the saints, but it was also a century of theological conflict and the century of French classicism. Europe was tipping toward recession, which meant that booksellers needed to offer the public the largest possible choice of books at the lowest possible price. In the era of the *Discourse on Method* (1637), it was no coincidence that many published titles included phrases like *Abrégé, Moyen court,* or *Méthode aisée.* The market needed new ideas, whether they came from the devotional and liturgical books that made up the bulk of the printers' business or from secular literature.[29]

This totally upset the rules of the publishing game. Like latter-day publishers, the booksellers of the time had ways to evaluate the market. The prestige of a preacher, the reputation of a confessor, an author's membership in a religious order or an organized religious current were all aids to success. It was also possible to run a "test" on a poet whose verse was beginning to find a hearing in fashionable circles by inserting some of his or her poems into one of the collective publications that took the place of our literary reviews. Similarly crowds flocking to see a new play attracted attention to its author. Still there were no guarantees of success, and the booksellers of the time already knew—and clearly explained—that only one out of ten of the works that they published had any chance of selling really well, enabling them to make up the losses they sustained on other books. Even at that early date publishers needed "big names." In that age they were Corneille, Madeleine de Scudéry, Guez de Balzac, and Voiture. After 1660 they were Molière, Racine, La Fontaine, and Boileau. The greatest drawing cards, however, were religious: Louis of Grenada, Francis de Sales, Le Moyne, and Le Nobletz. Works that bore their names moved fast at any price.[30]

Such authors' works were immediately and widely pirated, to the detriment of the original publisher and the author. Let us move to Grenoble on the eve of the Fronde to understand how book pirating worked.[31] Jean II Nicolas, the son of a Protestant peddler from Oisans, was a bookseller, but he also sold paper, parchment, and pens. He handled military supplies as well, but in that frontier region he managed to sell only one cannon. As treasurer general of the duc de Lesdiguière, the governor of the city of Grenoble, Nicolas dabbled in banking, even in usury, and on occasion he furnished cash to citizens of Grenoble who needed to go to Paris. All in all, he figured as a notable, and was named third *consul* of the city. He knew Molière, whose troupe toured the region. Still, bookselling remained his principal activity. His stock came from two centers, Geneva, which sent him Protestant works for the large Calvinist community in Grenoble and its environs, and Lyons, which relayed new books from Paris as well as furnishing its own publications. Soon, however, he also established a correspondence with a bookseller in Avignon, Jean Piot, who sent him pirated editions of popular theatrical works. Like all other booksellers, Nicolas operated by barter, so he needed something to offer his correspondents. Now and then he produced works of local interest and books written by local authors, one a life of Lesdiguières, who rose to be Constable of France, another a life of Bayard, the heroic "Chevalier sans peur et sans reproche." These somewhat specialized works failed to balance his accounts, so he tried exporting other products of the region such as paper from Dauphiné mills, gloves, and dog and deer hides. No great profits ensued. This trade was interrupted by the Fronde, and Nicolas did not return to it. The only solution to his problem lay in printing pirated editions. He and a colleague from Grenoble regularly provided the regional market with small duodecimo editions printed in pressruns of about one thousand copies of literary successes from Paris—works like Father Le Moyne's *Saint Louis,* Lucan's *Pharsalia* (in the Brébeuf translation), or Chapelain's *La Pucelle.*

A brief glance at a pirated edition of this sort is singularly enlightening. The tiny duodecimo volumes produced by Piot, printed on poor-quality paper and sold with rough paper covers, are not much to look at. Neither were they expensive: 7 sols, 6 deniers for Corneille's *Théodore vierge et martyr* whereas the copy of the original Paris quarto edition that Nicolas had bought, probably in order to use it for his own reprint, cost him 2 livres, 10 sols. Or take the case of *La Pucelle.* Following a tried and true commercial strategy, the publisher of this work, the Paris printer Augustin Courbé, gave this long-awaited poem a sumptuous in-folio edition embellished with engravings by Abraham Bosse, after Vignon. Their curiosity aroused, Nicolas's wealthier clients came into his shop to borrow the work, but only five of them kept the copy they had borrowed, paying between 13 and 20 livres, depending on the binding. When the duodecimo edition, also illustrated, arrived from Paris, Nicolas sold it at 3 livres the copy. But the Grenoble pirated edition had already begun to circulate in a duodecimo volume that was selling briskly for a modest 1 livre 10 sols. That settled the case.

These examples illustrate an ineluctable fact: henceforth reputations were made in Paris, and the booksellers of the capital had every interest in offering their new publications in a handsome edition at a high price, later progressively lowering both quality and sale price to reach a larger and larger public. The provincial printer interested in putting out a pirated edition, whose costs were less since he reproduced a text that had already been printed, had every reason to try to break into the market as soon as the first edition appeared. This meant that the Paris firms had to realize the better part of their profits from that first edition by offering it at the highest price that the market would bear, as, for example, 30 livres for the ten calfbound octavo volumes of Madeleine de Scudéry's *Clélie* in 1660, a sum equivalent to half the dowry of the wife of a journeyman printer.

Pirated editions were not an exclusively French phenomenon. A chronic disease of publishing, the practice reached the acute stage when a market for new books developed. Since it was not against the law to counterfeit a book originally published in another country, book piracy particularly affected regions where more than one state shared a linguistic area. It was particularly widespread in Italy and even more so in Germany. During the eighteenth century the major German booksellers—those who published the works of Leibniz, Lessing, and Goethe, most of whom were established in Berlin, Halle, and Leipzig—complained bitterly when their best publications were systematically pirated in the cities of southern Germany, Switzerland, and the Austrian Empire, where Joseph II, an enlightened despot, encouraged the system. We can understand why Enlightenment authors denounced what they considered a form of true commercial piracy that deprived them of the legitimate rewards of their labors.[32]

As in our own day, the printing presses of that age served to provide a large number of other print pieces besides books. We shall see later the role of occasional pieces of all sorts, pamphlets, and the earliest newspapers. Printers and booksellers had flocked to secondary centers during this period, often in response to an appeal from the local authorities. Their chief source of income was printing texts of a totally practical nature—print jobs for the city, administrative and judiciary documents, local or regional news sheets, but also primers, catechisms, and civility books for use in the parish schools, and even class texts for secondary schools. Since printers were in close touch with a broad public that was gaining an ever-larger familiarity with the written word, they knew how to evaluate the public's aspirations. In their function as retailers of learned books, they gradually came to realize that most works of that sort interested only a restricted elite; they were instrumental in the rise of the literature that is somewhat erroneously called "popular," and they created new circuits for book distribution.

This trend was universal, but the clearest example of it is the Bibliothèque bleue.[33] To recall its history: in the early years of the seventeenth century, the son of a master printer in Troyes, Nicolas Oudot, set up shop on his own. Whether or not he took inspiration from an earlier initiative, he gathered together old woodcuts that seemed outdated in comparison to the new copperplate engravings, and he used them to illustrate small-format books that he printed with close-set type, using worn fonts, on the poor-quality paper made in the region, covering his volumes with a rough blue paper. For his texts he drew on local hagiography, on traditional tales inspired by Scripture, and on a devotional literature popular among the clergy of the region, but he also offered a number of old chivalric romances and a variety of theatrical works. Above all, he was betting on the public's taste for Christian mythology and on the power of attraction of traditional tales. As years went by, one success followed another. Nicolas II Oudot, the founder's son, added Parisian *tabarinades* (farces) to the collection and recent works by Parisian writers teaching the arts of proper social com-

portment, conversation, and letter-writing. Other printers in Troyes—
Girardon, Febvre, and Briden—soon imitated the formula. These men
drew up an agreement with a group of Paris booksellers on the Quai des
Grands-Augustins and set out to conquer the capital. There are traces of
members of the Oudot family in Paris at the end of the century; other
printers preferred to go to Franche-Comté and even to the Ardennes. In
1722 the warehouses of the mother house in Troyes contained 40,000
small volumes tied up in packets of a dozen each, ready for sale for a few
deniers each, and 2,576 reams of printed sheets—enough to make up
350,000 octavo-sized books of 48 pages each. The Garnier family later
picked up where the Oudots had left off, and two inventories (in 1781 and
1789) show that their stocks were even larger.

All this had not been created *ex nihilo*. Typographers had always taken
traditional texts that the literati considered outmoded and relaunched them
at a low price to a humbler clientele of relative newcomers to reading.
Before the Oudots, the Bonfons firm in Paris, for example, had already
tested this formula. The Bibliothèque bleue borrowed some of its titles—
L'Art de mourir, for instance, and Aesop's *Fables*—from one or another of
these series. It even borrowed a certain number of its chivalric romances
from Vérard, and *Le Calendrier des bergers* and *La danse macabre* from Guy
Marchand. On occasion, it used books published in Lyons in the early
sixteenth century. The Bibliothèque bleue was an ambiguous collection,
however: it was enriched as the centuries went by with some literary borrowings that have been called popular but that were more accurately from
the burlesque genre; other choices such as Perrault's *Contes* were tales of a
genuinely popular origin but revised and reinterpreted by men of letters.
Along with books that are still famous today, the inventories of the Troyes
booksellers list large numbers of primers, collections of Christmas songs,
catechisms bearing the approval of local bishops, and civility books.[34] This
means that in the last analysis the Bibliothèque bleue aimed at furnishing
low-cost manuals of maximum edification and accessible to all who frequented or had frequented the parish schools in the east of France, a region
of early literacy. Given its success, it is hardly surprising that printers in
Rouen soon imitated the example of their Troyes colleagues by creating a
Norman Bibliothèque bleue aimed at a similar public, or that the same
thing occurred somewhat later in Liège and Limoges. These specialized
booksellers also offered almanacs, some of which, the *Messager boiteux* of
Liège for one, met with enormous success. The almanacs originally included astrological information and gave the dates of the fairs and the pil-

grimages in the region. In the eighteenth century they tended to become more diversified to show an increasingly open attitude toward the world outside, noting the most important events of the year just past.[35]

These little books could not be distributed through the usual networks, hence peddlers sold them from town to town. Peddlers had appeared in France as early as the sixteenth century: Albert Labarre noted their presence around Amiens between 1540 and 1560, where they sold small prints called *fatras,* and they undoubtedly were highly instrumental in circulating works relating to the Protestant Reformation, as were the militant peddlers who carried printed materials from Geneva. In the reign of Henry IV established booksellers complained of competition from notions sellers (*merciers*), some of whom must have been itinerant, and they persuaded the authorities to prohibit the *merciers* from selling books other than almanacs and books of hours. In the seventeenth century the books on the Bibliothèque bleue lists seem to have been sold by *mercerots* of this sort working a limited territory. Soon, however, another and more far-ranging form of peddling appeared. Merchants from Mont-sous-Vent in the diocese of Avranches, from Chamagnon in Lorraine, or from Monestier-lès-Briançon took to the road for an annual "campaign," following a set itinerary and selling books and engravings.[36]

The account books of one of these peddlers, a Norman named Noël Gille but known as Pistole, gives a good idea of their business.[37] These men often covered hundreds of kilometers, stopping at fairs and markets, at the gates of the châteaux, or in the town squares, offering for sale works that they had brought along, sometimes in a horse-drawn cart. Their stock included the familiar blue booklets and small devotional books for everyday use, but at times they carried merchandise of quite another kind: prohibited books, of course, but also major publications like Voltaire's *Oeuvres complètes.* Many peddlers eventually settled down, and some founded illustrious publishing dynasties. They continued to peddle their wares during the French Revolution, and they returned in force from Normandy to the gates of Paris under the Restoration. Their business took another growth spurt with the spread of literacy, as we can see from Jean-Claude Darmon's studies of the peddlers of Haute-Comminges. The *bons esprits* of the mid-nineteenth century often denounced peddlers' books, which did indeed often dabble in magic and purvey Bonapartist propaganda. This sort of literature died off only when the schoolmasters (the *hussards noirs*) of the Republic imposed the publications of Hachette and his ilk even in rural areas, offering a quite different ideology of the book, the Larousse ideology.

The blue booklets of the Bibliothèque bleue no more represented a distinct sector of the book trade than paperback books do today. Nearly all the peddlers who sold them also sold engravings and songs—a question to which I shall soon return. Many printers (in Lorraine, in Normandy, and in Avignon) specialized in reprints of best-selling devotional books, some of which reached truly impressive total pressruns. The account books of one bookseller and bookbinder from Langres, Pierre Héron, show just how books were sold in the age of the Enlightenment. Héron ordered books from Paris and Lyons for customers in Langres, a good-sized city, and its environs. For example, he sold three copies of Father Louis Moreri's *Grand dictionnaire historique* to local cutlers; he ordered a copy of the *Encyclopédie*, and he sold a good number of law books, even of theological works, albeit a few at a time. His principal suppliers were Monnoyer in Neuchâtel for devotional books and Garnier in Troyes for books from the Bibliothèque bleue lists, which together accounted for most of his sales. His best-selling title was a sort of book of hours of Jansenist inspiration, *L'Ange conducteur*, with 2,500 copies sold between 1756 and 1776. This merits a smile when we learn that Héron's wife's name was Denise Diderot and that she was a cousin of the philosopher. But then, Héron, like most of his colleagues, may also have traded in less orthodox works that he fails to mention.[38]

During the century and a half that preceded the French Revolution, distribution circuits (that have somewhat hastily been labeled "popular") devoted to a broadly based sale of low-priced books grew up throughout France. The phenomenon was universal, however: we can see it everywhere from England to Italy and from Sweden to Spain, and comparable phenomena can be found in seventeenth-century Japan and in modern Brazil. Moreover, certain works reappeared from one region of Europe to another. One such was the famous *Till Eulenspiegel*, probably first set down by the Strasbourg theologian Thomas Murner around 1515 and later circulated in Germany, Flanders, and France. Another example is the *Miroir des âmes*, or *Miroir de l'âme du pêcheur*, originally a French work, which has been attested in various versions throughout Europe and was later carried by Catholic missionaries to the Indies and South America.[39] Peddlers' practices differed considerably from one place to another. In England peddlers usually bought their stocks in London, moving out from there to country areas to sell ballads, small books, and almanacs; in Italy peddlers sold devotional works often written in verse. Avignon, Venice, and Brescia, the city of the Romanellis, provided books to southern Europe. Those were the cities to which the "Bisoards" (peddlers from Briançon) came to fill their packs, as did the "Esclavons" (Slavic inhabitants of the Venetian mainland), who traveled east to the Greek islands and as far as eastern Armenia and west to Spain and Portugal. The first book networks in South America were created by French booksellers from the Alps or from Normandy—among them, in the nineteenth century, one of the Garnier brothers. Finally, there were specialized presses often run by emigrés that produced similar forms of literature to attempt to help Armenians and Greeks conserve their religion and some form of national identity under Turkish domination.

In all societies texts and images multiply at a similar pace, and from the fifteenth to the nineteenth centuries engraving and typography followed parallel careers in Europe.

Like the printed book that caricatured, redefined, and modified its manuscript model, print illustrations had an ambiguous relationship with their models.[40] When it transcribes a work of art, an engraving appears to substitute for the real thing. But even when it has distorted their image it has contributed to the glory of some of the most famous works of art: we need only think of the vicissitudes of the *Mona Lisa*. It is only natural that many of the first engraving workshops (for copperplate engravings in particular) were organized around famous artists from Mantegna and Dürer to Rubens. Such artists often used the new technique to increase their celebrity and raise the prices their paintings could command, but they also helped to make engraving something else than an instrument for reproduction. With the aid of some talented engravers, they gave engraving its autonomy and its titles of nobility, and they did much to give it a new mission as a reflection of current happenings and real life.

Any printer of engravings was subject to somewhat different laws than those regulating the book publisher. By far the larger part of his investment went into the making of the drawing and the engraving of the plate, with the actual printing and the paper entailing only minimal expense. Nonetheless, he could not get an infinite number of prints from his plates. The first pulls had much greater value for collectors; plates soon wore down and showed a loss of quality; even woodcuts, although more durable, eventually wore out or broke.

The first markets for engravings were quite naturally the major commercial cities—Bruges very early on, later Augsburg, Nuremberg, Venice, and Florence. Even more than the printed book, the engraving was a bourgeois art par excellence, but it also appealed to a broadly varied public. Copperplate engravings signed by famous masters, executed in goldsmiths' circles, and printed in small quantities were obviously destined for a wealthy elite, whereas reproductions of the same plates in copies of highly varying quality were probably accessible to broader social circles.

Woodcuts could still be found everywhere. Usually made by anonymous artisans, they could be produced more rapidly and printed in larger numbers and were easier to copy. As the sixteenth century progressed they tended to loose their value for collectors. Woodcuts were already a propaganda tool when Dürer contributed to the emperor's glory by his depiction of the "Triumph of Maximilian I." Later they played an important role in spreading the Reformation—largely through Protestant-inspired caricatures—and even at that date they served to illustrate broadsheets and *canards* (satirical or sensational newssheets). As a form of popularization, woodcuts began in Germany but soon reached all of Europe. In France for instance artisans grouped in the rue Montorgueil around 1560 illustrated booklets on current happenings and even provided news reports (sold by street hawkers) of the latest news in the Wars of Religion.

Is it simple coincidence that only a few years earlier, around 1550, when Christophe Plantin was about to found his printshop there, Jérôme Cocx launched a revolution in the engravings market from Antwerp? Cocx, who had entertained Pieter Brueghel and Giorgio Ghisi of Mantua in his shop, took advantage of the artists who flocked to Antwerp and of the city's commercial prosperity to found the first large-scale enterprise for the publication of engravings. Breaking with the system in which artists printed and sold their own works, Cocx commissioned works from artists and introduced specialization. Thus the bottom of his plates bears a mention of the person who provided the idea ("inv." = *invenit*), of the one who drew the image ("del." = *delineavit*); of the painter ("pinx." = *pinxit*) and the engraver ("sculp." = *sculpsit*, or "inc." = *incidit*), but also of the publisher ("exc." = *excudit*) who owned the plate and the right to reproduce it.[41]

The Counter-Reformation was organizing its forces in just this period. When Antwerp was reconquered by the Spanish, Galle and Wiericx, Cocx's successors, became agents of a concerted propaganda, as did Plantin and others. Working under the direction of the Society of Jesus, they introduced a new religious imagery and their engravings circulated in copies by the million. By the end of the sixteenth century Flemish engravers also moved south to swell the ranks of their French colleagues. By then printers and merchants of copperplate engravings had set up shop in the rue Saint-Jacques near the booksellers and book printers, and lesser personages sold images on the quais or outside the cemetery of the Holy Innocents.

There was no rigorous division of labor in the engraver's trade. A good many engravers, particularly in Paris, also had a shop in which they sold their own works and those of a few colleagues, and there were also dynasties of great print sellers like the Langlois and Mariette families who might also be stationers and bookseller-publishers. Marianne Grivel's studies have shown that in the seventeenth century although nearly 30 percent of the works that have been conserved have a religious subject, portraits account for a good share of them (20 percent). The time had come when the faces of statesmen, great men, scholars, or the most famous artists could be familiar to everyone. Similarly, new fashions in dress, ornament, and decor were published without delay. Finally, while cartographers and sellers of mathematical instruments set up shop near the Tour de l'Horloge, peddlers sold almanacs and engravings of current events throughout the land.

Henceforth copperplate engravings reached a large public, and some of them sold at truly low prices. This meant that woodcuts, which portrayed reality with less precision, went out of style in Paris and clients deserted the image-makers of the rue Montorgueil. Was this change partly due to an increase in the number of wood engravers and *dominotiers* in the French provinces? Although Toulouse had a long tradition going back to 1465, the real rise of the imagery usually known as "popular" came only in the late sixteenth or the seventeenth century in a number of other cities such as Orléans, Chartres, Avignon, Le Puy, Epinal, Clermont, Limoges, and Bordeaux.[42] The spread of "popular" prints was a phenomenon comparable to the appearance of the Bibliothèque bleue in that it too was connected with the progress of literacy as well as with a more open attitude toward the outside world. A turning point seems to been reached in France in the late seventeenth and the early eighteenth centuries, giving a new impetus to business for book peddlers, nearly all of whom also sold images. Some, the Chamagnons for instance, were itinerant singers as well.

All through Europe distribution circuits were set up for images and booklets of this sort. Also throughout Europe we can see a difference between the ruder materials destined for small towns, villages, and even rural areas and the more up-to-date and "modern" books or images for sale in the cities. Everywhere a written culture and an imagery circulated in a range of forms whose hierarchy was symbolized in the quality and general aspect of the engravings as much as in the messages they transmitted. In the last analysis the distribution circuits for engravings seem to have been modeled on those of the book.

THE POWER STRUCTURE AND THE PRESS

When printing devised a cultural communication network modeled on that of commercial exchanges it was as if it had moved the literati of Europe into the same time frame, producing a phenomenon of "massification" in somewhat the same fashion as television in its early days. Everyone strove to sing the praises of the new art and glorify its inventors, giving rise to a theme that is still with us today. The desire to stimulate and broaden the market led booksellers to innovate ceaselessly and to diversify their wares, which means that they reached out over greater distances to reinforce a variety of intellectual solidarities. They produced an increasing number of works in the vernacular languages aimed at the greatest possible number of readers, and they invited scholars to pursue a written propaganda for the use of the less scholarly that often took up where oral propaganda— the sermon or the university debate—had left off. By contributing to the moral awakening of large numbers of people and by sharpening antagonism, this tendency encouraged the crystallization of heresies, while nationalism and class struggle waited on the distant horizon. One result was the organization of systems of censorship and repression.

At the same time, book folk turned to the authorities and asked them to arbitrate the conflicts that had grown up within their ranks, thus launching the slow process of the elaboration of complex legislation. Economics, politics, and religion were closely connected when it came to regulating the book trade, and rulers, who were more often arbiters than parties to the disputes, found they had to play an active role in the organization of book distribution circuits if they wanted to keep the public peace and maintain economic prosperity.

One cannot begin to comprehend the history of censorship in Western societies without some notion of the church's ideas concerning the discussion and diffusion of dogma. Until Gutenberg the church had censured ideas more than texts (symbolic exceptions aside) because it considered the book primarily as a working tool for the exclusive use of scholars. Thus it had concentrated on pursuing the preachers and had shown little concern for written propaganda. The church soon learned that the spread of heresy was regularly accompanied by the translation of sacred texts, and every time this happened it denounced the dangers of free interpretation of the Bible. Nonetheless, the church did not react when dynamic printers in southern Germany began putting out not only large numbers of edifying works but also Bibles in High German, nor when that movement reached Italy, France, the Low Countries, and Spain. Nor did professors at the University of Cologne, in northern Germany, express alarm when some typographers came to settle in their city (1464–65). No one was yet wary of the press. Early in 1478, however, a member of the clergy wrote a pamphlet denouncing maneuvers on the part of the city fathers against benefice-holders in the region, and the magistrates immediately countered with legal prosecution. The first censorship of a printed book was thus promoted by a civil power. Around the same time a sumptuously illustrated Bible in Low German was beginning to circulate in Cologne. It was a major publishing venture, launched from Nuremberg by the powerful Anton Koberger in partnership with the master of the emperor's mint. The doctors of the university, who were traditionalists and dominated by the Dominicans, took fright and turned to Rome for help.

The pope's response to their plea arrived in March 1479: henceforth, all printers, buyers, and readers of heretical books were to be chastised, either through ecclesiastical censure or in some other manner, and booksellers were to ask permission before launching a new work. [43] The book trade in Cologne was still complaining in 1501 of this system that hampered its activities. It was not an isolated case. In 1485 in Mainz the archbishop, Berthold of Henneberg, denounced improper use of the press and the avidity of booksellers. His criticism was aimed at translations of texts on canon law and liturgical works, especially missals, but also at works of the classical Greek and Latin authors. His monitory letter, repeated in 1486 and again in 1487, specified that authorization to print a book would be given by a four-member commission that included university professors from Erfurt.

Italy was next in line. In Venice, which had become the largest publishing center in Europe, the papal legate and archbishop of Treviso, Nicola Franco, prohibited the printing of books regarding the Catholic faith or ecclesiastical matters without previous authorization from the bishop or the vicar general. Papal intervention soon became more systematic: in 1501 Pope Alexander VI reinforced existing measures to forbid the typographers of the ecclesiastical provinces of Cologne, Mainz, Trier, and Magdeburg from printing or causing to be printed, under pain of excommunication, any piece of writing without the express and freely given permission of the bishop or his representative. And on 4 May 1515, during the Fifth Lateran Council, Pope Leo X published a new constitution prohibiting throughout all Christendom the publishing of any work without the authorization of one of two persons, the Vicar of His Holiness and the Master of the Sacred Palace at Rome; in other places, the bishop and the inquisitor.[44]

The Catholic Church had thus opted for prior censorship of the press even before Lutheranism exploded on the scene. What we have seen above of the history of heresies gives an insight to its point of view. The Protestant Reformation confirmed the church's outlook and led it to take positions at the Council of Trent that were to shape Western society for centuries to come.

From the church's point of view, what lay at the heart of the matter was the essential problem of the foundations of religion. Catholics and most of the reformers agreed that the apostles had not written (or "insinuated," as Cardinal Cervini said) all that Christ had taught, and that the Holy Spirit continued the work of Revelation after Christ left this earth. If this was the case, how was one to situate traditions in relation to Scripture? Must one hold, with Luther (and the post-Tridentine theologians), that traditions were an interpretation of Scripture? Also, given the perpetuity of traditions concerning dogma, how could one explain such changes in the Western church as the disappearance of prayer to the East, communion under two kinds, and the marriage of priests, or the consumption of meat from strangled animals? Like Luther, Tridentine Catholics held that the unity of Revelation resided in the living Christ and in the living reality of the Christian mystery, not in what had been transmitted either orally or in written form. Still, the Fathers of the Council declared in their decree of 1546 that "the fountain of all, both saving truth, and moral discipline" was contained "in the written books, and the unwritten traditions which, received by the Apostles from the mouth of Christ himself, from the Apostles themselves, the Holy Ghost dictating, have come down even unto us, transmitted as it were from hand to hand."[45]

This text is essential. The affirmation of the apostolic origin of traditions, the content of which is not made explicit, was combined with the idea that "the Church does not hold its authority from Scripture, nor Scripture its [authority] from the Church, but one and the other hold their authority from God—Scripture by divine inspiration, the Church by divine institution" (Edmond Ortigues). This proclaims the continued succession of the evangelic ministry from the apostles to the bishops (taken collectively), a succession that gives the bishops a divinely inspired mission and justifies the priesthood and the sacraments. Finally, the mention of doctrinal pertinence in connection with truth and moral discipline (in the formula *Tum ad fidem, tum ad mores pertinentes*) justifies the church's exercise of its function of magisterium and grants it the power to determine dogma.[46]

The Catholic religion, a religion of the book, was thus also a religion of a tradition, so the church considered it logical that it be designated by the supreme Power as the interpreter of the book and the guardian of a custom. The Tridentine doctors and the popes who followed their example when the Council of Trent closed in 1564 drew practical conclusions from these premises. The Mass continued to be said in Latin with the priest bearing the responsibility for furnishing any necessary explanations to the faithful. To nip controversy in the bud the Vulgate of St. Jerome was proclaimed the authentic document of Holy Scripture—that is, the most authentic version in the written tradition, other versions being available for consultation should its meaning need clarifying. Local liturgies, which the Protestants had so often denounced, were to be brought into line with a carefully revised Roman liturgy. The immense task of textual revision meant the publication of official editions: although the Sovereign Pontiff tended to reserve the monopoly to Paolo Manuzio, the work had to be shared and it brought immense amounts of business to the book trade.

At the same time Rome attempted to coordinate repressive policies that were burgeoning everywhere, beginning with the various versions of the Index that were springing up on all sides. Thus in 1564 Pius V, after mature reflection, put out an Index to replace the hastily drawn-up lists of Paul IV. A special congregation was created soon after to see to updating this "honors list" at regular intervals. The bull *Dominici gregis* (24 March 1564) laid down ten essential rules: all works of the principal heresiarchs were definitively prohibited, as were non-Christian books on religious topics, obscene and immoral works, and works on magic and judiciary astrology; translations of the Bible were not exactly prohibited, but the faithful were enjoined not to read them without the permission of the local ordinary or inquisitor, which permission would be granted only after consultation with the would-be reader's parish priest or confessor; controversial books were to be treated in a similar manner; the reading of classical Greek and Latin authors was tolerated because of the elegance and the purity of their language, but children were not to be exposed to them under any pretext (which meant that the era of expurgated versions was not far off); finally,

rule ten reiterated the obligation to obtain authorization before the publication of all works, and it called on the ordinaries in each locality to made
regular visits to the printshops and the booksellers' shops.[47]

Next the church needed to find ways to put its policy into effect, which
meant that it had to turn to the secular arm, thus to temporal authorities.

Ferdinand of Aragon and Isabella of Castile had completed the reconquest of Spain in the years in which printing was established in their kingdoms.[48] Henceforth religious minorities were to be assimilated. In 1478,
one year before prior censorship was established in Cologne, a new form
of inquisition appeared in Spain under the aegis of both the popes and the
Most Catholic sovereigns. Its courts, which were even installed in the New
World, did not disappear definitively until the nineteenth century. In the
years around 1500 the Spanish Inquisition burned immense amounts of
Jewish and Arabic books. The Spanish monarchs took their own precautions, however, and in 1502 they decreed that no book could leave the
presses of their kingdoms without their authorization or that of persons
designated by them, thus preventing the inquisitors from carrying out prior
censorship on their own authority. The monarchy never relinquished this
power. As late as 1558, Princess Joanna put out (in the name of Philip II)
a famous Pragmatic that established new rules for printers and booksellers:
manuscripts of all new books were to be presented to the Council of Castile
to be examined by qualified censors, who also retained the manuscript so
that they could check whether the published text conformed to it. Later, in
1627, the Council of Castile even claimed the right to examine all documents, even those of only a few pages, before they were printed.

As a matter of course these councils and commissions contained a
number of ecclesiastics. Nor were the church authorities inactive. They
sprinkled the first pages of published works with authorizations, particularly when the author was a member of a religious order. Henceforth the
publication of any book was preceded by lengthy formalities since the
theologian charged with reviewing a text took his time and made many
comments; it was also costly since it was advisable to offer each council
member a copy for his personal collection. Above all, although the Inquisition played no official role in the process of prior censorship, it did play
an active role in repressive censorship, and on occasion it seized books that
had been published with all the requisite authorizations. It drew up indexes that were veritable monuments of bibliography; it put ports under

surveillance to make sure that no "bad" books came in from outside; it burned a number of seized books and had its readers black out condemned passages in books censured *donec corrigantur*. This immense coercive effort undoubtedly hindered Lutheran propaganda and clipped the wings of certain forms of spirituality; it was less successful in the eighteenth century in combating Enlightenment ideas. Judgments of the Inquisition have varied: some have denounced its rigor, particularly toward widely circulated religious books, but others have noted its tolerance toward philosophical and scholarly publications and toward comic authors.

In France the alarm was sounded only in 1521, when Lutheran pamphlets began to spread.[49] The emotional reaction of the Faculty of Theology was immediately reflected in measures voted by the Parlement. At this first stage the king, Francis I, was torn between a desire to protect the humanist and evangelical movement and the need to prevent German heretical ideas from spreading in France. He ordered the Parlement to prohibit the publication of books on religion in the vernacular or in Latin without a permission given, after examination, by a member of the Faculty of Theology. A decree of the Parlement of 1532 stated that its judges were to visit printshops and booksellers' shops. Next the king stated, for example in his *Lettres patentes* of 17 March 1538, that no new book could be printed without his permission or the permission of "justice," and he later decreed (*Edict of Chateaubriant*, 27 June 1551) that the Parlement had to refer a work to competent theologians before granting a permission to publish. This proliferation of sometimes contradictory decisions indicates that in Gallican lands Paris university professors were considered logical choices as censors, but it also shows that the sovereign power was incapable of controlling everything that was published. If this was true in an active center like Paris, it was even truer in Lyons, where the church and the state had no such organ of control.

During this same era sovereigns and law courts were also urged to take action by people in the book trade, although for totally different reasons. Late in the fifteenth century printers who wanted to launch new publications began to demand rights to protect them against pirated editions. Venice led the way, but as early as the beginning of the sixteenth century demand for this sort of action was rising everywhere in the book trade. As with prior censorship, the various agencies of the state held competing powers. Rulers reserved to their own councils both the task of according permissions and the privilege of granting monopolies. As we have just seen, this is what happened in Spain in 1558. In France the king decreed (by the Edict of Nantes, 10 September 1563, followed by the Ordinance of Moulins, February 1566) that henceforth no book could be published without the *congé, permission, et privilège* guaranteed by the Grand Seal, hence granted by the chancellor. These measures, which were being promulgated in the same years that the Council of Trent was drawing up the rules of the Index, were obviously aimed at enabling the French sovereigns to have a personal say concerning the press.

The temporal authorities gradually became aware of the enormous task involved in publishing revised texts of Scripture, liturgical works, and the great works of the Christian tradition. They could not stand by and watch the monopoly for printing these works be reserved exclusively to the printer for the Holy See. Philip II of Spain obtained a derogation valid in his territories that permitted him to grant the task of updating liturgical books to the Hieronymite fathers of the Escorial, who edited them and jobbed out large commissions to a group of printers, working first through members of the Giunta family and later using Christophe Plantin. The kings of Spain made a general practice of such commissions, and they fixed the price of books at the same time that they granted publishing privileges and accorded exclusive rights to both private people and civil and religious communities such as the General Hospital of Madrid, the cathedral of Valladolid, and the monks of San Lorenzo del Real of the Escorial. Stripped of their legitimate profits, Spanish booksellers were left in a perpetually weak position in international competition.

The kings of France had a totally different attitude. Since they had never accepted the decrees of the Council of Trent in their kingdom, they granted a monopoly on printing books of reformed liturgy first to the bookseller Jacques Kerver, then to a booksellers' company, and they granted another company, which took as its emblem the ship of the City of Paris, a privilege to publish the principal works of the church Fathers. These powerful associations, which reorganized on several occasions, permitted the concentration of the most profitable parts of the book trade in the hands of only a few families, the most famous of which in the early seventeenth century was the Cramoisy family.[50]

During this time the book professions were evolving. Even in the finest hours of the Renaissance there were tensions between master typographers and their journeymen.[51] The journeymen, as we have seen, were subjected to a grueling work load, and they watched as their masters turned more and more to the unpaid labor of apprentices, whom the journeymen saw as future rivals in the labor market at a time when they themselves had to go from town to town and shop to shop in search of employment. Strikes of an almost modern nature broke out, chiefly in Paris (1539–43) and Lyons (1569–72). The Parlement and the king's council intervened to regulate the professions of the book trade, which led to the constitution of *communautés*—trade associations—the most important of which was the Parisian printers', booksellers', and binders' association, to which the Châtelet granted statutes in 1617. The *syndic* of this organization and his fellow-officers were quite naturally called upon to supervise the print-shops, thus becoming auxiliaries of the royal police. As if in spite of economic conditions, publishing prospered in this period when both the Counter-Reformation and the Catholic Renaissance encouraged reading, unauthorized peddlers proliferated, and access to master status remained to some extent open. Hence, as we have seen, the Paris book trade underwent a crisis of overproduction that began in the years from 1636 to 1640.

During that entire period prior censorship had remained totally ineffective since all the monarchy's efforts in that direction were countered by the claims of the doctors of the Sorbonne, who demanded the right to judge texts and admitted to no other censors than themselves. Richelieu himself encountered ferocious resistance when he attempted to name four doctors to pass on new books. Eventually Chancellor Séguier decided to have the officials of his services, the secretaries and the notaries of the king, review the manuscripts that were submitted to him. He inaugurated the long series of census registers that have come down to us, and he initiated the policy of systematic distribution to his protégés of privileges for older books that were in what we would now call the public domain. Did Richelieu imagine going even farther? There are indications that he did. By reorganizing the booksellers' companies and naming men he trusted as "printers to the king" (who thus enjoyed the lucrative publication of official acts), he occasioned the creation, under somewhat troubled conditions, of the Académie Française: its first secretary, Valentin Conrart, was also secretary to the king, and as such he was responsible for the chancery's granting of most of the privileges in the book trade. Thus one might well wonder whether Richelieu did not regard the new institution as a body of de facto censors. In 1639–40 he created the Imprimerie royale, the ancestor of France's Imprimerie nationale today, an organism that it was once suggested should hold the lucrative monopoly for publication of all French dictionaries and almanacs.[52]

Provincial presses, however, had no part in this system. Moreover, the lesser master printers and the bookbinders in Paris revolted against a policy

that favored the large booksellers, and they took over power in the corporation. Richelieu and Séguier reacted, ex officio, by appointing persons
who owed everything to them—among them Sébastien Cramoisy and Antoine Vitré—and charging them with reestablishing order. Next came the
Jansenist explosion. In the feverish climate that resulted, printers and
booksellers proliferated, and treatises and pamphlets published without
authorization were distributed openly (1643–44). Anarchy was the rule
by the time the Fronde broke out. At first the major booksellers rallied to
the support of their best customers, the members of Parlement, and they
tried to persuade the magistrates to approve the principle of granting privileges for older works (a policy to which the Parlement had traditionally
been hostile). The typographers, who were short of work, produced increasing numbers of Mazarinades and swelled the ranks of the rioters.[53]

In England the printing and sale of books was first developed by foreigners—Frenchmen for the most part—who made up two-thirds of the personnel of the book trade from 1476 to 1533. But the English gradually
learned the skills of the new profession, heretical books began to flood the
market, and Henry VIII broke with Rome. These events led to a protection-
ist policy that prohibited English printshops from accepting apprentices
from the Continent and from employing more than two foreign journeymen, and that prohibited Continental firms in England from importing
bound books, selling books at retail, or establishing new bookshops and
printshops. Toward the mid-century, the monarch granted master printers
who enjoyed the royal trust monopolies over entire categories of works:
liturgical works, Bibles, psalm books, catechisms, primers, almanacs, Latin
texts for school use, and even treatises on common law.[54] The relatively
restricted British market thus reserved to its own the publication of works
specific to its interests. This special situation encouraged a heightened
sense of association among the British booksellers. Already concentrated
in London, they joined forces in a strongly structured organization, the
Stationers' Company, which received its statutes in 1557. The surveillance
of the Stationers' Company was efficacious, and it long enjoyed a monopoly over most of the land, since outside the capital only the universities
of Oxford and Cambridge had an official right to have presses. The booksellers and the smaller printers, who held the numerical majority in the
assemblies of the Company, set out to get the better of the larger, privileged
printers. Backed by the Commons and by public opinion they won their

cause, and in 1603 and 1605 the king remitted or sold the contested privileges to the Company. The Stationers' Company had by then developed an original and coherent internal organization. They set up an "English stock," a society whose capital was divided into three overall parts corresponding to the three categories of master printers (assistants, liverymen, and yeomen). There was also a "Latin stock" made of Latin books that were traded at the Frankfurt fairs, and an "Irish stock" constituted from proceeds of the rights of the King's Printer in Ireland. The English stock, which still existed in the nineteenth century, guaranteed the predominance within the Company of a fairly large group of booksellers who shared out to printers substantial and relatively regular amounts of work. It maintained a degree of order in commercial procedures and encouraged cohesion within the English book trade.

The chief support of this cohesion was the copyright system. In order to combat pirate editions and eliminate disputes, booksellers and printers who published a text developed the habit of registering the title of the work and the name of its author with the Stationers' Company as a way of giving themselves permanent title to the work. The system functioned so well that by the sixteenth century it was generally acknowledged that proprietary rights to a work could be obtained not only by an official privilege, which was normally granted for a limited period, but also by a copyright (which could, incidentally, be sold). In certain periods, a copyright granted by the Company could enable the publisher to omit the formalities involved in requesting a permission.

England was no asylum of tolerance, however. In 1538, a proclamation forbade the publication of a book without the permission of the Privy Council, and the principle of prior censorship was reinforced in 1549, 1551, and 1559. As a general rule the "establishment"—officials of the crown and bishops—did its best to control production in times when religious differences stirred up incessant polemics. During the last quarter of the sixteenth century the Puritans launched veritable propaganda campaigns from the presses of Cambridge University, all the while proclaiming that the state should not intervene in matters of faith. In spite of the Puritans' powerful backing the Star Chamber decreed in 1586 that all works were to be submitted to the archbishop of Canterbury or the bishop of London before they could be registered with the Stationers' Company. The results of the vigilant surveillance of the church hierarchy were the rise of clandestine presses, an increase in Presbyterian propaganda from Scotland, and a massive importation of Protestant works from Holland. Pamphlets proliferated both in Stuart England and in the France of Marie de Médicis. In England they prompted a sharp reaction headed by Archbishop Laud, chief adviser to Charles I. Several authors had their ears, on occasion their nose, cut off, and in 1637 the Star Chamber decreed the reinstitution of prior approval, designating the persons to be consulted for each type of publication, tightening control over imported volumes, reinforcing the system of inspections, and forbidding book peddling. This did not stop the printing and distribution of books.

When Charles I was forced to call Parliament into session in 1640 after the failure of his first military operations, the press found itself suddenly freed of all constraints. Censors disappeared; new titles were no longer registered with the Stationers' Company. As in France during the Fronde, pamphlets and gazettes proliferated; Laud was tried. But the absence of regulation produced large numbers of unauthorized printshops and pirated editions. The House of Commons reacted, at first with moderation, but the Presbyterians and the Puritans who dominated the assembly and whose main concern was to curb the propaganda of their adversaries called for more severe controls. With the ordinance of 14 June 1643 the House of Commons reestablished both prior censorship and the Stationers' Company's control over publications, created importation licenses, and prohibited unauthorized publication of anything regarding the deliberations of the Chamber. England had simply changed censors, replacing the Anglican prelates and chaplains with the jurists, members of Parliament, schoolmasters, and ministers who had so often denounced the methods of the ecclesiastical censors. The new censors were particularly zealous in their pursuit of the royalist newspapers headquartered at Oxford, and of "Arminians," whom they suspected of Catholic sympathies. This reversal (which incidentally was predictable) led to the publication of Milton's *Areopagitica*, and the new censors had their chance to learn the lesson of the futility of coercion.[55]

After a period of relative toleration under Cromwell, the restoration of the Stuarts brought a return to draconian measures. The Stationers' Company lost its traditional powers, the Licensing Bill of 1662 set up a rigorous system of prior censorship, and Charles II created the post of Licenser and Surveyor of the Press and entrusted it to Sir Roger L'Estrange. Taking inspiration from the French model, L'Estrange used his authority to reduce the number of printers in London from between thirty-nine and fifty-nine under the Commonwealth to twenty. This drastic change had catastrophic results and prompted a new wave of pirated editions. Next came the Glorious Revolution in 1688. The Licensing Bill, extended several times, was abrogated in 1696, while Parliament worked on new legislative texts with prudent slowness. The Copyright Act of 1709 definitively abolished prior censorship, at least for books. It also granted exclusive rights for twenty-one years to works published before 1 April 1709 and granted rights for fourteen years to works published after that date, the right to be extended for another fourteen years if the author was living. This law, which abolished the perpetual rights of the traditional copyright, quite naturally set off a deluge of protest from the booksellers. In practice, however, it turned out to be a monument of liberalism, and it founded the modern notion of literary property. There is little doubt that it encouraged both freedom of expression and the astonishing growth of British publishing during the eighteenth century.[56]

The press had never been as free in France as it was immediately after the Fronde. The Jansenists, who had solid allies in the book world, managed, with the cooperation of Fouquet, to bring out Pascal's *Lettres provinciales* before Séguier could act. The Elzeviers and their imitators in Amsterdam and Brussels put out scandalmongering little books (for example about the illicit love affairs of the young Louis XIV) that were soon to be found all over Paris. Colbert was determined to impose the rule of order in Paris and elsewhere. After long deliberations during meetings of the Conscil de police, he set up an authoritarian policy that his successors continued without respite. The governing powers prohibited new promotions to master printer until further notice, first in Paris (1667), then in the provinces (1686). These measures reduced the number of printing establishments in the capital nearly by half (in principle, to thirty-six), and almost as stringently in the provinces. This concentration, which occurred during a recession, resulted in the creation of larger and better-equipped printshops that also were easier to keep an eye on. During this same period the Paris printers received constant visits from the commissioners of the Châtelet, while the lieutenant general of police, La Reynie, and his successor, d'Argenson, kept a particularly sharp watch over the book trade. Strict controls were set up at the gates of Paris and bales of books were carefully examined by the Chambre syndicale. Furthermore, books could enter into France only through certain specified cities where inspection stations were set up. Attempts were made to trace and dismantle the distribution systems for clandestine books. At the same time the system of official permissions was remodeled, extending the requirement of the *privilège* to include almanacs. Allies of the power structure were all the more systematically given preferential treatment for *privilèges* to publish older works, and extensions were conceded automatically. The result was that France instituted a de facto system of prior authorization and perpetual copyright just as England was abandoning theirs.

These policies quite naturally secreted a bureaucracy. A special bureau of the chancery was charged with powers for *juridiction gracieuse*—the granting of *privilèges*, or permissions to publish. This agency, set up under Louis XIV, was first headed, by direct appointment, by a close friend of the chancellor and Pontchartrain's nephew, Abbé Bignon. Later it was headed by Malesherbes, the son of Chancellor Lamoignon. On several occasions these directors of the book trade conducted inquiries regarding those under their jurisdiction, and high functionaries and men of letters with good connections at court were charged with the censorship of new books. During the same period a special section of the Conseil privé had responsibility for settling disputes within the book trade, and influential state council members, aided by brilliant young *maîtres des requêtes* on their way up in government careers, held what amounted to competitive examinations to name new master printers and served as a court of appeals that set sentences for book piracy and the publication and distribution of "bad books."[57] "Good behavior" and docility were encouraged. Grouped in their powerful community, the booksellers and the printers of Paris showed proof of both. With the Revocation of the Edict of Nantes the Paris bookseller-printers received considerable credits to help them print works aimed at new converts and were the obvious beneficiaries of *privilèges* and royal publishing orders. In the early eighteenth century they accumulated considerable fortunes. Under the Regency they put out the monumental publications of the Benedictines, and they encouraged business by introducing into France the English practice of financing publishing ventures by subscription. The book trade in Paris was a closed milieu in which masterships were a monopoly reserved for the sons or the sons-in-law of current masters. André-François Le Breton, the printer and chief publisher of the *Encyclopédie* and the first printer to the king, was a product of this harem system: his grandfather was Laurent d'Houry, who had married the chambermaid of Chancellor Le Tellier's wife, thus obtaining the *privilège* to publish the *Almanach royal*, an administrative publication equivalent to the *Bottin* of latter-day France.[58]

Thanks to such men, to the intellectual prestige of France, and to the talents of its typographers and engravers, Paris exported immense numbers of books during the Enlightenment. But any society that is too protected and too sure of the morrow tends to become petrified. Not only were the printers and booksellers of Paris detested by their workers and scorned by writers; they were also denounced by Malesherbes for lacking the spirit of enterprise.

The system that had been set up to prevent all hostile propaganda ended up, as such systems always do, reinforcing the existing balance of power. After the revocation of the Edict of Nantes, the elite of the Protestant intelligentsia from Jurieu to Bayle had gone into exile, where they fed the opposition to absolutism. Huguenot printers and booksellers also flocked to places of refuge, notably the Low Countries, where the dynamic atmosphere of those lands so close to England inspired the most gifted of the exiles to innovate.[59] The Desbordes family, who had been modest booksellers in Saumur, became large-scale publishers in Amsterdam. The Huguetan family, whose business had languished in Lyons, made an immense fortune. One of their number had been made a count of the Holy Roman Empire, and Louis XIV's dragoons kidnapped him to force him to give up the title. Something like an international cartel of French publishers was established outside France from Berlin to London and from Amsterdam to Geneva. It reflected the activities of a singularly diverse small Calvinist world in which heterodoxy flourished. Stimulated by the renewed prosperity of the empire, the entire periphery of France took part in this activity. From 1740 to 1775, enterprising businessmen of intellectual tastes behind whom there often lurked a strange fauna of literary adventurers founded new fortunes as publishers and propagandists for a "philosophical literature" by and large prohibited in France. This was true not only in Holland but also in England and the Belgian Low Countries, thanks to presses in Bouillon and Liège. In Geneva, when Gabriel and Philibert Cramer took over from the Chouet family, who had furnished books to the French Calvinists and inundated Iberian lands with Catholic publications distributed under false imprints, they sold off the Chouets' stocks to speculate on the talent of Voltaire. They launched Voltaire's new works, selling out their first editions in a few days and leaving it to the printers of pirated editions to reprint them in the various regions. The superior of the Collège de Neuchâtel and several notables kept four presses constantly at work. Their network was a veritable spider's web, and they corresponded with a large number of French men of letters and acted as both literary agents and distribution agents. They concentrated on exploiting current offerings more than on launching sensational works: for example, they reprinted the *Encyclopédie* but they also contracted with smugglers to carry into France works printed in Switzerland such as scandalous tales about the loves of Louis XV and Madame Du Barry.[60]

Booksellers and printers in the French provinces were both the victims and the stakes in this game. The preeminence of Paris, where literary reputations were made and broken, and the privileges that gave the capital not only a near monopoly on both new publications and existing works made their situation untenable. Even without support they did their best to make the system work. In his study of Rouen, Jean-Dominique Mellot introduces us into a strange world.[61] Printers were numerous but poorly equipped in this city of a long-standing literary and intellectual life and in a region of early literacy. Brilliant seconds to the Paris publishers in Corneille's day, under Louis XIV they had been obliged to shift to pirated editions, prohibited books, and peddlers' literature. They had long had a corporate organization, and their journeymen were often the sons of master printers and themselves licensed masters. The Rouen booksellers created their own copyright, and each printer recorded the titles that he intended to publish, thus avoiding local competition. As Rouen was a gateway to Paris, they were expert in the art of book smuggling. They were ferociously persecuted for these activities and, toward the end of the reign of Louis XIV, they only survived thanks to the complicity of men like Boisguilbert, the Rouen chief of police. When Boisguilbert was given the task of investigating *L'état présent des affaires de la France*, a clandestinely printed work that he himself had written, he responded to d'Argenson that no publication of the sort could be found. As for the members of the Parlement of Rouen, they pleaded the cause of their fellow citizens with Abbé Bignon, at the time the director of the book trade. That ecclesiastic, an "enlightened" spirit, a friend of Fontenelle's, a lover of good wine, and the father of a daughter, maintained amicable relations with booksellers in Holland, with whom he was in constant contact, and was aware of the disadvantages of the procedures that he himself had helped to put into place. He agreed to permit the Rouen printers, starting in 1709 at the latest, to print books that had already been published abroad; he kept a list written in his own hand of such books—books that were not downright scandalous but to which he could not grant an official *privilège*. When somewhat later the regent, Philippe d'Orléans, accepted the dedication of a new edition of Bayle's *Dictionnaire* (which was forbidden in France), Bignon's successor, Louis de Chauvelin, took the risk of seeing the work in everybody's hands and declared that he would prefer to have it printed within the kingdom rather than let money leave the country. This was the birth of the notion of tacit permission, an administrative imposture that authorized printers and booksellers to print and publish (with foreign or fantastic imprints) works on the censors' lists. A growing number of these works were registered with the chancery, and when the system of *dépôt légal* was instituted in 1537 a copy of each of these books was duly entered in exactly the same way as books published under a *privilège*.

The Rouen printers continued to show even greater audacity. It is hardly surprising that some of their number—members of the Malassis or the Jore families—figured prominently on the lists of prisoners in the Bastille or were sentenced to a variety of other punishments. The new ideas penetrated more and more deeply into French society as the century advanced. The first to be seduced by them were of course the members of an establishment that nonetheless did its best to maintain its privileges and prerogatives. Even in the beginning of the eighteenth century prominent people received visits from a new sort of canvasser who offered them—at high prices—manuscript copies of frankly scandalous texts. Soon some "peddlers" rose from this milieu to open a shop and begin publishing this sort of literature. Some became famous, one of them named Merlin whom Voltaire dubbed "Merlin the Enchanter." Eventually an entire network of tolerated booksellers profited from both a mounting prosperity and an evolution in ideas and mores.[62]

An incoherent situation had reached its height by the time Malesherbes was named director of the book trade. This son of the severe Chancellor Lamoignon had neither the qualities nor the defects that make adroit politicians and good police agents. A fine fellow but somewhat scatterbrained, he lacked the consistency to read a dossier attentively, and he seems to have been quite often misinformed. A student of Antoine-Laurent Jussieu's, Malesherbes might perhaps have been a good naturalist, but he often let his heart rule him rather than his reason. He was obliged to play a sort of double game with his father the chancellor (as some of his predecessors had done), and on several occasions he seems to have gone too far, failing to look closely enough at the manuscripts he allowed to be printed in France. For instance, after *Emile* had been published in France with a simple verbal authorization, Rousseau, whom he had intended to help, was exiled. Malesherbes was so little able to reconcile his sentiments and his principles that when he was first president of the Cour des aides he took the side of privilege during the affair of Maupeou's confrontations with the

Parlement. In spite of his natural timidity Malesherbes later took a heroic stand in defense of Louis XVI in an appearance before the Convention, after which fanatics whose nature differed totally from his own found him an obvious choice for àn expiatory victim and he ended his life on the scaffold.

The power structure had taken a position against the philosophes, whose works everyone wanted to read, that was becoming daily more untenable. While the closed caste of Paris printers and booksellers continued to make money without risk from the *privilèges* they had accumulated over the generations thanks to automatic extensions, innovation passed into the hands of "peddler" booksellers, who in theory worked clandestinely, but whom the authorities integrated into the official ranks of the book trade at regular intervals. Under Louis XVI, when it came time for sweeping reform the system of publishing *privilèges* was totally recast. Taking the English copyright law of 1709 as a model, the decrees of the Council of 1 August 1777 moved in the direction of a recognition of authors' rights by according authors a perpetual *privilège* when they printed and sold their own works. If they ceded a work to a bookseller, however, the *privilège* was reduced to the author's lifetime or a minimum of ten years after the author's death. By the same decrees, massive numbers of publications fell into a reconstituted public domain. The book trade in France benefited enormously.

An essential element was still missing. Nearly everywhere—in Germany as in France—writers denounced the patronage system and claimed the right to make a living from the fruits of their labors. Moreover, the gradual repatriation of the writings of the major philosophes (for which the Panckouckes could take credit) and the police measures taken on Vergennes's suggestion led to a decline of the publishing houses positioned outside France whose works had long invaded French territory. This did not prevent booksellers from setting up two sections in their shops, a public section for "good books" and another, more discreet, for books attacking the power structure and the royal family. The Revolution loomed. Censorship was to bloom again in the nineteenth century, but under new forms.

Seven

The Forms and Functions of Writing

Fifteenth–Eighteenth Centuries

The modern period, which our schoolbooks tell us began with the invention of printing and the great voyages of discovery and lasted until the French Revolution and the coming of the industrial revolution, was a period in which the written word, an instrument of power, began to be in general use throughout Europe. We need to turn next to the documents of that period to examine their functions and the forms they took.

THE INFLATION OF WRITTEN FORMS

The historian traditionally separates written culture into the age of the manuscript and the age of print, but a new procedure never eliminates its predecessor; it merely imposes a new division of labor. Gutenberg's invention was part of a broader context of an unceasing proliferation of writing and images.

The only way we can hope to measure that proliferation is through an evaluation of paper production. The history of the paper industry shows that paper mills constantly increased in number throughout Europe. Gradually every region attempted to produce enough paper to meet the demands of local consumption. By the end of the seventeenth century, technological advances permitted improvement in paper quality, and some papermakers experimented with using other raw materials than the traditional rags. We can sense progress, but unfortunately we cannot detail the rate of change. At best, we can attempt a rough approximation of French paper production during the Enlightenment, for which we have some figures thanks to information provided in Alix Gambier-Chevalier's study of surveys of the paper industry that were sponsored by the monarchy.[1]

According to Gambier-Chevalier, eighteenth-century France had some 750 paper mills and perhaps one thousand pulp vats. If we can estimate that each of these vats had an annual production capacity of two thousand reams of paper, this means that the roughly ten thousand workers who worked in the mills produced something like two million 500-sheet reams of paper. During the same period, the approximately one thousand presses in French printshops, combined with the presses of the *dominotiers* who put out games and the like and those of the copperplate engravers, used little more than 400,000–500,000 reams of paper. Taking into consideration paper for export (partially compensated by imports) and paper for such other uses as wrapping paper, we can calculate that French requirements for writing purposes amounted to at least one million reams—or 500,000,000 sheets—for an annual per capita consumption of some twenty sheets.

Thus the twenty-five million Frenchmen (men, women, and children) of the Enlightenment "consumed" an average of some 100 sheets each of standard note-sized paper (21×29.7 cm). This is not a great amount, particularly if we remember that government offices were already beginning to devour paper. It also speaks of the vast inequalities in societies of former times.

What could these sheets of paper be used for? We need to recall briefly the role of writing in the establishment of a European market. The chief problems here were to standardize transactions, arrange for billing and collection between places some distance apart and in places where wealth was distributed differently, and furnish capital to back enterprises that, taken singly, were risky. Italy had responded to these challenges in the thirteenth and fourteenth centuries by developing partnership contracts and insurance contracts, the bill of exchange, and double-entry bookkeeping. The exchange operations on which all wide-scale commerce depended had at first taken place at the great fairs in Lyons, Geneva, Antwerp, Genoa, and Frankfurt. Later, the need for public credit and the development of speculation exploiting differences in the supply of precious metals from one place to another prompted the rise of permanent exchanges, the first of which appeared in Antwerp in 1531. After that date an uninterrupted flood of bills of exchange circulated from one end of the Continent to the other. They covered transfers of funds to send merchandise, pay ecclesiastical taxes, and finance the military expenditures of the great states. Princely finances lacked organization, and in order to have funds when and were they needed them heads of state contracted with powerful moneylenders for short-term loans (constantly renewed) to pay for their sumptuary expenses, their political programs, and the upkeep of their armies. The popes of the fifteenth century turned to the Medici family; the Habsburgs had connections with the Fuggers (without whom Charles V would never have been elected emperor); Francis I relied on the bankers of Lyons, many of whom came from southern Germany and from Italy and who pooled their resources in an alliance called the Grand Parti. Such men had ways to make sure they would get their money back. Both the

Fuggers and the Medicis gained control of mines and commerce in ores. A representative of Jakob Fugger, who had recently financed the election of Albert of Brandenburg to the bishopric of Mainz, accompanied a famous indulgence preacher, Brother Tetzel, on his preaching missions, and the Augsburg banker and the Holy Father divided the proceeds from the sale of those tickets to heaven fifty-fifty! The Spanish monarchy, which every year eagerly awaited the return of its fleet of galleons loaded with American silver, had created a special type of exchange contract in Brussels—the famous *ascensios*—by which Genoese, Spanish, and German financiers guaranteed the Spanish crown ready cash deliverable on the various exchanges of Europe in return for the right to remove precious metals from the Iberian peninsula at times to be ascertained. This was how international financial exchanges in Europe came into being.[2]

The techniques that were used were nonetheless primitive. Limited advances took place in the late sixteenth century in a climate of bankruptcy and weak money, and in the seventeenth century during a period of scarce money and recession. Bills of exchange began to be endorsed, which meant they could be used as credit instruments. Soon banks began to accept deposits, at first to lessen the confusion that arose from the diversity of the many coins in circulation and from fluctuations in the relative values of gold and silver, but also to facilitate payments. The Bank of Venice was founded in 1584–85, the bank of Amsterdam, whose deposits were guaranteed by the municipal government, in 1609. Next the Dutch created corporations that issued stock, shares of which could be traded on the exchange, thus prompting the English and the French to create similar corporations.

From the bill of exchange to the letter of indulgence or the stock certificate, paper became a transferrable asset charged with multiple meanings. The financiers soon went much farther. Bankers at the medieval trade fairs had already given receipts to merchants who deposited funds with them from one fair to the next. The Venetians perfected this practice by rendering receipts made out to a merchant's name transferrable by endorsement. Next, the Bank of Venice delivered a standardized receipt prepared in varying amounts, payable to the bearer on sight and with interest. This instrument was the earliest form of paper money; it still resembled a cashier's receipt, and it was backed by precious metals that (in principle) were tucked away safely in the bank's coffers. Some noted that a respected establishment guaranteed by public authority could issue bills for a value higher than its precious metal reserves, thus earning a profit on its deposits. Sweden, whose copper money was cumbersome to carry about, led the way here in 1650. The Bank of England was founded in 1694 after a long gestation period. It was the first to issue real banknotes, engraved promissory notes in specific values that developed into negotiable instruments. This system, which was based on an act of faith and in one way or another on state guarantees, permitted England to lay the foundations of its national wealth. Addison and many other British writers of the eighteenth century praised the institution, and Berkeley called it a gold mine.[3]

This happened—once again—in a climate of crisis and bankruptcies. The invention of the banknote was extremely recent in the beginning of the eighteenth century, and when John Law introduced it into France it resulted in a failure. It took paper money more than a century to conquer the world. Like the law, paper money has some original sins; it still has some pernicious effects today. Still, the emergence of an economy based on pieces of paper imbued with a symbolic value was an essential stage in the history of writing.

It would be interesting to be able to trace the evolution of bookkeeping and accounting practices in merchant milieus from the fifteenth to the eighteenth centuries, but old registers keep a good many mysteries to themselves. We do know that treatises on accounting, published in quantity beginning in the later fifteenth century, testify to widespread use of a good many practices based on the use of double-entry bookkeeping.

The masters of this art (after the Italians) were the Flemish, and their theoretical treatises seem to have flooded France in the sixteenth century. The Germans were already developing methods of their own; the English and the Scots began to catch up; but the Spanish and the Portuguese were still marking time. After 1650 a number of more inclusive works were published. This was the age of Barrême and his *Comptes-faits,* a work that did much to help merchants with their accounts. It was also the age in which Jacques Savary offered French businessmen models for thirteen kinds of ledgers and explained that Colbert had intended to use double-entry bookkeeping in the public accounts of the land. That system reigned unchallenged until 1796, when Edward Thomas Jones in England suggested better procedures for handling the increasingly complex operations of the larger firms.[4]

The ledgers that have come down to us seem to prove that the principles proposed in a number of treatises were applied, at least among the great merchant traders and on occasion among the middle range. One such case was the firm of Christophe Plantin and his successors; another was the Société typographique de Neuchâtel, which in the eighteenth century kept painstaking accounts and whose directors sent some 250,000 letters in about a decade. It was not always the case. Daniel Defoe, whose many works included *The Complete English Tradesman* (1726), provides an example of a nearly illiterate man who used primitive accounting techniques but whose business nonetheless prospered. What we know of the business practices of some booksellers confirms that this was often the case. Similarly, merchants varied enormously in their mastery of writing, even in the eighteenth century, and weak literacy skills did little to hinder developing commerce. Cannot the same be said of the nineteenth century, when the bourgeoisie reigned triumphant, and even of times closer to our own?

To pass on to public writing, the great administrative, judiciary, and financial files that line the shelves of public archives are eloquent proof of how states made a growing use of writing to gain an increasingly systematic grip on Western societies. This is particularly true of France in the age of a developing absolute and administrative monarchy.

With increasing use of public records "the logic of writing" more and more tightly imposed its sometimes Kafkaesque logic. One instance of this was in counting and categorizing people. The recording of civil status appeared in France as early as the fourteenth century, and it soon became general practice. Registry was carried out by the clergy, who noted marriages, baptisms (not births), and burials (not deaths). As is always the case when the bureaucratic spirit reigns, "progress" often had seemingly unimportant origins. In France the reason behind the royal power's original move to record civil status in 1539, when it mandated the keeping of dual baptismal records, one copy to be deposited with the clerks of the courts of the *bailliages* and the *sénéchaussées*, was to make sure that candidates for ecclesiastical benefices were of canonical age. Temporal concerns soon joined spiritual ones, and the state supervised record-keeping in the interests of accuracy. Civic categorization was still embryonic—the identity card, which its inventors called a "passport," was created by the Convention. Nonetheless it was a first step toward a police universe. The church played its part. The decisions of the Council of Trent on the keeping of marriage registers were incontestably aimed at controlling the regularity of marriages, but they also served the purposes of counting Catholics and verifying religious practice.

1612 Pope Paul V, adopting methods advocated by St. Charles Borromeo, decreed that books must be kept on the state of parishioners' souls.
The French bishops adopted the practice and elaborated on it, to the point
of creating virtual card files on the sins and vices, but also the edifying
reading, of the faithful. Cardinal de Retz sent the clergy of Paris a model
for this sort of notation that prefigured card-sort techniques. When a certain Father Olier was named to the "difficult" parish of Saint-Sulpice, he
listed his parishioners by name, noted a number of details about them, and
revised his records every three months.[5] Except in Alsace the Revocation
of the Edict of Nantes punished Protestants who refused to convert to Catholicism or to emigrate by depriving them of their civil identity, hence of
legal existence. Those who refused to marry in the church were accused of
living in concubinage; if parents avoided having a child baptized his or her
birth was not recognized; the family of someone who died without receiving the last sacraments had to seek "alternate" ways to register the death.
Jews had an equally difficult time getting their civil status recognized until
the last years of the ancien régime, when measures were passed with a few
measures of tolerance for both Protestants and Jews.

There were already administrative networks set up in ways that strove to
be rational but that risked churning in a void. This is particularly striking in the history of prior censorship of books in eighteenth-century
France, the complex operations of which Robert Estivals has described so
knowledgeably.[6]

The granting of privilèges was the responsibility of the Bureau de la librairie of the royal chancery, an agency shaped by Abbé Bignon in 1700.

The first step in the process was the submission of a request for a permission (which gave the right to publish) and a privilège (which gave exclusive
rights to a text), along with a copy of the manuscript to be published. This
request was immediately registered in a large record book arranged in columns, where it was given an order number, the work's title was copied,
and the names of the person making the request and the author were
noted. Next, the director of the book trade (la librairie) named a censor,
whose name was duly inscribed in the same record book. When the censor
had turned in his report and given his opinion the latter was inscribed in
the register as well. All that remained to do was to note the decision to
grant or refuse the privilège in the last column of the register, in some cases
along with an indication of the length of time for which the privilege was
valid.

The manuscript was then returned to the applicant, initialed on every page. Next, the person who had requested the permission and the privilege had to have a letter patent drawn up and validated with an official seal, for which he of course paid a fee. This involved a new series of moves. These began, at least in some cases, with *feuilles de jugement*—"judgment papers"—bearing the information needed to draw up the letter. The redaction, verification, and validation of this act set off a process that is difficult to reconstruct. But even this was not enough. The *privilège* that had been obtained in this manner still had to be registered, both with the chancery and, for publicity reasons, with the Paris printers' and booksellers' Chambre syndicale. In earlier days this notice was simply summarized in the records of the Chambre, but later it was carefully copied in full in a stately hand into registers with fine parchment pages.

Then all the holder of the privilege still had to do was to deliver one copy of the freshly published book to be kept in a sort of *dépôt légal* in the king's library. If we add that every bale of books that entered Paris set off another series of registrations, we cannot but admire the diligence of the army of scriveners who attempted to supervise the reading matter of the French.

Despite the bureaucratic perfection of these systems, a majority of the books published in France or that penetrated into France avoided going through these procedures. In the age of the administrative monarchy, the principal result of proliferating regulations and probes was to furnish a pretext to create hundreds of posts that were lucrative for the governing elites and costly for the French people.

At the same time, writing continued to gain a firm hold in the domains of justice and taxation. The corridors of the Parlement were crowded with increasing numbers of *procureurs* who prepared dossiers for those who came to plead a case, and courts developed specialized offices with an entire staff of clerks, notaries, and secretaries. As if symbolically, the post of crier in the Palais de Justice was abolished by the ordinance on civic procedures of 1667, thus eliminating not only the functionary who, on specific days, read out the decisions that the courts had reached but also a rare survival of the oral tradition. The same ordinance further stifled traditional procedures by stipulating that extracts of summonses to official hearings would no longer be posted on the doors of churches and other public places but would be available from the clerks and notaries.

In an only partially literate society these many efforts had only imperfect results. Writing was superimposed on custom as if on an uneven and shaky terrain. The existence of innumerable special privileges and the government's inability to ascertain the wealth and the revenues of its subjects made for a dubious and arbitrary tax base, as Jean Guéroult has shown concerning the levying of *tailles* in the *généralité* of Paris between 1740 and 1787.[7]

The Conseil des finances set the *brevet des tailles* each year that stated the global sum to be paid by each *généralité*. In the *généralité* of Paris, the tax to be paid was then divided up, first among the various *élections,* then subdivided among the parishes. The latter's shares were determined on the basis of "horse rides" (*chevauchées*) made by treasurers of France and the *élus* (heads of the *élection*) to estimate the worth of the coming harvest, but the officials also took into account the opinions of the intendant and his subdelegates, who were often recruited among the *élus*. Once the decree covering the overall *généralité* had resulted in a list, it was printed on a form on which all parishioners' names were already entered, and the residents of every parish elected collectors who were responsible for drawing up a list of taxable households. Between 1738 and 1761, when the state decided to divide people's resources into three categories and apply a tax on "property," on "exploitation," or on "industry," these collectors, who were often close to illiterate, had to call on professionals to help them.

We can well imagine the number of special favors and the unjust practices that each step of this sort of procedure could create, and the importance of vertical connections that allowed persons of more modest status to call on the influence of more powerful people. Still, the fact that procedures were adopted in all these domains helped to break down the compartments into which society was divided, as can be seen in diplomatic and administrative correspondence and in the first printed statistics to appear in France in the seventeenth and especially the eighteenth century. The administration's efforts were often in vain: on many occasions tradition imposed continuing use of more primitive procedures. Despite heroic efforts, registration of civic identity led to dissimulation, and it was some time until legislative bodies kept a copy of record of their decisions. Recourse to writing made the incoherence of the existing system clear, but it did not correct it. Other sources of confusion were the coexistence of a multiform customary law and a written law, the unequal imposition of taxes among individuals and from one region to another, and overlapping jurisdictions. As a result, the breakdown of a compartmentalized world that writing helped to bring about made it even more evident to people of a logical turn of mind that only a revolution could impose the rule of the law on everyone.

But just what forms of writing penetrated into people's homes in that period? First there were notarial acts. Increased numbers of complaints about the incompetence of notaries in Germany in the late fifteenth and early sixteenth centuries point to a crisis of growth. State governments all over Europe attempted to put some order into this proliferation. In 1512 Emperor Maximilian, in a decree not always applied in practice, set rules for access to and the exercise of the notarial profession. The kings of Frances imposed the reign of the royal notary, in an attempt to limit the influence of the apostolic notaries in the Midi, and set what limits they could on the prerogatives of the seigneurial notaries. Financial pressures led the state to sell excessive numbers of notarial positions (prerevolutionary France had some fourteen thousand notaries, many of whom also exercised other functions) and to reserve the redaction of such acts as probate inventories to municipal clerks and court clerks. Private persons made increasing use of the services of the notaries and their competitors, and professional manuals remind us of the broad range of acts that they drew up. There were commercial acts such as contracts and agreements for the sale and transportation of commodities, credit arrangements such as rental contracts, but also documents reflecting the major events in private life such as apprenticeship contracts, marriage contracts, wills, and probate inventories. An interesting study could be written on the different ways in which people and regions regarded the intrusion of writing in such circumstances. In France Parisians had a probate inventory drawn up when the deceased left minor heirs, whereas in Lyons the court clerks of the *sénéchaussée* drew up an estate inventory only when there was litigation. An infinite variety of practices corresponded to a variety in traditions but also to different ways of thinking.[8]

Every family of some substance thus began to own "papers" that it kept with care and passed on from generation to generation. But, outside their business dealings, to what extent might individuals pick up a pen and write personal letters, to cite one example? It may be symptomatic that in the sixteenth century, the epistolary art rather than discourse was the focus of a great debate about prose. This debate still concerned a purely literary genre, and the first collection of letters in French—those of Etienne Pasquier—appeared only in 1583. For some time, however, merchants' letters had included occasional bits of family news, often awkwardly expressed, among their conventional commercial formulas. There are a few sets of personal letters, miraculously conserved, that leave quite a different impression. Jean de Coras, the Toulouse judge and a member of a humanist milieu, sent letters to his second wife. The affair of Martin Guerre, for which Coras served as presiding judge, reminds us how poorly information circulated in isolated rural societies. In the following century the success of the many novels that contained letters and of Voiture's *Lettres* reflected the desire of many women of privileged circles to learn how to write graceful missives. In Molière's *L'école des femmes* Arnolphe regrets that Agnès, a farmer's daughter, has learned to write—who knows where?—thus enabling her to dispatch notes to her suitor.[9]

This period also saw a proliferation of conversation manuals and works on the "Perfect Secretary" or the "Up-to-date Secretary" offering model letters for a wide variety of circumstances, to the point that some epistolary writers of the late seventeenth century regretted a decline in their art that they attributed to its popularity. In the eighteenth century the epistolary novel marked a new advance in the art of expressing one's sentiments through correspondence. Jacques Rychner has exhumed some astonishing documents written by journeymen typographers between 1765 and 1780,[10] and Mercier de Saint-Léger shows us woman servants and lackeys exchanging love notes just as their masters did.[11] These are admittedly exceptional cases, but when combined with other evidence they show that just prior to the French Revolution a good proportion of the population of French cities was beginning to have access to active forms of written culture.

There were also account books. A minor notable usually needed no more than a thick register to note a lifetime of extraordinary expenses, often adding a word on noteworthy events within his family or his city. He might also keep a small notebook in which he noted with particular care the trips that enlivened an otherwise monotonous existence. Such documents appeared early in Italy, they then became common in Germany, and they reached France and England in the sixteenth century. At times people also used the blank pages of almanacs to note accounts and information of various sorts, and in Protestant lands births and deaths were often entered on the end pages of the family Bible. In this fashion the "middle class" of officeholders and merchants gained an awareness of being rooted in time in an age when it became common practice to engrave dates on the faces of monuments. Personal notation increased slowly. On occasion, even when they were writing for themselves alone, the writers exhibited a certain restraint, refraining from setting down too clearly matters they deemed inappropriate or things that should not be common knowledge. Claude Paradin and the sire de Gouberville wrote in Greek when the first recounted escapades of the canons of Beaujeu and the second his own adventures. On the other end of the scale, certain Puritans, as if to purge themselves of at least the most admissible of their failings, might assiduously set down a full account of their relations with God in a form resembling genuine credit and debit accounting. In the late eighteenth century modest journeymen and artisans began to write their recollections and their reflections, at times even knocking at the door of the world of letters by daring to address a memoir to the academies.[12]

Administrative paperwork in those times cannot compare with that of our own day. Administrative structures were embryonic everywhere, even in the eighteenth century, and the times' most sophisticated written procedures would seem singularly sketchy today. Although the *minutes* of the decrees of the king's council were rapidly written on a loose sheet, they were regarded as authoritative, and the intendants, who had only a small staff, avoided all paperwork that was not indispensable. The juridical system often involved complicated written procedures—we need only think of the importance of the *procureurs*—and there were innumerable courts. Nonetheless, the registers of the Parlement, on whose parchment pages both royal decrees and its own decisions were entered in a ceremonious and elaborate hand, take up very little space in the national archives. Similarly, three or four bundles of documents or registers are enough to contain the records, noted year by year in a closely spaced hand, of the affairs of the largest notarial firms of Paris. Even the biggest commercial firms used only a relatively small amount of paper in the eighteenth century.

Still, all this activity shows that a new spirit was abroad. Once again the history of writing brings eloquent testimony to the advances of the written word. The growth of the great chanceries, which set the tone, had introduced a new model for writing, the *bâtarde* or "mixed" hand, while further to the south, a handful of intellectuals created the artificial and composite script known as "humanist." Despite the triumph of the humanist writing style in typography, the "mixed" hand continued to reign in a large number of governmental offices, but pressure to write more rapidly to increase the production of acts and documents introduced changes and modifications in the original model. As if stricken by galloping cursiveness, writing showed an acceleration of strokes applied to habits of *ductus* that still retained gothic underpinnings.[13] As a result there are few documents as difficult to decipher as the original drafts of acts of the sixteenth or early seventeenth centuries. Certain letters long remained fragmented, following the traditional system of foot-to-head connections inherited from antiquity, and certain words were reduced to a series of strokes. Furthermore, when the humanists and writers wrote in their national languages, whose dignity they proclaimed, they preferred their national scripts. Certain calligraphers attempted to canonize these scripts, and Robert Granjon gave typographical form to the French hand with the letter style known as *caractères de civilité*.

Except in some German lands that remained faithful to their traditional gothic script out of hostility to Rome, the disappearance of ancient habits encouraged the development of original and more legible writing styles. At the same time, writing masters, who taught calligraphy along with arithmetic and accounting, encouraged the use of a "financial" hand derived from the humanist script and originally designed to make accounts and balance sheets more readable. Handwriting showed an increasing tendency to follow a fixed canon, and a less choppy, more regular style developed. This reversal of previous tendencies occurred in France toward the mid-seventeenth century; it broke definitively with a tradition that had lasted nearly two thousand years, and it heralded modern writing styles. It incontestably reflected a desire to make manuscript texts, whose redaction and deciphering had long been reserved to specialists, accessible to everyone.

The historian, who has access to a broad range of texts, is surprised by the liberties taken by men of the seventeenth and especially of the eighteenth century with the presentation and the form of their private texts. After the Renaissance, calligraphy and even elegant handwriting became the business of copyists and accountants; spelling and punctuation had not yet acquired the rigidity they have today; and in an age in which conversation was an art in some circles, letter-writing style became more flexible and took on the accents of speech. Men high in the administration toward the end of the ancien régime, who on occasion wrote missives with their own hand, brought to letters a liberty of form and tone that today would be taken as nonchalance. Later a bourgeoisie of notables tended to mask its lack of savoir faire and spontaneity in an ostentatious respect for formulas that emphasized social difference. During the same age the art of writing a well-turned letter penned in the "English hand," which convent schools taught along with the rudiments of music, was one of the accomplishments that a young lady of "good" French society was expected to bring to marriage. In short, the art of fine writing embarked on a decline consummated much later with the appearance of the typewriter, the arrival of the secretary-typist, a return to compendia of formulas, and a depersonalization in hierarchical relations. That was all before the telephone instituted new kinds of personal relations.

FROM THE POSTER TO THE NEWSPAPER

Scholars have occasionally wondered whether Gutenberg and his counterparts intended to use the art of typography that they had invented to put out school grammars (the "Donatuses"), Psalm books, and Bibles, and to produce handbills, manuals to facilitate the work of administrative offices, or the many sorts of informational pieces aimed at the broadest possible public.

Such print pieces were often thrown away when they had been read, so they have only rarely come down to us. One such piece was the *occasionnel,* a newssheet about current events. The *occasionnels* on war with the Turks amounted to a genuine press campaign in Germany and central Europe in the fifteenth and sixteenth centuries; others recounted the exploits of the king's armies in the Italian wars. French printers, probably with the encouragement of the government, produced them in large numbers. There were also *canards,* slight publications in pamphlet form that told of astonishing events, miracles and diabolical manifestations, natural catastrophes and the passage of comets, or described "monsters." During the sixteenth century it became customary for sovereigns to have the texts of their decisions printed and distributed to those who needed to know of them. Later the various courts and still later the ecclesiastical authorities and local governments imitated their example. Finally, first sovereigns then leaders of political factions published circular letters in support of their policies.[14]

Although tens of examples of the 42-line Bible, which was probably put out in fewer than 500 copies, are still in existence, massive quantities of these ephemeral documents, which were never intended to be kept, have disappeared. Thus they retain their mystery: holding in one's hands a letter of indulgence printed in 1454 that has miraculously been preserved is an extraordinary experience. These first printed "certificates" bear blank spaces in which the name of the recipient and the amount of his payment could be filled in with pen and ink. What a saving in time for both the customer and the ecclesiastical authorities, who until then had to have specialized scribes, now freed for other tasks, to copy the same text endlessly. There were also the first printed publicity pieces—handbills prepared by early bookseller-publishers giving the list of their books and announcing the visit of an agent at a place and date to be filled in by hand.[15]

These brief notes remind us of the role that handbills and posters have played in all times and places when writing began to spread to the people. We need only recall the election propaganda painted on the walls of Pompeii. A complete, century-by-century survey of what decorated the walls of houses and covered the walls along the streets is an impossible dream. Pious images were to be seen everywhere, but in the houses of burghers and scholars in French cities of the seventeenth and eighteenth centuries one might also see a calendar or a *thèse illustrée,* a large poster illustrated by a well-known artist and stating the main arguments of a thesis. The bishop's most recent pastoral letter would be affixed to the church doors, and illustrated sheets describing the priest's acts when he said Mass or administered the sacraments hung in a good many sacristies. Mathematicians posted challenges to their colleagues at the gates of the colleges, or they displayed a proposed solution to a problem, as Pascal did for his treatise on conic sections. Streets were lined with death notices, notaries' announcements of sales, announcements of the decrees of the Parlement and edicts of the king, and notices of spectacles. One of the latter was an advertisement for bear fights and bull fights that left a blank for filling in the place and date of the spectacle. It was designed by the famous engraver Jean-Baptiste Papillon, according to whom these flyers were printed in tens of thousands of copies.[16]

Since the power structure controlled outside walls, in times of civic peace these documents recalled the ubiquity of public power. They could have a boomerang effect, however, as on several occasions during the seventeenth century. Notices posted up on market days announcing some perfectly anodyne measure could be read by troublemakers who presented them to illiterate peasants as announcements of new taxes that ran counter to established custom. This was the origin of a number of popular revolts.[17] To give another example of the force of public power, when a handbill (*placard*) appeared attacking a piece that Bayle had written against Father

Maimbourg, the lieutenant of police in Paris, La Reynie, who detested Maimbourg, had so many copies of it posted that it set all Paris laughing and, as is often the case, gave Bayle a good deal of positive publicity. On the other hand, when in the eighteenth century the public authorities began to mark the names of Paris streets with tin-plate plaques and to number the houses, the innumerable illiterates among the population, many of them recent arrivals from the country, must have felt some frustration.

In troubled times the opposition takes over the walls, as it did in inscriptions on the walls of the cathedral of Meaux in 1525, in the hand-written and mimeographed materials that circulated in Paris during the riots of May 1968, or in Beijing during the Cultural Revolution. The *placard* per excellence, however, was perhaps the one that gave its name to the "Affaire des placards" in 1534, several copies of which were found only some thirty years ago padding the sideboards of a book in the municipal library of Neuchâtel.[18] This modest sheet looks much like a page from a folio-sized book, but the shocking denunciation that it spread throughout Paris— starting with its first line, written in bold type, a salvo against the "horrible, great, and important abuses of the papal Mass"—had enormous repercussions. Nor should we forget, on a different level, the *placard* in which Robert Estienne gave his revised version of the Decalogue and proved that the doctors of the Sorbonne had been arguing on the basis of a text in which the two last commandments contained mistakes. For a final example, there were English ballads printed with an accompanying illustration that played an important part both in the religious quarrels of the sixteenth century and the disputes over freedom of the press in the eighteenth century.

There were also increasing numbers of the small print jobs known as *bilboquets*, which ranged from marriage or funeral announcements to tracts, commercial advertising circulars, or theater tickets. Above all, there were innumerable print pieces that, bound into volumes, often take up more space in the older French archives than actual books. Many of these pieces came from ecclesiastical sources, as with the 1665 articles by which the archbishop of Paris ordered the parish priests of his diocese to send him written reports on the state of their parishes. They might also originate from the civil powers, however, like the royal acts printed by the French monarchy and distributed to officeholders or hawked in the streets. There were also decrees of the parlements and the courts, distributed at the expense of the losing party, and *factums*—briefs for the accused—that were often quickly snapped up by a public always fond of human-interest items. The affair of the marquise de Brinvilliers, a famous poisoner, and the Diamond Necklace Affair are excellent examples of these.[19]

Still, these many pieces represented only a fraction of production in a constantly increasing use of print. There were also accounts of royal or princely entries and of public festivities, often illustrated and at times resembling modern reporting. *Canards*—occasional pieces on current news items—have already been mentioned. Political pieces deserve special mention: letters from rulers or party leaders to their followers, reports of an important event like the assassination of the duc de Guise during the Wars of Religion or the arrest of the princes during the Fronde. Whenever events reached a fever pitch, pamphlets of all descriptions flooded the streets. We need to distinguish carefully among these publications, however, as the term "pamphlet" could refer to very different things. Many pamphlets occasioned by wars and religious conflicts are really theological dissertations aimed at the learned. Similarly, as Richelieu rose to power his person and acts gave rise to true political treatises, and Pierre Jurieu's pamphlets, written following the revocation of the Edict of Nantes, were more like small volumes. During great national crises, a totally different sort of pamphlet appeared: genuine appeals to the people, often filled with personal attacks and the result of concerted action, distributed by other means than the usual channels of diffusion.[20]

Readers interested in the full range of pieces printed in France in the late sixteenth and early seventeenth centuries can find descriptions in the *Mémoires-journaux* of Pierre Taisan de L'Estoile or, for late seventeenth-century England, in Samuel Pepys's journal. It would be intriguing to know more precisely who were the readers of such pieces. *Les caquets de l'accouchée* (ca. 1620) seems to indicate that some ephemeral pieces reached a relatively cultivated audience that included presiding judges of the courts, wealthy merchants, and their wives. Similarly, the registers of the bookseller Jean Nicolas show clearly that only the notables of Grenoble were interested in the *mazarinades*.[21] Nearly everywhere, however, single sheets appeared bearing pictures or songs. We need to remember, though, that such pieces were always accompanied by the spoken word, whether in sermons given by monks in support of the Catholic League, in calls to order from the coadjutor's *crieurs* or the prince de Condé's *criailleurs*, in reading aloud within the bosom of the family or in the craftsman's shop, or in conversation and song in the tavern. How else are we to explain the many mass movements?

Although we have a good many posters and ephemeral print pieces, the ones we know are only a small part of what the presses put out. This explains the existence of well-established firms that have left us practically nothing. Denis Pallier has counted some one thousand pieces on the Catholic League published within a ten-year period; Hubert Carrier estimates that from five thousand to six thousand *mazarinades* appeared between 1649 and 1653, giving a daily average of twelve at certain times in Paris; Louis Desgraves sets at nearly ten thousand the number of controversial pieces printed in France between the promulgation and the revocation of the Edict of Nantes (1598–1685). This large production represents the activity of only a limited number of presses—only some twenty out of the 138 presses that were operating in Paris during the Fronde—which tends to confirm the large proportion of print matter that has disappeared forever. Studies on the question suggest that in eighteenth-century France one-third of the active presses did job work, which would have produced enough print matter to cover a good number of walls and make a host of labels, wedding announcements, and handbills, even though it would have been nothing in comparison to the flood of paper that submerges us today. England led the way in this domain: in the eighteenth century the compilers of the *Short Title Catalogue* took up the challenge of including the greatest possible number of "nonbooks" in their lists, and after painstaking inquiry among a considerable number of libraries and archives, they listed 250,000 pieces, even though they excluded job work proper and some fifty thousand theater posters. What is more, after 1750, at the dawn of the industrial revolution, this production grew at a dizzying pace. Tracts, time-tables, advertisements, prospectuses, and catalogues for all sorts of products were printed, at times in port cities on the Continent (in English), at times in the Antilles or the American colonies. There were also circular letters such as those put out by the Nonconformist churches. The declarations of great polemicists like John Wilkes were circulated in broadsheets through alternate distribution networks. Finally, political ballads had a new impact, and after 1764 elections prompted a near deluge of tracts and posters great and small. This print explosion was accomplished by new presses set up throughout the kingdom; it encouraged freedom of expression and, in the long run, the democratic spirit.[22]

During this same period regular correspondence written by hand began to shift to print. The periodical originated in newsletters by recognized "correspondents" that were sent at more or less fixed intervals to bankers like the Fuggers, major merchants, statesmen, and politicians and were later copied for a wider public. By the sixteenth century there were a number of such *nouvellistes* in Europe. Furthermore, printers very early produced almanacs and annuals that early in the seventeenth century took the name of *mercures*, the most famous of which was the *Mercure français* (1611). In Antwerp at about the same time (1604) Abraham Berhoeven was granted a monopoly by Archduke Albert and Archduchess Isabelle on publication of accounts of their future victories, and in 1605 Berhoeven launched the first periodical newssheet, the *Nieuwe Tindinghe*, first as a weekly and, after 1620, published three times a week. Soon after, gazettes of all sorts began to appear.

France was a latecomer to news publications. Richelieu had come to power with the aid of a pamphlet campaign; he attached particular importance to attacks against him from Antwerp by polemicists backing the supporters of Marie de Médicis and was even more sensitive to attacks from the Protestant faction. He may or may not have had a hand in granting one of his protégés, the physician Théophraste Renaudot, a monopoly for a weekly called *La Gazette*. Was the newssheet *Nouvelles extraordinaires de divers endroit*, put out by Jean Martin and Louis Vendosme, two Calvinist booksellers in Paris with connections in Holland and known only from issues published after the founding of the *Gazette*, started before Renaudot's newssheet or in response to it? Whichever came first, Renaudot cleverly exploited the situation. He furthered the interests of his periodical by creating the first publicity agency in France, the Bureau d'adresses, and he attempted to set up an information network in the form of provincial branches of his bureau. He also created a lecture series that offered a talk every Monday on "divers secrets and curiosities of the arts and sciences." Furthermore, the *Gazette* ran advertisements in the form of articles, although most of its advertising appeared in the newssheet of his Bureau d'adresses. Renaudot's enterprises were well received, and the *Gazette*, to which Louis XIII occasionally deigned to offer an anonymous contribution, met with notable success. Because it reached the provinces only after long delays and postal expenses were prohibitive, counterfeited versions had already skimmed the market when most of the genuine copies reached their destinations. The enterprising Renaudot responded by strengthening his own reprint facilities in the provinces, first in Rouen (1631) and Lyons (1633), then in Tours (1646) and in Toulouse (1673). The press runs of the *Gazette* were not very high: 1,200 for Paris and

500 for Bordeaux, but Grenoble received at least 200 copies, printed in Lyons, at the time of the Fronde (1649), many of which passed from hand to hand in a rental scheme that cost 6 livres a year rather than the 12 livres that a subscription cost. Sixteen new centers for printing the *Gazette* were created between 1686 and 1699 and nine others from 1702 to 1716. If we add that a number of specialized newssheets were launched in France during the same period and that the news press was growing rapidly in England, we can say that by that time modern journalism was born.[23]

The press created new political and intellectual solidarities. Scholars and men of letters—"the Republic of Letters"—were in the first ranks of this movement. In an age when knowledge itself was becoming nationalized, the letters in Latin that such men exchanged were no longer enough to circulate information on the new works that were appearing throughout Europe. Thus in France Colbert encouraged the founding (in 1665) of the *Journal des savants*, the first periodical that reviewed books, while in London the first issues of *Philosophical Transactions* appeared not long after. There were soon a number of similar periodicals—Bayle's *Nouvelles de la République des lettres*, for example, Jean Le Clerc's *Bibliothèque universelle et historique*, or the *Acta eruditorum* of Leibniz. Mere mention of these titles indicates that in a Europe henceforth sharply divided the literary press would play an essential role in structuring and diversifying opinion within the cultural elites.

For a more complete survey of the periodicals of the time, in all their diversity, the reader is referred to the histories of the press.[24] Let me simply add that such periodicals bore little resemblance to the modern newspaper. They offered a somewhat random selection of news items with no hint of the sensational. Moreover, the model of the book was so strong that the intention of both the editors and the readers of such periodicals was that they would be gathered together and bound as permanent volumes. The only newssheets that escaped that obsession were the advertising sheets that proliferated during the eighteenth century, particularly in the French provinces. Although the news periodical was a new arrival on the public scene it took an increasingly important place in political life, a topic to which I shall return.

BOOKS

At this same time, the book, written discourse in its most finished form, was gaining an extraordinary authority. Because it reflected the reason-

ing process and by its very organization conditioned that process, and because it canonized knowledge, the book more than ever appeared as a
symbolic object whose very possession conferred ownership of learning
and ideologies.

But the printed book also obeyed certain laws. The first was a standardization implicit in the serial production of any industrially manufactured
product. It was also subject to the laws of the market, which dictated that
the publisher must adapt his product to a potential public, although cost
imperatives might necessitate sacrificing the physical aspect and even the
accuracy of the final product.

This serially produced object rapidly differed from its initial model, the
manuscript, and took on characteristics of its own. The most evident sign
of that difference was certainly what Lucien Febvre called the "civic identity" of the book—its hallmark; its "label"—the history of which is traced
in *The Coming of the Book* and the major elements of which were the title
page (a form of publicity) and folio or page numbers.[25]

Let me limit my remarks here to recalling that at first printers simply
copied the *incipit* of the manuscript, in most cases devoting a few lines at
the head of the first page of text to the title of the work and the author's
name, and then repeated the same elements in a colophon at the end of
the volume, adding their own names and the date on which printing was
completed. Soon a separate title page appeared, first as a simple mention
of the title on the recto of the book's first leaf, which was originally left
blank, probably because a printed page might easily be smudged before the
work could be bound. Other elements were gradually added to the title
and the author's name: a laudatory phrase placed at the top of the title
page introduced author and title; the bookseller's mark was placed prominently at mid-page, and the foot of the page was reserved for his imprint.
This minor revolution had been completed by the last quarter the fifteenth
century.

At the same time, printers or booksellers needed to provide the binders
with some indication of the order of the leaves in a volume. At first they
noted the necessary information by hand in ink, but they soon found it
more expedient to print it on the sheets themselves. Thus a sign or a catch-
phrase was put at the foot of the page or the end of the signature, or a table
was placed at the end of the book summarizing the makeup of each signature or giving the word with which each signature began. Running
heads were introduced, and in the late fifteenth century printers began to

number folios (at first often inaccurately) at the head of each leaf. Pagination proper, which did not replace folio numbers for another fifty years or so, opened up new possibilities for indexing and reference and the modern table of contents became possible.

The first printers had attempted to imitate as closely as possible the script of the manuscripts they wanted to reproduce: in Rouen printers imitated the flamboyant bâtarde letters of the English chancery hand as a way to break into the English market. Cutting new dies demanded a high degree of technical skill and took a great deal of time, so typographers turned increasingly to specialists—often themselves booksellers—for matrices or fonts. They soon gave up using large numbers of ligatures and abbreviations because they cluttered the type case and slowed the compositors. As much as possible they continued to use certain typefaces for certain types of publication or to respect certain countries of origin, keeping to *lettres de formes* for liturgy, *lettres de somme* for theology, the bâtarde typefaces for vernacular languages, and roman fonts for the Latin classics and Italian authors.

Book design was also undergoing a gradual evolution. As long as their volumes competed with the copyists' books, typographers had not dared to modify the appearance of the page, but later they often tried to economize on paper by reducing the amount of white space on the page, shortening the height of the characters, and printing their lines closer together, at the risk of sacrificing clarity to density. This tended to favor gothic typefaces, with their heavier thick strokes and reduced height, over the slighter roman with its more elongated ascenders and descenders that usually required more paper to print any given text.

Thus before the sixteenth century roman characters remained an Italian specialty, as Italy's larger clientele was accustomed to humanistic script and pressruns seem to have been bigger. The first roman letters were produced in Venice by Nicolas Jenson, a Frenchman. Jenson's fine-quality letters produced somewhat black, uniform pages that much resembled their manuscript models. His classical editions circulated throughout Europe, to the point that Martin Lowry found a number of them in three libraries in Yorkshire.[26] Jenson soon found imitators and emulators in several other Italian cities. When Aldus Manutius arrived on the scene in the last years of the century, he created a new, more supple roman typeface (engraved by Francesco Griffo) so refined that his type cases contained several slightly different versions of some letters. Manutius also invented italics, a typeface in which he had accented letters made in imitation of Greek, which made the works of the great Latin authors easier to read.[27]

The roman typeface was slow to gain acceptance outside Italy, as the Germans, French, and English evidently thought it odd. The alphabets designed by Peter Schoeffer the Younger, the great Basel typefounder and the greatest specialist in roman typefaces outside Italy, were thick, with letters whose bodies were too large for the interlinear spaces. Even Josse Bade long continued to use thick-set gothic fonts for his titles, compacting his texts inside decorative woodcut frames of a style prefiguring Renaissance forms. He used small gothic characters for glosses and an undistinguished roman for the text.

How then can we explain the triumph of "foreign" roman typefaces over the various national letter styles in much of Europe after 1530? First, by the prestige of their origins and the prestige of the Latin texts for which they seemed a natural means of expression; also by the fact that they bore a genuine ideology. Poggio Bracciolini and Niccolò de' Niccoli wrote in an adaptation of Carolingian script, but great artists like Donatello and Ghirlandaio had begun to decorate their works with inscriptions imitated from those of imperial Rome. In an age in which people agreed with Leon Battista Alberti that there was a canon for all things, men like Francesco Filelfo, among other things a calligrapher and a close friend of Mantegna's, and later Luca Pacioli, who had consulted Piero della Francesca and worked with Leonardo da Vinci, undertook mathematical investigations of the ideal proportions for roman letters. Aldus himself may have relied on some of their conclusions when he had his roman capitals cut.[28]

During the Renaissance, letters, which expressed language, the vehicle of ideas, were thought to be linked with divinity in a Neoplatonic hierarchical order of things. Those outside Italy who were reflecting on the problems of writing must have been struck by these theories. One characteristic response came from Geoffrey Tory, who published a work in 1529 (written several years earlier) with a title that merits full citation: *Le Champfleury: l'art et science de la due et vraie proportion des lettres attiques, qu'on dit lettres romaines.*

Tory, a rector of a university college and a man of many talents, was a calligrapher, a painter, an engraver, a printer, and a "reader" (lecturer) in French at the Collège royal. He admired Italy, which he had visited twice and where he had studied drawing with the best masters. In his book he proclaims his admiration for the French language. Citing Strabo, he explains that the Latins simply borrowed their letters from the Greeks, distorting them in the process, and that before the Roman invasion Gaul had been a center of Greek culture. He adds that the idea for his book came to him after he had worked on the decoration of Jean Grolier's town house. Tory states that he wrote his book as a service to French artists engaged in the difficult task of reproducing roman letters in paintings, tapestries, stained-glass windows, and phylacteries. It is of little importance that Tory declares his hope to write on French letters one day, that the *Champfleury* itself is printed in a rather ugly roman typeface, or that he ends his work with models for perfectly harmonious gothic capitals.[29] In the aesthetic revolution that was sweeping the avant-garde of French society he had chosen his camp. At the same time Francis I was sponsoring the printing—also in roman characters—of translations of Latin authors, and Simon de Colines recut punches that had belonged to Henri I Estienne, whose widow he had married, to create characters with more body, thus giving his texts more space. Soon not only Colines, who gradually renewed his initial stock and in particular made admirable italics, but a long line of talented engravers of fine characters—Augereau and Garamond, later Granjon and Haultin—surpassed the models of their Italian masters and perfected a typography that was so simple that it must have seemed almost aggressive, as if it intended to drive through to the essence—the text.

The divorce between typographic characters and manuscript hands was at last final. It is surprising to realize that such a great change in reading habits could occur, in France at least, in less than a generation. French letters underwent an even more important change, however, in the codification of spelling, which these typographers inscribed into the steel of their punches. Publishers of classical texts, who used roman letters, had attempted a reform of Latin spelling and punctuation. In France Fichet and Heynlin, whose atelier could boast of only primitive humanistic resources, nonetheless did their best to make the works they brought out more readily accessible, and in a dedication at the head of one book that came from their presses Guillaume Fichet even congratulated his friend for having made the text so readable that even a child could follow it.[30] Later Josse Bade and Simon de Colines consistently used diphthongs and accents in their Latin texts.

Those who were attempting to codify a rapidly evolving French language ran into even more complex problems than the Italians had encountered in the age of Alberti or the Spanish in the age of Nebrija.[31] They needed not only to propose coherent grammatical rules and rethink the spelling of words that practice had overloaded with extra letters but also to make choices among forms and pronunciations that came from very different milieus and a number of major dialects. Thus it was important to devise graphic means for translating the sounds of spoken French with more precision than the traditional alphabet could achieve. Since any standardization of the sort could be effected only with the aid of the printing press, it was essential to have the necessary characters cut and to persuade both the typographers and the public to change their habits.

The publishers of traditional French texts seem to have begun by using accented letters, in imitation of Latin, to mark tonic syllables, in particular the closed *e* in stressed final position (as in *abbé*). The first move in this direction may have come from an Englishman, John Palsgrave, the author of a French grammar for English use. The decisive reform came from the extremely self-contained "micromilieu" of the humanist printers: men thoroughly familiar with Latin and its grammar who were protected by the king, close to the chancery and the royal courts, and who supported what one might call monarchic centralism. Behind them we can glimpse Clément Marot, the king's readers, and Marguerite de Navarre and her friends. At the center of this group was an extraordinary person, Robert Estienne, who had recently emerged from the tutelage of his step-father, Simon de Colines. An impassioned Latinist, Estienne had already conceived the program for his dictionaries: each Latin term or expression would figure in its various acceptations, next to which he would give the French equivalent. Since the French definitions would have to be written concisely and coherently, certain decisions had to be made and held to. Thus Estienne asked Claude Garamond not only to design characters on the model of Aldus Manutius' but also to engrave a set of signs that permitted a closer rendering of French. He used Garamond's typeface immediately for a Latin-French grammar entitled *In linguam gallicam Isagoge* (Paris: Robert Estienne, 1531), by Jacobus Sylvius, the Latinized name of the physician Jacques Du Bois. Next, after an edition of the *Miroir de l'âme pécheresse* of Marguerite de Navarre, Estienne published a *Briefve doctrine pour deuement escripre selon la propriété du language françoys* (1533), completed in 1540 by a brief treatise, *De la punctuation de la langue françoyse, plus accents d'icelle* by Etienne Dolet. All the diacritical marks that were eventually adopted in French—accent marks, the cedilla (probably invented by Geoffrey Tory), the diaeresis, the apostrophe—were proposed at that time, as was the differentiation between the vowel and consonant values of *i* and *u* (the letters *i* and *j*; *u* and *v*) and variant spellings to distinguish between the hard and soft pronunciations of *g* and *c*. The most difficult part of the project still remained to be accomplished, which was to change custom and tradition by attacking the spelling of the commonest words. Various camps formed immediately. In one camp there were phoneticians in search of printshops that would not only put their proposals into effect but even agree to engrave a totally new phonetic alphabet. Authors, in particular the poets of the Pléiade with Ronsard at their head, formed a second camp. They were ready to follow the phoneticians, but they often tended to be prisoners of their personal habits and eager to reserve a margin of liberty for themselves (notably for rhymes). Above all, they did not want to shock their public. The printers made up a third party. Some of them were tempted to follow the theoreticians, at least at first, but they soon tried to dampen the scholars' ardor in order to avoid sudden breaks with established procedures and keep a certain latitude in the written form of words that they found useful for line justification. The printers, like the poets, had no wish to upset their customers.

Standardizing French spelling was thus an extremely slow process. When Robert Estienne saw that the public found the grammars of Du Bois and the phonetician Meigret hard to use, he noted in his own *Grammaire*, published in Geneva not long before his death in 1557, that it was better to follow the customs practiced "in the courts of France, both of the King and of his parlement of Paris, also of his Chancery and Chambre des comptes: in which places the language is written and is pronounced in greater purity than in any other." Plantin in Antwerp and later the Elzeviers in Leiden and Amsterdam, printers who worked in a milieu and for a public for whom French was more a language of culture, felt more keenly the need to guide their readers (like Palsgrave before them). Thus their books, which circulated widely in France, made common use of the letters *j* and *v*, of acute accents, and of circumflex accents to replace the superfluous use of *s*. They did much to accustom readers to these innovations.

The French humanists were persuaded that a canon existed for everything and they had dreamed of setting absolute rules. Even though they were unaware that the eye and the mind are capable of grasping and identifying words globally, they were wise enough to retain the rules for mute letters that aid comprehension of meanings and functions. French spelling was not definitively fixed in printed texts until the mid-eighteenth century: as in so many other domains, the shift from custom to law was accomplished only gradually.

All this was not without consequences, however. In the dedication to his *Champfleury* Tory had called for a "noble heart" capable of bringing "rule" to the French language so that it would no longer be "changed and per-verted" every fifty years. Eternal illusion of "the logic of writing"! In re-ality, the revolution that had begun in the 1530s made a break inevitable between spoken language, where custom reigned, and written discourse with all its jurisconsults, legislators, and successive "laws" that sanctioned or selected and that slowly imposed a new logic. In the long run the adop-tion of roman characters sacralized the printed word, which is by vocation conservative and authoritarian. Official, learned French, henceforth pro-moted to the status of the national literary language, became regulated and even (with the Académie française, for example) became an affair of state (as in China). After Malherbe and Vaugelas, one result was classical French literature. Another was that oral traditions and the dialects gradually faded. Thus progress, perhaps beneficial from some points of view, inevitably brings keenly felt mutilations.

During this time other nations, each at its own pace, adopted roman characters and set out to unify its language, notably with the aid of certain widely read religious texts. Vernacular texts continued to be printed in the national script only in German lands, where the gothic had never lost its creative sap (we need only think of Dürer) and where the Protestant Ref-ormation had made everything that came from Rome suspicious. Further to the east, finally, Russian printers began to cut punches to print in the Russian alphabet, which Peter the Great subjected to authoritarian revi-sion. Inevitably these different options helped the nations of Europe to develop divergent ways of thinking.

Toward the mid-sixteenth century the printed book had acquired what continued to be its basic elements: title page, preliminary matter (increas-ingly often set in italics), text (set in roman), table of contents, index, and pagination.

We need only glance at the volumes conserved in our libraries to see that books continued to show an infinite diversity, that each one bears the stamp of its place of birth, its times, and its destined public, and that each is a reflection of how a text was regarded in its time.

We do not need to open the books to imagine who first bought them; the bindings tell us. The volumes that belonged to the great collectors of the French Renaissance have multicolored bindings at times decorated with geometrical designs and tracery that remind us it was incumbent on the ruler to honor great authors and fine editions with sumptuous covers.

A binding tells us less when it bears something like the famous device *Johannis Grolieri et amicorum* rather than the arms of a sovereign. A great personage in the state and a wealthy financier, Grolier was probably interested in supporting the policies of his king, for example by aiding the Aldine press, whose publications he bought in great number, thus promoting them in France. Grolier heeded his own personal taste above all, however, and his collection reminds us that harmony between the cover, the typography, and the text make the book a whole in which every element contributes to a global expression. The overelaborate bindings of the mid-seventeenth century frequent in the circle of Chancellor Séguier are out of harmony with the texts they dress. The same is true of the infinitely delicate bindings of the eighteenth century when they are placed on works of piety foreign to their spirit, bindings whose sole purpose was to celebrate the princesses who might read the work or to blend in with the setting in which such ladies lived and received visitors.

A great many works, especially in the seventeenth and eighteenth centuries, had morocco or calf bindings. Prominent among them are the large albums relating a princely entry, a festive occasion, or a ceremony. Distributed by the authorities to celebrate an official event, they were proclamations of a claim to loyalty and instruments of propaganda. The same holds true of the *Almanach royal,* an annual publication put out by the administration bearing decorations with hot-stamped gold leaf showing the arms of a minister, a member of the king's council, or an intendant. Then come a mass of bindings in the great libraries that bear the arms of a ruler, a minister, or some great personage. Such books give witness to an ostentatious possession of a culture but also of an intention to protect it. Decency, a sense of hierarchy, and wealth dictated that morocco bindings were for the ruler and the most powerful in the land, while humbler figures—even Fouquet—were content with calf.

On occasion there is a volume that stands out among the others in French collections, a volume whose wooden sides are covered in pigskin and whose cold-stamped decoration recalls French volumes of the early sixteenth century. When we open it we may find that it is printed in gothic type, bears a date from the late sixteenth century, and comes from Germany. Each nation lived at its own pace until the century of the Enlightenment. A connoisseur has little difficulty placing and dating every binding. All he or she has to do is examine the texture of the skin, which varies from age to age in fineness and treatment, and to look at the spine to see whether the cords stand out or lie flat, "à la grèque." Our expert will also need to remember that the spine was seldom decorated in the Renaissance, but that after, in the seventeenth century, it might show the title enlivened with fleurons, and in the eighteenth century it might have a title patch in a more brightly colored leather giving more information than before: the author's name, the title, and, if appropriate, a volume number.

Most of the books of the artisanal age were bound in much humbler fashion, however. Parchment was much used in German lands, for example. The dukes of Brunswick, great bibliophiles, were particularly fond of parchment bindings. In France current publications destined for provincial readers were nearly always covered in *basane,* a lower-grade parchment that was less elegant but more resistant than calf. And, as everyone knows, peddlers' books were covered with rough blue paper. In the late eighteenth century, to end the series, printers began to deliver novels and many other works unbound, with simple paper covers so that readers could have them bound if they wanted to keep them after reading them. In this way, the book tended to become an item of general consumption on the eve of the French Revolution.

The format of a volume could reflect its symbolic value and hint at its prospective public. Heavy folio volumes stated the durability of tradition and an intent to bring together in an exhaustive whole consecrated authors and the summas of religious, juridical, or secular knowledge. As the memory of written civilization, these were usually presented printed in two closely set columns per page, and they often included some critical apparatus and used typographical indices that aided the reader who wanted to consult them without reading them through. During the Renaissance printers used in-folio volumes to put out the first series of collected works of the authors of Christian and pagan antiquity. Such volumes reigned supreme, however, in two epochs, the century of the Catholic Reformation and the age of the Enlightenment. During the Catholic Reformation they were used for three polyglot editions of the Bible, but also the entire corpus of the Catholic tradition, the commentaries and summas of revised theology, and, more generally, the stock of works that a scholar had to know if only to refute them. This is why many of these enormous sets, bought systematically by ecclesiastical institutions, seem to have hardly ever been read or even consulted.

Gradually, though, the advance of nationalism and national languages prompted the appearance, particularly in France, of monumental works of another sort. Amyot translated the ancient classics. Soon the publication of the works of Ronsard in an edition of this sort, complete with notes and indices, symbolized the entry of the first French writer into the Parnassus of immortal authors. Soon the desire to glorify France and its tradition led French historians to write similar multivolume works, among them God-efroy's *Cérémonial français*, Mézeray's *Histoire de France*, or the Dupuy brothers' *Preuves des libertés de l'Eglise gallicane*. The crisis of the years from 1645 to 1665 interrupted the success of such works. The century of Louis XIV was not a learned age, and the great publishing projects reappeared en masse only with the Regency, when they benefited from the technique of publication by subscription introduced from England by the Benedictines of Saint-Maur. Tradition's arsenal was well garnished once more, both in France and in Italy. Soon, however, the vogue for dictionaries—works that surveyed a body of knowledge with the intent of deepening and enlarging it—began to challenge the closed set of traditional acquisitions by offering other summas that contradicted or reached beyond the older bodies of knowledge. Such works ranged from Bayle's *Dictionnaire historique et critique* to Diderot and d'Alembert's *Encyclopédie des arts et métiers*. Thus a new cultural project was launched under the patronage of the powerful and the wealthy, whose purchases were indispensable to enterprises of so large a scope.[32]

Throughout this period volumes in quarto format were a brilliant second to the folio volume. As the "literary" format the quarto lent itself to a certain solemnity. It was not overly ostentatious (for example when it offered verse printed in italics), and in the late sixteenth and the seventeenth centuries it served to consecrate living or recently deceased authors. Its finest hour came in the mid-seventeenth century with the decline of the folio volume, when it was used for the *belles infidèles* of the Jansenist translators and for famous editions of Vaugelas, Malherbe, Ménage, Balzac, and Voiture, as well as for the original editions of Corneille's plays. It later declined, however, and during his lifetime Racine was published only in duodecimo. Quartos were still used, however, to publish such ventures as Father Maimboug's histories of heresies or Bossuet's *Oraisons funèbres*. The quarto format was to be revitalized in the early eighteenth century, for example, for Gallican manuals or treatises on theology, which Joseph II had reprinted in his empire. Voltaire's *Henriade* was published in London in 1728 in a quarto edition, as was *Le siècle de Louis XIV* and Montesquieu's *Histoire de la grandeur et décadence des Romains*, and also a good many other books of the French philosophes that were published outside France but were nonetheless well received at court and among the great. Similarly the official edition of Molière with illustrations by Boucher was published in Paris in 1755–59 in the same noble but not ponderous format. The quarto edition of the *Encyclopédie,* less costly than the folio edition, enlarged the audience for that publication in a second phase of its history.

The intentions that lay behind the use of the octavo and the duodecimo formats were much more complex. Since these formats produced volumes that could be transported and manipulated easily they were also, in principle, less costly. The Aldine octavo editions were relatively expensive, however, and above all they supposed a notable familiarity with the great authors, whose works, printed in elegant italics, were neither glossed nor annotated. The duodecimo and 24 mo. editions of the Elzeviers and their imitators, conceived at a time when paper was scarce, bear equally little resemblance to modern paperbacks; they were closer to the modern editions of the French Bibliothèque de la Pléiade for a remarkable legibility in which technological prowess made up for small type. The small 18 mo. editions put out by Hubert Cazin (for one) during the next century were more characteristic. The miniaturization of a culture offers much to meditate on.

During the sixteenth century there was a large audience for certain illustrated octavo or duodecimo editions such as the emblem books, the vogue for which was started by Andrea Alciati, or such as *Les figures de la Bible* and the *Métamorphoses d'Ovide figurées* illustrated by Bernard Salomon for Jean I de Tournes, a book that had spawned a long series of imitations. It was also to be the case with books at the end of the ancien régime that were conceived as elegant objects. These books, designed to seduce the eye by their "gallant" text, their adorable vignettes, and the perfection of their page layout, could at times have an undeniable success: one example is the "Fermiers généraux" edition of La Fontaine's *Contes.* Often, however, as with Dorat's *Les baisers,* they have the charm of a ravishing but empty-headed beauty. The pirated editions of some of these works show them to have had a wider public than the handful of bibliophiles who originally created them for their personal delectation. In a society on the decline they may have contributed to the formation of cultural countermodels.

Octavo and duodecimo editions, the Maître Jacques—or Jack-of-all-trades—of publishing, served for the publication of the majority of literary texts, in particular those of "less noble" genres. Here too, however, the bookseller-publisher's choice of format did not always correspond to a desire to lower the price of the book. In the early seventeenth century, for instance, the volumes of *L'Astrée* and *Clélie,* printed in several thick volumes and with large type (with only some 1,200 characters to a page), sold for quite high prices (6 livres for each volume of *Clélie* in 1660). The *Lettres de la religieuse portugaise* (1675) had scarcely more than 750 characters per page. Such books may have been printed in this manner to facilitate reading by women unaccustomed to that activity. Above all, the booksellers of the time, sure of their public, were no more intent on lowering costs when dealing with a wealthy clientele than were their counterparts during the Restoration and the July Monarchy who sold novels with especially open typography and at extremely high prices for the most part aimed at the readership of the Cabinets de lecture.

There was also a quite different reason for the precipitous move toward smaller formats that began, in France as elsewhere, toward the mid-seventeenth century. In a period of crisis, when the booksellers were obliged to suspend the publication of large works and to fall back on "novelties," they shared the market with the publishers who pirated their editions. The pirates, who served a less wealthy provincial public, reduced page margins and formats in an attempt to reduce the per-copy price. Clandestine publishing grew, and it continued its tradition of using octavo or duodecimo formats. Small books could be transported more discreetly and hidden more easily, and perhaps their reduced size was a more enticing wrapping for the attractions of forbidden fruit.

Every published work has a prehistory, whether the work was printed from the author's manuscript or from a copy of the author's manuscript, with or without his or her permission. It could also be a reprint or a republication of a preexistent work. Computer techniques may perhaps help scholars show that European culture had periods of continuity and times of rupture, one of the clearest of which seems to have occurred around the 1650s.[33] Even in periods of apparent stability, however, traditional texts were ceaselessly revised, adapted, translated, and changed in their physical aspect to bring them into line with the spirit of the times and make them appeal to a specific public.

The presentation of written texts—one might say, the "staging" of the written work—never stopped evolving. Just as twelfth-century Romanesque churches covered with frescoes reflect a sensitivity and a conception of man's relationship with God that was expressed in quite different terms when Baroque decorations were added to those same churches during the seventeenth century, and in totally different terms after the Revolution when the churches were stripped down to skeletons of their former selves, and even later in another way after restorations of varying felicity, so each republished edition of a work expresses a successive vision of that text.

The title page of a book was a declaration of intent that reflects this evolving vision. When title pages first appeared, the booksellers' primary interest seems to have been to make sure there was enough material on it: as long as the gothic style lasted, it seemed to abhor a void. This meant that little attempt was made to emphasize the author's name or the title, and that for some time the title page publicized the work in lengthy and hyperbolic phrases in boldface type, often in two colors. This fashion, which continued for centuries in German lands, presupposed that typography was still based on the rhetoric of oral discourse. The great French humanist printers, who admired Roman inscriptions, reacted to this custom (at times aggressively) in much the same spirit as when they stripped texts of their traditional glosses. They took particular pains, for example, to let the word "Bible" stand alone at the head of the title page. On some occasions they succeeded brilliantly, as with Jean de Tournes' folio version of the Bible published in 1554, where the words "La Sainte Bible" emerge from the middle of the page in thick but supple characters several centimeters high. In other works—Robert Estienne's in particular—the printer's mark becomes extraordinarily prominent, as if to proclaim his self-satisfaction, pushing the title and the imprint to the head and the foot of the page. Was it in reaction to this that Michel Vascosan, who married one of Robert Estienne's daughters, sometimes left off his mark, as if to create a carefully calculated typographical balance between the two main elements separated only by a blank space? [34] Even among the greatest printers—Colines, the prince of elegant page layouts, and Robert Estienne himself—aesthetic considerations often took priority over text, leading to layouts in which unimportant words that happened to occupy a prominent place are given in large capital letters and terms bearing genuine information are stifled, printed in smaller capitals or lowercase letters. At times a word is even split in two and spread over two lines in the interests of harmonious line spacing. Such habits, which continued through the seventeenth century, and a fondness for lengthy formulaic titles show the continuing dominance of spoken rhetoric over typographic rhetoric. Typography was long in winning a place of its own.

The persistence of lengthy discourses on the title page (where we would look for concise information) is still not a complete definition of a sixteenth- or seventeenth-century book. The title page often mentioned a *privilège*, a *permission*, or official ecclesiastical approbation, the full text of which might be reproduced on a later page. Indeed, if one of these guarantees of orthodoxy were missing it was enough to arouse suspicion. The humanists were also in the habit of placing at the head of their works verse dedications sent by well-wishing friends to honor the publication—a form of publicity that enabled the reader to identify the circle from which the work had emerged. It was appropriate to place a new work under the protection of a ruler or a great personage, an homage that was long accompanied by offering that person a manuscript copy of the work or at least a copy printed on vellum or special paper and perhaps illuminated. In this way the author could thank a protector or solicit a reward (Erasmus often used this means); above all, the gesture was a profession of allegiance in the hope of gaining some measure of support. As a result dedications could be afflicted with enormous pomposity. When the king of France deigned to accept a dedication it was presented in the volume preceded by a scroll bearing the king's arms; the text would begin with large decorated initials and was usually printed in large-sized italic type. Custom dictated that the dedication end with the same formulas as a letter, thus symbolizing the existence of personal connection between the monarch and his writer.

All this seems to us pure formality. Nonetheless, the mention of a royal *privilège*, printed ostentatiously on the title page of a book printed by Robert Estienne or Etienne Dolet must have had a quite special resonance in the age of the Protestant Reformation. Similarly the solemn dedication of the third edition of Bayle's *Dictionnaire*, which the regent accepted (although in principle the work was banned in France) seemed both an act of defiance and a wise political move. In contrast, aggressively fantastic imprints on the title pages of many clandestine publications were certainly received as insolent challenges to the power structure, and foreign or fictitious imprints in editions printed in France, some even with tacit permission, show proof of governmental impotence.

These subtle changes operated as signs that enable us to penetrate into a somewhat Manichaean world in which books were the bearers of graces or sins but rarely seemed to carry an objective message. It was almost a revolutionary move for Voltaire to dedicate certain of his works published outside France to foreign rulers. This trend was completed when the traditional dedication was replaced by a foreword—an *Avis au lecteur*—

claiming to establish a direct relationship between the author and the reader and launching the book on its own without a protector.

The essential question lies in how the text was cast in physical form. Works had been divided into numbered "books" from late antiquity, they in turn had been divided into chapters, and various ways had been devised to indicate sections, sometimes by numbering them. In the twelfth and thirteenth centuries new procedures were invented to place glosses on the page and provide visual indications of the steps in scholastic argumentation. The Bible had been given chapters at that time (in principle, definitively), and its chapters had been divided into sections lettered from *a* to *f* or *g*, with the letters placed in the margins. Theologians and jurists—the kings of indexing techniques—devised a number of systems for retrieval and reference.[35]

As in other cases, the printers at first reproduced exactly what lay before their eyes in spite of the technical difficulties involved in certain layouts. They kept the traditional page layout of the works of the last Scholastics, but more often than not they skipped the step of having a rubricator underscore the marginal signs in different colors according to the structure of the argument. The printers made faithful reproductions of glossed texts, in particular the *Corpus juris civilis* and the *Corpus juris canonici*. As long as they published the traditional glosses, publishers in Lyons continued to produce books using chapters, headings, paragraphs, and the traditional system of references by incipit, replacing these with numbers only when the critical commentaries of the new school began to appear.[36]

The challenge to the traditional scholarly systems of reference thus came from the humanists, who imposed their numbering system and their rigid references on the great texts. The Bible was of course the first text to which they turned their attention. In 1509 Henri Estienne numbered the psalms and divided them into verses, following the liturgical dispositions of the early centuries of Christianity, in the *Psalterium quincuplex* of Lefèvre d'Etaples. Somewhat after Estienne the Roman edition of Pagninus borrowed the Jewish system of verses. The decisive move came— once more—from Robert Estienne, whose 1555 concordances introduced the numbering system still in use, which the Church of Rome eventually adopted. Next Jean Frellon in Lyons put the text of the Bible into paragraphs.[37]

Editions of classical authors and of the Fathers of the church were given similar treatment. The first selection among innumerable apocryphal pieces was made by the fifteenth-century booksellers who first compiled various authors' complete works. Advances came one by one, first in Basel in the time of Erasmus, next in Paris with Claude Chevallon and Charlotte Guillard, then in the Low Countries in the entourage of Christophe Plantin. Erasmus used a methodical presentation of the works of St. Augustine instead of the alphabetical order that Johann Amerbach had used. Publishers of ancient texts gradually began to present works in numbered *capitula* even when the scheme somewhat fragmented the author's thought. By the late sixteenth century this became accepted practice, and even today Plato and Plutarch's *Moralia* are cited following the pagination and numbering systems of Henri II Estienne's editions. Systematic numbering of the lines in verse works, in which Plantin played an important role, took longer to catch on.[38]

Sixteenth- and seventeenth-century editors found it a much harder task to give a clear and rational critical apparatus to the texts that they had untangled from their glosses. At first they used an enormous number of signs (letters, ciphers, and lemmas) to indicate textual variants or to explain certain terms and expressions, and they adopted a presentation *en hache* ("like an axe," with hanging indentations) and marginal notes to complete the footnotes. The modern, simple, but somewhat abrupt system of notes won over the philosophers' scrupulousness only in the late seventeenth century.[39]

The Renaissance scholars' efforts to produce accurate texts had singularly positive results. Vernacular works, however, continued to be printed as long discourses strung out over a great number of pages with no paragraphs or pauses. This choice was to some extent understandable in the case of "canonical" texts, which gradually came to have systems of reference markers introduced into them. Learned works in national languages often bore marginal headings or sidenotes, subtitles, and summaries, all of which served as something like a parallel argument. Still, the *De re navali* of Lazare de Baïf, a work that defined a number of terms and gave examples, was printed with no blank spaces. The works of Rabelais and Montaigne's *Essais* were printed with an equally dense page layout, which makes one realize that people of the time had a truly different conception both of the writing of a text and of its reception. It seems even odder to us that the tales and novellas of Boccaccio and Marguerite de Navarre were printed in solid blocks with no pauses, as were the long multivolume novels of the seventeenth century. Admittedly, many novelists took care to arrange pauses within their narrations by inserting letters or conversations. Still, although a letter may be announced by a title in *L'Astrée,* the same is not true in *Clélie* or *Le grand Cyrus,* which also present dialogue in such a way that it is hard to know who is speaking, between the *dit-il* that refers to one character and the *reprit-il* that refers to another. The only way to read this sort of work without losing track of the discourse was probably to closet oneself with it and murmur the text aloud, deciphering its extremely long passages, if not entire volumes, without stopping, an activity demanding a concentration that would indeed mean "losing oneself in a book."

Similarly, it was a long time before theatrical works in the national language (except perhaps in Italy) adopted the printed form to which we are accustomed today and which was based on editions of ancient drama. Both the page layout that we find familiar and the ways we read result from a long struggle, particularly where theatrical works are concerned, as Micheline Lecocq has shown.[40] Printing a dramatic work posed particularly complex problems because the reader had to be helped not only to understand the text but also to sense or imagine the flow of the action by the actors' exits and entrances, the tone of their speeches, and the stage business.

The basic division of a play into acts is a convention that seems to have come from Seneca, whereas the notion of scene seems to have been introduced by Donatus and Evantius in their commentaries on Terence. The idea was first taken up in fifteenth-century printed editions such as the Lyons Terence edited by Josse Bade and printed by Jean Trechsel (1493), in which every (unnumbered) scene is preceded by a note telling how many actors are on stage and what their names are. The Strasbourg edition of the same work by Johann Grüninger (1496) numbers the scenes. The practice was adopted for Italian comedy, first in Italy and then in France thanks to Charles Estienne's translations of the *Andria* of Terence (1542) and an Italian play, *Gl'Ingannati,* known in French as *La comédie du sacrifice* (1543). Charles Estienne, who composed several epistles and treatises on comedy, defined the notions of "act" and "scene" and launched a revival of the theater in France; his disciples later composed treatises on comedy and tragedy as introductions to their own dramatic works. After 1576 certain authors experimented with special typographical devices to show rapid speech (Gérard de Vivre, 1578), a battle (Beaubreuil, 1582), or impatience and anger (Larivey, 1579), but their experiments found no imitators.

This movement to divide plays into acts and scenes affected comedies first. It was only in the early seventeenth century that some uniformity was introduced into drama in printed form. After about 1600 acts and scenes were used more frequently and scenic indications increased. As time went on, scenes were broken down into smaller segments and more typographical devices were used to underscore the division. One, two, then three typographical ornaments were used to mark the beginning of acts and scenes, then the ends of acts as well, then the ends of both acts and scenes. Such markings were at first sporadic but they became increasingly systematic until each scene became a self-contained unit. At the same time stage directions increased: first monologues were noted, then exits and entrances, and finally stage business ("he whispers in her ear," "they disguise themselves," "they fight"). The layout began to overwhelm the text. One scene in Guillaume Colletet's *Cyminde* (Augustin Courbé and Antoine de Sommaville, 1641) contains two lines of text and a total of thirteen words, and in Corneille's *L'illusion comique* (François Targa, 1636) an entire quarto page is given over to a scene (2:9) that contains five one-line speeches. Establishing some sort of balance among scenes came only later.

The publishers of French classical theater followed procedures that had been created for the plays of ancient classical authors, but the quarto editions of Shakespeare's plays (published from 1594 to 1615) bore neither acts nor scenes. In the folio edition of 1623 thirty-three out of thirty-seven plays are divided into acts and nineteen among them into acts and scenes. It was only in the 1709 edition that all of Shakespeare's plays were divided into both acts and scenes. During this period English printers, more pragmatic than their French counterparts, observed no fixed rules. Their printed editions of plays often included a number of stage directions, but some publishers were strikingly negligent. Congreve's publishers, for example, first put out quarto volumes in which dialogue is printed one speech after another, with no indication of entrances and exits, on occasion not even giving the name of the character who is speaking. In 1710 Congreve's friend Jacob Tonson published a revised edition of Congreve's works in a much more elegant octavo edition. D. F. McKenzie has shown how apparently minor typographical changes gave these works a new dignity—the dignity of all-time "classics"—and incited the author to refine his style.[41]

When we study a publication we cannot dissociate the author's contribution and the aspect that the publisher gave the work. No one can claim to restore a famous text to its full, disembodied purity; every book is an instrument of communication that must be interpreted as a whole. But by the same token we need to ask why so many texts that we believe we appreciate were originally presented in a form that baffles us.

The answer is simple. Briefly, what mattered was status. Marc Fumaroli recalled some years ago that in the eyes of men of the Renaissance great writers were above all orators and men of action, as they had been in classical antiquity, and that this was true even though literary quarrels about prose centered on the art of the letter (a sign of the times) rather than on oratory. As we have seen there was no opposition between spoken and written discourse in a society in which people thronged to listen to a harangue, a sermon, or a homily and the spoken word was the only means of communication for a great many men and women.

Generalizations this broad are of course subject to reservations. In particular we need to distinguish between the attitude of Catholics and that of Protestants, imbued with the Book. We can understand why the learned considered the epic to be the finest genre, but also why all attempts to write an epic failed when the enormous scope of such a work composed by a single author and the development of the printing industry made the epic a learned and artificial composition. This explains the paradox that classical literature triumphed in France through genres that were considered secondary but that occupied a particularly significant position between the spoken word and letters. Court poetry and *poésie galante* were in fact originally written to be read within certain limited circles and they circulated, one copy generating another, for a long time before (sometimes) being published. The theater, a genre that was scorned at the beginning of the century, was primarily performance. In the century of Bossuet, the sermon was omnipresent. Thus for some time no one imagined that discourse could be cast in any other language, or follow any other rhetoric, than that of the spoken word.

The illustration of books in the sixteenth and seventeenth centuries reflects a comparable ambiguity. In the early sixteenth century a desire to make a self-sufficient entity of the title page had led to a fashion for frames. These could be a triumphal arch, a portico, or an *échafaud,* a scenic construction like those set up for a prince's solemn entry. One entered into the book as into a city or onto a theatrical stage set. Colines in his second career and, later, Plantin conformed to this fashion; Jean de Tournes kept to a purely ornamental decoration, but Luther's printers framed their title pages and decorated them with scenes from sacred history.

Eventually the image escaped the tyranny of the text and came into its own again. Tradition dates this movement from Aldus Manutius' publication in 1500 of the *Hypnerotomachia Polifilii,* a work probably written by a Dominican prior of dubious morals. This work, the story of a dream perhaps inspired by the technique of the arts of memory, is the most famous published work of all time. It charms the reader by both its typography and the quality of its illustrations, which are full of ruins, symbolic processions, and ancient allegories unfolding like a film. Written in an abstruse language that it claims to be a mixture of Italian and Latin, the work suggests a number of interpretations but never reveals all its mystery.[42] Next came a number of didactic booklets in which every page bore a small picture and a short explanatory text. The fashion for such works was launched by Andrea Alciati, an Italian jurist, whose *Emblemata* depicted such concepts as vices, virtues, and abstract qualities or scenes borrowed from mythology, each interpreted in a moralizing maxim. After that came booklets of "Figures de la Bible" and the *Métamorphoses d'Ovide figurées* launched by Jean de Tournes in Lyons. Beyond any doubt these small-sized works, which were translated into all languages and pleased an extremely broad public, responded to an enormous demand. Just as Geoffroy Tory was addressing not only typographers but everyone interested in the decorative arts, Alciati explained in a "Letter to the Reader" that his book, although composed for his own amusement, was also intended as a help for those who were seeking inspiration for the pewter hat-ornaments that were in vogue at the time. The illustrated emblems that the painter Bernard Salomon created for Jean de Tournes (followed by those of Salomon's rivals) soon appeared on pieces of furniture, enamels, and faience ware, as did the emblems in the series of copperplate engravings on the same themes published not long after in Antwerp.

Thus new forms of allegorical iconography arose, at first using mythology to reveal the secrets and the wisdom of classical antiquity. Emblem books had an immediate and astonishing vogue. The metalanguage that they elaborated called for codification; it was a sign of the times that people of the age also found Egyptian hieroglyphics intriguing. Cesare Ripa published his famous *Iconologie* in 1539, a veritable compendium of symbolic personifications that included Virtues, Vices, Love, Wisdom, Justice, and a broad range of other qualities, all defined with as much precision as an official description of international highway symbols today. For centuries painters, medalists, and artists drew inspiration from such figures. The cultivated public was also persuaded that the ancient fables bore eternal wisdom. In 1599 a secretary to the duc de Nevers, Blaise de Vigenère, compiled a manual for his employer's use, *Les images ou tableaux de platte peinture des deux Philostrate,* which he claimed was the translation of a work by two Alexandrian Sophists. A sumptuous edition of the work was published in 1614 with illustrations drawn by Antoine Caron, the court painter to the last of the Valois, shortly before his death in 1599. This work, like the temple of memory portrayed in its frontispiece, invited the French aristocracy (its evident audience) to meditate on scenes from the most famous ancient legends, offering edifying explanations and moralistic conclusions to go with them.

The appeal of works such as this is incomprehensible to us if we forget that the society of that age had a fondness for spectacles in which it was both subject and viewer, as in the innumerable ceremonies and processions in which each person acted, as if symbolically, to take his or her proper place in ordered rank. There were royal entries resembling the triumphs of classical antiquity, and on such occasions poets (Maurice Scève and Ronsard among them) invented constructions that were often carried out by artists who then provided illustrations for a book; there were engravings celebrating imaginary triumphs such as that of Maximilian I; there were funeral ceremonies and processions with decorated floats as in the obsequies of Charles V in Brussels described in the first work Plantin published in Antwerp. Soon court festivities and ballets drew inspiration for themes and costumes from the same collections, as did French classical theater with its many "machines" to provide scenic effects. During the funeral services of the seventeenth century, preachers recalled the virtues of the deceased, who was perched on his cenotaph halfway between heaven and earth in a church hung with draperies and decorated with emblems recalling his life and his merits. By the Baroque and the classical periods characters portrayed in books wore theatrical costumes: shepherds' garb and the costumes of pastoral drama for *L'Astrée,* for epics and novels the Roman or Turkish dress of the tragi-comedies and tragedies. Jacques Callot's *The Temptation of St. Anthony* depicts nothing less than a scene from an elaborately staged opera. Thus the written word had not yet acquired a direct hold on reality, and the heroes that it celebrated were viewed only through a form of scenic representation. This is hardly surprising in an age in which Louis XIV, the last of the Renaissance princes, could host a banquet dressed in the gaudy theatrical costume of a Roman emperor, surrounded by similarly garbed princely kin and his marshals.

The church of the Counter-Reformation used the same techniques, promoting an iconography that was both learned and broadly accessible. While the mystics called up mental images to help them approach God, as Ignatius of Loyola had taught in his *Spiritual Exercises,* an edifying style of illustration developed that tended toward the theatrical and was often inspired by the arts of memory and the art of emblems. It was a didactic style and a point of departure for meditations and spiritual flights toward God. In one of its ultimate forms it provided the great painted panels used during missionary campaigns to give visual form to the preacher's words and a concrete image of love of God or of Good and Evil.

The popularity of the allegorical image in the Baroque age charged the engraved title page with a new mission; at the same time, the printing of the copperplate engravings that were replacing woodcuts involved constraints that encouraged bookseller-publishers to concentrate their figured message on the engraved title page. Design was a simple matter as long as the main task of the title page was to glorify an author. A medallion representing Justus Lipsius or Ronsard being crowned by some illustrious or symbolic personage could be placed atop a triumphal arch whose sides were decorated with meditating figures of like inspiration. At the height of the Catholic Reformation ambitious compositions of another sort began to appear, for example, the soul's ascent toward the divine. Images of the sort often depicted the work's main topics in allegorical form, and Marc Fumaroli has shown that even treatises on rhetoric followed this fashion, as did tracts of both the Jesuits and their adversaries, who used similar images to illustrate their opposing views. Rubens made a good many allegorical drawings that include finer points whose meaning escapes us today. At times a marriage of text and image could enable symbolic language to become a form of total expression, as with the *Imago primi saeculi Societatis Iesu,* a work with exceptionally fine illustrations printed in 1640 by Plantin to celebrate the centennial of the Society of Jesus. An androgynous figure that could be interpreted in various ways stands above the title, which in turn is placed between six medallions, three to either side, showing the contents of the six parts of the work. Several pages of preliminary matter giving a gradual introduction to the body of the text are followed by a series of emblems with interpretative legends. Thus the work's first pages offer a singularly homogeneous whole with parts and subdivisions that might be compared to the various parts of a church; they explain the ideal, the objectives, and the action of the companions of St. Ignatius in a triumphal volume that in the final analysis resembles a festival book.[43]

That Tridentine Rome mistrusted this sort of language is well known. In these later years the *Imago primi saeculi* was somewhat antiquated, and it reflected its provincial origin. Richelieu wanted to prepare a counter-thrust to the prestigious compositions of the Flemish school that were being put out by his Spanish enemies. He called on Nicolas Poussin to illustrate three of the first works published by the Imprimerie royale, which he had recently created: a Virgil, a Horace, and a Bible. Poussin, a great artist, turned away from the complicated frontispieces of the Antwerp style to design simple images showing figures that are sculptural and, in Claude Mellan's engravings, somewhat glacial: Virgil being crowned by his Muse, Horace whose satirical mask is torn off by Apollo; and, for the Bible, two female figures, one veiled to represent the Old Testament, the other unveiled to represent the New Testament, surmounted by God the Father soaring in the heavens. These prestigious plates stand out for their noble conception, but the time for allegory had passed. Book illustrators deserted the sculptural model that had so often inspired them, and henceforth they turned toward the painters—just as Lodovico Carraccio was giving them a new conception of the painter's art.

❖

Since the Renaissance, illustrations of a totally different type and expressing a new form of thought had made their appearance.

In classical antiquity ancient writers had often complained of the difficulty of reproducing drawings exactly, with their colors, and it perhaps hindered their observations of nature and oriented their classifications toward more abstract forms of definition. Thus although Galen stated that the sick person must be the doctor's textbook, he probably knew little about anatomy since he had never performed dissections. Moreover, if some ancient texts had been accompanied by drawings, these had disappeared over time, which meant that the works of Dioscorides, Theophrastus, Galen, Ptolemy, Vitruvius, and Vegetius were known only through their texts. We know practically nothing about what ancient cartography might have been.

As is known, notable advances in the calculation of proportions and in optical perspective were made in the same age in which engraving and printing emerged. In the 1460s an artist went to the Holy Land to draw illustrations for two works published in Mainz, the *Gart der Gesundheit* printed by Schoeffer in 1485, which contained pictures of plants, and the *Peregrinatio in Terram Sanctam* printed by Breydenbach in 1486, which offered views of cities. At the same time Hartmann Schedel and his nephew, the promoters of the *Nuremberg Chronicles* (1493), collected a vast amount of iconographic documentation in order to show views of a number of European cities in their chronicle. Western sailors were discovering new worlds. A rhinoceros brought to Portugal was received with lively curiosity. The animal was offered to the pope but it died before reaching Rome, and Dürer made his famous engraving on the basis of descriptions that were sent to him. A new movement had nonetheless been launched. Conrad Gesner tramped through the Alps studying their fauna and Pierre Belon, who wanted to publish Theophrastus but found it difficult to understand his descriptions with no illustrations, set off, pencil in hand, for the Levant. Such ventures contributed to the great collections of observations that are the foundations of modern science. By 1612 some six thousand species of plants, ten times more than in Dioscorides, had been identified and named. Advances were not solely quantitative: when drawings were circulated and exchanged and notes were accumulated they provided a sort of "feedback" to correct any given author's inaccuracies and lacunae. The concrete representations that circulated everywhere in this manner were an even better invitation to awareness and imagination than words. Engravings inspired by Piero della Francesca showed the life of the earliest people—the discovery of fire, the construction of the first houses, and so forth—to illustrate the works of Vitruvius. Portraits of the aboriginal Americans were another fine subject for meditation. Belon placed the upright skeletons of a bird and a man side by side at the head of his *Traité des oiseaux,* and the illustrators of Vegetius' *Epitoma rei militaris* depicted the sometimes fantastic designs of engineers of their own times, from a diving bell or a sea-diver's suit to a pneumatic mattress. Thus images multiplied, reproductions of works of art and depictions of famous monuments circulated widely, and distant worlds were brought closer. As the historian of science Georges Sarton has pointed out, there were also pockets of resistance: the science of the age continued to be verbal and based on definitions, and Western Europe continued to took toward the Levant and the Holy Land more than toward the Americas. Some innovators feared that the image would itself serve as a screen to block out reality. Vesalius, who criticized Galen's inaccuracies and preached dissection, insisted that his book not be used to turn people away from direct study of the human body.[44]

It is understandable that when precise description was needed the copperplate engraving dethroned the more suggestive woodcut. Nonspecialists, however, long found it difficult to comprehend and analyze abstract figurative description. The works of Ptolemy had of course begun to be illustrated with maps showing distances from the Holy Land, but more concrete representations continued to be much more common than true maps. Chorography—city views from a nearby height or a bird's eye view of the islands of the Venetian lagoon—was preferred to strict cartography, even in the poems of Ronsard. The chief problem was to give maps an iconic language so that they could be read more easily, which is what Girolamo Cardano attempted to do. Modern cartography spread out from Flanders in the late sixteenth and early seventeenth centuries, when Plantin and his successors brought out first pocket atlases then the great Dutch atlases, volumes of maps whose legends were translated into various languages according to the needs of a market in full expansion. Maps were working tools for sailors, merchants, and soldiers, but henceforth they also figured in the libraries of men of letters. In France an ability to imagine abstract space seemed to accompany the technological revolution and the rapid growth of the monarchical army of the age of Mersenne and Richelieu. The many treatises on surveying, ballistics, and military science published at the time prove that nearly everywhere people were learning to plot space. The Carte du Tendre appeared in the same age, as did the maps of spiritual itineraries drawn up by Breton missionaries.

Everything seemed to connect. Poussin serves as a symbol for the end of the era of the allegorical frontispiece in France, which came a few years before Puritan England forbade theatrical representations and Milton composed his *Eikonoklastes*. Astronomic observatories proliferated, and symbolism took refuge in court festivities and funeral ceremonies. Father Claude-François Ménestrier, a Jesuit and the last theoretician of such ceremonies, wrote on the language of images—and one of his works was condemned by the church. He was describing the beauties of a dying form of thought, and he was writing in an age in which no one still believed in correspondences between the celestial world and the terrestrial world; a world in which the witch trials were over and writers were setting down fairy tales and adapting them to the customs of polite society. Jean Bérain opted for classical simplicity rather than the Baroque designs of Ménestrier for the funeral obsequies of Queen Marie-Thérèse in 1683.

During this same time La Fontaine was writing his *Fables*. Contemporary authors of second rank had often presented the same tales borrowed from Aesop, following the methods of emblematics by centering each fable on an image.[45] The language of the great fabulist was sufficient unto itself, however, and had no need of images. Henceforth, it was not the portrait of the author but the frontispiece that provided the only illustration in most books. Similarly, when Boileau wrote his *Art poétique*, fixing the rules of a rigorous art in which even rhymes were made to be read and criticizing the excesses of the Baroque rhetoric of the beginning of the century, he was preparing an epoch without poetry.

A true low point in the art of the book, the century of Louis XIV produced few innovations. Change occurred later and became evident in the age of the Enlightenment.

The first change was in the status of the book. The Sun King admitted only manuscripts in his *cabinet* in Versailles. He considered printing and engraving merely as ways to acquaint his subjects with the masterpieces with which he surrounded himself and the festivities he sponsored. Louis XV, on the other hand, learned to compose a text for printing at the same time as he learned to write, and the regent, Philippe d'Orléans, drew illustrations for an edition of *Daphnis et Chloé*. Madame de Pompadour engraved a frontispiece for *Rodogune* under Cochin's direction, and she had a printing press brought into her apartments in Versailles on which the *Tableau économique* of Quesnay, her physician, was printed with the collaboration of her royal lover. The princes of the blood and great lords also owned and used *presses de bureau*, typography was a topic for salon conversation, and bibliophiles followed with anxious attention the progress of works that they had commissioned. There was less interest in producing original works than in reproducing writing and drawing. Engraved texts imitated manuscript writing in luxury editions, and the younger Fournier, the leading typefounder of the time, strove to create typefaces inspired by contemporary calligraphy. Hence the fashion for engraving techniques that could create the illusion of drawings (from crayon manner to wash drawings) and the emergence of the first procedures for making color engravings, which were later to give painting such keen competition.[46]

The art of typography took on new life as well. Louis XIV's ministers had opened the way by commissioning Philippe Grandjean to create typefaces worthy of the Great Monarch for the Imprimerie royale. Grandjean chose to take inspiration from the royal calligraphers rather than wait for the commission charged by the Académie des sciences to calculate—yet another time—the ideal proportions for letters. He created characters that are striking for the horizontal serifs capping the lowercase *b*s, *d*s, and *i*s and that give the impression that the line is perfectly straight and that the vertical has become law. The *grandjean* typeface thus bore a relation to the chilly rigor of the colonnade of the Louvre conceived and built by Claude Perrault after Bernini's Baroque project was abandoned.[47] There were attempts to transfer rococo style to the printed page. Pierre-Simon Fournier, borrowing from Louis Luce, Grandjean's successor, used a great number of typographic ornaments to decorate (and overdecorate) his title pages and the first pages of his texts, but he also gave a suppleness to roman letters that made them resemble those of his British contemporary, William Caslon. Another Englishman and a former writing master, John Baskerville, worked with John Wattman to invent wove paper, using forms lined with fine metal mesh to produce a paper that gave new brilliance to luxury print jobs. Baskerville also made improvements in printers' ink and cut the rounded roman characters that bear his name and that were inspired by those of the Imprimerie royale.

The discovery of Pompeii had a widespread influence on styles in Europe during the years of the typographic revival that was accomplished in Madrid with Joaquim Ibarra and in Parma with Giambattista Bodoni. In France the Didots' style developed in stages from the reign of Louis XVI to the coronation of Napoleon. The new typography, with its geometric design, its sharp contrasts between thick and thin and between its blacker ink and the whiteness of wove paper, seemed to have taken inspiration from the rigidity of certain Roman inscriptions. The new typography was a conscious return to classical antiquity and a reaffirmation of order. In its most extreme forms (under the Consulate and the Empire) its letters were lined up like soldiers on parade. It was at its best in the publication of pompous editions of the great classics or for printing the *Code civil*, where it stood as an affirmation of eternal certitudes.

If France set the tone in typography, England took the initiative in renovating the title page. English printers had long respected a traditional layout in which the title of the work and the printer's imprint were set into a frame of ornamental bands. (On occasion the entire text was so framed.) Jacob Tonson changed all that by introducing a more sober presentation inspired by the appearance of classical works. Titles became simple and suggestive, and they offered an alternative: *Candide, ou De l'optimisme; Emile, ou De l'éducation,* and so forth. The Scottish printers, who were less committed to tradition than the London booksellers, put out uncluttered title pages that look quite modern.[48]

Page layout also changed. The paragraph conquered all. Paragraphs had of course appeared in sixteenth-century works, but they now became more common practice in print, beginning with legislative texts (in France, royal acts in particular). The paragraph was also used in books of natural history when a series of items was being described, and at times collections of philosophical or moral reflections used it as well. Some authors even numbered their paragraphs, as did Descartes in his *Traité des passions de l'âme*. The publisher of La Rochefoucauld's *Maximes* used the same system, but La Bruyère preferred to place at the head of each of his "characters" a reversed *D* recalling the sign used in the gothic tradition.

Systematic use of the paragraph was in fact the result of a gradual process. Amyot's translations of ancient classical authors were presented in compact blocks of print, but this was no longer true of the *belles infidèles* of the mid-seventeenth century and it was even less true of their successors of the end of the century. The term *alinéa* was officially introduced into the French language by Guez de Balzac in a letter written in 1644:

> At your leisure, you will copy for me (I beg of you) the Harangue of La Casa, because I want to put it in a preface at the end of the Lettres choisies. But I would like it if the copy were *ex vera recensione Capellani* and that he [the copyist] take the trouble to divide it into several sections or (to speak like Rocollet) *alinéas*, as are all my discourses, which is something that greatly aids the reader and handily untangles the confusion of species.[49]

Thus we can understand why Descartes' *Méditations* should have been published without paragraphs but the *Discours de la méthode* (printed in Holland) was printed with paragraphs, as was Pascal's *Lettres provinciales*, another work that relied on demonstration. The use of paragraphs was far from universal, especially in novels.

As a general rule, typographical innovations occurred in moments of rupture with tradition—first in the mid-seventeenth century, then in the early eighteenth century. Such innovations signaled the definitive triumph of white space over black type, and with Caslon and Fournier letters won a certain suppleness. Letters became more rounded with Baskerville, Bodoni, and the Didots, whose letters have more massive black parts but were in fact fewer to the page. In contrast, all elements peripheral to the text itself gave less firm information: running heads became less precise, marginal notes tended to disappear, and footnotes became less weighty. Although dictionaries proliferated, fewer books had an index. The times were no longer propitious for references. What is more, the text was now definitively divorced from the image, a separation from which it benefited, as demonstrated by the *Encyclopédie* and its separate volumes of plates. It is only fair to note that the priority that the *Encyclopédie* gave to discourse encouraged generalization and made the gaps in a sometimes outdated documentation less obvious. We should also keep in mind that both the encyclopedists who realized that monumental "Dictionary of the Sciences, Arts, and Trades" and the members of the higher echelons of society for whom it was designed were no more artisans than Marie-Antoinette was a shepherdess.

Thus the Enlightenment marked the moment of triumph of the text over the image, of a certain form of typographical rhetoric over the rhetoric of the spoken word, and of the serially produced object. The book that displayed its charms in its title was no longer coy about showing its price on the same page. The standardization of the book owed a good deal to the governing powers, particularly in France, and the book's new layout, which invited new forms of writing, guided reading and tended to suggest, if not to impose, an interpretation. Was this not the age of enlightened despotism? Beyond any doubt, the organization of the text into paragraphs and an emphasis on clarity facilitated fluent reading. It is less clear whether an interest in clarity was carried over to the general plan of the work. A cursory examination of tables of contents does not give that impression. We may have to wait for the industrial revolution for that to become a priority, and for the appearance of the newspaper and the arrival of a generation of people in a hurry.

Eight
The Book and Society

Historians of the book have long paid homage to statistics. By the same token, they have perhaps tended to neglect what Marshall McLuhan vociferously recalled when he asserted that the medium itself was the message, and only recently have they begun to scrutinize the book as an instrument of communication. Today historians are bringing new types of questions to this topic, first concerning the ways in which print materials have been appropriated and read within societies whose views of the written word—whose mental universe—has never stopped evolving and continues to do so, but also concerning the status and functions of the author and the author's career strategies. These will be the focus of a chapter that will lead us from the reader to the author.

APPRENTICESHIP IN READING

The appearance of a new communication technique hardly ever eliminates the ones that preceded it. The new technique simply imposes a new distribution of labor in the overall system that conditions the way people on the various levels of a society think.

It is difficult to reconstruct today the system that prevailed in the West in early modern times before the industrial revolution. Action played a much greater part in the transmission of knowledge and in the mechanisms of memorization than it does now. Since action taught automatic behavior patterns, it was predominantly conservative in both the traditional techniques and the social and religious attitudes that it passed on. Hence the importance of salutations, genuflections, and making the sign of the cross; hence the value given to symbolization of social order, as in respecting an order of march in processions on ceremonial occasions. Remembered gestures were coupled with remembered formulas, prayers, and chants. The priest, a man invested with a transcendent power, taught, explained, and judged. He also acted as an intermediary, as did the local lord and the notables, for the transmission of information and instructions from spiritual and temporal authorities to the population at large.

Those who had access to writing and who spoke the French of Paris enjoyed a certain prestige in the eyes of peasants who understood only their patois, a prestige shared, in the village, with the reader whom others could count on to decipher writing and, in the city, with the preacher, the magistrate, the lawyer, and the physician, all of whom held a seemingly inaccessible learning. Anyone who could master the art of the spoken word was invested with prestige, the tale teller, guardian of a particular form of oral memory, for instance, or the *beau parleur* who could dazzle with his "gift of gab." Such humble means of communication explain the importance of places in which sociability and exchange took place, not only the church but the village tavern, the blacksmith's forge, the workshop, and the market square; in the cities the courts, clubs and associations, and salons. In such places one could always hear talk about a newly arrived traveler or listen to someone who was "well informed"; one could also pick up hearsay, that many-mouthed monster, and hear mischievous calumny.[1]

The family played an essential role in this acculturation, whether in apprenticeships or in the perception of basic social models, in imparting notions of hierarchy, in relations with others, and in the division of labor between the sexes and among the generations. The image of the family cell reached up to the king and even to God, transmitting the principles of a stable world whose equilibrium came from tradition. It was a world in which everyone's place was predetermined by birth and change was considered somehow sinful.

Writing, long reserved to the clergy, had shattered some of the channels of transmission of the oral tradition—the most aristocratic ones, perhaps. Around 1340, from 45 to 50 percent of the children of Florence between the ages of six and thirteen were in school; in 1497, 70 percent of the 100,000 inhabitants of Valenciennes probably knew how to read.[2] These were exceptional cases, however, which, by a process of accumulation, produced new mental attitudes only in certain large cities or certain individuals. The manuscript did not have the force of penetration of print. Even the most cultivated of the literati remained immersed in the atmosphere that had formed them.

With the Renaissance, increasing communications, higher production figures, and a stronger state encouraged a growing use of writing; and with print, writing could penetrate society more broadly for the first time. To what extent Europeans were ready for this cultural revolution is what we need to examine next.

When the humanists set up culture as an autonomous force independent from both the church and the state, they denounced the outmoded methods of traditional schools that relied on mechanical memorization. From

Alberti on, they stressed the need for a reform in education, and Erasmus outlined its methods in his *De pueris statim instituendis*. Erasmus followed classical writers to state that one could command nature only by obeying its dictates. Parents and schoolmasters must thus heed the physical and emotional stage of development of their charges and adapt their methods accordingly. Like all pedagogues of his time, however, Erasmus was directly interested only in the formation of the orator (in the classical sense of the term). Only the study of the Latin language and Latin literature could teach the budding orator how words relate to things and could initiate him into the art of discourse that was indispensable for the government of the city. Children should begin their study of the language of Cicero at the age of seven and should learn to read Latin before they began to write, since writing was simply a technique. Unlike Vives, for example, Erasmus had little interest in mother tongues that lacked grammar and written rules: a child's surroundings and the streets would teach the vernacular.

The literati of the Renaissance were primarily interested in the formation of elites. They rejected Gerson's notion that the education of women was always suspect; their patrons included cultivated princesses, and many women in their circles were extremely learned. Nonetheless they viewed the education of the "second sex" as a means for providing the "first" with wives and mothers—or widows. Hence the greater part of the humanists' pedagogical efforts went into elaborating theories, writing manuals, and helping to found pilot projects such as the school that the powerful drapers' guild created at St. Paul's in London or the trilingual college in Louvain. Above all they aimed at placing humanists and humanistic methods in the secondary schools that city fathers were founding everywhere for the education of their own children and small numbers of other youngsters who showed particular promise.[3]

Whether the established religion was maintained or replaced in any one place, it long was the principal stimulus for the instruction of the population at large. We need to ask: to what extent did the Protestant Reformation and the Catholic Reformation contribute to the reorganization of schooling in the sixteenth century?

The reformers, who rejected the use of Latin as a sacred language, proclaimed that Scripture must be the sole foundation of dogma. That position led them to condemn traditional theological teachings and to embrace the notion that reading the Bible was the principal means for dissipating error. This was Luther's stance in the early phases of the movement that he launched. In the days when nothing seemed impossible he saw the father and family head as the perfect catechist: it was the father's task to explain and reinforce the lessons taught by the preachers. Every child, according to Luther's appeal to the Christian nobility of the German nation (*An den Christlichen Adel deutscher Nation,* 1520), should be introduced to the Gospels before the age of nine or ten, and Holy Scripture must be the prime focus of secondary studies. When Luther took on the task of translating Scripture he stated in the preface to his translation of the New Testament (1522) that all Christians ought to read daily the Gospel according to St. John or St. Paul's Epistle to the Romans.

Luther soon realized that dangers lurked in widespread reading of Scripture, and he became concerned that an explosion of the Catholic Church risked fragmenting the German communities. Were extremist preachers to be allowed to denounce education, empty the schools and universities, and declare that faith could be based on individual reading of the Bible in German? For both Luther and Melanchthon there could be no church without schools and the basis of all pedagogy must be humanist pedagogy. Thus Luther called on city governments to occupy the place left vacant by the Catholic Church and use some of the wealth seized from the abbeys and monasteries for a reorganization of the schools (1524).

Luther became a tireless advocate for schools.[4] He proclaimed that language is a gift of God that distinguishes humankind from the beasts and that Germans should cultivate their beautiful language, but he also denounced as illusory the notion that Scripture could be truly understood without a knowledge of the languages that had expressed it and stressed that the decadence of theology was a result of the theologians' ignorance of the true Latin language. Any real intellectual formation, he insisted, demanded a knowledge of Latin, Greek, and, when feasible, Hebrew. This sort of education was indispensable for anyone who wanted to participate in government, and even women should have enough education to instruct their children and their domestic servants. Luther emphasized the school's role in "social promotion," urging even the poorest families to make an effort to educate their children in order to provide the preachers, sacristans, and school-masters and -mistresses that the new church needed, and urging the authorities to oblige parents to give children who already worked one or two hours a day away from their tasks so that they could attend school.

All these efforts to improve education would be insufficient, however, if the bases of dogma were not clearly explained. Luther published his *Kleine Catechismus* (1529), with its two-tiered explanation in extremely clear terms of the Decalogue, the Credo, and the Pater and its formulas for the sacraments of Baptism and the Eucharist. Luther intended this booklet for the use of pastors and preachers; he saw it as a "Bible for the laity" that in its simplest version could be taught to the illiterate but that would also serve for students in the Latin schools as an introduction to the sacred texts that they would study later.

Luther's followers drew up a number of specific programs to aid rulers and city magistrates who were attempting to apply his principles. In Strasbourg Jakob Sturm, the "iron man" of the city, was named scholarch (inspector of schools) at the suggestion of the preachers Martin Bucer and Wolfgang Capito. Sturm founded Latin schools that combined to form a *gymnasium* directed by Sturm's homonym, Johannes Sturm, with a student body of 645 in 1545. This establishment offered the rudiments of a solid humanist formation to the six lower classes and two years of elementary theology, law, and medicine to its upper levels. Reputed to be one of the best schools of its time, it later became an academy (1566–68) then a university (1621). During the same period elementary education was provided in German schools—six boys' schools with 304 pupils and two girls' schools with 126 pupils in 1535. Thus Strasbourg, a prosperous city with a population of some twenty thousand, had one thousand young people in its schools—a figure that implies that a large number of children did not attend school.[5]

Nearly everywhere, then, the reformers worked in concert with the temporal authorities to prepare well-educated elites. In spite of incontestable gains, however, the Germany of Luther's day was not yet ready for universal literacy. The authorities paid less attention to German elementary schools than to higher education, and primary schools developed unevenly in the various regions, so in the final analysis their results were limited. On the eve of the Thirty Years War Lutheran visiting committees checking on the religious education of the faithful in the Rhineland noted that children did not always attend catechism classes on Sundays, and that when the children were interrogated they often responded by reciting orally taught formulas that they had not understood.[6] It is hardly surprising that a large number of superstitious practices flourished in these milieus.

England had a period of remarkable prosperity from 1520 to 1640. Its population doubled, and the population of London went from 60,000 to

450,000. The distribution of ecclesiastical holdings tripled the numbers of the landed gentry. It was a society that was renewing itself and growing in wealth and in which the elites were becoming aware that they had responsibilities, notably on the local level. Hence the "educational revolution" of the years from 1560 to 1640 about which much has been written.

According to W. K. Jordan's calculations, the number of elementary and grammar schools in the six counties that he studied passed from 35 schools in 1480 to 410 schools in 1660.[7] Thus there was a school for every twelve square miles and for every 45,000 inhabitants. Public schools with paid tuition—Eton, Winchester, Westminster, and other more modest schools— should be added to these figures, as Lawrence Stone has pointed out.[8] One should also add the Inns of Court, which dispensed practical juridical instruction, and the universities of Oxford and Cambridge, which took in a growing number of students during the early decades of the seventeenth century and had more than one thousand new registrants per year between 1620 and 1640.

All in all, the gentry and members of the propertied classes rushed their children into institutions of secondary and higher education, which around 1640 had a number of students they were not to equal until the early nineteenth century. The generation of the Long Parliament summoned in 1640 was one of the youngest and above all the best educated in English history, and its (often) Puritan schoolmasters had introduced it to classical democracy and a Ramist logic that taught thinking for one's self and veneration of the common law. By the same token, however, the schools produced a number of educated clergy and laity that seemed too high for a country whose administration had remained underdeveloped, and this resulted in frustrated ambitions and resentment. Still, the yeomen farmers, freeholders, and shopkeepers who had attended the elementary schools read the Bible, the Gospels in particular, which taught them the notion of equality. Primary schooling and Puritan schooling grew at the same pace, but elementary schooling only widened the gap between the various social categories. Although 60 percent of townspeople knew how to sign their names in 1642, the figure falls to 38 percent in rural parishes and under 20 percent in the north and the west of England. Only 23 percent of Scots could sign their names in 1638–43. This meant that at best three-fourths of the shepherds, fishermen, construction workers, and smallholders, two-thirds of village shopkeepers and craftsmen, and half of the masters in the clothing and textile trades could read a bit but were unable to write. The educational revolution in England, like its counterpart in German lands, remained incomplete in the mid-seventeenth century.

Meanwhile the Jesuits were setting to work in much the same fashion in the Catholic world. Although Ignatius of Loyola showed some reticence regarding schooling, he eventually came around to the idea that the conquest of souls required the formation of minds. The Jesuits did not reach out to found schools; rather, they responded to a universal need, agreeing to open a school at the invitation of a ruler, a bishop, or a city government when they were assured of revenues, a locale, and students. Their arrival at times prompted protests from already established institutions, and their quarrels with the University of Paris (which, not without reason, denounced their ultramontanism) are a familiar story. Well-prepared pedagogues and remarkable humanists, the Jesuits could make a text come alive better than anyone: they dramatized their teaching with theatrical performances that the entire city attended, and on occasion the quality of their instruction even attracted young Protestants. Their efforts seem massive when compared to the broad dispersion of Protestant education. As early as 1575 there were 125 Jesuit secondary schools; by 1640 the Jesuits were teaching some 15,000 students in 521 schools and headed a number of universities in cities from Poland to Spain. Everywhere they followed the rules laid out in the *Ratio studiorum* promulgated in 1585. Their basic education in grammar, belles-lettres, and rhetoric was divided into five classes and six years of instruction, after which they offered three years of philosophy and, for pupils studying for the priesthood, four years of theology.[9]

The Jesuits soon encountered imitators and competition in France and elsewhere, in mid-sized cities in particular. Flourishing *collèges* at times had over one thousand students. The fathers of the Society of Jesus also managed a number of grammar schools in which Latin was taught in smaller cities and towns. Thanks to their efforts the northeast of France had a denser network of secondary schools in 1650 than it had in the nineteenth century. The offspring of nobles, officeholders, and burghers sometimes found themselves in the minority in these schools among the sons of merchants, craftsmen, and workers who may have been at a disadvantage in the lower grades but in some instances turned out to be the most brilliant students. The young of the aristocracy began to join this movement after the mid-seventeenth century, arriving, accompanied by a tutor, at the schools of Clermont or La Flèche, or the Oratorians' school in

Juilly. Often they were also accompanied by a somewhat older comrade charged with helping them to keep up an "accelerated" pace, and at the age of fifteen or sixteen the young aristocrats moved on to a military academy, where they learned the arts of war but might also have relatively high-level instruction in mathematics. After finishing the *collège*, some of the Jesuits' students went on to study at a university, but although the professors in the faculties of theology and medicine offered substantive courses, the jurists usually preferred to sell diplomas that guaranteed little or no higher learning.[10]

There were over fifty thousand students registered in all French *collèges* around 1650 (some of whom had entered secondary schools with little or no preparation). That number remained fairly stable until the age of the Enlightenment. Thus French society gave priority to the formation of elites to fill the innumerable offices that the state had created in an attempt to increase its treasury—elites that would thus have access to the advantages connected with the various forms of participation in public life.

Gradually, however, Catholics and Protestants shifted their emphasis, working to develop a program for elementary education that would include the masses and acquaint them with true religion.

In lands subject to Rome this movement was spearheaded by religious congregations founded to promote charitable works. In the late sixteenth century the congregations were particularly active in regions such as Lorraine that were in contact with Protestantism. In France, particularly when the Calvinist school network was eliminated after the revocation of the Edict of Nantes, first the Compagnie du Saint-Sacrement (Company of the Most Blessed Sacrament) then the Aa—secret societies that arose from the Marian congregations founded by the Jesuits—worked to persuade prominent persons, prelates, and notables to reorganize parish schools and to found free schools (in principle) for the poor.

Teaching methods were traditional in these schools: the curriculum was divided so that students progressed from one clearly defined phase to another, moving from deciphering single letters to reading syllables, then words, and finally Latin texts. The schoolmasters worked with each child individually while the others kept busy as best they could. Taught in this manner, even the most gifted pupils needed at least three years to learn to read. Those who were still attending school next learned to write, in principle in two years. Necessary revisions to this program were gradually introduced by Charles Démia and Jean-Baptiste de La Salle and the Brothers of the Christian Schools, who reorganized the schools of Lyons (and elsewhere) and founded both seminaries for future schoolmasters and schools, which greatly increased in number during the eighteenth century. Henceforth French children learned to read in French; they were subject to strict discipline that included their movements and their posture, and they were divided into grade levels or "classes" so that all students in one class could work simultaneously. The acquisition of writing skills was still dissociated from learning to read, however, and instruction in arithmetic was so scant that future merchants had to go elsewhere to complete their training, usually to a writing master who also taught accounting.[11]

In 1877–79, at the height of a public debate concerning the school system, more than fifteen thousand primary-school teachers responded to a questionnaire distributed by *recteur* Louis Maggiolo on the progress of literacy that gives some indication of the success of these efforts.[12] The data in this survey were based on signatures in marriage records, so it might give a literacy rate higher than the number of people who could actually write, since some probably could write little more than their names, but certainly lower than the number of those who could read. The data also give greater weight to rural areas than to the cities. Nonetheless, the figures are significant: 29 percent of French men and 14 percent of French women signed the marriage registers in 1686–90; 47 percent of men and 27 percent of women could do so a century later (1786–90); and 75 percent of men and 61 percent of women did so in 1871–75. Furthermore, literacy advanced unevenly from one region to another: figures are highest for the eastern and northeastern regions of France, and for centuries an imaginary line drawn from Saint-Malo to Geneva separated northern France, where the population was better educated, from southern France, perhaps because in the regions of the Midi people spoke languages and dialects very different from Parisian French, but also quite certainly because these regions were in general less wealthy and more isolated. One exception was the Hautes-Alpes, whose astonishingly high literacy rate led the list for 1689–90 with a 45 percent of men and women who signed the marriage registers, a figure that later leveled off. The winter evenings were long in the mountains and the land was poor. Often without resources and obliged to emigrate, the inhabitants of the Briançon region traditionally turned to tutoring and schoolteaching in order to survive. Like many other mountain folk, they were also book peddlers—the famous *Bizoards*.

Literacy rates continued to vary greatly. People from comparable milieus were more apt to read and write in the larger cities, which were the seats of administrative offices, courts, and even universities, than in the merchant cities; more in towns than in rural areas. Despite the Counter-Reformation's efforts at forming Christian wives and mothers, there were fewer schools for girls. Some women from cultivated milieus who had been educated in convent schools became great readers, first of devotional books then, in the eighteenth century, of novels; women from a merchant background often learned to write in order to help their husbands, but when they did they had sometimes already been taught to read by their parents.

Religious activism found its most fertile terrain in Protestant countries, where the masses were urged to learn to read in order to understand the Bible. After 1560, when Catholics were eliminated from Scotland and the Church of Scotland was established, the Presbyterians showed an exemplary zeal for reading. John Knox's first tract on religious guidance contained a proposal for universal education that was confirmed by acts in 1646 and 1696. A network of elementary schools was created in which students could pursue relatively advanced studies, and some Scottish cities had Latin schools comparable to the English public schools. In 1587 the University of Edinburgh was added to the three other universities that had been founded in that small country during the preceding century. In like fashion, the Puritans embarked on the evangelization of Wales during the English Civil War, sending 150 preachers to do the job, creating sixty new schools and printing six thousand copies of the Bible and three thousand New Testaments in Welsh. Other Puritans in New England resolved that the children of domestic servants were to be educated, at the expense of the community if need be. Thus the figure for signatures on marriage registers rose from 25 percent in Scotland and 30 percent in England in 1640 to 60 percent (for men) in the two countries toward the mid-eighteenth century, reaching 30 percent for English women and 15 percent for Scottish women. These figures reflect an undeniable advance, but they seem relatively modest when contrasted with the figures for North America: 84 percent of New Englanders and 77 percent of Virginians signed their wills in 1787–97.[13]

Can we pinpoint the moments when this conquest of literacy that continued to the nineteenth century leveled off or accelerated? Lawrence Stone has attempted, with some temerity, to compare literacy figures for Scotland, England (including Wales), and France between 1600 and 1900.[14] England led at first, but literacy in Scotland began to rise around 1660, passed Scotland's neighbors, then tapered off around 1770. Figures

THE BOOK AND SOCIETY

for the north of France show that in 1786—90, 71 percent of men and 44 percent of women could sign their names, a higher percentage than for Scotland, England, and the Netherlands under Austrian rule, where signatures oscillated between 60 to 65 percent for men and 37 to 42 percent for women. The French Midi showed a considerable lag in the same period, with 27 percent of men and 12 percent of women who could sign their names.

Once again, it was when religion entered the picture that radical advances were made in the general movement for literacy. In the Protestant lands of Germany, ravaged by the Thirty Years War, and later in regions affected by renewed conflict during the wars with Holland, Lutheran burghers (in Hesse in particular) were furious when they contemplated princes who had become absolute rulers with courts that imitated the magnificence of the court of Louis XIV and patricians who spent ruinous sums on luxuries when some of the population was reduced to beggary. They felt that Christ had been forgotten and that the time had come for a Second Reformation to restore the church as the apostles had known it. They organized into conventicles and preached a return to Scripture. The princes took fright and persecuted such groups, but the Calvinist elector of Brandenburg welcomed them and established them in Halle in 1691—95. He thought their efforts to regroup his Lutheran subjects in line with the Calvinist model would give him an advantage over them. Although the Pietists encountered some resistance, they founded a number of hospitals; above all they founded schools in which Luther's *Kleine Catechismus* was a basic text and each new student received a Bible to be used for daily class work. The king of Prussia saw to it that equally rigorous methods were applied in the cadet school that he established in Berlin, and between 1725 and 1775 the rules of Pietist education were adopted in a great many Lutheran lands from Prussia to Baden, from Hanover to Hesse, and even in the German cities of Transylvania. In the century following its creation in 1711, the printshop founded in Halle circulated a million copies of the Bible and two million copies of the New Testament.[15]

Northern European regions that had seemed somewhat marginal made striking advances, although not without difficulty. Prussian peasants may indeed have begun to write their names during the eighteenth century (10 percent signed their names in 1750, 25 percent in 1765, and 40 percent in 1800), but reading often remained dissociated from writing. In Sweden the Lutheran Church launched a vast campaign to improve reading skills. According to a law passed in 1686 illiterates could neither take communion nor marry, and women on isolated farms worked under the supervision of their pastors to act as schoolmistresses for their families, with the result that 80 percent of the Swedish faithful could decipher a text, although only a limited elite knew how to write.[16] As always, access to the written word came by degrees.

In the Catholic countries of southern Europe, according to the still-fragmentary data available on literacy rates, Spain and Italy always lagged behind northern European lands, and in some periods literacy rates even fell. In 1850 Sweden led the list in Europe with only 10 percent of its population total illiterates; next came Prussia and Scotland (with 20 percent illiterates) followed by the other northern lands. Literacy rates in England and Wales had shown little change for a century (30 to 35 percent illiterates), France followed next (40 percent illiterates), then came the Austro-Hungarian Empire, including Galicia and Bukovina. Far behind them came Spain (75 percent illiterates) and Italy (80 percent) and the other Mediterranean and Balkan lands. In last position came Russia (90 to 95 percent illiterates).[17]

Like Spain, Italy, the cradle of humanism, entered the industrial age with three-quarters of its population illiterate, and some areas of southern France were no more advanced. Thus we see the same imbalance in literacy that we have seen in the book market. Mediterranean Europe, where agricultural techniques had not changed and population was stagnant, eventually became a closed world that lost out to the tightly knit area of ancient culture that included England, Scotland, part of Ireland, France (the north leading the south), the Low Countries, and the western portion of the German world. Further to the east, however, new fortunes were in the making during the age of enlightened despotism, and Poland was drawing up ambitious plans on the eve of its Third Partition in 1795. Meanwhile, the Russian elites looked to France.

Culture went where the wealth was. The development of a market economy always favors writing, and one of the greatest obstacles to literacy among the peoples of eastern and southern Europe long remained the closed life of peasant societies within great domains owned by an aristocracy originally trained (along with a handful of the bourgeoisie) by the Jesuits and the Piarists. Conversely, the circulation of men and goods, which increased connections and the exchange of information, generated progress in communication techniques (in the broad sense of the term).

Indeed from time immemorial literacy developed along land, river, and sea routes and concentrated where routes intersected. This happened in France in the fertile lands of Normandy and Champagne, where rural industry made up for the poverty of certain uplands, while the Massif Central, where peasants depended on a subsistence economy, remained a cultural desert. It is hardly surprising that the Enlightenment in Europe was concentrated in zones that had a well-developed network of dependable roads. In one sense schools were the product of wealth and of a population density of more than fifty people per square kilometer. Elementary instruction could also depend on the reaction of people faced with an isolation imposed on them by nature, as with the book peddlers who descended from hill country nearly everywhere in Europe, the Swedish farm wives who taught their families to read Scripture or Luther's catechism, and, even more, the men and women of the American colonies who set off to conquer a vast space clutching their Bibles. We also need to keep in mind the importance of the newspaper and experiments as odd as those of Prussian rulers who attracted an elite of Protestant exiles to their land and transformed their veterans into elementary-school teachers after they had learned their new trade in Berlin.

The shift to written culture always resulted from a desire or a willingness to break down the barriers of a compartmentalized society and a will to join a larger community. Linguistic considerations closely connected to the will of the governing powers played an important role as well. With printing, victory always went to the strongest forces, whose idiom the authorities used as a vehicle, ineluctably setting up a written language that contrasted with the diversity of spoken dialects. When that happened, the cultures embodied in the languages that had been thrust aside might show some resistance or foster brutal reactions, but they were threatened with near-extinction.

There is a danger of confusing causes and effects. François Furet and Jacques Ozouf have noted that Basque and Breton lands and the regions in which the langue d'oc was spoken always came at the lower end of literacy rankings in France, but they have also shown that it would a mistake to impute that position to the use of French in the schools. French was not used systematically in the school systems of France until the late nineteenth century, and the withdrawal of these communities into themselves was older: in an attempt to cleave to the mechanisms of the oral tradition they totally rejected a written culture that was imposed on them.[18]

The history of the Czech language shows similar reactions. When Bohemia was forcibly brought back within the Habsburg empire in 1620 several things combined to Germanize a nation with powerful traditions. During the eighteenth century the Bohemian nobility was decimated and replaced by a military aristocracy of German origin; a German minority that had been settled on the edges of a territory rich in mineral ores grew wealthy with the emergence of an industry that Maria Theresa made every attempt to encourage; under Joseph II use of the language of Vienna was mandatory in the various branches of the imperial administration. During this same time the Jesuits, who attempted to attract the masses by magnificent ceremonies and pilgrimages that borrowed from popular traditions, used Czech for basic instruction in the primary schools but later switched to German. As a result the "better society" of Bohemia tended to forget its own language, which degenerated to the point of becoming incomprehensible in certain documents emanating from the Diet, and the Czech peasantry kept its children out of the parish schools where they would learn a language that offered few opportunities for advancement. The schools changed only as a result of contact with the German colonies. Did this mean that Czech ceased to be a living written language? A threefold reaction occurred. First, the peasants revolted against a system that favored the nobility and tied them to the soil, and they obtained the suppression of feudal dues. Second, a handful of notables—parish priests and pedagogues—sought to reinvest the Czech language with dignity, a process aided by an accelerating industrialization that developed the cities of the land. Third, the emperors relaxed their policy of Germanization but remained faithful to the principle of enlightened despotism in attempts to develop the school system in their lands. This meant that Bohemians were by and large better educated than other Slavs who remained isolated.[19]

More widespread use of writing and the state's growing recourse to procedures dependent on writing encouraged the establishment of a lay elite of humanist culture. In eastern Europe this elite was recruited from among the nobility; in France it came from the bourgeoisie, and when offices tended to become hereditary it more resembled a caste. Priority was inevitably given to the formation of a relatively restricted elite, and, as always, the system was conceived to guarantee the replication of the group in power and assimilate the more gifted members of emerging forces. Could it have been otherwise?

It was not easy to pass from one world to another. In societies still immersed in orality, changes remained slow and gradual, as a glance at the full range of the ability to sign one's name attests. Some people were completely illiterate; others were near-literate and, like Lubin, Clitandre's valet in Molière's *Georges Dandin*, could decipher only the capital letters of inscriptions carved on certain walls. Some reader-writers could decipher a text out loud and write their names in block letters; some craftsmen and merchants who needed to write for business reasons could read only utilitarian documents such as posters, announcements, official texts, and perhaps a volume of the Bibliothèque bleue or a religious work. Then there were *précieuses* who had had some schooling, had learned to read from novels, and were learning to write a proper letter with the help of manuals like the *Secrétaire à la mode*. Finally, there were the Jesuits' former pupils who had access to what we would call the culture of letters.

We can imagine the tensions that such a range of skills could create. Roger Chartier has recalled (in a recent piece to which I am much indebted) [20] that in Shakespeare's *Henry VI*, part two, the clothier and rebel Jack Cade and his followers debate putting a law clerk to death because writing is the instrument of a justice and a power that they reject and, symbolically, because law clerks use and set down formulas Cade and his men take to be magical. The French revolutionaries who burned feudal titles in 1789 may perhaps reflect a similar attitude. On the other hand, scholars were capable of denouncing printing as an instrument for the prostitution of learning or, like certain Enlightenment philosophes, of doubting the usefulness of instruction for the people.

Gradually, however, the notion that the people must be educated began to gain ground. At first the justification for popular education was religious, as we have seen. Still, it is simplistic to state that children were taught reflexes that would make them into good Christians and obedient subjects. People of these times were highly receptive to reading when writing skills were not required, but they found themselves more and more in situations that called for writing as well. This means that the gradual shift from the world of orality to the society of writing that we have been examining led, in the final analysis, to something quite new—the unleashing of mechanisms that prompted a new view of self and a spirit of abstraction. Education may well have helped people to conceive of a unique and invisible God. In any event, it encouraged a logic of the act as well as a logic of the word, and also an ability to reach reasoned decisions and a higher measure of self-control. It is not by chance that there was concern in Venice in the fifteenth century that too many Venetian sailors were illiterate. The best sailors and the best soldiers of all ages have been those with the best education. One need only recall the spirit of enterprise of the Puritans, great Bible readers, or the many craftsmen in the fine arts who were Jacobins during the French Revolution and, later, leaders of the working class.

ACCESS TO THE BOOK

Even more than today, being able to read in no way implied access to even the simplest forms of book culture in societies in which most readers had only imperfectly mastered the techniques of reading, in which the penetration of the written word was only partial, and in which books were still relatively precious and rare objects.

Today's historians are less fortunate than the sociologists, who can investigate the psychological background of a representative sampling of living men and women. Historians can never be sure that they understand exactly how their ancestors read any given text in an environment that is—to say the least—difficult to reconstruct.

Probate inventories are the documents that tell us the most about readers in past times. Although they do not permit a reconstitution of what the deceased actually read, they at least give us the number and often the titles of the volumes they owned on their day of death. Christian Bec acquaints us with the book holdings of a group of fifteenth- and sixteenth-century Florentines who, at their death, left a child or children who became wards of the city.[21] A first surprise is that very few of these people owned books: 3.3 percent of them in 1413–53, 1.4 percent in 1467–1520, 4.6 percent in 1531–69, and 5.2 percent in 1570–1608. The appearance of printing thus brought little change in this group of people who owned books. Moreover, the proportion of small collections (fewer than ten volumes) long remained high: they account for at least 75 percent of all book holdings before 1520, 67.5 percent of collections in the mid-sixteenth century, and a little less than 50 percent of collections toward the end of the century. The number of libraries with more than fifty volumes increased from 6 percent of libraries in 1531–69 to 18 percent for the period 1570–1608. It is as if book culture remained the province of an extremely small minority of wealthier citizens. Among the works most often mentioned were books of piety such as the *Golden Legend*, texts of Marian devotion, lives of the saints and brief treatises on popular religion, and the works of St. Augustine. Although they are frequently listed in their own times, after the Council of Trent Savonarola and Machiavelli disappeared, from these inventories at least, as did the Bible. Among secular works the authors most cited were Boethius, Horace, Ovid, Plutarch, Livy, Valerius Maximus, and Virgil, and for more modern authors Dante, Petrarch, Boccaccio, Ariosto, and Pietro Bembo. There was very little that was new or that looked to the world beyond: Florence, where few books not of a popular nature were printed, remained true to its past.

In Spain of the Golden Age in the city of Valencia, 702 (more than one-fourth) of the 2,489 probate inventories for the years 1474-1560 that Philippe Berger has examined mentioned books.[22] Readers were in the minority among craftsmen and merchants but in the majority among nobles and even more so among physicians, judges, and the clergy, three categories that accounted for 75 percent of all volumes mentioned. In Spain as in Italy, the appearance of printing brought no revolutionary change in a city in which culture was already well established. Through time a minority of craftsmen stood out from the others, members of the liberal professions accumulated volumes, and the libraries of the nobility declined, although there were still noblewomen who read copiously.

Do these figures indicate that Valencia had a particularly intense book culture? Bartholomé Bennassar provides some enlightening figures from Valladolid.[23] That Castilian city was a relatively active center of printing where not only books of theology, law, and spirituality were printed but also humanist texts and chivalric romances. Some tradesmen and some of the wealthier merchants owned volumes: one shoemaker even owned twenty-five books and one merchant twenty-two (books of spirituality and novels). Still, three-fourths of the books were owned by *ledrados, hidalgos,* and churchmen. The learned remained faithful to Aristotle and to tradition, but they were increasingly influenced by humanism, thanks to the penetration of classical works, the great Italian authors, and—above all—Erasmus. They also sought books of spirituality and travel accounts. In strong contrast with Florence, the general picture is one of an open-mindedness and a high level of instruction among at least a small part of the population. A city where routes intersected, Valladolid was also the seat of the court of Castile, and it functioned for some time as the capital of the kingdom and was also the seat of a university.

Albert Labarre provides similar data on Amiens from 1503 to 1575.[24] Amiens, which was returned to the French crown in 1477, had an urban population, within the walls, of some twenty thousand souls, many of them shopkeepers and members of the "mechanical" trades. Of the 4,443 probate inventories drawn up during this period, 887 mention books, or a slightly smaller proportion than in Valencia. Among ecclesiastics, 143 out of a total of 196 inventories mention books, as do 129 of the 168 men of the law, all 33 members of the medical professions, and 38 out of 52 nobles, giving an overall figure of 344 out of 449 members of the privileged professions who mention books. The 109 who did not have books listed among their possessions may easily have owned a library that was removed from the estate's goods before the appraisers arrived. However, there were also more than four thousand inventories of the possessions of deceased from other social categories, only 543 of which mention books among the possessions of 261 merchants, 98 tradesmen, and 40 others, many of them burghers with an independent income or "masters" who had some university education. Also included among these 40 others were some women, the daughters and widows of noblemen or of men from the milieus of the law and the administration or medicine. We can identify some three thousand of the twelve thousand works mentioned (though not always described) in these data. More than half of the identifiable books—1,534, to be precise—are religious: 764 books of hours, 128 breviaries, 43 missals, 120 Bibles, 27 Psalters, a dozen books of extracts from Scripture, some 30 postillas, 42 copies of the *Golden Legend,* and some 50 works of the Fathers of the church, among them a dozen by St. Augustine. There were also books on the law (64), many of which were course books on civil and canon law, belles-lettres (396 titles, among them 19 works of Ovid, 17 of Cicero, 9 of Virgil, and 8 of Homer), arts and sciences (198, thanks to many books on medicine), and history (about 140, among them Valerius Maximus and 9 copies of the *La mer des histoires*). Fifty-eight nobles, persons from the worlds of the robe, medicine, and the church, and four merchants each owned more than fifty volumes, twenty-one of them owned more than 100 volumes, and one person owned as many as 500 volumes. It is in particular among the larger libraries that we can see traces of the humanistic spirit, as indicated by the presence of the 205 works by Greek and Latin authors noted above. Piety and liturgy accounted for nearly all the reading matter of the citizens of Amiens who owned only one or two books. These data clearly show that in Amiens during the Renaissance and the Reformation, as in Valencia and Valladolid, printed books were primarily reserved to clerics and servants of the temporal powers. In less exalted milieus, books, as if symbolically, seem to serve tradition in the form of a family book of hours, perhaps a Bible, a Psalter, or a copy of the *Golden Legend* or some other book that fell into the owner's hands perhaps by chance. One might well wonder how the Reformation managed to penetrate beyond the world of the literate if Labarre had not also mentioned the presence, both in the city and in its immediate surroundings, of notions-sellers who sold ABCs, books of hours, and "folderol" (*fatras*) that probably included some of the booklets and the calendars utilized for Protestant propaganda and intended to follow and reinforce preaching and oral propaganda.

During that same period the princes of Europe who wanted to attract humanists to their entourages created libraries after the Italian model.

The kings of France had shown the way. Charles VIII returned from Naples with books that he had commandeered from the library of the Aragonese rulers, and he brought back from Florence Janus Lascaris, Lorenzo de' Medici's librarian. Later, when Louis XII conquered Milan he brought back the rich collections of the Visconti and the Sforza rulers of that city which, together with the books of his father, the poet Charles d'Orléans, and the richly illuminated manuscripts of Louis de Bruges, seigneur of Gruthuysen, formed the original holdings of the King's Library. The library was installed in a gallery of the royal castle at Blois and it was further enriched by Francis I with works from his family collection, with works confiscated from the duc de Bourbon, ex-constable of France (who had inherited some of the treasures of the duc de Berry), and especially with Greek manuscripts that the scholars of his entourage needed for their studies. These works, sumptuously bound and divided between Blois and Fontainebleau, the principal residences of the court and the chancery, were placed under the care of Guillaume Budé and Pierre du Châtel, assisted by Lefèvre d'Etaples and Mellin de Saint-Gelais.

During the Reformation, the German princes adopted a similar policy. In Saxony, Julius of Brunswick, a champion of the Protestant cause and an admirer of French literature, acquired precious manuscripts from the abandoned monasteries and acquired books and autograph documents of Luther. Thus an illustrious collection was born, later augmented with care by a long line of book-loving dukes whom Leibniz and Lessing served as librarians in a library in Wolfenbüttel that served as a model for the German princes. During the Counter-Reformation the Catholic Church took the lead in the development of book collections, and the Vatican Library, backed up by its printing press, became a place of study where learned men and philologists could busy themselves with the revision of scriptural texts and the Roman liturgy. Soon after, Archbishop Federigo Borromeo

founded the Ambrosian Library in Milan and Philip II charged Hieronymite monks with the direction of the library that he founded in a desolate
valley near their monastery of the Escorial. Nearly everywhere in Europe—in particular in Spain, Flanders, and France—monasteries old and
new, universities of recent founding, and Jesuit or Oratorian secondary
schools created libraries in which the very order of the folio volumes reflected the solidity of a doctrine that had been revised during the Council
of Trent and that represented the sum total of human knowledge. The
works they acquired have come down to us in such good condition that
they seem never to have been read, even though the ones that were placed
on the Index *donec corrigantur* had been censored by carefully blacking out
the condemned passages. Some of these collections—those of the princes
in particular—were put to the service of genuine intellectual activity. In
Paris, for example, Father Petau, the founder of positive theology, and
Father Sirmond, the editor of the decrees of the councils, worked in the
Collège de Clermont, while Father Mersenne received scholars in the
Capuchin monastery of the Place Royal, Dom Luc d'Archery brought
together in Saint-Germain-des-Prés a model library that was used by Mabillon, Montfaucon, and their followers, and Father Léonard de Sainte-
Catherine grouped around him in the Abbey of Sainte-Geneviève a group
of learned clerics who engaged in rigorous critical discussions.[25]

Nowhere was this movement more intense than in the Paris of the
Catholic Reformation. A relatively weak monarchy produced a corresponding decline in the Bibliothèque du Roi, which for a century (1560–
1660) was housed in a series of temporary locales in the Latin Quarter and
was stripped of a part of its printed works in obscure circumstances. Leading ministers reacted to this decline, each in his own way. Richelieu, who
amassed an incredible number of paintings, antiquities, and sculptures in
the Palais-Royal, at Rueil, and in his châteaux in the provinces, seized the
library of the city of La Rochelle and brought together a large number of
volumes that he bequeathed to the Collège de Sorbonne at his death. Séguier created a library in two superimposed galleries with walls covered
with mosaics and ceilings painted by Simon Vouet. Unbeatable when it
came to pillage, Séguier brought back treasures from his expeditions in
Normandy to repress the revolt of the Va-Nu-Pieds. As part of his dream of
a reconciliation with the Eastern Christians he ordered systematic searches
for Greek manuscripts, even among the Turks, and he had the monks who
had served him as agents put into prison so that he would not have to pay
them. Finally, he arranged it so that he would have the right to pick what

pleased him from French print production by invoking the rule of *dépôt légal* (roughly, copyright copies). Mazarin, to end the list of ministers, established a library in his palace (subsequently the home of the Bibliothèque nationale) whose woodwork and decorations were moved after his death to the Collège des Quatre Nations, today the Palais de l'Institut. Before the Fronde that was the place where Gabriel Naudé, who had close connections with the Dupuy brothers, the curators of the Bibliothèque du Roi, held court at the center of a group of learned libertines, rationalists, Gallicans, and Machiavellians, all good servants of the king.

Collections were developed that proclaimed an immutable order even in their architecture and the decoration of the buildings that housed them, an order reflected in the arrangement of the volumes on the shelves and in the busts and portraits of the authors most revered by the master of the place. Such libraries served as a summation of knowledge, and their chief function was conservation. Asylums for both rediscovered treasures and more recent works, they were the instruments of a cultural policy, and they were open to the erudite and the learned, whose mission it was to promote that policy. Symbols of appropriation, they were in essence clerical. It is hardly surprising that the possession of a library, especially in Catholic lands, was invested with a very specific meaning. Very few craftsmen and merchants in France had even a few volumes. Nobles—*gens d'épée*—had books, but most book-owners in lay society were lawyers, physicians, and especially officials in the royal administration. Dynasties of *robins* (men "of the robe") had a book collection that was an essential part of their wealth and would be classed among their *propres* (exclusive and incontrovertible property) when they died. In the early seventeenth century there were more than a thousand such collections. These men, for whom the family's rise in society often went hand in hand with a humanist tradition represented in their books by Scripture, the Fathers of the church, the authors of classical antiquity, and Roman law, also succumbed to an attraction to history, ecclesiastical history at first but increasingly monarchical history, and to a marked interest in science in the age of the revolution brought on by mechanistic philosophy. Although such probate inventories give us little insight into the market for literary novelties, French authors such as Philippe de Commynes and Ronsard, but also Montaigne, Du Vair, and Charron, are nonetheless well represented.[26]

This rapid review does not mean, however, that libraries represented one unvarying stereotype. Medical libraries were a separate world where the shelves for religious books, exceptions aside, were singularly bare. Law libraries reflected Stoic and Gallican thought and Seneca, Tacitus, and Justus Lipsius shared shelf space with St. Augustine, Pierre Pithou, and the Dupuy brothers. The presence of Spanish spiritual writers and Jesuit authors, on the other hand, attested to an ultramontane sensibility. Men active in public finance were more likely to be modernists and interested in the exact sciences, and the king's secretaries, often parvenus, affected costly books and garish bindings. If we except lawyers and physicians, there was a hierarchy in libraries that normally corresponded to the hierarchy of offices and wealth. For example, one could not be the first president of a royal law court without possessing a large collection managed by a secretary-librarian that occupied a space in which several copyists worked to gather materials at least in part related to the patron's profession.

Inventories, which emphasize larger works and collections built up over generations, are normally an inadequate measure of the penetration of recent literary works. Still we can glean some information from the records of the bookseller Jean II Nicolas, who ran a shop in Grenoble between 1645 and 1668. Just what were the reading tastes of the elites of the city, Catholic and Protestant, who formed the better part of his clientele? First of course they read religious works—Bibles, New Testaments, Psalters, or paraphrases of Scripture—but also catechisms and sermons among the Protestants and books of devotion and spirituality among the Catholics. Both groups followed current events—the execution of Charles I of England or the arrest of the Grand Condé—and at the height of the Fronde *La Gazette* had a circulation of more than two hundred copies bought or rented from Nicolas's *cabinet de lecture.* Latin erudition no longer sold well (our notables' collections were already full of the works of Latin authors), but new literary works in French were snapped up as soon as they appeared. This was also true of the novels of Mlle de Scudéry and the poetry of Voiture, which was particularly popular among female customers. The plays of Corneille sold ten at a time in low-priced pirated editions, while the Grenoble literati admired Balzac, La Mothe Le Vayer, and Hobbes, and those among them who kept up a massive correspondence within the republic of letters introduced their circles to the writings of Descartes, Mersenne, Pascal, and Spinoza. Nicolas's customers included members of the Company of the Holy Sacrament, whose ultramontane sentiments are evident in the works they bought, but there were also utter libertines such as the Abbé de Saint-Firmin, the presumed author of *Aloysia Sigea,* an erotic masterpiece published in Grenoble somewhat later, probably with the complicity of Nicolas's son.

Thus we see interests open to the greater world beyond, but on the part of people of a narrowly defined society: craftspeople and merchants almost never figure on the pages of Nicolas's account books. Such people may have paid cash to buy the ABCs and readers that their children needed for the elementary school; they may also have bought from notions-sellers who carried that sort of publication along with low-cost books of hours and even a few chapbooks. Similarly, the *procureurs* who regularly bought paper in Nicolas's shop only exceptionally bought a book. Thus in Grenoble as elsewhere ownership of books seems to have been related to wealth and profession. Moreover, in Grenoble as in Paris, the *premier president* of the court provided a model for others that he himself had received from higher-placed persons and that was echoed all the way down the line to the city's *huissier* whose wife and sister aped the *précieuses*. Clearly, in mid-seventeenth century-France scholarly written culture, and more particularly classical literature, served to cement bonds among the elite, as opposed to the rest of the population.[27]

On the other side of the Channel, England's rupture with Rome had led to the seizure of the wealth of the Catholic clergy, in particular of the monasteries. The traditional network of libraries was nearly destroyed; only the libraries in the colleges of Oxford and Cambridge were left intact, and both they and the cathedral libraries were undergoing an astonishing growth. However, the sale of ecclesiastical holdings, followed by the alienation, under the Stuarts, of a large portion of the Crown lands, brought on widespread land transfers and reinforced the power of landed proprietors in a country that had no homogeneous category comparable to the administrative bourgeoisie and the *noblesse de robe* in France. Hence the role played by a particularly dynamic middle class that included wealthy craftsmen, merchants, the richer yeomen, and the greater part of the gentry.

Thus far only a portion of the history of private libraries in England has been written. Peter Clark has written about Kent, in the far southeast of England,[28] and in his study he mentions important collections already existent in the late sixteenth century. Certain of these collections belonged to aristocrats like the Cobdens and the Sidneys; on occasion, to lesser lords. As far as one can judge, these libraries included a good proportion of new literary works. Men of law, physicians, grammar-school teachers, and members of the clergy also owned hundreds of volumes in which the law, the sciences, and theology predominated, according to the owner's taste. A broader sampling might perhaps show that these men did not conform to the Continental model. In the three Kent towns that Clark has studied in depth, Canterbury (from five to six thousand inhabitants), Faversham, and Maidstone (about two thousand inhabitants each), books seem at first glance to have been broadly distributed. In 1560 there were books in roughly one house out of ten; half of the houses had books on the eve of the Civil War in 1640. This extraordinary advance seems to have been accompanied by a greater familiarity with reading, given that the volumes tended to move from the great hall or the study to the bedroom and even the kitchen.

By this time a good many yeomen, tradesmen, and merchants read the Bible, books of piety, or John Foxe's *Actes and Monuments* and (on occasion) works of jurisprudence. Except among the very rich, literature seems singularly absent from their lists. It is also surprising not to see chivalric romances, popular tales, the *Shepherd's Calendar,* and ballads, whose popularity is attested by their many surviving contemporary texts. Such publications may have seemed of too little value to have attracted the appraiser's attention.

Kent was of course not the whole of England. Books penetrated the areas of commercial exchange, and country folk remained overwhelmingly illiterate. In any event, the middle classes wanted to read books, the Bible (thanks to the influence of the Puritans) first among them. The Restoration slowed this movement but it later regained even greater momentum. It is hardly surprising that even in that age the British excelled at creating the infrastructure of a community. University and school libraries were built up in record time, and in the eighteenth century the British Museum grew out of Parliament's acquisition of private collections, to which bequests from George II and George III were added. It is important to note that the first municipal libraries in England were created in the early seventeenth century out of subsidies from merchants. Cafés and libraries began to rent out books (fashionable novels, for the most part) in the early eighteenth century, and private societies organized lending libraries that offered somewhat more difficult fare. Both sorts of library often opened a reading room in which books and periodicals could be consulted.

Paul Kaufman has estimated that some six hundred libraries and lending libraries were in operation in England around 1790 and that they served a total clientele of fifty thousand persons. Subscription customers (a system that was already well developed) of the London and provincial press should be added to that figure. The advertisements in such works show that a great many new literary works were available in the many provincial libraries. At the same time English peddlers did an even more thriving business than their French counterparts in abridged versions of such famous novels as *Robinson Crusoe* or *Gulliver's Travels*. Beginning in the 1740s John Wesley and the Methodists made concerted and well-organized efforts to circulate "good books," abridged and simplified, for instance, *Paradise Lost* and *The Pilgrim's Progress*. The Methodists founded a press in London, the Methodist Book Room, and they distributed pamphlets and booklets in their chapels and encouraged at least one former shoemaker to sell low-priced used books. During this same age political tracts and publicity pieces began to be omnipresent in British society.[29]

There is nothing to prove that even the simplest books found readers below the lower echelons of the middle class in an age in which many English men and women remained illiterate. In Puritan circles the notion slowly gained strength that the instruction given in the grammar schools (based on the study of Latin) was poorly adapted to the times. Provincial periodicals began to fill with announcements for the opening of private schools in which studies were based on a good knowledge of English, and the account books of one printer, Charles Ackers, show that between 1730 and 1758 his printshop produced 27,500 copies of one English grammar.[30] The schoolmasters taught reading and elementary rhetoric from such works, which were compilations of extracts from secondary authors. Gradually a new public formed; a public already accustomed by family tradition to reading the Bible or a pious work as they gathered in the evening. That public could already spell out the ballads posted on the walls of the home or read chapbooks, but henceforth it developed a taste for other texts and other forms of reading. Women moved on to *L'Astrée, Le Grand Cyrus*, or *Pamela*; men preferred drama or poetry. As the century drew to a close, reading continued to spread to the humbler categories of a society in which everyone—but city dwellers in particular—felt surrounded by written culture.

The Thirty Years War had pushed Germany to the point of near collapse, but when hostilities ended German lands underwent a new beginning. A good many German princes, now freed of all constraint, became absolute sovereigns and refashioned their courts to follow the French model, taking the lead in a movement that spread through much of Europe. French artists were commissioned to construct and decorate scaled-down versions of the château of Versailles, while the aristocracy throughout Europe adopted the French language and read French literature, to the enormous profit of French writers and their bookseller-publishers. German princes (Frederick II for one) thought that their compatriots lacked wit and did their best to attract French men of letters to their courts. That most German rulers gave no encouragement to German letters in the age of the *Aufklärung* and of *Sturm und Drang* explains why the most prestigious German writers flocked to Weimar, a decidedly secondary court. The middle classes had no such prejudices. The Reformation had accustomed them to reading the Bible, canticles, and pious works, which meant that in the early eighteenth century a considerable proportion of people owned religious books in cities like Frankfurt, Tübingen, or Speyer. Thanks to the influence of the Pietists, they typically read more works of devotion than works of theology, and, as in England, devotional reading encouraged a shift toward secular works, the sentimental novel in particular. Quite understandably, even in Catholic regions belles-lettres, history, and law overtook theological works in the production boom of the late seventeenth century.[31]

In this way a specifically middle-class literature came into being. The question is, however, to what extent did it reach the more modest levels of the middle classes? One can of course find traces of common people who knew, directly or indirectly, certain works or certain authors, but the inventories seem to show, somewhat paradoxically, that reading declined among tradespeople toward the end of the century. Once again, everything points to an emergent middle class dominated by pastors and professionals that imposed its ideas on the rest of the nation.

In Enlightenment France the humanist model was now a mere memory. Nonetheless the collections of the aristocrats and the officeholders prospered. On the eve of the Revolution the large private homes that bordered the better streets of Besançon contained hundreds of thousands of books.[32] Whatever their political opinions might have been, the owners of these collections were interested in scientific and technological progress and followed the work of the philosophes. One example is the maréchal de Croÿ, a man who showed little inclination for remaking society and whose journal Marie-Pierre Dion has studied.[33] These were the milieus from which the subscribers to the original edition of the *Encyclopédie* were recruited—and without subscribers that costly edition of Diderot's monumental undertaking could never have gotten beyond the planning stage.

Furthermore, all the studies of émigrés' libraries show that even they were children of the Enlightenment in spite of their diversity. Few of them, however, were ready to see their privileges challenged, not the least of which was to have handsomely bound examples of the most up-to-date culture, including its most aggressive forms, stamped with their crests on the shelves of their town houses and their châteaux.

One wonders to what extent the French counterparts of the British and German middle classes, who provided their writers with the better part of their audience, participated in this movement. Michel Marion's study of private libraries in Paris in the mid-eighteenth century offers a first response.[34] Of four thousand probate inventories drawn up between 1750 and 1759, only 841 mentioned at least one book, which put Parisians far behind the Germans. Of the people thus identified as readers, 60 were clergy, 226 nobles of "the robe" and "the sword," and 120 belonged to the professional middle class. The 435 others belonged to categories ranging from the merchant to the domestic servant, a figure that might be misleading unless we note that only 17.5 percent of the deceased who were the members of the Third Estate owned books, as against 44.5 percent of nobles (books in their Paris residences alone) and 62.5 percent of clergy (who also had access to religious libraries). What is more, burghers, merchants, and craftsmen usually owned only a few volumes.

Was Paris an exceptional case? If we follow Jean Quéniart to the northwest of France we shall see that although most of the clergy owned a certain number of books of Tridentine (and often Jansenist) inspiration—an undeniable progress—the libraries of laypeople evolved more unevenly.[35] At the end of the seventeenth century readers were proportionally more numerous in the region's two large cities, Rennes (32 percent of testators) and Rouen (40 percent). Thirty years later the proportion of probate inventories that mentioned books showed a gain of ten percentage points everywhere, but between 1725–30 and 1755–60 the only towns in which these figures were still rising were Quimper (which reached 37 percent) and, even more strikingly, Le Mans, Caen, and Rouen (more than 50 percent of testators with books). After 1760 the figures decline everywhere but in Rouen, which reached 63 percent just before the Revolution.

There may of course have been circumstances that hindered one city—illiterate country folk flocking into the city, for instance—or benefited another, but two other facts deserve mention. First, there was a sharp decline in the number of religious books toward the middle of the century in nearly all collections; second, during the later eighteenth century there was a de-

cline in the number of book owners in general that coincides with what
we have already seen in certain German cities. Readers in the lower social
categories seem to become "detached" from the rest, while other readers'
collections grew. Everywhere men "of the robe," officeholders, and lawyers owned libraries that typically reached several hundred volumes and
included a good number of classical texts. In the early eighteenth century
the titled nobility seems to have been won over to book culture, although
some country squires dropped out just before the Revolution. The professional bourgeoisie that at first followed the traditional model of the "robe"
later began to show an interest in new works. Early in the century books
can be found in the possession of some day-workers, craftsmen, merchants,
and wholesalers. At the beginning of this period collections were modest
and dominated by devotional works. Later a series of breaks occurred. "Libraries" of fewer than ten volumes became less numerous; next a new
model appeared in a social group ranging from the masters of certain
trades to wholesale merchants. Religion was somewhat eclipsed and libraries showed, first, increasing numbers of works from a professional literature (Savary's *Le parfait négociant* for example), then works of history
(often of foreign lands), and finally works of literature and novels. Such
collections seemed to repudiate classical conceptions and alternate between the interests of the autodidact and a desire for escapist literature and
entertainment.[36]

The few volumes that a merchant owned cannot be compared with the
collections of a lawyer or a magistrate. Also, probate inventories do not
tell us the whole story. Like similar documents elsewhere, they fail to
mention the many peddlers' books and books of devotion printed in provincial printshops and sold by booksellers and notions-sellers even in the
smallest towns. Nor do such inventories take into account the almanacs,
which gradually abandoned astrological predictions in favor of yearly summaries of political events, or the growing periodical press, or the announcements and handbills printed in the larger cities. They also omit
pamphlets, particularly the ones that criticized the mores of the royal
family and its entourage, which were circulated in large numbers in prerevolutionary France by presses in such smaller cities as Neuchâtel. Still,
the printing trade was a good deal more dynamic in Germany and England
than in France in the latter eighteenth century, and lending libraries, for
example, developed in France only under the Restoration. Hence in France
much more clearly than elsewhere book culture was a sort of privilege
primarily reserved to the higher classes of society; to some extent it ex-

cluded merchants and craftsmen even though they spent their daily lives surrounded with writing.

For a long time the book had only a limited place within social communication systems. Authors and readers were still conditioned by other forms of culture and other ways to represent the world and society that were based in traditions that we find difficult to grasp but that often played an important role in both the composition and the reception of textual messages.

We should not forget the debt that printing owed to what is commonly called folklore—that is, the oral literature of all ages (that of the Renaissance in particular). Mikhail Bakhtin has reminded us, for instance, of all that Rabelais owed to comic popular culture and carnival laughter. That same vein was exploited, directly or indirectly, in the literature of folly, for example in Sebastian Brant's *Ship of Fools,* in Erasmus's *In Praise of Folly,* or in the *Epistole obscurorum virorum* that ridiculed the theologians of Cologne. The debts that Cervantes, Shakespeare, Lope de Vega, Tirso de Molina, Guevara, Quevedo, and many others owed to such sources are well known. Traces of these traditions can often be seen when book people gathered. In Lyons, for example, the major booksellers took an active part in such official city celebrations as royal entries, where learned and popular themes mixed, and typographical workers were long the major organizers of public mockery. Robert Darnton has shown that journeyman typographers in eighteenth-century Paris were imbued with much the same spirit.[37]

How, then, were books received, and what might the members of societies with mental outlooks so different from our own have retained from them?

First, we need to recall from our own experiences with the Third World that it is useless to open schools in closed societies that feel no need to know how to read and write. There is little doubt that Champagne, for example, owed its advance in literacy to the fact that it was a crossroads. Furthermore, the learning of social circles of high literacy has never easily penetrated an illiterate society. The chief result of the Protestant pastors' efforts to teach the Lutheran catechism to the peasants of the Rhineland in the late sixteenth century was that after long hours of mechanical repetition the peasants could recite garbled snatches of texts that they were unable to understand. Schools were not much help: in Catholic societies schools long attempted to teach children to decipher the Latin texts indispensable for elementary worship, beginning with prayers and psalms. As late as the eighteenth century this was all the young Restif de la Bretonne had learned at school, and he had to discover by himself, perched high in a tree, that he could also read the French contained in a book that he had borrowed from his father's modest library. A child could develop his curiosity and his taste for reading only if his home environment, later his socioprofessional environment, incited him to read. The motivation was usually religious: many parents seem to have taught their sons and daughters to read as a way of passing on their own faith. Here commentary (on the Bible in particular) that connected a text with daily life probably was a primordial influence in the child's intellectual awakening. Hence the importance of collective reading aloud of sacred texts in Puritan milieus and on occasion in Catholic lands among certain Jansenists. In some cases (as with Jean-Jacques Rousseau) the child immersed in a milieu in which reading took place knew how to read so early that it seemed to him that he had never had to learn to read. Learning to read might also come at a much later age. A good many shepherds seem to have taught their fellow-shepherds, and the same seems to have happened among shoemakers. Soldiers might also teach their comrades to read: this happened (perhaps for religious reasons) among Wallenstein's troops, but also in the French royal army, at least among soldiers in the "scientific" branches of service for whom a minimum of book learning was useful. It was even truer among Napoleon's troops, for whom learning to read and write was a prerequisite to promotion to corporal.[38]

Voyages and moves forced young people who left their original setting to confront a different world and seek an education. Circumstances often intervened either to help or hinder their development, and some have left accounts that indicate that books were not such rare objects that a person determined to procure them could not borrow them (for example from the parish priest) to forge an embryonic culture that could be developed later, perhaps after a move to a larger city.

There are a few exceptional documents that help us to understand what the encounter of persons like these with written culture might have been like. One such person was Menocchio, a miller in Friuli tried for heresy in the latter sixteenth century (a charge for which he eventually was burned at the stake), whose career Carlo Ginzburg has reconstructed. Menocchio seems to have owned or borrowed religious books that had a wide circulation at the time, among them a Bible in the vernacular, *Il Fioretto della*

Bibbia, the *Rosario della gloriosa Vergine Maria,* and a translation of the *Golden Legend.* The headstrong Menocchio was so little capable of receiving information that he would retain only one detail or one word, or he would take an image in its most concrete sense. He would then apply to these motley acquisitions the lore of a nonliterate cultural tradition, thus creating a wholly personal but coherent system of his own. Recently exhumed autobiographies and journals present self-taught persons bringing together bits of knowledge that they have accumulated in a series of chance occurrences and classifying them according to half-assimilated norms. At times these diarists uncritically juxtapose fantastic pieces of information transmitted to them in writing; at other times they do their best—almost desperately—to bring to bear on their gleanings a critical spirit sharpened by their many experiences.

These narratives concern exceptional cases, but they help us to image what might have been the ways in which written texts were received in milieus of traditional culture. When one member of a group read aloud it might have made some listeners feel that they were being thrust into a new universe, and even though they had not totally grasped the story line they might remember some elements—perhaps a name that they later gave a child or that they used as a pet name for a friend. For lack of a recognized context a reader unable to write might have no greater grasp of the story than his hearers, but because he necessarily compared his patois with the printed language his framework of reference expanded. He could truly analyze a work only to the extent that he could write enough to become an "author" himself. Some such "authors" even set down their life histories despite their scant acquaintance with the rules of grammar and their resistance to systematic spelling rules.[39]

Can we try to reconstruct the reading matter of the many men and women whose first initiation to reading, and eventually writing, came in this manner? Peddlers' books come immediately to mind: they appeared in all lands in largely similar forms, and they seem to have been designed to give a minimum of instruction to a world of semi-notables, to acquaint them with proper comportment in society, and to offer them escapist literature. Such publications, presented in short chapters preceded by titles that summarized the chapter's contents, reduced the narratives to a series of actions that often "telescoped" the plot and transcribed it in a periodically simplified and modernized vocabulary.

It would be instructive to know how people read these works. Their pages presented massed blocks of type printed in characters with such poor definition that a first reading must have been singularly difficult. But were they not perhaps primarily designed to be reread? The reports sent to Abbé Grégoire during the French Revolution tell us that the peasants closeted themselves at home for long hours when they read. We can imagine them following the text with a finger, as they had been taught at school, and perhaps mumbling it aloud. One might wonder how they made the transition from one chapter to another: did they try to pick up the thread of the story? Did they return to previous episodes that touched on the same themes? In any event, we know that they could recite long passages from such books by heart, which meant that they doubtless could recreate the stories and tell them in a much more lively fashion than when they read them aloud. Still, to judge by changes in the almanacs, which by the eighteenth century no longer focused on astrological predictions but summarized the principal events of the year, this particular public seems to have had a different attitude toward the book and toward the outside world.[40]

When we turn to the reading matter of clerics, theologians, humanists, and scholars we need only open the heavy folio volumes that transmitted ancient tradition—both Christian and pagan—to understand that these volumes were conceived to be analyzed line by line, even interrogated on specific points with the aid of their tables of contents and indexes. Such texts were physical "places" in which an entire chain of interpretations converged: they were presented at the center of glosses by which the *auctor*, the annotator (or annotators) whose interpretations surrounded the text, imposed a reading of the work. With the humanist printers this vise loosened: they were more interested in making available the original work in an accurate text provided with devices to facilitate consultation. By that time the reader also had dictionaries that reviewed the various meanings of any term or expression. Thus the literati often read with pen in hand and became their own glossators, sprinkling the margins of the works they read with annotations. When they wrote works of their own they provided a mosaic of citations.

The number and the long career of such publications aimed at transmitting tradition, now restored to its original form rather than being adapted to new times, pose a problem. To what extent did printers publish the learned publications in Greek of Jacques Toussaint or Pierre Danès for a large public? Or were such works intended to bear witness by their simple existence? How many readers were there, other than the few members of the republic of letters protected by the sovereign, for the learned works published in large number in the early seventeenth century by the Wechels in Frankfurt? Does it mean anything that by this time only the first pages of many of these much-printed volumes were peppered with annotations? [41]

It would also be interesting to know precisely how the techniques of reading and consulting such volumes evolved from the fourteenth to the eighteenth centuries. Before the invention of printing the most literate form of scholarly reading consisted in establishing one's own carefully revised copy. Petrarch devoutly kissed his copy of Virgil before opening it; Erasmus did the same for his Cicero, and in the evening, when he had finished his day's work, Machiavelli put on his best clothes to read his favorite authors. The ecstasy that overcame these men during long evenings spent reading the great classics is a *topos* of humanism. Montaigne, who rejected the display of explicit citations in his *Essays,* went to the opposite extreme when he described himself in his library on the top floor of his tower, a room sixteen feet in diameter lined with books housed on five-tiered shelves. Like many of his contemporaries, Montaigne considered reading a fatiguing exercise that made the mind work while it "tied down" and "saddened" the body. He tells us that he liked to walk about as he read, supervising his household through the three windows that brought light into the room, and that he even contemplated adding a balcony outside his library. Did Montaigne take notes? He described himself seizing one book, then another—a Plutarch, then a Seneca with which he felt more at ease—but also on occasion "registering" or dictating his "dreams"—that is, his *Essays.* [42]

There were of course other and more cursory ways to read the same works. One Venetian senator, for example, thanks Aldus Manutius for having given him one of his small, portable publications printed in italics because he could then read Lucian between two sessions of the city council. Several humanists tell us they read during the long horseback rides that were an inevitable part of travel at the time. How much affectation was there in such statements? Were the innumerable duodecimo publications of the Elzeviers and their imitators published and bought in the seventeenth century for assiduous reading or to show familiarity with great texts? We know that sixteenth- and seventeenth-century scholars were sufficiently imbued with the Latin language and Latin culture to be able to compose works that might have a flamboyant style, but such works are always more or less redolent of the school exercise put to the service of a language that had remained unchanged for centuries. The spectacle of the neo-Latin poets, whom their contemporaries compared to the greatest authors of classical antiquity but who wrote in Latin with no sense of the rhythms of the language, makes one wonder. A form of tradition that had outlived its time became ossified just when rulers, grandees, and churches were building libraries in the form of temples (soon, of necropoli) in an attempt to conserve monuments of the past arranged in a time-honored order. The unceasing, massive publication of such works, flowing like the outpouring of words in the works themselves, ran counter to more sequential presentation in modern historical works whose rhythms were based on chapters corresponding to epochs and reigns.

The evolution of devotional reading is even more interesting. The basic book of prayer (and in many houses the only book) had long been the book of hours. It enabled the worshiper to address his or her Creator alone and in a properly meditative frame of mind. It was composed of a mosaic of familiar texts intended to aid the elevation of the soul, but the calendar that it included and its alphabetical arrangement also contained a good deal of practical advice, popular medical advice in particular. When the book of hours was richly illustrated, its pages echoed the lessons of the sculptures and the frescoes in churches, and its many pictures made it useful to members of the household who could not read.

New ways of praying appeared within the Catholic world with the reawakening of religious sentiment in the late sixteenth and the seventeenth centuries. Ignatius of Loyola invited the pious to apply all their faculties to seeking contact with the Other World by creating a precise place in the mind where the mind and the imagination could concentrate on the topic of meditation (a technique that resembled the methods of the arts of memory and that had inspired the contemporary fashion for emblem books). With St. Teresa of Avila, that place became a Castle of the Soul made of diamond and clear crystal to which the bride of Christ could escape and return to her Master. The book—an object that the typographer's art had placed in everyone's hands—was to be a material presence in this often desperate quest. It was a "place" that made dialogue possible; it was not designed to provide knowledge but to be a signifier for the Other. The reading of a book marked the threshold of meditation; it offered a path to solitude and a means for establishing a relationship. The reader did not retain all of a text but rather assimilated fragments, even isolated words that he plucked out of their context and that then inhabited him as he lost himself, as if in a dream in which the book dissolved into contemplation (Michel de Certeau).

This sort of spiritual quest arose (not coincidentally) at a time when tradition seemed opaque, destroyed, and humiliated. It developed quite spontaneously within social categories that had been marginalized by socioeconomic change or ruined by wars (Michel de Certeau). Rather than rejecting the ruins or the corruption that surrounded them, the mystics made them their home, an asylum in which they sought their passion in a present with no past and no assurance of a future. In face of the uncertainties that burdened their system of reference the intellectuals who helped to found these practices often went out of their way to consult witnesses who belittled their learning—hence the great number of biographies of poor girls or illiterates.[43]

These new uses of the book elicited a new reading matter. A text was no longer used for deep study and analysis but as an aid to achieving an awakening or an escape that was somehow a point of departure for an individual adventure inspired by a desire for self-annihilation. Not surprisingly, images figured prominently at the head of so many books of devotion: this was the age in which the Sisters of St. Teresa, when Bérulle brought them to Paris, taught French women (whose prayers they thought singularly abstract) to form an image in their minds. When the spiritual authors came to setting down methods to guide the spiritual progress of their brothers and sisters they took care to present a clear and easily accessible text well spaced out on a page with generous margins, and the voluminous pedagogical literature of the time used all the modern procedures for laying out a text.[44]

Reading matter evolved in due course. Since Ramus, in fact, the schemata of logical order had been reconstituted on sheets of paper. Advances in cartography also taught an increasingly large public how to read space. With the arrival of the mechanistic revolution the officers of the royal French army found they needed to learn mathematics, geometry in particular. Women, nobles, and magistrates made up a large portion of the reading public for the classics. They repudiated the erudite tradition and demanded other means of access to all forms of knowledge. Little wonder that so many books (not only devotional works) included terms such as "short means" or "easy method" in their titles.[45]

Toward the mid-seventeenth century it became customary to arrange texts into paragraphs,[46] and that minor revolution was accompanied, in the late seventeenth and especially in the eighteenth century, by the triumph of extensive over intensive reading (of the Bible or some other treasured volume) as it had been practiced in many circles and many lands.

THE INTELLECTUAL FIELD AND THE STRATEGY OF THE AUTHOR

Unlike their Anglo-Saxon colleagues, French historians have long shown little interest in studying the organization and the operation of intellectual milieus. The first to react was Jean-Paul Sartre, who asked the essential questions in his *Qu'est-ce que la littérature?* Then the sociologists, notably Pierre Bourdieu and his students, studied "intellectual fields." More recently the dossier has been notably enlarged by some remarkable studies by Italian scholars.[47]

Bourdieu suggests, first, that intellectual life takes place as if in a magnetic field in which creative people occupy specific positions that are determined by lines of force corresponding to their social situations and to the relations that they establish, and second, that the notion of "symbolic capital" plays an important role in an economy of cultural goods in large part founded on a denial of "economism." If we admit these premises we can state (according to Bourdieu) that as human activity became differentiated, intellectual life gradually became organized in Western Europe in a particular type of society in opposition to the religious, political, and economic powers—that is, to the various institutions that claimed to legislate in cultural matters in the name of an authority that was not properly speaking intellectual.

The various stages of this slow evolution need to be distinguished. For example one might see intellectual life as long being dominated by the church and the aristocracy, but even at that stage there was intense and autonomous intellectual activity. Theologians in particular were already developing their theories within the framework of the medieval university and within a system that was in many ways comparable to the modern intellectual field and its different procedures for achieving legitimacy. As we have seen, within the limits set by the ecclesiastical institution, censorship was relatively lax, and condemnations were followed by concrete action only when debate overflowed the closed arena in which the learned clashed in comparative liberty. Ecclesiastics then, like intellectuals today, could choose to play the role of "priest" and guardian of tradition by seeking a primarily institutional success, or they could play the role of "prophet" through their lessons, disputations, and sermons. Their strategies differed little from those of *homo academicus* today. Nor is there any doubt that the aristocracy played an important role where vernacular literature—poetry in particular—was concerned. Still, we need to keep in mind that most of the authors of those times were the products of clerical milieus, whose ideology they adapted, and that forms of contestation already existed in the fabliaux.

The progress of writing in state administrations and in the exercise of justice soon made the overall picture more complex; at the same time men of culture, particularly in Italy, occupied an essential place in the direction of public affairs just when the conflicts between Guelphs and Ghibellines incited all factions to seek arguments to give legitimacy to their positions.[48] Other men of culture, exiles for the most part, were forced to stand at a distance from real society and to try to regain their footing by proposing a theory and an ethics of power. For instance, when Brunetto Latini, formerly a redactor-notary in the chancery of Florence, was living in Paris he wrote a sort of encyclopedia, *Li livres dou trésor,* which he wrote in French in the interest of reaching a broader public. Latini ends this work with a description of the ideal municipal magistrate watching vigilantly day and night over the common good. Dante was another magistrate who was exiled and obliged to take refuge with princes and tyrants; he set himself up as a judge of his contemporaries, argued in favor of a universal monarchy, and, in *Il convivio,* proposed a definition of nobility that implied a disinterested quest for *virtù,* with all that the term implied in the way of intellectual aptitude and moral stature. Petrarch, the son of a notary and a man who preferred to regard himself as an Italian more than as a citizen of Florence, claimed the right to judge society and criticize the power structure, although without contesting its legitimacy. Finally, Boccaccio, the illegitimate son of a merchant, proclaimed the precariousness of power and gave a realistic view of the world of his time.

A new breed of intellectual emerged. In the age of the chancellors Coluccio Salutati (1351–1406) and Leonardo Bruni (1370–1444), such men developed a form of civic humanism in Florence. The products of a merchant bourgeoisie, they proposed an ideal of active participation in economic and political life and devotion to the homeland. Increasingly, they relegated the study of law to a secondary position, proclaiming themselves the heirs of the ancient classical orators and professing an unlimited admiration for Cicero. Their Latin culture was a capital essential to funding

their prestige. Total independence, however, proved possible only for extremely short periods of time; the ideal that such men pursued weakened
before the rise of tyrannies, and the new generations of the latter half of
the fifteenth century tended to become less active in public life and less
likely to be the courtiers of a patron or a ruler. When they did join a court,
the best of them—Ariosto, for example, with the Este—demanded that the
master they served leave them room for free exercise of their critical functions. Their best hope for even a relative independence lay in the legitimacy
that they earned in the eyes of the cultivated world and the opinion of men
of letters—a legitimacy that gave any governing power good reason to win
them over. Following an example set by Petrarch, they made it their business to found relational networks that might often take the concrete form
of a circle in which thought-provoking dialogue could thrive.

Such circles often crystallized around an initiator, a patron, a prominent
family, even an enlightened ruler, or they sprang up to pursue a shared
goal. They gave rise to some of the "micromilieus" that are always the
founding nucleus of any republic of letters. The circle might be informal,
as was the Platonic Academy that developed in Florence around Marsilio
Ficino, a protégé first of Cosimo de' Medici, then of Lorenzo the Magnificent, and that eventually triumphed over the Aristotelians grouped around
John Argyropoulos, the director of the *studium* of Florence. Or the circle
might resemble a sort of lay confraternity, as did the Accademia Marciana
of Venice, it might form around a school, or the school itself might offer
public lectures.

A number of academies sprang up in fifteenth- and sixteenth-century
Italy. They tended to become institutionalized either by developing a ritual
that included the adoption of academic pseudonyms and holding banquets
now and then or by adopting statutes stipulating rules of operation and
criteria for admission. As always, however, such systems were closely dependent upon the governing powers. The Platonic Academy dissolved in
the age of Savonarola: few of its members remained loyal to the Medici
when they were no longer in power, and even Marsilio Ficino denied his
former masters. Later, Machiavelli, who had been called to important
public functions by the democratic government that followed Savonarola's
dictatorship, found himself out of favor when the Medicis returned, when
his fall from grace led him to write *The Prince*. By that time Italy no longer
controlled its own destiny, and Castiglione wrote *Il cortegiano* (printed in
1528) as an idealized representation of an ephemeral phenomenon and a
message to the nobility throughout Europe. Finally, in Florence under

Duke Cosimo I, the Accademia degli Umidi became a prototype for a growing number of multipurpose state cultural organisms in the service of absolutism.

Still, while Italy fell under foreign rule, humanism conquered Europe in one of those *translationes studiorum* to which we have become accustomed in the history of written culture. This transfer coincided with the emergence of a merchant bourgeoisie that provided towns and cities with patrician dynasties and states with administrators. Learned correspondence came back into fashion, providing an opportunity to put stylistic exercises into practice and to exchange ideas and information. On occasion these long-distance relations, which often traveled the same routes as commerce, turned into genuine friendships and prepared halting places on the long voyages that the men of the time often made. Public opinion solidified around acknowledged leaders whose positions strengthened rulers' reputations and carried weight in both literary quarrels and political and religious controversies.[49]

This network had its bastions and its bridgeheads. In Germany recently created universities less marked by Scholasticism than the older ones soon (often very soon) became centers for the diffusion of the new ideas. Johann Wessel, who had trained in Italy, introduced the study of Greek at Heidelberg in the mid-fifteenth century, and Martianus Rufus, who had been influenced by Florentine Platonism, built up a humanist circle at Erfurt. The early typographers often studied at the Faculty of Arts of such universities. Italy's lessons soon found eager listeners in the universities of Oxford and Cambridge, and Padua, a center for a free interpretation of Aristotelianism, attracted large numbers of foreign students. The traditionalistic universities, Cologne and even Paris, remained strongholds of the customary forms of reasoning. The partisans of innovation often sought support from rulers or high-placed persons, and the innovators frequently found advocates to plead their cause in chancery circles in such men as Thomas More in England, Guillaume Budé in France, and many others—powerful figures who could aid an intellectual's career and smooth over resistance by persuading their royal masters to undertake such initiatives as the creation by Francis I, by royal fiat, of endowed positions as "royal readers."

Printing presses had originally been used largely for the reproduction of consecrated texts. Compared to the many "producers of texts" who drew works from the available stock of manuscripts and edited them for print, there were very few "intellectuals" or "professional" writers. Nonetheless, the new art circulated the same texts throughout Europe, thus reinforcing the position of those few and giving their reputation a broader base. This was true of Erasmus, who rapidly obtained a fame even more brilliant than Petrarch's and who achieved a status equaled only by Voltaire's during the Enlightenment.

The circles that emerged around the humanist printers represent the best example of the intellectual "micromilieus" that lie at the base of all creative endeavors. Such circles crystallized the innovative activities of specific groups; by publishing their books, the humanist printers provided them with an all-European base. The printers also provided legitimacy: it brought as much prestige to be published by Johann Froben around 1520 or by Robert Estienne around 1540 as it did in France to be published by Gallimard between the two world wars. Nonetheless, princely protection and patronage continued to have an enormous importance in that small world. Although men such as Amerbach and Froben in Basel (and even more, Gryphe and de Tournes in Lyons) seem emanations of bourgeois milieus, Aldus Manutius dreamed of finding moral and financial support for his academy and his Greek editions by placing them under the direct protection of the emperor, the pope, or lesser rulers in the hope of furthering his program for the cultural and moral renewal of Italy. Similarly, without the protection of Marguerite de Navarre and Francis I, the Paris humanists could never have grouped around Robert Estienne and his printshop and around the royal "readers." Nearly all the French humanists and writers of the Renaissance lived in the shadow of protectors who were to some extent close to the sovereign and who, in some cases, had aided them in their youth and continued to support them. Such protectors were often prelate-diplomats of Italianate tastes such as Cardinal de Tournon, the two Du Bellay brothers, and Cardinals de Guise and de Lorraine; or they might be prominent political figures such as the *connétable* Anne de Montmorency, not to mention lesser fry that included leaders of the many provincial intellectual circles in France, particularly in the southwest.

Sketching out the career strategies of writers of this period is not a difficult task. We might look, for example, at the *Apollon de collège* dear to Lucien Febvre.[50] These secondary-school directors were the rank and file of humanism; they turned out enormous quantities of neo-Latin verse full of echoes of the great authors of antiquity. Good fellows all, they exchanged hyperbolic praise, thus providing one another with free publicity. Consecration in their eyes was to have a collection of their writings, headed by verse written by their friends, published by Gryphe. A vain and hypersensitive lot, they were quick to pick a quarrel—which gave rise to more writings, followed by a reconciliation celebrated in yet more writing.

Etienne Dolet's career offers a good introduction to this milieu. The son of an Orléans burgher, Dolet began his studies in Paris at the age of twelve; there he learned to venerate Cicero, whom he later defended against Erasmus in a famous literary controversy. Dolet then went to Padua, where he attended Pomponazzi's lectures, after which he became secretary to Jean de Langeac, bishop of Limoges and ambassador of the king of France to Venice. Jean de Pins, a diplomat and a friend of Jean de Langeac, took Dolet under his wing when Dolet returned to France. Next Dolet went to study law in Toulouse in order to increase his chances of finding a position. Just at that moment the Parlement of Toulouse sentenced Jean de Caturce, a monk converted to Lutheranism, to burn at the stake. Dolet, who had been elected a representative of the Nation de France in Toulouse, saw this as his big chance, and he gave two eloquent speeches against intolerance. He was imprisoned but then freed thanks to the efforts of his protectors. In poor health and forced to give up his political ambitions, Dolet went to Lyons, where Jean de Boyssonne, a liberal jurist and the acknowledged leader of the humanist circle of Toulouse, recommended him to Sébastien Gryphe. Dolet was made welcome by literary circles in Lyons, and he earned his living as a proofreader and literary adviser for Gryphe. Dolet then determined to conquer fame with the aid of the printing press and to seek revenge for his past humiliations. Always a violent man, he killed a painter in a brawl. Luckily his patrons and comrades did not abandon him: he rushed to Paris and, thanks to influential aid, notably from Marguerite de Navarre, he obtained the king's pardon. The event was celebrated with a banquet. Even more, Cardinal de Tournon approached Francis I on his behalf, and the king granted Dolet a privilege that seems astonishing, given that it came on the heels of the *Affaire des placards,* when Protestant handbills placed in Paris, at court, and even in the king's chamber had challenged royal authority. The king granted Dolet a license to print whatever he wished for a period of ten years, subject only to the control of the *prévot* of Paris and the *sénéchal* of Lyons. On the instigation of Guillaume Du Bellay, Hélouin Dullin, a *procureur* at the Parlement of Rouen who had been compromised in the *Affaire des placards,* obtained enough funds for Dolet to set up a printshop. Now that he was well settled, Dolet complained that everyone had abandoned him during his trials and he behaved abominably, even to his friends. He seemed to lose control, publishing more and more suspect books in French. The Parlement ordered his arrest on several occasions, he was imprisoned repeatedly, and eventually he was burned at the stake in the Place Maubert.[51]

With Dolet's death the time for public displays of audacity had passed. And after Francis I's death Robert Estienne himself was advised by no less a person than Henry II not to publish Bibles. He fled to Geneva. As in Florence a century earlier, a period of relative liberty had lasted only as long as there was internal peace and the reign of an enlightened ruler. Humanism was not dead, however: it abandoned grand, all-embracing schemes to become philological, critical, and (soon) Stoic. It took on different forms in Protestant lands, where publishers concentrated on Greek and Latin classics, and in Catholic lands, where they preferred the Fathers of the church. Humanism also turned toward the sciences: first toward the natural sciences in the Low Countries; then, from Poland and Denmark to Italy, toward astronomy as well; finally, starting in France, toward mathematics and the physics of mechanistic philosophy. Humanism eventually gave rise to various forms of national erudition tinged with propaganda.

As with all intellectual movements, humanism won the day the moment it stopped being militant. In reality, it had followed the trajectory of the social category whose aspirations it symbolized—the merchant bourgeoisie, which took only a few generations to place its offspring in positions of command in the state. The bourgeoisie triumphed when administrative office in France became hereditary, thus creating a new social category of royal officeholders and nobility "of the robe." Unlike the old aristocratic families, the new class claimed as its heritage a culture rooted in Greco-Latin antiquity. Henceforth the intellectuals who were the standard-bearers of that tradition became the men of the hour: they clustered around the innumerable libraries that were being founded by rulers and their ministers; in Protestant lands in particular they invaded the universities. The University of Leiden, founded by William of Orange to reward the city for its resistance to the Spanish troops, became a center of European thought. We can find prominent humanist intellectuals in the northern Low Countries, where religious diversity encouraged tolerance and where Descartes was to compose his *Discourse on Method*. In France humanist intellectuals held important offices, often occupying key posts obtained through powerful influences. In the provincial courts they figured as the king's men. When French scholars turned their thoughts to their own antiquities and their own history they tended to be intellectually Machiavellian, Gallican, and libertine, especially if they were librarians, historiographers, or geographers of the king. During the same period the Benedictines of Saint-Maur organized religious and national research centers, and the Jesuits were also actively engaged in scholarship.[52]

This small intellectual world was of course subjected to pressures of many sorts. It was nonetheless a community that underlay all intellectual life, and it guaranteed letters a certain coherence independent of national frontiers by its use of Latin and by books published in that language of learning, but also by the system of *peregrinatio academica* as students (Protestant students in particular) went from one university to another. Above all, incessant correspondence guaranteed a degree of coherence, symbolized by such figures as Peiresc, a senator at the Parlement of Aix in the early seventeenth century who was baptized the *procureur* of the republic of letters, or Mersenne, the Capuchin friar of the Place des Vosges through whose hands passed the better part of the information exchanged among European scholars in the mid-seventeenth century. This system allowed intellectuals, Catholic and Protestant, to share points of view and suggestions in mutual respect and as among equals. We need only think of the correspondence between Bossuet and Leibniz. The result was the creation of a tribunal of enlightened opinion that expressed itself cautiously but that rulers did well to treat with respect. Although this structure began to disintegrate with the decline of Latin and the rise of the national languages (accompanied by the appearance of publications giving bibliographical information), still it survived long enough to prepare the century of the Enlightenment.

At the beginning of the seventeenth century a newcomer—the writer—began to occupy the center of the stage in France.[53]

In order to gain admittance to the world of letters, national languages had to overcome obstacles of various sorts. For example, although Tuscan had gradually won enough prestige to dominate the other Italian dialects, Italian authors continued to write their works in the language of the court that they frequented. Their works continued to circulate by being read aloud from manuscript copies. The laws of the market dictated that the booksellers who wanted to publish such works had to "rewrite" them to make them accessible throughout Italy. Venetian print shops had professional "rewrite men." We can guess the authors' reactions to such highhanded treatment of their texts. Bembo, who resigned himself to the process, stressed that the sole aim of such publications was to make available to a broader audience works that had been composed in traditional circles, and Castiglione provided a long explanatory preface in the same vein for the published edition of *Il cortegiano*. [54]

In England poetry was queen at the Tudor court, where Anne Boleyn and a number of other eminent figures wrote verse. A man would prefer to be seen as a servant of the king and a courtier than as a writer, and authors of modest extraction normally had a noble patron, which meant that they had to adopt concepts and forms pleasing to their patrons, "correcting" their works at the patrons' suggestions. Poetry became a sort of collective game, and at royal celebrations it gave a sense of coherence to the elite of the kingdom. Great lords evidently considered it indecent to prostitute the verses composed for such festive occasions by giving them to the press, and poets who yielded to the temptation to do so (Spenser, for one) risked not only their master's displeasure but comparison to popular balladeers whose poems were hawked at fairs. [55]

The situation was more complex in France, where a larger virtual public had been identified earlier. Clément Marot was the perfect example of the poet in a court in which princes and princesses might turn their hand to rhyming. Still, the entourage of Marguerite de Navarre showed no scorn for the printing press, and Marot himself published a revised edition of the *Roman de la Rose*, printed by Galliot Du Pré. In Lyons poetry soon flourished in predominantly bourgeois circles, and Jean de Tournes (like Gilles Corrozet and Denis Janot in Paris) published a number of editions of Ovid's *Metamorphoses* and emblem books aimed at a vast audience. The strategy of the poets of the Pléiade is particularly interesting. Most of them came from families closely connected to the royal court. Ronsard had been a page and had been obliged to renounce his hopes for a military or diplomatic career because of his early deafness. Du Bellay belonged to the poor branch of an illustrious family, and Lazare de Baïf was the son of an ambassador. They pursued "accelerated" studies, at an age somewhat older than the norm, with Dorat at the Collège du Coqueret. Unlike the official court poet, Mellin de Saint-Gelais, whose works were handwritten for presentation to great personages, the Pléiade poets used print to establish their reputations. Du Bellay published his *Défense et illustration de la langue française*, a topical work, and Ronsard followed his example for his *Odes* and his *Amours*, published within the four-year period between 1549 and 1553. This early preference for print helps us understand the ambiguity of Ronsard's attitudes: he first joined the humanists in preaching a radical reform of spelling but soon retreated from his initially rigid position, and he advised poets to read their works aloud—better, to sing them—as a way to gauge their effectiveness. Recognized as France's leading poet, Ronsard circulated portions of his *Franciade* as they were written, long before they were published, but he used print to circulate the poems he had just composed. During the Wars of Religion he wrote in defense of royal policies, but between 1570 and 1580 he participated with less than full enthusiasm in the activities of the Italian-style academies that were created within the royal entourage, apologizing before he read his prepared discourse that he was no orator.[56]

After Ronsard's death, Desportes returned to the traditional ways to circulate his verse, and Catherine de Médicis had them copied by the royal calligraphers. Still later, Malherbe did his best to gain advancement first with the great lords then at the royal court, while he and other poets worked to refine and enlarge the court's vocabulary. The poets of the Wars of Religion and the Baroque age, soldiers or adventurers, were typically just as dependent on noble or royal patronage, and both Théophile de Viau's rough language and his refinements were reflections of the vocabulary and the tastes of the aristocratic youth who were his first audience. Multi-author publications, a common genre of the period, circulated the writings of the best-known authors, but until the time of Voiture the press did little but popularize works that sprang from one "micromilieu" or another. This meant that until the Fronde the professional "poet" continued to be a member of the domestic staff of a great personage whom he served as secretary, whose love-notes he wrote, and for whom he wrote polemical pamphlets in troubled times.

When theater became fashionable it started a process of fusion among publics that had previously existed side by side without blending. The old mystery plays had gradually stopped being performed, and other sorts of spectacle had gained in popularity—court drama in the Italian style, religious dramas presented in the schools and *collèges* (on occasion before a large audience), farce, and the *tableaux vivants* prepared for princely entries.

Amateur groups soon formed in connection with educational, religious, and municipal institutions. Some groups became professional, notably in England, where troupes of actors toured the land and even hazarded an occasional excursion to the Continent. Performances were given in a space temporarily adapted to theatrical use: outdoors, in the hall of a palace, in a church, or in a tennis court. Later certain cities—Madrid in 1574 and London in 1578—had spaces designed for theatricals. A motley throng attended the performances of any given play. In the *corrales* of Madrid as in London theaters aristocrats, royal officeholders, and notables occupied the galleries and the boxes, while a more mixed public that included a large number of tradespeople crowded the open pit. A comedy by Lope de Vega might be performed first in the capital, then in provincial towns, then in villages; originally by professional actors and eventually by amateurs who had bought a copy of the manuscript. Still, theatrical troupes were wise—when it was not a legal obligation, as in England—to place themselves under the protection of a ruler or an important noble who could defend them from the hostility of certain groups or institutions and help to attract a more elegant public. Such persons might even deign to take an active part in writing a play or preparing a performance.

The first concern of both authors and actors was to satisfy the tastes of their protectors, but they also had to take into account the royal officeholders and notables who made up the better part of the audience and remember to provide the sort of repartee that won them the sympathies of the pit. Spectators of such different sorts did not always understand or appreciate any given topic in the same way. Still, it is undeniable that drama played an important role in creating shared forms of awareness, particularly concerning nationalism, social rank, and the concept of monarchy.[57]

Thus a new sort of author, the playwright, appeared. There were two ways in which a playwright could earn a living: he could follow the traditional path and seek royal protection, or he could hope for a more popular success through collaboration with a theatrical entrepreneur, commercializing his own activities along with those of the troupe that he served. Often a playwright would try to do both. Lope de Vega, for instance, spoke through a buffoon in one of his plays to appeal to the generosity of the duke of Alba, but he also write for the general public. This dual appeal worked in much the same way as the strategy of an author who published a work dedicated to a patron but also offered it to several other people in the hope of remuneration, while his bookseller attempted to sell the work to the broadest possible public.

A vogue for the theater came comparatively late in France but produced much the same effects. A theatrical performance that brought together in one place and for the same purpose members of the aristocracy, of the world of the administration, and of the body of city notables exposed these varied groups to one ideology. More than in other lands and despite what some scholars have held, the French classical theater undoubtedly excluded tradespeople and shopkeepers from its audience; they went instead to the shows on the Pont-Neuf in the seventeenth century and to the theaters at the fairground a century later.

One problem to be resolved was to find a literature that would be accessible to the varied groups that had begun to come together in this manner. Authors of epics—a popular genre in France at the time—made a valiant attempt to make the epic accessible. All of them failed, from Ronsard to Chapelain. In reality, the time of the novel had come: novels that ranged from *Les histoires tragiques,* Belleforest's translation of the *Novelle* of Matteo Bandello, to Cervantes's *Don Quixote* or to the picaresque novels of Quevedo and, in France, from Honoré d'Urfé's *L'Astrée* to Madeleine de Scudérie's *Clélie* and *Le Grand Cyrus.* At least in France, such works brought sizable earnings to their authors, which means that they were the first "best-sellers" of modern times.[58]

The passion for the theater that flared nearly everywhere in Europe in the late sixteenth and early seventeenth centuries reflected a change in European society. The aristocracy was gradually losing its power and wealth, while the emergent bourgeoisie was becoming more and more firmly established. In France hereditary offices helped to create a strong and stable social category. Henceforth the notables who attended the same theatrical spectacles participated in the same culture. Cliques and the old loyalties still had their full importance, but the age became one of congregations, confraternities, circles, and salons in which pious or worldly people of similar religious or literary sensibilities could meet. A network of *précieux* salons sprang up throughout France, as well as a more fragmented network of academies that brought together the learned and the lettered.

It was an intellectual climate in which humanists and scholars still enjoyed prestige and always were given priority when posts and pensions came available. But at the same time, the vast public that opened up before the booksellers' eyes demanded translations of the essential works of the classical authors and the Fathers of the church and, even more, original religious and literary works. Criticism was out of fashion: what sold was mysticism and the flights of fancy of Baroque literature. Most writers were still clerics (although some made their careers exclusively in secular letters), but the proportion of lay authors steadily increased. Some authors were born into the lesser nobility or into families that held government posts. Often they came from a family in which others had made their living by their pen. They were poets, dramatists, or novelists; their numbers included some men of modest extraction who were connected with a nascent journalism, polygraphs who wrote on commission books of popularized history or philosophy, letter-writing manuals and *secrétaires à la mode*, or conversation books to teach the art of writing and expressing oneself as an *honnête homme*.

These newcomers still had to find ways to survive and get ahead. Those at the bottom of the authorial ladder lived on advances from their bookseller-publishers. Dramatic authors were paid per performance, thus their economic position was somewhat better. These were merely expedients, though. Until the Fronde, the writer's greatest resource remained patronage and the client-patron relationship. Great lords were unfortunately not always overly generous with the poets in their service (as Sorel's *Francion* tells us). Authors' prefaces often point to the example of Maecenas and compare the illustrious (or less illustrious) person to whom their work is dedicated to heroes and demigods of antiquity, exaggerating his deeds, his wisdom, his valor, or more simply his generosity. Thus when they speak of the transaction as one of reciprocal gift, they inflate their own talent. This explains the pomposity of a great many dedications, but it also explains others that are more modest, such as Racine's dedication of *Andromaque*, in which he reminds Madame (Henrietta Anne, duchesse d'Orléans) that the idea for the play was originally hers. All that brought in little money, however. As in our own day, authors were perpetually in search of a pension or an employment that would assure them both respect and stable revenues. Everything depended on the amount of esteem that an author had acquired, but the "reputation-makers" were already chary of popular success. Corneille learned that lesson after *Le Cid*. A better tactic was to gain an introduction into the salons, to have one's wit and one's verse admired there, and thereby to become more widely known and enjoy the liberalities of some great personage. This was how Chapelain received an annual pension of 3,000 livres for *La Pucelle* from the duc de Longueville, a descendent of Dunois.[59]

Authors had also developed the habit of comparing points of view, discussing literary theory, and studying together the problems posed by a language undergoing rapid change when they met during the periodic sessions of their "academies." Thus just when the term "writer" was being invented, the notion of a learned man was also undergoing adjustment. Booksellers began to gather together the best of the poems in circulation and publish them in collective anthologies something like an irregularly published literary revue, a phenomenon that has led Alain Viala to date the appearance of the first "literary field" from this period.[60] At this point Richelieu appeared on the scene. A "prince in purple" who made himself the center of all activities, Richelieu claimed to write plays through a ghost writer, and when he had gained political control he took care not to alienate the two great learned academies respected by the entire *respublica litteraria* gathered around the Dupuy brothers and around Mersenne (Marc Fumaroli). Still, Richelieu could not remain indifferent to a new sort of man of letters intent on pleasing public opinion, many of whom were in the service of his adversaries. The result, as is known, was the creation of the Académie française, whose original members came from the group that met unobtrusively at the house of Valentin Conrart, secretary to the king with particular responsibilities in the chancery for drafting permissions to publish. Loyal supporters of Richelieu and men of letters carefully chosen from among the most prominent coteries were soon added to the original group. The enterprise, a part of a more general policy of the guidance of thought, did not immediately inspire enthusiasm in those who were summoned to be its members. Furthermore, the Parlement de Paris only agreed to register the letters patent creating the Académie after being promised that the new group would examine only such works as would be submitted to it by the authors themselves.[61] Nonetheless, the foundation of a new institution whose task was to lay down the law concerning language and to support the established powers was the death knell of the old humanist ideal of the man of letters as adviser to the prince, and it marked the triumph of a rhetoric of glorification of the monarch and his ministers.

Louis XIV carried the patronage system to its logical conclusion. After the Fronde, the great lords of the realm gave up playing the patron and attention focused on the court of the young ruler. Colbert, the organizer of the royal glory, set about improving the efficacy of censorship and assuring his master a chorus of praise from Europe's most illustrious authors. After consultation with Chapelain, ninety authors, French and foreign, were picked to receive pensions, but the stipends were delivered regularly only for ten years or so and stopped altogether after another ten years. Still, official support of academies continued. The founding of a "little academy" in 1663 and of the Académie des Sciences in 1665 gave further impetus to the fragmentation of the humanistic intellectual field. Academies were founded in the larger provincial cities, where their members solicited the approval of the local power-brokers—the bishop, the governor, or the royal intendant—and sought affiliation with one of the Paris academies. In their meetings all the members of such academies were, in principle, equal, but there were subtle differences between the great lord seated among the honorary members and the lawyer or the physician elected as an associate. At least all members demonstrated their participation in a common culture—the culture of Paris, behind which there lurked the shadow of the monarchy. Everything in the academic session was directed toward the glorification of the sovereign and his ministers, especially on the feast of St. Louis, the most solemn occasion of the year. Although rhetoric was their chief concern, the academies soon displayed an interest in scientific and technological advances. They made a special effort to unearth talent in young men whose careers their more powerful members aided. Nonetheless, the academies of the early eighteenth century remained instruments for the promotion of service to the established order, and the system was so successful that the enlightened despots and potentates of Germany founded their own academies and recruited French (or French-speaking) men of letters and learning to set the proper tone in them.[62]

The way that the writer was represented in the social imagination changed. Although the figure of the pedant or the unkempt poet continued to exist in satires or in discourses addressed to a patron, a quite different set of images evoked the "free republic of minds" and glorified the author as an *honnête homme* who devoted his life to celebration of the monarchy. Racine declared that posterity equates the excellent poet with the great general. However, the system soon proved unable to sustain this image. It had seemed to fit in well with the ambitions of the monarchy during the first part of the personal reign of Louis XIV, when the king gave his protection to Molière on the occasion of the dispute over *Tartuffe* and when Boileau and Racine were "removed from the state of literature" and promoted to the rank of historiographers to the king, after which Racine wrote tragedies only for the young ladies of Saint-Cyr. The status of most authors continued to be a hybrid affair: they could continue to seek a patron, as La Bruyère did with the Condés, or they might turn to their booksellers for a living. As royal pensions declined and ecclesiastical benefices began to be granted to men of letters of dubious talent and morality, the leaders of the Jansenist faction and the Protestant intellectuals were forced into exile, where they took up their pens to protest and to defend their positions. Many became journalists, contributing to the development of what we would have to call an opposition press outside France. A challenge to absolutism by appealing to public opinion began to be profitable.

In the meantime the Restoration had injected new energy into court life in Great Britain. A number of gentlemen who dabbled in literature themselves protected authors, dramatists in particular. Later, the Glorious Revolution of 1688 and the struggles between Whigs and Tories led the contending factions to recruit to their cause men of letters capable of influencing public opinion. Patronage was never more active than in the period in which the earl of Dorset snatched the young Matthew Prior from the tutelage of the wine merchant who had employed him and sent him to school, in which John Somers helped Locke to become wealthy, took Addison out of the secondary school in which he was teaching, and aided Matthew Tindal, or in which Charles Montagu arranged for pensions and positions for Addison, Congreve, and Newton.[63]

After the death of Queen Anne the Hanoverian dynasty took little interest in English letters and patrons became scarce. A modern press developed with the parliamentary regime, however, and an increasingly large public demanded books. Soon the copyright law of 1709 spurred the production of new works and a throng of newcomers arrived in Grubb Street, the booksellers' street. Although well educated, these men had neither wealth nor social status, and they were looking for employment. Politicians (Walpole among them) spent notable sums for propaganda, and on occasion they hired one of these new writers to write a lethal pamphlet. They might also garner a translation, or a publisher who lacked ready copy might contract with them for a work, dictating its title, subject matter, and length. Pope was only the first to denounce the miserable condition of the Grubb Street writers. London nonetheless had a number of enterprising publishers who paid authors sizable sums and gave English literature its "Augustan age." Men of letters began to abandon their traditional strategy. Many of course continued to dream of a wealthy patron and a more brilliant social position, as did Congreve (1670–1729). At the same time, however, a new breed of writers, the journalists, emerged.

The most illustrious of the journalists was Daniel Defoe. Defoe first studied for the Presbyterian ministry. He became a merchant, but when he went bankrupt with 17,000 pounds in debts he set to writing in order to earn his living and feed his family, putting himself at the service of various political factions. Changes of ministry and dynastic quarrels soon led him to play a double and even a triple game, and he became acquainted with both prison and the pillory. He wrote a considerable number of works, but financial independence came only when he was almost sixty and began to write novels and *Robinson Crusoe* and *Moll Flanders* gave him a degree of ease.

Jonathan Swift (1667–1745) had a totally different attitude. After an unhappy childhood, Swift went to court in the retinue of Sir William Temple, a distant relative whom he served as secretary. He eventually won a reputation at court as a satirist for the Tory cause. Tory influence helped him to a parish in Ireland, then to become dean of St. Patrick's, Dublin, but he was never named bishop. After the fall of his political friends, he was left with a modest post and was obliged to live in semi-exile. Despite his misfortune he published a large number of works under a pseudonym. He refused all patronage in order to safeguard his independence and he wanted no money from his writings. Only his friend Pope could persuade him to accept earnings from *Gulliver's Travels*.

New things were stirring in literary life in England. Dryden (1631–1700) had a brilliant career at the court of Charles II and was named poet laureate and historiographer to the king. He lost his laureate's crown and, at the fall of James II, his pension. When Dryden converted to Roman Catholicism he turned his hand to translation, notably of Virgil, and was still well regarded by his aristocratic friends. During the same age many authors began to publish collections of letters and translations that were sold by subscription, a form of collective patronage that enabled the more illustrious among them to earn sizable sums without becoming too dependent on a bookseller. Above all, there were increasing numbers of cafés and clubs in which prominent personalities, booksellers, writers, and merchants of like interests could find kindred souls. Alexander Pope (1688–1744) had a remarkable career as "poet of the age" in this climate. Physically deformed but highly talented, Pope was at ease in aristocratic circles, but he found public office closed to him since he was a Roman Catholic and fully intended to remain one. By conviction a Tory, Pope avoided political involvement, and he refused pensions in order to preserve his dignity and his independence, although on occasion he agreed to correct his verse on the request of his noble friends. These friends helped to assure his reputation, and three of them went so far as to put their names to the second edition of the *Dunciad*, which contained the key to the persons attacked in the work, thus putting an end to any eventual suit for libel. In spite of its high price, the subscription for his translation of Homer was a triumph.

In this way certain men of letters attempted to reconcile the esteem of connoisseurs with public success. As in our own day this could be done only if the author wrote for a distinguished review and had his works brought out by a well-known publisher. Samuel Johnson (1709–84) was the prime example of this. An essayist and voluminous writer whose two most famous works, the *Lives of the Poets* and the *Dictionary of the English Language,* were obviously designed to help the emergent middle class appropriate new values, Johnson went so far as to compare his booksellers with patrons and to criticize traditional patronage. He continued to be harassed by financial problems until Lord Bute, the prime minister under George III, settled an annual pension of 300 pounds on him, payable by the state.[64]

In France during the first part of the eighteenth century everything in the world of letters seemed organized, regulated, and provided for: the academic system was operating well under the guidance of Abbé Bignon, an enlightened high commissioner with close connections to Fontenelle,[65] who personally saw to it that the most interesting papers from provincial academies were transmitted to the Académie des Sciences. The King's Library, over which Bignon reigned and where scholars passing through Paris were welcomed with solemnity, was at the time interested in acquiring works in oriental languages, Chinese in particular. The library lodged both the Académie des Sciences and the editorial committee of the *Journal des savants,* more than ever the organ of the official point of view. The director of the library was also responsible for assigning every new work to a competent examiner for censorship. Many of these censors were openminded men, and their constant preoccupation was to avoid having a work published with royal approval stir up a tempest within one or another of the pressure groups that surrounded the monarchy. Their relations with their colleagues, whose works they judged, were in general amicable, and all things considered their position was somewhat comparable to that of the elected or appointed members of similar French institutions in our own day.

More than ever, the power structure (or structures) worked to distribute

pensions and sinecures to learned men engaged in traditional studies and
to upcoming men of letters whose allegiance the monarchy sought to gain.
More than ever the financiers and farmers general who were the great
personages of the land followed the state's example. Aristocratic salons and
coteries were open to authors, although early in the century authors were
on occasion treated highhandedly at such gatherings (as in the case of Voltaire's beating at the hands of the Chevalier de Rohan's lackeys). But a
reaction took place as the figure of the man of letters acquired authority,
and Marie-Antoinette reminded one of her following who complained of
the "bonhomme Sedaine" that she and the king always addressed a writer
as "Monsieur."

Between the seventeenth century and the eighteenth the French language became the language of courts throughout Europe, French artists
were well received everywhere, and French literature was a precious commodity in which the elites of all Europe intended to have a share. All these
factors should have strengthened publishing in France and enabled French
writers to win an independence on the English model, but censorship and
the absence of international agreements complicated the situation, and the
book market, fragmented as early as the seventeenth century, broke into a
set of parallel circuits. These conditions led the Paris booksellers to form a
closed circle, with the complicity of the state. They had formed the habit
of avoiding all risks and refused to pay high prices for manuscripts, arguing
the dangers of pirated editions. One hardly dares imagine what Le Breton
and his associates would have earned if they had retained proprietary
rights to the *Encyclopédie* after its first publication. What would a philosophe have been if he had been richly paid by his bookseller-publishers?
And what would his indignant protests against injustice and social inequality have been worth? In this period, which Sartre called the one stroke of
luck and the lost paradise of French writers, the ambiguity of the authors'
status, the favors but also the humiliations that they received from the
great, and even their straitened circumstances (we need only think of Diderot or Rousseau) were all converted into symbolic capital. There never
has been a comparable antagonism between the real public for politically
engaged writers—a privileged public that included the many émigrés who
subscribed to the first edition of the *Encyclopédie*—and the potential public
for such writers—the public that the official networks of the book trade
did not win over in time but that, during the Revolution, so often invoked
the names of Voltaire and Rousseau without always knowing their works.
It was a curious epoch, in which Frederick II or Catherine the Great of

Russia could welcome Voltaire and Diderot on a footing of false equality, and in which such writers could seem to dictate policy to enlightened despots who, for all their enlightenment, reigned no less despotically. It was an epoch in which the French elite, which no longer believed in the values that founded its power, asked those who attacked that power to breathe an air of liberty into that same elite and provide it with a reflective awareness that it subsequently found it hard to live up to (Jean-Paul Sartre).[66] That elite, unable to join forces with its oppressors, was denounced in the very books that it admired; its ranks divided, it gave free rein in its reading matter to flights of generosity that had consequences it could not foresee. This is what happened to Malesherbes, the friend of the philosophes, when he became president of the Cour des Aides and defended the privileges of the members of that court by participating in the resistance against the Maupeou Parlement.

The literary field had never lent itself to more subtle strategies.[67] The philosophes maneuvered here like masters. They accepted the pensions offered by the power establishment as long as they were a recognition of their worth, and they denounced them indignantly the minute they threatened to become instruments of control. The greatest trap that could be laid for a philosophe was to grant him permission to print a work, since the public might take this as a sign of connivance with the power structure. The philosophes were better off when they could launch a work with great fanfare but have it printed clandestinely, after which any condemnation (particularly from the church) would be free publicity. In certain cases it was an even better tactic to restrain the audacity of one's printed text and circulate more aggressive writings in manuscript copies that hit the mark all the more efficiently because they circulated among leaders and were aimed at the head of the society they wanted to overthrow.

Society was changing fast and the system set up by the monarchy was falling to pieces. The cafés, the *sociétés de pensée,* and Freemasonry all competed with and duplicated the efforts of the academies. The number of children receiving traditional instruction in secondary schools remained roughly stable, but elementary instruction was growing and various forms of technical education were developing. The publishers of the traditional book trade were overwhelmed by newcomers. Thanks to the efforts of Charles-Joseph Panckoucke, the works of the philosophes, until that time prohibited in France, were published one after another. Provincial booksellers had one section for official publications and another for increasingly aggressive works published clandestinely. A smaller proportion of the works that were published were by well-known authors, and French writers were proportionally fewer than English or German writers. Academic competitions revealed claims that were expressed in nontraditional forms. Everywhere literary adventurers acted as self-appointed experts for the publishers, the booksellers, and the public. This was the moment of "gutter Rousseaus," to use Robert Darnton's term, who attacked persons rather than the system and denounced the immorality of the court and the royal family. The French Revolution was not far off. Still the German bourgeoisie found spokesmen who grouped around Goethe at the court of Weimar, a court too poor to have an academy "à la française" like the one in Berlin headed by disciples of the great French philosophers. Soon, in a Germany trampled by the troops of the French Revolution and the Empire, intellectuals backed by a market unified by the Leipzig fairs would at last address the German nation.

OTHER WORLDS*

In spite of the compartmentalization imposed by censorship, by multiple states, and by heresies, the circuits of the printed word, which paralleled those of commercial exchanges, wove a coherent cultural network throughout Western Europe. They permitted the affirmation of a homogeneous culture springing from a common Latin and Christian substratum within peoples who used the same system of writing, spoke languages of the same linguistic family, and used the same dominant languages—Latin, then to a limited extent Italian and Spanish, later French, while English awaited its turn—for intellectual exchange.

European printers began very early to engrave characters that would enable them to publish works written in other languages, and the populations who used those scripts either continued to use their own methods of typography or adopted Western techniques. We need to ask to what ends and to what effect they did so.

The case of printed Hebrew is a fairly simple story, at least in appearance.[68] In spite of the Diaspora and the variety of languages that Jews spoke in their daily lives, they maintained the homogeneity of their culture and the purity of their religion thanks to their practice of a learned language, Hebrew, for prayer and study. Indefatigable copyists, they enthu-

*This section was written with the aid of François Dupuigneret Desroussilles and, for the Slavic portion, Matei Cazacu, both of whom I thank.

siastically welcomed the invention of printing and saluted it, without re-
striction, as a "holy work." Except in such specific liturgical uses as reading
the Torah, printed texts quite naturally replaced manuscripts. It is not
known whether there were already Jews among those who printed texts
in Avignon between 1444 and 1447 under Waldfoghel's direction, but
there were almost certainly Jews who learned the new art from the first
typographers in Mainz. Soon printshops were set up in the two great centers of high Jewish culture, Italy, where the first dated book was printed in
Reggio Calabria in 1475, and the Iberian peninsula, in 1475 or 1476 in
Spain and in 1487 in Portugal. In 1492, when Spain banished from its
territory Jews faithful to their religion and Portugal followed suit in 1497,
a number of Jewish printers took refuge in Italy, thus giving a new impetus
to Italy's already flourishing printing trade in Hebrew. One example among
many was the small city of Soncino, not far from Mantua; another was the
great printshop of Daniel Bomberg in Venice, where the Babylonian Talmud and the Jerusalem Talmud were printed. Other Jewish printers were
welcomed into the Ottoman Empire by Sultan Bajazet II: the Ibn Nahmias
brothers (active between 1493 or 1503 and 1530) founded an important
printshop in Constantinople, launching a print production in Hebrew that
continued almost without interruption to the early nineteenth century. In
the first decades of the sixteenth century important centers of Jewish printing were created in Bohemia (Prague, 1512), in Poland (Krakow, 1534),
and in the Mediterranean basin in Salonika, where Jews made up half the
population until the Greek conquest in 1912, and more ephemerally in
Morocco (Fez, 1516–21) and in Egypt, where two works were printed in
Hebrew in Cairo in 1557. Finally, a Jewish printer from Prague who had
worked in Constantinople, Isaac Ashkenazy, created the first typographical
workshop in the Near East in Galilee (Safad, 1577).

The status of printing among the various Christian communities of the Ottoman Empire—Greeks, Armenians, Slavs, or Eastern Christians—was
more complex. All these groups made use of printing to defend their cultural independence, but they encountered opposition both from the Ottoman government, which found this ferment of autonomy disruptive, and
from the Western Christian powers, which hoped to bring them back into
the fold of the Roman Church or convert them to Protestantism. As a general rule, they had to buy their supplies in continental Europe.

In Venice specialized printshops produced Greek texts not for European humanists (as did Aldus Manutius or Zacharias Callierges) but for the Greeks of the Venetian colonies and the territories under Ottoman domination.[69] Thus nearly all the liturgical works needed for the Orthodox cult were printed in Venice between 1521 and 1545, for the most part by the large firm of the Nicolini da Sabbio brothers and their Greek collaborators. The classic Greek bibliography by Legrand states that 79 percent of the production of printed Greek books before 1790 originated in Venice. The hostility of the Ottoman rulers was not the only impediment to the development of a Greek typographical industry in the Ottoman Empire: until the seventeenth century a large part of the Orthodox clergy, particularly in Constantinople, mistrusted the new art. In the Venetian colonies (Crete and the Ionian Islands in particular), where a high level of literacy and culture (attested by icons and magnificent manuscripts filled with paintings) and a degree of economic prosperity might make one expect to see Greek printing firms, the traditional policy of the Republic of Venice to protect its own industries explains the lack of any local typographical industry.

Unlike the Greek clergy, the Armenian clergy helped to found a number of printshops in the sixteenth and seventeenth centuries.[70] Because the Ottoman government tolerated the printing of Armenian books only in Constantinople and only during certain periods, Armenian priests and bishops were sent to the West to establish printshops to provide books for the entire diaspora. These printshops were financed by the merchant bourgeoisie of the Armenian colonies of Europe, who served as middlemen for an international trade with merchants in the Philippines, China, Indonesia, India, and Persia. The largest of these colonies—Livorno, Marseille, Venice, and Amsterdam—were thus the first to have Armenian printshops (Venice, 1511; Livorno, 1643; Amsterdam, 1658; Marseille, 1672). Their pressruns were at times astonishingly high, and they had the benefit of an exceptional network, both ecclesiastical and commercial, to distribute their books. Print was clearly instrumental in the conservation of the Armenian cultural heritage.

Arabic-speaking Christians who lived under Turkish domination were hindered by the prohibition to print in Arabic or in Turkish mentioned by a traveler, Nicolas de Nicolay, in 1551 ("en turc ou en arabe ne leur est permis d'imprimer"). The first print editions in Melchite Arabic date only from the early eighteenth century and come from the Danubian principalities, far from the center of the Ottoman Empire.

Western Christians could not be indifferent to the existence of these Christian minorities. Rome dreamed of gathering in the various scattered communities of Arabic-speaking Christians surrounded by Islam, and after the Reformation the same communities were disputed between Catholics and Protestants. To further these ends close connections were established between European scholars and certain Eastern men of letters, the Maronites in particular. Early in the seventeenth century the papacy created an Eastern printshop in Rome under the aegis of the Congregation for the Propagation of the Faith (the *De Propaganda Fide*). This press used the handsome characters that Robert Granjon had engraved for Cardinal Ferdinando de' Medici, and it produced a number of editions of sacred texts, catechisms, and apologetic works for Arabic-speaking Christians. Some time later in Paris Antoine Vitré used a typeface created under the direction of Savary de Brèves, the French ambassador to Constantinople and later to Rome, to produce similar works for free distribution by the missionaries whom Père Joseph was urging to set out for those far-off lands. This same period was an active one for the Protestant printers of the Low Countries, where Eastern scholars were numerous, in particular at the University of Leiden. In 1620 the Netherlands ambassador offered the patriarch of Constantinople, who rallied to Protestantism, a partial text of the Bible in Arabic. Calvinists later aided the founding of an Arabic printshop in Constantinople itself. These enterprises were immediately denounced by the French ambassador, whom the Sublime Porte recognized as the representative of Catholicism. The English and the Dutch responded immediately by denouncing the activities of Catholic missionaries who were distributing works hostile to the religion of Islam. A quarrel ensued that the Ottoman government settled by deposing the patriarch, Cyril, and putting an end to Protestant propaganda.

The Christian communities of the Ottoman Empire undoubtedly viewed print as a means for reinforcing their cohesion. Rome intervened to the extent that typography enabled the Roman Church to replace faulty manuscripts with revised texts and to propagate right doctrine among Eastern Christians. Even the Maronites, who were working to strengthen their ties with the papacy, showed displeasure at these hegemonic moves by setting up a printshop of their own in Mount Lebanon. As for the Armenian Church, it was closely supervised by the Catholic authorities, in France in particular. At least European scholars gained increased contact with their Oriental counterparts, and the French monarchy, in its desire to end the schism with the Eastern Orthodox Church and to replace Protestant learning with Catholic, used the presses of the Imprimerie royale to print the great collection of texts known as the Byzantine collection of the Louvre.

In all these conflicts the Ottoman government acted as moderator, but it proved skilled at setting Christians against one another and Jews against Christians. The important question that remains is why that great state— which in other domains was by no means closed to technological inno- vation, as proven by the excellent cannons it soon made—consistently opposed printing texts in Arabic characters. The explanations that are usu- ally advanced—explanations of a general cultural nature that put varying stress on a fear that writing would be desacralized by print—seem utterly unsatisfactory.

The development of the printing industry in Slavic lands offers a picture of particular complexity thanks to the diversity of political regimes, religions, and above all alphabets in those lands. The Latin alphabet was used to print, first, works in Latin and, later, works in Czech and Polish, but there were also the Glagolitic alphabet used by Croatian Catholics and the Cyril- lic alphabet adopted by Eastern Orthodox Bulgars, Serbs, Ukrainians, Rus- sians, and Romanians.[71]

Slavic printing in Glagolitic characters originated in Venice, where a *Sluzebnik* (or *Leitourgikon*) was published in 1483, followed by missals and breviaries, all printed by Andrea Torresani, the future father-in-law and associate of Aldus Manutius. After 1494 some attempts were made to cre- ate printshops in Croatia itself, first in Senj in 1508, then, after 1530, in Rijeka (Fiume). The work of these firms was almost totally liturgical (reli- gious, at any rate), and it had strong competition from manuscript works that were better adapted to the diversity of local liturgical customs. Religion also dictated the output of a printshop founded to provide Protestant pro- paganda that was set up in Tübingen between 1560 and 1564 by Baron Hans von Ungnad and that printed the great Lutheran texts in Glagolitic characters.

The earliest texts printed in Cyrillic characters circulated among the Eastern Orthodox southern Slavs in a zone under Venetian influence (the Venetians still considered the Adriatic "their gulf" and jealously defended their control of it). In 1493 the Crnojevich rulers of Montenegro set up a printshop in Cetinje, the capital city. Its presses and typefaces were bought in Venice and it operated under the direction of a famous monk, Macarios, who had learned typography in that same city. The Montenegro printery produced six liturgical works in three years, but its activities were cut short in 1496 by the Turkish occupation. After that date the centers of printing in Cyrillic shifted from one place to another according to the vicissitudes of the hostilities between Venice and the Ottoman Empire in the Balkans. Macarios attempted to continue his publishing activities in Walachia between 1508 and 1512, after which Bozidar Vukovic, a Montenegran, dominated printing in Cyrillic for several decades. Vukovic owned a large printshop in Venice, where in the sixteenth century he produced some thirty Latin and Slavic works. To guarantee the canonicity of liturgical works he jobbed out work to a number of small print works in Orthodox monasteries. It was a precarious business, though. From the mid-sixteenth century, the consolidation of Ottoman power meant that the only way that printing in Cyrillic could survive was through the establishment of a center of production in a land that was on friendly terms with the Turks but that had a powerful Orthodox hierarchy. Walachia was the only Slavic land that fitted that description. There, an extraordinary personage, Dimitrie Liubavici, printed liturgical books between 1544 and 1551. In the seventeenth and eighteenth centuries, following an eclipse of over a century, the principal episcopal cities of Walachia had printshops that operated under the direct control of the ecclesiastical authorities and that produced works in both Slavonian and Romanian. As in Croatia, Protestant propagandists were active in Walachia. In the sixteenth century, after a large portion of the population of Transylvania had converted to Protestantism, Lutheran Saxons settled in Transylvania, the municipal governments of Sibiu and Braçov encouraged printing, and their cities became important centers of production for Protestant literature in Slavic and in Romanian.

Among the eastern Slavs—Ukrainians and Russians—only sporadic attempts were made to set up printshops before the late sixteenth century. The first known printshop was founded in Krakow in 1491 by a German, Szwajpolt Fiol. A purely commercial enterprise, it later furnished books to the Orthodox Ruthenians who made up the greater part of the population of the Grand Duchy of Lithuania and it was closed by the Lithuanian Catholic hierarchy after only a few months of activity. Similarly, a Byelorussian named Prantsish Skaryna printed a Bible in Slavonian in Prague in 1517–19 and an Acts of the Apostles in Vilna in 1525. Seven books were published in Moscow between 1550 and 1560 by a printshop about which we know nothing. It was not until 1563 that Czar Ivan IV ("the Terrible") founded the first stable Cyrillic printshop in Moscow, known as *Pecatnyj dvor,* or the "Print House." Although the master printer, Ivan Fedorov, was chased from Moscow by a revolt of copyists and clergy (he took refuge in Lithuania), the printshop, which was moved from the capital city to the village of Sloboda Alexandrovskaja, had produced some five hundred titles by the late seventeenth century. Even though the printshop had been founded by the political establishment, all but seven of these works were religious. The most important of the fifteen or so printshops in the Ukraine in the seventeenth century—one run by Ruthenian friars in Lvov and another in the Monastery of the Grottos in Kiev—were controlled by religious authorities. Religious in its contents, controlled by and for the most part produced by the Orthodox Church, the eastern Slavic printed book supported tradition more than it did ferment.

The modern Slavic printed book really dates from the early eighteenth century, when Peter the Great, who previously ordered maps and books in Russian printed in Amsterdam, decided in 1711 to make a symbolic break with the past and to found a printing establishment in St. Petersburg, the new capital of the empire. Soon there were presses printing in Russian for the Senate, the Naval Academy, and above all the Academy of Science. These printshops, challenging the authority of the Holy See, specialized in the publication of books of science and erudition in Russian but also in Latin, German, and French. After the death of Peter the Great, the Holy Synod managed to take back control of publishing until the reign of Catherine the Great, who freed printing from its state monopoly. In 1783 private printshops were authorized and they flourished throughout the empire. The number of books printed increased rapidly, rising from 139 works in 1762 to 479 in 1788. In reaction to the French Revolution and out of fear of "Jacobin ideas," Catherine reversed her liberal policy, and in 1796 one of her last acts as sovereign was to close all private printing firms and create censorship offices in Moscow, St. Petersburg, and the principal ports of the Russian Empire. Controls were to some extent relaxed under the reign of Alexander I (1801–25), who once again authorized private printshops, but before the 1917 revolution printing in Russia continued under a regime of draconian severity in which all books and even articles in periodicals were subject to prior censorship.

All in all, although one cannot say that the Slavic world refused printing, books printed in the national languages were confined to a limited subject matter and subjected to the political and religious authorities. The Russian elites read works in German or French.

Printing in the Far East was dominated by China.[72] Although the Chinese incontestably invented xylography, scholars are still debating the date of that invention. Similarly, the physical conditions of book production and the specifics of quantities printed and circulation are known only through vague indications in the works themselves or from literary sources. It should be stressed, following the great English sinologist Joseph Needham, that xylography was first developed for the use of religious minorities— Buddhists for the most part—who wanted multiple copies of devotional images and pious booklets. The story of the Diamond Sutra is familiar: this is the famous scroll dated 868 brought back to the British Museum from the Caves of the Thousand Buddhas near Tun-huang by Aurel Stein, along with several thousand other ancient Chinese manuscripts. As early as the thirteenth century private printing establishments appeared in the great urban centers of China, but only in the sixteenth century can we speak of the development of a genuine print industry. Although the Chinese had a form of movable type, the nonalphabetic characters of the Chinese language made woodcuts better adapted to the purposes of mechanical duplication. Wood engraving was a technique that was not only simple and inexpensive but also particularly well adapted to Chinese ideograms. The only notable expenses were for paper, ink, and wood, plus the costs of transposition from a manuscript original, engraving and printing the blocks, and assembling the leaves. No costly and cumbersome press was needed for impressions taken by rubbing, and all the tools required for printing could be carried on a man's back. Once the blocks were engraved, one man could print several thousand sheets per day unaided, and the plates could be recut for later pulls.

In the Ch'ing dynasty (1644–1911), the graphics industry was both quite specialized and very diverse. Men of letters produced learned works printed by the large establishments in the coastal cities of the Yangtze delta, Nanking, Souchow, and Hangchow. The printing of popular works was concentrated in southern China, and such works were distributed through the regional branches of the major booksellers.

The development of a large xylographic industry in the sixteenth century increased the circulation of the great novels of the eighteenth century.

There also were collections of poetry from the various regions, large collections of popular songs, short stories, word games, and even all sorts of piquant tales centering on the imperial family. Moralizing booklets were printed, as were almanacs and popular encyclopedias, letter-writing manuals and models for various sorts of documents, arithmetic textbooks, and even "comic strips" in color. In the early nineteenth century popular newspapers (*xinwenzhi*) were printed from clay or wax blocks (which could be reused) and sold for a few coins on the street corners. These broadsheets served to complement the official gazettes that contained lists of appointments to government office and notices pertaining to affairs of state.

The large number of texts available may perhaps explain the high degree of literacy reached by the Chinese people under the Ch'ing dynasty. According to Evelyn Rawski, the leading specialist on the question, it can be estimated that at the end of the nineteenth century between 30 and 45 percent of the male population of China was literate.

In Japan as in China, the beginnings of printing were connected with the beginnings of Buddhism,[73] as indicated by the history of the Hyaku-mato-dharani, the first known printed books. When in 764 the empress Kōken defeated the Confucians and returned to the throne under the name of Shōtoku, she ordered the making of a million *stupa*—small wooden pagodas containing slim woodcut scrolls on which formulas of thanksgiving were printed—to be distributed among ten great temples. Tens of thousands of these scrolls have come down to us. These miniature "books" were of course not designed to be read, which again raises the question of the religious value of manuscripts and printed texts. In the Far East the ascetic act par excellence was to copy a religious text by hand and offer it to a temple. The essence of the original offering was thought to persist even when it was reproduced in another form and in a large number of copies. Thus we can understand that it was acceptable to burn a sacred text in poor condition, not to destroy it but to send it on its way to the supernatural world in the more subtle form of smoke. This attitude is comparable to the Jewish or Muslim practice of burying sacred texts, as opposed to the Latin and Greek practice of washing off the leaves of manuscript Bibles in order to reuse the parchment.

After the colossal enterprise of the million charms nothing was printed in Japan for over two hundred years. In the eleventh century the nobles of the Kyoto region once again ordered print materials in extremely varied numbers (from one to a thousand copies) that bore prayers and offerings for the repose of the souls of the dead or for the coming of rain. At the same time Buddhist texts for the instruction of monks were published in the temples around Nara. Printing was not secularized and did not really develop until the Edo period (late sixteenth to early seventeenth centuries), when the merchant bourgeoisie occupied a dominant place in Japanese society and forced the country's opening to the world.

That was the moment when Christian missionaries—the Society of Jesus in particular—were admitted into Japan. As they had done in Goa, Macao, and Manila, the Jesuits established presses in Kazusa (1590), Amakusa (1592), and Nagasaki (1597). Following a program so orderly that it seemed preestablished, they printed works first in Latin, then in romanized Japanese (probably for the use of young missionaries), and then in kana (simple syllabaries for the mass of the converts), in hiragana for the governing classes, and in kanji, the writing system of the scholars. At the same time the Japanese themselves adopted a system for printing with movable metal characters that they had brought back from an expedition in Korea in 1592–93. In 1597, after several attempts to print with these characters, the emperor commanded characters to be cut out of wood (which was easier to work than metal) and ordered the printing of a number of prestigious books. Following his example, the Tokugawa shoguns had several works printed for the use of warriors, and the Buddhist temples embraced the new procedures. Moreover, the various professions of the book trade were organized, first in Kyoto, then in Osaka and in Edo, on the initiative of patrons but also increasingly often thanks to the backing of wealthy burghers eager to invest in a new product.

There has been much discussion on just what urged the Japanese to use movable characters (*kokatsubijan*) for roughly fifty years. While the publications of missionaries, who for the most part printed works in syllabary characters, reached sizable pressruns of as many as 1,500 copies, the Japanese printers concentrated on using the full resources of kanji, which was still possible as long as they limited their editions to 100 or 150 copies printed for an aristocratic clientele. As soon as they wanted to print in greater numbers they found it impossible to stock enough characters to compose new forms while the previous forms were still locked up and awaiting further pressings. Their solution was to return to xylographic printing, which made larger press runs possible—at times as many as three thousand copies for a "best-seller"—but which also lent itself to calligraphic inventiveness and to illustration.

We need to insist on the true cultural revolution that took place in Japan.

Previously, printed texts, nearly all produced within the Buddhist temples, were written in Chinese. Henceforth printing could also be done in Japanese, and the number of works available to the public seems to have been considerable, given that one bookseller in 1671 had 3,874 titles to offer his clients. As in the West, the printed book had become "merchandise" just when the literacy rate in Japan—at least where the simplest sorts of writing were concerned—reached a level comparable to that of European lands.

$\mathcal{N}\!ine$
The Industrial Era

During the Enlightenment, European economy had a new beginning. It coincided with the revolutions: the American Revolution, which signaled that a new world had come of age, the French Revolution, which was political, and the English Revolution, which was industrial.

Once again, an end to major epidemics and an increase in population launched sweeping changes. Rising curves in every sector reflected growth in Europe between 1730 and 1760. The development of a road system in Europe, then a system of canals, helped to break down the compartmentalization of society, but although technological innovation was much praised in the age of the *Encyclopédie*, in this first phase its effect was gradual. Innovation was aimed at increasing profits, but it almost automatically prompted further innovation and advances in related sectors.

Increased amounts of energy were needed to effect change of this kind, and Europe looked to its coal mines to provide it. The mines needed machinery to counter water seepage and make the coal seams easier to exploit. In England in 1698 Thomas Savery patented a system that used a steam engine to pump out mines; later Savery, Thomas Newcomen, and John Calley worked together, and Newcomen and Calley developed a steam-powered piston-driven engine that launched the steam engine's long career. (Denis Papin was also experimenting with steam-powered engines between 1705 and 1707.) Newcomen's machine responded to a need, and it was an instant success in England. James Watt separated the condenser and the cylinder, thus increasing the engine's work capacity, and the double-acting engine that he later invented was the first industrial motor (1775–84). Such engines long served only to pump water, but in 1769 Nicolas-Joseph Cugnot invented the first steam-driven self-propelled vehicle, a three-wheeled artillery tractor. When the British economy "took off" the steam engine enabled British manufacturers to mechanize their factories. In the late seventeenth century English collieries had already begun to use coal carts that ran on a system of wooden rails to move the coal from the mines, switching to metal rails around 1730. The steam locomotive was born of the combination of these techniques (1804). The first railroad line open to travelers (Stockton to Darlington) was inaugurated in 1825, and in 1829 George Stephenson's "Rocket" sped along the

Liverpool-Manchester line at thirty miles an hour. In France, colliery lo-
comotives were transporting coal the twenty-one kilometers from Andre-
zieux to Saint-Etienne in 1827, the line from Saint-Etienne to Lyons was
opened in 1831, and the Paris-Saint-Germain passenger line opened in
1837. Railroad fever gripped England, then Germany, France, and the rest
of the Continent. Tens of thousands of kilometers of rail were laid in fifty
years, at times passing over viaducts and bridges that were true works of
art. The appearance of the railroad in a region was nearly always followed
by its industrialization.[1]

Thus some of the old barriers were shattered in the most dynamic part
of Western Europe. Important advances were also made in marine trans-
port. The idea of using steam power to propel ships, with the aid of gigantic
paddlewheels, had occurred to people in the late eighteenth century. Then
the propeller was invented (1832), and the first iron ships appeared.
Coastal steamers were widely used, and when the steam-powered ocean
liner little by little replaced the sailing ship, ocean crossings became a more
common occurrence.

In a world in which distances were diminishing, financial speculation
was increasing, and everyone felt himself more immediately concerned by
news from afar, information needed to pass more rapidly and more de-
pendably. Modern postal systems were organized, taking advantage of the
increasing number of railroad lines, and between 1840 and 1849 the
postage stamp was adopted nearly everywhere. The electric telegraph (to
which I shall return) replaced the visual telegraph system invented by
Claude Chappe during the French Revolution, much advancing the railroad industry and later contributing greatly to the rise of the periodical
press.

At the same time, Europe was undergoing vast social changes. Between
1800 and 1914 the population of Europe rose from 250,000,000 to
400,000,000 (emigration not taken into consideration), a rise that was the
principal impulse behind the industrial revolution. Between 1850 and
1914 the population of Germany increased 96 percent; the populations of
the Austro-Hungarian Empire and the United Kingdom rose 66 percent,
while the population of Russia increased 126 percent. Thanks to a declining birthrate that was to have serious consequences for the nation, population growth in France was somewhat slower. This increase meant that
large numbers of peasants whom the land could no longer support mi-
grated to the cities, where they provided industrialists with the low-cost
manpower they needed. In 1800 there were only twenty-two cities of more

than 100,000 inhabitants in all Europe; in 1850 there were forty-seven, twenty-one of them in England alone. London's population rose from 960,000 to 2,300,000; the population of Paris rose from 547,000 to 1,000,000; Roubaix quadrupled its population, which went from 8,000 in 1812 to 34,000 in 1831; Mulhouse tripled its population; Cologne reached a population of 92,000 in 1848. The figures rise even more steeply after that date, so that in 1914 there were 182 European cities with a population of over 100,000, some fifty of them in England and nearly as many in Germany.

Social upheaval accompanied these changes. The aristocracy continued to play an essential role in certain countries (Russia and Spain), but a business bourgeoisie (liberal by definition) and the middle classes in general were gaining more and more influence. The city was a place of striking contrasts, offering a spectacle of flagrant material success but also of human misery. The city stimulated ambitions, desires, and resentment. The development of industry in cities was encouraged by a higher standard of living and lower food prices (made possible by new techniques and large-scale production methods); it was just as true, however, that the new industrial cities and the peripheries of the major older cities resembled concentration camps where uprooted peasants lived massed together in squalor.

Until around 1850 the movement for literacy examined above received considerable encouragement from the revolution in communications and from social upheaval. In France, where the Revolution had made education its standard-bearer in its struggle against the old world (François Furet), civil authorities, who picked up where the religious authorities had left off, regarded schools as a means for better integrating citizens into society. The city proletariat, many of whose leaders came from the world of printing and engraving, saw education as a way of becoming masters of their fate and of giving their children a less precarious future. Hence the appearance of an ideology of the school that gave both German and French schoolmasters great moral support and helped them to fashion in their image generations of children who absorbed their ideals and aspirations.

According to François Furet and Jacques Ozouf, the French Revolution had very little effect on the gains in literacy that had already begun in France, and the Maggiolo investigation revealed trends that were completely independent of political events. The map of literacy in France and its changes over time reflect social development. During the eighteenth century literacy made progress in the middle levels of society; in the nineteenth century it conquered the lower levels. For obvious reasons, literacy increased in the cities earlier than in rural areas, primarily because cities contained a great many men of the law, merchants, and craftsmen. Advances might be masked by the arrival of illiterate rustics, but the literacy rate soon rebounded because it was increasingly difficult to live in the cities and towns without at least a minimal education, and the urban elites offered an omnipresent model. The regional imbalance between the "two Frances" simply reflected differences in their stage of development. The enormous change that the nineteenth century brought was to couple the teaching of reading and the teaching of writing: henceforth any child who had attended primary school could not only decipher a text but also hold a pen and write at least a few words.[2]

The mechanisms of literacy were enormously complex, and it is a daunting task to attempt to draw any general conclusions regarding any one country. Etienne François has compared the situation in France and in Prussia on the basis of census figures for 1820 and 1867 (for France) and for 1846 and 1864 (for Prussia), and he has noted that between those dates school attendance rates rose from 47.5 percent to 70.4 percent in France and from 78 percent to 85 percent in Prussia.[3] Thus Prussia was incontestably ahead of France in literacy. Nonetheless, a region-by-region analysis showed François that both countries contained areas of lesser literacy. Be that as it may, illiteracy became increasingly residual in the more advanced countries of Europe, and in the latter part of the nineteenth century France and England, which had lagged behind Scotland, moved at roughly the same pace to catch up. Around 1900 census figures show that illiterates made up less than 10 percent of the population in France, England, and Germany, while in Belgium 12 percent of the population was illiterate and in the Austro-Hungarian Empire (where figures vary greatly from one ethnic group to another) 22 percent of the people were illiterate. Italy joined the group of more literate countries only just before World War I, and in Russia 50 percent of the population achieved literacy only at the turn of the century.[4] Thus the great revolutions seem to have broken out—in England in the seventeenth century, in France toward the end of the eighteenth century, and in Russia in the early twentieth century—at the moment when the literacy rate reached or passed 50 percent. Nonetheless, it long continued to be true that many of the children who went through the primary schools emerged without much more than a limited education that they had little means for developing—hence the continued importance, in many regions and until quite recent times, of mechanisms for oral transmission. At least everyone (or nearly everyone) could decipher a practical text and write a few words, and increasing numbers could learn about current events—at least on occasion—by reading a newspaper. Access to books remained for the most part elitist, a question to which I shall return.

PRINTING ADAPTS TO THE INDUSTRIAL AGE

The industrial revolution thus coincided with a long-term disequilibrium that had violent consequences, and its technological advances varied from one set of particular circumstances to another. In some lands and certain periods, for example, increased population and increased revenues created an expanding market and encouraged investment. When that occurred two successive processes were set in motion. First, capitalists attempted to increase production through the use of more powerful machines. When the market was saturated, a scarcity of fresh capital led to a search for more economical production methods. On occasion a weak market might induce entrepreneurs to innovate by increasing production as a way to lower prices and thus stimulate demand. Such variations in strategy were particularly noticeable in the publishing world. Moreover, the various countries of Europe underwent their industrial revolutions at different rates. The first takeoff in the late eighteenth and early nineteenth centuries started in Great Britain and from there spread to the United States, France, Belgium, and Switzerland. In a later stage from 1840 to 1860, when the first railroad systems were being established, Germany spearheaded the movement to industrialize, and it continued to advance at an accelerated rate in spite of brief periods of stagnation between 1870 and 1880. Industrialism also continued to advance in North America, but it slacked off in northwest European lands (especially in England) until the upswing (particularly in France) just before World War I. Between 1860 and 1913 industrialization reached the lands of eastern Europe, Russia in particular. Thus specific economic situations were in perpetual evolution, and each country displayed a unique array of cleavages and disparities that were reflected in attitudes toward the newspaper and the book.[5]

These were the conditions under which printing underwent a total change. One technological advance inexorably followed another, working to eliminate bottlenecks and to increase the rate of production of texts.

The first problem was to find a paper supply adequate to growing demands that an increased use of writing prompted. In the eighteenth century wide use of the cylindrical paper mill and the appearance of wove paper signaled a new departure. Around 1789, Nicolas-Louis Robert, an engineer and printer who worked with Pierre-François Didot in his paper works at Essonnes, had an idea for a procedure for producing paper much more rapidly than with the traditional vat. In that same year Robert took out a patent for a machine that would produce paper in a continuous strip that could be rolled onto a drum as it emerged. In 1801, Didot Saint-Léger, Pierre-François Didot's son, set up business in England with his brother-in-law, John Gamble, who took out a patent in the same year for an enormous paper-making machine 3.70 meters wide and 13.70 meters long. The two men began to manufacture their machines in 1805, and in 1814 they started making similar machines in France. What was innovative about their machines was not so much that they produced paper in a continuous web (in fact, some machines produced sheets) as that the various stages of paper manufacturing were gradually incorporated into a single piece of machinery. This gave an infinitely higher rate of production than with traditional procedures, and it enabled the manufacturer to replace a specialized and traditionally restive personnel with a small number of mechanics and an unskilled work force of women and children.[6]

Born in England, the paper-making machine set off to conquer the Continent. France had four paper works equipped with such machinery in 1827 and twelve in 1835; by that date Germany had five or six. The next problem was to feed these hungry machines. The usual supplies of rags were no longer sufficient. As early as the eighteenth century people had experimented with using various sorts of vegetable pulp to make paper, and in the nineteenth century a number of substances—straw, alfalfa, wood—were tried as substitutes for rags. In 1844 a Saxon master weaver, Gottfried Keller, created a machine for grinding down logs to make what is called "groundwood" or "mechanical pulp." He ceded his patent to Heinrich Völter, the director of a paperworks in Bautzen, who improved the procedure with the aid of a mechanic named Voith. At this stage, however, wood was no more than a promising complement to other materials; it became the dominant material only when ways were found to separate the fibers by slicing the wood with the grain and to "cook" the pulp by breaking it down chemically. When this became possible around 1860, the Western world could think that its supply of raw materials was inexhaustible. Paper production increased sixfold in Germany and fourfold in France between 1875 and 1908. Attempts were also made to lower costs, which meant that in Germany in 1912 raw materials represented only 12 percent of the cost price of a book as opposed to 30 percent in 1870. Replacing gelatin size with a less expensive and faster-drying resin size, improved procedures for bleaching rag or mechanical pulp, the use of chemicals to dissolve the lignin that binds wood fibers, and procedures for making chemical pulps produced papers that had a fine appearance but that aged poorly.[7] Thus the conservation of posters and newspapers printed after 1875 requires infinite precautions, and 75,000 of the two million books of that period conserved in the Bibliothèque nationale in Paris have been permanently lost, 580,000 others are in danger in the short term, and 600,000 will be at risk soon. The book had become a commodity; our civilization entrusts its memory to a vehicle as fragile as the papyrus of the ancient world, and the massive destruction of the forests that furnish woodpulp now poses increasingly urgent problems. Whether we like it or not, the time is fast approaching when we will have to find a new medium for the transmission and conservation of most written messages.[8]

The mechanical aspects of printing also underwent increasingly revolutionary innovation. Attempts had been made during the latter part of the eighteenth century to increase the production of the screw handpress. Around 1772 a typefounder in Basel, Wilhelm Haas, built a press mounted on a stone base to give it a better footing and ran the pressing screw through a metal arc rather than the traditional double horizontal beams. Between 1781 and 1783, Laurent Anisson and François-Ambroise Didot perfected presses that could print an entire form at one pull, and later Philippe-Denis Pierre replaced the press-bar with a rocking-lever. Finally, presses began to be made entirely out of iron, the most famous of which was designed in 1795 by Charles Stanhope with the aid of his engineer, Robert Walker.[9]

Printing needed to be done faster and faster to satisfy the public's demand for newspapers, which increased in both numbers and circulation throughout the century, and to meet the commercial demand for publicity materials of all sorts. The next revolutionary changes in printing were thus the use of rollers or cylinders, the integration of the various printing operations into a single machine and one continuous process, and the use of steam power.[10]

The use of a cylindrical roller instead of a platen was perhaps first inspired by the presses used for copperplate engravings. I might recall that in 1784 Valentin Haüy had used a cylinder to print embossed characters in relief for the use of the blind. In 1790 an English physician, William Nicholson, invented a roller system to replace the oakum- or wool-filled leather-covered ink ball that had served printers for inking their forms since the fifteenth century. Rollers were also used in the paper-making machinery perfected in England in the early nineteenth century.

The man who contributed the most to the revolution in printing presses was a German, Friedrich Koenig, who worked in England from 1806 to 1816 before returning to his native land. This new Gutenberg first improved the inking process, using Nicholson's inking cylinder and devising an ink feeder with a tank and four superimposed cylinders to transfer the ink to the form. Next, he replaced the traditional platen with an impression cylinder. Using these same principles, he built two steam-powered mechanical presses for *The Times* of London with oscillating rollers, also driven by steam, capable of printing 1,100 sheets of newsprint per hour. Next he connected two presses so they could print both sides of the sheet at once without human aid. This system, improved on several occasions (notably by Ambrose Applegath and Edward Cowper), raised output to roughly 7,000 sheets per hour by 1827. Use of the new machinery spread slowly, however, and until around 1830 many mechanical presses still depended on human muscle power.

In an age when typographers' pay was rising, printers were also seeking to use procedures for making clichés and stereotypes as a way to avoid recomposing a text each time it was reprinted. When labor was cheap and character fonts costly, many printers recomposed a book for every reprinting and only a few printers of books of hours kept forms for reuse. Forms were cumbersome to keep, however, and if their quoins loosened the type risked pieing. It seems that some Dutch typographers attempted to solder composed type together at the base, as Firmin Didot did in 1795 for Callet's *Table de logarithmes,* a frequently reprinted work. Louis-Etienne Herhan then thought of casting a page in one block from a matrix or a set of matrices, a process known as stereography. Type molds had been known in Paris in the late seventeenth century, however, when lead plates with characters in relief were used for the calendars that appeared at the heads of liturgical books. Similar experiments were made in Scotland and in Germany, and in 1784 François Hoffman, an Alsatian, opened a "stereotype" print shop in Paris, obtained an exclusive *privilège* for the process, and produced a large number of works.

The need to protect paper banknotes (in particular, Revolutionary *assignats*) from counterfeits led to further experimentation, but stereotype reproduction was practical only for more frequent and larger pressruns, which meant that stereotypy was not practiced on a large scale until the early nineteenth century. Until the 1830s in England and the 1840s in France, printers used plaster of paris molds that, under normal conditions, could be used only once, but printers were already perfecting procedures for making matrices of "flong," a heat-resistant material somewhat like papier mâché. Procedures for electrotype printing came next.

All these procedures were undeniable improvements, but newspaper circulation demanded an even greater hourly rate of production. Hence the rotary press. Eighteenth-century textile printers had shown the way by devising machines to pass bolts of cloth between two cylinders, one that provided pressure and the other that bore an intaglio design to be imprinted. Nicholson had already thought of using a similar technique for typography, but it required the print form to be curved. Richard March Hoe, an American, devised a way to attach type to a large cylinder, keeping the lines of type tight with wedge-shaped separator rules. This astonishing machine did service in English-speaking lands in the mid-nineteenth century, after which the appearance of flong, which could be bent to form curved stereotypes that fit the cylinder perfectly, led to the simpler solution of passing a web of paper between two cylinders, an impression cylinder and a cylinder bearing the material to be printed. Thus there appeared a new generation of enormous machines that only quite recently have become outmoded.[11]

The revolution in printing machinery had been accomplished. Such machines remained too costly as long as they were powered by steam, which required a cumbersome infrastructure, but when they began to be equipped, first with gas motors, then with electric motors, it became feasible to use them in more modest printshops.

It was soon obvious that if a newspaper wanted to be first with the news it not only had to have its copies printed as rapidly as possible but its texts had to be composed without delay. In London during the last years of the eighteenth century the compositors of the *Times* used fonts made up of syllables rather than separate letters, a system that demanded a singularly complicated case. Next someone had the idea of using a keyboard to make characters that would fall out of the machine along a slot into a composing stick.

This technique was used in 1822 in the United States and from 1855 on in France (the first typewriter was not commercially available until 1873) but it was a cumbersome system and only a temporary solution to the problem. In 1845 Gérard de Nerval suggested a method that was to have a brilliant future: a compositor-founder that would use molten metal to make type—letters and signs—as needed and line them up.[12] Linotype was perfected in 1886 by an American of German origin, Ottmar Mergenthaler, and another American, Tolbert Lanston, invented the Monotype machine in 1887–88.

The basic idea of the Linotype machine is to create a metal block or slug containing a line of type. Pressing the keys on a keyboard accesses matrices that fall into a magazine inside the machine like type sorts on a composing stick. Wedges are inserted to fill out and justify the line. The line of type matrices is then sent to a sort of mold into which a jet of molten type metal is injected and the line is cast in one piece. The matrices and the spacing wedges then drop into a sorting box to be returned to their places and the slug drops to join others on the galley.

A Monotype machine uses a three-hundred-key keyboard connected with a justification drum. As the key for each sign is struck, a hole is made on a continuous paper tape. When the operator reaches the end of a line a bell rings, which signals the operator either to split up the word being written or strike the justification key, which will calculate and provide the amount of space needed to fill the line (to "justify" it) and thus to give an even margin. When the text has been written, the perforated tape is placed in another machine that reads the tape and casts the signs one by one from molten type metal, letting each line fall automatically into the galley when it is cast.

These machines were much faster than manual composition: an operator could set five to seven thousand characters per hour with the Linotype or the Monotype machines, and casting machines could process eleven thousand characters per hour. With their appearance toward the end of the nineteenth century and with their widespread use for printing books in the early twentieth century the mechanization of the graphic chain was complete.

During this same period there was an even more important revolution in copying and reproducing images.

Engraving long seemed a largely autonomous art that gave an account of the real world with lines and dots. During the Enlightenment pictorial representation came into fashion and reproduction techniques diversified. Commerce in prints expanded, and artists and technicians sought to offer the broader public works that gave the illusion of pencil drawings, tinted drawings, watercolors, and even oil paintings, enlarging the use of procedures often known in the preceding century and prompting the rise of engravings in color.

One of the new techniques that blossomed in the early industrial age was the mezzotint, a technique that required roughening the surface of a copper plate with a serrated-edged tool called a rocker or a cradle to produce a background that would print as a slightly variegated dark area, on which the artist could burnish lighter-toned areas. Another popular technique was the aquatint, an etching process using applications of acid to bite into a varnished plate that had been grained or crackled by a dusting of powdered resin. A third technique, crayon engraving or crayon manner, used a pointed stippling tool and serrated wheels to give the impression of pencil drawings.

The first known mezzotint was done in Amsterdam in 1642 by Ludwig von Siegen, a native of Kassel. Prince Rupert is reputed to have introduced the technique into England during the Restoration, and in the following century it helped to popularize relatively inexpensive and often political images. It reached its peak of popularity around 1780 with reproductions of the works of Sir Joshua Reynolds. The aquatint, invented in 1650 by Jan Van de Velde, was widely used to imitate the wash drawing and the watercolor, the crayon manner was in use nearly everywhere in the mid-eighteenth century, and after 1773 a Florentine, Francesco Bartolozzi, assured the success of stippled engraving.

Colored prints were all the rage. Some artists—Bartolozzi, for one—used a stencil and pounce, and in 1722 Jakob Christoph Le Blon, in Frankfurt, began to use a series of plates, each with a primary color (blue, red, yellow), often with an additional bister plate for lines and shadings, to produce an image that imitated painting. After 1741 the various members of the Gautier-Dagoty clan contributed to popularizing this method.

Thus techniques were perfected at the beginning of the industrial revolution that would later serve for photomechanical reproduction: three- and four-color reproduction, and even decomposing an image into a series of points, which prefigured the ruled halftone screen.[13]

The last years of the eighteenth century also brought innovations to engraving techniques that would revolutionize prints and, in the early nineteenth century, enlarge their audience. In 1775 Thomas Bewick won a prize in London for a woodcut made from a block of wood cut perpendicular to the grain rather than with it, as was customary. By using small cubes taken from the heart of a fine-grained wood (box, for example), binding them together tightly to form a block, and polishing them well, one had a working surface as resistant as metal that would accept extremely fine-cut lines.

Such techniques were possible only when finer grades of paper became available, either wove paper, which John Baskerville had perfected, or, even better, rice paper. End-grain woodcuts required care during the printing process but they enabled text and image to be printed side by side and they withstood long pressruns. The technique was used constantly in books and periodicals throughout the nineteenth century. Each engraving demanded long and delicate labor on the part of specialized craftsmen, however, and when time was short (as when depictions of news events were needed) a number of workers had to collaborate to engrave portions of the design on wooden cubes later assembled to reconstitute the whole image.

In 1796 Aloys Senefelder, a needy musician in Munich who was searching for a way to reproduce his compositions inexpensively, discovered the properties of the lithographic stone.[14] In lithography a grease-based ink is used to draw on a porous limestone surface. The stone is washed with a syrupy solution of gum arabic and nitric acid, and when the stone is inked with a roller, only the drawn portions retain the ink. One advantage of this technique is that it permits the artist direct and nearly total freedom of expression. Its freedom made it an excellent medium for caricatures and theatrical posters (those of Toulouse-Lautrec come immediately to mind) since decorative handwritten text could be printed along with the image. It was also a rapid and inexpensive way to produce announcements, invitations, and publicity pieces of all sorts.

From the start, techniques of engraving evolved to achieve a better representation of reality. For people in the eighteenth century and until the appearance of photography and photomechanical techniques, this necessarily implied the imitation of drawing and even of painting.

Even in the Renaissance people had dreamed of reproducing exactly what lay before their eyes. Leonardo da Vinci, for instance, described the principles of the camera obscura in 1519, and many artists of his time used it to study problems of perspective. A camera obscura was used to observe an eclipse of the sun at Louvain in 1544. In the mid-sixteenth century the luminosity of the image was augmented by fitting a convex lens and a diaphragm to the aperture.[15]

In the eighteenth century, painters like Canaletto often used the camera obscura to trace an image, and portraitists used it to outline the subject's profile for an engraving. The age's increasing passion for images created a thriving industry for optically accurate views. French and English scientists (Jacques-Alexandre Charles, Sir Humphrey Davy, and Thomas Wedgwood, for example) attempted to obtain images on sensitized papers coated with silver chloride but were unable to fix them (1780–1802), and in England William Hyde Wollaston invented the camera lucida with which images reflected through a glass prism could be projected onto paper.

Photography was finally perfected in a climate of economic boom and rapid technological advance by men who in some ways recall Gutenberg. Like Gutenberg, Joseph-Nicéphore Niepce and his brother Claude were born inventors, and they devised, in rapid succession, an internal combustion engine, a hydrostatic pump, and procedures for extracting sugar from sugar beets. The rise and success of lithography attracted Joseph-Nicéphore to the graphic arts, but because he had little skill in drawing he at first reproduced both images and real scenes, using silver chloride as his predecessors had done. He then copied a portrait of Pius VII, using a bitumen-coated glass plate. Niepce next experimented with a coated pewter plate and an acid solution that eliminated the coating where it had been exposed to light. The result was a negative resembling an etching, but the image required hand finishing (portrait of Cardinal d'Amboise, 1824). In 1826 he succeeded in reproducing the landscape outside his window using an eight-hour exposure time.

In that same year, Niepce established contact with Louis-Jacques Mandé-Daguerre, a painter of theatrical scenery who, together with Charles Marie Bouton, created the diorama, an optical show made by throwing changing lights on large sheets of cloth to give the illusion of perspective and movement. After some hesitation, the two men joined forces (1829). Daguerre brought his experience with the camera obscura to the partnership, and after Niepce's death in 1833 Daguerre and his son Isidore continued the research. Thus the "daguerreotype" was born; it was presented to the Académie des Sciences in 1839, and was widely used in both France and America.

What Daguerre did was to find a way to imprint an image on a silver-plated copper plate treated with iodine vapor, then to develop the latent image by fuming the plate with mercury vapor, which left droplets of mercury on the exposed portions of the plate, and finally to fix the resulting image with a salt solution. By 1851 exposure time had been reduced from eight hours to one minute. This technique produced only one image on metal. During the same period, others—Hippolyte Bayard in France and William Henry Fox Talbot in England—were attempting to print images on paper, and in 1841 Talbot patented the "calotype," or "talbotype," a process that produced a less clear image than the daguerreotype but that had the advantage of offering a negative that could print multiple positive images on paper. The use of a glass plate for the negative and Frederick Scott Archer's invention, in 1851, of the wet collodion process made photography more generally accessible.

Photographic prints required the use of a special paper, however, and one negative could serve for only a limited number of prints. Moreover, the prints did not last well, although that did not prevent publishers like Blanquart-Evrard from publishing books illustrated with tipped-in photographs. Artists were often asked to do lithographic renderings of photographs. Books and newspapers long continued to be illustrated by wood engravings, and stereotypes were often used to obtain a larger number of good prints and to speed up printing. A number of inventors—Armand Fizeau, Edouard Baldus, Charles Nègre, Claude Niepce de Saint-Victor, Walter Bentley Woodbury, Alphonse Poitevin, and many others—worked to perfect techniques for stereotyping images for printing. In France, Firmin Gillot, who was trained as a lithographer, built on the work of Tissier, a chemist, to develop a process (patented in 1850) for "throwing" drawings "into relief" and transferring them from a lithographer's stone or transfer paper to a zinc plate by means of an acid wash. Gillot's son returned to the work of Niepce de Saint-Victor and improved the process by using photographic instead of manual transfer. Thus line photogravure was possible in 1875, but it could not yet render shading or middletones. Soon Talbot thought of using two layers of black gauze as a screen, but the invention of the halftone screen in typographic reproduction is generally credited to Burnett, thanks to his article in the *Photographic Journal* in 1855. It took some thirty years for the process to be perfected, when Ottmar Mergenthaler, born in Germany but a naturalized American, and Frederick E. Ives, also an American, made mechanically ruled crossline screens that could reproduce middletones and shadings by concentrating or spacing out juxtaposed dots. In 1891 two brothers in Philadelphia, Max and Louis Levy, began to manufacture halftone screens. Halftone photoengraving was immediately and widely used for newspaper illustration.

Researchers returned to the technique of Le Blon and the Gautier-Dagoty family to perfect color photogravure. One of these was Charles Cros, who theorized about three-color photography as early as 1867 (and published his theories in 1869), and who experimented with the registration of sound and invented a "paleophone." Another was Louis Ducos du Hauron, who made Cros's theories about color photography practicable. The first three-color photographs appeared in France and Germany between 1870 and 1880.

By the end of the nineteenth century photomechanical techniques for the reproduction of images, the result of this long evolution, were in general use in the press.

❖

The development of modern printing processes took over a century. From 1760 to 1830 England led the way. It was in London in the late eighteenth century that the demi-luxury print industry got its start. The first metal presses were English, as were the first papermaking machines. It was in England that Keonig first perfected his steam-driven press. Finally, it was the English who first attempted to lower the price of books. The first duplication technique, lithography, came from Germany, as did the chromolithograph later.

During this period all operations of the printing process were still largely artisanal. In Paris in particular, papermaking machines and mechanical presses were usually operated by human labor, even in the most advanced firms. It was only between 1830 and 1860, when Germany and the United States gradually took the lead, that real change took place, and the true revolution came only after 1875 with the appearance of woodpulp paper, Linotype and Monotype machines that combined type-casting and composition, and photomechanical printing processes.

A few figures, borrowed from Frédéric Barbier's pioneering dissertation, can serve to show the scope of this change.

The most significant data concern paper production.[16] In 1800 in Saxony, which was admittedly a privileged case, 800 workers working in 80 paper mills that had a total of 90 vats produced 800 tons of paper. During the second half of the century the traditional paper works were gradually replaced by modern machinery. In 1900, 15,427 workers produced 228,000 tons of paper. It might be objected that this was an exceptional case, but statistics tell us that France produced 500,000 quintals (hundredweights) of paper in 1875, and in 1909, after woodpulp paper had been introduced, reached an annual production of 6,000,000 quintals. During the same period annual production in the German Empire went from 2,300,000 to 13,500,000 quintals. This represents an annual consumption at the turn of the twentieth century of 15 quintals of paper for every French citizen and of 20 quintals for every German, or a twentyfold to a fiftyfold increase within a little more than a century. The industrial revolution saw to the omnipresence of the written word.

Typographic shops, which were often founded or modernized with financial backing from paper manufacturers, multiplied at a similar pace. Change was particularly swift in Germany, where there were 18,000 employees and workers in the print industry in 1849, 46,000 in 1875, 116,000 in 1895, 134,000 in 1907, and 224,000 in 1913. Printshop establishments diversified, ranging from small shops to shops that worked for the news press and had enormous rotary presses that consumed huge amounts of paper. By now, however, it was immense factories run like commercial empires that handled the greater part of production.

One example of these was the Berger-Levrault firm founded in Strasbourg in the late seventeenth century. The firm served as the printer for the Army of the Rhine, and during the First Empire it set out to conquer the German market. Things went slowly at first for family reasons, but the firm had a new start in 1850 under two young and enterprising directors, Oscar Berger-Levrault and Jules Norberg. The new directors acquired modern printing presses and other machinery, including the first two machines for founding type introduced into France. They made other improvements, for example, carts that ran on railroad tracks, machines that helped to speed up paper calendering and the preparation of stiffened paper for job printing, and folding machines from Switzerland (1859). They specialized in administrative publications, in particular for the French army. Just before the Franco-Prussian War in 1870–71 they rebuilt their works, but when Germany annexed Alsace-Lorraine in 1879, Berger-Levrault and Norberg decided to remain in France, so they purchased 15,000 square meters of land in Nancy on which to build a new factory. Their new works, built all on one floor, formed a rectangle 88 meters long and 50 meters wide, plus the annexes. The main part of this structure was divided lengthwise into four large galleries for composition, general printing, binding and paper storage, and administrative print jobs and book printing. Foremen stationed on walkways supervised the workers, and the offices, which were grouped together across the entire south end of the building and raised some two feet above the rest, overlooked the shops through glass doors and windows. The complex also included a modern type foundry, shops for stereotypy and electroplating, for lithography, for calendering and drying paper, a repair shop, and a woodworking shop. Each component of this complex was positioned with time-saving in mind, with special attention to flow through the various operations, particularly by the use of the wheeled carts on rails. By 1877 the firm, which had employed only 150 people in 1855, was employing 404 people working ten hours a day (somewhat better than the customary twelve) whose salary had risen 40 percent in twenty years. Among them were 84 compositors (composition was still done by hand), 103 printers, and 8 foremen and proofreaders, aided by 41 master workers, workers, and young girls who worked on ruling, drying, and finishing sheets of paper, 74 binders, 17 foundrymen and stereotpyists, 17 lithographers, and 9 mechanics and woodworkers, plus 52 warehousemen and men of all work. Aside from administrative and military documents (which consumed an average of 160 tons of paper per year) and a large amount of job printing, the Berger-Levrault firm printed 1,114 sheets a year for periodical publications and 701 sheets for works of a variety of sorts, plus a total of 7,261,850 sheets printed on both sides and bound within their walls and another 2,433,575 sheets for volumes reprinted from stereotypes.[17]

One could cite a number of examples of other large factories such as the Martial-Ardent works in Limoges, which specialized in industrial bindings, absorbed other printshops (some quite large ones) and put out a series of prize books with brightly colored bindings.[18] The heart of such large works was an enormous steam engine located in the basement and carefully separated from the workshops, in case of accident, which drove an often impressive set of mechanical presses.

One might well wonder what motivated entrepreneurs in the paper and printing industries to use powerful machines that integrated activities hitherto done by specialized workers. The usual answer is that rising salaries led to mechanization. Some studies even specify that mechanization was often set off by a desire to eliminate specialized workers who thought themselves sufficiently indispensable to challenge their employers.[19] Whether such specialized workers were eliminated or not, the typographers retained their independence of thought and soon showed proof of maturity. It is true that during the Revolution of 1830 print workers in Paris broke up the first mechanical presses imported from England, but they fought royal absolutism side by side with their employers. Aware of the dangers of technological obsolescence, they soon learned to help one another and were leaders in movements for mutual aid and in the trade-union movement. Compositors, who were indeed long irreplaceable and were the elite of their profession, often played a leadership role in the world of labor. They objected vehemently to the employment of women and children, but on occasion they came to an agreement with their employers for action in common. For their part, employers enthusiastically practiced paternalism (at least during the later nineteenth century), providing lodging for the more stable and more highly skilled of their personnel in buildings they had built near the print works, heading mutual aid societies, and helping to found hospitals and schools. Thus print workers, who were relatively well paid, were often regarded as well-off in comparison to the greater mass of the proletariat.

Until the early twentieth century capitalists were more than willing to invest in what appeared to be an expanding market for print. Nonetheless, complex and costly machinery upset all the relationships among the various types of printing. The bulk of the presses' work was now newspapers, government work, and advertising, and increases in fixed costs obliged the industry to work for long pressruns. This meant that redoubled efforts had to be made to enlarge the book market, and the book, a medium whose vocation had been largely elitist, henceforth tended to lose importance from an economic viewpoint.

THE AGE OF THE NEWSPAPER

The eighteenth century had been the age of the book; the nineteenth was the age of the newspaper.[20]

From their first appearance in the seventeenth century, periodicals never ceased to exert an increasing influence on public opinion. Almanacs were published in large numbers, and a specialized press grew up that included not only literary, learned, bibliographical, and medical publications but also gazettes for public announcements and advertising. Yet the authorities of that age found it extremely difficult to grant the news press the margin of liberty indispensable for it to flourish and treat the weightier topics. England was the first to set an example. After the Glorious Revolution and the abolition of the Licensing Act, brilliant and aggressive publicists orchestrated the quarrels between Whigs and Tories and made the fortune of sometimes ephemeral periodicals. The first true daily newspaper, the *Daily Courant*, was first published in 1702, and between 1712 and 1757 the combined circulation of English newspapers increased eightfold. The governing classes took fright when they saw newspaper reading begin to make headway among the people, and in 1712 Parliament passed a newspaper Stamp Act that taxed every copy of newspapers. Next it taxed advertising gazettes, which were already numerous. Taxation—with periodic raises in the tax rates—long held back the growth of the periodical press in Great Britain.

The government also attempted to control the insolence of the pamphleteers by sending them to prison or putting them in the stocks. Although Parliament wanted to keep its deliberations and votes secret, the number of "leaks" was so overwhelming that in 1771, after much resistance, its members were forced to grant the press the right to report on debates. Not long after, the famous remark, attributed to Edmund Burke, was made of the parliamentary journalists seated in the gallery listening to the proceedings, "You are the fourth estate."

War with the American colonies brought even greater numbers of newspapers and pamphlets, and attacks on the government prompted Lord Mansfield to support the removal of questions involving the press from trial by jury (since juries were independent of government control) and placed under the jurisdiction of a judge ordinary. The Libel Act, voted in 1792, guaranteed genuine freedom to printers and booksellers, at the same time authorizing legal redress against journalists whose attacks passed the bounds of the normal violence of the day.

As the British economy picked up, new advances were made in the press. In 1785 John Walter, a Scot who was a printer and bookseller in London, launched a daily that he intended to keep independent of parties and accessible to all, *The Daily Universal Register*, which changed its name to *The Times* in 1788. At nearly the same time a second Scot, James Perry, took over *The Morning Chronicle*, a paper of Whig sympathies, and a third Scot, Daniel Stuart, became owner of *The Morning Post*, a Tory paper. Sunday papers made their appearance, and the provincial news press was growing fast. A climate of competition launched a race for news. The *Times* made its reputation during the Napoleonic wars, when it even sent foreign correspondents to the Continent, while its technical staff developed a system of syllabic type in an attempt to gain time in composition.

The total combined annual circulation of London newspapers rose from 9,464,790 copies sold in the year 1760 to 24,424,713 copies in 1811, and 29,387,843 copies in 1820. There were still misgivings about newspapers in some quarters. When peace returned to Europe after 1815 the Tory government, concerned about mounting radicalism and noting that the *Political Register* had lowered its subscription price by a shilling in order to make the paper more accessible to the working classes, imposed payment of a surety bond on newspapers and raised the rate of the stamp tax. These measures favored the hegemony of the *Times* and brought a degree of stagnation to the press in England during the early nineteenth century. The French press, however, grew remarkably under the July Monarchy.[21]

The French periodical press had developed considerably during the eighteenth century, both inside and outside the borders of the kingdom, but royal censorship hindered all free expression. Everyone knows the famous monologue that Beaumarchais put into the mouth of Figaro in *Le Mariage de Figaro*, which was written only a few years after the decrees of 1777 had brought some flexibility into the rules for permission to publish but retained prior censorship. Figaro declares:

> One day, tired of feeding an obscure guest, they threw me out into the street, and since a man must eat even when out of jail, I sharpen my quill once more and ask people what is in the news. I am told that during my retreat at public expense, free trade and a free press have been established in Madrid, so that, provided I do not write about the government, or about religion, or politics, or morals, or those in power, or public bodies, or the Opera, or the other state theatres, or about anybody who is active in anything, I can print whatever I want with perfect freedom under the supervision of two or three censors. To take advantage of such sweet liberty, I let it be known that I am starting a periodical, and to make sure that I am not treading on anybody's heels, I call it *The Useless Journal*. Mercy! No sooner done than I see a thousand poor devils of subsidized hacks in arms against me. I am put down and once again unemployed.[22]

On the eve of the French Revolution, the men who registered their grievances in the *cahiers de doléance* demanded total liberty of the press. Newspapers and pamphlets were flooding off the presses without preliminary authorization. The government was powerless to control this extraordinary outburst; when it attempted to prohibit publication of Mirabeau's *Etats généraux*, Mirabeau, who had just been elected as a deputy, responded by changing the title of his pamphlet to *Lettres du comte de Mirabeau à ses commettans* (Letters of Count Mirabeau to His Constituents). When the guilds were abolished, a host of small typographical workshops sprang up (in Paris at least) and even more newspapers, occasional pieces, pamphlets, and tracts were printed.

Freedom of the press was thus written into events before it was recognized in texts. The Constituent Assembly attempted to establish the principle of a free press with the Declaration of the Rights of Man and Citizen. Their chief problem was to decide whether or not to retain prior censorship. In the end, article XIX of that document specified that "the free communication of ideas and opinions is one of the most precious of the rights of man; every citizen then can freely speak, write, and print, subject to responsibility for the abuse of this freedom in the cases determined by law." Several months later, on 3 September 1791, the Constitution submitted to the king specified:

> Article 17. No man can be questioned or prosecuted on account of writings which he shall have caused to be printed or published upon any matter whatsoever, unless he may have intentionally instigated disobedience to the law, contempt for the constituted authorities, resistance to their acts, or any of the acts declared crimes or offences by the law.
> Article 18. No one can be tried either by civil or criminal process for written, printed, or published facts, unless it has been recognized and declared by a jury: 1st, whether there is an offence in the writing denounced; 2d, whether the prosecuted person is guilty.[23]

Need we add that these were only pious vows? With the Revolution, the number of both newspapers and pamphlets had considerably increased. The periodicals that reported the debates of the assemblies (or rather, what was heard by the stenographers charged with taking notes in that tumultuous age without microphones) played an essential role. The leaders of the Revolution were often militant journalists: we need only think of Camille Desmoulins, Marat, and Hébert, among others. After a period of relative liberty, however, the fall of the monarchy broke the balance of power among political tendencies. From that point on the parties in power tended to consider illegal the positions of any who expressed opposition to the regime of the moment and its politics. This meant, as Jules Janin noted, that freedom of the press was devoured by its own excesses, and that the Directory was not the last regime to subject journalists to massive repression.[24]

Napoleon Bonaparte, who owed some of his popularity among his soldiers to the newspapers he created for them, was quite aware of the power of the press. When he became First Consul, he set about putting the press to his service. By a decree of 27 Nivôse Year VIII (17 January 1800), he winnowed the 73 newspapers published in Paris (not counting scientific and literary journals and advertising gazettes) down to 13. Next, he set up a censorship bureau under Joseph Fouché, the minister of police, and attempted to reestablish prior censorship. When Napoleon became emperor he went even farther: he had the *Journal des débats* seized and renamed it *Le Journal de l'Empire* (1805), and in 1811 he authorized only four newspapers but confiscated all their property. He also ordered the 170 papers still being published in the provinces to discuss no political questions on their own initiative but to print extracts from *Le Moniteur,* the regime's mouthpiece and a paper that had operated as an official journal of record since 1799 but that also contained articles of general interest. In 1810 Napoleon reduced the numbers of provincial newspapers to one per département.[25]

The newspapers of that age look odd to our eyes. Like most of the newssheets of the ancien régime, revolutionary periodicals appeared in octavo format and were conceived as parts of an annual volume. *Le Moniteur universel,* however, and the *Journal des débats* (later the *Journal de l'Empire*) adopted a folio format and printed their articles in columns. The periodical with the best layout was without doubt *Le Moniteur.* The various members of the Panckoucke family who published it put more effort than their competitors into presenting information clearly. They also ran regular features: political news occupied page one, followed by *variétés* (cultural events), and so forth. Newspapers tended to follow a set order, with foreign news placed first, unlike papers today, which give priority to the most sensational "story." Word of the executions of Louis XVI and Marie-Antoinette was given in the body of the newspapers with no headline, and one paper reported Napoleon's death in the middle of the first page as a one-column item with a headline in ten-point light italics (Raymond Manevy).[26]

Articles were often composed in the order in which news arrived, which meant that the latest news was placed on the last page. However, in an age in which the only time-saving device was the Chappe telegraph, news was slow to arrive and journalists could afford to take a moment to reflect. Thus the coup d'état of 18 Brumaire was reported in the papers on 20 Brumaire, not at the head of page one but in the third column in the section headed *République française,* following news from abroad and reports on military activities. *Le Journal de l'Empire* reported the victory at Austerlitz fifteen days after the battle and on the third page (however, a Bulletin of the Grande Armée had already given word of it).

The emperor never offered news items to the publishers of these newssheets, but he read them regularly. He did express surprise at the mediocrity of the articles they printed, and he suggested that they organize debates on safe subjects like the comparative merits of French and Italian music. His attitude changed completely during the Hundred Days: in an attempt to rally the support of the liberals and to show his opposition to Louis XVIII, who, in spite of the Charter, had reestablished prior censorship, Napoleon proclaimed freedom of the press, abolished prior censorship, and put lawsuits involving the press under trial by jury (article 163 of the Additional Act). Hence during the Hundred Days newspapers enjoyed freedom of expression, and in that short period the emperor went so far as to declare, "My son will reign with freedom of the press: it is a necessary evil."

French society remained traditional under the Restoration. The electoral body was singularly small (eighty thousand voters, most of them property owners), peasants still made up the overwhelming majority of the population, and the liberal bourgeoisie was prevented from wielding power. Communication was still slow and fragmented. Under such conditions, the relatively high price of newspapers made them accessible to a restricted minority only, and many potential readers went to the cafés or the *cabinets de lecture* to consult newspapers, if they were not reduced to giving them up altogether.[27]

Nonetheless, newspaper editors had every intention of giving their opinion on a wide range of topics, and the many and active pamphleteers of the time already held a formidable power in a divided society passionately involved in politics. Under Louis XVIII at least, the monarchy attempted to carry out a policy of relative tolerance, but even he found the aggressive attitude of the opposition journalists unbearable, and when a crisis loomed he viewed the press as an instrument of perversion that threatened to set off an explosion among the masses. The problems posed by freedom of the press prompted heated debate, and the king's attitude fluctuated with circumstances. There were periodic returns to authorizations to print and prior censorship, certain offenses were removed from jury trial, stamp taxes were reestablished, and surety bonds were set so high that it became impossible to launch a periodical without the backing of wealthy patrons. These measures quite naturally exasperated the liberal bourgeoisie, spearheaded by journalists, printers, and booksellers.

An already tense situation worsened when Charles X attempted to turn back the clock. This became clear when Joseph Villèle, president of the Council, attempted to put through a law that would have subjected all printed matter to previous submission (five days prior to publication in the case of newspapers) before it could be put on sale. *Le Moniteur* called this proposal a "law of justice and love," but it aroused such protest that the minister was obliged to retire it. Two years later, however, the king replaced the relatively liberal Martignac with the ultraroyalist Polignac, seconded by General Bourmont, who had betrayed Napoleon on the eve of Waterloo. The fury of the opposition press knew no bounds, and a small group of men led by Jacques Lafitte and that included the booksellers Sautelet, Bossange, and Jacques Renouard (the son of another great bookseller, Antoine-Augustin Renouard) launched an opposition newspaper, *Le National*, entrusting editorial responsibilities to two southerners, Adolphe Thiers and François Mignet, and Armand Carrel.[28] The king and the new president of the Council responded to the increasing attacks on their policies by dissolving the Chamber of Deputies and enacting four ordinances, the first of which decreed that newspapers must have authorization to publish (renewable every three years), adding that the presses and the type fonts used to publish any unauthorized papers would be seized (25 July 1830). This lit the powder keg, brought on the July Revolution ("Les Trois Glorieuses," 27–29 July 1830), the fall of Charles X, and the proclamation of Louis-Philippe, duc d'Orléans, as regent of the kingdom and then king of the French.

This was a striking confirmation of the power of the press. The affair was conducted, however, by an extremely small nucleus of determined men risking their all, and it came at a time when most booksellers—like many other businessmen—were bankrupt or on the verge of bankruptcy and counted on the establishment of a regime more favorable to their interests as a way out of their troubles. It seems astonishing to us that the victorious newspapers had a circulation that was extremely small by modern standards: a letter of the prefect of police to Casimir Périer notes as remarkable that the leading periodicals published in Paris went from a circulation of 61,000 in 1830 to an average of 77,500 in the three first months of 1831. In the liberal press in the same periods, the circulation of *Le Constitutionnel* went from 18,600 to 23,300; *Le Courrier français* from 5,490 to 8,750; *Le Temps* from 5,150 to 8,500; *Le National* from 2,320 to 3,280.[29] The press revolution was still to come.

❖

The effects of the industrial revolution began to be felt after 1830 and even more after 1840. Henceforth, the time had come for industrialization, speculation, and the accumulation of wealth, thus providing a climate that strengthened the liberal bourgeoisie and led to the rapid emergence of a middle class passionately involved in politics and avid for news.

At the same time, outlets needed to be found for the new products made by assembly-line methods whose prices were forced down by the adoption of new technologies every time the market lagged. Lithography flourished, along with chromolithography, which could be used to print large runs of attractive posters, sale catalogues, and advertisements, as well as the usual invitations and announcements.

Some of the more enterprising bourgeois embarked on the task of restructuring the press, gradually making it more accessible by opening it up to advertising. Emile de Girardin may not have been the father of the transformations that ensued, but he remains their symbol.

Born in 1806 the natural (and unrecognized) son of comte Alexandre de Girardin, who was at the time captain and commander of a regiment of the imperial horse guard, and a married woman, Emile was brought up in secret under the name of Emile Delamothe by a friend of his mother's, first in Paris, then in the Orne, where he learned to read from the parish priest of the village and only irregularly dipped into the history books in the library in the château of his protectress. He returned to Paris, where he did little for some years until he wrote an autobiographical novel, *Emile,* and boldly took the name of Emile de Girardin. Sensing instinctively the transformation that was in the making, he decided that journalism could assure him the fortune and fame he craved in order to blot out the memory of his early poverty and the stigma of his illegitimate birth. An ambitious and seemingly cold and calculating man, Girardin was capable of incredible boldness once he had made a decision. He was to encounter striking success in his chosen profession.

He and a friend decided to start a periodical, but since they lacked capital, the weekly was entitled *Le Voleur* (The Thief) and it reprinted the best articles that had appeared elsewhere during the week, saving editorial costs. The operation earned Girardin a duel and a scratch on the shoulder, but it also brought its founders 50,000 francs a year.

The following year, 1829, when Emile de Girardin was only twenty-three, he created another weekly, *La Mode,* which became the voice of an aristocratic and worldly *tout-Paris*. This time the periodical had contributors as brilliant as Balzac and Dumas. Above all, it was illustrated by such artists as Gavarni.

After this promising start Girardin married the charming Delphine Gay, whose mother had a literary salon and who, at the age of twenty, was regarded as a national poetess and the muse of a nascent Romanticism (1830). Girardin went on from one audacious move to another; he was equally successful at founding newspapers and publishing houses that put out inexpensive books, and he was elected to the Chamber of Deputies.[30]

In an age in which large-circulation publications were being founded everywhere, Girardin's spectacular successes encouraged him to become the theoretician of a mass press, and he discovered that he had a vocation to educate the public, whose rise he linked to the development of primary education.

If this educational goal was to be realized, the subscription price of periodicals needed to be low. A conservative publication, *Le Journal général de la France*, had been launched on 15 March 1836 at a subscription price of 48 francs instead of the customary 80 francs, just as Girardin was negotiating with another journalist, Armand Dutacq, to found a low-cost daily. When the two men failed to reach an agreement they started two competing papers, *La Presse* and *Le Siècle*, which first appeared on the same day, 1 July 1836, and sold for the same subscription price of 40 francs—a price that did not cover their costs but that was feasible if circulation figures were sufficiently high to attract the sizable revenues that could now be earned from advertising. Girardin described how this worked in the first issue of *La Presse:*

> The return from announcements being proportional to the number of subscribers, the subscription price must be lowered to the extreme in order to raise the number of subscribers to the highest possible level. It is up to the advertisers to pay for the paper. . . . At the price of 40 francs per year, ten thousand subscribers will be easier to acquire than a mere one thousand would be at a price of 80 francs. *La Presse* will have gone beyond this number within six months. This is our opinion, founded on experience and on a study and a profound knowledge of the periodical press.

Girardin's calculations proved correct. At the end of six months, *La Presse* had 10,000 subscribers and soon reached 20,000, while *Le Siècle*, which had chosen the more comfortable position of an opposition paper, reached a circulation of 40,000 only after some years. Other papers soon followed

Girardin's example, and in 1846 the twenty-five dailies published in Paris had a combined circulation of some 180,000 subscribers.

Today we can measure the effects of the revolution that began at that time. As the creator of the modern news press, Girardin has been accused of infecting it with all its vices. His duel may be symbolic. It opposed Emile de Girardin, a businessman who adjusted the opinions of his paper according to their profitability and who was even suspected of having sold out his paper to the power structure for two months on the promise—never fulfilled—that his father would be ennobled, and Armand Carrel, a graduate of Saint-Cyr, a Bonapartist, a member of the Carbonari, and a man devoted to liberty. It was Carrel who was killed.

But it was not enough simply to lower the price of a paper to reach the large circulation figures that the publishers wanted; readers had to be attracted and kept.

In order to do so, Emile de Girardin and his imitators turned to the most famous writers of the day. Some wrote a column, but most serialized novels that often contributed enormously to the success of the dailies. This was how Chateaubriand's *Mémoires d'outre-tombe* was first published, as were Victor Hugo's *Le Rhin* and Lamartine's *Les Confidences* and *L'Histoire des Girondins*. The greatest successes were probably the novels addressed to a female readership such as Balzac's *Scènes de la vie privée*, published in *La Presse*, or Dumas's *Capitaine Paul*, which added 5,000 subscribers to the list of *Le Siècle*. Similarly, Eugène Sue's *Les mystères de Paris* filled the coffers of the *Journal des débats*, while his *Le juif errant* helped *Le Constitutionnel* to sell 20,000 extra copies. The fashion for serial novels spread to other countries, and there were innumerable "mysteries" in imitation of the Paris original.

Thus the press offered writers new forms of activity and literature was put to the service of advertising. This inevitably brought on a gradual change in forms of writing, and authors became less interested in expressing their personal sentiments and convictions and more intent on attracting readers by offering them a reflection of their own universe and their own fantasies.

Images had multiplied along with texts. The appearance of lithography had brought about a genuine revolution in illustration: original works by artists could now be reproduced in multiple copies, which perfectly fitted the bourgeois spirit of the age. Lithography was soon used to make large numbers of landscapes, views of famous monuments, and reproductions of works of art. It enabled Delacroix, for example, to make his famous series of illustrations for Goethe's *Faust,* and it lay behind the monumental publishing venture of the *Voyages pittoresques et romantiques dans l'Ancienne France* of Taylor and Nodier, volumes of which continued to be published throughout the century. It helped pictures to invade the periodical. In France Girardin used lithography to illustrate *La Mode* (1829), but above all it encouraged the rise of political and satirical caricatures, leading to the appearance in 1832 of two satirical journals, *La Caricature* and *Le Charivari,* that featured the talents of Philippon and Daumier. Lithography still could not conveniently be used except as a separate plate, which meant that wood engraving was the technique most widely used. Wood engraving allowed printers to combine texts and their illustrations on the same page, printing them on the same press, and in the long run it proved more economical, even though it required armies of engravers working not only on documentary illustration but also on the satirical works of the most famous artists. Wood engraving was used to launch low-cost illustrated periodicals, in England in 1830 with the *Penny Magazine,* then in Germany in 1833 with the *Pfennig Magazin,* which later had a circulation of hundreds of thousands of copies.[31]

Next came the era of the "Illustrateds": *The Illustrated London News,* a sixteen-page periodical printed with three columns per page and twelve small illustrations (1842), then *L'Illustration* in Paris and the *Illustrierte Zeitung* of Leipzig (1843). Finally, the famous *Fliegende Blätter* (1844) published caricatures on topics of current interest in Germany, and *Punch* began its long career in England.

By 1850 the future was clear. The elimination of "taxes on knowledge" gave the British press a new start, and in the vast expanse of the United States newspapers had an essential role to play. Nearly everywhere periodicals set out to win the largest possible readership. The industrial revolution was a circulation revolution—the circulation of people, of objects, and of news, aided by railroads, steamships, and the electric telegraph—that launched the bourgeoisie of Europe on its conquest of the world. It prompted the rise of new forms of communication by texts and images that broadened horizons and transmitted information with ever-greater speed. This meant that competition among the big dailies increasingly took the form of a fight to be the first to provide their readers with information. The English at first led in news-gathering: the *Times* placed correspondents in the larger cities of Europe and had news sent by special couriers who on occasion were paid by John Walter himself. In 1837 the *Times,* in agreement with two other papers, obtained word of the Sepoy mutiny in India in record time by having dispatches carried by sea to the Gulf of Suez then by camel back to Alexandria to a waiting ship. Soon, however, the English found worthy rivals in the Americans. James Gordon Bennett, a native of Scotland and the publisher of *The Morning Herald*, was the first to send a packet boat to meet ships arriving from Europe so as to scoop the other papers on news from the Continent.[32]

In a new world in which rapid communication was being established but the communication network still had large gaps, a new figure, the reporter, played an important part in the race to be the first with the news. One of these was William Howard Russell. During the Crimean War Russell wrote articles for the *Times* of London denouncing official mismanagement and the sorry situation in the British hospital services. His articles contributed to the fall of the Aberdeen cabinet, and heads of state treated him as a power to be handled with care. There was also Archibald Forbes, a Scot, who followed the German army during its campaigns in 1870 and 1871 and wrote cool-headed dispatches under fire for *The Daily News* in the "telegraphic" style he helped to popularize.

When it became obvious that the press was becoming industrialized, agencies were formed for the collection and sale of news. In 1832 Correspondance Garnier in Paris lithographed extracts from foreign newspapers, adding news and, after 1840, reports from a German correspondent. When Charles Havas bought the firm he renamed it Agence Havas, and he utilized the telegraph, pigeons, and all other new means of communication to speed information to his subscribers. One of Havas's men moved to England, adopted the name Paul Julius von Reuter, and founded the agency in London that soon became the greatest in Britain. In Germany the Wolff Agency was founded in 1849. The support of the Prussian government helped it to grow after 1860, and it soon functioned as the semiofficial agency of the German Empire.[33]

In spite of its many advances, the periodical press in Europe during the early nineteenth century reached only a minority of notables and members of the middle classes. The only exceptions were short-lived newspapers inspired by the workers' movement, whose influence was out of proportion to their limited circulation and means.

Attempts had been made to found workers' newspapers. In Great Britain, where an exorbitant stamp tax increased the price of papers, the Socialist printer Henry Hetherington, choosing a moment in which the struggle for reform of the electoral law was at its height (1831), launched a weekly, *The Poor Man's Guardian*, that declared itself in its motto, "A weekly newspaper for the people established counter to law to try the power of Might against Right." The government responded by arresting and sentencing a number of peddlers who carried the paper, and Hetherington had to give up after a long struggle.

Around the same time, a workers' press developed in Lyons. The most famous of its newspapers was *L'Echo de la fabrique*. Founded in 1831 and financed by mutual aid societies, it served as a cover for a number of underground organizations. The paper's principal editor, Marius Chastaing, preached trade solidarity. Uniting the working class proved a task as yet too difficult, and Chastaing give up *L'Echo de la fabrique* in 1845 in order to found a monthly, *La Tribune lyonnaise*, but two years later, in 1847, it had only 300 subscribers. Another periodical, *La Glaneuse*, championed radical ideas in the early days of the July Monarchy, but it disappeared fairly soon, after costly lawsuits, leaving only *Le Précurseur*, which managed to survive with the support of the Société des droits de l'Homme (Tudesq). These periodicals give a notion of both the dynamism of the labor movement and of the difficulties it had in creating some sort of structure for itself.

In Prussia, where Frederick William IV seemed favorable to liberal ideas and attempted to relax censorship (1841), a group of Cologne burghers founded the *Rheinische Zeitung* and hired Karl Marx as its editor. Soon recognized as an excellent journalist, Marx took up the defense of the proletariat and the downtrodden, with the result that his paper was suppressed in 1843. The situation changed with the Revolution of 1848, and the *Neue Rheinische Zeitung* under Marx's leadership had as many as 6,000 subscribers. He was eventually expelled from Prussia, however.

The events of 1848 gave rise to papers of all tendencies whose existence was agitated and short. This was particularly true in France, as André-Jean Tudesq has shown. In a first phase newspapers of democratic sympathies multiplied. Next there came a reshuffling of the most prominent periodicals, and the new ones that appeared were often aimed at the new class of voters. After the "June Days," however, the Cavaignac government opted for reaction. A number of periodicals stopped publication, and La Mennais, unable to pay the required security deposit, announced the demise of *Le Peuple constituant* on 11 July 1848. He stated, "*Le Peuple constituant* began with the Republic; it ends with the Republic. For what we see is certainly not the Republic; it is not even anything that has a name. Today you need gold, much gold, in order to enjoy the right to speak: we are not rich enough. Silence to the poor!" Subsequently, a number of newspaper people were arrested or deported and their newspapers or revues were suppressed in the coup d'état of 2 December 1851. The Second Empire simply completed, perfected, and applied the arsenal of repressive weapons that it had inherited.

Already, however, a totally different kind of mass press was developing in the United States.[34] The printer-journalist had appeared early in America, where he served to connect a widely scattered population to the world beyond. Newspapers normally had quite low circulation figures. In 1833, however, Benjamin Henry Day set the per copy price of the newspaper he founded, the New York Sun, at a modest one cent at a time when New York papers normally cost six cents. The Sun's daily circulation rose to 5,000 within six months, to 10,000 within a year, and reached 19,000 by 1835. The New York Herald had a daily circulation of 33,000 in 1849. Later Horace Greeley's Tribune and Henry Jarvis Raymond's New York Times (1851) competed with their two precursors.

Benjamin Day achieved high circulation figures by appealing to an unsophisticated public, relying not on the serial novel, as on the Continent, but on sensationalism and detailed accounts of bloody domestic dramas. James Gordon Bennett sought a more cultivated public with reports on what was going on at the Opera, on Wall Street, or in the national conventions of religious sects. He sent reporters to interview the families of people involved in some newsworthy event, and he maintained foreign correspondents in all the European capitals. The New York Times specialized in instructive articles, for instance publishing a series of articles on daily life and race relations in the South just before the outbreak of the Civil War.

In 1850 there were 240 dailies in the United States with a total daily circulation of 750,000. The Mexican War (1846–48) and then the Civil War (1861–65) occasioned special reporting that increased sales, and American economic development after the Civil War encouraged entrepreneurs like William Randolph Hearst and Joseph Pulitzer to launch newspapers that returned to the per copy price of one penny. Every large city soon had its press, and before long newspaper chains were organized that furnished the entire United States not only with local news but also with news about the country as a whole and the world. By 1910 there were 2,340 dailies in the United States with a combined daily circulation of 24,000,000 copies.

In Europe the French, whose economy was expanding at a slower rate than England's or Germany's, proved particularly open to new ventures. After a period of total freedom of the press during the Second Republic, the French press was again subject to prior authorization from 1852 to 1868. It nonetheless developed considerably, and it even enjoyed relative freedom under the liberal Empire and the parliamentary Empire. As a result the overall circulation of daily newspapers in Paris rose from 150,000 in 1852 to one million in 1870, and dailies and political weeklies published in the provinces doubled their circulation between 1853 and 1870, when they reached 900,000 copies. The press in France was subjected to fairly strict regulation after 1870, but after 1881 it benefited from a law considered a monument of liberalism.

The French legislators attempted to guarantee a maximum of liberty to newspapers. The law eliminated all prior authorization and control. Henceforth the only formalities needed to put out a book were to publish the name of its printer or, for a periodical, to give the name of the director who held legal responsibility. When a person was mentioned by name in a periodical publication, he or she could exercise a right to respond and demand that a rectification or response of equal length be printed in the same place and in the same size of type. Opinion was no longer a criminal offense, although the law provided for certain offenses under common law that a journal might commit, such as libel, defamation of character, or incitement to crime. In the same spirit, the law punished falsehood only when inaccuracies were published in bad faith or when public order was disturbed. Press offenses were subject to trial by jury, except for defamation, which was judged by the criminal courts. Finally, if a lawsuit was instituted, the publisher of the paper (often a figurehead) or the publisher of a book was held responsible; the author could be answerable only for complicity.

The newspaper in France never held a greater sway over the masses than during the early years of the Third Republic (1871–1914) when the politically active press was at its height. Most journalists took sides in the bitter controversies opposing royalists and republicans: during the crisis of 1877, Adrien Hébrard, the publisher of *Le Temps*, Pierre Jourda of *Le Siècle*, Jules Bapst of *Les Débats*, Edmont About of *Dix-Neuvième Siècle*, Auguste Vacquerie of *Le Rappel*, the aging Emile de Girardin, still at the helm of *La France* and *Le Petit Journal*, all rallied around Gambetta, and they played an important role in the fall of Mac-Mahon. Similarly, French newspaper editors exerted considerable influence at the time of Boulangism and during the Panama scandal. The finest hour of the political press came with the Dreyfus affair: we all know the story of Emile Zola's famous article, "J'accuse!" in Clemenceau's *L'Aurore*. [35]

The power of the press in that age can be understood only when we recall that the newspaper was the only instrument of mass communication. Without the newspaper, Boulanger's popularity could never have spread through all of France and the Dreyfus affair would not have been national in scope. For a long time most newspapers had only a limited circulation. Although a circulation of 50,000 was considered very large under the Second Empire, in the period of the Boulangist movement *La Lanterne* in Rochefort and *La Presse*, the official party organ, reached circulations of 100,000 and even 200,000.

As in America, however, the great mass of the population in France, which was by that time literate, demanded another type of information. They found it in the prodigious growth of another and much more profitable sort of newspaper, the general nonpolitical daily.

The financier Polydore Milhaud took an important step in this direction when he set the price of *Le Petit Journal*, which he founded in 1863, at only one sou. His excellent editorial team included Edmond About and Francisque Sarcey and the even more famous reporter Timothée Trimm. Holding that the role of a newspaper publisher was not to dictate a political line but to guarantee circulation, Milhaud used all the tricks of publicity to launch his daily and stated that one had to have the courage to be foolish to increase circulation. His detractors claimed that he had stooped at nothing to achieve a daily circulation of 83,000 copies. *Le Petit Journal* reached its full strength after Milhaud's death in 1871, when Hippolyte Marinoni and Emile de Girardin took it over. In 1877 its circulation reached 500,000, and later it was the first French paper to reach one million. It soon met a formidable competitor in *Le Petit Parisien*, founded in 1876 and (after 1888) directed by Jean Dupuy, who served as a government minister on several occasions. Dupuy not only developed the paper's sports page and sought out good serial novels (by Ponson du Terrail, Gaboriau, and Michel Zévaco); he also encouraged his engineer, Jules Dierrey, to design rotary presses that could print six and eventually ten pages (although Marinoni's *Le Petit Journal* was still doing well with its four pages). *Le Petit Parisien*'s circulation rose to 1,550,000 just before World War I. In 1896 *Le Matin* passed into the hands of Henry Poidatz, a financier, and Maurice Bunau-Varilla, a contractor who specialized in public works. After 1903 it expanded further under Bunau-Varilla alone, who (according to Raymond Manevy) posed as a champion of justice, virtue, and truth, but in reality cultivated sensationalism and devoted a large amount of space to air meets and automobile races. Henri de Jouvenel and Gaston Leroux (the creator of Rouletabille, the hero of a popular crime series) helped the paper to reach a circulation of 650,000 in 1907 and 900,000 in 1914. The fourth large daily, *Le Journal,* which had begun as a satirical paper, had a prime objective of making the greatest names of literature available to all purses, and it managed to gather a brilliant list of contributors. First Catulle Mendès then Henri de Régnier edited the literary section, which published Lucien Descaves, Tristan Bernard, Abel Hermant, Henri Lavedan, Jules Claretie, Victor Margueritte, Jean Richepin, and many others. *Le Journal* also had a team of crack reporters and sportswriters whose names were equally famous at the time.[36]

Le Matin and *Le Journal* served a more middle-class readership than *Le Petit Journal* or *Le Petit Parisien*. Their high pressruns made them subject to costly remainders. *Le Matin* engaged in some campaigns (even on topics of secondary importance) that lost it as many as 100,000 or 200,000 readers who went over to *Le Journal*—readers whom it had to win back gradually. It is obvious that these dailies systematically avoided taking too clear a position on political questions so as not to irritate a public as diverse as it was large. The publishers of these papers preferred to feature sports and human-interest stories that catered to the tastes of their readership.

During the same period increased advertising and bitter competition led to lowering the price of a daily newspaper to one half-penny in England in 1855. Some forty years later, Alfred Harmsworth, who became Viscount Northcliffe in 1906 and won the nickname of "the Napoleon of the press," set the price of the *Daily Mail* at a half-penny, and it reached a circulation of 200,000 two months after it first appeared in 1896. Soon after, the *Daily Express* followed suit, and it soon passed into the hands of a Canadian familiar with American advertising methods, the future Lord Beaverbrook.

After promulgation in 1874 of the law unifying supervision of the press in Germany, the German press made considerable advances but in a decentralized empire it remained fragmented. Newspapers in the largest city in each region and even in smaller towns were strengthened by the law, but before 1914 Germany had no national newspapers as powerful as the French and English papers.

The period was the golden age of the French press. Henceforth the big dailies required sophisticated machinery, not only enormous rotary presses but also composing machines and facilities for making halftone illustrations. Still, the collection and distribution of news became increasingly complex. As it often happens, the only big daily newspapers that long survived were backed by powerful financiers and had large pressruns. One natural result was a concentration that began even before World War I and that was particularly striking in the United States.

The impact of this scandal-mongering press aimed at high circulation figures and increasingly subservient to advertising raises some questions. Henceforth the newspapers that emphasized "serious" news—the *Times* in London and *Le Temps* in France—risked becoming something like confidential news sources. There was a new opinion-press that developed (notably in France) that played an important role after the war.

The Socialist press, as we have seen, was unable to find a stable structural base, but it nonetheless had a profound influence on thought. *Le Socialiste,* for example, the organ of the workers' party, published the first translation (by Laura Lafargue, Karl Marx's daughter) of *The Communist Manifesto* to be approved by Engels (1885). The text was picked up by several local newspapers—*Le Déshérité* of Roanne, *La Défense des ouvriers* of Montluçon, *Le Réveil du forçat* of Roubaix, and *La Défense des travailleurs* of Reims—which also reprinted several pages of *Le Socialiste* along with articles and news items of local interest. In 1904 Jaurès founded *L'Humanité* and the following year, after the Congress of Unity (April 1905), it became the official organ of the SFIO. Under Jaurès's direction *L'Humanité* published documented investigations of the financial establishment and articles protesting loans to Russia, the war in Morocco, and other issues. The paper had a brilliant staff of editors, writers, and contributors that included such names as René Viviani, Aristide Briand, and Albert Thomas, as well as Jules Guesde, Paul Lafargue and Edouard Vaillant, Octave Mirabeau, Tristan Bernard, Gustave Lanson, Georges Lecompte, Abel Hermant, Jules Renard, and Anatole France. Still, it took the full prestige and energy of the paper's founder to keep *L'Humanité* from going under within a few years.

During this same period, Charles Maurras elaborated the doctrine of integral nationalism, and Léon Vaugeois, Léon Daudet, and Bernard de Vézins founded *L'Action française*. This newspaper, which exerted a profound influence in rightist milieus in France and was directed for more than thirty years by the same editorial team, never had a high circulation. The same was true of the periodicals backed by the Christian Democrats, *Le Sillon, La Démocratie,* and later *L'Aube*. [37]

The late nineteenth and early twentieth century was the golden age of the daily press, still unrivaled in the dissemination of information. The use of advertising had enabled papers to multiply, although France lagged be-hind other European countries in this regard, its large-circulation dailies usually having no more than twelve pages up till World War I. The German papers and especially the English and American papers, however, had al-ready begun to expand.

At least in the big cities, the newspapers succeeded in reaching the gen-eral population, whose cultural and educational level was often low. The price they paid to do so was a constant effort to adapt to their readers' tastes, disapproving anything that might divide or shock their public and pushing aside other problems. Newspapers and other periodicals also tended to diversify. The local and regional press, which was closer to its public and offered it information of immediate interest, grew by leaps and bounds in the United States and in Germany but also in France. Since the nineteenth century was also a great age for literary and learned reviews, the press structured opinion on a variety of social levels.

The way that newspapers presented their information evolved only slowly. We can of course easily distinguish low-cost newspapers printed on poor paper from the more costly papers published for a wealthier reader-ship, but on the whole they all give today's readers an impression of gray-ness and uniformity. With the exception of certain specialized publications, the overwhelming majority of the newspapers put out in 1900 had no illustrations other than line drawings. Their first page normally began with an article that was continued over several columns. Articles that did not finish on one page were carried over to the head of the next page, but with no systematic reference to the page where the reader could find the con-tinuation. The articles seemed more interested in appealing to reason and curiosity than in stirring their readers' emotions.[38] Since readers were less hurried than they are today, there was no attempt to extract the essence of the news in a headline and subheads. Finally, columns designed to make the average reader reflect—*la chronique*—were often signed by a well-known name. The newspaper was not yet designed to be read quickly. Things began to change, however, in the early years of the twentieth cen-tury. Headlines began to appear, in particular in the popular press, and improvements in photogravure made it possible for illustrations to give an immediate account of important happenings. There was already a weekly, *L'Excelsior* (a distant ancestor of *Paris-Soir* today), based on the principle that a picture informs better and is more pleasing than a long discourse.

One might well ask to what extent the long struggle to liberate the press from the yoke of politics facilitated the development of a truly independent press. The answer would require a good many reservations, to say the least. It is true that the reading of a printed text, a newspaper in particular, has never led its readers to change their deeply held opinions. Nonetheless news and the way the news is written, the way a prominent person is presented, judgments made about the policies of a country, or the denunciation of real or imaginary scandals can make opinion evolve in one direction or in another. Financial news can shift the trend of speculative investment. The editors and publishers of the opinion-press (whose circulation remained relatively small) were almost automatically obliged to appeal to private capital in order to survive, and such support is rarely disinterested.

On the other hand popular newspapers with a low copy price and a high circulation were slaves to advertising. Hence the appearance of specialized intermediaries (whose activities Pierre Albert has described in *L'histoire générale de la presse française*) [39] who charged a fee for using their good offices and guaranteed a bank or an industry a "good press" in a specified number of papers and for a particular matter. The "publicity" they assured in this manner was not always apparent, and the sums paid often remained in the hands of someone along the chain of command. Over a fifteen-year period the Crédit Foncier spent 60 million francs (22 million of which went directly to newspapers) in an attempt to create a favorable climate for loans it hoped to make, and it did so with the acquiescence of certain ministers of finance who were happy not to have to use their own secret funds. It is hardly surprising that the accusations of corruption in the Panama affair touched a good many French newspapers as well as members of Parlement.

The affair of loans to Russia, well publicized since that time thanks to the Soviet government's publication of a number of documents from the Czarist archives, was much more serious. Russia, eager for access to French savings (the well-known *bas de laine* in which the French were reputed to keep gold), first distributed modest sums to publicize and prepare the successful negotiation of these loans. The payments grew higher in 1901 and 1902, on the request of the head of the brokers' association, who was concerned to see public sentiment turning against the loans, and they rose still more in 1905 during the Russo-Japanese war and the October Revolution. The distribution of this manna continued for some time with the accord of the French government, and in 1913 no less a person than Raymond Poincaré, at the time president of the Council, and his minister of finance, Reinhold Klotz, even asked the Russians to distribute large sums to a certain number of radical newspapers in order to facilitate the vote on military laws and to help out the government in a delicate situation.[40]

The Response of the Book

During the nineteenth century the newspaper managed to adapt to the demands of a society that was arriving at full literacy. The periodical press demanded ever more powerful and more advanced machinery capable of furnishing the same product in greater quantity, faster, and cheaper. How did the book, which until that time had served relatively small elites, respond to this challenge?

Great Britain offers one answer to that question. We should note, without repeating what has already been said about Britain's precocious demographic and economic development, that this growth was accompanied by a proliferation of printed matter of all sorts, newspapers and prospectuses, books and tracts, but also print engravings. Artisanal engraving techniques underwent notable improvement in England, as seen, for example, in the mezzotint or in Thomas Bewick's invention of end-grain wood engraving (1773). England also had the first all-metal press in Europe, developed by Lord Stanhope in 1799, then the first machine press, invented by Friedrich Koenig and put into service by the *Times* in 1813–14. Early nineteenth-century England also had the first machines to make paper (which were based on a French idea, however), machines that helped respond to a growing paper shortage caused by both progress in writing and a dwindling supply of raw materials.

Book publishing in England at this time was organized around two centers, London and Edinburgh, and the publisher was beginning to be distinct from the bookseller. Powerful firms published both periodicals and books. It is striking to see the same names on the honor roll of great publishers from the eighteenth to the nineteenth centuries and to today: Longman, Rivington, Constable and Murray; later, Blackwood, Chambers, Nelson, Macmillan, Black, and Black and Cassel. Publishing was so successful that its leading figures found it difficult to adjust to the industrial revolution. Was it not better to continue to offer recent works to a narrow audience willing to pay a high price rather than seek to win over a mass of potential readers, social newcomers who often had limited cultural baggage and limited means? At the end of the eighteenth century British booksellers continued to address a public of perhaps some eighty thousand readers. Increased readership was also blocked by the fact that the leading publishers opted to enforce the perpetual copyright on their lists in spite of the copyright law of 1709. Pirated editions from Scotland and Ireland helped to lower prices, however, some enterprising publishers put out low-priced reprints of works that had fallen into the public domain, and realistic booksellers began to sell overstock at cut prices rather than destroy their remainders, as was the custom. These were all marginal initiatives, however, in comparison with the practices of the book-trade "establishment." Traveling libraries became popular, as did subscription lending libraries that, for a modest cost, made new works more readily available to the middle classes. Not only the traditional chapbooks but also series of low-cost books that were inspired by a lively religious proselytism and, after the French Revolution, by political radicalism also met with enormous success.

The Methodists were among those who offered new readers other reading matter than the traditional peddlers' books or ballads. Reading was as important for them as it was for the Scots Presbyterians. After 1740 the Methodist Book Room in London served as headquarters for the distribution of a host of works, and, in an effort to make such works better known, Charles Wesley himself condensed and adapted *The Pilgrim's Progress, Paradise Lost,* and Henry Brooke's *Fool of Quality,* rebaptized for the occasion *The History of Henry, Count of Moreland.* The Methodists' lists remained small, however, and (except for Welsey's works) their selections were often somewhat narrow-minded. It was another fifty years before the masses again became the target of printed propaganda on a grand scale. At the outbreak of the French Revolution Edmund Burke published his *Reflections on the Revolution in France* (1790) denouncing the excesses committed on the Continent. This pamphlet of conservative inspiration was enormously successful (30,000 copies sold), and it was followed by responses from the radicals, the most famous of which was Thomas Paine's *The Rights of Man* (1791), which was printed in hundreds of thousands of copies if not over a million in the next few years. The religious activists were just as upset as members of the governing classes to find works like Paine's among the more traditional chapbooks in peddlers' bundles. The actress, playwright, and evangelist Hannah More headed a movement to develop a popular literature that would promote the security of the nation and the glory of God, the "Cheap Repository Tracts," a long list of booklets sold in the thousands by peddlers and booksellers at a modest price between a half-penny and a penny and a half. Almost immediately a number of religious societies launched similar initiatives. Among the most famous of these were the Religious Tract Society founded in 1799, which printed

314,000 tracts in 1804, Drummond's Tract Depository Society based in Scotland in Stirling, and the British and Foreign Bible Society, which distributed some two and a half million copies of the Bible and the New Testament between 1804 and 1819. In other words, massive amounts of books were involved.

The established publishers began to show an interest in low-cost books when all this religious proselytizing led Lord Brougham, Charles Knight, and others to found the Society for the Diffusion of Useful Knowledge, which aimed at providing materials to adults interested in completing their education. In 1827 the society launched a collection, the *Library of Useful Knowledge,* that offered a series of booklets, at sixpence apiece, whose thirty-two closely printed pages provided a text that was the equivalent of one hundred normal pages and offered scientific and utilitarian information. The society later added another series, the *Library of Entertaining Knowledge,* to develop more general cultural notions. Finally, the same society launched a *Penny Cyclopaedia* and the famous *Penny Magazine,* which were enormously successful at a time when the rest of the book trade in England was already in crisis (Richard D. Altick).[41]

The success of Sir Walter Scott's novels, which were sold during the first decades of the nineteenth century at prices as high as 31s. 6d., simply demonstrates that an elite readership that remained limited in number had grown wealthier. No one had any interest in lowering prices as long as he still had customers. This was all the more true because books continued to be made by traditional methods that permitted little cost-cutting, and the power structure, suspicious of radical propaganda, retained the "taxes on knowledge" that made both books and newspapers more expensive.

This situation did not even begin to change until 1825−30. After a first alert in 1819, the British economy and then the European economy underwent periods of crisis and panic that had dramatic results for entrepreneurs (1825−26, 1829−32, 1837−42, and 1847−48). The economy zigzagged between inflation and deflation. Sales of books, held to be a luxury item, declined and bankruptcies were common. It is hardly surprising that the biggest publishing firms in both London and Edinburgh reacted by putting out collections of thickly printed, paperbound works that sold for 5 shillings rather than the usual 10s. 6d. Even this low price was too high for most of the "white-collar" workers who peopled the offices, and new books, novels in particular, continued to be put out at higher prices. Lending libraries and subscription libraries flourished.

The market needed stimulating. The middle classes reacted favorably to the installment sale of books, which was inaugurated with Dickens's *Pick-wick Papers*, sold at 1 shilling the installment (1836–37). A low-priced illustrated press also developed after 1830–32, as we have seen. Next, during the 1848 crisis, the publisher W. H. Smith opened his first railroad station bookstall and stocked it with inexpensive books. These various efforts were primarily aimed at the middle classes, and they were soon surpassed by attempts to address the mass of laborers. Edward Lloyd imitated periodicals such as the *Sunday Times*, beginning quite early to use rotary presses and introducing serialized novels into his two publications, *The Penny Sunday Times* and *The Police Gazette*. Installment novels at one or two pennies the installment proliferated, and the "Penny Bloods" that Lloyd launched in 1836 offered a vast public a glimpse into the lives of famous thieves, stories of pirates of all nations, a gallery of horrors, and more. This was a commercial literature that could not fail to irritate right-thinking souls: in the 1860s it incited the Religious Tract Society to put out two weeklies of a quite different sort, *The Boy's Own Paper*, which soon reached a pressrun of 500,000, and *The Girl's Own Paper*, which proved equally successful.[42]

The competition for low prices did not stop there. The major publishing firms put out increasing numbers of economical collections, works that often were designed to be read on trains, and they soon found themselves looking for new texts or attempting to sign up recent literary successes for these series. Thus a change that had begun in a period of crisis forced the big firms to shift their publishing strategies in much in the same way that Penguin Books and the first pocket books, a century later, were the offspring of the economic crisis of the 1930s.[43]

To return to France, during the Enlightenment the French book had conquered Europe.[44] During the final years of the ancien régime Charles-Joseph Panckoucke had begun to create a press empire, and he contributed much to the repatriation of the major works of the philosophes, which until then had been printed outside France. The Paris book trade had no reason to envy London, but the French Revolution put an end to its prosperity. The Revolution suspended the publication of religious books, ecclesiastical libraries were seized, the traditional reading public was eliminated, and their collections were seized or dispersed. The Revolution eventually dreamed of making those sequestered books available to the nation, but it neglected to renew the stock of that enormous list of works. Many booksellers and printers profited from the new situation to become notables, which meant that they deserted their bookshops and their workshops. The number of typographic establishments increased greatly, however, rising (so we are told), from fewer than fifty to some three hundred fifty, although most of these were modest printshops that put out more tracts and pamphlets than books and newspapers and that used simple single-sheet presses with a relatively small platen. Thus Bonaparte had little difficulty in reducing this artificially inflated number to eighty presses.

Everything that had survived from the ancien régime now seemed outmoded. A few booksellers, particularly under the Empire, continued to circulate their catalogues to a Europe under Napoleonic domination. Martin Bossange, who in spite of the blockade had contracted to exchange books for exotic products from England, preferred to throw his unsalable merchandise into the Channel even before it reached Dover.[45]

The Revolution and the Empire did little to encourage the revival of the French book trade. It was no time for either literature or reading, and the masters of the hour were usually military men or bourgeois of little refinement. Presses served above all to print official forms, legislative texts, and utilitarian works. The former Imprimerie royale became the Imprimerie nationale, abandoned its original mission, and was transformed into a working printshop in the service of a triumphant law and financial paperwork. The reign of the Didot family began—rigorous and impeccable typographers who were lodged in the Louvre in the quarters that the former Imprimerie royale had outgrown now that it was an official establishment. The Didots adapted to the taste of the day and printed frigid and solemn editions of the great classical texts in the style of David (who had been a foreman in the firm). Like the works printed by Bodoni, their rival in Parma, their publications graced the libraries of dignitaries of the imperial regime who had better things to do than to read publications so sumptuous that one wonders if they were ever really meant to be read.

New life came to the book trade with the Restoration.[46] After the troubles and confiscation of goods during the Revolution, the first task was to fill château and town-house libraries that had been emptied of their contents with collections that reflected the flattering image that their proprietors wished to give of themselves. Hence the appearance of great publishing collections. Such ventures were often realized by the descendants of publishing dynasties that had survived many a storm, the Didots and the Panckouckes first among them. The Didots were papermakers, printers, and booksellers: they were prominent figures who were treated with respect by all those in power. They put out monumental publications, each one of which was made up of a number of large-format volumes: *Les ruines de Pompéi, Les monuments de l'Egypte et de la Nubie, Les voyages de l'Inde,* and *Les oeuvres complètes de Piranèse,* not to mention a Greek library in fifty octavo volumes. They imposed their pompous style on all French books. In the late Empire the Panckouckes, who published *Le Moniteur,* the official journal, offered a collection of books on French victories and conquests. Next they published a Latin-French collection, a *Dictionnaire des sciences médicales,* a *Biographie médicale,* a *Flore médicale,* and a *Barreau français.* Other firms such as those of the Renouards and the Delalains in Paris, the Levraults in Strasbourg, and the Aubanels in Avignon were run by dynasties of learned booksellers who were heirs to the traditions of the ancien régime. Families of more recent wealth joined them: the Baudouins, whose founding father printed the poster that marked the beginning of the coup d'état of 18 Brumaire, and the Michauds, correspondents of Louis XVIII in Paris under the Empire, the eldest of whom was elected to the Académie française when the allied troops entered the capital. There were a number of memoirs, bibliographical dictionaries, and authors' complete works that were sold by subscription, a method that the Baudouins and the Michauds used to launch publications of a quite different inspiration. At the same time booksellers such as Desoer, Lefèvre, and their competitors brought out new editions of the great classics and of the philosophes, whose presence on their lists justified the new wealth of many newcomers. Since provincial France lacked structured distribution networks, the Paris firms hired traveling salesmen who sold their costly publications throughout France. The flow of these luxury books soon abated, however, and with the depression of 1830–48 dried up completely.

Innovation became mandatory, and necessity proved a boon to publishing in France. In the days when the ranks of the book trade had thinned, imperial stalwarts (often ex-army officers) became involved in publishing, as did some lawyers and professors, Désiré Dalloz, for example, who published law texts. Peddlers from the Cotentin and elsewhere had also flocked to Paris, at first offering meager stocks by the city gates or on the boulevards. Soon they moved into bookstalls, gathering in the neighborhood of the Palais Royal, whose arcades were lined with shops. This gradually became the headquarters for the latest books. Around 1830 the book world in Paris was a picturesque mix that included the ancestors of many of the great publishing dynasties of today.

Romanticism had arrived. In 1818 the publisher Henri Nicolle accepted

Lamartine's *Méditations* (which had been refused by Firmin Didot), and he sold out the first printing so rapidly that six others followed by the end of the year. An eighth printing appeared in 1832 under Nicolle's successor, Charles Gosselin, bringing the total number of copies in circulation to twenty thousand. The biggest publisher of the Restoration, however, was Charles Ladvocat, a man whose prospectus presented him as the publisher of Chateaubriand, Byron, Shakespeare, Schiller, and others. In 1822 Ladvocat published a collection of masterpieces of foreign drama that introduced a vast public to English, Spanish, and Italian theater. The popularity of Romantic authors was not instantaneous, however: the first printing of Victor Hugo's *Han d'Islande* when it was published in 1823 was 1,200 copies, and the novel sold very slowly, and Bossange and Gosselin felt impelled to add "second edition" to their catalogue listing of *Les Orientales* when they had sold only 320 copies in six months.

In reality both fiction and poetry were too costly for most potential buyers. Like their English counterparts, the French middle class read such works in one of the many *cabinets de lecture* that were springing up everywhere.[47] Bookseller-publishers catered to this market by supplying novels printed in large type and with well-spaced lines that they printed in limited numbers to ensure quick sale but at a price still beyond the reach of the ordinary reader, thus assuring the *maîtres de lecture* who managed the *cabinets de lecture* something like a monopoly. Hard times from 1826 to 1848 that spread from England to France forced one Paris bookseller after another into bankruptcy, since the booksellers operated on credit and were not selling their stocks. The situation became dramatic for all French booksellers when Bossange, the biggest exporter of French books, went out of business. As in London, the Paris booksellers' only hope was to stimulate the market. Taking a hint from Ladvocat, French booksellers began to publicize their latest offerings by posters, handbills, and *publicité rédactionnelle*—newspaper articles that were really advertising inserts in disguise. They also attempted to rejuvenate famous works with illustrated editions that used wood engravings, lithographs, or steel engravings, and to increase sales by serial publication that stretched out payment. As in England, French publishers also began to use machine binding and mechanical presses to print books, while the new papermaking machinery made possible a greater variety of formats.

The booksellers of the July Monarchy also made every attempt to enlarge their public by diversifying their production and seeking the best balance between quality and price. Alexandre Paulin, for example, published

Lesage's *Gil Blas* in an edition that was quite closely printed but included six hundred engravings after Gigoux, selling the work in twenty-four installments at 50 centimes apiece. He sold fifteen thousand copies within a few years, launching a fashion. Paulin's successor, Jules Hetzel, used industrial printing methods to produce illustrated children's books and a book of hours of very high quality. Léon Curmer was best known for the most famous illustrated book of the Romantic period, *Paul et Virginie*, published with illustrations by Tony Johannot, Eugène Isabey, and Jean Meissonier, on which Curmer spared no pains. Nonetheless, the bulk of his business came from religious books ranging in price from 5 francs for a mourner's book to 1,000 francs for a sumptuous missal. He was also one of the first publishers to make systematic use of chromolithography. In France as in England, book publishers competed to lower their prices in much the same way that Emile de Girardin and his competitors slashed the price of daily newspapers. Gervais Charpentier inaugurated a "library" with a promising future with Brillat-Savarin's *Physiologie du goût* in a new format, the octodecimo "jésus," whose somewhat close-set lines provided twice as much text as a traditional octavo volume for half the price: 3.50 francs. Charpentier later contracted to use the same format to publish the best novels of Balzac and works of George Sand, Alfred de Musset, and Alfred de Vigny. It also served for works of Homer, Goethe, Shakespeare, and the French classics of the seventeenth and eighteenth centuries, not to mention the first edition of works by André Chénier.

These relatively well-made publications still did not reach a public of petits-bourgeois, craftsmen, or workers (who earned little more than 4 francs per day). Hence the development of low-priced illustrated periodicals such as *Le Journal des connaissances utiles,* a 32-page monthly first published in 1832 by Girardin and sold for a subscription price of only 4 francs a year, or *Le Magasin pittoresque,* a 6- to 8-page weekly with many illustrations that cost only 2 sous the copy. In 1848, when Gustave Havard published an unabridged quarto *Manon Lescaut* illustrated with woodcuts and printed with two closely spaced columns to the page that sold for a price of only 20 centimes, the age of the *roman à quatre sous*—the fourpenny novel—had come. Contrary to his British counterparts (and to his credit), Havard published famous works for low prices. By 1856 he had put out some six thousand installments, each printed in at least ten thousand copies, representing a total of some sixty million high-quality books.[48]

This technological and commercial evolution was accompanied by radical changes in the professions of the book trade. Between 1835 and 1845 a new figure, the publisher, became distinct from the retail bookseller. His special functions included supervising the manufacture of the books that he put on the market and serving as strategist and intermediary among the public, the authors, the typographers, and all the other people who contributed to the production of books.

The French book trade thus emerged entirely transformed after the difficult years between 1830 and 1850. A selection process had taken place among the newcomers, and those who survived were the ones who had enough funds to live through adversity, who were clever enough to withdraw in time from risky operations, and whose strategy included the acquisition of the stocks of their bankrupt competitors. This is exactly how the Garnier brothers and the Lévy brothers built their fortunes.[49]

The Garniers were sons of a butcher from Lingreville, in the Cotentin; the Lévys were the children of a peddler from Phalsbourg, in Lorraine, who came to Paris during the crisis of 1825–26 to try to improve his fortunes. Both sets of brothers learned their trade selling on the boulevards, and the Lévy brothers even sold notions along with newspapers and books and rented out opera glasses at the doors of the theaters. One of the four Garnier brothers went to Rio de Janeiro, where he became the head of a large press agency and made a fortune in real estate, while Hippolyte, Auguste, and Pierre Garnier established their headquarters in a bookstall in the Palais-Royal. They had probably had little schooling: one police report judged the "intelligence" of Hippolyte no higher than might be expected in a book dealer. He had an instinct for public relations, however, and a real talent for business. He also turned out to be a peerless speculator, whether in stocks, real-estate properties, or interest-bearing loans. After buying out the stock of several well-known booksellers between 1841 and 1848, Hippolyte and Auguste Garnier signed contracts with Musset, Jules Sandeau, Théophile Gautier, and, above all, Sainte-Beuve, whose principal publishers they became. Next, the Garniers settled into the former Hôtel du Gouvernement militaire on the corner of the rue des Saints-Pères and the rue de Lille, where they launched a collection of masterworks of literature that established their reputation. During the same period Michel Lévy, who had attended a consistory school and later the Conservatory of Dramatic Art (when the family finances permitted it), was obliged to give up the idea of becoming an actor to help his father manage a *cabinet de lecture* that the elder Lévy had opened in 1836 on rue Marie-Stuart. Michel continued to peddle books near the Bibliothèque royale until he finally moved indoors into a shed constructed at 1 rue Vivienne. Always passionately fond of the theater—the famous tragedienne Rachel, a childhood friend, played a great role in his life—Lévy published opera libretti in association with the Widow Jonas, bought out advertising gazettes, and managed to sign up famous authors to write for the Opéra, the Opéra-Comique, and the boulevard theaters. This was the start of a theater collection in the "English" octodecimo format, to which Lévy later added an illustrated collection of contemporary drama in quarto format. He took care to establish close relations with a number of authors and, like Hetzel and Hachette, he launched collections at prices that ranged from 1 franc to 3.20 francs and, like Charpentier, he carefully supervised their distribution to the provincial bookstores. Perhaps Lévy's outstanding attribute was an infallible flair for best-sellers: he brought out Baudelaire's translation, published as *Histoires extraordinaires*, of an obscure American named Edgar Allan Poe, Flaubert's *Madame Bovary*, and the *Vie de Jésus* of Ernest Renan, whom he sought out when Renan lived in a garret and had published only a few signed articles.

None of the conquering bourgeois who founded powerful publishing dynasties between 1830 and 1848 had the breadth of Louis Hachette.[50] The son of a seamstress in the Lycée Louis-le-Grand, Hachette was accepted into the Ecole Normale, which at the time was politically suspect and about to be closed. He and all his classmates were prohibited from teaching by Monseigneur de Frayssinous, the Grand Master of the University. He next studied law and made his living as a teaching assistant at the Lagneau school and by doing private tutoring. In 1827 he bought out a publisher's stock that included a few good titles, such as Eugène Burnouf's translation of Cicero's *Orations Against Catiline* and the *Annales du concours général*. His device, *Sic quoque docebo*, stated his intentions, which were to prepare the future by creating the pedagogical materials necessary for a revision of teaching within a program appropriate to the ideology of the liberal bourgeoisie. This required a considerable investment. His marriage with a lawyer's daughter brought him some capital, but above all he managed to win the confidence of three wealthy notaries (one of whom, Henri Bréton, a legitimist deputy from 1815 to 1827, became connected with Hachette's family), and he obtained advances from the Rousseau and Moisant bank. This enabled Hachette to commission the best writers available to compile a Greek dictionary and a Latin dictionary and to edit a series of the Greek and Latin classics. He also began to publish a collection of manuals for use in the primary schools. The crisis of 1832 nearly wiped him out, but he was saved by a "friendly hand"—Henri Bréton. In 1835, Guizot, who had become minister of education, sent Hachette an order for 500,000 copies of his *Alphabet des écoles,* 100,000 copies of *Le livret élémentaire de lecture,* 40,000 copies of Vernier's *Arithmétique,* another 40,000 copies of Meissas's *Géographie,* and 44,000 copies of the *Petite histoire de France* of Mme de Saint-Ouen. Hachette remained in close touch with his former comrades at the Ecole Normale, among them Emile Littré, whom he commissioned to compile his famous dictionary; he kept up connections with the school inspectors; he founded periodicals to keep in contact with both primary teachers and secondary-school professors. He used these contacts to put pressure on the authorities and to get funds allocated for schools when budgets came up for a vote, and he was so successful that under the more authoritarian Empire he was considered a sort of independent state whose power needed to be curtailed. This did not keep Hachette's publications from reaching enormous circulation figures: 2,276,708 copies of Mme de Saint-Ouen's *La Petite histoire de France* were sold between 1834 and 1880, to cite only one work. A prime example of the conquering bourgeoisie, in 1838 Hachette founded the Librairie Centrale de la Méditerranée in Algiers in the hope of contributing to the introduction of French culture in Algeria and the knowledge of Arab culture in France. In passing, he bought up vast tracts of land in the Mitidja that his descendants sold off at a good price. In 1851–52 Hachette proposed to the French railroad system the creation of a network of bookstalls in railroad stations like the ones he had seen in England. Although the Algerian project finally came to naught, the Bibliothèque des Chemins de Fer that Louis Hachette published succeeded beyond his fondest dreams. The collection took its place among the others he had created in a system that permitted him to move a work into a lower-priced collection when it had exhausted its sales potential at a higher price.

By 1848 Louis Hachette occupied the block between the rue Sarrazin and the boulevard Saint-Germain that is still the firm's headquarters. He also increased his real-estate investments (Jean-Yves Mollier). He was a wealthy man, as were the Garnier brothers, Michel Lévy, and many other publishers. Those of the young entrepreneurs of 1830 who had survived the crisis had become well-established notables by 1848. They had also taken on the attitudes of notables. Although the book world played an active role in preparing the way for the Revolution of 1830 and Louis Hachette, for one, unhesitatingly took up arms against the monarchy of Charles X during the Trois Glorieuses, in 1848 most book people held back, and Louis Hachette was not the only publisher who joined the forces of law and order to repress violence during the "June Days."

Business was more than ever the order of the day under the Second

Empire. Immense printing plants had developed, as we have seen. Periodicals and administrative documents proliferated more rapidly than books, but the number of titles published every year grew astonishingly. Master printers often launched collections just to keep their presses busy. To counter the concentration of forces in Paris, provincial publishers specialized in one specific category of books. Prize books were one of these. Their physical aspect was more important than their text: the Martial-Ardant firm in Limoges put out volumes with tooled and gilded board covers featuring chromolithographs, while the Mame family in Tours specialized in covers with red boards.

There was little latitude for improvisation, and publishers sought to offer new products that corresponded to a latent demand. This was what made Pierre Larousse so successful.[51] An innkeeper's son and a graduate of the Ecole Normale de Versailles, Larousse taught for two years in the village of his birth before he went to Paris, where for some years he lived a somewhat disorderly life (like many other publishers in their early years). He lived with a young woman whom he married only in 1871, he admired Béranger, and he apparently professed republican sentiments tinged with socialism. His attitude during the 1848 revolution is not known; he was perhaps present (as he later stated) when the deputy Jean-Baptiste Baudin was killed on 3 December 1851. Larousse had already published his *Lexicologie des écoles primaires* at his own expense when he had the good luck to meet another schoolteacher from Burgundy, Augustin Boyer, who shared his ideas and had a good head for business. The two men set up a corporation and sold shares of stock to attract the capital they needed to carry out their plans. The many French grammars that they published reached enormous printings; above all, they put out a *Nouveau Dictionnaire de la langue française* (the ancestor of the *Petit Larousse*), and the famous *Dictionnaire du XIXe siècle*. Thus a solid and powerful publishing house was born.

During this same time the most imaginative and inventive of the publishers of the period of Romanticism, Jules Hetzel, who had been ruined just before the 1848 revolution, had participated actively in the revolution, and had been exiled after the coup d'état of 2 December, returned to Paris. On his return, Hetzel made several imprudent but profitable moves: he published Prodhon's *La guerre et la paix*, which the Garnier brothers, in their new respectability, had not dared publish, the *Mémoires* of Pierre-Louis Canel, a former head of the Paris police, and Michelet's *La Sorcière*, which Louis Hachette and Laurent Pagnerre had rejected. Hetzel was threatened with lawsuits, but his business was thriving and he obtained the license that officially welcomed him back into the publishing world in Paris. From then on he became more "serious." In 1863, the year in which Michel Lévy published Renan's *Vie de Jésus*, Gervais Charpentier put out Gautier's *Le Capitaine Fracasse*, and Hachette brought out Fromentin's *Dominique*, Hetzel published Jules Verne's *Cinq semaines en ballon* and Erckmann and Chatrian's *Madame Thérèse, ou les volontaires de 1792*. Hetzel shared with Louis Hachette the books of Comtesse de Ségur, the leading author of young people's books. He sought to protect his financial position by incorporating his firm and entering into associations with the powerful paper mills of the Marais, with Charles Lahure, a prominent book printer, and with a number of friends, Jean Macé among them (1868).

After this period the race to lower prices accelerated in an increasingly slow market, and in 1905 Arthème II Fayard launched a Moderne Bibliothèque with pressruns of 100,000 copies that offered the complete works of the great authors at 95 centimes the volume. Fayard later inaugurated his great collection of Livres Populaires with Charles Mérouvel's 700-page *Chaste et flétrie*, over 300,000 copies of which had been printed before the outbreak of war in 1914. Publishing in France had been in crisis since 1894, however, in part because of the meteoric rise of low-cost periodicals, but also because the French economy was losing ground to the rising strength of the German Empire, a situation that had consequences for the intellectual orientation of both countries, as we shall see.

One need only compare a French book of the Enlightenment with a German book of the *Aufklärung* to note that the latter is a more obviously "popular" book. This in itself indicates the advantage that publishing in French enjoyed. French-language works reached a large market of wealthy people in France itself, and French culture had conquered the courts of Europe, whereas in a fragmented Germany books in the national language appealed above all to a bourgeois and academic public.

German-language books were already proving an indispensable bond for the German people, and German booksellers compensated for the dispersion of their customers and what they saw as the endemic disease of pirated editions printed in a nearby state by concentrating their business dealings in Leipzig, where wholesale booksellers had their warehouses and filled orders that came in from retail booksellers.[52]

The industrial revolution enabled the Germans to catch up with impressive speed. Frédéric Barbier has shown how a number of socioeconomic factors worked increasingly in their favor: a relatively stagnant population in France contrasted with demographic expansion on the other side of the

Rhine; an urbanization that increased more rapidly in Germany; a standard of living that rose faster there; a more advanced school system; the advance of technical education. The Empire under William I and William II was not only a land of barracks but also a land of schools.

In this rapidly expanding country, where culture and wealth were unevenly distributed from one region to another and a conglomeration of different religions and traditions coexisted, booksellers were able to make a virtue of the dispersion that had long seemed their greatest weakness. In the capital cities, great and small, in the university towns, in the industrial metropolis, and in the country towns, a division of labor within the book world was more necessary than ever. Publishing (*Verlagsbuchhandlung*) was carefully distinguished from distribution (*Sortimentsbuchhandlung*), street peddling (*Kolportagesbuchhandlung*), and retail selling for cash payment (*Barsortiment*). Under this system, booksellers who sold their own publications and others' were highly respected in their towns and cities, where they ranked with professors, who were traditionally better-respected in Germany than in France. Booksellers were connected through book wholesale houses and sales agents, who were now established not only in Leipzig but also in Berlin and Stuttgart. German booksellers had the benefit of an expanding market; the heirs to a learned tradition, they were treated as professionals, often spoke several languages, and were methodically prepared by special courses and internships, often abroad. The founders of modern professional bibliography, they took control in international trade, especially with France.

These traditions, this sense of organization, the sheer size of a growing demand, and the Germans' desire to give a nation back its history explain the orientation of the German book trade: the most evident early bestseller was an encyclopedia, the *Konversations-lexicon* published by Friedrich Arnold Brockhaus (1772–1823), a text that was distributed in ceaselessly updated editions in sizable enough numbers to warrant the use of mechanical presses and to require new methods of distribution. Soon the dynamism of Wurtemburg booksellers like the Cottas helped Stuttgart to rival Leipzig and Munich, and a number of editions of the German classics were published in Stuttgart: Goethe and Schiller, but also Heinrich von Kleist, Fichte, Jean-Paul, Humboldt, and many others. Early in the nineteenth century, however, other enterprising publishers sensed that the market could be broadened. A financier with the soul of a pirate, Joseph Meyer, launched a *Grosse Konversationslexicon* inspired by Brockhaus's encyclopedia, and it reached its sixth edition in twenty volumes in 1907–9. Stating that the German classics were the property of the nation, Meyer refused to acquiesce to the copyright laws, and he put out low-cost pirated editions at 2 groschen the volume. This earned him the hostility of the major booksellers in Germany, and he left Gotha in 1828 to avoid lawsuits, settling in Hildburghausen, the minuscule capital city of a neighboring principality, where he created a veritable book factory with seventy handpresses and ten mechanical presses. In order to avoid seizures he used the mails to distribute his books directly to his customers.

Another powerful publishing firm that was headed by men who enjoyed a prominent position in the community was that of the Cotta family, one member of which represented the book trade at the Congress of Vienna. Soon such men created illustrated weeklies with large circulations in imitation of the French weeklies. Keil, for example, created the *Gartenlaube*, a periodical modeled after the *Pfennig Magazin* launched in Leipzig by Bossange in 1839, and by 1861 the *Gartenlaube* had a circulation of 100,000, peaking in 1881 at 378,000.

There were also important changes in literary publishing. In 1835 the Bundestag reduced the time span of copyright protection for literary works to the ten years following the death of the author. A transitional measure later provided that the rights of authors who had died before 9 November 1837 would expire and the works fall into the public domain on 9 November 1867. This meant that immediately after that date a throng of "libraries" of low-priced editions of the great national classics came on the market, the most famous of which was the Universal Bibliothek of Anton Philip Reclam (1806–96). This was followed, from 1880 to 1896, by a return to the quality book, as in other countries.

The situation of the publishing world in Germany and in France during this period seems radically different. In German lands the book trade developed a structure that relied on a series of intermediaries, and German publishers found new outlets, for example among the Germans who emigrated to Pennsylvania. During the same period the international status of the French book gradually declined. German publishing had been and remained decentralized; the concentration of French publishing houses not only in Paris but in certain parts of Paris made the rest of France a desert where knowledgeable booksellers were few and books might easily be sold along with humbler household items in bazaars and notions shops. Still, Frédéric Barbier's statistics prove that French publishers nearly kept up with their German counterparts even though the French market was expanding much more slowly. French publishers, who often seemed like illiterate adventurers in comparison with their learned colleagues across the Rhine, maintained their position only by innovating. They explored all the possibilities and all the potential publics, ceaselessly exploiting new publishing genres and working to lower prices. This meant that the book penetrated French society much more deeply than in Germany.

FROM THE AUTHOR TO THE READER

The industrial revolution, which evolved at the same time as nationalism and the rise of literacy in the West, put printed matter into everyone's hands—though not necessarily the book or even the newspaper. It is hardly surprising that it also created new cultural solidarities, or that these solidarities were henceforth national in character. This means that there were observable differences between publishing policies and strategies in Great Britain, Germany, and France.

Even before the Protestant Reformation, the English considered the book to be a boon because it gave the individual personal knowledge of the divine Word. Thus the English were early and enthusiastic supporters of collective "libraries," and many nineteenth-century British publishers took a moral satisfaction in doing good works by disseminating knowledge and in moralizing the contents of the works they published. They saw the book as an exceptionally favored object and an instrument of knowledge sure to individualize and glorify nations certain of their destiny. The Germans were also in large part children of the Protestant Reformation and also a people who traditionally revered the book, but their situation was totally different. They needed to connect the nation they were striving to create with the illustrious past of the Germanic Holy Roman Empire, with all the universalism it implied, but they also needed to guarantee coherence to a social reality of increasing complexity in a land in which the break between economic evolution and social and political structures was striking. The mission of German publishers, as Frédéric Barbier has so clearly seen, was to create prestige. Publishers supported the power structure, using their books and their impeccable organization to proclaim the superiority of German culture and the deep-seated unity of their new nation.

The history of libraries clearly reflects opposing conceptions of book culture in Anglo-Saxon and Germanic lands.[53] In English-speaking lands most libraries were originally founded by private groups, hence they reflected extremely general interests. In German lands libraries developed out of princely and university collections, which meant that they were above all learned: the masses had little share in them until the "popular" libraries of the early twentieth century. In France, the sheer numbers of ecclesiastical collections and such of the émigrés books as were deemed useful to the community that were annexed during the Revolution gave the state an impossible mission. The revolutionaries' successors sifted through these books from another age, but they forgot that culture is constantly renewed. The bourgeoisie attempted to take over where the former aristocracy had left off and to rule over culture and politics alike, but (unlike in England) they neglected to create public libraries. Gradually, however, the French government realized, in its effort to develop the school system, that schools needed libraries; at the same time the French working class was choosing its leaders, awakening, and beginning to organize libraries as well. All that came too late. The collapse of the book trade in 1894, the meteoric rise of the large-circulation news press, and the stagnation that gripped French society in the two decades before World War I obliterated the policies that had been developed earlier.

Throughout the nineteenth century, as we have seen, things worked to encourage the sale and the reading of books, now products of mass distribution. The French Revolution had established the principle of the responsible citizen who ought to have a minimum of schooling, but it had done nothing to create the infrastructure for that schooling. A population shift toward the cities and the need for a more skilled labor force contributed greatly to the spread of literacy. At the same time, a rise in the standard of living allowed a greater proportion of the population to acquire low-priced books and periodicals, particularly in the more industrialized countries. A good many families now had at home a few school texts, some novels, and illustrated revues rather than the devotional literature of yesteryear. Personal libraries and home offices proliferated, physicians and barristers found it even more indispensable to display their knowledge than under the ancien régime, and furniture specially designed to hold books began to be made.

People read in many ways, however. Solitary silent reading, a contributing factor to individualism, existed. But so did a number of forms of group reading that ranged from reading aloud in a salon or in a small circle of people who saw themselves as cultivated, to collective reading interrupted by commentary among workers, or to reading in the home, now not necessarily by the father and family head but often by a schoolchild. It was an age of autodidacts.

The social status of an author was totally different from what it had been during the eighteenth century. Beginning in the early nineteenth century in Great Britain, with the July Monarchy in France, and somewhat later in Germany, the reading public had grown constantly. When Sir Walter Scott was already immensely popular in Great Britain and Goethe had become something like a prophet in Germany, the Romantic movement in France, which originated in émigré or royalist circles, had only a limited audience. Later, however, innovative writers who soon saw themselves as the spokesmen of the people reached an increasingly large public, achieving what Paul Bénichou has called "the anointing of the poet." [54] This was how Romantic authors of the great generation maintained a balance between literature and economics. In a still unorganized market, authors moved blithely from one publisher to another, driving hard bargains for rights to a work in a specified format and for a limited period only. Serial publication increased the earnings of the most famous writers. The authors of popular theatrical works and novels often made a good living, and on both sides of the Channel a career in literature attracted young people eager for success. [55] Still, the bloody consequences of the June Days (23–26 June 1848), followed by the coup d'état of 2 December, dashed many hopes. Many authors felt alienated from both the people and the new power structure. Parnassians and Symbolists opted for an elitist literature, but under the Third Republic realists and naturalists continued to try to reach a broader public, even when they had to make use of the news press—as did Zola—to reach more readers.

In reality, the vast public that gained access to reading at this time often appreciated classics hallowed by tradition—in France, La Fontaine, for example—or their old schoolbooks more than recent authors. They also loved serial novels: in France *Les Misérables* and the acknowledged masterworks of the *littérature à quatre sous* and in England Dickens's latest novels. Writers needed to diversity their strategies. It also became general practice for an author to earn royalties in the form of a percentage of the sale price of each copy sold. Some authors continued to seek the high circulation figures made possible by serialized novels and popular novels, but that "industrialized" literature demanded greater and greater concessions to public taste. There was as much of a gulf between Dumas or Eugène Sue and Paul Féval or Charles Mérouvel as there was in England between Dickens and the writers of penny dreadfuls. Many authors aimed at the middle, which in France meant a public of some fifty thousand readers who could make an author's reputation. That public might suddenly expand, as for Renan's

Vie de Jésus or Zola's novels. Finally, the poets wrote for extremely limited circles, although some of them—Verlaine, for one—found themselves suddenly in the limelight on the literary stage.

Lest these few generalizations be misleading, let me note that writers pinned their hopes on the revenues that their works might bring them, and toward the middle of the century their hopes were often realized. But a throng of younger authors soon made their situation difficult, and they still had to rely on the salons and the personalities or the critics who could make or break a reputation. Or else they found they had to sacrifice to the tastes of a public already attuned to the newspaper's more easily accessible form of reading. Publishing was also becoming a less profitable sector of activity for its backers. All this meant that most book authors continued to have another profession. Religious literature accounted for a diminishing proportion of the works published, and many authors were university professors (especially in Germany), some were physicians, even state employees. And of course some were journalists, a rather special variety of the man of letters. The basic problem remains in our own day.

A word or two still needs to be said about the essential objects: documents, written and printed, and books in particular. This epoch, which saw the triumph of the bourgeoisie, also cultivated beautiful handwriting, legislated on correct spelling, and valued the art of letter-writing, which was carefully taught to marriageable young women of "good family." The age demanded well-kept accounts, it developed bookkeeping, and it improved postal service. Stamped envelopes appeared during this period, and later postcards. Above all, modern publicity made its appearance with lithographed handbills and colored posters intended to catch the eye of the crowd with their bright colors, striking images, and aggressive typography. Paper had completely changed in texture and general aspect. Most papers produced after wood pulp became almost universally used, newsprint in particular, have not withstood the test of time.

The book as well underwent a radical change in its appearance.[56] It was often richly illustrated, particularly in the Romantic age. Steel plates came to be preferred over copper plates for engraved illustrations because they gave a finer image, and lithography was used for illustrations of current events that were often gathered into albums. The use of end-grain wood permitted the wood-engraved vignettes printed with the text to be read like a film paralleling the story, and the comic strip (about which more later) was born with the humorous drawings of Rodolphe Töpffer. The cinema was not far off. Still, the book format typical of the Didots long continued its reign, somewhat enlivened by the use of a copperplate engraving or an exotic type style on the title page. It is characteristic of the reaction that occurred in the mid-nineteenth century that printers of the early years of the Second Empire, rather than innovating, returned to traditional typography and took their inspiration from the seventeenth-century books printed by the Elzeviers, much sought-after by the bibliophiles of the age.

Nineteenth-century books were totally different from books of the preceding century. At first they often had attractive board covers, but paper covers soon became the rule.[57] For use in high-quality books papermakers developed a thick white paper that made type look inscribed. Authors and publishers seem to have made an effort to clarify the structure of the works they published by adding a table of contents. There were drawbacks to the changes: the use of mechanical presses might have catastrophic results, as the champions of traditional methods were quick to point out. Furthermore, the use of rotary presses designed to print other things besides books facilitated the production of large numbers of copies at an extremely low price, but they used such high pressure that the text sometimes seems graven into the paper. The works produced in this period bear the same relationship to their ancestors of the artisanal age of printing as copies of old pieces of furniture do to their originals. Books of the period were no longer treasures to be carefully saved but simple consumer items. Thus many of the innumerable editions that came from the presses of the time seem to have disappeared entirely, swallowed up by time. When photomechanical procedures became the rule in book publishing, the bibliophiles' reaction was to commission luxury editions crafted by the best artisans available, illustrated by major artists, and printed by hand on vat-made paper.[58] The art of fine bindings was also further developed for a public of wealthy book lovers.

If we place side by side the books produced by the great industrial printing firms of Europe we can see that as each nation experienced a growing sense of nationalism it asserted its individual sensitivity through its graphics and its books. This is particularly striking in works published in Latin, which were international by definition and imposed the same rules on all publishers. After the crisis that began in the decade between 1880 and 1890 the book became a commodity for mass distribution, and as populations became increasingly literate it aimed (in vain) at reaching the broadest possible public. Thus far, however, the schools taught only the rudiments, and those who decry the ignorance of today's schoolchildren would have been horrified by the low level of the instruction that was given then to the majority of the population, who still lived in a relatively closed universe. Hence the immense success of daily newspapers and periodicals: access to them seemed easy, and they offered a window to the world beyond. All this was of course well before the arrival of the new means of communication.

THE CONQUEST OF THE WORLD

The typographical industry set out to conquer the world during these years, and two giants, Russia and the United States, already loomed large at either side of Europe.*

In Russia illiteracy remained a major obstacle to advances in the typographical industry until well into the twentieth century.[59] We have little accurate information on the literacy rate among the Russian population before the first general census in the Empire in 1897. We can estimate, though, that at best one man out of six in the rural population (which was 90 percent of the whole population) was basically literate toward the mid-nineteenth century. In 1897, 21 percent of the total population of the Empire declared they could read and write. The figure rises to 32 percent of males over eight years of age. Fifty-four percent of city-dwellers within this group were literate, as were 19 percent of people in rural areas. We should keep in mind that these figures do not represent any demonstrated ability to write but reflect the respondents' opinion that they could do so. In reality, the gap between Russia and the most industrialized country in Europe, England, was enormous in the early twentieth century. During the general elections in England and Wales in 1910, only 17 percent of voters are listed as illiterate, whereas in 1913 the average literacy rate in the Russian Empire was only 28 percent, a figure equivalent to the proportion of English men and women who did *not* know how to read in the mid-nineteenth century.

The growth in literacy in Russia between 1897 and the Russian Revolution can be measured by using the census of 1920 as a basis for comparison. The literacy rate for males rose from 32 to 42 percent; for females,

*The text of this section was written in cooperation with François Dupuigrenet Desroussilles and, for the Far East, Jean-Pierre Drège, both of whom I thank.

from 13 to 25 percent. Although this increase is of the greatest importance in any analysis of the participation of the working world in the Revolution, one cannot deny that the literacy rate was low. In the Russian army 50 percent of the reservists were considered literate on the eve of World War I, yet foreign observers were struck by the fact that common soldiers almost never wrote their own letters but had to ask a noncommissioned or commissioned officer to write for them. Most enlisted men had not seen a book since they were eight or nine years old, when they had attended school for a year or two. Illiteracy in imperial Russia was not limited to the peasantry or the common people: in 1897, 28 percent of the nobility, the state bureaucracy, and the clergy were classed as illiterate.

On the eve of the Russian Revolution a cultural gulf continued to separate a cultivated elite from the great illiterate mass of the population. This situation was expressed in literature in the idealized image of the illiterate peasant in Dostoyevsky, Turgenev, or Tolstoy, for instance in the dialogue between Platon Karataev and the aristocrat Pierre Bezukhov in *War and Peace*. Lenin, the son of a school inspector, was particularly aware of this problem. Fascinated and frightened by the *stikiia*, the spontaneity of the illiterate Russian peasant (which is exactly what Tolstoy admired in Platon Karataev), Lenin soon set out to lead the masses to *soznatel'nost* (self-awareness), without which they could never be the protagonists of their own history. "Politics," he wrote, "does not exist for someone who cannot read." Paradoxically, it was precisely the force of *stikiia* that enabled the Bolsheviks to seize power. In all the films and photographs of 1917 one is struck by the number of slogans and colorful banners designed for the illiterate and the semiliterate and by the role of oral propaganda. More decisive than the 200,000 copies of *Pravda*, only half of which were distributed outside St. Petersburg in April 1917, was the role of all the soldiers, sailors, postal employees, and railroad workers who returned to their villages after the success of the October Revolution. We might say that as the Revolution unfolded it widened the gap between a cultivated elite and the illiterate masses. To cite only one example: in 1923 Moscow and St. Petersburg published 30 percent of the newspapers of the Soviet Union but they accounted for 90 percent of the distribution of newspapers.

In an early phase corresponding roughly to the civil war, the Bolsheviks launched a campaign for adult literacy, accompanied by a propaganda campaign. A decree in 1919 made school attendance obligatory for the entire illiterate population between the ages of eight and fifty. Despite the extreme difficulties of the period, we can estimate that some five million people learned to read and write between October 1917 and the end of the civil war. During a second period, the time of the NEP, propaganda was less emphasized and the campaign for literacy was entrusted to a semi-independent organization. In spite of all these efforts, the 1926 census shows that although 76 percent of the inhabitants of cities and towns knew how to read and write, only 45 percent of the rural population could do so. Among the reasons given for this relative failure was that it was difficult for a child to attend school in wartime (in 1926 only 50 percent of children attended school), which reestablished illiteracy at the base of the age pyramid. The production of books and newspapers had certainly increased as compared to the period before 1914—2,700,000 copies of 859 news-papers were sold in 1913 as against 9,400,000 copies of 1,197 papers in 1928—but the paper shortage was so acute that the poet Yesenin, unable to publish even his shorter lyrics, wrote them on the walls of a monastery. Roger Pethybridge has shown that for a time Russia went back to being a predominantly oral culture. When the poor showings of the 1926 census were made known during the winter of 1927–28, new and alarming data were added to them: among the population between the ages of sixteen and thirty-five there were sixteen million illiterates and thirty to forty mil-lion semi-illiterates, and five million children between the ages of twelve and sixteen were illiterate as well. This situation made it difficult to carry out the massive industrialization of the country that was the major objec-tive of the first Five Year Plan, which required skilled manpower.

Under Stalin, the party considered literacy an absolute priority. From 1930 on, a central agency closely dependent on the government took con-trol of a new campaign in which literacy and propaganda were closely connected, as they had been during the civil war. Thanks to the return of peace, financial resources were more easily available, and when the entire party was mobilized to work for literacy durable results were swiftly won. At the time of the 1939 census, 81 percent of the population over the age of nine and 89 percent of the population between nine and forty-nine years of age could read and write. In thirty years Soviet power had led the peoples of the U.S.S.R. to the literacy level that most European countries had reached at the end of the nineteenth century after at least a century of effort.

This was certainly the greatest literacy campaign ever undertaken, but we should keep in mind that it was originally conceived as a precondition to the industrialization of the U.S.S.R., not as a cultural process. Furthermore, the imposition of a regime of draconian censorship and the submission of printed matter to the imperatives of authoritative planning set barriers all around that literacy. For Stalin, control over the newly literate masses was much more important than control over the intelligentsia of Moscow and Leningrad. After Peter the Great and Catherine II, who had challenged the religious authorities by keeping printing for the use of a restricted and cultivated elite, Soviet power permitted the mass of the population—for the first time—to have a direct and personal relationship with the printed word. It restricted the use of that word, however, at times dramatically.

After the American colonies won their independence from Great Britain and until the Civil War, the development of printing in the United States accompanied the vast westward movement of the pioneers.[60] As the colonists moved into Kentucky and toward the frontier and then the citizens of the new nation moved into the Northwest Territory and what soon became Ohio they carried printing presses in their wagons and on their flatboats. Most of these people came from countries of northern Europe whose populations had long been literate, and they were used to regarding printing as a power to be dealt with, much like church or school. Newspapers and books soon began to be published in the new territories. Tennessee had a newspaper in 1701, as did Ohio in 1793, before statehood. In 1808 the first printshop west of the Mississippi was established in St. Louis. Samuel Bangs, a native of Baltimore, set up a printshop in Galveston in 1817, and he made a decisive contribution to Texas' war to win independence from Mexico. In 1846 a printshop was founded in San Francisco, and when the Gold Rush came in 1849 it was ready to serve the new demand. On the eve of the Civil War the entire United States was well served by a dense network of printing establishments that made the newspaper, if not the book, a common object in daily life. Three territories had printing presses well before they were admitted to the union: Montana in 1862, Wyoming in 1863, and North Dakota in 1864.

The big cities of the East Coast were expanding rapidly, and between 1820 and 1852 they produced at least 24,000 book titles, or as many as during the entire period from 1639 to 1791. In 1850, 486 periodicals were published in the United States, not including daily newspapers. The better part of book production was concentrated (still between 1820 and 1852) in New York (which had 345 publishing firms), Philadelphia (198), Boston (147), and Baltimore (32),but the Middle West began to show its strength, and there were 25 book publishing firms in Cincinnati.

The decades following the Civil War saw sweeping changes in American publishing. The great firms founded in the early nineteenth century—Harper, Putnam, Appleton, and Scribner—still existed, but they were changing from smaller family-run businesses into huge organizations that dominated American publishing through the mid-twentieth century. All these firms were general publishers who attempted to cover the greatest possible number of genres and disciplines, leaving only school and university or purely professional publishing to specialized firms. Geographically New York clearly led the list of book publishers, and Boston and Philadelphia soon specialized in university and professional books. Outside of these three cities, the only publishing firms of national scope were in Cincinnati and Chicago.

In the early twentieth century new waves of immigrants—Italians, Germans, Scandinavians, Russians, and Central European Jews—brought changes to the programs of American publishers interested in responding to the demands of new readers. In 1915 Alfred A. Knopf offered a sizable catalogue of European literature (Russian, German, and Scandinavian in particular). In the same period some American firms became so large that they began to dominate the world market for books in English. Doubleday, for instance, which was founded in 1897, took over the great London publishing house of Heinemann. Until 1929 one can speak of a boom in American publishing, notably with the founding of Harcourt, Brace & Howe in 1914, Simon & Schuster in 1926, and Random House in 1927.

From the start, the immensity of the American territory posed the problem of distribution on a scale new in the history of the book. As the famous itinerant bookseller Parson Weems wrote to the Philadelphia printer-publisher, Mathew Carey, "I'm the one who leads the charge in our squadron." After 1840 rotary presses enabled newspaper publishers to produce books that were sold as a supplement to the newspaper at one-tenth the bookstore price for the same titles: in 1850 English novels in openly pirated editions cost six and a half cents as a newspaper supplement and sixty-five cents in a regular edition.

To combat this competition, publishers attempted to modernize their systems for selling to bookstores. Each firm had salesmen responsible for large territories. There was one Harper representative for all of New England, half the Midwest, or the entire Pacific Coast. In 1914, however, these sales-people visited only 3,501 retail distributors, or one bookstore for every 28,000 inhabitants of the territory. Rural areas were completely neglected, which means that most books were not bought in a bookstore. Just before World War I, 90 percent of the books sold in the United States were sold by subscription, by door-to-door sales, or by mail. To cite one example, in September 1910 Harper spent $12,000 on its bookstore sales, $15,000 on subscription sales, and $9,000 on mail-order sales, and these expenditures were more evenly distributed than in most publishing firms.

The relative weakness of bookstore sales was long to remain one of the basic characteristics of the history of the book in the United States, as was the subordination of the book to the newspaper and the magazine, even well before the invasion of the new media of radio and television.

Western penetration into urban China in the mid-nineteenth century brought slow but radical change to Chinese printing and publishing. Until that time economic structures and the technical processes used in publishing had hardly evolved since the Sung dynasty. Three traditional types of printed matter shared the market: official publications that emanated from imperial or local administrative offices, private editions put out by collectors and bibliophiles, and booksellers' editions that might be called commercial. The various techniques for printing with movable type made of terracotta, wood, copper, and even porcelain had long hung fire, and in comparison to xylography they never represented more than a very small part of print production. The traditional forms of printing and publishing survived to the late nineteenth and early twentieth centuries.

During the latter half of the nineteenth century, attempts to modernize and industrialize China led to a movement to imitate Western methods, which in turn created a need for educational and technical works. These spawned translation bureaus and agencies for publishing and disseminating Western knowledge.

Another element in the Westernization of China, perhaps more decisive for print production, was the role of missionaries, Protestant missionaries in particular. Such men carried out the first successful attempts to apply typography to the Chinese language, importing type fonts from Europe and America. Lithography also had a certain success. The missionaries produced school manuals as well as religious publications. In the early twentieth century these technological transformations and the new educational orientation made possible the establishment of publishing houses that soon became the largest in China.

The slow advance of printing in China cannot be compared to the progress of Japan under the Meiji dynasty beginning in 1867. At the same time European printing techniques began to spread throughout the world in a complex history that I cannot trace here, even briefly: the formation of a capital of written culture long remained a form of ancestral wealth that helped assure European lands a certain form of preeminence over the rest of the world—even over America, where the United States only slowly rid itself of the cultural yoke of its European heritage. Europe's secret was new techniques.

When print completed its conquest of the world in the early twentieth century the creative capacity of the book and its force of penetration were already lessened. We can perhaps get to the root of this seeming contradiction with the help of Jean-Yves Mollier's important and extremely well-documented work on the relationship between finance and letters in French publishing between 1880 and 1920.[61] The founders of the modern publishing dynasties—former booksellers who managed to survive and prosper under bitter competition—reigned over a specific sector of printing, publishing, or distribution by agreeing (as far as possible) to share the market and share the authors whom they attempted to put under contract. They built up a sizable capital, but in an attempt to limit their risks, as Mollier says, they "invested in many domains, all the while adopting a multimedia strategy, trying to include in their businesses press operations, theatrical organizations, and press agencies, and to solidify the whole by means of a diversified portfolio." Having made their fortunes in a limited span of years, these captains of the press industry hastened to adopt the life-style and the taste for privacy of the milieu they had joined. They were partisans of order and, when the opportunity arose they pursued a matrimonial strategy that often linked them with the world of high finance. However, they could not avoid a separation between the social capital of their firm and the rest of their wealth, nor could they prevent their wealth from being divided among their descendants. Thus their situation worsened as the book market shrank and they underwent a series of crises in the three final decades of the nineteenth century. This meant that the great publishing families, who long before had acquired lands and houses and, for the more dynamic among them, bonds and especially stocks, turned increasingly toward the attractive speculative investments available in that age. When this led them to limit their investments in the family business, they prevented the firm from lowering production costs and broadening its markets, forced it into a wait-and-see attitude that left it exposed to competitors, and obliged it to compensate for lower revenues by imposing draconian conditions on authors. Thus it was the authors, as always full of illusions and poorly armed to defend themselves, who were the ultimate victims of the troubled times before the turn of the century.

These strategies differed only in scale from those of the bookseller-publishers of preceding ages from Jean Petit to Sébastien Cramoisy or Le Breton, and they seem to have been shared by all the dynasties of the conquering bourgeoisie.[62] We need to note, however, the ambiguity of the position of these imaginative and active persons who were intimately involved in the intellectual life of their times and often operated to stimulate it—an ambiguity that they concealed under a stereotyped editorial discourse.[63]

All in all, these attitudes seem to me merely to illustrate the evolution of the economy at the turn of the century. During the last third of the nineteenth century, Western society as a whole swung toward a new logic that might be qualified as "industrial" and that combined mass consumption and mass production. The corollary of this new logic was that it was an age in which Western Europe was achieving literacy, the development of "cultural" consumption, increased political participation, and a growing demand for information. In spite of a number of things that distorted this picture and in spite of special economic situations, the trend everywhere and in all domains was to produce in large quantities in order to broaden the market while reducing costs, which would bring sale prices down as well. In our context, this meant the success of low-priced popular periodicals whose reading level was better adapted to the vast public that now needed to be conquered. It also meant the rise of press magnates, most of whom came to publishing from other sectors but who had a passion for power in all its forms, as well as a proliferation of people in journalism, with the overlap between the news press and book publishing that we are familiar with today. At the same time, the sheer amount of capital needed for a profitable and aggressive industrial strategy tended more and more to exceed the financial capabilities of even a very wealthy family. This is probably what brought on the most fundamental and radical change in the domain of the book: after 1870 the world of publishers was replaced by the world of publishing houses, with their specialized personnel and their diversified services. This change in scale gradually turned the family business into the corporation. By the same token, it brought on a penetration of the publishing world by outside elements, notably banks.[64]

This penetration operated at a different pace from one country to another. The size of the German market during the Empire and the importance of cartels explain why this phenomenon was more noticeable in the more innovative publishing centers, especially in Stuttgart with the Deutsche Verlagsanstalt. Overlapping families and firms and a community of interests among the worlds of high finance, power, the newspapers, and publishing also played their role. In France the economic situation and the exportation of capital slowed this change, and although institutions such as the Union Commercial, the Crédit Commercial de France, and Paribas launched similar moves fairly early, they remained relatively small in scope.

These were the circumstances under which the book, which had become a commercial entity less attractive to investors and was, in the final analysis, elitist by vocation, ceased its conquests and began a retreat before the periodical press—until other and more formidable rivals appeared on the scene.

$\mathscr{T}en$
Beyond Writing

The changes that our own century has brought to writing would require more than an entire volume if they were treated in the same detail as changes in the past. We all know the pitfalls that await historians who try to write of their own time as they do of the past. Nonetheless, I need to recall a few facts and mention the inevitable questions that advances in communications systems raise in our society.

THE "RISING TIDE" OF PAPER

In face of growing demand, cheaper paper and increased paper production encouraged written communication and made paper the universal writing material of the nineteenth and twentieth centuries. I cannot possibly trace here all that our civilization has derived from the use of paper. We need think only of advances in accounting techniques, of the role that paper money plays in our society, of passports and identity cards, of the innumerable questionnaires we are asked to fill out, of our obligation to declare and justify our revenues, of the enormous amount of paper required by governmental agencies such as Social Security (in France and elsewhere), or of all the many other documents that living in contemporary society demands.

These many uses of paper relegate the book to a secondary level in print statistics, particularly when book-paper consumption is compared to the use of paper in the commercial communications that take up so much space in our letter boxes that we seldom bother to read them.

This enormous increase in paper consumption is connected with an expanded service sector and a proliferation of writing, which in turn are linked to the particularly rapid rise of bureaucracies. In keeping with the expansion of the service sector, the number of state employees in France rose from 150,000 under the July Monarchy to 300,000 at the end of the Second Empire. On the eve of World War I in 1914 the figure stood at

This chapter was written by Bruno Delmas and Henri-Jean Martin on the basis of documentation in large part gathered by Bruno Delmas.

646,000, and today it has reached roughly 4,300,000, local administrations and public services included, or 20 percent of the active population of France.[1] The increase in personnel is particularly striking in the central offices of the administration that serve the public indirectly, unlike public instruction, the postal service, or the army. In the context that interests us here, this change can be symbolized by the appearance of the steel pen nib, then of the fountain pen, and finally of the typewriter.[2]

The better part of the work of this central core of the state administration is gathering, treating, and circulating data. The concrete result is generally the creation of documents on paper, a phenomenon that could not have expanded so enormously if the industrial revolution had not produced an equally rapid rise in paper production. The pace of that rise can be schematized for France, using production figures for 1938 as base 100:

1802-12	1825-4	1865-74	1885-94	1904-13
2	4	8	33	45

During those same years office workers switched from the goose quill pen to the metal pen nib when glazed paper made it possible to write with a harder implement. The public school system was a leading consumer of steel pen nibs, but pens replaced quills more slowly in the administration, where both were used up to World War I.

There was also an inevitable increase in the number of administrative publications. Although the government printing office—named the Imprimerie royale, impériale, or nationale as regimes changed—took an increasing role in the production of such texts, private firms always handled the majority of the print jobs, and the official journals were printed by the state printers only in 1881. Day after day some convenient way had to be found not only to print these large jobs but also the documents produced by all the various branches of government. One solution was machines for rapid reproduction. Lithography was used, then zincography, and the many processes and devices for duplication and photoreproduction, all of which became increasingly economical and efficient.

The greatest revolution in this domain was the typewriter. As early as the beginning of the nineteenth century astonishing and ingenious prototypes had appeared on both sides of the Atlantic (Georges Ribeill). They attracted much attention at the various world's fairs of the 1850s and the 1860s, and they were contemporary with the first composing machines, which also used a keyboard. Remington, the gun manufacturer, began to produce typewriters commercially in 1873, and soon a number of brands and conceptions competed for the market. Some machines lined up their type characters on a sliding metal strip; others set them in a curve with a shuttle mechanism; on some typewriters separate characters were struck on a flat surface; on others, on a cylinder, and so forth. The typewriter using separate characters on type bars striking on a cylinder soon dominated the market. Because adjacent striking bars tended to jam when struck rapidly, manufacturers abandoned the alphabetical placement of letters on the keyboard in favor of the left-to-right "qwerty" disposition that takes into account the frequency and sequence of letters in English. American typewriters made this the standard keyboard layout, and only in the last decade of the nineteenth century did French typewriters begin to change, and in 1901 Albert Navarre and a team of twenty experts devised a French "zhjay" keyboard. French typists were already accustomed to the international keyboard, whose "azerty" disposition differed only slightly from the American. After 1890 side-strike type bars that enabled the typist to see what was being typed and carbon paper facilitated widespread use of the typewriter.[3]

Acceptance of this revolutionary device paralleled the growing use of stenography, making it easier to dictate letters and leading to the replacement of *expéditionnaires*—"letter senders"—with secretaries and typists. At the same time, a vastly increased production led to a new formalism. The diplomatics of modern documents (a discipline in formation) should provide singular insights into the minds of those who governed (and still govern) us.

Equally sweeping changes were taking place in typography and in the coupling of text and image. Typographical practices were once again revolutionized. The first innovation was the invention of photomechanical procedures for polychrome printing using the three basic colors (trichromy) and borrowing from color selection processes first realized in photography by Charles Cros and Louis Ducos du Hauron in 1867. The second innovation was photogravure, a distant relative of intaglio printing and the result of long efforts and gradual improvements. A special copper drum gridded with "cells" of varying depth permitted the reproduction of a colored image rendered in fine detail that could be printed with the text. Between the two world wars photogravure was used for high-quality color illustrations in "prestige" advertising and plates for art books and such luxury magazines as *L'Illustration*. Lithography, which in 1896 still accounted for one-fourth of the graphics printing in the Paris metropolitan area (notably for commercial printed matter, labels, and wrapping papers), gradually engendered offset printing, a technique with a brilliant future. Characteristically, offset printing arose from a need for attractive imprints for wrappings and metal boxes. As early as 1868, Hippolyte Marinoni perfected a procedure for replacing a lithographic stone with a flexible zinc plate that could be fitted to a print cylinder. In 1875 Robert Barclay and J. Doyle Fry solved the problem of the rapid wear of the zinc plate by using a rubber-covered cylinder to transfer the image from the plate cylinder to the impression cylinder. Our latest printing technique and the one that tends to replace all others was thus born of the demands of marketing. The first offset presses capable of printing on paper appeared only in 1904, however, and the process came into general use only after World War II.[4]

Techniques such as these consummated the marriage of text and image that had begun in the Romantic era. They tended to make all books into picture books, and they contributed to the rise of the comic strip.[5]

One can trace the long history of the Italian *fumetti*—so called from the speech that emerges like puffs of smoke from the characters' mouths—or of the American "comics" or "funnies," but the father of the French *bande dessinée* is usually considered to have been Rodolphe Töpffer, born in Geneva in 1799. Töpffer, a professor and school principal who wrote well-received works (*Voyages en zig-zag*, 1843), was much influenced by the dramatic and narrative aspects of the engravings of Hogarth and Rowlandson, but he long hesitated to publish his own "stories in prints": *Les amours de M. Vieubois* was composed in 1827 but published ten years later, *Les voyages du docteur Festus*, which Goethe particularly liked, appeared in 1829. He also produced *L'histoire de M. Cryptogame* and several other series. Töpffer was unusual in using the "English hand" (italics), a form of calligraphy quite uncommon at the time. Above all he established a close connection between text and image. As he explained in *L'histoire de M. Jabot* (1837), "Each of these drawings is accompanied by one or two lines of text. Without this text the drawings would have only an obscure meaning; the text without the drawings would mean nothing at all; the whole, together, forms a sort of novel, a book that speaks directly to the eyes [and] expresses itself by representation, not by narrative."

The *bande dessinée* thus began in the same age as the Romantic illustrated book and photography. After Töpffer came Gustave Doré, who was only fifteen when he composed *Travaux d'Hercule* (1847), a work followed by many other series. The genre inspired a number of other authors, among them the famous Christophe, whose *La famille Fenouillard*, *Le sapeur Cam-*

embert, and *Le savant Cosinus* were all published serially between 1889 and 1899. Next the United States took the lead, and comic strips began to appear in newspapers' Sunday supplements. James Swinnerton's *The Little Bears and Tigers* first appeared in 1892, a strip that had no text under the images and resembled caricature more than the French *bande dessinée.* The first modern comic strip was *The Yellow Kid,* launched in the Pulitzer press's *Sunday World* and run in the Hearst press's *American Humanist.* It recounted the adventures of a bald ragamuffin with big ears and vaguely asiatic features dressed in a long yellow robe whose bright color added much to the strip's popularity.

After 1907 comic strips proliferated in American newspapers: one example is Martin Branner's *Winnie Winkle,* exported to France in 1913, where it became the popular Bicot. The genre evolved in 1929 with Hal Foster's *Tarzan,* then with *Mandrake the Magician* (1934), *Prince Valiant* (1937), and others. Until *Zig et Puce* the European *bande dessinée* kept the traditional style of placing the text under the images rather than using speech balloons. *Le Journal de Mickey* gave the genre a boost and did much to acquaint Europe with the American strips. The most popular strips of the next generation were Belgian: *Spirou* (1938) and *Tintin* (1946). The *bande dessinée* gradually evolved in such periodicals as *Pilote* (1959), *Hara Kiri* (1960) and its companion publication *Charlie mensuel* (1960), and later in publications connected with the "underground movement" such as *L'écho des savanes, Mormoil* (1970), *Métal hurlant,* and *Fluide glacial* (1975). Italian, English, and Spanish strips also took on new energy.

The new printing procedures freed typography from its long-established models. The noble letters inspired by ancient inscriptions gave way to whimsical, baroque, and attention-grabbing letters popularized by billboards. Daily newspapers made increasing use of aggressive headlines. In France *Paris Soir* dominated its age and attracted readers with its massive page-one headlines (made possible by continuing news stories on later pages), its attention-getting pictures, and its horoscopes.

There were important changes in book publishing as well. Information was proliferating, and it circulated faster in a world in which communications media were developing and accelerating. Newspapers had to solve a variety of problems. The various distribution agencies—news dealers, area wholesalers, delivery services—appeared to be all-powerful in both the periodical press and book publishing. News agencies that select and sell news but also furnish background files, pictures, and prefabricated texts multiplied constantly. Henceforth the newspaper had to be attractive to potential advertisers. When we add that the machinery required to produce printed pages more efficiently and better was constantly improved and ever more complicated, it is understandable that the major press organs in all countries tended to become concentrated in a few hands. As "opinion" papers began to catch on and show a profit, the increased advertising that brought them success eventually drowned out their editorials, which became more and more neutral as the audience for such papers broadened.

Modern book publishing followed a comparable route.[6] The publisher stood at the center of a network that connected the production forces (the printers), the writers, and the public. A publisher who was also a printer drew the better part of his revenues from printing advertising materials, administrative publications, and circulars, with publishing representing only a secondary activity. This made innovation out of the question. The best a firm could do was to offer the traditional fare in well-presented books aimed at book-club membership. At times a firm's strength came from a specialized clientele (as with textbooks) or from an efficient distribution system. Bringing out truly original works mattered less than attaining the largest possible printings. Children's books, particularly board-covered storybooks, provide a classic example of this.[7]

These practices have now led to some particularly worrisome current phenomena (well described by Philippe Schuwer). Working out the story and illustrations for children's books in a comic-strip format involves exceptionally high investments, as does printing them. Publishers often have to plan for versions in three or four languages for which the three color-films used for the illustrations can be reused, requiring a new version of only the black film that contains the text. This means, however, that tales specific to one nation are eliminated in favor of internationalized stories or ones from the most powerful tradition, which is of course the Anglo-Saxon. It also means that translators have to fit their text into the space available in the speech balloons, regardless of the brevity or prolixity of their language.

There is nothing exceptional about this situation, of course. French children now and for generations to come are fated to admire the exploits of the Union cavalry during the Civil War, American cowboys of the heroic Far West, or American soldiers in recent wars. The same young people are surprised and would be quick to denounce the chauvinism of a French film presenting Napoleon's cavalry or the trials of the *poilus* of the 1914–18 war in that manner. They become accustomed at an early age to admiring the energy of a "hero"—even a gangster—who has "worked hard" and made large amounts of money, and they understand only the most superficial aspects of stories that take place in a landscape and a social setting that only those who know the United States can evaluate.

The truly creative sectors of the publishing industry can be found, as always, in small-scale publishing enterprises constrained to innovate, even to scandalize, in order to carve out a niche for themselves. Such firms find it mandatory to cultivate authors capable of attracting attention in narrowly focused areas. A prime example of this in France was the group gathered around the *Nouvelle revue française* and that included André Gide, Jacques Copeau, Jean Schlumberger, André Ruytens, Henri Ghéon, and Michel Arnauld. They appealed to Gaston Gallimard, who was not yet a publisher, to put out their works, and Gallimard soon made his mark, founded a dynasty, and reached the pinnacle of the publishing profession. For one success story, however, there were many publishers and innovative presses that failed but did much for letters—firms like La Sirène or Le Sans Pareil, whose careers Pascal Fouché has described.[8]

In both France and England the publishing world had difficulty recovering from a crisis brought on by an overproduction of titles, by inflated pressruns from 1890 to 1914, and by World War I. Readership in France tended to collapse, and in spite of a relative upswing between 1920 and 1930 both books and daily newspapers operated in an atmosphere of crisis between the two world wars. Nothing indicates that the situation was any better in other countries. Henceforth newspapers concentrated increasingly on their less noble tasks—tasks that they had always performed but which were broadened by the growth in advertising. The book underwent a brilliant revival after 1960, as we shall see, but first we need to examine to what extent its supremacy was to be challenged by the appearance of new media.

THE NEW MEDIA

A growing use of paper masked a second phenomenon, the rise of multiform new media. At first the appearance of new media was closely connected with the industrial revolution.[9] Isolated advances were made on individual initiatives by somewhat marginal figures, but basically that revolution was the child of electricity.

A first step, taken early, was rapid and long-distance transmission of messages.[10] The long road from the telegraph to telecommunications began in 1792, when Claude Chappe, whose brother was a deputy, suggested that the Legislative Assembly back an "aerial telegraph." His project was in essence an improvement on the old system of fire signals from one height to another: he used a series of towers with a staff on top bearing a movable central member and two movable side arms that could be put in different positions, each corresponding to a number that conveyed a word. The first line of towers was built from Paris to Lille in 1794, and by 1850 this visual telegraph system covered 4,000 kilometers and performed a number of services in France. Around 1830 the British experimented with using electricity for telegraphic communication, and in 1834 in Göttingen Karl Friedrich Gauss and Wilhelm Weber installed a line 3 kilometers long for a remote electromagnetic signal system. Next, the American Samuel Morse, who was already well known as a painter, invented the code that bears his name and, in 1837, constructed the first telegraph to function with a system of coded electric signals. Rapid advances were made from that date on. In 1844 a line was completed over the 375 miles from Washington to Baltimore; by 1852 the British had over 3,750 miles of lines in their telegraph system. The French telegraph system was reserved for administrative communications until 1851; soon after it became available to the public, business and commercial uses accounted for three-fourths of its activity. The first teleprinter to print incoming messages directly was put into service in Paris in 1860.

From that date on, the new system of communication kept pace with the railroads, for which it was indispensable. It also played an essential role in the life of nations, as shown by the Ems dispatch that launched the Franco-Prussian War. In 1907 Edouard Belin succeeded in transmitting images by wire with an electric device that he called the *bélinographe,* and in 1930 the Telex network (Teletypewriter Exchange) appeared. Telex service was made available in France in 1946; it had some 100 subscribers in 1950, 1,000 by 1956, 10,000 in 1966, 60,000 in 1975, and 135,000 in 1986. Today the Telex service is the primary world-wide communication network using writing since it gives more than 1,600,000 subscribers throughout the globe an opportunity to exchange written communications twenty-four hours a day.

Electricity also made long-distance sound transmission possible. In 1854 François-Charles Bourseul sketched out the principles of the transmission of sound in a series of articles, but it was an American of Scottish birth,

Alexander Graham Bell, and another American, Elisha Gray, who separately and simultaneously invented the telephone in 1876. A private company obtained a monopoly for the device in the United States, and by 1881 it had 123,000 subscribers. When Bell's patents fell into the public domain in 1894, several companies exploited them in the United States and in England, but in Germany the telephone system was a state monopoly and France had three telephone companies as early as 1881. These three were eventually merged into the Compagnie Générale du Téléphone, which rapidly established networks separate from the telegraph wires in major commercial cities, port cities in particular. The French proved relatively resistant to this form of communication, however, and a telephone had to be installed almost by force in the official residence of President Jules Grévy.

Between 1883 and 1887 the French government created telephone exchanges in twenty-five cities, beginning with Reims. In 1885 the first telephone booths were opened in the post offices, rebaptized "bureaux de postes et télégraphes." Also in 1885 long-distance connections were established from Paris to Rouen and Le Havre, followed in 1886 by the Paris-Reims line and the Lille-Roubaix-Tourcoing line, then by connections between Paris and Brussels in 1887, Paris and London in 1891, and London and New York in 1927. After these rapid and promising beginnings, the Chamber of Deputies decided in 1889 to withdraw the concession of telephone services from the private sector and the telephone became a state monopoly and public service.

The invention of the automatic selector in 1889 led to the installation of the first automatic telephone exchange in the United States in 1892. Similar equipment was introduced into France in 1913 in Nice and, in 1921, in Orléans. Telephone service developed slowly in France, and the French had to wait until 1925 before the Ministère des Postes et Télégraphes, which had been in existence since 1879, changed its title to the Ministère des Postes, Télégraphes et Téléphones (PTT) of today. France could count 12,000 telephones in 1889, 70,000 in 1912, 400,000 in 1924, 1,000,000 in 1946, 1,750,000 in 1955, 4,300,000 in 1970, and more than 24,000,000 in 1988.

During this same time, other technologies were evolving that combined individual use and mass distribution.

❖

Devices for recording and transmitting sound were among these.[11] Léon Scott de Martinville took out a patent in 1857 for a device he called a "phonotographe" (phonautograph) that served to study and analyze the timbre of musical instruments and the voice. In 1877 Charles Cros submitted a sealed packet to the Académie des Sciences describing a procedure for using photogravure to transfer the trace obtained by the phonautograph to a more permanent support. Thomas Edison, however, was the first to produce a working phonograph, a hand-cranked machine using a cylinder. For the first time humankind could "record" and play back sounds, the human voice in particular. The cylinder survived until 1919, when it was replaced by the disk, invented in 1900, and when electricity was applied to recording further improvements came swiftly. As we all know, the traditional shellac record was in turn replaced by the vinyl plastic microgroove "long-playing" record around 1945, which was in turn largely supplanted after 1983 by the compact disk, which is based on the totally different technology of a digital pulse code "scored" by a laser beam. Magnetic recording was an idea that Valdemar Poulsen had used in 1898 in his wire "telegraphone," the ancestor of the tape recorder (1935). Tape recording developed rapidly during the 1950s, in particular with the widespread use of cassette tape recorders.

The notion that movement could be recorded and reproduced arose very early in the milieus of the theater and public spectacles.[12] Joseph Plateau produced a "phénakistiscope" that functioned much like a stroboscope to give an effect of motion by rapidly passing simple images behind a viewing slot (1829–33). Later Emile Reynaud invented a "praxinoscope" (1876), a toy that showed brief animated scenes by reflecting images off mirrored prisms. Raynaud perfected this device and opened an "optical theater" that offered fairly long projections of animated drawings (1892–1900). During those same years, an astronomer, Jules Janssen, experimented with ways to take serial photographic observations of the passage of Venus in front of the Sun (1874), and Etienne-Jules Marey, a professor at the Collège de France, worked on the cinematic recording of physiological phenomena. Edison, who knew of Marey's work, claimed the invention of the kinetoscope (1894) that his collaborator Dickson, had devised. This was a box fitted with an eyepiece with a crank that turned a continuous loop of flexible film containing single photographic frames. Seen through a revolving mechanism with a shutter, these gave an illusion of movement. At about the same time, the Lumière brothers realized their "cinématographe" and made notable improvements in photographic film. Louis Lumière gave the first demonstration of their projector in the basement of the Café de Paris in 1895, thus launching public film performances that at times (with Georges Méliès, who produced and directed more than four thousand films) resembled carnival shows. Moving pictures were further developed in France by Charles Pathé and Léon Gaumont with the help of such people as the engineer Gabriel Martin, who made a number of improvements in electrical equipment. In the meantime the popularity of motion pictures had spread to Anglo-Saxon lands. During World War I American motion picture production expanded rapidly and led the world market after the founding of studios in the Los Angeles suburb of Hollywood. Henceforth America drained off Europe's creative talent and became the chief producer of motion pictures, an industry that the French may have been wrong to sell off so willingly. With the arrival of radio the public was dissatisfied with the silent cinema, and the motion picture industry reacted by producing films with musical accompaniment. Next Warner Brothers introduced the "talkies," and Fox launched news films. Finally, the appearance of color motion pictures in the 1930s helped the film industry to retain its public and—soon—to withstand competition from television.

In 1864 a Scot, James Clerk Maxwell, worked out the theory of the transmission of electromagnetic waves: vibrations moving through space with no physical support.[13] The world had to wait twenty years, however, until a German, Heinrich Hertz, brought experimental proof to Maxwell's theories. It was then noted that Hertzian (or radioelectric) waves could leap across long distances and be captured on the way by a number of receivers. The work of Michael Faraday (1845), Maxwell (1864–73), Hertz (1887), Edouard-Eugène Branly (1890), Aleksandr Stepanovich Popov (1896), and Guglielmo Marconi led to the development of the wireless telegraph.

It was Marconi who perfected the procedures for using electromagnetic waves for sending telegraphic messages over long distances. In 1896 he succeeded in transmitting three kilometers across the Bay of La Spezia and in the following year twelve miles across the Bristol Channel. A. C. H. Slaby in Germany succeeded in transmitting first over 21, then 48 kilometers, and in France Eugène Ducretet established wireless telegraphic communication between the Pantheon and the third level of the Eiffel

Tower. In 1899 Marconi transmitted across the English Channel from Dover to Wimereux and in 1901 across the Atlantic. Henceforth wireless telegraphy was in use everywhere and was particularly useful for transmitting distress calls from ships at sea. Military telegraphy also underwent notable advances in France between 1914 and 1918 under the direction of General Ferrié.

Soon vacuum electron tubes, pioneered by an English electrical engineer, Sir John Ambrose Fleming in 1904 and improved by Lee De Forest with his grid-triode vacuum tube (1907), permitted the emission of radio waves at fixed frequencies and high power. Such devices, which detected oscillations between the tips of the antennae and amplified the frequencies, proved an ideal aid to wireless telegraphy.

Unlike Edouard Branly, Marconi did not limit his thinking about wireless telegraphy to military applications and disasters at sea, and he realized that it could serve to transmit music and the spoken word. The microphone appeared in 1912 and with it the idea of radio transmission, which took on its current form after World War I.

Early experimental radio transmission aroused great interest in the general public, and crystal sets for broadcasting and receiving were relatively easy to make. In its early days radio was a paradise for amateurs, but in 1920 the first radio station in the United States appeared in Pittsburgh. In the following year France had a station broadcasting from the Eiffel Tower in Paris. The major European countries differed in the ways they regulated broadcasting stations and, later, networks. Although all agreed that there must be orderly sharing of wavelengths if chaos was to be avoided, some countries privileged private initiative and others opted for a state monopoly. In the United States the Radio Act of 1927 provided for granting licenses to broadcast, but it also privileged commercial interests and prompted the rise of networks that are still in operation, NBC (the National Broadcasting Company) and CBS (the Columbia Broadcasting System). These networks lived on advertising, but in the American fashion they compensated for this with an ethics of duty. Truth was not to be sacrificed to profits, the news was to be given honestly, commentators were named, and morbid and sensational news items were declared taboo.

The British chose a quite different solution. The BBC (British Broadcasting Corporation) was created and licensed in 1923 as a for-profit private corporation that served as a holding company for six large companies. The BBC and the government shared revenues from a tax on radio receivers, and the importation of foreign-made receivers was prohibited. According to its contracts with the government (renewable every ten years) the BBC was obliged to use news agencies so as to reduce its competition with the print press and to maintain eight transmitters, thus blanketing the British Isles. Since the radio was considered a public service, advertising was prohibited, and high standards of morality and broadcast quality were imposed. The BBC had a news program as early as 1925; it also had a system for polling listeners and attempted to include controversy in its programs. In 1937 there were as many as 8,300,000 radio sets in Great Britain, or twice the number owned by the French.[14]

In France the radio industry was founded on the principle of universal coexistence. The Compagnie de Télégraphie et Téléphonie Sans Fil, which was created in 1912 and included sizable amounts of German capital in its funding, was seized during World War I. The company was revived in 1922 with the help of the Marconi Company, and it founded an independent station, Radio-Paris; at the same time the state founded Radio-Tour Eiffel. This dual private and public status was authorized by a decree in 1923, but the law specified that "free" radio stations needed to request authorization before taking to the air waves. Stations gradually increased in number. Laurent Eynac, Minister of the PTT, established a radio tax in 1933. Jean Mistler bought out Radio-Paris, and Georges Mandel worked to provide an infrastructure for provincial stations. French radio was regulated by law in 1937, when there were eighteen nationwide and eighteen provincial stations dependent on the state, the liveliest of which was perhaps Radio-Toulouse, but also private stations such as the Poste Parisien, Radio-Cité, and Radio-Ile-de-France.

Even in those early days, the radio's impact on the masses could pose problems. In 1922 a private station, Radiola, began to specialize in news and music, as English stations were already doing. In 1925 Maurice Privat launched a news program in France on Radio-Tour Eiffel with the support of the former president of the Republic, Raymond Poincaré. Next, Radio Journal de France appeared, an agency that provided news and special programs to the various government-owned stations. Journalistic ethics demanded strict objectivity: when the news press was reviewed, the reviewers had to include both *L'Humanité* and *L'Action Française*, although they spent most of their time reviewing the dailies with the largest readership. The Popular Front placed Radio Journal under the aegis of a bureau that handled all the information services of the state. A weekly of the far

Left, *Radio libre*, launched a campaign to purge the radio of government influence, but in 1938 reaction set in. These quarrels were a good deal less clamorous, however, than those of more recent years.

Politicians found that they needed to become knowledgeable about using the media. They learned to change their declamatory style in public speeches to a more intimate tone. The success of Franklin Roosevelt's "New Deal" was thought in great part due to his "fireside chats." In France André Tardieu, who campaigned systematically against the Popular Front, never learned to speak with the necessary measure, Léon Blum sounded too vague and too intellectual, and the Radicals, who were too well accustomed to oratory more appropriate at county fairs, were leery of the microphone. Adolph Hitler, however, used it to perfection.

The new media made extraordinary advances after World War II. By that time, television was by no means an unknown technique.[15] After a number of others, Boris Rosing (1905) and A. A. Campbell-Swinton (1911) laid down the theoretical foundations that resulted in the transmission of televised images by John Logie Baird in 1926 and René Barthélemy in 1931. France had its first regularly scheduled television program in 1935, England had scheduled programs in 1936, and by 1941 eighteen licenses for telecasting had been granted in the United States. The most rapid development in the number of televised programs occurred in the United States between 1948 and 1950, with the result that by the 1960s, 88 percent of American homes contained a television set. In France the real development of television occurred after 1949, and telecasting reached everywhere in France by 1961. The first color telecast in France came in 1963. A second network was created in 1964, a third in 1973, and three new networks were added in 1984 and 1985.

Satellite communications, which opened the way to vastly expanded intercontinental exchanges, began in the United States in 1962 with Telstar and in Japan in 1964; with the launching of the Early Bird and Molnya satellites in 1965 international telecommunications increased by 25 percent, doubling the previous rate of increase. Today 165 countries use the worldwide Intelstat network and a dozen more use Intersputnik; regional satellites (Arabsat, TV-sat and Telecom I) and dozens of others of national scope interconnect urban telephone networks and distribute programs to radio-relay and cable television companies. Cable television, launched in the United States in 1963, made its first appearance in France in Grenoble in 1972 and is fast being installed in a number of French cities.

In the last analysis, however, it was data-processing machines that brought the most profound changes to society. Data handling by electric and electronic means was preceded by a long history of the mechanical treatment of information.[16]

The abacus was long used as an aid to memory in calculation, but in times nearer to our own several types of machines were developed that were particularly adapted for that purpose. A first step was John Napier's discovery of logarithms in 1614, which led to the invention of the slide rule. Next came the first calculating machine, invented by Pascal in 1642, which could perform additions and subtractions. In 1673 Leibniz created a calculating device that could do all four arithmetical operations. These inventions were not followed up until 1820, when Charles-Xavier Thomas created his "arithmometer," an adding machine that came into general use late in the nineteenth century. Adding machines were constantly improved, incorporating some of the feature of typewriters, and after 1910 typewriters were made that incorporated bookkeeping functions. Some calculating machines involved printers that produced results on paper tape, at first mechanically and later electrically, and after the 1970s these were increasingly replaced by electronic calculators.

Automatic devices for the mechanical reproduction of information fed into them by means of perforated cards or toothed cylinders also had a long history in such devices as music boxes, barrel organs and street pianos, and player pianos. In 1728 a native of Lyons named Falcon devised a system for guiding a mechanical weaving loom by means of perforated cards whose holes created patterns in the woven cloth by directing the shuttle over or under the warp thread. Jacques Vaucanson made improvements in this invention in 1750, and in 1801 Joseph-Marie Jacquard made Falcon's system commercially feasible by automating the weaving operation and devising ways to reproduce textile designs. In 1833 a British mathematician, Charles Babbage, who had been experimenting since 1812, perfected a calculating machine and forerunner of the modern computer that he called an "analytic engine." His "engine" had a memory, could do calculations, and worked by sequential commands. Once the sequence was defined by means of punched cards, the machine could execute the operation automatically, and the sequence could be changed by changing the cards. The memory elements were toothed wheels; the arithmetic elements were mechanical; data could be entered either by means of punched cards or hand-positioned frames, and the results could be had either in the form of punched cards or printed pages or could be read from the characters on the frames.

Later Hermann Hollerith turned punched cards to a new use by reversing the process, using them for automatic treatment of the data encoded on them rather than for guiding the machine. In 1881 he used punched cards to automate the collection of census data in the United States, an operation that took two and a half years. To accomplish this task Hollerith built two machines, a perforator to register information by punching holes to correspond to the encoded data, and an electric sorting machine that could group the punched cards according to common characteristics or put them in a stipulated order. The eighty-column card he created for this purpose was used in computing until the early 1980s. The machines that Hollerith invented attracted the attention of a number of manufacturing firms, and in 1895 he himself founded the Tabulating Machine Company, the successor of which became International Business Machines (IBM) in 1922.

The card-sorting procedures made possible by such machines relied on a reasoning tool—logical calculation—that made available all possible combinations and relations among propositions. It was the work in symbolic logic of George Boole (1815–64) and Augustus De Morgan (1806–71) that permitted clear definition of the three basic operations of modern logic. Their work was completed by Georg Cantor (1845–1918), a pioneer in set theory, the basis for the modern mathematical techniques underlying such procedures.

The development of increasingly reliable mechanical, then electromechanical, and finally electromagnetic computing devices permitted Howard Hathaway Aiken and his team at Harvard University to produce the Harvard Mark I computer, which used electromagnetic circuits and a continuous perforated paper tape instead of electrically punched cards. John Presper Eckert, Jr., and John William Mauchly, working at the Moore School of Engineering at the University of Pennsylvania, produced the ENIAC (Electronic Numerical Integrator and Computer) in 1945, sponsored, like the Mark I, by the United States Army. This was a more powerful and faster computer than the Mark I because its internal functions were totally electronic. It depended on external cables to connect its various components; input and output were by punched cards.[17]

The basic idea underlying today's computers—registering instructions onto the memory of a calculator in order to process data—first appeared in a paper by the American mathematician John von Neumann in 1945. Not only could instructions be put into memory, but the use of binary numbers much enhanced computer capacity. The computers of the first generation, EDVAC and EDSAC, were based on these principles.

Further advances were made in speed, dependability, and ease of use. Beginning in 1951 Remington Rand produced forty-six UNIVAC I computers, a decimal computer that used mercury for memory storage and provided output on magnetic tape. In France, Bull produced the Gamma 3, more than a thousand of which had been sold by 1953; the IBM 701 was a binary computer that used Williams tubes for memory numbers; the WHIRLWIND I, developed at MIT, was the first computer to use a random access magnetic core main memory. The commercialization of computers began with the UNIVAC I, followed by the IBM 650, well over a thousand of which were sold. These models differed from the earlier ones, which operated with punched cards, in that the program could be stored in memory, in the case of the IBM 650, using a rotating magnetic drum. The circuits of the mainframe used electronic vacuum tubes that permitted a speed of calculation of from one to two thousand operations per second, but the tubes were fragile. People began to realize that computers could be used on a broad scale for other purposes than military and scientific applications, and new technological "generations"—an over-simplifying but convenient term for expressing technological advances—followed the first generation of computers of the 1950s.

After about 1958 computers of the "second generation" operated on transistors rather than by electronic vacuum tubes and electromagnetic circuits. The transistor was more compact, it lasted longer (in theory, nearly forever), and it permitted faster operations than vacuum tubes, reducing operating time from millionths of a second to billionths of a second. The magnetic drums of the main memory were replaced by more economical and faster-operating ferrite cores. The first six models of computers using transistors were delivered toward the end of 1959, and over the lifetime of the IBM 1401 that came out in September of that year, the company sold between 15,000 and 20,000 units. The third-generation computers, which were introduced in 1963, used miniaturized electronic components—

planar integrated circuits that could perform millions of operations per second—in the central processing unit, thus reducing transmission time even further. Computers became faster, cheaper, and more modular in their design, and software became increasingly important.

The next development was the minicomputer. By 1965 IBM was marketing its S/360 models, and Bull-General Electric put out their series 50 in 1966. The wide-scale use of integrated circuits in microprocessors (1971) helped to produce central processing units of extremely small size and led to the microcomputers of the fourth generation in the early 1970s. This revolution was more properly industrial than technological because the price of the CPU was by then one-hundredth of what it had been ten years earlier. Speed of operation increased, and modular design enabled the manufacturers not only to continue to incorporate improvements but also to offer "custom made" systems that varied in memory capacity, set-up, the nature and capacity of input and output, and the amount of auxiliary memory.

Generational advances in software accompanied technological improvements in hardware. Furthermore, mini- and microcomputers, first used for scientific calculation and then for all sorts of management tasks, developed along with their larger counterparts. Henceforth administrative and business offices were computerized at an accelerating rate: the French government used 484 computers in 1970 and 4,224 in 1981; the numbers of computer programmers and operators rose from 7,000 to 81,000 persons in the same time period. In 1986, 68,000 computers were in operation in France. The market broadened as well: late in 1983, more than one-half of small- and mid-sized businesses in France were computerized, as compared to 36 percent just the previous year. Needless to say, record-keeping applications and personal data-processing as we now know them also appeared in the late 1970s.

All in all, the nineteenth century was indeed the century of the communications revolution, when the all-conquering machine substituted for human beings and their tools and took over a good many human tasks involved in the reproduction, transmission, and treatment of information—that is, in the various forms and uses of writing. But the late nineteenth century was also the beginning of the reign of electricity, which presented the advantage of satisfying two hitherto irreconcilable needs: the need to inscribe messages on a physical material and the need to liberate those messages from that physical medium during the transfer or the treatment of information. Henceforth electricity profoundly transformed a number of mechanical means created to satisfy a specific need—the telegraph, office machines—and made possible electric telegraphy, data processing, and magnetic recording. Electricity also led to the development of new means of communication such as the telephone, the radio, and television.

The universal use of electricity as a carrier, an energy source, and the basic principle in these devices soon permitted the various parts of the computer system (the central processing unit and the peripherals) to be integrated into one "machine," then enabled the tasks performed by different machines to be integrated into one unit.

The essential turning point in this evolution was surely the merging of data processing and telecommunications in the automatic data-transfer techniques known in French as *la télématique*, a term coined by Simon Nora and Alain Minc in their *Rapport sur l'informatisation de la société: La télématique*.

"Telematics" got its start in the 1940s, when IBM devised a way to generate and read supply lists for the United States Army, using telephone lines to relay information from punched cards generated by one keypunch machine to a similar unit on the receiving end that produced identical punched cards. As computer capacity increased and the integration of peripheral functions improved, data-processing techniques assured better connections between them.

An early application for the new techniques was an aerial defense and offense system that used a radar network to plot the movement of aircraft. Any information detected was immediately transmitted to a central computer, which processed the data in real time and responded immediately, thus permitting rapid action. Programs such as this laid the groundwork for other systems of aerial surveillance such as SAGE (Semi-Automatic Ground Environment) in the years of the Cold War and in support of the Strategic Air Command.

Civilian systems in the image of the military ones were developed to manage specific data bases such as commercial airline reservations. One of these was the SABRE (Semi-Automatic Business Research Environment) system created in 1959. Large mainframe computers were used to set up these commercial systems, adapting them and supplementing them with equipment and software to handle multiple remote communications tasks.

The central processing unit was reserved for data processing, while external memory on disks permitted storage of both input and output. Programs were developed that took into account both these new possibilities and changing and multiform needs.

During the 1960s communications peripherals and software became an integral part of the system. Multiprogramming became possible, permitting multitasking and the seemingly simultaneous processing of more than one data set, which is the essence of "telematics."

In a first phase the merged technologies of the processing and transmission of information were constrained by systems that had been developed for use in one place and that depended upon means of communication that had been created for other purposes (the telephone and the telex, for example). The rapid expansion of both the industry and user needs led to the development of new data-processing systems made up of increasingly separated elements and to the appearance of communications networks dedicated to the transmission of data.

These new networks marked a turning point: conceived for remote data transmission and the tasks it did best, they made possible considerably enlarged capacities for communication among data-processing components. Batch processing permitted the creation of such new communication services as airlines reservations and tourist videotex systems, text transmission, and phototelegraphy.

The first packet-switching communications network was the experimental ARPA network in the United States in 1968. This network permitted communication and the sharing of resources among nearly one hundred heterogeneous computer systems with ninety-four "nodes" at eighty-eight sites, in universities and research laboratories for the most part. In France, the Cyclades network, first conceived in 1972 as an experimental prototype connecting some twenty participating centers, became fully operative in 1975.

The shift to large-scale commercial public networks was rapid. In the United States, TELENET, the first public communication network to use packet switching was put into service in 1975, and in France the TRANS-PAC system of the Direction générale des télécommunications was operative by late 1978 and is currently available for use throughout France. By the beginning of 1986 it had 31,300 outlets in France, and by the end of that year it was connected with fifty foreign networks, for the most part European, American, and Japanese.

Today remote data-processing occupies a preponderant place in the field and is constantly increasing its capacity for integrating and absorbing all the other techniques for gathering, processing, storing, and communicating information. It responds to a need to put the data-processing capabilities of the computers within the reach of the greatest number of users.

These developments have created a similar increase in data banks, remote data-processing and data-retrieval systems, and the information networks, an increase that affects all domains of modern life. To cite one example, TELETEL, the French videotex system put into place in 1981–82, now offers the public more than three thousand data-retrieval and financial services, and the number of transactions processed rose from 136,000,000 in 1978 to 790,000,000 in 1986.

In the United States the exponential growth and the pervasiveness of data-processing techniques in all aspects of daily and professional life—the bank card is proof enough of this—prompted a new development in the late 1970s. The success of Apple computers (whose early profits served to finance rock concerts) was a part of that new development, along with all the industry, which, for the first time, put the new data-processing and communication techniques within the reach of everyone. [18]

These revolutionary developments have done much to achieve a complete restructuring of the publishing industry. Between the two world wars bank investment in publishing ventures in France were carefully focused and limited in scope, in spite of some signs of greater interest around 1930. Immediately after World War II and until the mid-1960s, Spanish, Portuguese, and Swiss banks began to invest in the large French publishing firms, taking a 5 to 10 percent interest in the firms. These investments aroused the curiosity of French bankers in a sector of the economy that was by then undergoing a strong revival, but their involvement remained limited. After the brief economic downswing in 1974, however, a quite different movement was launched when investors realized that the communications industry was fast becoming one of the largest sectors of the economy. Large corporations such as Matra and profitable press groups like the CEP (Compagnie Européenne de Publications) sought to diversify their holdings and extend them to include businesses with a promising future. Turning initially to banks for backing, they acquired controlling interests in companies that later became integrated into communications groups with a broad range of data-processing and communications activities—so broad, in fact, that one might wonder if these components will ever enjoy the mutual enhancement being sought. These firms have sought more than ever to realize the highest possible profits in the shortest time, even at the price of neglecting long-term planning. The publishing houses, themselves targets of speculation, have stressed massive circulation figures and enormous pressruns. By the same token, the profitability of a book is now gauged over one or two years, just the opposite of long-standing policies in such firms as Gallimard. This sort of attitude might make one fear that the book, now in competition with so many other media, might cease to play its traditional role in intellectual innovation. As has always been the case, however, new firms have accepted the challenge of creativity at high financial risk. We see once again that since printing was invented the mechanisms of book publishing have remained by and large the same.

Nonetheless, the market share of the book as a means for the transmission of information and knowledge seems to have regressed, particularly when we consider the growth of information and communication media that treat enormous quantities of material, mobilize considerable equipment (satellites, for example), and require a capital investment on a totally different level of magnitude from that of traditional book publishing.

Can this basic picture help us to draw any general conclusions about the universe that the most recent media are bringing to pass? We need first to stress what those media have given us before going to ask what we have lost by them.

The audiovisual media that are based on the capturing and transmission of sounds and images do not involve deciphering special encoding: pictures and music are an immediately accessible and universal means of communication. By the same token, the last forty years do seem to have ushered in a change that has negative aspects for writing as we know it; the entire symbolic system that has been elaborated in the last thousand years has been challenged by the very instruments that were created thanks to the aid of writing. This becomes clear if we compare the evolution of various "languages" and their modes of presentation.

In the first of these languages, music, one cannot help being struck by the emancipation of the voice and the liberation of auditory memory.[19] At first music was a natural part of the oral tradition. Even today many who sing or play popular or religious music cannot read music, let alone write it. In a number of civilizations that practice writing—the Moslem world and Far Eastern civilizations, for example—music is still seldom written down. Thus musical writing—musical notation—is specific to Western Europe. It is also the end product of a very long history.

Musical notation originated in the signs that accompanied poetic texts in ancient Greece and served to jog the performer's memory. Only a very limited number of specialists were aware of them. This "ancient musical notation" disappeared in the age of Boethius (480–525) and Cassiodorus (480–575), after which the traditional monody of the Western churches was transmitted orally. Isidore of Seville (ca. 570–636) stated that "music cannot be written." Nonetheless, the tradition of noting chants continued in Byzantium, where several different systems of signs succeeded one another, and the habit of adding signs to a text as an aid to musical memory reappeared in northern France during the Carolingian renaissance in the mid-ninth century. Several parallel systems developed for the memorization of the Gregorian plainchant that accompanied religious texts. These notations were derived from the script then in use, the Carolingian minuscule, and they followed principles stated in the works of the Latin grammarians, notably the *De accentibus* of Priscian and Donatus (fourth century). The signs, or neumes, were written between the lines of text as accent marks or points on an imaginary or indicated line. A short line slanting up toward the right meant that the voice rose in pitch; a descending slant (or often just a point) meant that it fell. This was simply a mnemonic device to recall the inflections of the voice and did not indicate either the duration or the absolute pitch of the note. It was a new writing system born of divergence from another writing system.

This quite rudimentary code was gradually improved. Between the late tenth and the early eleventh centuries a vertical line was added to situate neumes pertaining to one syllable in relation to one another, and the neumes were carefully spaced along the line of written text to as to give a notion of pitch values for the entire line. The code governing lines and neumes later became more diversified and more complex, and eventually various codes for noting plainsong developed in monasteries and cathedrals, although these were not observed either regularly or assiduously and the chants continued to be learned by rote. It took a century before manuscript copyists began to write literary texts that took musical notation into account by spacing out the lines, using abbreviations and breaking the phrase to follow the melodic line. Various schools used different techniques (the use of letters, for example) to note the melodic line more precisely, and one Benedictine, Guido of Arezzo (962–1031), systematized this procedure by creating a full alphabetic notation. The staff, which had begun with one line, soon moved on to use two lines, and eventually four lines, two of which were colored.

This slow evolution of a system for the memorization of melody seems to us somewhat incomplete, since neither rhythm nor the parts of the accompanying instruments were noted. Nonetheless it was a dynamic first step that created conditions propitious to the development of polyphonic music, at which point musical notation became an absolute necessity. From its beginnings as simple ornamentation of Gregorian chant in the age of Hucbald, the Benedictine abbot of Saint-Michel, polyphonic music developed rapidly in thirteenth-century Paris, the period of the School of Notre-Dame, perhaps thanks to a process of adaptation similar to the one we have just seen.

Polyphony brought another dimension to music, and because of it notation no longer functioned simply as an imprecise aid to memory and a prop to the oral tradition. The extreme complexity of polyphonic music made writing obligatory: only with written music could each independent voice line be coordinated with the other voices to form a harmonic whole and produce the desired effect, and writing was even more necessary when several vocal lines were juxtaposed. A true writing system, musical notation gradually developed conventional signs to express nearly all the parameters of musical language. In return, it imposed quite particular constraints on the written text. It empowered the musician to act on sounds—that is, it furnished a working tool for composition that has never ceased to be improved. In quite unique ways musical notation not only shaped the creation of music in the West for centuries but also encouraged its rapid development. The oral tradition continued to play a large role in religious music and popular music.

During the Renaissance musical notation included instrumental accompaniment as well as voices. New possibilities stimulated the creation of new musical instruments and their perfection as tools and machines for making music. Music itself evolved in the direction of an increasing complexity in sound production. Many innovations during the eighteenth and nineteenth centuries added to the complexity of instrumental techniques, hence to the complexity of musical notation. Sébastien Erard (1752–1831), for example, made improvements in the action of the harp in 1814 and in the striking mechanism of piano keys in 1821; wind instruments such as the transverse flute and the oboe and some brass instruments were redesigned; Adolphe Sax invented the saxophone; Aristide Cavaillé-Coll

(1811–99) introduced "distinctive voicing" to the organ to create the Romantic symphonic organ. One might well wonder whether musical instruments, which offer much broader possibilities than the human voice, did not gradually reduce the voice's share of and role in music. Music was becoming emancipated from its dependence on the voice just as the musical score liberated the performer's memory. Moreover, the orchestra included more musicians and instruments, and the technique required to play each instrument grew more complex and demanding. In the mid-twentieth century musical notation improved in precision in order to make the written score reflect the expressive qualities the composer had in mind. By the same token, improvisation declined, and the interpreter's role began to be reduced to simple execution.

It is hardly surprising that the twentieth century was characterized by a search for new and more expressive sounds and by a breakdown of the traditional system of notation. A search for new sonorities and new musical languages necessarily involved the creation of new instruments and a new and synthetic music. It also led to a proliferation of signs. The traditional system of musical notation seemed to be disintegrating, and the lack of a universally accepted system for encoding sounds poses serious problems for composers today, while interpreters are often constrained to learn a new code before they can perform a new work. Furthermore, the traditional system is incapable of giving an adequate account of the new musical landscape created by electronic instruments and techniques or by compositions that include sonic phenomena that used to be called "noise." Traditional notation is powerless to note this new "solfège of the sound object" (as Pierre Schaeffer has called it), and no new system has succeeded in predominating because none has grasped the full complexity of all the sound information that must be processed simultaneously.

The invention of sound recording by Charles Cros and Thomas Edison in 1877, followed, toward the end of the century, by the commercial success of cylinder and disk recordings, and by the development of radio transmission after World War I, gave full force to the oral tradition. Writing lost some of its importance while two seemingly opposite trends arose: improvisation was rediscovered in jazz and in non-European forms of music, and forms of musical pictography appeared in which graphics told the interpreter what general direction to go in rather than translating the desired execution note for note. The question arises of whether it would be possible (and even desirable) to create a new system of notation, and whether computer-assisted composition and even more direct transcription and the electronic conversion of gesture and motion directly into sound are signs of a mutation, a renascence, or an end.

To sum up, in the Carolingian age Western European civilization began to shape a unique kind of musical writing that enabled musicians to avoid repetition and improvisation. The system that was created favored a new sort of musical creation, on which it imposed constraints of rigor and analysis. It prompted the appearance of constructions more elaborate than memory alone could produce, and it permitted the criticism of finished works in the interest of improving future compositions. The shift to writing also emphasized the role of the composer, the author of the score, and it reduced the role of the interpreter. Today, however, musical notation has failed to keep pace with composition, and we can see a return to the oral tradition, whose drawbacks are eliminated by sophisticated recording techniques. With electronic music we can also see the advent of a new notation, dissociated from recording, in which writing is no longer necessarily opposed to orality. New instruments, new sounds, a new notation, new music, new ways of listening, a new culture. By the same token, music of the oral tradition, popular and religious, is tending to disappear along with its instruments, whose sonic possibilities are now inadequate. Classical music seems in decline.

Another language in which the hand and memory—visual memory this time—have undergone vast changes is figured language.

Graphic language addresses sight just as spoken language addresses hearing. Like spoken language, it is a privileged means for analyzing and describing objects and for processing, communicating, and storing information concerning them. When pictorial representation is promoted to the rank of a writing code, however, it becomes a unique mode of communication that requires initiation because the meaning of the signs is not immediately evident.

Images, as we have seen, preceded writing in the systems of communication that mankind has elaborated, and a number of ancient writing systems grew out of pictures. The transfer into writing of what one can see, with all the imperatives of analysis and method that task supposes, has had considerable consequences for the evolution of Western European society, thanks to the practical utility of figures and representations. Pictures offer the opportunity to integrate into a set of signs a much larger amount of information than an equivalent amount of text can furnish. Unlike music, for which a limited number of notation systems have been created, pictorial representation has inspired as many writing systems as there are fields of knowledge to be explored, analyzed, and described. Unlike linear writing, it is inscribed in a two-dimensional, even a three-dimensional world, thus it offers incomparable possibilities for the integration of data. I should not need to repeat the Chinese proverb that a single image is worth a thousand words.

The use of pictorial representation to create new scholarly writing codes gave a new impulse to the search for knowledge. One of the advantages of the Western system of writing was that it had managed to transfer from the text to pictures the information that it wanted to conserve or treat when a text alone proved incapable of describing something. This dialogue between text and image has made a large contribution to the development of contemporary science and technology. Indeed, words present ambiguities and are often powerless to describe briefly—that is, economically—the thing observed. In many cases pictorial representation has substituted for narrative and has evolved and grown more accurate in response to need. In cartography, for example, we can follow the changes as merchants' and navigators' portolans were filled in with more accurate detail, pushing monsters and chimeras to the edges of the known world. First in the portolans and then on maps, we can see gains in knowledge about the earth keeping pace with the elaboration of an increasingly precise and more fully articulated language for the representation of geographical phenomena. Printing encouraged the standardization of conventions, as Father François de Dainville showed in a work on geographers' language. These advances, enhanced by improved instruments for observation and measurement and aided by systematic geographical surveys (such as the ones that resulted in the Cassinis' topographical maps of France, published in 1793) further aided the development of that language.

In every scientific and technological field advances were accompanied by the application of pictorial representation and the image. These drawings and images consistently improved in quality in the modern age and in the nineteenth century with printing.

Medicine and the natural sciences are typical examples of the domains in which pictorial representation progressively supplemented texts. Throughout the Middle Ages the scholarly tradition relied on descriptions in ancient Greek texts, known in Arabic and Latin translations, for the transmission of medical lore and knowledge about the botany of herbs and simples.

Such translations (which varied greatly in accuracy) altered the texts of Hippocrates and Galen, but also those of Avicenna and Mesuë. Pliny complained that illustrations of plants that varied in shape and color from one copy to another were useless for botanical classification. If imperfectly translated notions and descriptions were to be understood, they needed generous glosses, commentaries, and examples to remedy their ambiguity and obscurity. In the Renaissance, when engraving made it possible to use illustrations in these texts to give more exact and more numerous depictions of organs and plants, great strides were made in the extension and transmission of knowledge. Illustration much reduced the role of scholastic glosses, which disappeared in the early modern age. It also enhanced the enormous importance for anatomical science of the *De humani corporis fabrica* of Vesalius (1542). Pictorial description encouraged observation and a thirst for knowledge that constant advances in the magnifying glass and, later, the microscope whetted and attempted to satisfy.

Engineering profited from pictorial representation as well. Mechanical engineers, following the lead of Villard de Honnecourt's *Album* (thirteenth century) and Leonardo da Vinci, cultivated technical drawing, which developed in France among architects (Philibert Delorme, ca. 1510–70), shipbuilders, military engineers and experts in fortification (Vauban), and civil engineers (Trudaine, Perronet, and the engineers of the Ponts et chaussées).

All this activity, in which instruments for observation, techniques of description, and a need for practical knowledge spurred one another on to further achievements, climaxed in the great achievements of the eighteenth century, chief among them Buffon's *Histoire naturelle,* a monumental work printed by the Imprimerie royale (1744–89), or the *Encyclopédie* of d'Alembert and Diderot (1751–72), whose volumes of plates provided systematic and detailed depictions of technologies and trades, often in their traditional forms. Such efforts continued into the nineteenth century, gaining in precision and diversity, particularly with the expansion of industrial design, the use of patents, and engineers' drawings. Mechanical drawing was applied to a growing number of objects, and the problem of integrating increasing amounts of data onto a surface that remained two-dimensional was aided by descriptive geometry, which permitted better renderings of three-dimensional objects than a perspective drawing or a bird's-eye view could give.

In certain fields graphic aids were invented when a language that had initially been adequate failed to adapt. One of the clearest examples of this is chemistry, as François Dagognet has shown in his *Tableaux et langages de la chimie* (1969). One might think, a priori, that chemistry, which studies the nature and the properties of chemical substances and compounds, would have no need of pictorial representation to describe these phenomena and could make do simply with naming them. Nothing could be further from the truth. When alchemists had identified and utilized only a few hundred substances, they could designate them and distinguish between them by using phrases, vernacular terms, obscure idiomatic expressions, and proper names. Memory could hold them all. But when the number of known substances had reached a thousand, the alchemists' descriptive tools proved impracticable, imprecise, and overly complicated. Description was no longer adequate; a limit had been reached. Since all bodies are composed of the same basic elements, late-eighteenth-century chemists thought they could get around this difficulty by categorizing the elements by their composition and situating them in a table, thus moving them into a two-dimensional world and creating a new nomenclature by combination of the elements in the table. This achievement was the work of Lavoisier and his collaborators. The system was an evolving one that permitted the unambiguous designation of newly discovered substances as they related to other elements. The word became an idea: it met and described an order and it enabled the science of chemistry to progress.

The number of identified chemical compounds continued to increase, and science has passed from a thousand known elements to several thousand increasingly complex substances. The system of the table of elements, with its scholarly terminology, became insufficient for economical and clear description of the new state of knowledge. It was too unwieldy; a new threshold had been reached. New words were of course still created to designate new compounds, but in order to utilize, distinguish between, and study them, their chemical structure was depicted, and it was immediately clear that this depiction was both easier to read and more accurate. Chemistry could continue to progress. Today, however, this system is once again reaching its limits, as there are now more than seven million known chemical compounds. The spoken and written word cannot even count and describe them: doing so would require twenty years. What is more, chemists often use different terms to designate and write compounds, which produces a high degree of linguistic confusion. New systems have been created, but none seems adequate. The only solution is three-dimensional representation, which frees science from the task and the need for writing, pictorialization, and notation.

The development of printing, industrial printing in particular, has made an enormous contribution to the utilization of writing in all its forms. The art of typography has created a model of communication—the model of the multiple document—that has been imposed on all the new writing materials and systems for the diffusion of writing. The need for multiple copies lay behind most systems of mechanical writing at their first appearance, leading the inventors of those systems to discoveries that in turn produced many other new developments. In order to take hold and to thrive, those discoveries needed to resolve the problem of the production and distribution of multiple copies. Hence the rise of the many modern techniques for graphic reproduction.

The industrial age ushered in the age of machines—machines to retrieve and record data, to produce, reproduce, process, transfer, and distribute information and documents. This universal but heterogeneous mechanization has transformed not only humankind's relation to writing but also the traditional role of the written word. It has augmented and diversified the mass of documents produced and data received, and it poses new questions about the vast accumulation of data to process or communicate.

When engraving techniques proved inadequate to a greatly increased use of pictorial representation, photography appeared. It was an invention that had unforeseen and considerable consequences. Photography, originally a procedure whose use was limited to a handful of specialists, spread to the public at large when it became easier to use (Kodak, 1888). No longer a tool uniquely for professionals, it became an instrument for both amateurs and scholars and technicians. Now anyone could create images.[20]

Both photographic techniques and traditional imaging techniques worked to put onto the market increasing numbers of documents whose use did not require the need for knowledge of any special code, writing included. The new images soon invaded books, some of which were made up exclusively of images. It became fashionable to announce the death of the book. Since photography had beaten drawing and painting at their own game, they were forced to exploit new and different paths. Art went the way of a surrealism and a hyperrealism that attempted to compete with photography on its own terrain; or else art went the way of impressionism, then cubism, and finally abstract (or, more accurately, nonfigurative) art, a term that clearly states art's radical difference from photography. Above all, however, the new images totally changed the transmission of information: photography was in fact a new type of information that had a tremendous impact on the public at large and on collective behavior, as Nadar (1820–1910) once noted, commenting on a human-interest news item. It was remarked that with a weakened traditional culture, photography could produce an appearance of truth that made it a perfect instrument for the manipulation of public opinion among a public unaware of such tricks. It is in fact true that the photographic image, saturated with information, lends itself more than other medium to this sort of operation.[21]

These criticisms aside, photographic and other procedures now enable us to record, write about, and know phenomena that have until now been imperceptible or unknown. They enable science to make extraordinary progress. For example, photography and the cinema offer extraordinary possibilities for the analysis of invisible phenomena thanks to ultraviolet, infrared, or X-ray films, discovered as early as 1895 and now routinely used in radiology. Enormous strides have also been made in micro- and macrophotography and in aerial photography.

I might also mention other procedures for creating documents that involve figuration. The collection of scientific and technical data uses a number of other machines and produces a variety of graphic documents that are not strictly pictorial. For instance there are innumerable measuring and recording devices: thermometers, barometers, hygrometers, seismographs, anemometers, marigraphs, and so forth. The number and use of such devices increased still further with the development of electrical recording devices, beginning in the early days of electromechanical measurement in 1845 and leading, to cite only a few examples, to the electronic endoscope and the megaloscope, and eventually to the electrocardiograph (1887) and the electroencephalograph (1929).

These new domains produced (and continue to produce) considerable quantities of documents, graphic records that can be read only with scientific training and, often, the mastery of a particular code. Today holography permits three-dimensional images that are much more satisfactory than the old stereoscopic images. Now, with echography, the CAT scanner, nuclear magnetic resonance imagers, and spectrometers, computerized numerical data can be obtained that can be converted into synthetic images.

All these developments led to the most singular discovery that humankind has ever made—that the universe was written in a mathematical language. Thus writing systems and the most abstract schemata are simulations of reality and even the only approach to that reality. Furthermore, it seems that certain forms of simulation or interrogation permit the perception of hidden reality. What began as simply a convenient way to commit speech and vision to memory has engendered an embryonic explanation, now within our grasp, of the mechanics of the universe.

I need to add a word on scientific language and the emancipation of the brain and the intelligence.[22]

As the centuries passed, written discourse in the strict sense, with its full freight of rhetoric, was more and more clearly inadequate to deal with advances in knowledge. Today we are faced with a dizzying increase in the numbers of audio and visual documents, and technical progress in these fields (often originally thanks to isolated individuals) has reached a scale and been put to uses that could not have been imagined in the beginning. When they were confronted by a new need, people responded. Each response (and they came in no ordered sequence) accelerated the increase in information produced and utilized in a certain time and a certain domain. But those responses also fitted into an overall framework in which specialists used increasingly diversified codes that made up a singularly complex whole. In this qualitative and quantitative cognitive evolution, specialists regularly arrived at thresholds that obliged them to change their systems of representation.

A revolution of this scope obviously affected many people and faced them with wrenching changes in the writing codes, languages, cultures, systems, and machines to which they had barely become accustomed. They were particularly disoriented by the extraordinary variety and heterogeneity of new systems, machines, and techniques, whose perpetual evolution created endless problems for the very persons whose tasks they were supposed to facilitate. As things stand today, technology requires still new procedures and new means if it is to function well—which means new systems for remote data-processing. This is already happening. A single code is being imposed on the many languages and writing codes that the various systems have engendered. This code is the language of the machines, the digital binary code that fuels data-processing technology today. It permits the "reading" of writing (by scanners or in graphic form in tables), voice recognition and the recognition of actions and physical phenomena, data-processing, data storage on tapes, cassettes, or disks, remote electronic transfer to other machines, and retrieval on monitor screens or in printed "hard copy." Today these techniques seem to offer a way to surmount an ever-increasing flood of data and a hope for solving the prob-

lem of multiple codes, reducing communication costs, and integrating the
many functions that have hitherto been separate because they used techniques derived from different and incompatible sources.

In this way manual systems were replaced by instruments, when the
need arose, then by machines. These innovations have contributed to humankind's definitive liberation from an apprenticeship in codes, from the
tasks of writing by hand and from handwork, from long and tedious ma-
nipulations to process data, from transporting heavy documents, and from
the constraints of distance and time. Today the accumulation of all these
machines and all these procedures has produced what is usually called the
"information explosion." A few figures will suffice to show the acceleration
in the production of documents that the combined effects of such changes
have brought on since the mid-century.

In one century all the means and facilities that industrial society has put,
successively or simultaneously, at the disposition of humankind have
changed radically. Communication, which was once faulty, scarce, slow,
expensive, and limited gradually became more accessible and finally abundant, varied, rapid, and, all things considered, inexpensive. We have gone
from penury to abundance and even superabundance. According to studies
in the United States and elsewhere, the number of reviews and scientific
and technical journals has grown enormously: in 1750 ten such periodicals were published; in 1800 the number rose to 100; in 1850 there were
1,000; in 1900, 10,000, in 1950, 100,000. There were nearly 500,000 in
the late 1980s. Journals are admittedly an approximate and inaccurate
gauge but they nonetheless correspond to a reality: we can state and many
studies confirm that the number of documents produced is growing expo-
nentially. To cite another example, the number of sound recordings (records, tapes, cassettes, etc.) sold in France rose from 62,000,000 in 1970 to
144,000,000 in 1980. Other examples might be given to reinforce the same
point: all the figures show strong growth, even when one technique re-
gresses to the profit of another that incorporates a technological improvement, as with long-playing records and compact disks.

Postal service offers an even more striking example, as the statistics for
the French postal system show. The French system processed 64,000,000
letters in 1830 and 40,000,000 pieces of printed matter and packages; in
1850 these figures rose, respectively, to 160,000,000 and 94,000,000; in
1870, to 285,000,000 and 348,000,000 million; in 1890 to 748,000,000
and 1,015,000,000; in 1910 to 1,541,000,000 and 2,217,000,000; in
1930 to 1,738,000,000 and 4,543,000,000; in 1950 to 1,936,000,000 and

2,114,000,000; in 1970 to 6,031,000,000 and 2,229,000,000; and in 1982 to 8,557,000,000 and 3,323,000,000. In 1858, when electric telegraphy was introduced, there were 350,000 telegraphic communications; in 1870, there were 5,000,000; in 1890, 24,000,000, without counting some 7,000,000 telephonic communications. In 1890 the figures for telegrams and telephone communications begin to be reversed, giving 45,000,000 telegrams to 264,000,000 telephone calls; in 1930 these same figures reached 29,000,000 and 831,000,000, respectively; in 1950, 15,000,000 and 1,537,000,000; and in 1985, 10,000,000 and several billions. The telephone has replaced the telegram for a great many uses and is fast developing new ones. Well before the modernization of the French telephone system in 1970 and well before the Minitel (a device with a small monitor screen and a modem hookup), telephone communication expanded in an extraordinary manner. In 1983 there were 120,000 Minitels in operation and in 1988 the number had risen to nearly 4,000,000. Between 1985 and 1988 communication hours rose from 15,000,000 to 75,000,000.

Similar remarks could be made concerning the audiovisual media. Although circulation figures for daily newspapers in France remained nearly stable (9,500,000 copies in 1914; 10,400,000 in 1984), the number of radios rose between 1965 and 1983 from 15,000,000 to 47,000,000. Although the number of cinema admissions continues to fall (423,000,000 in 1947; 370,000,000 in 1950; 259,000,000 in 1965; 162,000,000 in 1986), the number of television sets owned has risen from 6,000,000 in 1965 to over 20,000,000 in 1983. Annual radio broadcast hours in France reached a total of 28,741 hours before legislation on local radio broadcasting and telecasting was passed in 1979, and annual transmission hours for French television rose between 1975 and 1985 from 8,089 hours to 13,003 hours. In 1964 every French person over the age of fifteen watched an average of 55 minutes of television per day; by 1981 that figure had risen to 132 minutes per day, not counting another 163 minutes of radio listening—and these figures do not take into account viewers and listeners under fifteen! This amounts to nearly five hours per day for the reception of other kinds of knowledge, and particularly of another culture, than the ones transmitted by traditional means, notably by reading. These remarks are roughly applicable to the other industrialized countries.

One might easily imagine that the book, which seemed to be imperiled between 1930 and 1950, would be condemned to oblivion by this irruption of new media. Not so. Publishing in France may never have enjoyed better health and never have had a more varied, numerous, and curious public than between 1950 and 1980. There has never been a larger reading public. The ready availability of word-processing programs has done much to facilitate writing tasks for authors and to decentralize many aspects of printing. Now a writer willing to give up the direct contact with words offered by writing by hand can give his or her publisher easily revised diskettes that take the place of the manuscript for composition of a work. Some ten years ago there was an advertisement featuring Balzac that boasted of these capabilities. The relatively long time required to write a book and transfer it to print keep it from being the principal instrument for publicizing topical questions, recent discoveries, and new ideas. New writing materials have been available for some time: microphotography and the resulting microfilm and microfiches facilitate the publication and reprinting of annual compilations and, in France, of the *Journal officiel* at a much reduced cost. Today the optical disk (laser disk), the video disk, and the CD-ROM permit the reprinting and updating of entire encyclopedias. Soon print will no longer be used for reference works or for telephone books, which can easily be updated with the new procedures and which increasing numbers of subscribers have made heavier and more unwieldy every year. One might ask whether the proliferation of means has not prompted a "brain drain" into the new means of communication.

We have also entered the age of the ephemeral. Knowledge and news, but also the materials on which they are circulated, have become transitory. Parchment and rag paper, which defied the ravages of time, have been replaced in the last century by materials that self-destruct: woodpulp paper, whose acidity has condemned to dust many of the works in our national libraries; color slides and color photographs, whose pigments fade; magnetic tapes and video tapes that lose definition in ten to thirty years. For the moment only microfilm has resisted. What witness will we leave of our times?

New techniques and new media will be substituted for printing, but printing will not disappear. Television, after all, has not killed posters and billboards. It even seems clear that within our data-hungry society writing will continue to develop even though its relative share in the realm of communication gradually diminishes. We may have to wait only a generation, however, before printed matter represents less than half of all the media in use. Nonetheless, we need to ask whether the book will remain the noblest instrument of communication; whether there will continue to be writers willing to devote months and even years of their time and energy to sharing their thoughts and experiences with the public; whether, for example, the poets of tomorrow will not prefer to express themselves in videoclips rather than on sheets of paper.

It would be unthinkable to end this analysis without a few words on the impact of these technological and cultural phenomena on men and women and on how society functions. Some years ago Marshall McLuhan introduced a notion that has become familiar to us all: thanks to the new media the entire world has become a global village. McLuhan's works had the incontestible merit of recasting some important questions, ones on which our society would do well to reflect. The new situation in which we find ourselves, however, is extremely complex. Admittedly, the first appearance of a new means of communication has always prompted a certain "massi-fication," but mass enthusiasm has always been followed by a settling period in which each medium has found its role by creating new solidarities within public opinion. The final result has been increased possibilities, as in the recent expansion of a specialized press when television tended to take the place of the nonspecialized newspaper.

I need not insist on these much-discussed topics. A question more essential to our purposes here is to ask to what extent do the new information media permit the formation of a truly independent opinion.

One case in point is the way in which major political events and social phenomena are shown on television with a seemingly "neutral" presentation but one that never clearly separates fact from commentary. We should not forget that for many reasons (in particular, because on-site reporting is time-consuming and expensive), the written and spoken news media tend to reproduce news that emanates from the five major worldwide agencies closely connected with a major state—the United States, the Soviet Union, Great Britain, and France—or from agencies with connections to smaller countries or even to liberation movements. We also need to keep in mind that news is an exceptionally malleable entity: in a particular newspaper an apparently objective headline can be deadly; the way a television angle is shot is not always innocent; word choice can be given a special thrust. To take one example, announcing that someone has been "assassinated" or that he has been "executed" give a quite different impression.

The sheer number and the important role of the mechanisms involved tend to reduce the independence of information even more. Although the written press still assumes, albeit with increasing difficulty, its function as a "counterpower," television requires such enormous sums of money that the state is often tempted to dictate policy—in nations that have state-owned channels—or to influence programming, with all the risks to freedom of information that implies. This is of course the normal practice under totalitarian governments, but it has also tended to be true in a number of other countries when television was introduced. In France, that moment coincided with the advent of the Fifth Republic, when the government deemed it necessary to have access to means for defending its policies at a time when it found the greater part of the written press hostile to it. Subsequent attempts to leave the opposition some means of expression within the framework of a governmental monopoly have produced debatable results, and it is too early to measure the consequences of the French government's recent policy of media privatization. In England, state television and private television have shared viewers for a longer time, while in Italy, until the recent explosion of private channels, television was divided among the political parties in proportion to their electoral strength. Television is entirely private in the United States, although there is a network of public television channels that operates on grants from governmental agencies and foundations and on viewer contributions.

Privatization appears to some extent to be a way to hold state omnipotence at bay; in return, it makes television a slave to publicity, hence to viewer ratings. Examples from countries other than France seem to indicate that in the long run privatization can lead to dividing up viewership, thus to a balance among tendencies. Be that as it may, it is clear that publicity now rules our society. It has taught everyone, politicians included, the power of the slogan, the carefully crafted formula, and the striking or evocative image. The news that "sticks in the mind" is the news that interests the public. To the general public today a bloody crime is much more striking than the long-term consequences of a declining birthrate in the West, a problem that is seldom mentioned.

We inhabit a new world, thus a new climate with new cultures. American values, positive and negative, penetrate everywhere, thanks to American "know-how" but also to widespread use of the English language. Japan mass-produces animated cartoons based on a cultural confusion. An avalanche of changes and innovations is counterbalanced (or compensated for?) by forgetting the past and national cultures, even when their loss is bitterly resented. People have never shown a greater interest in history, but secondary-school students learn only about the most recent past. One cannot do everything.

It is perhaps too early to know what psychological effects our societies will feel from the deluge of images and sounds, or from a "show business" presentation of news that appeals more to feelings than to reason and that fails to provide the distance offered by the written word. No one denies that our modern means of communication make us aware of all the problems that are posed by coexisting societies living on our shrinking globe as if in different epochs. But to what extent will this awareness help us to resolve those thorny problems? And with what result?

A study should be made (although it would be difficult and perhaps impolitic to carry it out) of the microcosms in which news "products" subsequently offered for public consumption are tried and tested. To what extent do the decision makers—writers of all sorts, journalists—escape from the closed worlds in which such plots are hatched? To what extent are such people inspired, consciously or unconsciously, by an ideology that they may dissimulate, for career purposes or by conviction, and that they feel they do not have the right to proclaim openly, even if it would enlighten their public? To what extent are they motivated by a desire to throw light on essential problems? Or are they simply seeking to please the majority? Do they guide opinion or follow it? These are questions that I feel impelled to pose at the end of this book. The historian feels himself at something of a loss before them. Modern technologies have made possible and encouraged the emergence of a fourth power—the power of information—whether that power is exercised over the public by and in the media or by and within the state administration.

The proliferation of administrative forms and questionnaires in our societies has been much discussed. It raises two problems: the first is that of the excessive size of administrations whose internal operations are increasingly complex; the second is that of the administration's relationship to the individual in an age in which the rapid development of data-processing techniques, the relative ease with which data banks can be interconnected, and the expansion of telecommunications all pose a threat to privacy. Furthermore, these technological advances have come at a time when such powerful new means of communication raise the perpetual problem of excessive state power and of the power of more or less anonymous groups to use disinformation, deny pluralism, and threaten to lead our democratic societies into rampant totalitarianism.

These dangers—which have often been denounced—have led to the constitution of a sheaf of new institutions, new jurisdictions, and even new magistracies and embryonic counterpowers whose aim is to defend individual freedom from systems that are being set up and that contain a force for integration and cultural and social conditioning unprecedented in the annals of writing. These new agencies are not all of the same kind, nor have they the same tasks. A few deserve mention.

In the United States between the two world wars the rapid accumulation of the papers of congressional agencies and committees and the opening (in 1934) of the National Archives led, in 1948, to the creation of the Federal Records Administration. Other nations as well sought to bring order to the administrative forms and questionnaires that were proliferating in anarchical fashion, to simplify them, and to reduce their number. In France, the Centre d'enregistrement et de révision des formulaires administratifs (CERFA) was set up in 1966, when it launched the gargantuan task of first reviewing all existing documents then examining documents in the planning stage in order to make them uniform on the national scale. In 1985, thanks to the work of this agency, 294 pieces of printed matter put out by local offices of the Ministère de l'éducation nationale were reduced to one form, thus merging or eliminating hundreds of documents. In twenty years France has reduced its paperwork from some twenty thousand forms to around ten thousand and has replaced innumerable printed forms of local origin with nationalized forms. One result is that since the health care form for French Social Security was standardized in 1978 a total of over 400,000,000 copies have been used. Similar efforts were made by the Commission de coordination de la documentation administrative.

In 1973 Le Médiateur, an independent authority, was created and empowered to receive and investigate citizen complaints against the administration and its jurisdictional decisions. A similar law on 17 July 1978 founded a Commission d'accès aux documents administratifs to determine the rights of citizens to examine administrative records.

The greatest threat to the citizen's liberties, however, probably comes from the growing administrative abuse of files. France, a land with a centrist tradition, offers abundant proofs of this. The French still recall the *affaire des fiches* in 1904, in which General André, the minister of war, was forced to resign when it was discovered that his office was keeping files on officers' political and religious affiliations. Between the two world wars the keeping and use of files hit a new high, thanks to the development of mechanical card-sort machines. In 1941 a system of punched cards enabled René Carmille to draw up a complete list of potential combatants, and when the Germans occupied French territory they made the use of a national identity card obligatory. The French have continued to use personal identification cards, but the English and the Americans have shown systematic hostility to this form of registration. After World War II INSEE (Institut national de la statistique et des études économiques) created a nationwide data bank, a personal identify file whose numbering system was subsequently used for the Social Security system. Data was at first compiled by hand in regional offices, but from 1970 to 1973 the agency was computerized and its national headquarters was established in Nantes. Name files have increased in France at a dizzying pace; an apparently irreversible movement had been launched. These files inspired fabulous ojects but they also set off violent reactions. In 1971 the Safari project (Système automatique pour les fichiers administratifs et le répertoire des individus) was created with the aim of establishing connections among all existing administrative files, thus constituting one vast directory of individuals. The thought of being able to pass on such information to future colleagues, if posterity can still access it, is enough to set a historian to dreaming, but the citizen might rightly tremble at the thought of procedures that threatened to make public property of his or her private life and to bring about a complete alienation from a state that knows more about individuals than they themselves do.

Public reaction to the extension of such computerized files made people everywhere aware of their threat to individual freedoms. In the 1960s the United States led the reaction, and Sweden and Germany joined them in the 1970s. During this same time the French government changed Article 3 of the Code Civil to guarantee respect for a privacy threatened in modern society, and in 1974 it created the famous Commission Informatique et Liberté. The work of that commission resulted in a bill formulated in 1976 and voted into law on 6 January 1978 regulating the use of automatized data banks involving named individuals (the law was later extended to nonautomated data as well). Notably, this law guaranteed the concerned individual's right of access to files and the right of rectification. The final step was the creation of a controlling agency, the Commission nationale de l'informatique et des libertés (CNIL). The commission was conceived as an independent administrative authority; its deliberations were published in the *Journal officiel* and its members, who had lifetime appointments, had full regulatory powers. The CNIL had jurisdiction over all existent files and over the creation of further files, and it had the power to evaluate the appropriateness of any potential public documentation of this sort. It also could order the destruction of such files, and it was charged with establishing norms for ordinary administrative documents. From its inception to 1985 the CNIL has received from the public over thirty thousand declarations and requests for an opinion regarding, for instance, the files of INSEE (a data bank with some 55,000,000 entries), voter files (35,000,000 entries), the computerized central files of telephone subscribers (24,000,000 entries), the list of customers of the EDF-GDF, the state electric and gas companies (25,000,000 entries), the list for the income tax "short form" (20,000,000 entries), judicial conviction records (1,500,000 entries), and the files of the Aide Sociale (600,000 entries).

There was also concern in France about the accuracy and independence of reporting and the expression of a plurality of views on French television and radio, but also about equal opportunities of expression for an array of cultures, beliefs, and currents of thought and opinion. The state, which at the time had a monopoly of the media, was led first to create an independent supervisory agency and then, as we have seen, to withdraw gradually from telecasting. Milestones in this slow process were the creation of the ORTF (Office de la Radiodiffusion Télévision Française) in 1964 and the founding of an advisory body, the Haut conseil de l'audiovisuel, in 1972. The Haute autorité de la communication audiovisuelle, which was organized on the model of the Conseil constitutionnel, was established in 1982. Its role was in principle much broader than that of its predecessor, since it was not simply to interpret the law but also to give guidance to the various news services and organisms and define the norms that regulated them. In 1986 it was replaced by the Commission nationale de la communication et des libertés (CNCL), which was enlarged to include members designated by the high courts (the Conseil d'Etat, the Cour des comptes, etc.) and drawn from prestigious institutions such as the Académie Française. The CNCL was in turn replaced by a Conseil supérieur de l'audiovisuel endowed with broader powers over the media.

The French will undoubtedly long continue to debate what effect such organisms can have, whatever form they take, and the relations that their members might or might not be cultivating with the political leadership of the moment. The efficacy of such bodies will depend on the reactions of the people whose liberties they are charged with defending. This means that all citizens must have a schooling and a cultural initiation that will permit them not only to handle modern communication tools and to serve modern societies but also to safeguard their freedom. They will need to have instilled in them forms of the critical spirit that will allow them to

perceive the workings of publicity and propaganda, that will enable them
to form independent judgments, and that will help them to a real grasp
of the world and of problems outside their own immediate sphere. They
will need to be taught their duties, not only their rights. This implies scientific and technical instruction but also a "sense of the city" and a taste
for liberty. Whether we like it or not, it implies a return to forms of humanism—admittedly imperfect, open to criticism, and reserved to a minority—that we long called our own and that our world has been too quick
to renounce. It also implies the invention of new forms of humanism that,
when all is said and done, seem to me to rely necessarily on a critical
awareness of the past. Much is at stake: any society that loses its liberty
in the modern world runs the strong risk of not regaining it for a long
time. There are means for exerting pressure on the individual and for integrating him or her into a totalitarian system—means that rely on the
technology of today's computerized systems and that are so powerful that
they threaten a return to a closed world and a univocal society.

After a period of anarchical growth, the gradual "electrification" of the
many procedures for the treatment and distribution of information created
a technological system that is now unified by electronics. For an equivalent
to the scope and consequences of this phenomenon we need to look back
to the Neolithic revolution, the age when language and property made
their first appearance. Information is now an inexhaustible source of
wealth that can be shared endlessly, like the bread in the parable of the
loaves and fishes. It will reach beyond the technological considerations that
merely constrain its modes to challenge law, custom, behavior patterns,
beliefs, and cultures. In fact, it is already doing so.

Today we are at the heart of these changes; tossed back and forth as if
between a wave and its backwash by the appearance, first of the news
press, then of the cinema, the radio, and television, we neglect other phenomena. Above all, we fail to see the tide moving beneath those waves.

We humans find ourselves in such a new and rapidly changing situation
that we risk becoming "destabilized." At first men had tools that were extensions of their hands; next they had machines that took the place of
those tools and accomplished complex tasks and functions but remained
subservient to human will. Now we often delegate decisions to automatic
devices that think for us according to seemingly rational criteria, whereas
they should be programmed as an aid to help us organize and manage

human societies. In France we now have an elaborate system of signs and traffic lights on urban throughways to control entry, inform the motorist of traffic conditions, limit speed, and regulate collective behavior. This is what can happen when we delegate our power of decision, of imposing order, and of subjecting events to the rule of law. Computer-driven program trading was in part responsible for the stock market crash of 19 October 1987.

The emerging society is making use of increasingly complex mechanisms; it is creating an increasingly artificial civilization and placing humankind in a more and more dependent position. We are becoming increasingly liberated from nature's constraints and from what we take to be nature's imperfections, weaknesses, and fragilities, but also from the forms of freedom that nature grants us. We gain in efficiency, in well-being, and in some forms of security. We are ceaselessly and simultaneously winning and losing liberties and responsibilities.

Cultural transformations are on the scale of these vast phenomena. Juxtaposed local cultures, the basis of an agreement to live in mutual respect, are disappearing under the influence of the audiovisual media as we move toward a uniform mass culture. Dialects and local languages are disappearing—although not without violent reactions that may provide unforeseen challenges to the state—to the profit of the few great international languages. A new diversity is developing on top of this uniform substratum—a diversity based on professional competence and speaking professional jargon, and the oral tradition is finding a role for itself in scientific meetings, academic conferences, and the new Tower of Babel of "universities without walls." When the computer is as widely distributed as radio and television sets we may perhaps witness the return of writing.

There has also been considerable economic and social change. What is going to remain of the old Indo-European triad of the priest, the soldier, and the peasant? After several millennia of existence, the rural world and the peasant have disappeared, as has the workers' world after only a few centuries of existence. A growing and already considerable share of economic activity is taken up by professions that did not even exist fifty years ago. Henceforth the "information trades" will occupy more than half of the active population of industrially developed countries.

New spaces and new liberties have opened up now that instantaneous access to data and to interconnected data systems is possible. The time is near when everyone will have access to knowledge; ways to bring mankind together are already opening up. Information permits more active individual participation and facilitates the redistribution of power (for example, in the broader use of the referendum). It also facilitates a stronger social control. This redistribution of power must remain within the reach of everyone, for these new techniques also permit a concentration of power and the manipulation of public opinion. We have seen this happen with polling, which is now better supervised than it used to be. But what are we to think of the polls taken "live" on television that never disclose the source of the poll, its full results, or its sampling methods?

The future is full of promise and perils. It seems imperative to reinforce, extend, perfect, and broaden the control mechanisms that have been put into place in the last fifteen years. These mechanisms cannot do everything, but they can clarify the situation and they can keep vigilant watch. The various movements for civil rights, in spite of their ambiguity, taught a similar vigilance. Beyond technology and institutions, however, there are human beings. We have to be taught to manage this abundance of information and this gift of freedom—that is, we must be better prepared and taught that the end of human society is the human person. Not in the material sense, as the subject of economics and history, but as a moral and spiritual being; as an active force, and, in the last analysis, the master of human history.

Conclusion

Writing: An Ongoing Process

We have seen that writing is a means of communication requiring both a long apprenticeship and a quite special effort of participation. How and why was it imposed on the world?

The notion bears repeating: writing is nothing by itself. It serves little purpose to introduce writing techniques into closed societies; at best they will just use them to immobilize and set down sacred words as secrets that give an oligarchy its power. The use of writing cannot develop spontaneously until small groups fuse and organize into a society. It is probable that primitive forms of graphic expression vanished without a trace for lack of just that sort of motivation. Similarly, nothing indicates that the incomplete experience of the Amerindians would have gone much further if it had not been interrupted by the Spanish conquest. Certain parts of the globe, however—China, Mesopotamia, Egypt—gave rise to dynamic writing systems destined for a great future. The original motivation of these creations matters little: were they a new way of interrogating the gods? Or did they reflect a desire to classify people and things? In any event, their rise corresponded to the start of brilliant civilizations, to the accumulation of wealth, and to accelerated communications. It is undeniable that writing, a means for dominating space, sprang from the availability of capital; it is equally undeniable that it quite naturally became a tool for accumulating information about past times and for storing knowledge. This was true even before writing became the symbol and creator of wealth with the bill of exchange, the banknote, and eventually the magnetic credit card.

All around the regions where "the logic of writing" had arisen other peoples began to awaken and new sources of prosperity appeared. When scribes from long-standing cultures passed into the service of younger nations, they (or their students) created systems that were simpler and more direct; systems less respectful of tradition, not as rich in connotations, but more easily assimilated. This is what happened in the West, where alphabets marked the end of a long process. It also happened in the East, where Japan simplified the repertory of Chinese ideograms and completed them with syllabaries, and where the Koreans created an alphabet, retaining Chinese ideograms because the new system seemed meager to them. This mechanism shows that "progress"—or efficiency—was the province of newcomers and "barbarians." In the West at least, restorations and innovations in writing normally occurred during the crises that preceded a regeneration. This happened in Rome when the crisis of the third century was accompanied by a revolution in the *ductus;* it happened again in the eighth century when the invention of Carolingian minuscule preceded the emergence of the Carolingian empire. The same can be said for the fourteenth and early fifteenth centuries with the appearance of the humanistic hand. This dual process is even clearer in the appearance of printing, a "catch-up" operation carried out on the eve of the great Renaissance by the Germanic peoples, masters in the arts of metallurgy, in a Europe whose center of gravity was shifting eastward.

Since it appeared and developed in specific historical circumstances, writing was by no means the inspired invention of some demiurge. Whatever the system adopted, it was only a bastard artifice born of the symbolism of the image and spoken discourse. The signs that were aligned by the human hand were nothing by themselves. What mattered was the resonance that seeing them prompted in those who deciphered them on the basis of their own previous experience. The loyalty of the peoples of the Far East to their ideograms and their relative indifference to the creation of texts as we conceive them have advantages that are not easy to analyze, particularly since we find it difficult to sense how much of the difference between their way of reasoning and their sensibilities and our own is due to the structure of their languages and their graphic systems. Unlike the Eastern systems, our alphabet, which lays claim to phonetism, offers only a vague reflection of languages, whose evolution it lags behind. Furthermore, our eye normally seizes only a global image of each word, an image that the brain recognizes as it would an ideogram. This means that writing may very well draw its essential values from its very ambiguities, even during the mysterious alchemy that corresponds to the act of reading and that takes place in the mind of each one of us. The simplification of a graphic system in societies in search of efficiency does not always bring an enrichment.

It has been customary to boast of the virtues of such mutations and to glorify writing's powers of liberation, as the cult of Gutenberg demonstrates. Others have denounced writing as an instrument of servitude. Thus the moment has come to attempt to define, in harmony with the spirit of "history and decadence" of the collection in which this work was originally published, not only what writing has brought to humankind but also what we have lost by it.

By transforming the flow of the spoken word into a series of signs inscribed on the two dimensions of a clay tablet, a waxed board, or, later, a sheet of papyrus or paper, writing has enabled man to analyze discourse by decomposing it; it has sharpened his ability to distinguish between words and has taught him to define them better by drawing up lists. Grammar then seemed the mother of all the arts, and logic permitted the drawing up of the rules of the logic of writing. Once spoken discourse had been visualized and had become an object of observation it revealed its snares. Then rhetoric taught the orator how to manipulate of the sentiments of his listeners and dialectics offered the philosopher procedures for seeking to attain objective truth. At the same time calculation made astonishingly rapid progress and man learned to draw geometrical figures and derive mathematical laws from them. Eventually the accumulation of a store of knowledge and observations that now no longer became distorted by being passed from mouth to mouth led to the rise of the critical spirit. The appearance of alphabets undoubtedly played an essential role in this process. In societies dominated by the art of oratory alphabets made writing an aid to remembering the spoken word, and they helped to make classical Greece and the Mediterranean basin in the time of Jesus the highest centers of culture and thought the world has ever known. Everywhere, however, writing secreted a language that was in some ways autonomous. After all, did not ideograms enable the Chinese to find a common language even when their spoken tongues were so different that they could not understand one another? And was not the written language par excellence in the West a learned language, Latin, that long served as a model for the writing of "vulgar" spoken languages and for works written in those languages? The present work has followed the stages of the slow revolution that completed the divorce, in Europe, between the written word and the spoken word as it was worked out in different ways of reading and different ways of writing a text. We have seen ways of reading become ways of skimming texts and thus of consulting them more efficiently. We have also seen ways of reading that operated to make a text one's own. It is interesting to note, for example, that the practice of silent reading by the laity in the later Middle Ages helped the faithful to put less stress on collective prayer and to give up a certain magic inherent in the word in order to internalize and individualize their dialogue with God. Later, printing and the rise of schools undeniably contributed to breaking down the compartmentalization of society. The process was slow; in the last analysis it was a form of enrichment and liberation.

All progress (but just what is "progress?") has its drawbacks, as our own generation has paid a price to learn. Some particularly serious charges have been leveled against writing. Did it not obliterate traditional societies' mechanisms of memorization and replace them with a form of artificial memory that Plato denounced (albeit in somewhat ambiguous terms)? Did it not dry up the sources of true poetry, sources that primitive societies thought inspired by the gods? It is certainly not a coincidence that the most beautiful human songs that have come down to us—in Europe, the Homeric poems and the medieval epics—are legacies that societies without writing, hence without history, have bequeathed to societies of writing. Similarly, when men adopted writing they renounced placing their contracts and their agreements under the watchful eyes of the gods in favor of the guarantee of temporal powers. At that point, law tended to replace custom, at least in appearance. Writing became an instrument of domination within societies that, by abandoning continuity, condemned themselves to an incessant series of revisions, each one of which prompted a rupture in a now fragmented time.

Another of the original sins charged against writing is that even in the ancient Middle East the use of ideograms led to the scribes' domination over a hierarchical society. From that moment on, the masters of the stylus or the pen were responsible for giving the sovereign's decrees concrete form; as if by an ineluctable mechanism, real power was usurped, at first by the scribe, then by the "secretary" (in the Renaissance sense of "keeper of the secrets") of the ruler, and from the "secretary" to the high-placed graduate of the best schools (in France the *énarque*). What is more, the man of writing learned a dual language, and written discourse was at times used to mask or distort perceptible reality by using forms of rhetoric that were not always to his credit. Written discourse incited the individual to adopt a cold view of the world and of his fellows, a view detached from contingencies and repressing sensitivity; it found its most characteristic form in the administrative style still being perfected today in a flood of anonymous, unsigned, computer-generated letters. When what was generated was an unreal logic, written discourse could pass from the ridiculous to the odious. To end the list of the sins of writing, we should not forget that access to texts has always been one of the least evenly distributed things in this world. The scribe, the cleric, or the man of letters has never had much in common with those, in any age, who could only decipher a word or two or just write their names, or who today can only leaf through an illustrated magazine. The fact that, with printing, books became a commodity with a price attached to them shows in what direction this hierarchization has always operated.

We should not let these few reflections make us forget what the culture of writing has brought to societies of all times. To return for a moment to the documents whose history has been traced here: we have seen clay tablets that stored information based on accumulated acquisitions of knowledge; Egyptian papyri that brilliantly married image and text; ancient scrolls visualizing, like films, the words of times past and written in a rapid or a ceremonious hand; medieval manuscripts, works for study crammed with information or illuminated books such as books of hours whose sumptuousness solemnizes a message written in a search for God; printed books of the artisanal age that attained a marvelous clarity during the age of humanism, each one of which has its own personality; books of the industrial period, increasingly conceived as consumer goods but subjected to rigid norms to facilitate both their manufacture and their accessibility. All these many forms testify to a long history during which written communication ceaselessly sought more standardized and less flamboyant ways to reach a greater public, but during which the book has always appeared as the best means for giving human thought its most perfect form.

Will the same be true tomorrow? Let me offer a few simple observations. In all societies communication between human beings has made up a complex whole in which a natural division of labor occurred, and the current communication revolution only continues and broadens earlier revolutions. On every occasion, oral communication (and communication by images) has developed along with writing in a world of expanding cities and accelerating exchanges. And now, in the last few decades, a society of simultaneity has come to be organized, as if it were a logical point of arrival. The true novelty of this perhaps lies in humanity's ability not only to keep in memory a written text, with all its permanence, and transmit it over space but rather in the fact that we have also learned to transmit the image in all its movement and sound in all its instantaneousness. As always, however, the appearance of new procedures has modified the division of labor. More than ever, but in a more constraining and more aggressive manner, all culture has now become a commodity. Furthermore, with the rise of publicity and with the controversy over the objectivity of the news media, the skepticism we feel concerning the mass media and our fears concerning the future of our freedoms are totally justifiable.

In this new situation writing plays its part by means of more and more powerful machines that perhaps exaggerate its faults. The book will doubtless take on a new look in the years to come. As a consequence of new constraints and a new standardization it may also offer other forms of logic. The greatest problem is to know whether it will be able to continue to preserve its character as something complete and permanent and whether it can retain its force of penetration in a universe of the immediate whose reactions are conditioned by more powerful and direct means of communication. The men and women still among us who drew their learning from the culture of yesteryear—a culture based on Greece and Rome—and who, after all, belong to the generations who realized the most fabulous technological revolution since the Neolithic age doubtless react to the forms of culture invading their universe with much the same sentiments as the learned men in Boethius' days when they heard the chants of the warriors and the Germanic poets at the court of Theodoric. Conscious of their mission, these last of the ancients wrote texts that became the legacy of the classical world; in anticipation of a future rebirth they did their utmost to preserve the works they held most dear. After many centuries, a Renaissance, the result of a long process of hybridization, finally came. It may well be the mission of our own generation to help our descendants to understand that technological progress does not necessarily imply unthinking rejection of what the past has brought us.

Notes

Chapter One

1. Gabriel Camps, *La préhistoire. A la recherche du Paradis perdu* (Paris: Perrin, 1982).

2. André Leroi-Gourhan, *Le geste et la parole*, 2 vols. (Paris: Albin Michel, 1965; reprint, 1982).

3. Geneviève Calame-Griaule, *Ethnologie et langage. La parole chez les Dogon,* Actes du colloque international de l'Université de Paris VII, 22–24 April 1980 (Paris: Institut d'ethnologie, Musée de l'homme, 1986), available in English as *Words and the Dogon World,* trans. Dierdre LaPin (Philadelphia: Institute for the Study of Human Issues, 1986). See also Anne-Marie Christin, "Le Sujet de l'écriture ou le partenaire silencieux," *Littoral. Revue de psychanalyse. 7/8; l'Instance de la lettre* (February 1983): 209–31. For what follows, see *Naissance de l'écriture. Cunéiformes et hiéroglyphes,* Exposition, Galeries nationales du Grand Palais, 7 May–9 August 1982 (Paris: Ministère de la Culture, Editions de la Réunion des musées nationaux, 1982). More generally, see also James G. Février, *Histoire de l'écriture,* new rev. ed., 2 vols. (Paris: Payot, 1959; 2d ed. 1988); Marcel Cohen, *La grande invention de l'écriture et son évolution,* 3 vols. (Paris: Imprimerie Nationale, 1958).

4. Jean Bottéro, *Mésopotamie. L'écriture, la raison et les dieux* (Paris: Gallimard, 1987), available in English as *Mesopotamia: Writing, Reasoning, and the Gods,* trans. Zainab Bahrani and Marc Van De Meiroop (Chicago: University of Chicago Press, 1992). I thank M. Bottéro for providing me with the manuscript text of a course that he has given on this topic. See also René Labat, "L'écriture cunéiforme et la civilisation mésopotamienne," in *L'écriture et la psychologie des peuples,* Centre internationale de Synthèse, XXIIe semaine (Paris: A. Colin, 1963), 23–92; Jean Bottéro, "De l'aide-mémoire à l'écriture," in *Ecritures: Systèmes idéographiques et pratiques expressives,* Actes du colloque international de l'Université de Paris VII, 22–24 April 1980 (Paris: Sycomore, 1982), 13–39; Jean-Marie Durand, "Trois approches de la notion d'idéogramme sumérien," *Ecritures II* (Paris: Sycomore, 1985), 25–42; Durand, "Diffusion et pratique des écritures cunéiformes au Proche-Orient ancien," in *L'espace et la lettre* (Paris: Union Générale d'Edition, 1978), 13–60; Pierre Amiet, "Comptabilité et écriture archaïque à Suse et en Mésopotamie," in *L'espace et la lettre,* 39–60. See also *Naissance de l'écriture,* esp. p. 144 on the diffusion of cuneiform writing.

5. Jean-Marie Durand, "L'écriture cunéiforme," in *Atlas des littératures* (Paris: Encyclopaedia universalis, 1990), 130. See also note 4.

6. Jean Bottéro, "Les noms de Marduck," in Maria de Jong Ellis, ed., *Essays on the Ancient Near East in Memory of Jacob Joel Finkelstein* (Hamden, Conn.: Archon Books, for the Connecticut Academy of Arts and Sciences, 1977), 5–28.

7. For the appearance of writing in Egypt, see, in particular: Jean Sainte-Fare-

Carnot, "Les hiéroglyphes. L'évolution des écritures égyptiennes," in *L'écriture et la psychologie des peuples*, 51–72; Pascal Vernus, "L'écriture de l'Egypte ancienne," in *L'espace et la lettre*, 61–78; Catherine Chadefaud, "Egypte pharaonique: de l'expression picturale à l'écriture égyptienne," *Ecritures: Systèmes idéologiques*, 81–101; Pascal Vernus, "Espace et idéologie dans l'écriture égyptienne," in *Ecritures: Systèmes idéologiques*, 81–98, esp. pp. 92–93.

8. J. T. Hooker, *Reading the Past: Ancient Writing From Cuneiform to the Alphabet* (Berkeley: University of California Press, 1990), 110.

9. Vernus, "L'écriture de l'Egypte ancienne," 70–71.

10. Février, *Histoire de l'écriture*, 69–72; Léon Vandermeersch, *Wangdao, ou La Voie royale*, 2 vols. (Paris: Ecole française d'Extrême-Orient, 1977–80), 2:473–93; Vandermeersch, "Ecriture et langue écrite en Chine," in *Ecritures: Systèmes idéologiques*, 255–70; Jacques Gernet, "La Chine, aspects et fonctions de l'écriture," in *Ecriture et la psychologie des peuples*, 29–49; Vivianne Alleton, *L'écriture chinoise* (Paris: Presses Universitaires de France, 1978, 4th ed. rev., 1984).

11. Vandermeersch, "Ecriture et langue écrite en Chine," 256ff. See also Vandermeersch, *Wangdao, ou La Voie royale*, 473–93.

12. Alleton, *L'écriture chinoise*, 473–93.

13. Anne-Marie Christin, "Le Sujet de l'écriture ou le partenaire silencieux."

14. Sir John Eric Sidney Thompson, *The Rise and Fall of Maya Civilization*, 2d ed. enl. (Norman, Okla.: University of Oklahoma Press, 1966); Paul Gendrop, *Les mayas*, (Paris: Presses Universitaires de France, 1978); Frederick A. Peterson, *Ancient Mexico: An Introduction to the Pre-Hispanic Cultures* (London: Allen & Unwin, 1959; New York: Capricorn Books, 1962); Donald Robertson, *Mexican Manuscript Paintings of the Early Colonial Period: The Metropolitan Schools* (New Haven: Yale University Press, 1959); Charles E. Dibble, "Writing in Central Mexico," in Gordon F. Ekholm and Ignacio Bernal, eds., *Handbook of Middle American Indians: Archaeology of Northern Mesoamerica*, 16 vols. (Austin: University of Texas Press, 1964–76), vol. 10, pt. 1, 322–32; Joaquín Galarza, *Lienzos de Chiepetlan* (Mexico City: Mission archéologique et ethnologique française au Mexique, 1972); Serge Gruzinski, *La colonisation de l'imaginaire. Sociétés indigènes et occidentalisation dans le Mexique espagnol, XVIe–XVIIIe siècle* (Paris: Gallimard, 1988); William H. Prescott, *The History of the Conquest of Mexico* (New York: Harper & Bros., 1843; abridged and ed. C. Harvey Gardiner [Chicago: University of Chicago Press, 1966]).

15. "Naissance et formation de l'alphabet au Proche-Orient," in *Naissance de l'écriture. Cunéiformes et hiéroglyphes*, 172–95.

16. Emmanuel Laroche, "L'Asie mineure. Les Hittites, peuple à double écriture," in *L'écriture et la psychologie des peuples*, 103–12.

17. Olivier Masson, "La civilisation égéenne. Les écritures crétoises et mycéniennes," in *L'écriture et la psychologie des peuples*, 93–100.

18. Michael Ventris and John Chadwick, *Documents in Mycenaean Greek* (Cambridge: Cambridge University Press, 1956), 2d ed. rev., John Chadwick, ed. (Cambridge: Cambridge University Press, 1973), with bibliography; Chadwick, *The Decipherment of Linear B*, 2d ed. (London: Cambridge University Press, 1967), reprinted 1970, 1990; *The Cambridge Ancient History*, 3d rev. ed., 12 vols. (Cambridge: Cambridge University Press, 1970–), vol. 2, pt. 2, *History of the Middle East and the*

Aegean Region c. 1380–1000 B.C., chap. 29(a), "The Prehistory of the Greek Language," 805–19; L. R. Palmer and John Chadwick, eds., *Proceedings of the Cambridge Colloquium on Mycenaean Studies* (Cambridge: Cambridge University Press, 1966); Chadwick, *The Mycenaean World* (Cambridge and New York: Cambridge University Press, 1976). See also John Chadwick, J. T. Killen, and J. P. Olivier, *The Knossos Tablets, A Transliteration*, 4th ed. (Cambridge: Cambridge University Press, 1971), and especially the first part of a large venture, J. Chadwick, L. Godart, J. T. Killen, J. P. Olivier, A. Sacconi, I. A. Sakellarakis, *Corpus of Mycenaean Inscriptions from Knossos* (Cambridge and New York: Cambridge University Press; Rome: Edizioni dell'Ateneo, 1986), vol. 1 (nos. 1–1063), vol. 88 of *Incunabula Graeca*.

19. Maurice Sznycer, "L'origine de l'alphabet sémitique," in *L'espace et la lettre*, 79–124.

20. Ibid., 97ff.

21. Maxime Rodinson, "Le monde islamique et l'extension de l'écriture arabe," in *L'écriture et la psychologie des peuples*, 263–74; Cohen, *La Grande Invention de l'écriture*, 1 : 182–86.

22. Alphonse Dain, "L'écriture grecque du VIIIe siècle avant notre ère à la fin de la civilisation byzantine," in *L'écriture et la psychologie des peuples*, 167–80; Février, *Histoire de l'écriture*, 384ff.; Michel Lejeune, *Phonétique historique du mycénien et du grec ancien* (Paris: Klincksieck, 1972). Concerning Greek alphabetic writing, see esp. Margherita Guarducci, *Epigrafia greca*, 3 vols. (Rome: Istituto poligrafico dello stato, 1967–74), vol. 1, *Caratteri e storia della disciplina. La scrittura greca dalle origini all'età imperiale*; Lilian Hamilton Jeffery, *The Local Scripts of Archaic Greece. A Study of the Origin of the Greek Alphabet and Its Development from the Eighth to the Fifth Centuries B.C.* (Oxford: Clarendon Press, 1961, 1963).

23. Mario Lombardo, "Marchands, économie et techniques d'écriture," in Marcel Détienne, ed., *Les savoirs de l'écriture: en Grèce ancienne* (Lille: Presses universitaires de Lille, 1988), 166.

24. Marcel Détienne, "L'écriture et ses nouveaux objects intellectuels en Grèce," in Détienne, ed., *Les savoirs de l'écriture: en Grèce ancienne*, 22–25.

25. Gernet, "La Chine," 347.

26. Raymond Bloch, "Etrusques et Romains. Problèmes et histoire de l'écriture," in *L'écriture et la psychologie des peuples*, 186–96.

27. Cohen, *La grande invention de l'écriture*, 131, 172–80.

28. Friederich Heyer, *Die Kirche Armeniens* (Stuttgart: Evangelisches Verlagswerk, 1978); *The Teaching of Saint Gregory: An Early Armenian Catechism*, Robert W. Thomson, trans. and commentary (Cambridge, Mass.: Harvard University Press, 1970); Maghak'ia Ormanian, *L'Eglise arménienne: son histoire, sa doctrine, son régime, sa discipline . . .* (Antelias: Catholicossat Arménien de Cilicie, 1954), available in English as *The Church of Armenia . . .* , trans. G. Marcar Gregory; ed. Terenig Poladian, 2d rev. ed. (London: Mowbray, 1955); Serge Mouraviev, "Les caractères daniéliens (identification et reconstruction)" and "Les caractères mestrobiens (leur genèse reconstituée)," *Revue des études arméniennes* n.s. 14 (1980): 55–85 and 87–111; Paul Peeters, "Pour l'histoire des origines de l'alphabet arménien," *Revue des études arméniennes*, 9 (1929): 203–37; Gorioun, *Biographie de saint Mesrob*, trans. Jean-Raphael Emine, in Victor Langlois, ed., *Collection des historiens anciens et*

modernes de l'Arménie, 2 vols. (Paris: Firmin fils & cie, Didot frères, 1861–69), 2:9–16; Nicolas Adontz, *La Bible arménienne et sa portée historique* (Paris: E. Leroux, 1938), 47–63, a work published on the occasion of the fifteenth centenary of the Armenian translation of the Bible; Hakob Anasyan, *Biblia sacra* (Yerevan: Académie des sciences, Institut d'histoire, 1976), which contains a very full bibliography.

29. "Lettre d'Antoine Meillet," in *La Bible arménienne et sa portée historique,* 18.

30. André Vaillant, "L'écriture cyrillique et son extension," in *L'écriture et la psychologie des peuples,* 301–11; Francis I. Dvornik, *Byzantine Missions Among the Slavs: Ss. Constantine-Cyril and Methodius* (New Brunswick: Rutgers University Press, 1970); J. Hahn, *Kyrillo Methodiguiche Bible* (Munich: 1973); Dimitri Obolensky, "Cyrille et Méthode et la christianisation des Slaves," in *Byzantium and the Slavs: Collected Studies* (London: Variorum reprints, 1971), 587–609; Obolensky, *The Byzantine Commonwealth: Eastern Europe, 500–1453* (London: Weidenfeld and Nicolson; New York: Praeger, 1971); Riccardo Picchio, "Slave ecclésiastique, slavons et rédactions," in *To Honour Roman Jakobson. Essays on the Occasion of his Seventieth Birthday,* 3 vols., *Janua linguarum,* series maior, 31–33 (The Hague: Mouton, 1967), 2:1527–44; André Poppé, "Dans la Russie médiévale, Xe–XIIe siècle. Ecriture et culture," *Annales E.S.C.* 16 (1961), 1:12–35; Ivan Dujcev, "Protostoria dell'alfabeto slavo," in *Paleografia, diplomatica e archivistica, studi in onore di Giovanni Battelli* (Rome: Edizioni di Storia e Letteratura, 1979), 1:231–49.

CHAPTER TWO

1. René Labat, "L'écriture cunéiforme et la civilisation mésopotamienne," in *L'écriture et la psychologie des peuples* (Paris: A. Colin, 1963), 80–81.

2. Quoted in ibid, 81.

3. Paolo Matthiae, "Ebla à l'époque d'Akkad, archéologie et histoire," *Académie des Inscriptions et Belles-Lettres. Compte rendu des séances* (1976): 190–215; Matthiae, "Le palais royal proto-syrien d'Ebla, nouvelles recherches à Tell Marikh," ibid. (1977): 148–74, available in English as "Preliminary Remarks on the Royal Palace of Ebla," in *Communiqué of the Italian Archaeological Mission to Syria . . .* (Malibu: Undena Publications, 1978). Issues of the *Compte rendu des séances* of the same Academy for 1979, 1981, 1982, and 1986 contain other communications by the same author of less interest for our purposes. See also Matthiae, "The Archives of the Royal Palace G of Ebla: Distribution and Arrangement of the Tablets According to Archaeological Evidence," and Alfonso Archi, "The Archive of Ebla," in Klaas R. Veenjof, ed., *The Cuneiform Archives and Libraries,* Papers Read at the 30e Rencontre Assyriologique Internationale, Leiden, 4–8 July 1983 (Leiden: Nederlands Historisch-Archaeologisch Instituut te Istanbul, 1986), 53–71 and 72–86, respectively.

4. Guillaume Cardascia, *Les archives des Murašû. Une famille d'hommes d'affaires babyloniens à l'époque perse (453–403 av. J.C.* (Paris: Imprimerie nationale, 1951).

5. Naphtali Lewis, *Papyrus in Classical Antiquity* (Oxford: Clarendon Press, 1974). See also Pliny the Elder, *Historia naturalis* 1.13.74–82; L. D. Reynolds and N. G. Wilson, *Scribes and Scholars: A Guide to the Transmission of Greek and Latin Literature* (London: Oxford University Press, 1968).

6. Alphonse Dain, "L'écriture grecque du VIIIe siècle avant notre ère à la fin de la civilisation byzantine," in *L'écriture et la psychologie des peuples*, 167–80, esp. p. 174. See also Ovid, *Ars amatoria* 3.469–72 and 613–25, passages in which Ovid suggests that a servant could bear a message from her mistress to a lover written on her back, thus eluding the surveillance of a jealous husband or guardian.

7. Marcel Détienne, "L'écriture et ses nouveaux objets intellectuels en Grèce," in Détienne, ed., *Les savoirs de l'écriture: En Grèce ancienne* (Lille: Presses universitaires de Lille, 1988), 7–26, esp. p. 14.

8. Claude Nicolet, *Le métier de citoyen dans la Rome républicaine* (Paris: 1976), 517–18, quoted from *The World of the Citizen in Republican Rome*, trans. P. S. Falla (Berkeley and Los Angeles: University of California Press, 1980), 390–91.

9. Mireille Corbier, "L'Urbs. Espace urbain et histoire (Ier siècle av. J.-C.–IIIe siècle ap. J.-C.," *Actes du colloque international CNRS*, 8–12 May 1985 (Rome: Ecole française de Rome, 1987), 27–60. Robert Etienne, *La vie quotidienne à Pompéi*, 2d ed. rev. and corr. (Paris: Hachette, 1977); Marcello Gigante, *Civiltà delle forme letterarie nell'antica Pompei* (Naples: Bibliopolis, 1979); Robert Marichal, *L'occupation romaine de la Basse-Egypte. Le statut des auxilia: P. Berlin 6.866 et P. Lond 116-Fay* (Paris: E. Droz, 1945).

10. Eric Gardiner Turner, *Athenian Books in the Fourth and Fifth Centuries B.C.* . . . (London: published for University College, London, by H. K. Lewis, 1952); Sir Frederick George Kenyon, *Books and Readers in Ancient Greece and Rome*, 4 vols. (Oxford: Clarendon Press, 1932; 2d ed. 1951).

11. R. Reed, *Ancient Skins, Parchments, and Leathers* (London and New York: Seminar Press, 1972); Jean Vezin, "La réalisation matérielle des manuscrits latins pendant le Haut Moyen Age," *Codicologia*, 2 (1978): 18–20.

12. Pan Jixin, "Zhongguo zaozhi jushu shigao," *Wenwu chubanshe* (Beijing) (1979), summarized by Jean-Pierre Drège in *Bulletin de l'Ecole française d'Extrême-Orient*, 71 (1982): 264–66.

13. Jean-Marie Durand, "Espace et écriture en cunéiforme," in *Ecritures, systèmes idéographiques et pratiques expressives*, Actes du colloque international de l'Université de Paris VII, 22–24 April 1980 (Paris: Sycomore, 1982), 51–63, esp. p. 60; Joseph Needham, ed., *Science and Civilization in China*, 6 vols. (Cambridge: Cambridge University Press, 1985), vol. 5, pt. 1, *Paper and Printing*, ed. Tsien Tsuen-Hsuin.

14. Durand, "Espace et écriture en cunéiforme," 55.

15. Pierre Vernus, "Espace et idéologie dans l'écriture égyptienne," in *Ecritures, systèmes idéographiques*, 101–14. See also various sections of *Naissance de l'écriture. Cunéiformes et hiéroglyphes*, Exposition Galeries nationales du Grand Palais 7 May–9 August 1982 (Paris: Ministère de la culture, Réunion de Musées nationaux, 1982): Bernadette Letellier, "Les écritures cursives: l'écriture hiératique," 154–61; Jean-Louis de Cenival, "Hiératique anormal et démotique," 62–63; Jean Leclant, "La diffusion des écritures égyptiennes: le méroïtique: une écriture africaine proche de l'égyptien," 163–64.

16. Letellier, "Les écritures cursives: L'écriture hiératique," and Cenival, "Hiératique anormal et démotique."

17. Viviane Alleton, *L'écriture chinoise* (Paris: Presses Universitaires de France, 1976), 25ff.

18. Ibid., 61–62, 111–14.

19. James G. Février, "Les Sémites et l'alphabet," in *L'écriture et la psychologie des peuples*, 122.

20. Rudolf Wolfgang Müller, "L'époque gréco-romaine," in Mohammed A. Hussein, ed., *Les origines du livre. Du papyrus au codex*, trans. Rodolphe Savoie (Leipzig: Edition Leipzig, 1975), 49–50, 68.

21. Alfonse Dain, *Les manuscrits*, new ed., Jean Irigoin, ed. (Paris: Belles lettres, 1975), 109–13.

22. Müller, "L'époque gréco-romaine," 51.

23. See Rudolf Wolfgang Müller, *Rhetorische und syntaktische Interpunktion. Untersuchungen zur Pausenbezeichnung im antiken Latein*, inaugural lecture, Tübingen, 1964; E. Otha Wingo, *Latin Punctuation in the Classical Age*, Janua linguarum series practica, 133 (The Hague: Mouton, 1972); J. Moreau-Maréchal, "Recherches sur la ponctuation," *Scriptorium* 22 (1968): 56–66; Jean Vezin, "La division en paragraphes dans les manuscrits de la basse antiquité et du Haut Moyen Age," in Roger Laufer, ed., *La notion de paragraphe* (Paris: Editions du CNRS, 1985).

24. This study is still unpublished, but see Pascale Bourgain, "Qu'est-ce qu'un vers au Moyen Age?" *Bibliothèque de l'Ecole des Chartes*, 147 (1989): 231–82.

25. Wilhelm Schubart, *Das Buch bei den Griechen und Römern* (1907), 3d ed., ed. Eberhard Paul (Heidelberg: L. Schneider, 1962); Kenyon, *Books and Readers in Ancient Greece and Rome*; Wilhelm Wattenbach, *Das Schriftwesen im Mittelalter*, 3d ed. (Leipzig: S. Hirzel, 1896).

26. Jean Mallon, "Quel est le plus ancien exemple connu d'un manuscrit latin en forme de codex?" *Emerita* 17 (1949): 1–8; Mallon, *Paléographie romaine* (Madrid: Consejo Superior de Investigaciones Cientificas, 1952), 77-80; C. H. Roberts, "The Codex," *Proceedings of the British Academy*, 40 (1954): 169–204; Jean Vezin, "La réalisation matérielle des manuscrits latins," 23–38; Dain, *Les manuscrits*, 116–17.

27. See various sections in chap. 5, "Les scribes," in *Naissance de l'écriture*: Béatrice André-Leicknam, 324–38; Christiane Ziegler, 340–43; Dominique Benazeth, 343–57. See also Dain, *Les manuscrits*, 23–25.

28. Jean Vezin, "La fabrication du manuscrit," in Henri-Jean Martin and Roger Chartier, gen. eds., *Histoire de l'édition française*, 4 vols. (Paris: Promodis, 1982–86), vol. 1, *Le livre conquérant: Du Moyen Age au milieu du XVIIe siècle*, 25–47, esp. p. 33.

29. Olivier Guyotjeannin, review of Bernhard Bischoff, *Paléographie de l'Antiquité romaine et du Moyen Age occidental* in *Bibliothèque de l'Ecole des Chartes*, 144 (1986): 387–90.

30. Robert Marichal, "L'écriture latine et la civilisation occidentale du Ier au XVIe siècle," in *L'écriture et la psychologie des peuples*, 203–4, figures, p. 205.

31. Emmanuel Poulle, "Une histoire de l'écriture," *Bibliothèque de l'Ecole des Chartes*, 135 (1977): 137–44 (the review of Mallon's 1976 film). See also Mallon, *Paléographie romaine*; Mallon, *De l'écriture: recueil d'études publiées de 1937 à 1981* (Paris: Editions du CNRS, 1982).

32. Marichal, "L'écriture latine," 209.

33. Mallon, *Paléographie romaine.*
34. Poulle, "Une histoire de l'écriture."
35. Marichal, "L'écriture latine," 212−23.
36. Poulle, "Une histoire de l'écriture."
37. Joseph Balogh, "Voces paginarum," *Philologus,* 82 (1926−27): 84−100. For the interpretation of the texts exhumed by Balogh, see Bernard M. Knox, "Silent Reading in Antiquity," *Greek, Roman and Byzantine Studies,* 9, 4 (1968): 421−35.
38. Armando Petrucci, "Lire au Moyen Age," *Mélanges de l'Ecole française de Rome. Moyen Age, Temps moderns,* 96, 2 (1984): 603−16, quotation p. 604.
39. Henri-Irénée Marrou, *Histoire de l'éducation dans l'Antiquité,* new ed., 2 vols. (Paris: Editions du Seuil, 1981), vol. 2, *Le monde romain,* 69−70.
40. Jean Leclercq, *L'amour des lettres et le désir de Dieu: Initiation aux auteurs monastiques du Moyen Age* (Paris: Editions du Cerf, 1957), 21−22, 72−73, quoted from *The Love of Learning and the Desire for God: A Study of Monastic Culture,* trans. Catharine Misrahi, 3d ed. (New York: Fordham University Press, 1982), 19, 90.

CHAPTER THREE

1. Elena Cassin, "Symboles de cession immobilière dans l'ancien droit mésopotamien," *L'Année sociologique* (1952): 108ff.; Georges Tessier, *La diplomatique,* new rev. ed. (Paris: Presses Universitaires de France, 1967), 12.
2. Elena Cassin, "Le sceau. Un fait de civilisation dans la Mésopotamie ancienne," *Annales E.S.C.* 15 (1960): 742−51; Wilhelm Eilers, "Réflexions sur les origines du droit en Mésopotamie," *Revue historique du droit français* (1973): 13−22.
3. Dominique Charpin, "Le geste, la parole et l'écrit dans la vie juridique en Babylonie ancienne," in *Ecritures, système idéographique et pratique expressive,* Actes du colloque international de l'Université de Paris VII, 22−24 April 1980 (Paris: Sycomore, 1982), 65−74.
4. Henri Levy-Bruhl, "L'écriture et le droit," in *L'écriture et la psychologie des peuples* (Paris: A. Colin, 1963), 329. See also Paul Ourliac and Jehan de Malafosse, *Histoire du droit privé,* 2 vols. (Paris: Presses Universitaires de France, 1961), 1:18, 37, 43 (2d rev. ed. 1969); Alberto Maffi, "Ecriture et pratique juridique dans 'la Grèce classique'," in Marcel Détienne, ed., *Les savoirs de l'écriture: En Grèce ancienne* (Lille: Presses universitaires de Lille, 1988), 204−5.
5. Paul-Frédéric Girard, *Manuel élémentaire de droit romain* (Paris: A. Rousseau, 1906), 938−39; Alain de Boüard, *Manuel de diplomatique française et pontificale,* 2 vols. (Paris: Editions Auguste Picard, 1929−48), 2:48−53.
6. Levy-Bruhl, "L'écriture et le droit," 325−26.
7. Jean Gaudemet, *Institutions de l'Antiquité* (Paris: 1967), 18−22.
8. Eilers, "Réflexions sur les origines du droit," 208.
9. Emile Szlechter, "La 'loi' en Mésopotamie," *Revue internationale du droit de l'Antiquité,* 11 (1965): 55−77; Szlechter, "La loi et la coutume, manifestation d'autorité et source d'enseignement dans l'Antiquité orientale," *Travaux et recherches de l'Institut de droit comparé de l'Université de Paris,* 23 (1962): 5−11.
10. Louis Gernet, *Recherches sur le développement de la pensée juridique et morale en Grèce (Etude de sémantique)* (Paris: Ernest Leroux, 1917); Gernet, *Anthropologie de la*

Grèce antique (Paris: F. Maspero, 1968), available in English as *The Anthropology of Ancient Greece*, trans. John Hamilton and Blaise Nagy (Baltimore: Johns Hopkins University Press, 1981). See also Jean Imbert, "La loi et la coutume, manifestation d'autorité et source d'enseignement dans l'Antiquité orientale," *Travaux et recherches de l'Institut de droit comparé de l'Université de Paris*, 23 (1962): 13–33.

11. Gaudemet, *Institutions de l'Antiquité*, 185–90.

12. Georges Dumézil, *Jupiter, Mars, Quirinus: Essai sur la conception indo-européen de la société et sur les origines de Rome* (Paris: Gallimard, 1941); Dumézil, *La religion romaine archaïque* (Paris: Payot, 1966), available in English as *Archaic Roman Religion*, trans. Philip Krapp (Chicago: University of Chicago Press, 1970); Raymond Bloch, *Les origines de Rome*, 7th ed. (Paris: Presses Universitaires de France, 1978), available in English as *The Origins of Rome* (London: Thames & Hudson; New York: Praeger, 1960); Bloch, *Tite-Live et les premiers siècles de Rome* (Paris: Belles lettres, 1965).

13. Girard, *Manuel élémentaire de droit romain*, 19–28; Jean Bayet, *Histoire politique et psychologique de la religion romaine* (Paris: Payot, 1957); André Piganiol, *Essai sur les origines de Rome* (Paris: Fontemoing et cie., M. Boccard, successeur, 1916).

14. Gaudemet, *Institutions de l'Antiquité*, 588–605.

15. Ibid., 732–89.

16. G. S. Kirk, *The Songs of Homer* (Cambridge: Cambridge University Press, 1962); Alan John Bayard Wace and Frank H. Stubbings, eds., *A Companion to Homer* (London: Macmillan; New York: St. Martin's Press, 1962); Albin Lesky, "Homeros," in vol. 1 of the supplement to Pauly and Wissowa, *Real-Encyclopädie; Archaelogia homerica, Die Denkmaler und das frühgriechische Epos*, Band III, Kapitel X; Alfred Heubeck, *Kleine Schriften zur griechischen Sprache und Literatur* (Erlangen: Universitätsbund Erlangen-Nürnberg, 1984), pt. 3, *Homer und die Schrift*, 126–84, esp. "Schriftlichkeit in Homerischer Zeit." See also Jacqueline de Romilly, *Homère* (Paris: Presses Universitaires de France, 1985).

17. A. B. Lord, *The Singer of Tales* (Cambridge, Mass.: Harvard University Press, 1960; New York: Atheneum, 1970); Milman Parry, *The Making of Homeric Verse*, ed. Adam Parry (Oxford: Clarendon Press, 1971).

18. Paul Mazon, with Pierre Chantraine, Paul Collart, and René Langumier, *Introduction à l'Iliade* (Paris: Belles lettres, 1942).

19. Jacqueline de Romilly, *Histoire et raison chez Thucydide*, 2d ed. (Paris: Belles lettres, 1967).

20. Dumézil, *La religion romaine archaïque*, 19–20; Bloch, *Tite-Live et les premiers siècles de Rome*; Bloch, *Les origines de Rome*.

21. Dumézil, *La religion romaine archaïque*, quoted from *Archaic Roman Religion*, 19–20.

22. Jean Collart, *Varron, grammairien latin* (Paris: Belles lettres, 1954).

23. Jérôme Carcopino, *Virgile et les origines d'Ostie*, 2d ed. (Paris: Presses Universitaires de France, 1968); Jean-Marie André, *Mécène, essai de biographie spirituelle* (Paris: Belles lettres, 1967).

24. Jack Goody, *La raison graphique: la domestication de la pensée sauvage* (Paris: Editions de Minuit, 1979), a translation of his *The Domestication of the Savage Mind* (Cambridge and New York: Cambridge University Press, 1977).

25. Goody, *La raison graphique*, 38.

26. Ferdinand de Saussure, *Cours de linguistique générale* (Paris: 1978), 45, quoted from *Course in General Linguistics*, ed. Charles Bally and Albert Sechehaye in collaboration with Albert Riedlinger, trans. Wade Baskin (New York, Toronto, London: McGraw-Hill, 1966), 23−24.

27. Goody, *La raison graphique*, 149−76, *Domestication of the Savage Mind*, 74−111; René Labat, in René Taton, gen. ed., *Histoire générale des sciences*, 3 vols. in 4 pts. (Paris: Presses universitaires de France, 1957−64), 1:85−89, available in English as *History of Science*, trans. A. J. Pomerans, 4 vols. (New York: Basic Books, 1963−66).

28. Jean Bottéro, "Les noms de Marduck," in Maria de Jong Ellis, ed., *Essays on the Ancient Near East in Memory of Jacob Joel Finkelstein* (Hamden, Conn.: Archon Books for the Connecticut Academy of Arts and Sciences, 1977), 5−28.

29. For a somewhat similar approach to Babylonian and Greek competence in arithmetical calculation, see Eric Alfred Havelock, *Aux origines de la civilisation écrite en Occident, étude de psychologie historique* (Paris: Maspero, Découverte, 1981), 96−97. See also Havelock, *The Literate Revolution in Greece and Its Cultural Consequences* (Princeton: Princeton University Press, 1982), and *The Muse Learns to Write: Reflections on Orality and Literacy From Antiquity to the Present* (New Haven: Yale University Press, 1986).

30. Bottéro, "Les noms de Marduck."

31. Jacques Gernet, *Chine et christianisme: Action et réaction* (Paris: Gallimard, 1982), 322−33.

32. Jean-Pierre Vernant, *Mythes et pensée chez les Grecs: Etudes de psychologie historique*, 2d ed. rev. and aug. (Paris: Découverte, 1985), 53−54, quoted from *Myth and Thought Among the Greeks* (London and Boston: Routledge & Kegan Paul, 1983), 77.

33. Havelock, *Aux origines de la civilisation écrite*, 9.

34. Plato, *Phaedrus* 274e, quoted from *Plato's Phaedrus*, trans. with intro. and commentary by R. Hackforth (Cambridge: Cambridge University Press, 1952).

35. Ibid., 275d, e.

36. Plato, *Republic* 3.396, quoted from *The Republic of Plato*, trans. and ed. Francis MacDonald Cornford (London: Oxford University Press, 1941).

37. For a clearer view of the Sophists, see Léon Robin, *La pensée grecque et les origines de la pensée scientifique*, 2d ed. (Paris: Albin Michel, 1973), 157−76, available in English as *Greek Thought and the Origins of the Scientific Spirit* (London: K. Paul, Trench, Trubner & Co.; New York: Knopf, 1928).

38. Plato, *Phaedrus* 265d, e; 266b.

39. My thanks to Professor Hans Georg Gadamer for permitting me to consult the text of a lecture on Plato and writing presented in Bologna in 1985.

40. Léon Robin, *Aristote* (Paris: Presses Universitaires de France, 1944), 31−70.

41. Pierre Aubenque, "Aristote et le langage," *Études classiques, Annales de la Faculté des lettres et sciences humaines d'Aix*, vol. 43, no. 2 (1967): 85−105; Robin, *La pensée grecque*, 282−84.

42. Serrus quoted in Aubenque, "Aristote et le langage," 88. See also Emile Benveniste, "Catégories de pensée et catégories de langage," in his *Problèmes de*

linguistique générale, 2 vols. (Paris: Gallimard, 1966–74), 1:63–74, available in English as *Problems in General Linguistics,* trans. Mary Elizabeth Meek (Coral Gables, Fla.: University of Miami Press, 1971).

43. Léon Brunschvicg, *Les âges de l'intelligence* (Paris: F. Alcan, 1934, 1969). See also Aubenque, "Aristote et le langage," 89, 103–5 (on Benveniste's study).

44. Alain Michel, *Rhétorique et philosophie chez Cicéron: essai sur les fondements philosophiques de l'art de persuader* (Paris: Presses Universitaires de France, 1960).

45. André, *Mécène, essai de biographie spirituelle.*

46. Jérôme Carcopino, *La vie quotidienne à Rome à l'apogée de l'Empire* (Paris: Hachette,1939), 228–34, available in English as *Daily Life in Ancient Rome: The People and the City at the Height of the Empire,* ed. Henry T. Rowell, trans. E. O. Lorimer (New Haven: Yale University Press, 1940); Anne-Marie Guillemin, *Pline et la vie littéraire de son temps* (Paris: Belles lettres, 1929), 44–45; Pierre Grimal, *La civilisation latine,* 5th ed. (Paris: Arthaud, 1960), available in English as *The Civilization of Rome,* trans. W. S. Maguinness (New York: Simon and Schuster, 1963); Ludwig Friedländer, *Moeurs romaines,* 4 vols. (1854–74), available in English as *Roman Life and Manners in the Early Empire,* trans. Leonard A. Magnus, 4 vols. (London: G. Routledge & Sons; New York: E. P. Dutton, 1908–13).

47. Henry Bardon, *Les empereurs et les lettres latines d'Auguste à Adrien* (Paris: Belles lettres, 1968); Jean Gagé, *Les classes sociales dans l'Empire romain* (Paris: Payot, 1964).

48. Alain Michel, *Le "Dialogue des orateurs" de Tacite et la philosophie de Cicéron* (Paris: C. Klincksieck, 1962); Pierre Grimal, *Sénèque ou la conscience de l'Empire* (Paris: Belles lettres, 1979), 416–17.

49. Gage, *Les classes sociales dans l'Empire romain,* 88–89.

50. E. Patrick Parks, *The Roman Rhetorical Schools as a Preparation for the Courts Under the Early Empire* (Baltimore: Johns Hopkins University Press, 1945).

51. Henri-Irénée Marrou, *Histoire de l'éducation dans l'Antiquité,* 2 vols. (Paris: Editions du Seuil, 1948; new ed. 1981).

52. Serge Sauneron, *Les prêtres de l'ancienne Egypte* (Paris: Editions du Seuil, 1957, 116–33; rev. ed., Paris: Perséa, 1988).

53. The best Bibles to consult are the Jerusalem Bible and *La Bible TOB: Traduction oecuménique,* new ed. (Paris: Editions du Cerf/Société biblique Française, 1988). See also Adolphe Lods, *Histoire de la littérature hébraïque et juive* (Paris: Payot, 1950); André Neher, *L'essence du prophétisme* (Paris: Presses Universitaires de France, 1955); André Robert and André Feuillet, eds., *Introduction à la Bible,* 2 vols. (Tournai: Desclée, 1957–59); Wilfred Harrington, *Nouvelle introduction à la Bible,* trans. J. Winandy (Paris: Editions du Seuil, 1971); André Feuillet, *Etudes d'exégèse et de théologie biblique* (Paris: Gabalda, 1975, 1983); Hilaire Duesberg, *Les scribes inspirés: Introduction aux livres sapientiaux de la Bible,* 2 vols. (Paris: Desclée de Brouwer, 1938–39); Roland de Vaux, *Les institutions de l'Ancien Testament,* 2 vols. (Paris: Editions du Cerf, 1958); Edmond Jacob, *L'Ancien Testament* (Paris: Presses universitaires de France, 1967; 5th ed. 1988); Pierre Grelot, "La formation de l'Ancien Testament," in Robert and Feuillet, eds., *Introduction à la Bible,* 2d ed. rev., 4 vols. (Paris: Desclée, 1973–77), vol. 2, *Introduction critique à l'Ancien Testament.*

54. Oscar Cullmann, *Le Nouveau Testament* (Paris: Presses Universitaires de

France, 1966, 1982), available in English as *The New Testament: An Introduction for the General Reader* (Philadelphia: Westminster Press, 1968).

55. Berthold Altaner, *Patrologie; Leben, Schriften und Lehre der Kirchenväter* (Freiburg: Herder, 1951).

56. Yves Congar, *La tradition et les traditions: Essai théologique*, 2 vols. (Paris: Fayard, 1960–63), available in English as *Tradition and Traditions: An Historical and a Theological Essay*, trans. Michael Naseby and Thomas Rainborough (London: Burns & Oates; New York: Macmillan, 1966).

57. Congar, *La tradition et les traditions*, 1:48, quoted from *Tradition and Traditions*, 32–33.

58. Régis Blachère, *Introduction au Coran*, 2d ed. (Paris: Editions Besson et Chantemerle, 1959); Blachère, *Le Coran (al-Qor'ân)* (Paris: Librairie Orientale et Américaine, G. & P. Maisonneuve, M. Besson, 1958).

CHAPTER FOUR

1. Pierre Riché, *Education et culture dans l'Occident barbare, VIe-VIIIe siècle* (Paris: Editions du Seuil, 1962), available in English as *Education and Culture in the Barbarian West, Sixth Through Eighth Centuries*, trans. John J. Contreni (Columbia, S.C.: University of South Carolina Press, 1976); Riché, *Ecoles et enseignement dans le Haut Moyen Age: fin du Ve siècle–milieu du XIe siècle* (Paris: Picard, 1979). For the nature of the law and for a bibliography, see Lucien Musset, *Les invasions. Les vagues germaniques* (Paris: Presses Universitaires de France, 1969), 278–81, available in English as *The German Invasions: The Making of Europe, A.D. 400–600*, trans. Edward and Columba James (University Park, Pa.: Pennsylvania State University Press, 1975).

2. Lucien Musset and Fernand Mossé, *Introduction à la runologie* (Paris: Aubier Montaigne, 1965); Mossé, *Manuel de la langue gotique: Grammaire, textes, glossaire*, 2d ed., rev. and enl. (Paris: Editions Montaigne, 1956); Hellmut Rosenfeld, "Buch, Schrift und lateinische Sprachkenntnis bei den Germanen vor der christlischen Mission," *Rheinisches Museum für Philologie* 95 (1952): 193–209.

3. Max Ludwig Laistner, *Thought and Letters in Western Europe A.D. 500 to 900*, 2d ed. (New York: L. MacVeagh, The Dial Press, 1931; Ithaca: Cornell University Press, 1966); Jean Leclercq, *L'amour des lettres et le désir de Dieu: Initiation aux auteurs monastiques du Moyen Age* (Paris: Editions du Cerf, 1957), available in English as *The Love of Learning and the Desire for God: A Study of Monastic Culture*, trans. Catharine Misrahi, 3d ed. (New York: Fordham University Press, 1982); C. E. Stevens, *Sidonius Apollinaris and His Age* (Oxford: Clarendon Press, 1933); James Joseph O'Donnell, *Cassiodorus* (Berkeley: University of California Press, 1979); Margaret T. Gibson, ed., *Boethius, His Life, Thought, and Influence* (Oxford: Blackwell, 1981–); R. Plate, *Geschichte der Gotischen Literatur* (Berlin and Bonn: Dümmler, 1931); Susanne Teillet, *Des Goths à la nation gothique: Les origines de l'idée de nation en Occident du Ve au VIIe siècle* (Paris: Belles lettres, 1984); *I Goti in Occidente: problemi*, Settimane di studio del Centro italiano di studi sull'alto medioevo, 3 vols. (Spoleto: Centro di studi, 1956).

4. Pierre Courcelle, *Histoire littéraire des grandes invasions germaniques* (Paris: Hachette, 1948), 178.

5. Riché, *Education et culture*, 112–17. On oral and written tradition concerning contracts, Robert Fossier has said: "These two traditions of the written diverge only on the level of method; as for the content, they both spring from a mentality solidly established in the minds of the peoples of the West, both in the Western period and in the Middle Ages: the contractual aspect of any human relationship and its corollary, mutual respect of the contract. There is no question here of consideration, nor of value judgments [but] simply a statement of fact: an engagement involves reciprocal obligations, breaking it is ranked at the level of bad things. We are so impregnated with that concept that we put the blame on any other behavior, qualified as amoral. This is not the place to enumerate the rude awakenings undergone by Europeans in Asia or in Islam as a consequence of this false judgment" (Robert Fossier, *Histoire sociale de l'Occident médiéval* [Paris: Armand Colin, 1970], 139).

6. Jacques Fontaine, *Isidore de Séville et la culture classique dans l'Espagne wisigothique* (Paris: Etudes Augustiniennes, 1959).

7. Riché, *Education et culture*, 236–50.

8. Georges Tessier, *La diplomatique*, new rev. ed., (Paris: Presses Universitaires de France, 1967), 111; Alain de Boüard, *Manuel de diplomatique française et pontificale*, 2 vols. (Paris: Auguste Picard, 1929–48), vol. 2, *L'acte privé*, 68–94, 106–7.

9. Gregory of Tours, *Histoire de France*, trans. and ed. Robert Latouche (Paris: Belles lettres, 1963–65), 2:222–23 (book 9, chapter 30); Riché, *Education et culture*, 268–69.

10. *Règle de saint Benoît*, intro., trans., and notes Adalbert de Vogué, 7 vols. (Paris: Editions du Cerf, 1972), 2:222–23.

11. Pierre Paul Courcelle, *Les lettres grecques en Occident de Macrobe à Cassiodore* (Paris: E. de Boccard, 1943), 313–88, available in English as *Late Latin Writers and Their Greek Sources*, trans. Harry E. Wedeck (Cambridge, Mass.: Harvard University Press, 1969). See also Riché, *Education et culture*, 205–12.

12. Riché, *Education et culture*, 42–44; Claudio Leonardi, "Il venerabilis Beda e la cultura del secolo VIII," in *Problemi dell'Occidente nel secolo VIII*, Settimane di studio del Centro italiano di studi sull'alto medioevo, 20 (Spoleto: Centro italiano di studi, 1973), 603–58.

13. Emile Lesne, *Histoire de la propriété ecclésiastique en France*, 6 vols. (Paris: Champion; Lille: René Giard, 1940), vol. 4, *Les livres, "scriptoria" et bibliothèques du commencement du VIIIe à la fin du XIe siècle*, reprint ed. (New York: Johnson Reprint Corp., 1964). See also Remigo Sabbadini, *Le scoperte dei codici latini e greci nei secoli XIV e XV*, 2 vols. (Florence: Sansoni, 1967); Philippe Wolff, *Histoire de la pensée européenne*, 6 vols. (Paris: Editions du Seuil, 1971), vol. 1, *L'éveil intellectuel de l'Europe*, 22; L. D. Reynolds and N. G. Wilson, *D'Homère à Erasme. La transmission des classiques grecs et latins*, new ed. rev. and enl., trans. C. Bertrand (Paris: Editions du CNRS, 1988), a translation into French of *Scribes and Scholars: A Guide to the Transmission of Greek and Latin Literature* (London: Oxford University Press, 1968). The text of the *Fifth Decade* (books 41–45) of the *Annals* from the Lorsch manuscript was discovered by Simon Grynaeus and transmitted to Erasmus, who used it in his edition of Livy (Basel: Froben, 1531).

14. Arthur Jean Kleinclausz, *Alcuin* (Paris: Belles lettres, 1948); Wolff, *Histoire de la pensée européenne*, 1:8–86.

15. Einhard, *Vita Caroli*, 25, available in various translations in English. One is *Einhard's Life of Charlemagne*, ed. H. W. Gartrod and R. B. Mowat (Oxford: Clarendon Press, 1925). See also Pierre Riché, *La vie quotidienne dans l'Empire carolingien* (Paris: Hachette, 1973), 244–45, available in English as *Daily Life in the World of Charlemagne*, trans. Jo Anne McNamara (Philadelphia: University of Pennsylvania Press, 1978); Riché, *Ecoles et enseignement*, 69–76.

16. François L. Ganshof, "Charlemagne et l'usage de l'écrit en matière administrative," *Le Moyen Age* 57 (1951): 1–25; Ganshof, "Recherches sur les capitulaires," *Revue d'histoire du droit français et étranger* (1958).

17. Georges Tessier, *Diplomatique royale française* (Paris: A. & J. Picard, 1962), 39–57.

18. Cyrille Vogel, "La réforme liturgique sous Charlemagne," in *Karl der Grosse; Lebenswerk und Nachleben*, 5 vols. (Düsseldorf: L. Schwann, 1966–68), 2:217–32.

19. Bernhard Bischoff, "Panorama der handschriften-überlieferung aus der Zeit Karls des Grossen," in *Karl der Grosse; Lebenswerk und Nachleben*, 2:233–54.

20. Bernhard Bischoff, *Paläographie des römischen Altertums und des abendländischen Mittelalters* (Berlin: E. Schmidt, 1979), available in French as *Paléographie de l'Antiquité romaine au Moyen Age occidental*, trans. A. Astma and Jean Vezin (Paris: 1986), and in English as *Latin Paleography: Antiquity and the Middle Ages*, trans. Dáibbí ó Cróinin and David Ganz (Cambridge and New York: Cambridge University Press, 1990); Bischoff, "La minuscule caroline et le renouveau culturel sous Charlemagne," trans. Colette Jeudy, *Institut de Recherche et d'Histoire des Textes. Bulletin*, 15 (1967–68): 333–36.; Robert Marichal, "L'écriture latine et la civilisation occidentale du Ier au XVIe siècle," in *L'écriture et la psychologie des peuples* (Paris: Armand Colin, 1963), 199ff.

21. Georges Duby, *Le temps des cathédrales. L'art et la société, 980–1420* (Paris: Gallimard, 1976), 24–27, available in English as *The Age of the Cathedrals: Art and Society, 980–1420*, trans. Eleanor Levieux and Barbara Thompson (Chicago: University of Chicago Press, 1981); Wolff, *Histoire de la pensée européenne*, 1:87–155.

22. Raoul Glaber, *Historiae*, in *Raoul Glaber: Les cinq livres de ses histoires*, ed. Maurice Prou (Paris: Auguste Picard, 1886).

23. Duby, *Le temps des cathédrales*, 97–98.

24. Robert Fossier, *Enfance de l'Europe: Xe–XIIx siècle: aspects économiques et sociaux*, 2 vols. (Paris: Presses Universitaires de France, 1982), 1:441–47.

25. De Boüard, *Manuel de diplomatique française et pontificale*, 2:153–82; Mario Amelotti and Giorgio Costamagna, *Alle origini del notariato italiano* (Rome: Consiglio nazionale del notariato, 1975); Federico Melis, *Guida della mostra internazionale di storia della Banca secoli XIII–XVI* . . . (Siena, 1972); Armando Petrucci, *Notarii. Documenti per la storia del notariato italiano* (Milan: Giuffrè, 1950, 1965).

26. Tessier, *La diplomatique*, 115–26; Mattia Moresco and Gian Piero Bognetti, *Per l'edizione dei notai liguri del sec. XII* (Genoa: R. Deputazione di storia patria per la Liguria, 1938); Robert-Henri Bautier, in *Manuel d'archivistique, théorie et pratiques des archives publiques en france* (Paris: SEVPEN, 1970), 380–84.

27. Melis, *Guida della mostra*; Raymond De Roover, *L'évolution de la lettre de change, XIVe–XVIIIe siècle* (Paris: Armand Colin, 1953).

28. For the oldest French acts written in *langue d'oc* and *langue d'oil*, see Clovis

Félix Brunel, *Les plus anciennes chartes en langue provençale* (Paris: Auguste Picard, 1926); Jacques Monfrin, preface to *Documents linguistiques de la France (série française)*, (Paris: Editions du CNRS), vol. 1, *Chartes en langue française antérieures à 1271 conservées dans le département de Haute-Marne*, Jean-Gabriel Gigot, ed., (1974), xli, xlv; Pascale Bourgain and Jacques Monfrin, "L'emploi de la langue vulgaire dans la littérature et dans les actes," in *La France de Philippe Auguste, le temps des mutations*, Colloque du CNRS 602, Paris, 29 September–4 October 1980 (Paris: Editions du CNRS, 1982), 765–82.

29. Tessier, *Diplomatique royale française* (Paris: Picard, 1962), 125–76; Bernard Guenée, *L'Occident aux XIVe et XVe siècles: Les états* (Paris: Presses Universitaires de France, 1971), pp. 181–84, 190–93, available in English as *States and Rulers in Later Medieval Europe*, trans. Juliet Vale (Oxford and New York: Blackwell, 1985). See also Jacques Monfrin, "Le mode de tradition des actes écrits et les études de dialectologie," *Revue de linguistique romane*, 32 (1968): 17–47.

30. For bibliography concerning the *Domesday Book*, see R. C. Van Caenegem with F. L. Ganshof, *Guide to the Sources of Medieval History*, 2 vols. (Amsterdam, New York, Oxford: North-Holland Publishing Co., 1978), 1: 96–97. See also M. T. Clanchy, *From Memory to Written Record: England, 1066–1367* (Cambridge, Mass.: Harvard University Press, 1979).

31. Tessier, *La diplomatique*, 30–52; Tessier, *Diplomatique royale française*.

32. Tessier, *La diplomatique*, 36–38.

33. Ibid., 49.

34. Ibid, 104.

35. Tessier, *Manuel de diplomatique française et pontificale*, 268–94; Tessier, *La diplomatique*, 53–80.

36. Robert-Henri Bautier, "Recherches sur la chancellerie royale au temps de Philippe VI," *Bibliothèque de l'Ecole des chartes*, 112 (1964): 89–176; 125 (1965): 313–459.

37. Ibid.

38. Michel Fleury and Louis Henry, *Des registres paroissiaux à l'histoire de la population, manuel de dépouillement et d'exploitation de l'état civil ancien* (Paris: Editions de l'Institut national d'études démographiques, 1956).

39. Henri Pirenne, "L'instruction des marchands au Moyen Age," *Annales d'histoire économique et sociale* (1929): 13–28.

40. Emmanuel Poulle, "Pour une histoire de l'écriture," *Bibliothèque de l'Ecole des chartes*, 135 (1977): 137–44.

41. Stephen d'Irsay, *Histoire des universités françaises et étrangères des origines à nos jours*, 2 vols. (Paris: Auguste Picard, 1933–35); d'Irsay, *L'Université de Bologne et la pénétration des droits romain et canonique en Suisse aux XIIIe et XIVe siècles* (Geneva: Droz, 1955).

42. Paul Fournier, "Un tournant dans l'histoire du droit," *Revue d'histoire du droit* (1917); Paul Fournier and Gabriel Le Bras, *Histoire des collections canoniques en Occident depuis les fausses décrétales jusqu'au Décret de Gratien*, 2 vols. (Paris: Recueil Sirey, 1931–33; reprint, Aalen: Scientia-Veriag, 1972).

43. Jean Leclercq, *Pierre le Vénérable* (Paris: Editions de Fontenelle, 1946); José María Millas-Vallicrosa, "La corriente de las traducciones cientificas de origen

oriental hasta fines del siglo XIII," *Cahiers d'histoire mondiale/Journal of World History/Cuadernos de Historia Mundial,* 2 (1954): 395–428; Richard Lemay, "Dans l'Espagne du XIIe siècle. Les traductions de l'arabe au latin," *Annales ESC,* 18 (1963): 639–65; Guy Beaujouan, "La science dans l'Occident médiéval chrétien," in René Taton, gen. ed., *Histoire générale des sciences,* 2 vols. (Paris: Presses Universitaires de France, 1957), vol. 1, pt. 1, 530–34; F. Van Steenbergen, *Aristote en Occident: les origines de l'aristotélisme parisien* (Louvain: Editions universitaires, 1947).

44. Beaujouan, "La science dans l'Occident médiéval."

45. Jacques Le Goff, *Les intellectuels au Moyen Age* (Paris: Editions du Seuil, 1957); Jacques Verger, *Les universités au Moyen Age* (Paris: Presses Universitaires de France, 1973); Emile Lesne, *Histoire de la propriété ecclésiastique en France,* vol. 5, *Les écoles de la fin du VIIIe à la fin du XIIe siècle;* G. Pare, A. Brunet, and P. Tremblay, *La Renaissance du XIIe siècle. Les écoles et l'enseignement* (Paris: J. Vrin; Ottowa: Institut d'études médiévales, 1933); Gordon Leff, *Paris and Oxford Universities in the Thirteenth and Fourteenth Centuries* (New York: Wiley, 1968); Jacques Verger, ed., *Histoire des universités de France* (Toulouse: Privat, 1986).

46. Etienne Gilson, *La philosophie au Moyen Age, des origines patristiques à la fin du XIVe siècle,* 2d ed. rev. and enl. (Paris: Payot, 1944), 278–96; Joseph de Ghellinck, *Le mouvement théologique du XIIe siècle: Etudes, recherches et documents,* 2d ed. enl. (Paris: J. Gabalda; Bruges: Editions "De Tempel," 1948); Etienne Gilson, *Héloïse et Abélard,* 3d ed. (Paris: J. Vrin, 1964), available in English as *Heloise and Abelard,* trans. L. K. Shook (London: Hollis & Carter, 1953; Ann Arbor: University of Michigan Press, 1960); Jean Jolivet, *Abélard, ou, la philosophie dans le langage* (Paris: Seghers, 1969); Jolivet, *Arts du langage et théologie chez Abélard* (Paris: Seghers, J. Vrin, 1982).

47. Etienne Gilson, *La théologie mystique de saint Bernard,* 2d ed. (Paris: J. Vrin, 1947), available in English as *The Mystical Theology of St. Bernard,* trans. A. H. Downes (Kalamazoo: Cistercian Publications, 1990); Jean Leclercq, *Saint Bernard et l'esprit cistercien* (Paris: Editions du Seuil, 1966), available in English as *Bernard of Clairvaux and the Cistercian Spirit,* trans. Claire Lavoie (Kalamazoo: Cistercian Publications, 1976); Leclercq, *Etudes sur saint Bernard et le texte de ses écrits* (Rome: Apud Curiam Generalem Sacri Ordinis Cisterciensis, 1955); Leclercq, "Saint Bernard et ses secrétaires," *Revue bénédictine,* 61 (1951): 208–29.

48. Palémon Glorieux, "L'enseignement au Moyen Age. Techniques et méthodes en usage à la Faculté de théologie de Paris au XIIIe siècle," *Archives d'histoire doctrinale et littéraire du Moyen Age,* 35 (1968): 65–186. On the *Quaestiones,* see also Bernard C. Bazán, John F. Wippel, Gérard Fransen, and Danielle Jacquart, *Les questions disputées et les questions quodlibétiques dans les Facultés de théologie, de droit et de médecine* (Tournhout: Brépols, 1985).

49. Marichal, "L'écriture latine et la civilisation occidentale," 236. On St. Thomas's working methods, see Antoine Dondaine, *Secrétaires de saint Thomas,* 2 vols. (Rome: Editori di S. Tommaso, S. Sabina, 1956).

50. Mary A. and Richard H. Rouse, "La naissance des index," in Henri-Jean Martin and Roger Chartier, gen. eds., *Histoire de l'édition française,* 4 vols. (Paris: Promodis, 1982–86), vol. 1, *Le livre conquérant: Du Moyen Age au milieu du XVIIe siècle,* 77–88; R. H. Rouse, "L'évolution des attitudes envers l'autorité écrite: le

développement des instruments de travail au XIIIe siècle," in *Culture et travail intellectuel dans l'Occident médiéval* (Paris: Editions du CNRS, 1981), 115–44.

51. Paul Delalain, *Etude sur le libraire parisien du XIIIe au XIVe siècle, d'après les documents publiés dans le cartulaire de l'Université de Paris* (Paris: Delalain frères, 1891); Jean Destrez, *La pecia dans les manuscrits universitaires du XIIIe et du XIVe siècle* (Paris: J. Vautrain, 1935); Guy Fink-Errera, "Une institution du monde médiéval: la pecia," *Revue philosophique de Louvain*, 60 (1962): 184–243, esp. pp. 240ff.

52. Philippe Wolff, *Les origines linguistiques de l'Europe occidentale* (Paris: Hachette, 1970); Charles Camproux, *Les langues romanes*, 2d ed. (Paris: Presses Universitaires de France, 1979); Walther von Wartburg, *La fragmentation linguistique de la Romania* (Paris: Klincksieck, 1967), French translation of his *Die Ausgliederung der romanischen Sprachräume* (Bern: A. Francke, 1950).

53. Nithard, *Histoire des fils de Louis de Pieux [Historiarum libri IV]*, ed. and trans. Philippe Lauer (Paris: H. Champion, 1926), 103–7.

54. Julius Caesar, *De bello gallico* 1.29; 4.14. See also Camille Louis Jullian, *Histoire de la Gaule*, 8 vols. (Paris: Hachette, 1908–26), 2:375–79.

55. Albert Fuchs, *Les débuts de la littérature allemande du VIIe au XIIe siècle* (Paris: Belles lettres, 1952).

56. Snorri Sturluson, *Edda*, ed. Anne Holtsmark and J. Helguson (Copenhagen: 1980), available in a number of editions in English, for example, *Edda/Snorri Sturluson*, trans. and intro. Anthony Faulkes (London: Dent, 1987); Gustav Neckel, ed., *Edda: Die Lieder des Codex Regius nebst verwandten Denkmälern* (Heidelberg: Winter, 1982); Felix Wagner, *Les poèmes héroïques de l'Edda et la Saga de Völsungs* (Paris: E. Leroux, 1929). There is a good summary of the question in Frédéric Durand, *Les littératures scandinaves* (Paris: Presses Universitaires de France, 1974), 7–19. See also Georges Dumézil, *Les dieux des Germains: Essai sur la formation de la religion scandinave* (Paris: Presses Universitaires de France, 1959), available in English as *Gods of the Ancient Northmen*, ed. Einar Haugen (Berkeley: University of California Press, 1973).

57. Henry Sweet, ed., *The Oldest English Texts* (London: Early English Text Society, N. Trübner & Co., 1885); Florence Elizabeth Harmer, *The Anglo-Saxon Writs* (Manchester: Manchester University Press, 1952).

58. H. Leclercq, s.v. "Cantilène," in Fernand Cabrol, ed., *Dictionnaire d'archéologie chrétienne et de liturgie*, 15 vols. in 29 (Paris: Letouzey et Ané, 1907–53), II, 2, cols. 1973–75; Fuchs, *Débuts de la littérature Allemande*. On the writing of the oldest French texts, see Guy de Poerck, "Les plus anciens textes de la langue française comme témoins de l'époque," *Revue de linguistique romane*, 27 (1963): 1–34; Jacques Monfrin, "Des premières apparitions du français dans les manuscrits à la constitution des grands recueils des XIIe–XIVe siècles," in Emmanuèle Baumgartner and Nicole Boulestreau, eds., *La présentation du livre*, Colloque, Nanterre, 4–6 December 1985 (Nanterre: Centre de recherches du Département de français de Paris X-Nanterre, 1987), 295–312.

59. Jean Rychner, *Les chansons de geste: Essai sur l'art épique des jongleurs* (Geneva: E. Droz, 1955). See also Joël W. Grisward, *Archéologie de l'épopée médiévale.*

Structures trifonctionnelles et mythes indo-européens dans le cycle des Narbonnais (Paris: Payot, 1981).

60. Edmond Faral, *Les jongleurs en France au Moyen Age* (Paris: H. Champion, 1910).

61. Léon Gauthier, *Les épopées françaises: Etude sur les origines et l'histoire de la littérature*, 2d ed., 4 vols. (Paris: Société générale de librairie catholique, 1878–82); Gaston Paris, *La littérature française au Moyen Age (XIe–XVe siècle)*, 3d ed. (Paris: Hachette, 1905); Philip August Becker, *Grundriss der alfranzösischen Literatur* (Heidelberg: C. Winter, 1907; Joseph Bédier, *Les légendes épiques: Recherches sur la formation des chansons de geste*, 4 vols. (Paris: H. Champion, 1908–13); Ramón Menéndez Pidal, *La Chanson de Roland et la tradition épique des Francs*, trans. Irénée-Marcel Cluzel, 2d ed. rev. (Paris: A. and J. Picard, 1960); Menéndez Pidal, *Poesía juglaresca y orígenes de las literaturas románicas: problemas de historia literaria y cultural* (Madrid: Instituto de Estudios Políticos, 1957), 6th ed. corr. and aug. of his *Poesia juglaresca y juglares: aspectos de la historia literaria y cultural de España* (Madrid, 1924); René Louis, *Epopée française et carolingienne* (Saragossa: 1956); Italo Siciliano, *Les chansons de geste et l'épopée: Mythes, histoire, poèmes* (Turin: Società internazionale editrice, 1968); *La technique littéraire des chansons de geste*, Actes du colloque international tenu à Liège, September 1957 (Paris: Belles lettres, 1959).

62. Reto R. Bezzola, *Les origines et la formation de la littérature courtoise en Occident (500–1200)*, 3 vols. in 5 (Paris: E. Champion, 1944–63); Henri-Irénée Marrou, *Les troubadours*, new enl. ed. (Paris: Editions du Seuil, 1971); Alfred Jeanroy, *Les origines de la poésie lyrique en France* (Paris: Hachette, 1889); Jean Frappier, *La poésie lyrique en France aux XIIe et XIIIe siècles*, 2 vols. (Paris: Centre de documentation universitaire, 1952).

63. Erich Köhler, "Observations historiques et sociologiques sur la poésie des troubadours," *Cahiers de civilisation médiévale X–XII siècles* (1964): 27–51; Köhler, *Ideal und Wirklichkeit in der höfischen Epik: Studien zur Form der Frühen Artus- und Gral-dichtung* (Tübingen: M. Niemeyer, 1956; 1970), in French translation as *L'aventure chevaleresque. Idéal et réalité dans le roman courtois* (Paris: Gallimard, 1974); Christiane Marchello-Nizia, "Amour courtois, société masculine et figures de pouvoir," *Annales E.S.C.*, 36 (1981): 909–81. See also René Nelli, *L'érotique des troubadours* (Toulouse: Privat, 1963, reprint 1984); Marie Ungureanu, *La bourgeoisie naissante: Société et littérature bourgeoises d'Arras*, Memoires de la Commission des monuments historiques du Pas-de-Calais, vol. 8, no. 1 (Arras: Imprimerie Centrale de l'Artois, 1955); Dominique Boutet and Armand Strubel, *Littérature, politique et société dans la France du Moyen Age* (Paris: Presses Universitaires de France, 1979).

64. Edmond Faral, *Recherches sur les sources latines des contes et romans courtois du Moyen Age* (Paris: E. Champion, 1913); Hidéichi Matsubara, "A propos du Dit de l'Unicorne . . . ," *Etudes de langue et le littérature françaises*, 22 (1973): 1–10; Matsubara, "Un conte japonais parallèle au *Lai de l'oiselet*," in Hans R. Runte et al., eds., *Jean Misrahi Memorial Volume: Studies in Medieval Literature* (Columbia S.C.: French Literature Publications Co., 1977), 197ff.

65. Edmond Faral, *La légende arthurienne: Etudes et documents*, 3 vols. (Paris: H.

Champion, 1929); Karl Otto Brogsitter, *Artusepik* (Stuttgart: J. B. Metzler, 1965); Roger Sherman Loomis, ed., *Arthurian Literature in the Middle Ages. A Collaborative History* (Oxford: Clarendon Press, 1959); Thomas Parry, *Hanes Llenyddiaeth Gymraeg* (Caerdydd: Gwasg Prifysgol Cymru, 1944), available in English as *A History of Welsh Literature*, trans. H. Idris Bell (Oxford: Clarendon Press, 1955).

66. Maurice Colleville and Ernest Tonnelat, *La Chanson des Nibelungen* (Paris: Aubier-Montaigne, 1958); Ernest Tonnelat, *La Chanson des Nibelungen: Etude sur la composition et la formation du poème épique* (Paris: Belles lettres, 1926).

67. Paul Zumthor, *Langue et technique poétiques à l'époque romane (XIe–XIIIe siècle)* (Paris: Librairie C. Klinckseick, 1963); Zumthor, *Introduction à la poésie orale* (Paris: Editions du Seuil, 1983), available in English as *Oral Poetry: An Introduction*, trans. Kathryn Murphy-Judy (Minneapolis: University of Minnesota Press, 1990); Zumthor, "Observations sur l'écriture médiévale. Extrait d'un livre en préparation sur les traditions orales du Moyen Age européen," *Cultura Neolatina*, 45 (1985): 149–70.

68. Ferdinand Lot, *Etude sur le Lancelot en prose* (Paris: H. Champion, 1954); Cedric Edward Pickford, *L'évolution du roman arthurien en prose vers la fin du Moyen Age* (Paris: A. Nizet, 1960).

69. Bernhard Bischoff, Gerard Isaac Lieftinck, and Giulio Battelli, eds., *Nomenclature des écritures livresques du Xe au XVIe siècle*, Premier colloque international de paléolographie latine, Paris, 28–30 April 1953 (Paris: Editions du CNRS, 1954).

70. István Hajnal, *L'enseignement de l'écriture aux universités médiévales*, 2d ed. rev. and corr. (Budapest: Académie des Sciences de Hongrie, 1959).

71. See, for example, Jacques Stiennon, *Paléographie du Moyen Age* (Paris: A. Colin, 1973); Bischoff, *Paläographie des römischen Altertums* (*Latin Paleography: Antiquity and the Middle Ages.*)

72. For an example of learned correspondence of the Carolingian period, see Loup de Ferrière (Lupus Servatus, abbot of Ferrières), *Correspondance*, ed. and trans. Léon Levillain, 2 vols. (Paris: vol. 1, H. Champion, 1927; vol. 2, Belles lettres, 1935). See also, in particular, Paul Edouard Didier Riant, "Inventaire critique des lettres historiques de croisade," *Archives de l'Orient latin*, 1 (1881): 1–224 (often supposed letters); Gerbert (Pope Sylvester II), *Lettres de Gerbert*, ed. Julien Havet (Paris: Auguste Picard, 1889); Peter Abelard, *Lettres d'Abélard et d'Héloïse*, trans. Octave Gréard, 2d ed. (Paris: Garnier, 1875), available in English in several translations, among them *The Letters of Abelard and Heloise*, trans. Betty Radice (Harmondsworth: Penguin, 1975); Peter the Venerable, *The Letters of Peter the Venerable*, ed. Giles Constable (Cambridge, Mass.: Harvard University Press, 1967); St. Bernard, "Lettres," ed. Jean Leclercq, *Studi medievali*, 3d ser., 12 (1971): 1–74; Leclercq, "Le genre épistolaire au Moyen Age," *Revue du Moyen Age latin*, 2 (1946): 64–70.

73. Ludwig von Rockinger, *Briefsteller und Formelbücher des eilften bis vierzehnten Jahrhunderts*, 2 vols. (Munich: G. Franz, 1863–64); Charles Victor Langlois, *Formulaire de lettres du XIIe, du XIIIe et du XIVe siècle*, 6 nos. in 1 vol. (Paris: Imprimerie nationale, 1890–97).

74. Armando Sapori, *Le Marchand italien au Moyen Age* (Paris: A. Colin, 1952),

available in English as *The Italian Merchant in the Middle Ages*, trans. Patricia Ann Kennen (New York: Norton: 1970).

75. Yves Renouard, "Comment les papes d'Avignon expédiaient leur courrier," *Etudes d'histoire médiévale* (1968): 739–64.

76. François J. M. Olivier-Martin, *Histoire de la coutume de la prévôté et vicomté de Paris*, 2 vols. (Paris: E. Leroux, 1922–30).

77. Paul Génicot, *La loi*, (Turnhout: Brepols, 1977; 2d ed. 1985).

78. Guenée, *L'Occident aux XIVe et XVe siècles*, 168–76.

79. Ibid., 176.

80. Henri-Jean Martin, "Culture écrite et culture orale, culture savante et culture populaire dans la France d'Ancien Régime," *Journal des savants*, July–December (1975): 225–84, reprinted in Martin, *Le livre français sous l'Ancien Régime* (Paris: Promodis/Editions du Cercle de la Librairie, 1987), 149–86.

81. Paul Perdrizet, *Etude sur le Speculum Humanae Salvationis* (Paris: H. Champion, 1908); Duby, *Le temps des cathédrales*, 98.

82. *Dictionnaire de théologie catholique*, 15 vols. in 30 (Paris: Letouzey et Ané, 1903–50), s.v. "Censure doctrinale," vol. 2, pt. 2, cols. 2101–13 (H. Quilliet); "Censures ecclésiastiques," ibid., cols. 2113–36 (T. Ortolan); "Traditeur," vol. 15, pt. 1, cols. 1250–52 (E. Amann).

83. *Dictionnaire de théologie catholique*, s.v. "Origène," vol. 11, pt. 2, cols. 1490–1566 (G. Bardy); "Origénisme," ibid., cols. 1566–87 (G. Fritz) (on the censorship and disappearance of Origen's works).

84. Isidore Loeb, "La controverse de 1240 sur le Talmud," *Revue des études juives*, 1, 2, and 3 (1880–81); Judah M. Rosenthal, "The Talmud on Trial: The Disputation at Paris in the Year 1240," *Jewish Quarterly Review*, 47 (1956–67): 58–76; 145–69; Solomon Grayzel, *The Church and the Jews in the XIIIth Century* (Philadelphia: The Dropsie College for Hebrew and Cognate Learning, 1933).

85. George B. Flahiff, "Ecclesiastical Censorship of Books in the Twelfth Century," *Mediaeval Studies*, 4(1942): 1–22; A. Hayen, "Le Concile de Reims et l'erreur théologique de Gilbert de La Porrée," *Archives d'histoire doctrinale et littéraire du Moyen Age* (1935–36): 29–102; M. H. Vicaire, "Les Porrétains et l'avicennisme avant 1215," *Revue des sciences philosophiques et théologiques*, 26 (1937): 449–82.

86. Gabriel Théry, *Autour du décret de 1210*, 2 vols. (Le Saulchoir, Kern: Revue des sciences philosophiques et théologiques, 1925–26), vol. 1, *David de Dinant*.

87. Roland Hissette, *Enquête sur les 219 articles condamnés à Paris le 7 mars 1277* (Louvain: Publications Universitaires, 1977); Hissette, "Albert le Grand et Thomas d'Aquin dans la censure parisienne du 7 mars 1277," in Albert Zimmerman, ed., *Studien zur mittelalterlichen Geistesgeschichte und ihren Quellen* (Berlin and New York: De Gruyter, 1982). On the *correctiones* published by the authors and their disciples in their own defense, see L. Hödl, "Geistesgeschichtliche und Literarkritische Erhebungen zum Korrektorienstreit (1277–1287)," *Recherches de théologie ancienne et médiévale*, 33 (1966): 81–114. See also Léopold Delisle, "Livres d'images destinés à l'instruction religieuse et aux exercices de piété des laïques," *Histoire littéraire de la France*, 38 vols. (Paris: Imprimerie nationale, 1733–1944), 31:211ff. The essential problem of sermons lies outside the framework of the present work; on that

subject, see, for example, Marie Magdeleine Davy, *Les sermons universitaires parisiens de 1230 à 1231: Contribution à l'histoire de la prédication médiévale* (Paris: J. Vrin, 1931); Michel Zink, *La prédication en langue romane: Avant 1300* (Paris: H. Champion, 1976).

88. Jean Duvernoy, *Le Catharisme* 2 vols. (Toulouse: Privat, 1976–79), vol. 1, *La religion des cathares;* vol. 2, *L'histoire des cathares.*

89. Amedeo Molinár and Giovanni Gonnet, *Les Vaudois au Moyen Age* (Turin: Claudiana, 1974).

90. Emmanuel Le Roy Ladurie, *Montaillou, village occitan de 1294 à 1324* (Paris: Gallimard, 1975; ed. rev. and corr. 1982), available in English as *Montaillou, The Promised Land of Error,* trans. Barbara Bray (New York: Vintage Books, 1979).

91. Marie-Thérèse d'Alverny, "Un fragment du procès des Amauriciens," *Archives d'histoire doctrinale et littéraire du Moyen Age,* 18 (1950–51): 325–36.

92. Herbert Brook Workman, *John Wyclif: A Study of the English Medieval Church,* 2 vols. (Oxford: Clarendon Press, 1926); John Adam Robson, *Wyclif and the Oxford Schools: The Relation of the "Summa de ente" to Scholastic Debates at Oxford in the Later Fourteenth Century* (Cambridge: Cambridge University Press, 1961). See also Pierre Chaunu, *Le temps des Réformes. La crise de la chrétienté. L'éclatement, 1250–1550* (Paris: Fayard, 1975), 262–75.

93. M. E. Aston, "Lollardy and Sedition, 1381–1431," *Past and Present* (1960): 1–44.

94. Joseph Henry Dahmus, *The Prosecution of John Wyclif* (New Haven: Yale University Press, 1952).

95. Josef Macek, *Le mouvement hussite en Bohême,* 2d ed. enl. (Prague: Orbis, 1958), available in English as *The Hussite Movement in Bohemia,* trans. Vilém Fried and Ian Milner, 2d ed. enl. (Prague: Orbis, 1958); Macek, "Jean Hus et son époque," *Historica,* 13 (1966): 51–80; Matthew Spinka, *John Hus: A Biography* (Princeton: Princeton University Press, 1968): Paul de Vooght, *L'hérésie de Jean Huss,* Bibliothèque de la Revue d'histoire ecclésiastique, fasc. 34 (Louvain: Bureaux de la revue, 1960); Howard Kaminsky, *A History of the Hussite Revolution* (Prague, 1958, Berkeley: University of California Press, 1967); Chaunu, *Le temps des Réformes,* 278–86. There is a summary of the question in Guenée, *L'Occident aux XIVe et XVe siècles,* 317–32.

CHAPTER FIVE

1. Pierre Léon, gen. ed., *Histoire économique et sociale du monde,* 6 vols. (Paris: Armand Colin, 1977–78), vol. 1, *L'ouverture du monde, XIVe–XVIe siècle,* Bartolomé Bennassar and Pierre Chaunu, eds., 429–48, 361–92, 493–514. See also Henri-Jean Martin, "La révolution de l'imprimé," in Henri-Jean Martin and Roger Chartier, gen. eds., *Histoire de l'édition française,* 4 vols. (Paris: Promodis, 1982–86), vol. 1, *Le livre conquérant, Du Moyen Age au milieu du XVIIe siècle,* Henri-Jean Martin and Roger Chartier, eds., 145–61.

2. Bertrand Gille, "Les XVe et XVIe siècles en Occident," in Maurice Daumas, ed., *Histoire générale des techniques,* 5 vols. (Paris: Presses Universitaires de France, 1962–79), vol. 2, *Les premières étapes du machinisme,* 27–37, 47–73; Bertrand Gille, ed., *Histoire des techniques. Techniques et civilisations, techniques et sciences* (Paris:

Gallimard, 1978), esp. pp. 1–120, available in English as *History of Techniques*, 2 vols. (New York: Gordon and Breach, 1986); Wolfgang Von Stromer, "Eine 'industrielle Revolution' des Spätmittelalters?" in Ulrich Troitzsch and Gabriele Wohlauf, *Technik-Geschichte: Historische Beiträge und neuere Ansätze* (Frankfurt: Suhrkamp, 1980), 105–38.

3. Carla Bozzolo, Dominique Coq, and Ezio Ornato, "La production du livre en quelques pays d'Europe occidentale aux XIVe et XVe siècles," *Scrittura e civiltà*, 8 (1984): 129–59; Ezio Ornato, "Les conditions de production et de diffusion du livre médiéval (XIIIe–XVe siècle), quelques considérations générales," *Culture et idéologie dans la genèse de l'Etat moderne*, Actes de la Table Ronde, Rome, 15–17 October 1984 (Rome: Ecole française de Rome, 1985), 57–84.

4. For the inventory of the chapter library in Bayeux in 1444, see E. Deslandres, "Manuscripts de la bibliothèque du chapitre de Bayeux," in *Catalogue général des manuscrits des bibliothèques publiques de France* (Paris: E. Plon, 1866–), vol. 10 (1889), 272–93, reprinted in *Bulletin d'archéologie du Comité des travaux historiques et scientifiques* (1896): 396ff.; Auguste Castan, "La bibliothèque de l'abbaye de Saint-Claude du Jura. Esquisse de son histoire," *Bibliothèque de l'Ecole des chartes*, 50 (1889): 301–54; Henri Auguste Omont, "Inventaire des manuscrits de Cîteaux par l'abbé Jean de Cirey," *Catalogue général des manuscrits des bibliothèques publiques de France* (1889): 339–52; André Vernet, *La bibliothèque de l'abbaye de Clairvaux du XIIe au XVIIIe siècle* (Paris: Editions du CNRS, 1979).

5. Alfred Franklin, *La Sorbonne, ses origines, sa bibliothèque*, 3 vols. (Paris: 1867–73) (the title of the 2d edition of his *Les anciennes bibliothèques de Paris*); Léopold Delisle, *Le Cabinet des manuscrits de la Bibliothèque impériale/nationale*, 3 vols. (Paris: Imprimerie impériale/nationale, 1968–81), 2:142–208; Berthold Louis Ullman, "The Library of Sorbonne," *The Septentrional Celebration of the Founding of Sorbonne College in the University of Paris* (Chapel Hill: Duke University Press, 1953), 33–47; Palémon Glorieux, *Aux origines de la Sorbonne*, 2 vols. (Paris: Vrin, 1965–66), vol. 1, *Robert de Sorbon, l'homme, le collège, les documents*; Richard H. Rouse, "The Early Library of the Sorbonne," *Scriptorium*, 21 (1967): 42–71, 227–51; André Tuillier, "La Bibliothèque de la Sorbonne médiévale et ses livres enchaînés," *Mélanges de la bibliothèque de la Sorbonne*, 2 (1981): 7–41.

6. Henri-Marie Feret, "Vie intellectuelle et scolaire de l'ordre des Frères prêcheurs," *Archives historiques des Dominicains*, 5 (1946): 5–37; Kenneth William Humphreys, *The Book Provisions of the Medieval Friars, 1215–1400* (Amsterdam, Erasmus Booksellers, 1964).

7. Martin, "La révolution de l'imprimé," 145–61. For a more detailed study on the topic, see *Histoire des bibliothèques françaises*, 3 vols. (Paris: Promodis/Editions du cercle de la Librairie, 1988–91), vol. 1, *Les bibliothèques médiévales du VIe siècle à 1530*, ed. André Vernet (1989).

8. Armando Sapori, *Le marchand italien au Moyen Age* (Paris: A. Colin, 1952), available in English as *The Italian Merchant in the Middle Ages*, trans. Patricia Anne Kennen (New York: Norton, 1970).

9. On this topic, see, in particular, André Chastel, *Art et humanisme à Florence au temps de Laurent le Magnifique: Etudes sur la Renaissance et l'humanisme platonicien* (Paris: Presses Universitaires de France, 1959).

10. Jeanne Bignami-Odier, *La Bibliothèque vaticane de Sixte IV à Pie XI: Recherches sur l'histoire des collections de manuscrits* (Vatican City: Biblioteca apostolica vaticana, 1973).

11. Pearl Kibre, "The Intellectual Interests Reflected in Libraries of the XIVth and XVth Centuries," *Journal of the History of Ideas*, 7 (1946): 257–97; Joseph de Ghellinck, "Les bibliothèques médiévales," *Nouvelle revue théologique*, 65 (1938): 36–55.

12. Enrico Frizzi, *Di Vespasiano da Bisticci e delle sue Biografie* (Pisa: Reale Scuola normale superiore di Pisa, 1880); Giuseppe Maria Cagni, *Vespasiano da Bisticci e il suo epistolario* (Rome: Edizioni di storia e letteratura, 1969).

13. Berthod Louis Ullman, *The Origin and Development of Humanistic Script* (Rome: Edizioni di storia e letteratura, 1960); Harry Graham Carter, *A View of Early Typography to About 1600* (Oxford: Clarendon Press, 1969).

14. Paul Saenger, "Manières de lire médiévales," in Martin and Chartier, gen. eds., *Histoire de l'édition française*, 1:131–44.

15. Christian Bec, *Les marchands écrivains: Affaires et humanisme à Florence, 1375–1434* (Paris and The Hague: Mouton, 1967); Bec, *Les livres des Florentins (1413–1608)* (Florence: L. S. Olschki, 1984).

16. Henri Bresc, *Livre et société en Sicile (1299–1499)* (Palermo: Luxograph, 1971); Bresc, "La diffusion du livre en Sicile à la fin du Moyen Age: Note complémentaire," *Bollettino del Centro di studi filologici e linguistici siciliani*, 1 (1973); Bresc, "La culture patricienne entre jurisprudence, humanisme et chevalerie: Palerme, 1440–1470," *Bollettino del Centro di studi filologici e linguistici siciliani*, 13 (1977): 205–21.

17. Carmen Batlle, "Las bibliotecas de los ciudanos de Barcelona en el siglo XV," in *Livres et lecture en Espagne et en France sous l'Ancien Régime*, colloque de la Casa de Velázques, 1982 (Paris: A.D.P.F, 1981), 15–35, and Philippe Berger, "La lecture à Valence de 1474 à 1560: Evolution des comportements en fonction des milieux sociaux," in ibid., 97–110.

18. Bernard Guenée, *L'Occident aux XIVe et XVe siècles: Les états* (Paris: Presses Universitaires de France, 1971), 95–204, 2d ed. rev. and enl. 1981, available in English as *States and Rulers in Later Medieval Europe*, trans. Juliet Vale (Oxford and New York: Blackwell, 1985).

19. Sylvette Guilbert, "Les écoles rurales de Champagne au XVe siècle: enseignement et promotion social," *Annales de l'Est* (1982): 121–47. See also Alain Derville, "L'alphabétisation du peuple à la fin du Moyen Age," *Revue du Nord*, special number, *Liber Amicorum. Mélanges offerts à Louis Trénard*, 66 (1984): 760–76; P. Pierrard, "L'écolâtrie de Saint Jean et l'enseignement à Valenciennes des origines au début du XVIIe siècle," *Mémoires du Cercle archéologique et historique de Valenciennes*, 3 (1957): 29–143.

20. Gilbert Ouy, "L'humanisme et les mutations politiques et sociales en France au XIVe et XVe siècle," in *L'humanisme français au début de la Renaissance*, Actes du Colloque international de Tours (XIVe stage) (Paris: J. Vrin, 1973), 27–44.

21. Ibid., 30–31.

22. Berthold Louis Ullman, *The Humanism of Coluccio Salutati* (Padua: Editrice Antenore, 1963).

23. Françoise Autrand, "Les librairies des gens du Parlement au temps de Charles VI," *Annales E.S.C.*, 28 (1973): 1219–44.

24. Etienne Gilson, *La philosophie au Moyen Age: Des origines patristiques à la fin du XVe siècle*, 2d ed. rev. and enl. (Paris: Payot, 1944), 633–56.

25. Stephen d'Irsay, *Histoire des universités françaises et étrangères des origines à nos jours*, 2 vols. (Paris: Auguste Picard, 1933–35), vol. 1; Hastings Rashdall, *The Universities in Europe in the Middle Ages*, new ed., ed. F. M. Powicke and A. B. Emden, 3 vols. (Oxford: Clarendon Press, 1936).

26. Palémon Glorieux, "Gerson et les Chartreux," *Recherches de philosophie ancienne et médiévale*, 29 (1961): 115–53; Veronika Gerz-Von Bühren, *La tradition de l'oeuvre de Jean Gerson chez les chartreux* (Paris: Editions du CNRS, 1973), vol. 1, *La Chartreuse de Bâle*; Geneviève Hasenohr, "Aperçu sur la diffusion et la réception de la littérature de spiritualité de langue française au dernier siècle du Moyen Age," in Norbert Richard Wolf, ed., *Wissensorganisierende und wissensvermittelnde Literatur im Mittelalter: Perspektiven ihrer Erforschung*, Colloquium 5–7 December 1985, Wiesbaden (Wiesbaden: L. Reichert, 1987), 57–90.

27. Hasenohr, "Aperçu sur la diffusion et la réception."

28. Regnerus Richardus Post, *The Modern Devotion, Confrontation with Reformation and Humanism* (Leyden: E. J. Brill, 1968); Albert Hyma, *The Brethren of the Common Life* (Grand Rapids: Eerdmans, 1950); W. M. Landen, "The Beginnings of Devotio Moderna in Germany," *Research Studies of the State College of Washington* (1981): 161–202, 221–53, (1984): 57–75; Paul Adam, *L'humanisme à Sélestat: L'école, les humanistes, la bibliothèque* (1962), 5th ed. (Sélestat: Société des amis de la bibliothèque de Sélestat, 1987).

29. Fritz Milkau, ed., *Handbuch der Bibliothekswissenschaft*, 2d ed., ed. Georg Leyh (Leipzig: O. Harrassowitz, 1931–40), vol. 3, *Geischichte der Bibliotheken* (1957), vol. 2, pt. 1, passim; Paul Joachim Georg Lehmann, ed., *Mittelalterliche Bibliothekskataloge Deutschlands und der Schweiz*, 4 vols. (Munich: C. H. Beck, 1918–79); Theodor Gottlieb, *Mittelalterliche Bibliothekskatakoge Oesterreichs* 5 vols. (Vienna, Cologne, Graz: Hermann Böhlaus, 1974), vol. 1; A. Derolez, *Corpus catalogorum Belgii* (Brussels: Paleis der Academiën, 1966).

30. Ezio Ornato, "Les conditions de production et de diffusion du livre médiéval"; Carla Bozzolo and Ezio Ornato, *Pour une histoire du livre manuscrit au Moyen Age. Trois essais de codicologie quantitative* (Paris: Editions du CNRS, 1980–83); Bozzolo and Ornato, "Les fluctuations de la production manuscrite à la lumière de l'histoire de la fin du Moyen Age français," *Bulletin philologique et historique (jusqu'à 1610) du Comité des travaux historiques et scientifiques* (1979): 62–75.

31. Paulus Volk, ed., *Die Generalkapitels-Rezesse der Bursfelder Kongregation*, 3 vols. (Siegburg: Respublica-Verlag, 1955–59); Erwin Iserloh, *Reform der Kirche bei Nikolaus von Kues* (Wiesbaden: F. Steiner, 1965); Paulus Volk, *Fünfthundert Jahre Bursfelder Kongregation: Eine Jubiläumsgabe* (Münster: Regensbergsche Verlagsbuchhandlung, 1950).

32. Milkau, ed., *Handbuch der Bibliothekswissenschaft*, 3: 537–40.

33. Lucien Febvre and Henri-Jean Martin, *L'apparition du livre* (1958), 2d ed. (Paris: A. Michel,1971), 39–60, available in English as *The Coming of the Book: The Impact of Printing, 1450–1800*, trans. David Gerard, ed. Geoffrey Nowell-Smith and

David Wootton, new ed. (London: N.L.B., 1976; London and New York: Verso, 1990); Anne Basanoff, *Itinerario della carta dall'Oriente all'Occidente e sua diffusione in Europa*, trans. Valentina Bianconcini (Milan: Edizioni il Polifilo, 1965). Concerning the appearance of paper in China, see in particular, Pan Juxin, *Zongguo zoozhi jishu shigao* (History of Technology and of Paper in China), *Beijing Wenwu chubanshe* (1979), summarized by Jean-Pierre Drège in *Bulletin de l'Ecole française d'Extrême-Orient*, 71 (1982): 263–66. For artisanal paper-making in the Middle East and in the Mediterranean basin, see Jean Irigoin, "Les débuts de l'emploi du papier à Byzance," *Byzantinische Zeitschrift*, 46 (1953): 324–29; Irigoin, "Les types de forme utilisés dans l'Orient méditerranéen (Syrie, Egypte) du XIe au XIVe siècle," *Papier Geschichte*, 13 (1963): 18–21; Irigoin, "Les origines du papier en Italie," ibid., 62–67; Irigoin, "Les filigranes de Fabriano (noms de papetiers) dans les manuscrits grecs du début du XIVe siècle," *Scriptorium*, 12 (1958): 44–50; Irigoin, "L'introduction du papier italien en Espagne," *Papiergeschichte*, 10 (1960): 29–32; Irigoin, "La datation du papier italien des XIIIe et XIVe siècles," *Papier Geschichte*, 18 (1968): 49–52.

34. For a description of its advance, see Febvre and Martin, *L'apparition du livre*, 2d ed., and for the principal studies published before 1970 on centers of paper production (too numerous to mention here), see ibid., 480–82. Italian archives have thus far been poorly exploited, and they doubtless contain much information on the growth of the paper industry in the West from its inception in Fabriano. On the first Italian papers (aside from the admirable studies of Jean Irigoin cited in the previous note), see Andrea Federico Gasparinetti, "Paper, Papermakers and Papermills of Fabriano," the English translation and new version of an article first published in 1938 and now available in Aurelio and Augusto Zonghi and Andrea Federico Gasparinetti, *Zonghi's Watermarks* (Hilversum: Paper Publications Society, 1953), 63–81.

35. Febvre and Martin, *L'apparition du livre*, 2d ed., 59–60.

36. On all these topics, see Thomas Francis Carter, *The Invention of Printing in China and Its Spread Westward* (New York: Columbia University Press, 1931); Jean-Pierre Drège, Mitchiko Ishigami-Iagolnitzer, and Marcel Cohen, eds., *Le livre et l'imprimerie en Extrême-Orient et en Asie du Sud*, Actes du colloque organisé à Paris du 9 au 11 mars 1983 (Bordeaux: Bibliophiles de Guyenne, 1987); Paul Pelliot, *Les débuts de l'imprimerie en Chine* (Paris: Imprimerie nationale, Librairie d'Amérique et d'Orient Adrien Maisonneuve, 1953), 11.

37. As an introduction to this corpus, see Wilhelm Ludwig Schreiber, *Manuel de l'amateur de la gravure sur bois et sur métal au XVe siècle*, 8 vols. (Berlin: A. Cohn successeurs; Leipzig: O. Harrassowitz, 1891–1911), vol. 4, *Catalogue des livres xylographiques et xylochorographiques* (1902).

38. Lieselotte Esther Stamm, "Buchmalerei in Serie: Zur Frühgeschichte der Vervielfältigungskunst," *Zeitschrift für Schweizerische Archäologie und Kunstgeschichte, Revue suisse d'art et d'archéologie, Rivista svizzera d'arte e d'archeologia* 40, 2 (1983): 128–35, which describes techniques developed around 1410–20 in the region of Basel for reproducing popular images rapidly.

39. Michèle Hébert, *Bibliothèque nationale, Cabinet des estampes. Inventaire des gravures des écoles du Nord, 1440–1530*, 2 vols. (Paris: Bibliothèque nationale,

1982–83); Max Lehrs, *Geschichte und kritische Katalog des deutschen niederländischen und französischen Kupferstichs im XV. Jahrhundert*, 9 vols. (Vienna: Gesellschaft für Vervielfältisende Kunst, 1908–34; Liechtenstein, Nendeln: Kraus Reprint, 1969).

40. Febvre and Martin, *Apparition du livre*, 2d ed., 86–101.

41. On Gutenberg's role in the invention of printing, see especially Aloys Leonhard Ruppel, *Johannes Gutenberg, sein Leben und sein Werk*, 3d ed. (Nieuwkoop: B. De Graaf, 1967); Hans Widmann, ed., *Der gegenwärtige Stand der Gutenberg-Forschung* (Stuttgart: A. Hiersemann, 1972); Charles Mortet, *Les origines et les débuts de l'imprimerie* (Paris: Société française de bibliographie, 1922); Jacques Guignard, *Gutenberg et son oeuvre* (Paris: Editions Estienne, 1960; 2d ed. rev., 1963); Martin, "La révolution de l'imprimerie," 145–61. On the questions that follow, see two excellent recent summaries: Albert Kapr, *Johannes Gutenberg. Persönlichkeit und Leistung* (Munich: C. H. Beck, 1987); Guy Bechtel, *Gutenberg et l'invention de l'imprimerie. Une enquête* (Paris: Fayard, 1992).

42. *Cologne Chronicle* (J. Koelhoff, 1499), GW 6688, Goff, C 176. See also Severina Corsten, *Die Kölnische Chronik von 1499* (Hamburg: Witten, 1982). Quotation taken from Guignard, *Gutenberg et son oeuvre*, 18, and here adapted from Febvre and Martin, *The Coming of the Book*, 53.

43. Aside from the Cologne Chronicle, see the memoirs of Jean Le Robert, abbot of Saint-Aubert de Cambrai, conserved in the archives of Lille, in which he mentions a Latin Doctrinal *getté en mole*, two copies of which are said to have been bought in Bruges in January 1445 (1446, new style) and in 1451. It is impossible to tell whether these books were printed with movable type or from metal plates. On this topic, see Mortet, *Les origines et les débuts de l'imprimerie*, 24n.2; 43n.5. On the "manner of Holland," see Gottfried Zedler, *Von Coster zu Gutenberg: Der holländische früdruck und die erfindung des buchdrucks* (Leipzig: K. W. Hiersemann, 1921). The thesis that the Dutch used sand-casting to make characters has been refuted, notably by Rudolf Juchhoff, "Was bleibt von den holländischen Ansprüchen auf die Erfindung der Typographie?" *Gutenberg Jahrbuch* (1950): 128–33. There is a useful summary in Victor Scholderer, "The Invention of Printing," reprinted in Dennis E. Rhodes, ed., *Fifty Essays on Fifteenth- and Sixteenth-Century Bibliography* (Amsterdam: M. Herzberger, 1966), 156–68.

44. On the Strasbourg trial, see Karl Schorbach, "Neue Strassburger Gutenbergfunde," in *Gutenberg-festschrift, zur Feier des 25 iaehrigen Bestehens des Gutenbergmuseums in Mainz* (Mainz: Verlag der Gutenberg-gesellschaft, 1925), 130–43 (an edition taken from an eighteenth-century copy, the original having been destroyed during the siege of Strasbourg in 1870–71). The French translation in Léon Laborde, *Débuts de l'imprimerie à Strasbourg* (Paris: Techener, 1840), quotation, 33–35, is incorrect on several points: see George Duncan Painter, *Studies in Fifteenth-Century Printing* (London: Pindar Press, 1984), 49.

45. For an interpretation of Gutenberg's backers and his activities in Strasbourg, see Wolfgang von Stromer, "Eine industrielle Revolution des Spätmittelalters," in Troitzch and Wolhauf, eds., *Technikgeschichte*, 105–17; von Stromer, "Hans Friedel von Seckingen, der Bankier der Strassburger Gutenberg-Gesellschaften," *Gutenberg Jahrbuch* (1983): 45–48.

46. Pierre Henri Requin, *L'imprimerie à Avignon en 1444* (Paris: Auguste Picard,

1890); Requin, "Documents inédits sur les origines de la typographie," *Bulletin de philologie et d'histoire du Ministère de l'Instruction publique* (Paris: 1890), 328−50; Wolfgang von Stromer, "Zur 'ars artificialiter scribendi' und weiteren 'Kunsten' der Waldfoghel aus Prague und Girard Ferose aus Trier, Nuremberg, 1433−1444, und Avignon, 1444−1446," *Technikgeschichte* 49 (1982): 279−89.

47. Paul Needham, "Johann Gutenberg and the Catholicon Press," *The Papers of the Bibliographical Society of America*, 76, 4 (1982): 395−456; W. J. Partridge, "The Type Setting and Printing of the Mainz Catholicon," *The Book Collector*, 35 (1986): 21−52.

48. Seymour de Ricci, *Catalogue raisonné des premières impressions de Mayence (1445−1467)* (Mainz: Gutenberg-gesellschaft, 1911).

49. Bertrand Gille, *Ingénieurs de la Renaissance* (Paris: Hermann, 1964), available in English as *Engineers of the Renaissance* (Cambridge, Mass.: MIT Press, 1966).

50. Drège, Ishigami-Iagolnitzer, and Cohen, eds., *Le livre et l'imprimerie en Extrême-Orient et en Asie du Sud;* Hee-Jae Lee, *La typographie corréenne au XVe siècle* (Paris: Editions du CNRS, 1987).

51. Pow-key Sohn, *Early Korean Typography* (Seoul: The Korean Library Science Research Institute, 1971).

52. Febvre and Martin, *L'apparition du livre*, 2d ed., 260−61, 266−67. See also K. Dachs and W. Schmidt, "Wie viele Inkunabelausgaben gibt es wirklich," *Bibliotheksforum Bayern*, 2 (1974): 83−95. Since the publication of the second edition of *L'apparition du livre*, the specialists have revised their estimate of the number of incunabula, now thought to be some 27,000 editions rather than 40,000.

53. Rabelais, *Pantagruel* (Lyons, 1532), chap. 8. See Rabelais, *Oeuvres*, Abel Lefranc, ed., 4 vols. (Paris: H. et H. Champion, 1912−22), 3:103 and notes 44−47.

54. Victor Hugo, *Notre-Dame de Paris; Les travailleurs de la mer*, ed. Jacques Seebacher and Yves Gohin (Paris: Gallimard, 1975), esp. the introduction to the second edition, 5−8. Quotation taken from *Notre-Dame de Paris*, trans. Jessie Haynes (New York: P. F. Collier & Son, 1902). See also Philippe Van Tieghem, *Dictionnaire de Victor Hugo* (Paris: Larousse, 1969), 161−64.

55. Ferdinand Geldner, *Die Buchdruckerkunst im alten Bamberg, 1458/59 bis 1519* (Bamberg: Miesenbach, 1964); Horst Kunze, *Geschichte der Buchillustration in deutschland: Das 15. Jahrhundert* (Leipzig: Insel Verlag, 1975).

56. Arthur M. Hind, *An Introduction to a History of Woodcut with a Detailed Survey of Work Done in the Fifteenth Century*, 2 vols. (Boston and New York: Houghton Mifflin, 1935; reprint, New York: Dover Press, 1963), 1:79−84, 91, 211, 279.

57. On this topic, see the studies of the Quanticod team directed by Ezio Ornato, in particular, Carla Bozzolo, Dominique Coq, Denis Muzerelle, and Ezio Ornato, "Noir et blanc: premiers résultats d'une enquête sur la mise en page dans le livre médiéval," in *Il libro e il testo*, Cesare Questa and Renato Raffaelli, eds., Atti del convegno internazionale, Urbino, 20−23 September 1982 (Urbino: Università degli studi, distrib. Edizioni quattro venti, 1984), 195−221, with graphs; Ornato et al., "Page savante, page vulgaire: étude comparative de la mise en page des livres en latin et en français écrits ou imprimés en France au XVe siècle," in Emmanuèle Baumgartner and Nicole Boulestreau, eds., *La présentation du livre*, Actes du col-

loque de Paris X-Nanterre (4, 5, 6 December 1985) (Paris: Centre de recherches du Département de français de Paris X-Nanterre, 1987), 121–33.

CHAPTER SIX

1. Ferdinand Geldner, *Die deutschen Inkunabeldrucker,* 2 vols. (Stuttgart: A. Hiersemann, 1968–70).

2. Jeanne-Marie Dureau, "Les premiers ateliers français," in Henri-Jean Martin and Roger Chartier, eds., *Histoire de l'édition française,* 4 vols. (Paris: Promodis, 1982–86), vol. 1, *Le livre conquérant, du Moyen Age au milieu du XVIIe siècle,* 163–75; Jeanne Veyrin-Forrer, "Aux origines de l'imprimerie française. L'atelier de la Sorbonne et ses mécènes," in *L'art du livre à l'Imprimerie nationale* (Paris: Imprimerie nationale, 1973), 32–53. The chronology of Heynlin's voyages should be revised in light of Robert Marichal, *Le livre des Prieurs de Sorbonne: 1431–1485* (Paris: Aux amateurs des livres, 1987).

3. Henri-Jean Martin, *Livre, pouvoirs et société à Paris au XVIIe siècle (1598–1701)* 2 vols.(Paris and Geneva: Droz, 1969).

4. For the mechanisms of the book trade in Germany, see Hans Widmann, *Der deutsche Buchhandel in Urkunden und Quellen,* 2 vols. (Hamburg: E. Hauswedell, 1965).

5. Charles Perrat, "Barthélemy Buyer et les débuts de l'imprimerie à Lyon," *Bibliothèque d'humanisme et renaissance,* 10 (1935): 103–21, 349–87; Henri-Jean Martin, "Le rôle de l'imprimerie lyonnaise dans le premier humanisme français," in *L'humanisme français au début de la Renaissance,* Stage international d'études, 14, Tours (Paris: J. Vrin, 1973), reprinted in Martin, *Le livre français sous l'Ancien Régime* (Paris: Promodis, Editions du Cercle de la librairie, 1987), 29–39; Martin *Le siècle d'or de l'imprimerie lyonnaise* (Lyons: Editions du Chêne, 1970).

6. Henri-Jean Martin, "Comment mesurer un succès littéraire. Le problème des tirages," in Giles Barber et al., *La bibliographie matérielle,* Table Ronde du CNRS organisée par Jacques Petit, présentée par Roger Laufer (Paris: Editions du CNRS, 1983), reprinted in Martin, *Le livre français sous l'Ancien Régime,* 209–26. On the production capacities of a printshop, see also Philip Gaskell, *A New Introduction to Bibliography* (New York: Oxford University Press, 1972), 163–70.

7. Gaskell, *A New Introduction to Bibliography,* 162.

8. Martin, "Comment mesurer un succès littéraire."

9. See Lucien Febvre and Henri-Jean Martin, *L'apparition du livre,* 2d ed. (Paris: Albin Michel, 1971), 247–50, available in English as *The Coming of the Book: The Impact of Printing, 1450–1800,* trans. David Gerard, ed. Geoffrey Nowell-Smith and David Wootton, new ed. (London: NLB, 1976; London and New York: Verso, 1990).

10. Ferdinand Geldner, "Das Rechnungsbuch des Speyrer Druckerrn Verlegers und Grossbuchhändlers Peter Drach," *Archiv für Geschichte des Buchwesens* 5 (1962): 1–197.

11. For example in the case of the failure of the Cramoisy brothers, see Henri-Jean Martin, "Un grand éditeur parisien au XVIIe siècle: Sébastien Cramoisy," *Gutenberg Jahrbuch* (1957): 179–88, reprinted in Martin, *Le livre français sous l'Ancien Régime,* 55–67.

12. Martin Lowry, *The World of Aldus Manutius: Business and Scholarship in Renaissance Venice* (Ithaca: Cornell University Press, 1979).

13. Philippe Renouard, *Bibliographie des impressions et des oeuvres de Josse Badius Ascensius, imprimeur et humaniste, 1462–1535 . . . avec une notice biographique*, 3 vols. (Paris: E. Paul et fils et Guillemin, 1908).

14. Henry-Jean Martin, "Publishing Conditions and Strategies in Ancien Regime France," in Kenneth E. Carpenter, ed., *Books and Society in History*, Papers of the Association of College and Research Libraries Rare Books and Manuscripts Preconference, 24–28 June 1980, Boston Mass. (New York and London: R. R. Bowker, 1983), 41–47.

15. Febvre and Martin, *L'apparition du livre*, 195–96; Jean François Gilmont, "La fabrication des livres dans la Genève de Calvin," in Jean-Daniel Candaux and Bernard Lescaze, eds., *Cinq siècles d'imprimerie genevoise*, Actes du colloque international sur l'histoire de l'imprimerie et du livre à Genève, 27–30 April 1978, 2 vols. (Geneva: Société d'histoire et d'archéologie, 1980–81).

16. Martin, *Livre, pouvoirs et société à Paris*; Henri-Jean Martin, "La prééminence de l'imprimerie parisienne," in Martin and Chartier, gen. eds., *Histoire de l'édition française*, vol 2, *Le livre triomphant (1660–1830)*, 262–81; Jean Quéniart, "L'anémie provinciale," in ibid., 282–93.

17. Claude Lanette-Claverie, "Les Tours de France des imprimeurs et libraires à la fin du XVIIe siècle," *Revue française du livre* (1971): 207–34; Jacques Rychner, *Genève et ses typographes vus de Neuchâtel, 1770–1780* (Geneva: Braillard, 1984).

18. *Anecdotes typographiques, où l'on voit la description des coutumes, moeurs et usages singuliers des compagnons imprimeurs, by Nicolas Contat dit Le Brun (1762); Le misère des apprentis by Defresne (1710)*, ed. Giles Barber, Oxford Bibliographical Society Publications, n.s., 20 (Oxford: Oxford Bibliographical Society, 1980); Robert Darnton, *The Great Cat Massacre and Other Episodes in French Cultural History* (New York: Random House, Basic Books, 1984), 75–104.

19. Karl Gustav Schwetschke, *Codex nundinarius Germaniae litteratae* (1850), 2 vols. in 1 (Nieuwkoop: B. de Graaf, 1963); Henri Estienne, *The Frankfort Book Fair. The Francofordiense Emporium of Henri Estienne*, ed. James Westfall Thompson (1911) (New York: Burt Franklin, 1968).

20. Martin, *Livre, pouvoirs et société à Paris*, 27–31, 303–5.

21. Rudolf Blum, "Vor- und Frühgeschichte der nationalen Allgemeinbibliographie," *Archiv für Geschichte des Buchwesens* 2, 2–3 (1960): 233–303.

22. Henri-Jean Martin, "Stratégies éditoriales et conjonctures dans la France d'Ancien Régime," in *Livre et lecture en Espagne et en France sous l'Ancien Régime*, Colloque de la Casa de Velázquez, Madrid, 17–19 November 1980 (Paris: A.D.P.F., 1981); Martin, "Publishing Conditions and Strategies in Ancient Regime France," 43–67.

23. Febvre and Martin, *L'apparition du livre*, 373–74.

24. Lucien Febvre, *Le problème de l'incroyance au XVIe siècle. La religion de Rabelais*, rev. ed. (Paris: A. Michel, 1947), 19–104, available in English as *The Problem of Unbelief in the Sixteenth Century: The Religion of Rabelais*, trans. Beatrice Gottlieb (Cambridge, Mass.: Harvard University Press, 1982).

25. Heimo Reinitzer, *Biblia deutsch. Luthers Bibelübersetzung und ihre Tradition,* Wolfenbüttel, Herzog August Bibliothek (Hamburg: Wittig, 1983).

26. Martin, *Livre, pouvoirs et société,* esp. pp. 6–19, 99–189. For southern Germany, see also Hans-Joachim Koppitz, "The Two Bookmarkets in Germany in the Seventeenth and Eighteenth Centuries," in *Le livre dans les sociétés préindustrielles,* Actes du premier colloque du Centre de recherches néo-Helléniques (Athens: Centre de Recherches néo-Helléniques. Fondation nationale de la recherche scientifique, 1982), 77–94.

27. H. L. Schaepfer, "Laurent de Normandie," in Gabrielle Berthoud et al., *Aspects de la propagande religieuse* (Geneva: E. Droz, 1957), 176–230.

28. Georges Bonnant, "La librairie genevoise au Portugal du XVIe au XVIIIe siècle," *Geneva,* n.s., 3 (1955): 183–200; Bonnant, "La librairie genevoise en Italie jusqu'à la fin du XVIIIe siècle," ibid., 15 (1967): 117–60; Bonnant, "La librairie genevoise en Allemagne jusqu'à la fin du XVIIIe siècle," ibid., 25 (1977): 121–51; Bonnant, "La librairie genevoise dans les Provinces-Unies et les Pays-Bas méridionaux jusqu'à la fin du XVIIIe siècle," ibid., 31 (1983): 67–88.

29. Martin, *Livre, pouvoirs et société,* 597–638.

30. Alain Viala, *Naissance de l'écrivain. Sociologie de la littérature à l'âge classique* (Paris: Editions de Minuit, 1985).

31. Henri-Jean Martin and Anne-Marie Lecocq, with Hubert Carrier and Anne Sauvy, *Livres et lecteurs à Grenoble: Les registres du libraire Nicolas (1645–1668),* 2 vols. (Geneva: Droz; Paris: Minard; Champion, 1977).

32. Reinhard Wittmann, "Der gerechtfertige Nachdrucker. Nachdruck und litteratisches Leben im achtzehnten Jahrhundert," in Giles Barber and Bernard Fabian, eds., *Buch und Buchhandel in Europa im achtzehnten Jahrhundert. The Book and the Book Trade in Eighteenth-Century Europe,* Proceedings of the Fifth Wolfenbüttler Symposium, 1–3 November 1977 (Hamburg: Hauswedell, 1981), 293–320.

33. Robert Mandrou, *De la culture populaire aux XVIIe et XVIIIe siècles: La Bibliothèque bleue de Troyes,* 2d ed. rev. (Paris: Stock 1975; Imago, 1985); Roger Chartier, "Stratégies éditoriales et lectures populaires," in Martin and Chartier, gen. eds., *Histoire de l'édition française,* 1:585–602, available in English as "Publishing Strategies and What the People Read, 1530–1660," in Chartier, *The Cultural Uses of Print in Early Modern France,* trans. Lydia G. Cochrane (Princeton: Princeton University Press, 1987), 145–82.

34. Alfred Morin, *Catalogue descriptif de la Bibliothèque bleue de Troyes (almanachs exclus)* (Geneva: Droz, 1974); Henri-Jean Martin, "Culture écrite et culture orale, culture savante et culture populaire dans la France d'Ancien Régime," *Journal des savants,* July–December (1975): 225–84, reprinted in Martin, *Le livre français sous l'Ancien Régime* (Paris: Promodis/Editions du Cercle de la librairie, 1987), 149–86; Jean-Luc Marais, "Littérature et culture populaire aux XVIIe et XVIIIe siècles. Réponses et questions," *Annales de Bretagne des pays de l'Ouest* (1980): 65–105.

35. Geneviève Bollème, *Les almanachs populaires aux XVIIe et XVIIIe siècles. Essai d'histoire sociale* (Paris and The Hague: Mouton, 1969).

36. Martin, "Culture écrite et culture orale"; Pierre Casselle, "Recherches sur les marchands d'estampes parisiens d'origine cotentinoise à la fin de l'Ancien Ré-

gime," Secrétariat d'Etat aux universités. Comité des travaux historiques et scientifiques, *Bulletin d'histoire moderne et contemporaine* 11 (1978): 75−91; Jean-Jacques Darmon, *Le colportage de librairie en France sous le Second Empire, grands colporteurs et culture populaire* (Paris: Plon, 1970).

37. Anne Sauvy, "Noël Gille dit Pistole, marchand forain libraire roulant par la France," *Bulletin des bibliothèques de France* (1967): 177−90.

38. Michèle Marsol, "Un oublié: Pierre Héron 'marchand libraire' à Langres-en-Bassigny, 1756−1776," Secrétariat d'Etat aux universités. Comité des travaux historiques et scientifiques, *Bulletin d'histoire moderne et contemporaine* 11 (1978): 33−74.

39. Anne Sauvy-Wilkinson, *Le miroir du coeur: quatre siècles d'images savantes et populaires* (Paris: Editions du Cerf, 1989).

40. On engravings, see Michel Melot et al., *L'estampe: Histoire d'un art* (Geneva: Skira, 1981), available in English as *Prints: History of an Art* (Geneva: Skira; New York: Rizzoli, 1981); William Mills Ivins, *Prints and Visual Communication* (Cambridge, Mass.: Harvard University Press, 1953); A. Hyatt Mayor, *Prints and People: A Social History of Printed Pictures* (New York: Metropolitan Museum of Art, distribution New York Graphic Society, 1971).

41. Marianne Grivel, *Le commerce de l'estampe à Paris au XVIIe siècle* (Geneva: Librairie Droz, 1986); Maxime Préaud et al., *Dictionnaire des éditeurs d'estampes à Paris sous l'Ancien Régime* (Paris: Promodis, Editions du Cercle de la Librairie, 1987).

42. On "popular" engravings, see Jean Adhémar, "La rue Montorgueil et la formation d'un groupe d'imagiers parisiens au XVIe siècle," *Bulletin de la Société archéologique, historique et artistique. Le vieux papier,* 21, 167, (April, 1954): 23−34; Adhémar, "Hypothèses sur la formation des imagiers provinciaux français du XVIIe et du XVIIIe siècle," *Arts et traditions populaires* (1955): 208−10; Pierre-Louis Duchartre et René Saulnier, *L'imagerie populaire. Les Images de toutes les provinces françaises du XVe siècle au Second Empire, les complaintes, contes, chansons, légendes qui ont inspiré les imagiers* (Paris: Librairie de France, 1925); Jean Gaston, *Les images des confréries parisiennes avant la Révolution* (Paris: Marty, 1910).

43. Otto Zaretzky, *Der erste Kölner Zensurprozess* (Cologne: M. DuMont-Schaubert, 1906); *Die Kölner Bibel 1478/1479. Studien zur Entstellung und Illustrierung der ersten niederdeutschen Bibel* (Amsterdam: Buijten and Schipperheim; Hamburg: Wittig, 1979).

44. George Haven Putnam, *The Censorship of the Church of Rome and Its Influence Upon the Production and Distribution of Literature,* 2 vols. (New York and London: G. P. Putnam's Sons, 1906−7), 2:77−80; *Dictionnaire de théologie catholique,* 15 vols. (Paris: Letouzey et Ané, 1903−50), "Censure des livres"; Antonio Rotondò, "La censura ecclesiastica e la cultura," in Ruggiero Romano and Corrado Vivanti, ed., *Storia d'Italia,* 6 vols. (Turin: Einaudi, 1972−77), vol. 5, pt. 2, *I documenti,* 1399−1492.

45. Quoted from *The Canons and Decrees of the Sacred and Oecumenical Council of Trent,* trans. J. Waterworth (London: C. Dolman, 1848), 18.

46. Edmond Ortigues, *Religion du livre et religions de la coutume* (Paris: Sycomore, 1981).

47. Franz Heinrich Reusch, *Der Index der verbotenen Bücher*, 2 vols. in 1 (Bonn: Verlag von M. Cohen & Sohn, 1883−85). This work is being completed by a remarkable collection put out by the University of Sherbrooke, Quebec, Canada, which is publishing the Renaissance indexes one by one. The volumes that have appeared so far are: *Index de l'Université de Louvain, 1546, 1550, 1558*, ed. J. M. de Bujanda, with René Davignon, Ela Stanek (Sherbrooke: University of Sherbrooke, Centre d'études de la Renaissance, 1986), *Index de Venise, 1549, Venise et Milan, 1554*, eds. de Bujanda, Davignon, Stanek (Sherbrooke: Centre d'études de la Renaissance, 1987), *Index de Rome, 1557, 1559, 1564: les premiers index romains et l'index du Concile de Trent*, eds. de Bujanda, Davignon, Stanek (Sherbrooke: Centre d'études de la Renaissance, 1990).

48. Bartolomé Bennassar et al., *L'Inquisition espagnole, XVe−XIXe siècle* (Paris: Hachette, 1979; Verbiers: Les nouvelles éditions Marabout, 1983).

49. Francis M. Higman, "Le levain de l'Evangile," in Martin and Chartier, gen. eds., *Histoire de l'édition française*, 1 : 305−26; Higman, *Censorship and the Sorbonne, A French Bibliographical Study of Books Censured by the Faculty of Theology of the University of Paris, 1520−1551* (Geneva: Droz, 1979); James K. Farge, *Orthodoxy and Reform in Early Reformation France: The Faculty of Theology of Paris, 1500−1543* (Leiden: E. J. Brill, 1985). See also chap. 4, above.

50. Martin, *Livre, pouvoirs et société*; Denis Pallier, "Les impressions de la Contre-Réforme en France et l'apparition des grandes compagnies de libraires parisiens," *Revue française d'histoire du livre* 31 (1981): 215−74.

51. Henri Hauser, *Ouvriers du temps passé (XVe−XVIe siècles* (1899), 5th ed. (Paris: F. Alcan, 1927), 177ff.; Febvre and Martin, *L'apparition du livre*, 199−201.

52. J.-M. Grinevald, "Richelieu et l'Imprimerie royale," in Chancellerie des universités de Paris et Académie française, *Richelieu et le monde de l'Esprit*, exhibition, Sorbonne, November 1985 (Paris: Imprimerie nationale, 1985), 237−48.

53. Martin, *Livre, pouvoirs et société*, 555−96. On Mazarinades, see Hubert Carrier, *La Presse de la Fronde (1648−1653): Les Mazarinades*, 2 vols. (Geneva: Librairie Droz, 1989−91), vol. 1, *La conquête de l'opinion;* vol. 2, *Les hommes du livre.*

54. On these topics, see H. S. Bennett, *English Books and Readers, 1475 to 1557* (1954), 2d ed. (Cambridge: Cambridge University Press, 1969); Bennett, *English Books and Readers, 1558 to 1603* (Cambridge: Cambridge University Press, 1965); Bennett, *English Books and Readers, 1603 to 1640* (Cambridge: Cambridge University Press, 1970); Colin Clair, *A History of Printing in Britain* (London: Cassell, 1965).

55. John Milton, *Areopagitica: A Speech of John Milton for the Liberty of unlicenc'd printing, to the Parliament of England*. See also the works cited in the following notes.

56. Laurence Hanson, *Government and the Press, 1695−1763* (London: Oxford University Press, H. Milford, 1936).

57. Daniel Roche, "La censure" and "La police du livre," in Martin and Chartier, gen. eds., *Histoire de l'édition française*, 2 : 76−83, 84−93.

58. Daniel Roche, "Les éditeurs de l'*Encyclopédie*," in Martin and Chartier, eds., *Histoire de l'édition française*, 2 : 194−97; Marie-Anne Merland and Jeanne Reyniers, "La fortune d'André-François Le Breton," *Revue française d'histoire du livre* (1979): 61−90.

59. Christiane Berkvens-Stevelink, "L'édition française en Hollande," in Martin and Chartier, gen. eds., *Histoire de l'édition française,* 2:316–25, and bibliography, 627–28.

60. Robert Darnton, "Le livre prohibé aux frontières: Neuchâtel," in Martin and Chartier, gen. eds., *Histoire de l'édition française,* 2:342–61, and bibliography, 628; Darnton, *The Business of Enlightenment: A Publishing History of the Encyclopédie, 1775–1800* (Cambridge, Mass.: Belknap Press of Harvard University Press, 1979).

61. Jean-Dominique Mellot, "La vie du livre à Rouen sous Louis XIV (1643–1715)," *Ecole nationale des Chartes. Position des thèses soutenues par les élèves de la promotion de 1985 pour obtenir le diplôme d'archiviste-paléographe* (Paris: Ecoles des Chartes, 1985), 95–106.

62. Henri-Jean Martin, "La prééminence de la librairie parisienne," in Martin and Chartier, gen. eds., *Histoire de l'édition française,* 2:263–81.

CHAPTER SEVEN

1. Alix Gambier-Chevalier, "L'industrie papetière en France au XVIIIe siècle: étude économique d'après les archives du Contrôle général des finances et des intendances," *Ecole des Chartes: positions des thèses soutenues par les élèves de la promotion de 1961 . . .* (Paris: Ecole des Chartes, 1961): 33–36.

2. Jean Delumeau, *La civilisation de la Renaissance: Le livre de la promotion de l'Occident. L'Age d'or de l'art* (Paris: Arthaud, 1967; new ed., 1984), 229–82; Richard Ehrenberg, *Das Zeitalter der Fugger: Gild Kapital und Creditverker im 16. Jahrhundert,* 2 vols. (Iena: G. Fisher, 1922), in French trans. as *Le siècle des Fugger* (Paris: SEVPEN, 1955), and available in English as *Capital and Finance in the Age of the Renaissance: A Study of the Fuggers and Their Connections,* trans. H. M. Lucas (London: J. Cape; New York: Harcourt Brace, 1929); Raymond De Roover, *The Rise and the Decline of the Medici Bank (1337–1494)* (Cambridge, Mass.: University of Harvard Press, 1963; New York: W. W. Norton, 1966).

3. Andreas Michael Andreades, *Histoire de la Banque d'Angleterre: Ses origines, sa fondation, son développement,* 2 vols. (Paris: A. Rousseau, 1904), available in English as *History of the Bank of England,* trans. Christabel Meredith (London: P. S. King & Son, 1909; 3d ed., 1935). On the history of promissory notes, which fall beyond the scope of this work, see Jean Lafaurie, *Les assignats et les papier-monnaies émis par l'Etat au XVIIIe siècle* (Paris: Léopard d'or, 1981).

4. Ernest Stevelinck, *La comptabilité à travers les âges,* exposition catalogue, Bibliothèque Albert Ier de Belgique, introduction by Raymond De Roover (Brussels: Bibliothèque Albert Ier, 1970).

5. Michel Fleury and Louis Henry, *Nouveau manuel de dépouillement et d'exploitation de l'Etat civil ancien,* 3d ed. rev. (Paris: Editions de l'institut national d'études démographiques, 1985), 4–18; Georges Couton and Henri-Jean Martin, "Une source d'histoire sociale: Le Registre de l'état des âmes," *Revue d'histoire économique et sociale,* 45 (1967): 244–53.

6. Robert Estivals, *La statistique bibliographique de la France sous la Monarchie au XVIIIe siècle* (Paris and The Hague: Mouton/De Gruyter, 1965).

7. Jean Guéroult, "La taille dans la région parisienne au XVIIIe siècle d'après le fonds de l'élection de Paris aux Archives nationales," *Mémoires publiés par la Fédéra-*

tion des sociétés historiques et archéologiques de Paris et de l'Ile de France 13 (1962): 145–360.

8. On the history of the notarial profession, see the review *Gnomon*, published by the Chambre des notaires.

9. Molière, *L'école des femmes*, III.4. For Jean de Coras and Martin Guerre, see Natalie Zemon Davis, Jean-Claude Carrière, and Daniel Vigne, *Le Retour de Martin Guerre* (Paris: Laffont, 1982) and Natalie Zemon Davis, *The Return of Martin Guerre* (Cambridge, Mass. and London: Harvard University Press, 1983).

10. Jacques Rychner, *Genève et ses typographes vus de Neuchâtel, 1770–1780* (Geneva: Braillard, 1984).

11. Daniel Roche, *Le peuple de Paris, esssai sur la culture populaire au XVIIIe siècle* (Paris: Aubier Montaigne, 1981), 242–77, available in English as *The People of Paris: An Essay in Popular Culture in the Eighteenth Century*, trans. Marie Evans and Gwynne Lewis (Berkeley: University of California Press, 1987).

12. On this topic, see Anne Fillon, *Louis Simon étaminier (1740–1820) dans son village du Haut-Maine au siècle des Lumières*, Dissertation de troisième cycle, Université du Maine, 1982, 2 vols. (Le Mans: Centre Universitaire de l'Education Permanente, 1984); Alain Lottin, *Chavatte, ouvrier lillois: Un contemporain de Louis XIV* (Paris: Flammarion, 1979).

13. On this topic, see Emmanuel Poulle, *Paléographie des écritures cursives en France du XVe au XVIIe siècle: Recueil de fac-similés de documents parisiens* (Geneva: Droz, 1966).

14. Jean-Paul Seguin, "L'information en France avant la fin du XVe siècle," *Arts et traditions populaires* 4 (1956): 309–30; 1 (1957): 46–74. See also note 20.

15. Konrad Burger, ed., *Buchhandelerzeigen des 15. Jahrhunderts* (Leipzig: K. W. Hiersemann, 1907). On the oldest known placards, see *Einblattdrucke des XV. Jahrhunderts, ein bibliographisches Verzeichnis* (Halle: Karras, 1914).

16. Maurice Audin, *Musée lyonnais de l'Imprimerie et de la Banque*, exposition, June 1964–April 1965, Lyons, 1964, no. 27.

17. Yves-Marie Bercé, *Fête et révolte: Des mentalités populaires du XVIe au XVIIIe siècle. Essai* (Paris: Hachette, 1976).

18. Gabrielle Berthoud, "Pierre de Vingle, l'imprimeur de Farel," in *Aspects de la propagande religieuse* (Geneva: Droz, 1957), 38–78.

19. Augustin Corda, continued by A. Trudon Des Ormes, *Catalogue des factums et d'autres documents judiciaires antérieurs à 1790*, 10 vols. (Paris: E. Plon, Nourrit et Cie., 1890–1936).

20. Jean-Pierre Seguin, *L'information en France de Louis XII à Henri II: Etude et bibliographie* (Geneva: Droz, 1961); Seguin, *L'information en France avant le périodique, 517 canards imprimés entre 1529 et 1631* (Paris: G. P. Maisonneuve et Larose, 1964); Hubert Carrier, *La Presse de la Fronde (1648–1653): Les mazarinades*, 2 vols. (Geneva: Droz, 1989–91), vol. 1, *La conquête de l'opinion;* vol. 2, *Les hommes du livre;* Christian Jouhaud, *Mazarinades. La Fronde des mots* (Paris: Aubier, 1985).

21. Henri-Jean Martin and Anne-Marie Lecocq, with the collaboration of Hubert Carrier and Anne Sauvy, *Livres et lecteurs à Grenoble: Les registres du libraire Nicolas, 1645–1668*, Histoire et civilisation du livre, 10, 2 vols. (Geneva: Droz; Paris: Champion; Minard, 1977); Martin, *Livre, pouvoirs et société à Paris au XVIIe siècle*

(1598–1701), Histoire et civilisation du livre, 3, 2 vols. (Geneva and Paris: Droz, 1969), esp. 1:253–75. For a more general view of the reception of printed matter, see Roger Chartier, *Lectures et lecteurs dans la France d'Ancien Régime* (Paris: Editions du Seuil, 1987), much of which is available in English as *The Cultural Uses of Print in Early Modern France,* trans. Lydia G. Cochrane (Princeton: Princeton University Press, 1987); Chartier, ed., *Les usages de l'imprimé (XVe–XVIe siècle)* (Paris: Fayard, 1986), available in English as *The Culture of Print: Power and the Uses of Print in Early Modern Europe,* trans. Lydia G. Cochrane (Princeton: Princeton University Press, 1989); Michèle Fogel, "Propagande, communication, publication: points de vue et demande d'enquête pour la France des XVIe–XVIIe siècles," in *Culture et idéologie dans la genèse de l'Etat moderne,* Actes de la table ronde organisée par le CNRS et l'Ecole française de Rome, Rome, 15–17 October 1984 (Rome: L'Ecole française de Rome, 1985), 325–36.

22. See Denis Pallier, *Recherches sur l'imprimerie à Paris pendant la Ligue (1585–1594)* (Geneva: Droz, 1976); Louis Desgraves, *Répertoire des ouvrages de controverse entre catholiques et protestants en France, 1598–1628,* Histoire et civilisation du livre, 14, 15, 2 vols. (Geneva: Droz, 1984–85); R. C. Alston, "The Eighteenth-Century Non-Book. Observations on the Printed Ephemera," in *Buch und Buchhandel in Europa im achtsehnten Jahrhundert/The Book and the Book Trade in Eighteenth-Century Europe,* Proceedings of the Fifth Wolfenbüttler Symposium, 1–3 November 1977 (Hamburg: Hauswedell, 1981), 343–58.

23. See Gilles Feyel *La "Gazette" en province à travers ses réimpressions, 1631–1752: Une recherche analytique de la diffusion d'un ancien périodique dans toute la France* (Amsterdam: Holland University Press, 1982); *Théophraste Renaudot, l'homme, le médecin, le journaliste, 1586–1986,* Colloque, Université de Paris II, 29 November 1986 (Paris: Institut français de presse et des sciences de l'information, 1987).

24. Georges Weill, *Le journal, origines, évolution et rôle de la presse périodique* (Paris: La renaissance du livre, 1934); Claude Bellanger et al., *Histoire générale de la presse française,* 5 vols. (Paris: Presses Universitaires de France, 1969–76), vol. 1, *Des origines à 1814.*

25. Lucien Febvre and Henri-Jean Martin, *L'apparition du livre,* 2d ed. (Paris: Albin Michel, 1958), 122–27, available in English as *The Coming of the Book: The Impact of Printing 1450–1800,* new ed., trans. David Gerard, ed. Geoffrey Nowell-Smith and David Wootton (London: NLB, 1976; New York: Verso, 1990).

26. Martin Lowry, "The Arrival and Use of Continental Printed Books in Yorkist England," in Henri-Jean Martin and Pierre Aquilon, eds., *Le livre dans l'Europe de la Renaissance,* Actes du XXVIIIe colloque international d'études humanistes de Tours, 1985 (Paris: Promodis/Cercle de la Librairie, 1988), 449–57.

27. Martin Lowry, *The World of Aldus Manutius, Business and Scholarship in Renaissance Venice* (Ithaca: Cornell University Press, 1979); Nicolas Barker, *Aldus Manutius: Mercantile Empire of the Intellect* (Los Angeles: Department of Special Collections, University Research Library, University of California, Los Angeles, 1989).

28. Giovanni Battista Verini, *Luminario; or, the Third Chapter of the Liber elementorum litterarum on the Construction of Roman Capitals,* trans. A. F. Johnson, introduction Stanley Morison (Cambridge, Mass.: Harvard College Library, 1947).

29. Henri-Jean Martin, "Au commencement était le signe," in Henri-Jean Martin and Roger Chartier, gen. eds., *Histoire de l'édition française*, 4 vols. (Paris: Promodis, 1982–86), vol. 1, *Le livre conquérant: Du Moyen Age au milieu du XVIIe siècle*, 463–77.

30. Jeanne Veyrin-Forrer, "Aux origines de l'imprimerie française: L'atelier de la Sorbonne et ses mécènes, 1470–1473," in *L'art du livre à l'imprimerie nationale* (Paris: Imprimerie nationale, 1973), 117–29.

31. Charles Beaulieux, *Histoire de l'orthographe*, 2 vols. (Paris: Champion, 1927); Nina Catach, *L'orthographe française à l'époque de la Renaissance: auteurs, imprimeurs, ateliers d'imprimerie* (Geneva: Droz, 1968).

32. Henri-Jean Martin, *Livre, pouvoirs et société à Paris au XVIIe siècle*; Martin, "La tradition perpétuée," in Martin and Chartier, gen. eds., *Histoire de l'édition française*, vol. 2, *Le livre triomphant, 1660–1830*, 174–85.

33. Martin, *Livre, pouvoirs et société à Paris*, 959–66.

34. Roger Laufer, "L'espace visuel du livre ancien," in Martin and Chartier, gen. eds., *Histoire de l'édition française*, 1: 479–97.

35. Richard H. and Mary A. Rouse, "La naissance des index," in Martin and Chartier, gen. eds., *Histoire de l'édition française*, 1 : 77–86.

36. Michel Reulos, *Comment transcrire et interpréter les références juridiques (droit romain, droit canonique et droit coutumier) contenues dans les ouvrages du XVIe siècle* (Geneva: Droz, 1985).

37. Laufer, "L'espace visuel du livre ancien," 495.

38. On this subject, see the contribution of Pierre Petitmengin to Martin and Aquilon eds., *Le livre dans l'Europe de la Renaissance*.

39. Ibid.

40. Micheline Lecocq, study in preparation on the publication of dramatic works in France during the sixteenth and seventeenth centuries; Henri-Jean Martin, "Pour une histoire de la lecture," in his *Le livre français sous l'Ancien Régime*, 227–46.

41. D. F. McKenzie, "Typography and Meanings of Words: The Case of William Congreve," in *Buch und Buchhandel: The Book and the Book Trade*, 81–126.

42. For more on the *Hypnerotomachia Polifilii*, see Lowry, *The World of Aldus Manutius*, 118–25, 135–36, and its accompanying bibliographies.

43. Marc Fumaroli, "Baroque et classicisme: l'Imago Primi Saeculi (1640) et ses adversaires," in Alphonse Vermeylen, ed., *Questionnement du baroque* (Louvain: Nauwelaerts/Université Catholique de Louvain, 1986), 74–111.

44. On this subject, see Elizabeth L. Eisenstein, *The Printing Revolution in Early Modern Europe* (Cambridge and New York: Cambridge University Press, 1983).

45. Georges Couton, *La poétique de La Fontaine. Deux études: La Fontaine et l'art des emblèmes, Du pensum aux "Fables"* (Paris: Presses Universitaires de France, 1957).

46. Michel Melot et al., *L'estampe* (Geneva: Skira, 1981), available in English as *Prints: History of an Art* (Geneva: Skira; New York: Rizzoli, 1981).

47. André James, *La réforme de la typographie royale sous Louis XIV: Le Grandjean* (Paris: Librairie P. Jammes, 1961), reprinted as *La naissance d'un caractère, le grandjean* (Paris: Promodis, 1985); Rémy Peignot, "L'esprit des lettres," in *De plomb,*

d'encre et de lumière: Essai sur la typographie et la communication écrite (Paris: Imprimerie nationale, 1982), 69–164.

48. Nicolas Barker, "Typography and the Meaning of Words: The Revolution in the Layout of Books in the Eighteenth Century," in *Buch und Buchhandel: The Book and the Book Trade,* 127–66.

49. Jean-Louis Guez de Balzac, *Lettres,* ed. Philippe Tamizey de Larroque (Paris: Imprimerie nationale, 1873), 578. I am indebted to Mme Paule Koch for this reference. See also Henri-Jean Martin, "En conclusion provisoire," in his *Le livre français sous l'Ancien Régime,* 247–60.

CHAPTER EIGHT

1. Daniel Roche, "La circulation de l'information à travers la France d'Ancien Régime," in *Les systèmes de communication,* Colloque, Université de Paris-Sorbonne, Institut de recherches sur les civilisations de l'Occident moderne, Paris, 1982 (Paris: Presses de l'Université de Paris-Sorbonne), 25–42.

2. Armando Sapori, *Le marchand italien au Moyen Age* (Paris: A. Colin, 1952), available in English as *The Italian Merchant in the Middle Ages,* trans. Patricia Anne Kennen (New York: Norton, 1970); Alain Derville, "L'alphabétisation du peuple à la fin du Moyen Age," *Revue du Nord,* vol. 66, nos. 261–62, *Liber Amicorum: Mélanges offers à Louis Trénard* (1984): 760–76. For Valenciennes, see also Hélène Servant, "Culture et société à Valenciennes dans la deuxième moitié du XVe siècle (vers 1440–1507), thesis, *Ecole nationale des chartes, Positions des thèses soutenues par les élèves de la promotion de 1989* (Paris: Ecole des Chartes, 1989), 183–94.

3. Jean-Claude Margolin, "L'éducation à l'époque des grands humanistes" and "L'éducation au temps de la Contre-Reforme," in Gaston Mialeret and Jean Vial, eds., *Histoire mondiale de l'éducation,* 4 vols. (Paris: Presses Universitaires de France, 1981), vol. 2, *De 1515 à 1815,* 167–91; 213–32.

4. Richard Gawsthrop and Gerald Strauss, "Protestantism and Literacy in Early Modern Germany," *Past and Present* 104 (1984): 31–55; Gerald Strauss, *Luther's House of Learning. Indoctrination of the Young in the German Reformation* (Baltimore: Johns Hopkins University Press, 1978), pp. 108–31.

5. Marc Lienhard, "Le rayonnement de Strasbourg dans l'Europe protestante: Le Gymnase et les problèmes de l'éducation de la jeunesse," in Georges Livet and Francis Rapp, eds., *Histoire de Strasbourg des origines à nos jours,* 4 vols. (Strasbourg: Editions des Dernières nouvelles de Strasbourg, 1982), vol. 2, *Strasbourg des grandes invasions au XVIe siècle,* 406–10.

6. Bernard Vögler, "La vie religieuse en pays rhénan dans la seconde moitié du XVIe siècle (1556–1619)," Thesis, Faculté de Lettres, Paris IV, 1972 (Lille: Services de reproduction des thèses de L'Université de Lille 3, 1974), esp. pp. 796–99, published as *Le clergé protestant rhénan au siècle de la Réforme: 1555–1619* (Strasbourg: Association des publications près les universités de Strasbourg; distribution Paris: Ophrys, 1976).

7. W. K. Jordan, *The Charities of Rural England, 1480–1660: The Aspirations and the Achievements of the Rural Society* (London: Allen & Unwin, 1961).

8. Lawrence Stone, "The Educational Revolution in England, 1560–1640," *Past and Present* 28 (1964): 41–80.

9. François de Dainville, *La naissance de l'humanisme moderne* (Paris: Beauchesne, 1940; reprint Paris: Slatkine, 1969); Dainville, *L'éducation des jésuites: XVIe–XVIIe siècles,* ed. Marie-Madeleine Compère (Paris: Editions de Minuit, 1978).

10. Roger Chartier, Dominique Julia, Marie-Madeleine Compère, *L'éducation en France du XVIe au XVIIe siècle* (Paris: SEDES, 1976).

11. Ibid, 114–46.

12. Michel Fleury and Pierre Valmary, "Les progrès de l'instruction élémentaire de Louis XIV à Napoléon III d'après l'enquête de Louis Maggiolo (1877–1879)," *Populations* 12 (1957): 71–93; François Furet and Jacques Ozouf, eds., *Lire et écrire, l'alphabétisation des Français de Calvin à Jules Ferry,* 2 vols. (Paris: Editions de Minuit, 1977).

13. Rab Houston, "The Literacy Myth? Illiteracy in Scotland 1630–1750," *Past and Present* 96 (1982): 81–102; Kenneth C. Lockridge, *Literacy in Colonial New England: An Enquiry into the Social Context of Literacy in the Early Modern West* (New York: Norton, 1974); David D. Hall, Introduction, "The Use of Literacy in New England, 1600–1850," in William L. Joyce, ed., *Printing and Society in Early America* (Worcester: American Antiquarian Society, 1983), 1–47.

14. Lawrence Stone, "Literacy and Education in England, 1640–1900," *Past and Present* 42 (1969): 61–139. On the same subject, see also R. S. Schofield, "Dimensions of Illiteracy, 1750–1850," *Explorations in Economic History* 10 (1973): 437–54.

15. On this topic, see Gérald Duverdier, "L'imprimerie catholique en Inde jusqu'en 1850," in *Le livre et l'imprimerie en Extrême-Orient et en Asie du Sud,* ed. Jean-Pierre Drège, Mitchiko Ishigami-Iagolnitzer, and Monique Cohen (Bordeaux: Société des bibliophiles de Guyenne, 1986), 295–320.

16. Gawsthrop and Strauss, "Protestantism and Literacy in Early Modern Germany," 31–55.

17. Carlo M. Cipolla, *Literacy and Development in the West* (Baltimore: Johns Hopkins University Press, 1969).

18. Furet and Ozouf, *Lire et écrire,* 344–48.

19. Josef Macek and Robert Mandrou, *Histoire de la Bohême: Des origines à 1918* (Paris: Fayard, 1984), 277–86.

20. Roger Chartier, "Les pratiques de l'écrit," in Philippe Ariès and Georges Duby, gen. eds., *Histoire de la vie privée,* 5 vols. (Paris: Editions du Seuil, 1985–87), vol. 3, *De la Renaissance aux Lumières,* ed. Roger Chartier, available in English as "The Practical Impact of Writing," in *A History of Private Life* (Cambridge, Mass.: Belknap Press of Harvard University Press, 1987–), vol. 3, *Passions of the Renaissance,* trans. Arthur Goldhammer, 111–59.

21. Christian Bec, *Les livres des Florentins (1413–1608)* (Florence: L. S. Olschki, 1984).

22. Philippe Berger, "La lecture à Valence de 1474 à 1560. Evolution des comportements en fonction des milieux sociaux," in *Livre et lecture en Espagne et en France sous l'Ancien Régime,* Colloque de la Casa de Velázquez, Madrid, 17–19 November 1980 (Paris: A.D.P.F., 1981), 97–107.

23. Bartholomé Bennassar, *Valladolid au siècle d'or: Une ville de Castille et sa campagne au XVIe siècle* (Paris and The Hague: Mouton, 1967).

24. Albert Labarre, *Le livre dans la vie amiénoise du seizième siècle. L'enseignement des inventaires après décès, 1505–1576* (Paris: Béatrice Nauwelaerts; Louvain: Editions Nauwelaerts, 1971).

25. *Handbuch der Bibliothekswissenschaft, begründet von Fritz Milkau, 2. verm. und verb. Aufl. hrsg. von Georg Leyh,* 2 vols. (Wiesbaden: O. Harrassowitz, 1950–57), vol. 2, *Geschichte der Bibliotheken im alten Orient;* Anthony Robert Alwyn Hobson, *Great Libraries* (London: Weidenfeld & Nicolson; New York: Putnam, 1970); Simone Balayé, *La Bibliothèque nationale, des origines à 1800* (Geneva: Droz, 1988).

26. Henri-Jean Martin, *Livre, pouvoirs et société à Paris au XVIIe siècle (1598–1701),* 2 vols. (Paris and Geneva: Droz, 1969), 1:474–554, 2:922–58.

27. Henri-Jean Martin and Anne-Marie Lecocq, with the collaboration of Hubert Carrier and Anne Sauvy, *Livres et lecteurs à Grenoble: Les registres du libraire Nicolas, 1645–1668,* 2 vols. (Geneva: Droz; Paris: Champion; Minard, 1977), 3–121, reprinted in part in Martin, *Le livre français sous l'Ancien Régime* (Paris: Promodis/Editions du Cercle de la Librairie, 1987), 187–208.

28. Peter Clark, "The Ownership of Books in England, 1560–1640: The Example of Some Kentish Townfolk," in Lawrence Stone, ed., *Schooling and Society: Studies in the History of Education* (Baltimore: Johns Hopkins University Press, 1976), 95–111.

29. Richard D. Altick, *The English Common Reader: A Social History of the Mass Reading Public, 1800–1900* (Chicago and London: University of Chicago Press, 1957), 35–38, 117–22.

30. D. F. McKenzie and J. C. Roos, *A Ledger of Charles Ackers, Printer of The London Magazine* (London: Oxford University Press for the Oxford Bibliographical Society, 1968).

31. Walter Wittmann, *Beruf und Buch im 18. Jahrhundert: Ein Beitrag zur Erfassung und Gliederung der Leserschaft im 18. Jahrhundert . . . ,* inaugural dissertation, Frankfurt am Main, 1934, photoreproduction of copy in Universitätsbibliothek, Frankfurt am Main (Bochum-Langendreer, H. Pöppinghaus, 1934); Hildegard Neumann, *Der Bücherbesitz der Tübinger Bürger von 1750 bis 1850* (Munich: H. Neumann, 1978); Etienne François, "Livre, confession et société urbaine en Allemagne au XVIIIe siècle: L'exemple de Spire," *Revue d'histoire moderne et contemporaine* 29 (1982): 353–75. See also the classic works of Rolf Engelsing concerning "periodization" in manners of reading: Rolf Engelsing, "Die Perioden der Lesergeschichte in der Neuzeit. Das statistische Ausmass und die sociokulturelle Bedeutung der Lektüre," *Archiv für Geschichte des Buchwesens* 10 (1969): 945–1002; Engelsing, *Der Bürger als Leser. Lesergeschichte in Deutschland, 1500–1800* (Stuttgart: Metzler, 1974). I might also mention John A. McCarthy, "Lektüre und Lesertypologie im 18. Jahrhundert (1730–1770): Ein Beitrag zur Lesergeschichte am Beispiel Wolfenbüttels," *Internationales Archiv für Sozialgeschichte der deutschen Literatur,* 8 (1983): 35–82; Albert Ward, *Book Production: Fiction and the German Reading Public, 1740–1910* (Oxford: Clarendon Press, 1970); Rudolf Schenda, *Volk ohne Buch: Studien zur Sozialgeschichte der populären Lesestoffe, 1770–1910* (Frankfurt am Main: Klostermann, 1970).

32. Paul-Marie Grinevald, "Recherches sur les bibliothèques de Besançon à la veille de la Révolution française," Thèse de 3e cycle, Université de Paris-I, 1980.

33. Marie-Pierre Dion, *Emmanuel de Croÿ, 1718–1784, itinéraire intellectuel et réussite nobiliaire au siècle des lumières* (Brussels: Université de Bruxelles, 1987).

34. Michel Marion, *Recherches sur les bibliothèques privées à Paris au milieu du XVIIIe siècle 1750–1759* (Paris: Bibliothèque nationale, 1978).

35. Jean Quéniart, *Culture et société urbaines dans la France de l'Ouest au XVIIIe siècle* (Paris: Klinksieck, 1978).

36. Roger Chartier and Daniel Roche, "Les pratiques urbaines de l'imprimerie," in Henri-Jean Martin and Roger Chartier, gen. eds., *Histoire de l'édition française*, 4 vols. (Paris: Promodis, 1982–86), vol. 2, *Le livre triomphant, 1660–1830*, 402–29, article available in English as "Urban Reading Practices, 1660–1780," in Chartier, *The Cultural Uses of Print in Early Modern France*, trans. Lydia G. Cochrane (Princeton: Princeton University Press, 1987), 183–239. See also Daniel Roche, "Noblesse et culture dans la France du XVIIIe siècle: Les lectures de la noblesse," in *Buche und Sammler: Private und öffentliche Bibliotheken im 18. Jahrhundert*, Colloquium d'Arbeitsstelle 18. Jahrhundert, Gesemthochschule Wuppertal, Universität Münster, Düsseldorf, 26–28 September 1977 (Heidelberg: Winter, 1979), 9–27.

37. Robert Darnton, *The Great Cat Massacre and Other Episodes in French Cultural History* (New York: Basic Books, 1984; Vintage Books, 1985), 75–104.

38. On this topic and, more generally, on what follows, see the works of Roger Chartier and his team. In particular, see Roger Chartier, *Lectures et lecteurs dans la France d'Ancien Régime* (Paris: Editions du Seuil, 1987), much of which appears in English as Chartier, *The Cultural Uses of Print in Early Modern France*, trans. Lydia G. Cochrane (Princeton: Princeton University Press, 1987); Chartier, ed., *Les usages de l'imprimé (XVe–XVIe siècle)* (Paris: Fayard, 1986), available in English as *The Culture of Print: Power and the Uses of Print in Early Modern Europe* (Cambridge: Polity Press, distribution Oxford: Basil Blackwell, 1989; Princeton: Princeton University Press, 1989).

39. Carlo Ginzburg, *Il formaggio e i vermi. Il cosmo di un mugnaio del '500* (Turin: Einaudi, 1981), available in English as *The Cheese and the Worms: The Cosmos of a Sixteenth-Century Miller*, trans. John and Anne Tedeschi (Baltimore: Johns Hopkins University Press, 1980; New York: Penguin Books, 1982); Valentin Jamerey Duval, *Mémoires: Enfance et éducation d'un paysan au XVIIIe siècle*, preface by Jean-Marie Goulemot (Paris: Sycomore, 1981); Anne Fillon, *Louis Simon, étaminier 1740–1820 dans son village du Haut-Maine au siècle des Lumières*, 2 vols. (Le Mans: Centre Universitaire d'Education permanente, 1984), Dissertation de troisième cycle, Université du Maine, 1982.

40. *Lettres à Grégoire sur les patois de France (1790–1794)*, introduction and notes by Augustin Louis Gazier (Paris: A. Durand et Pedon-Lauriel, 1880); Michel de Certeau, Dominique Julia, Jacques Revel, *Une politique de la langue: La Révolution française et les patois: l'enquête de Grégoire* (Paris: Gallimard, 1975), esp. pp. 190–92; Geneviève Bollème, *Les almanachs populaires aux XVIIe et XVIIIe siècles. Essai d'histoire sociale* (Paris and The Hague: Mouton, 1969).

41. Ian MacLean, "L'économie du livre érudit: le cas Wechel (1572–1627)," in Henri-Jean Martin and Pierre Aquilon, eds., *Le livre dans l'Europe de la Renaissance*, Actes du XXVIIIe colloque international d'études humanistes de Tours (Paris: Promodis/Cercle de la librairie, 1988), 230–39.

42. Christian Bec, *Machiavel* (Paris: Balland, 1985), 367–70 (translation of a letter of Machiavelli's); Michel de Montaigne, *Essays*, bk. 3, chap. 3; bk. 9, chap. 10.

43. Michel de Certeau, "La lecture absolue (Théorie et pratique des mystiques chrétiens, XVIe–XVIIe siècle)," in Lucien Dällenbach and Jean Ricardou, eds., *Problèmes actuels de la lecture* (Paris: Clancier-Guénaud, 1982), 65–80; Certeau, "L'énonciation mystique," *Recherches de science religieuse* 64 (1979): 183–215.

44. Marc Fumaroli, *L'âge de l'éloquence: Rhétorique et "res literaria," de la Renaissance au seuil de l'époque classique* (Geneva: Droz; Paris: Champion, 1980).

45. Martin, *Livre, pouvoirs et société*, 613–61, 959–66.

46. Martin, *Le livre français sous l'Ancien Régime*, 257.

47. Jean-Paul Sartre, *Qu'est-ce que la littérature?* (Paris: Gallimard, 1948, 1985), available in English as *What Is Literature?*, trans. Bernard Frechtman (New York: Philosophical Library, 1949); Pierre Bourdieu, "Champs intellectuels et projet créateur," *Les Temps modernes* 246 (1966): 866–75; Bourdieu, "Le marché des biens symboliques," *L'année sociologique* 22 (1971): 49–126; Alberto Asor Rosa, ed., *Letteratura italiana*, 8 vols. in 13 (Turin: G. Einaudi, 1984–91), vol. 1, *Il letterato e le istituzioni;* vol. 2, *Produzione e consumo.*

48. Franco Gaeta, "Dal commune alla corte rinascimentale," in Asor Rosa, ed., *Letteratura italiana*, 1 : 149–255.

49. On the Republic of Letters, see Paul Dibon, "L'Université de Leyde et la République des Lettres au XVIIe siècle," *Quaerendo* 5, 1 (1975): 5–38; Dibon, "Les échanges épistolaires dans l'Europe savante du XVIIe siècle," *Revue internationale de synthèse* 97 (1976): 31–50; Dibon, "Communication in the Respublica literaria in the 17th Century," in *Res Publica litterarum: Studies in the Classical Tradition* (September 1978): 43–55.

50. Lucien Febvre, *Le problème de l'incroyance au XVIe siècle: La religion de Rabelais* (Paris: Albin Michel, 1947; 1968), 1–104, available in English as *The Problem of Unbelief in the Sixteenth Century: The Religion of Rabelais*, trans. Beatrice Gottlieb (Cambridge, Mass.: Harvard University Press, 1982).

51. Claude Longeon, *Bibliographie des oeuvres d'Etienne Dolet, écrivain, éditeur et imprimeur* (Geneva: Droz, 1980).

52. René Pintard, *Le libertinage érudit dans la première moitié du XVIIe siècle*, 2 vols. (Paris: Boivin, 1943; reprint Geneva and Paris: Slatkine, 1983); Orest Ranum, *Artisans of Glory: Writers and Historical Thought in Seventeenth-Century France* (Chapel Hill, N.C.: University of North Carolina Press, 1980).

53. Alain Viala, *Naissance de l'écrivain: Sociologie de la littérature à l'âge classique* (Paris: Editions de Minuit, 1985).

54. Giovanni Ghinassi, "Fasi dell'elucubrazione del Cortegiano," *Studi di filologia italiana* 25 (1967): 155–96.

55. John Whiteside Saunders, *The Profession of English Letters* (London: Routledge and Kegan Paul, Toronto: University of Toronto Press, 1964), 25–67.

56. The best guide on these topics is *Ronsard. La trompette et la lyre*, Catalogue d'exposition, Galerie Mansart, 12 June–15 September 1985 (Paris: Bibliothèque nationale, 1985).

57. Jean Jacquot, Elie Konigson, Marcel Oddon, eds., *Dramaturgie et société. Rap-*

ports entre l'oeuvre théâtrale, son interprétation et son public aux XVIe et XVIIe siècles, Colloque CNRS, Nancy, 14–21 April 1967, 2 vols. (Paris: Editions du CNRS, 1968).

58. Martin, *Livre, pouvoirs et société*, 637–38.

59. Viala, *Naissance de l'écrivain*, 60–83.

60. Ibid., 152–76.

61. Martin, *Livre, pouvoirs et société*, 467–71; Marc Fumaroli, "Le Cardinal de Richelieu fondateur de l'Académie française," in *Richelieu et le monde de l'esprit*, exposition, Sorbonne, November 1985 (Paris: Imprimerie nationale, 1985), 217–36.

62. Daniel Roche, *Le siècle des Lumières en province: Académies et académiciens provinciaux, 1680–1789*, 2 vols. (Paris and The Hague: Mouton/De Gruyter, 1978).

63. Arthur Simons Collins, *Authorship in the Days of Johnson: Being a Study of the Relation Between Author, Patron, Publisher and Public, 1726–1780* (London: Robert Holden, 1927; New York: E. P. Dutton, 1929); Collins, *The Profession of Letters: A Study of the Relation of Author to Patron, Publisher and Public, 1780–1832* (London: Routledge & Sons, 1928; New York: E. P. Dutton, 1929).

64. Collins, *Authorship in the Days of Johnson*; R. W. Chapman, *Authors and Booksellers in Johnson's England*, 2d ed., 1954; Saunders, *The Profession of English Letters*.

65. Françoise Bléchet, "Recherches sur l'abbé Bignon (1662–1743), académicien et bibliothécaire, d'après sa correspondance," *Ecole nationale des chartes. Positions des thèses soutenues par les élèves de la Promotion de 1974*, 21–28; Bléchet, "Le rôle de l'abbé Bignon dans l'activité des sociétés savantes au XVIIIe siècle," in *Les sociétés savantes: Leur histoire*, Actes du 100e congrès national des sociétés savantes, Paris, 1975, Histoire moderne et contemporaine et Histoire des sciences (Paris: Bibliothèque nationale, 1976), 31–42; Bléchet, "L'abbé Bignon: Bibliothécaire du Roy et les milieux savants en France au début du XVIIIe siècle," in *Buch und Sammler: Private und öffentliche Bibliotheken im 18. Jahrhundert*, Colloquium der Arbeitsstelle 18. Jahrhundert Gesamthochschule Wuppertal Universität Münster, Düsseldorf, 26–28 September 1977 (Heidelberg: Carl Winter, 1979), 53–66; Balayé, *La bibliothèque nationale.*

66. Sartre, *Qu'est-ce que la littérature?*, 124–28 (Paris: Gallimard, 1975).

67. Roche, *Le siècle des Lumières en province*; Suzanne Tucoo-Chala, *Charles-Joseph Panckoucke et la librairie française, 1736–1798* (Pau: Marrimpouey jeune, 1977), originally presented as the author's thesis, Lille III, 1975; Robert Darnton, *Literary Underground of the Old Regime* (Cambridge, Mass.: Harvard University Press, 1982).

68. *Le livre dans les sociétés préindustrielles*, Actes du premier colloque international du Centre de recherches néohelléniques (Athens: Centre de recherches néohelléniques, 1982); Alexandre Lorian, "L'imprimerie hébraïque (1470–1550): Ateliers chrétiens et ateliers juifs," in Martin and Aquilon, eds., *Le livre dans l'Europe de la Renaissance*, 219–39.

69. *To Elleniko Biblio, 1476–1830* (Athens: Ethnikè Trapezatès Ellados, 1986).

70. Raymond H. Kevorkian, *Catalogue des "incunables" arméniens (1511/1695), ou, Chronique de l'imprimerie arménienne* (Geneva: P. Cramer, 1986); *Le livre et le Liban jusqu'à 1900*, exposition catalogue, Camille Aboussouan, ed. (Paris: UNESCO/AGECOOP, 1982).

71. From the enormous bibliography on this topic, let me mention: Ion-Radu Mircea, "Considérations sur les premières oeuvres imprimées à charactères cyrilliques," *Bulletin de l'Association internationale d'études du sud-est européen* 10 (1972): 111–20; Virgil Molin, "Venise, berceau de l'imprimerie glagolitique et cyrillique," *Studi veneziani* 8 (1966): 347–445; Matei Cazacu, "Dimitrie Ljubavič (vers 1520–1564) et les premiers contacts entre l'orthodoxie et la Réforme," in XVI. Internationaler Byzantinistenkongress, Akten II, 6 (1982), *Jahrbuch der Österreichischen Byzantinistik*, 32, 6 (1982): 89–99; Ludovic Demény, "La tradition de l'imprimerie de Macarios de Valachie dans l'imprimerie sud-slave du XVIe siècle," *Bulletin de l'association internationale d'études du sud-est européen* 8 (1970): 87–97; C. M. Hotimsky, "Book Publishing in Russia," in Joseph L. Wieczynski, ed., *The Modern Encyclopedia of Russian and Soviet History*, 54 vols. (Gulf Breeze, Fla.: Academic International Press, 1976–), 5:111–15; K. A. Papmehl, *Freedom and Expression in Eighteenth-Century Russia* (The Hague: Martinus Nijhoff, 1971); Marianna Tax Choldin, *A Fence Around the Empire: Russian Censorship of Western Ideas Under the Tsars* (Durham, N.C.: Duke University Press, 1985).

72. Jean Pierre Drège, Mitchiko Ishigami-Iagolnitzer, Marcel Cohen, eds., *Le livre et l'imprimerie en Extrême-Orient et en Asie du Sud*, Actes du colloque organisé à Paris, 9–11 March 1983 (Bordeaux: Société des bibliophiles de Guyenne, 1987); Evelyn Sakakida Rawski, *Education and Popular Literacy in Ch'ing China* (Ann Arbor: University of Michigan Press, 1979). On the beginnings of the periodical press, see Roswell Sessions Britton, *The Chinese Periodical Press, 1800–1912* (Shanghai, 1933; reprint, Taipei: Ch'eng-wen Publishing Co., 1966).

73. David G. Chibbett, *The History of Japanese Printing and Book Illustration* (Tokyo: Kodansha International, distribution New York: Harper & Row, 1977).

CHAPTER NINE

1. Pierre Léon, ed., *Histoire économique et sociale du monde*, 6 vols. (Paris: Armand Colin, 1977–78), vol. 3, *Inerties et révolutions, 1730–1840*, Louis Bergeron, ed.

2. François Furet and Jacques Ozouf, eds., *Lire et écrire, l'alphabétisation des Français de Calvin à Jules Ferry*, 2 vols. (Paris: Editions de Minuit, 1977), esp. 1:349–62.

3. Etienne François, "Premiers jalons en vue d'une approche comparée de l'alphabétisation en France et en Allemagne," in Philippe Joutard and Jean Lecuir, eds., *Histoire sociale, sensibilités collectives et mentalités. Mélanges Robert Mandrou* (Paris: Presses Universitaires de France, 1985), 481–94; Frédéric Barbier, "Livre, économie et société industrielles en Allemagne et en France au XIXe siècle (1840–1914)," Thèse, Doctorat ès lettres, Paris IV, 1986, forthcoming, chapter 1.

4. Carlo M. Cipolla, *Literacy and Development in the West* (Baltimore: Johns Hopkins University Press, 1969).

5. Léon, ed., *Histoire économique et sociale du monde*, vol. 4, *La domination du capitalisme, 1840–1914*, Gilbert Garrier, ed., 80–98, 148–66.

6. Robert Henderson Clapperton, *The Paper-Making Machine, Its Invention, Evolution, and Development* (Oxford and New York: Pergamon Press, 1967); Philip Gaskell, *A New Introduction to Bibliography* (New York: Oxford University Press, 1972), 216–34; Marie-Lise Tsagouria, "L'évolution des techniques de fabrication

du papier de 1791 à 1871," Ecole nationale des chartes, *Position des thèses soutenues par les élèves de la promotion de 1987*, 199–203.

7. Barbier, "Livre, économie, et société."

8. On this subject, see the annual reports put out by the director of the Bibliothèque nationale in Paris. For an introductory history to the Bibliothèque nationale, see Bruno Blasselle, *La Bibliothèque nationale* (Paris: Presses Universitaires de France, 1989).

9. Marius Audin, *Histoire de l'imprimerie par l'image*, 4 vols. (Paris: H. Jonquières, 1972), 1:222–36.

10. Barbier, "Livre, économie et société."

11. Audin, *Histoire de l'imprimerie par l'image*, 1: 247–53, 315–30.

12. Ibid., 317–18.

13. Ibid, 203–7.

14. Ibid, 270–74. For the history of lithography, see also Michael Henker, Karlheinz Scherr, Elmar Stolpe, *Von Senefelder zu Daumier: Die anfänge der lithographischen Kunst* (New York, Munich, London, Paris: Saur, 1988). Corinne Bouquin contributed to the section on France.

15. Beaumont Newhall, *The History of Photography: From 1839 to the Present*, rev. ed. (New York: Museum of Modern Art, distributed New York Graphic Society Books, 1982); Isabelle Jammes, *Blanquart-Evrard et les origines de l'édition photographique française: Catalogue raisonné des albums photographiques édités, 1851–1855*, Histoire et civilisation du livre, 12 (Paris and Geneva: Droz, 1981); Sylvie Aubenas, "Alphonse Poitevin (1819–1882), photographe et inventeur. La naissance des procédés de reproduction photographique et de la photographie inaltérable," thesis, Ecole des chartes, 1988, *Ecole nationale des chartes. Positions des thèses soutenues par les élèves de la promotion de 1988* (Paris: Ecole des Chartes, 1988), 19–30.

16. Barbier, "Livre, économie et société industrielles."

17. Frédéric Barbier, *Trois cents ans de librairie et d'imprimerie: Berger-Levrault, 1676–1830*, Histoire et civilisation du livre, 11 (Geneva: Droz, 1979).

18. Sophie Malavieille, *Relieures et cartonnages d'éditeur en France au XIXe siècle, 1815–1865* (Paris: Promodis, 1985).

19. Barbier, "Livre, économie et société industrielles."

20. Georges Weill, *Le journal: Origines, évolution et role de la presse périodique* (Paris: La Renaissance du Livre, 1934); Pierre Albert and Fernand Terrou, *Histoire de la presse*, 5th ed. (Paris: Presses Universitaires de France, 1986); Claude Bellanger, Jacques Godechot, Pierre Guiral, and Fernand Terrou, eds., *Histoire générale de la presse française*, 5 vols. (Paris: Presses Universitaires de France, 1969–76).

21. Weill, *Le Journal: Origines, évolution et rôle de la presse périodique*, 62–85; Albert and Terrou, *Histoire de la presse*, 14–16.

22. Beaumarchais, *Le Mariage de Figaro*, 5.3; trans. Jacques Barzun and quoted from *Phaedra and Figaro*, trans. Robert Lowell and Jacques Barzun (New York: Farrar, Straus and Cudahy, 1961.

23. Quotations from the Declaration of the Rights of Man and the Citizen and from the Constitution of 1791 are taken from Frank Maloy Anderson, *The Consti-*

tutions and Other Select Documents Illustrative of the History of France (Minneapolis: H. W. Wilson, 1904).

24. Raymond Manevy, *La Révolution et la liberté de la presse* (Paris: Editions Estienne, 1965).

25. Henri Welschinger, *La censure sous le Premier Empire* (Paris: Charavay frères, 1882); Jacques Godechot, "La presse française sous la Révolution et l'Empire," in Bellanger et al., eds., *Histoire générale de la presse française*, 1 : 403 – 557.

26. Raymond Manevy, *L'évolution de la présentation de la presse quotidienne* (Paris: Editions Estienne, 1956).

27. Charles Ledré, *La presse à l'assaut de la monarchie 1815 – 1848* (Paris: A. Colin, 1960).

28. Odile and Henri-Jean Martin, "Le monde des éditeurs," in Henri-Jean Martin and Roger Chartier, gen. eds., *Histoire de l'édition française*, 4 vols. (Paris: Promodis, 1982 – 86), vol. 3, *Le temps des éditeurs: Du Romanticisme à la Belle Epoque*, 174 – 75.

29. Bellanger et al., eds., *Histoire générale de la presse française*, 2: 99 – 100.

30. Maurice Reclus, *Emile de Girardin, le créateur de la presse moderne* (Paris: Hachette, 1934).

31. Weill, *Le Journal, origines, évolution et rôle de la presse périodique*, 198.

32. Ibid., 199 – 200.

33. Pierre Frédérix, *Un siècle de chasse aux nouvelles. De l'Agence Havas à l'Agence France-Presse (1835 – 1959)* (Paris: Flammarion, 1959); André-Jean Tudesq, "La presse provinciale de 1814 à 1848," in Bellanger et al., eds., *Histoire générale de la presse française*, 2: 149 – 206; Weill, *Le journal, origines, évolution et rôle de la presse périodique*, 216 – 17.

34. Albert and Terrou, *Histoire de la presse*, 51 – 52.

35. Pierre Albert, "La presse française de 1871 à 1940," in Bellanger et al., eds., *Histoire générale de la presse française*, 3: 135 – 622.

36. On this period, see Francine Amaury, *Histoire du plus grand quotidien de la IIIe République, le "Petit Parisien" 1876 – 1944*, 2 vols. (Paris: Presses Universitaires de France, 1972).

37. Henri-Jean Martin, *Le livre et la civilisation écrite* (Paris: Bibliothèque nationale, 1970), 3d installment, 44 – 47.

38. Manevy, *L'évolution de la présentation de la presse quotidienne.*

39. Albert, "La presse française de 1871 à 1904," 258 – 93.

40. Ibid.

41. On the English book in the nineteenth century, see Marjorie Plant, *The English Book Trade: An Economic History of the Making and Sale of Books*, 3d ed. (London: G. Allen & Unwin, 1974); Gaskell, *A New Introduction to Bibliography;* Asa Briggs, ed., *Essays in the History of Publishing in Celebration of the 250th Anniversary of the House of Longman, 1724 – 1974* (London: Longman, 1974); Richard D. Altick, *The English Common Reader: A Social History of the Mass Reading Public, 1800 – 1900* (Chicago and London: University of Chicago Press, 1957).

42. Altick, *The English Common Reader.*

43. Hans Schmoller, "The Paperback Revolution," in *Essays in the History of Publishing*, 282 – 318.

44. For France during this period, see Martin and Chartier, gen. eds., *Histoire de l'édition française*, vol. 3, *Le Temps des éditeurs. Du Romanticisme à la Belle Epoque*.

45. David Bellos, "La conjoncture de la production," in Martin and Chartier, gen. eds., *Histoire de l'édition française*, vol. 2, *Le livre triomphant, 1660–1830*, 552–57; H. Lanzac, *Martin Bossange* (Paris, 1865).

46. Martin and Martin, "Le monde des éditeurs," 158–215. See also Jean-Yves Mollier, *L'argent et les lettres. Histoire du capitalisme d'édition, 1880–1920* (Paris: Fayard, 1988).

47. Nicole Felkay, *Balzac et ses éditeurs, 1822–1837, essai sur la librairie romantique* (Paris: Promodis/Editions du Cercle de la librairie, 1987).

48. Claude Witkowski, *Monographie des éditions populaires: Les romans à quatre sous, les publications illustrées à 20 centimes* (Paris: J. J. Pauvert, 1982).

49. Jean-Yves Mollier, *Michel et Calmann Lévy, ou, la Naissance de l'édition moderne, 1836–1891* (Paris: Calmann-Lévy, 1984).

50. Jean Mistler, *La Librairie Hachette de 1826 à nos jours* (Paris: Hachette, 1965) See also Mollier, *L'argent et les lettres*.

51. André Rétif, *Pierre Larousse et son oeuvre (1817–1875)* (Paris: Larousse, 1975). See also Mollier, *L'argent et les lettres*.

52. Johann Adolphe Goldfriedrich and Friederich Kapp, eds., *Geschichte des deutschen Buchhandels*, 4 vols. (Leipzig: Börsenverein der deutschen Buchhändler, 1886–1913); Barbier, "Livre, économie et société industrielles."

53. On this subject, see, in particular, Jean Hassenforder, *Développement comparé des bibliothèques publiques en France, en Grande-Bretagne et aux Etats-Unis dans la seconde moitié du XIXe siècle (1850–1914)* (Paris: Cercle de la Librairie, 1967).

54. Paul Bénichou, *Le sacre de l'écrivain, 1750–1830, essai sur l'avènement d'un pouvoir spirituel laïque dans la France moderne* (Paris: Corti, 1973, 1985); Bénichou, *Le temps des prophètes. Doctrines de l'âge romantique* (Paris: Gallimard, 1977).

55. Christophe Charle, "Le champ de production littéraire," in Martin and Chartier, gen. eds., *Histoire de l'édition française*, 3: 126–57.

56. Michel Melot, "Le texte et l'image," in Martin and Chartier, gen. eds., *Histoire de l'édition française*, 3:286–311; Ségolène Le Men, "La vignette et la lettre," in ibid., 312–27; Jean Watelet, "La presse illustrée," in ibid., 328–41; Gérard Blanchard, "La typographie française de 1830 à 1885," in ibid., 318–19.

57. Malavielle, *Relieures et cartonnages d'éditeur*.

58. Antoine Coron, "Livres de luxe," in Martin and Chartier, gen. eds, *Histoire de l'édition française*, vol. 4, *Le livre concurrencé, 1900–1950*, 408–37; François Chapon, *Le peintre et le livre, l'âge d'or du livre illustré en France, 1870–1970* (Paris: Flammarion, 1988); Jammes, *Blanquart-Evrard et les origines de l'édition photographique française;* Aubenas, "Alphonse Poitevin (1819–1882), photographe et inventeur," 19–30.

59. Ben Eklof, "Schooling and Literacy in Late Imperial Russia," in Daniel P. Resnick, ed., *Literacy in Historical Perspective* (Washington, D. C.: Library of Congress, 1983), 105–28; Roger William Pethybridge, *The Social Prelude to Stalinism* (London: Macmillan, 1974); Pethybridge, "Spontaneity and Illiteracy in 1917," in Ralph Carter Elwood, ed., *Reconsiderations on the Russian Revolution*, Selected Papers

in the Humanities from the Banft International Conference, 1974 (Cambridge, Mass.: Slavica Publishers, 1976), 81–100.

60. Hellmut Lehmann-Haupt, in collaboration with Ruth Shepard Grannis and Lawrence C. Wroth, *The Book in America: A History of the Making, the Selling, and the Collecting of Books in the United States* (New York: R. R. Bowker, 1939, rev. ed. enl. 1952); John Tebbel, "Publishers and Booksellers, the Perennial Odd Couple," in John Y. Cole, ed., *Responsibilities of the American Book Community* (Washington, D. C.: Library of Congress, 1981), 50–59; William L. Joyce, David D. Hall, R. D. Brown, eds., *Printing and Society in Early America* (Worcester: American Antiquarian Society, 1983); David D. Hall, John B. Honch, eds., *Needs and Opportunities in the History of the Book: America, 1639–1876* (Worcester: American Antiquarian Society, 1987).

61. Mollier, *L'argent et les lettres. Histoire du capitalisme d'édition, 1880–1920.*

62. Henri-Jean Martin, "Publishing Conditions and Strategy in Ancien Régime France," in Kenneth E. Carpenter, ed., *Books and Society in History,* Papers of the Association of College and Research Libraries Rare Books and Manuscripts preconference, 24–28 June 1980, Boston (New York: R. R. Bowker, 1983), 43–68.

63. Jacques Breton, *Le livre français contemporain. Manuel de bibliologie,* 2 vols. (Malakoff: Solin, 1988), 1:190–98.

64. Mollier, *L'argent et les lettres,* esp. pp. 485–93.

CHAPTER TEN

1. Ecole pratique des Hautes Etudes, IVe section, *Histoire de l'administration française depuis 1800,* Actes du colloque organisé le 4 mars 1972 par l'Institut français des sciences administratives et la IVe section de l'Ecole pratique des Hautes Etudes (Geneva: Droz, 1975).

2. Bruno Delmas, "Révolution industrielle et mutation administrative. L'innovation dans l'administration française au XIXe siècle," *Histoire, économie et société* 4 (1985): 205–32; *La machine à écrire hier et demain,* Institut d'étude du livre, Colloque des 23–24 October 1980 (Paris: Solin, 1982), presented by Roger Laufer, esp. Bruno Delmas, "L'introduction de la machine à écrire dans l'administration française de 1880 à 1920," 19–28; Georges Ribeill, "Aperçu historique sur le travail de dactylographie," 29–53; René Ponot, "Pica, élite et les autres, ou les caractères de la machine à écrire," 143–54; Gérard Blanchard, "De la casse au clavier," 179–94; Pierre Schaeffer, "Deux reflexions à propos de la machine à écrire," 279–82.

3. *La machine à écrire hier et demain.*

4. Marius Audin, *Histoire de l'imprimerie par l'image,* 4 vols. (Paris: H. Jonquières, 1972), 324–32; Daniel Renoult, "Les nouvelles possibilités techniques: Le triomphe de la mécanique," in Henri-Jean Martin and Roger Chartier, gen. eds., *Histoire de l'édition française,* 4 vols. (Paris: Promodis, 1982–86), vol. 4, *Le livre concurrencé 1900–1950,* 36–57.

5. Auguste Blondel and Paul Mirabaud, *Rodolphe Töpffer: L'écrivain, l'artiste et l'homme* (Paris: Hachette, 1886; reprint Paris: Slatkine, 1976); Pierre Courthion, *Genève ou le portrait des Töpffer* (Paris: B. Grasset, 1936); Gérard Blanchard, *La bande*

dessinée, histoire des histoires en image, de la préhistoire à nos jours (Paris: L'inter, 1969); Georges Sadoul, *Panorama de la bande dessinée* (Paris: Editions J'ai lu, 1976).

6. Jacques Breton, *Le livre français contemporain. Manuel de bibliologie*, 2 vols. (Malakoff: Solin, 1988); Robert Estivals, *Le livre dans le monde, 1971–1981. Introduction à la bibliologie politique internationale* (Paris: Editions Retz, 1983).

7. On this subject, see Philippe Schuwer, *Editeurs aujourd'hui* (Paris: Retz, 1987).

8. Pascal Fouché, *Au Sans Pareil*, 2d ed. rev. (Paris: IMEC, 1989); Fouché, *La Sirène* (Paris: Bibliothèque de littérature française contemporaine de l'Université Paris 7, 1984); Fouché, "L'édition littéraire, 1914–1950," in Martin and Chartier, gen. eds., *Histoire de l'édition française*, 4: 188–240.

9. The variety and scope of the topics taken up in this section do not permit specific citation of all the works consulted. For technical aspects, let me mention Maurice Daumas, ed., *Histoire générale des techniques*, 5 vols. (Paris: Presses Universitaires de France, 1962–79), vols. 3, 4, and 5; Bertrand Gille, ed., *Histoire des techniques*, Encyclopédie de la Pléiade, 2 vols. (Paris: Gallimard, 1978), vol. 1, *Techniques et civilisations*, vol. 2, *Techniques et sciences*, available in English as *History of Techniques*, 2 vols. (New York: Gordon and Breach, 1986); and, for recent developments, the publications of *Techniques de l'ingénieur*. Most of the statistical data have been drawn from recent volumes published by the Institut national de la statistique et des études économiques (INSEE, *Annuaire statistique de la France*), from UNESCO surveys, or from Dominique and Michèle Frémy, eds., *Quid 1988* (Paris: Laffont, 1987). See also *Annuaire statistique de la France, résumé rétrospectif* (Paris: INSEE, 1966), and Francis Balle, *Medias et société*, 4th ed. (Paris: Montchrestien, 1988). On a number of specific topics the volumes in the Que sais-je? series have been utilized, notably Pierre Albert and André Jean Tudesq, *Histoire de la radio et de la télévision* (Paris: Presses Universitaires de France, 1981), and Pierre Mathelot, *La télématique* (Paris: Presses Universitaires de France, 1985).

10. Catherine Bertho, *Télégraphes et téléphones, de Valmy au microprocesseur* (Paris: Livre de Poche, 1981); Louis Leprince-Ringuet, *L'aventure de l'électricité* (Paris: Flammarion, 1983); Catherine Bertho, ed., *Histoire des télécommunications en France* (Toulouse: Erès, 1984).

11. Pierre Gilotaux, *Les disques*, 2d ed. (Paris: Presses Universitaires de France, 1971).

12. Georges Sadoul with the collaboration of Bernard Eisenschitz, *Histoire générale du cinéma*, 6 vols. (Paris: Denoël, 1973–75); Jean Mitry, *Histoire du cinéma: Art et industrie*, 5 vols. (Paris: Editions universitaires, 1967–68); Philippe d'Hugues and Dominique Muller, *Gaumont, 90 ans de cinéma* (Paris: Ramsay, Cinémathèque française, 1986).

13. Pierre Miquel, *Histoire de la radio et de la télévision* (Paris: Perrin, 1984).

14. Ibid.

15. Ibid.

16. G. Elgozy, "Origines de l'informatique," *Techniques de l'ingénieur* (1970).

17. Pierre Davous, "Historique des ordinateurs" in *Techniques de l'ingénieur*. See also Raymond Moch, "Le tournant informatique," a document used in Simon Nora and Alain Minc, *L'informatisation de la société, Rapport à M. le Président de la Répu-*

blique (Paris: Editions du Seuil, 1978). This article is mentioned but not provided in Supporting Document 1, "The Turning Point in Data Processing," in the English translation of Nora and Minc, *The Computerization of Society: A Report to the President of France* (Cambridge, Mass., and London: MIT Press, 1980).

18. Philippe Breton, *Histoire de l'informatique* (Paris: Découverte, 1987); J. J. Trottin, "Téléinformatique," *Techniques de l'ingénieur.* See also Bruno Lussato, *Le défi informatique* (Paris: Fayard, 1981; Hachette-Pluriel, 1982); Lussato, *Le dossier de la micro-informatique* (Paris: Organisation, 1980); Bruno Lussato and Gérald Messadié, *Bouillon de culture* (Paris: Laffont, 1986); Jean-Jacques Salomon and André Lebeau, *L'écrivain public et l'ordinateur: Mirages du développement* (Paris: Hachette, 1988).

19. Jacques Chailley, *La musique et le signe* (Lausanne: Rencontre; Paris: Hachette, 1967; Plan-de-Tour: Aujourd'hui, 1985); A. Machabey, *La notation musicale,* 3d ed. (Paris: Presses Universitaires de France, 1971); Marc Honegger, ed., *Dictionnaire de la musique,* 4 vols. (Paris: Bordas, 1970–76), vol. 3, *Science de la musique: Formes, technique, instruments,* in particular, Michel Huglo and Manfred Kelkel, s.v. "Notation"; Jacques Chailley, "Notation musicale," in Marc Vignal, ed., *Dictionnaire de la musique* (Paris: Larousse, 1982).

20. André Delmas, "Anatomic Imaging: Its Advantages and Disadvantages," *Surgical and Radiologic Anatomy* 10 (1988): 3–4; François Dagognet, *Tableaux et langages de la chimie* (Paris: Editions du Seuil, 1969); Abraham Moles and Elisabeth Rohmer, *L'image communication fonctionnelle* (Paris: Casterman, 1981); Jacques Bertin, *La graphique et le traitement graphique de l'information* (Paris: Flammarion, 1977), available in English as *Graphs and Graphic Information-Processing,* trans. William J. Bery and Paul Scott (Berlin and New York: de Gruyter, 1981); Jean Prinet, Roger Bellone, Ginette Bléry, *La photographie,* 10th ed. (Paris: Presses Universitaires de France, 1989).

21. Alain Jaubert, *Le commissariat aux archives: Les photos qui falsifient l'histoire* (Paris: Barrault, 1986), available in English as *Making People Disappear: An Amazing Chronicle of Photographic Deception* (Washington: Pergamon Press, Brassey's International Defense Publishers, 1989); Gérard Le Marec, *Les photos truquées, un siècle de propagande par l'image* (Paris: Atlas, 1985).

22. For the problems that are rapidly raised here, see not only the *Annuaire statistique de la France,* published by the Institut national de la statistique et des études économiques (INSEE), especially the retrospective summary from 1966, but also Jean Cazeneuve, *La société de l'ubiquité* (Paris: Denoël, Gonthier, 1972); Francis Balle, *Médias et société,* 4th ed. (Paris: Monchrestien, 1988), available in English as *The Media Revolution in America and Western Europe,* ed. Everett M. Rogers, Francis Balle (Norwood, N.J.: Ablex Publishing Corp, 1985); Jean Cluzel, *La télévision après six réformes* (Paris: J. C. Lattes, 1988); Georges Anderla, *L'information en 1985: Une étude prévisionnelle des besoins et des ressources* (Paris: Organisation de coopération et de développement économiques, 1973); Jean Louis Missika and Dominique Wolton, *La folle du logis, la télévision dans les sociétés démocratiques* (Paris: Gallimard, 1983); Alain Masson, *Mainmise sur l'enfance: Genèse de la normatique* (Paris: Payot, 1980); André Vitalis, *Informatique, pouvoir et libertés,* 2d ed. (Paris: Economica, 1988).

Index